Lecture Notes in Computer Science 8662

Commenced Publication in 1973
Founding and Former Series Editors:
Gerhard Goos, Juris Hartmanis, and Jan van Leeuwen

Robert C.-H. Hsu   Shangguang Wang (Eds.)

Internet of Vehicles – Technologies and Services

First International Conference, IOV 2014
Beijing, China, September 1-3, 2014
Proceedings

 Springer

Volume Editors

Robert C.-H. Hsu
Chung Hua University
707, Sec. 2, WuFu Road, Hsinchu, Taiwan 30012, R.O.C.
E-mail: robertchh@gmail.com

Shangguang Wang
Beijing University of Posts and Telecommunications
Box 187#, No. 10, Xi Tu Cheng Road, Beijing 100876, China
E-mail: sgwang@bupt.edu.cn

ISSN 0302-9743   e-ISSN 1611-3349
ISBN 978-3-319-11166-7   e-ISBN 978-3-319-11167-4
DOI 10.1007/978-3-319-11167-4
Springer Cham Heidelberg New York Dordrecht London

Library of Congress Control Number: 2014947343

LNCS Sublibrary: SL 3 – Information Systems and Application, incl. Internet/Web and HCI

Typesetting: Camera-ready by author, data conversion by Scientific Publishing Services, Chennai, India

Printed on acid-free paper

Springer is part of Springer Science+Business Media (www.springer.com)

Preface

This volume contains the proceedings of IOV 2014, the First International Conference on Internet of Vehicles, which was held in Beijing, China, during September 1–3, 2014.

Internet of Vehicles (IOV) is emerging as an important part of the smart or intelligent cities being proposed and developed around the world. IOV is a complex integrated network system that interconnects people within and around vehicles, intelligent systems on board vehicles, and various cyber-physical systems in urban environments. IOV goes beyond telematics, vehicle ad hoc networks, and intelligent transportation, by integrating vehicles, sensors, and mobile devices into a global network to enable various services to be delivered to vehicular and transportation systems, and to people on board and around vehicles, using contemporary computing techniques such as swarm intelligent computing, crowd sensing and crowd sourcing, social computing, and cloud computing. IOV 2014 played an important role for researchers and industry practitioners to exchange information regarding advancements in the state of art and practice of IOV architectures, protocols, services, and applications, as well as to identify emerging research topics and define the future directions of IOV.

This year, the technical program of IOV 2014 drew from a large number of submissions: 160 papers submitted from 30 countries representing four regions — Asia Pacific, Europe, North and South America. In the first stage, all papers submitted were screened for their relevance and general submission requirements. These manuscripts then underwent a rigorous peer-review process with at least three reviewers, coordinated by the international Program Committee. The Program Committee accepted 41 papers out of 160 submissions, resulting in an acceptance rate of 25.6%. The accepted papers provide research contributions in a wide range of research topics including telematics, wireless communication networks, services and applications, social information systems, swarm intelligence, economics for IOV, modeling and simulation, as well as cloud computing and big data. We believe that this volume not only presents novel and interesting ideas but also that it will stimulate future research in the area of IOV.

Organizing conferences with a large number of submissions requires a lot of hard work and dedication from many people. We would like to take this opportunity to thank the numerous people whose time and efforts made this conference possible and ensured its high-quality. We wish to thank the authors for submitting high-quality papers that contributed to the conference technical program. We wish to express our deepest gratitude to all Program Committee members and external reviewers for their excellent job in the paper review process. Without their help, this program would not be possible. We appreciate the participation of the keynote speakers, Prof. Chung-Ming Huang and Prof. David

Taniar; their speeches greatly benefitted the audience. Special thanks go to the entire local Arrangements Committee for their help in making the conference a wonderful success. We take this opportunity to thank all the presenters, session chairs, and participants for their presence at the conference, many of whom traveled long distances to attend this conference and make their valuable contributions. Last but not least, we would like to express our gratitude to all the organizations that supported our efforts to bring the conference to fruition. We are grateful to Springer for publishing these proceedings.

We are proud to have the authors sharing their research with you, fellow members of the technical community, through IOV 2014 and these proceedings. We hope that you enjoy the IOV 2014 proceedings.

September 2014

Robert C.-H. Hsu
Victor Leung
Shangguang Wang
Zibin Zheng

Organization

IOV 2014 was organized by Beijing University of Posts and Telecommunications, State Key Laboratory of Networking and Switching Technology, and sponsored by the Beijing Natural Science Foundation. It was held in cooperation with *Lecture Notes in Computer Science* (LNCS) and *Communications in Computer and Information Science* (CCIS) of Springer.

Executive Committee

2014 International Conference on Internet of Vehicles (IOV 2014)

Honorary Chair

Fangchun Yang	Beijing University of Posts and Telecommunications, China

General Co-chairs

Robert C.-H. Hsu	Chung Hua University, Taiwan
Victor C.M. Leung	The University of British Columbia, Canada

Program Committee Chairs

Shangguang Wang	Beijing University of Posts and Telecommunications, China
Zibin Zheng	The Chinese University of Hong Kong, Hong Kong, SAR China

Program Vice-Chairs

Akihiko Tozawa	IBM Tokyo Research Laboratory, Japan
Benot Parrein	Universit de Nantes, France
Chau Yuen	Singapore Univeresity of Technology and Design, Singapore
Chu-Hsing Lin	Tunghai University, Taiwan
Cong Wang	City University of Hong Kong, Hong Kong, SAR China
Daqiang Zhang	Tongji University, China
Feng Wang	University of Mississippi, USA
Jiong Jin	Swinburne University of Technology, Australia

Publicity Co-chairs

Shoji Kasahara	Nara Institute of Science and Technology, Japan
Vicente Milanes	Inria, France

Yu Chen   Binghamton University, USA
Jun Li   University of Sydney, Australia

Steering Committee

Robert C.-H. Hsu   Chung Hua University, Taiwan (Chair)
Shangguang Wang   Beijing University of Posts and
                                   Telecommunications, China (Vice Chair)
Victor C.M. Leung   The University of British Columbia, Canada
Jianhua Ma   Hosei University, Japan
David Taniar   Monash University, Australia

Technical Program Committee

Abdelmajid Khelil   Huawei European Research Center, Germany
Abderrahmane Lakas   UAE University, UAE
Abderrazak Bannari   University of Ottawa, Canada
Abderrazek Abdaoui   Qatar University, Qatar
Ado Silva   University of Aveiro, Portugal
Ai-Chun Pang   National Taiwan University, Taiwan
Akihiko Tozawa   IBM Tokyo Research Laboratory, Japan
Ala Al-Fuqaha   Western Michigan University, USA
Alessio Botta   University of Naples, Italy
Alexandre Santos   University of Minho, Portugal
Ali Abu-El Humos   Jackson State University, USA
Anthony Lo   Delft University of Technology,
                                   The Netherlands
Antonio J.R. Neves   University of Aveiro, Portugal
Aravind Kailas   UNC Charlotte, USA
Azzam Mourad   Lebanese American University, Lebanon
Behrouz Maham   University of Tehran, Iran
Benot Parrein   Universit de Nantes, France
Bernd E. Wolfinger   University of Hamburg, Germany
Bing-Hong Liu   National Kaohsiung University of Applied
                                   Sciences, Taiwan
Cailian Chen   Shanghai Jiao Tong University, China
Carlos T. Calafate   Universitat Politcnica de Valncia, Spain
Carsten Rcker   RWTH Aachen University, Germany
Cathryn Peoples   University of Ulster, UK
Chau Yuen   Singapore Univeresity of Technology and
                                   Design, Singapore
Chengnian Long   Shanghai Jiao Tong University, China
Chengwen Zhang   Harbin Institute of Technology, China
Chin-Long Wey   National Chiao Tung University, Taiwan
Chonho Lee   Nanyang Technological University, Singapore

Christian Prehofer   Fortiss, Germany
Chuan-Ming Liu   National Taipei University of Technology,
                                         Taiwan
Chu-Hsing Lin   Tunghai University, Taiwan
Claudio Estevez   University of Chile, Chile
Cliff C. Zou   University of Central Florida, USA
Cong Tang   Peking Univeristy, China
Cong Wang   City University of Hong Kong, Hong Kong,
                                         SAR China
Constandinos Mavromoustakis University of Nicosia, Cyprus
Constantine Kotropoulos   Aristotle University of Thessaloniki, Greece
Costas Busch   Louisiana State University, USA
Dalila B. Megherbi   University of Massachusetts, USA
Danda B. Rawat   Georgia Southern University, USA
Daqiang Zhang   Tongji University, China
Dario Vieira   EFREI, France
Daxin Tian   Beihang University, China
Dimitrios Koukopoulos   University of Patras, Greece
Domenico Ciuonzo   Second University of Naples, Italy
Donghyun (David) Kim   North Carolina Central University, USA
Dongliang Duan   University of Wyoming, USA
Enzo Mingozzi   University of Pisa, Italy
Esa Hyyti   Aalto University, Finland
Eva Marn Tordera   Universitat Politècnica de Catalunya, Spain
Feng Wang   University of Mississippi, USA
Franois-Xavier Coudoux   University of Valenciennes, France
Francis Lau   University of Hong Kong, Hong Kong,
                                         SAR China
George A. Tsihrintzis   University of Piraeus, Greece
George Caridakis   National Technical University of Athens,
                                         Greece
Georgios Kambourakis   University of the Aegean, Greece
Gerard Parr   University of Ulster, UK
Ghassan M. Kraidy   Notre Dame University, Lebanon
Giacomo Verticale   Politecnico di Milano, Italy
Guoqiang Mao   The University of Technology Sydney, Australia
Guoqiang Wang   Yahoo! Inc., USA
Gustavo Marfia   University of Bologna, Italy
Hafiz Malik   University of Michigan, USA
Hai Jin   Huazhong University of Science and
                                         Technology, China
Haitao (Tony) Xia   IEEE Data Storage Technical Committee
                                         Chair, USA
Han-Shin Jo   Hanbat National University, Korea

Hassan Hossein Nia	University of Extremadura, Spain
Henri Nicolas	Université Bordeaux 1, France
Hong (Jeffrey) Nie	University of Northern Iowa, USA
Hung-Min Sun	National Tsing Hua University, Taiwan
Hung-Yu Wei	National Taiwan University, Taiwan
Ibrahim Kamel	University of Sharjah, UAE
Ignacio Soto	Universidad Carlos III de Madrid, Spain
Ing-Chau Chang	National Changhua University of Education, Taiwan
Jana Dittmann	University of Magdeburg, Germany
Javier Rubio-Loyola	Tamaulipas, Mexico
Jean-Pierre Richard	Ecole Centrale de Lille, France
Jenq-Haur Wang	National Taipei University of Technology, Taiwan
Jenq-Neng Hwang	University of Washington, USA
Jeremy Blum	D.Sc., The Pennsylvania State University, USA
Jia-Chin Lin	National Central University, Taiwan
Jingon Joung	Institute for Infocomm Research, Singapore
Jinwei Wang	Nanjing University of Information Science and Technology, China
Jiong Jin	Swinburne University of Technology, Australia
Joel Rodrigues	University of Beira Interior, Portugal
John D. McGegor	Clemson University, USA
Jose Saldana	University of Zaragoza, Spain
Jos Soler	Technical University of Denmark, Denmark
Ju Wang	Virginia State University, USA
Juan-Carlos Cano	Universitat Politecnica de Valencia, Spain
Jukka K. Nurminen	Aalto University, Finland
Jun Li	University of Sydney, Australia
Junmin Wang	Ohio State University, USA
Kamesh Namuduri	University of North Texas, USA
Kan ZHeng	Beijing University of Posts and Telecommunications, China
Khalil Ibrahimi	IBN-Tofail University, Kenitra, Morocco
Laszlo G. Nyul	University of Szeged, Hungary
Lei Liu	University of California, Davis, USA
Lei Shu	Guangdong University of Petrochemical Technology, China
Leonardo Militano	Mediterranea University of Reggio Calabria, Italy
Lingfeng Wang	The University of Toledo, USA
Linghe Kong	SUTD Singapore University of Technology and Design, Singapore

Lisimachos P. Kondi	University of Ioannina, Greece
Ljiljana Trajkovic	Simon Fraser University, Canada
Lu Peng	Louisiana State University, USA
Luca Caviglione	National Research Council, Italy
Luca Reggiani	Informazione e Bioingegneria, Italy
Manohara Pai M.M.	Manipal University, India
Marco Listanti	University "Sapienza" of Rome, Italy
Maryline Chetto	Université de Nantes, France
Massimiliano Comisso	University of Trieste, Italy
Mehmet Celenk	Ohio University, USA
Mengjun Xie	University of Arkansas at Little Rock, USA
Miguel L´pez-Bentez	University of Liverpool, UK
Ming-Hsuan Yang	University of California at Merced, USA
Minseok Kwon	Rochester Institute of Technology, USA
Momin Uppal	Lahore University of Management Sciences, Pakistan
Mon-Yen Luo	National Kaohsiung University of Applied Sciences, Taiwan
Muhammad Khurram Khan	King Saud University, Saudi Arabia
Mujdat Soyturk	Marmara University, Turkey
Murtuza Jadliwala	Wichita State University, USA
Mu-Song Chen	Da-Yeh University, Taiwan
Na Li	Northwest Missouri State University, USA
Naixue Xiong	Colorado Technical University, USA
Nary Subramanian	The University of Texas at Tyler, USA
Natarajan Meghanathan	Jackson State University, USA
Ngai-Man Cheung	Singapore University of Technology and Design, Singapore
Nikolaos Papandreou	IBM Research-Zurich, Switzerland
Nitin Maslekar	NEC Laboratories Europe, Germany
Oscar Esparza	Universitat Politcnica de Catalunya, Spain
Pan Li	Mississippi State University, USA
Paolo Carbone	University of Perugia, Italy
Pascal Lorenz	University of Haute Alsace, France
Peng Zhang	University of Connecticut, USA
Qing Yang	Montana State University, USA
Rachid Outbib	University of Aix-Marseille, France
Rajarshi Mahapatra	Rockwell Collins India, India
Rajgopal Kannan	Louisiana State University, USA
Ramin Yahyapour	University of Gttingen, Germany
Razvan Stanica	INSA Lyon, France
Redha M. Radaydeh	Alfaisal University, Saudi Arabia
Rui Lopes	Lisbon University Institute & Instituto Telecomunicações, Portugal

Seng W. Loke	La Trobe University, Australia
Sergio Rapuano	University of Sannio, Italy
Shaohua Wu	Harbin Institute of Technology Shenhen Graduate School, China
Sherali Zeadally	University of Kentucky, USA
Shinfeng D. Lin	National Dong Hwa University, Taiwan
Shingchern D. You	National Taipei University of Technology, Taiwan
Shin-Ming Cheng	National Taiwan University of Science and Technology, Taiwan
Shiqiang Wang	Imperial College London, UK
Shoji Kasahara	Nara Institute of Science and Technology, Japan
Shujun Li	University of Surrey, UK
Sokratis K. Katsikas	University of Piraeus, Greece
Soufiene Djahel	University College Dublin, Ireland
Stefan Mangold	Disney Research, Switzerland
Stefan Poslad	Queen Mary University of London, UK
Suat Ozdemir	Gazi University, Turkey
Theodoros A. Tsiftsis	Technological Educational Institute of Central Greece, Greece
Theofilos Chrysikos	University of Patras, Greece
Thinagaran Perumal	Universiti Putra Malaysia, Malaysia
Thomas D. Lagkas	The University of Sheffield International Faculty, Greece
Thomas Little	Boston University, USA
Thomas M. Chen	City University London, UK
Tie (Tony) Luo	Institute for Infocomm Research, Singapore
Vicente Milanes	Inria, France
Vincenzo Piuri	Universitá degli Studi di Milano, Italy
Wang Jin	Soochow University, China
Wei Liu	University of Sheffield, UK
Wei Yuan	Huazhong University of Science and Technology, China
Wen Chen	Shanghai Jiao Tong University, China
Wen-Yen Lin	Chang Gung University, Taiwan
Winston Seah	Victoria University of Wellington, New Zealand
Woong Cho	Jungwon University, Korea
Wuxu Peng	Texas State University, USA
Xavi Masip-Bruin	Universitat Politecnica de Catalunya, Spain
Xiangqian Chen	Florida International University, USA
Xinming Huang	Worcester Polytechnic Institute, USA
Xu Chen	University of Gttingen, Germany
Yan Zhang	Simula Research Laboratory, Norway

Yang Song	IBM Research, USA
Yanmin Zhu	Shanghai Jiao Tong University, China
Yantai Shu	Tianjin University, China
Yasir Zaki	United Arab Emirates
Yi Wei	Microsoft, USA
Yi Xie	Sun Yat-Sen University, China
Yiming Ji	University of South Carolina, USA
Yiqing Zhou	Chinese Academy of Science, China
You-Chiun Wang	National Sun Yat-sen University, Taiwan
Yu Cai	Michigan Technological University, USA
Yu Chen	Binghamton University, SUNY, USA
Yuan-Cheng Lai	National Taiwan University of Science and Technology, Taiwan
Yueh-Min Huang	National Cheng Kung University, Taiwan
Yufeng Wang	New Jersey Institute of Technology, Newark, USA
Yuh-Shyan Chen	National Taipei University, Taiwan
Yunchuan Sun	Beijing Normal University, China
Zbigniew Dziong	University of Quebec, Canada
Zhe Chen	Northeastern University, China
Zheng Yan	Aalto University, Finland
Zhiguo Ding	Newcastle University, UK
Zhiguo Shi	Zhejiang University, China

2014 International Symposium on Cloud and Service Computing (SC2 2014)

Honorary Chair

Fangchun Yang	Beijing University of Posts and Telecommunications, China

General Chair

Robert C.-H. Hsu	Chung Hua University, Taiwan
Cho-Li Wang	The University of Hong Kong, Hong Kong
Sherali Zeadally	University of Kentucky, USA

Program Chair

Shangguang Wang	Beijing University of Posts and Telecommunications, China
Hung-Chang Hsiao	National Cheng Kung University, Taiwan
Anthony Lo	Delft University of Technology, The Netherlands

Publicity Chair

Wenguang Chen	Tsinghua University, China
Xiaofei Liao	HUST, China
Sheng-Lung Peng	National Dong Hua University, Taiwan
Lei Liu	University of California, Davis, USA
Henri Nicolas	Université Bordeaux 1, France

Program Committee

Alessio Botta	University of Napoli, Italy
Yu Cai	Michigan Technological University, USA
Jiannong Cao	Hong Kong Polytechnic University, Hong Kong
Paolo Carbone	Engineering Department, University of Perugia, Italy
Luca Caviglione	National Research Council, Italy
Lin-Huang Chang	National Taichung University, Taiwan
Jerry H. Chang	National Center for High-performance Computing, Taiwan
Yue-Shan Chang	National Taipei University, Taiwan
Yao-Chung Chang	National Taitung University, Taiwan
Juan-Carlos Cano	Universitat Politecnica de Valencia, Spain
Ngai-Man Cheung	Singapore University of Technology and Design, Singapore
Zhe Chen	Northeastern University, China
Mu-Song Chen	Da-Yeh University, Taiwan
Cailian Chen	Shanghai Jiao Tong University, China
Lung-Pin Chen	Tunghai University, Taiwan
Tzung-Shi Chen	National University of Tainan, Taiwan
Thomas M. Chen	City University London, UK
Shin-Ming Cheng	National Taiwan University of Science and Technology, Taiwan
Theofilos Chrysikos	University of Patras, Greece
Yeh-Ching Chung	National Tsing Hua University, Taiwan
Domenico Ciuonzo	Second University of Naples, Italy
Massimiliano Comisso	University of Trieste, Italy
Jana Dittmann	University of Magdeburg, Germany
Dongliang Duan	University of Wyoming, USA
Zbigniew Dziong	University of Quebec, Canada
Kuo-Chan Huang	National Taichung University, Taiwan
Chungming Huang	National Cheng-Kung University, Taiwan
Fang-Rong Hsu	Feng Chia University, Taiwan
Esa Hyytiä	Aalto University, Finland
Khalil Ibrahimi	IBN-Tofail University-Faculty of Sciences, Kenitra, Morocco
Fuu-Cheng Jiang	Tunghai University, Taiwan

Jiong Jin	Swinburne University of Technology, Australia
Hai Jin	Huazhong University of Science and Technology, China
Aravind Kailas	UNC Charlotte, USA
Georgios Kambourakis	University of the Aegean, Greece
Ibrahim Kamel	University of Sharjah, UAE
Rajgopal Kannan	Louisiana State University, USA
Muhammad Khurram Khan	King Saud University, Saudi Arabia
Abdelmajid Khelil	Huawei European Research Center, Germany
Donghyun (David) Kim	North Carolina Central University, USA
Dimitrios Koukopoulos	University of Patras, Greece
Minseok Kwon	Rochester Institute of Technology, USA
Thomas D. Lagkas	The University of Sheffield International Faculty, Greece
Kuan-Chou Lai	National Taichung University, Taiwan
Abderrahmane Lakas	UAE University, UAE
Guanling Lee	National Dong Hwa University, Taiwan
Che-Rung Lee	National Tsing Hua University, Taiwan
Marco Listanti	University "Sapienza" Roma, Italy
Chuan-Ming Liu	National Taipei University of Technology, Taiwan
Wei Liu	University of Sheffield, UK
Lei Liu	University of California, Davis, USA
Bing-Hong Liu	National Kaohsiung University of Applied Sciences, Taiwan
Kuan-Ching Li	Providence University, Taiwan
Na Li	Northwest Missouri State University, USA
Pascal Lorenz	University of Haute Alsace, France
Anthony Lo	Delft University of Technology, The Netherlands
Miguel López-Benítez	University of Liverpool, United Kingdom
Mon-Yen Luo	National Kaohsiung University of Applied Sciences, Taiwan
Behrouz Maham	University of Tehran, Iran
Stefan Mangold	Disney Research, Switzerland
Gustavo Marfia	University of Bologna, Italy
Nitin Maslekar	NEC Laboratories Europe, Germany
Constandinos Mavromoustakis	University of Nicosia, Cyprus
John D. McGegor	Clemson University, USA
Natarajan Meghanathan	Jackson State University, USA
Dalila B. Megherbi	University of Massachusetts, USA
Azzam Mourad	Lebanese American University, Lebanon
Henri Nicolas	Université Bordeaux 1, France
Ai-Chun Pang	National Taiwan University, Taiwan

Chau Yuen	Singapore Univeresity of Technology and Design, Singapore
Sherali Zeadally	University of Kentucky, USA
Daqiang Zhang	Tongji University, China
Kan Zheng	Beijing University of Posts and Telecommunications, China
Yanmin Zhu	Shanghai Jiao Tong University, China

Table of Contents

IOV Systems and Applications

Wireless Communications, Ad-Hoc and Sensor Networks

Security, Privacy, IoT and Big Data Intelligence

Cloud and Services Computing

A Novel Routing Protocol Based on Mobile Social Networks and Internet of Vehicles

Hao Wu, Hengliang Tang, and Lan Dong

State Key Laboratory of Rail Traffic Control and Safety,
Beijing Jiaotong University, Beijing, 100044
{hwu,10120151,donglan}@bjtu.edu.cn

Abstract. IOV (Internet of Vehicles) has received extensive attention recently as a part of ITS (Intelligent Transportation System). Due to various factors, such as high speed, road condition and traffic flow, the routing protocol becomes one of the important challenging problems in IOV. In this paper, we first present a mobility model at intersection and analysis it by the use of Markov method. On the basis of the mobility model, we propose a novel routing protocol in which the mobile social temporary relationship between vehicles has been considered for the urban transportation environment. Finally, the simulation results show that the packet delivery ratio and the average end-to-end delay of the proposed protocol are better than the traditional protocols.

Keywords: Routing Protocol, Internet of Vehicles, Mobility Model.

1   Introduction

As a part of Intelligent Transportation System (ITS), Internet of Vehicles (IOV) has been recently attracting an increasing attention from both research and industry communities so as to provide an effective solution to exchange safety messages between vehicles and avoid traffic jams [1].

The network structure of IOV mainly includes four components: OBU(On-Broad Unit), RSU(Road-Side Unit), CC(Control Center) and Internet, as shown in Fig.1. The OBU has GPS positioning module, vehicle state parameter acquisition module, the V2V (Vehicle-to-Vehicle) communication module, the V2R (Vehicle-to-Road) communication module and input/output devices. RSUs deployed along with the roads are responsible for the communication between vehicles and infrastructure, therefore the OBUs could exchange the traffic information with CC within the coverage area. Through Internet or satellites, the messages could be broadcasted more widely and meanwhile more information could be acquired.

An increasing number of car manufacturers are equipping vehicles with onboard computing and wireless communication devices, in-car sensors, and the global positioning system (GPS) which may be used for the deployment of large-scale vehicular networks. Whereas, due to various kinds of factors, such as high speed, dynamic topology, road condition and traffic flow, the design of routing protocols becomes one

R.C.-H. Hsu and W. Shangguang (Eds.): IOV 2014, LNCS 8662, pp. 1–10, 2014.
© Springer International Publishing Switzerland 2014

of the important challenging problems in IOV [2]. On the other side, vehicles are not isolated, so temporary social relationship between vehicles has also brought advantage for routing selection.

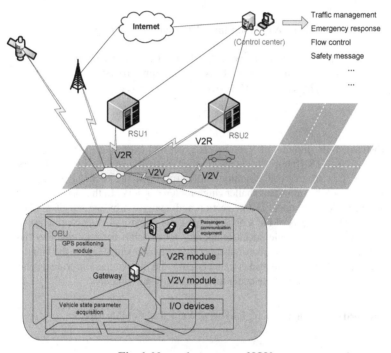

Fig. 1. Network structure of IOV

Mobile social networking is social networking where individuals with similar interests converse and connect with one another through their mobile devices [3], like Facebook or Wechat. Mobile social networking occurs in virtual communities, and it has a bright application prospect. The mobile social network based on vehicle communications may set up the inherent links between vehicles and drivers through coupling the license plate number with driver's phone number without having to build a new vehicle network. The network architecture is simple and easy to realize the communication between vehicles. According to the regularity of the movement of cars in urban cities, this paper presents a layered network structure and a group routing protocol based on mobile social relationship between vehicles, which is called MSGR (Mobile Social Group Routing) protocol. Different from the traditional group routing, our protocol depends on both the geographic information and the movement of vehicles behavior. Through the novel grouping method based on temporary social relationship between vehicle nodes, it can effectively reduce the routing delay, especially at the intersections in urban environment.

The rest of the paper is organized as follows: Section 2 describes the related works of mobility models and routing protocols in IOV. A mobility model at intersections is given and analysis in Section 3. And a novel routing strategy is proposed in Section 4, the simulation results and analysis are also discussed in this part, and Section 5 concludes the paper.

2   Related Works

2.1   Mobility Models of IOV

Since a strong interaction has been defined between the network protocol and vehicular mobility, the mobility model is a critical aspect in simulation studies of IOV.

Globally, vehicular mobility models may be classified into four different classes: *Synthetic Models* wrapping all models based on mathematical models, *Survey-based Models* extracting mobility patterns from surveys, *Trace-based Models* generating mobility patterns from real mobility traces, and finally *Traffic Simulators-based Models*, where the vehicular mobility traces are extracted from a detailed traffic simulator[4].

It is important to use a realistic mobility model so that results from the simulation can correctly reflect the real-world performance of IOV[5]. A realistic mobility model should consist of a realistic topological map which reflects different densities of roads and different categories of streets with various speed limits. Another important parameter should be modeled is the obstacles. Many previous studies [5], [6] have shown that a realistic mobility model with sufficient level of details is critical for accurate network simulation results. We found that realistic vehicular mobility model at intersections has rarely been studied.

2.2   Routing Protocols for IOV

Recently, researchers have proposed different routing algorithms[7-12] for IOV from the point of view of different characteristics, many routing protocols have been developed for Mobile Ad Hoc Networks (MANETs), and some of them can be applied directly to VANETs, such as GPSR (Greedy Perimeter Stateless Routing) and DSR (Dynamic Source Routing) [7],[8]. DSR is a classic on-demand routing protocol based on source routing, however, due to the delay is relatively increased, it is not suitable for real-time safety message transmission. GPSR forwards packets by greedy algorithm based on geographical position, whereas this algorithm is easy to lead to the routing void, i.e. the distance of all neighbors are farther than the node, but at this time the routing process is not over.

According to the characteristics of highly dynamic topology and frequently disconnected network, authors in literature [9],[10]and [11] proposed some novel protocols based on the connection, in view of communication between vehicles in city and highway environment. In literature [12] the author proposed a method called Long Lifetime Anypaths (LLA) providing stable communication paths. The mainly addressed the problem of stability of anypath communications in VANET networks in the presence of inter-vehicle link failures being result of vehicles mobility. However, those routing algorithms do not consider the temporary relationship between vehicles.

3   Vehicular Mobility Model at Intersection

3.1   Intersection Model

Usually, an intersection can be divided by two parts: horizontal-street and vertical-street. Considering a typical case in actual urban traffic, we establish a vehicular mobility model at intersection in urban road traffic as follows. In our mobility model, horizontal-street stands for the East-West direction and vertical-street stands for the South-North direction. Each direction has three lanes, a total of six lanes. In order to facilitate description, the streets are assumed as grids that have regular shape. Fig.2 shows the model.

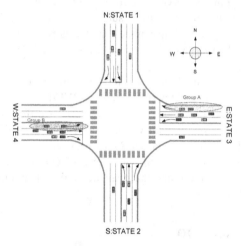

Fig. 2. Vehicular mobility model at intersection

Mobile nodes can move along the grid of the topology map, and at the intersections of the streets, the mobile nodes choose to turn right or left or go forward (remain unchanged) with a certain probability. The speed of mobile nodes in a certain moment is related with the previous moment. In addition, the speed of vehicles in the same lane also is related with each other.

As shown in Fig. 2, intersection is divided into four directions, east, west in horizontal direction and north, south in vertical direction. Vehicles in every direction are divided into three groups and they are set to D = {left, right, straight}, which means turning left, turning right and going straight respectively. So a intersection can be divided into twelve groups, which are set to M= {N→E, N→S, N→W, S→W, S→N, S→E, W→N, W→E, W→S, E→S, E→W, E→N}. The corresponding transition probability P_{ij} represents the radio of the vehicles in one group (i→j) to the total vehicles coming from direction i. For example, P_{NS} represents the radio of the vehicles from north to south to the total vehicles from north .Therefore, P_{NE}+ P_{NS} +P_{NW}=1. At the same time, the vehicles with the same destination are called groups with a high social relationship.

In order to simplify the modeling, assuming there are N mobile nodes in the model area, distributed randomly in the lanes within the model area, each node has the same signal transmission range and the same speed. The model complies with limited steps of execution in discrete time and the transition of limited state in the system according to the different probability, so it can be modeled as a Discrete Time Markov Chains (DTMCs). The streets are bidirectional and the intersections are regulated by means of traffic lights. At each intersection, the vehicles will choose its next direction following a Markov chain whose probabilities are calculated based on road segments attraction weights. The attraction weights usually are obtained by observed data.

3.2 Markov Process Analysis

Markov analysis method is widely applied to many fields, such as: market prediction and traffic transition prediction. In this paper, we use this method to predict traffic situation at signalized intersections.

Discrete Time Markov Chains Model can be defined as $(S, P, X(0))$. S corresponds to the state space, P is a matrix representing transition probabilities from one state to another, and $X(0)$ is the initial probability distribution of the states in S.

$$
\begin{bmatrix} X_1^{(k+1)} \\ X_2^{(k+1)} \\ \vdots \\ X_n^{(k+1)} \end{bmatrix}^T = \begin{bmatrix} X_1^{(k)} \\ X_2^{(k)} \\ \vdots \\ X_n^{(k)} \end{bmatrix}^T \begin{bmatrix} P_{11} & P_{12} & \cdots & P_{1n} \\ P_{21} & P_{22} & \cdots & P_{2n} \\ \vdots & \vdots & \vdots & \vdots \\ P_{n1} & P_{n2} & \cdots & P_{nn} \end{bmatrix} \tag{1}
$$

Where $k=1, 2, \ldots m$, m is the total transition steps.

In our mobility model, there are four states which classified by directions, S_1 is the north state, S_2 is the south state, S_3 is the east state and S_4 is the west state. We collected the traffic observed data at an intersection of Sidaokou in Beijing during a particular period. According to the statistics data, we calculated the transfer probability of vehicles at the intersection. Suppose P_{ij} represents the transition probability from State i to State j $(i,j=1,2,3,4)$, then the transition probability matrix P obtained as follows:

$$
P = \begin{bmatrix} 0 & P_{NS} & P_{NE} & P_{NW} \\ P_{SN} & 0 & P_{SE} & P_{SW} \\ P_{EN} & P_{ES} & 0 & P_{EW} \\ P_{WN} & P_{WS} & P_{WE} & 0 \end{bmatrix} = \begin{bmatrix} 0 & P_{12} & P_{13} & P_{14} \\ P_{21} & 0 & P_{23} & P_{24} \\ P_{31} & P_{32} & 0 & P_{34} \\ P_{41} & P_{42} & P_{43} & 0 \end{bmatrix} = \begin{bmatrix} 0 & 0.70 & 0.15 & 0.15 \\ 0.60 & 0 & 0.10 & 0.30 \\ 0.25 & 0.40 & 0 & 0.35 \\ 0.35 & 0.30 & 0.35 & 0 \end{bmatrix} \tag{2}
$$

Fig. 3 is the Markov probability transition diagram at a certain intersection. Furthermore, according to equation (1) and (2), it can be deduced as follows.

$$
\begin{bmatrix} \delta_1^{(k)} \\ \delta_2^{(k)} \\ \delta_3^{(k)} \\ \delta_4^{(k)} \end{bmatrix}^T = \begin{bmatrix} \delta_1^{(k-1)} \\ \delta_2^{(k-1)} \\ \delta_3^{(k-1)} \\ \delta_4^{(k-1)} \end{bmatrix}^T P = \ldots = \begin{bmatrix} \delta_1^{(0)} \\ \delta_2^{(0)} \\ \delta_3^{(0)} \\ \delta_4^{(0)} \end{bmatrix}^T P^k = \begin{bmatrix} \delta_1^{(0)} \\ \delta_2^{(0)} \\ \delta_3^{(0)} \\ \delta_4^{(0)} \end{bmatrix}^T \begin{bmatrix} 0 & P_{12} & P_{13} & P_{14} \\ P_{21} & 0 & P_{23} & P_{24} \\ P_{31} & P_{32} & 0 & P_{34} \\ P_{41} & P_{42} & P_{43} & 0 \end{bmatrix}^k \tag{3}
$$

where $k=1,2,3,...m$. $\delta_i^{(k)}$ represents the TFO (Traffic Flow Occupancy) of the vehicles driving to direction i of the next k cycles in the future, where $i= 1, 2, 3, 4$. And TFO means the probability density of traffic flow.

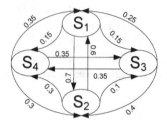

Fig. 3. Markov State Transition Diagram

3.3   Model Validation

Based on the analysis in 3.2, the predicted values of TFO within several cycles can be calculated. On the other hand, we have statistics the observed data in the same cycles, and compared the observed values to the predicted values for four states. The results are shown as Fig. 4. During the validation, it has been chosen 10 cycles to illustrate the values, and one cycle is 5 minutes.

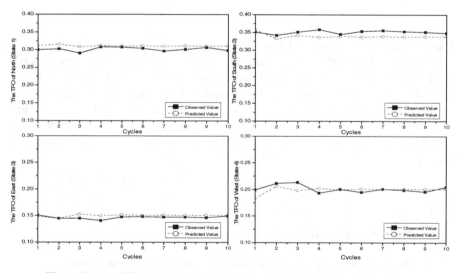

Fig. 4. Observed Values and Predicted Values of TFO for Different Directions

From the comparison it is obvious that the maximum error is not greater than 10%, therefore the Markov analysis method is feasible for the traffic situation at intersections in urban environment.

4   Routing Protocol

4.1   Description of MSGR Protocol

According to the regularity of the movement of vehicles in urban environment, this paper proposes a layered network structure and a group routing protocol based on mobile social temporary relationship between vehicles, which is called MSGR (Mobile Social Group Routing) protocol. Since the grouping method can be applied to routing strategies based on the location in urban environment, the basic idea of traditional method is to classify the nodes of network within the range of certain geographical location as a group. However, in this paper, we present a different and novel grouping method based on the temporary social relationship between vehicle nodes. The method depends on both the geographic information and the movement of vehicles behavior. For example, the nodes with a similar movement behavior in a certain range or the nodes with the same direction at a intersection have a higher probability to be considered as a group, as shown in Fig. 2, the vehicles in Group A and Group B have the same moving direction after crossing the intersection, so the priority of routing between these two groups is higher than other groups. In fact, these two groups will combine a new group after their turning. This grouping is dynamic by their temporary social relationships, so the routing should consider the special relationship between the vehicles. These close relations could communicate with each other with a higher priority. The grouping routing algorithm can reduce hops between the nodes of IOV and overhead of data transmission, meanwhile it can make the function of nodes more explicit and the management of network more convenient.

MSGR can find a route to the destination node with a high density of vehicles. It mainly contains three modules.

(I) *Grouping*, the vehicle nodes are grouped according to both the geographical location information and the temporary mobile social relationship, based on the mobility model in section 3, we assume that the vehicle can be divided into 12 groups, vehicle nodes within a group may communicate with a higher priority.

(II) *Next intersection choice*, when selecting the next intersection, as in equation (4), a transmitting node or intermediate node calculates a weight of each candidate intersection based on the number of vehicles and the distance to the destination node;

$$\text{Weight } (N_i) = a \times (1 - D_p) + b \times T_n / T_c \tag{4}$$

Where, N_i means the next candidate intersection; a and b represent the weight factor of the distance and vehicle traffic, $a+b=1$; D_p determines the relative distance between the candidate intersection to the destination node; T_n represents the total vehicles between the candidate intersection to the destination node; T_c represents the total vehicles between the current intersection to the destination node.

(III) *Multiple attributes decision*, in order to transmit data between two intersections, the next forwarding node, which has the maximum value of UC_i, is chosen by the multiple attributes decision mechanism. UC_i represents a comprehensive utility value of distance, direction, speed, velocity and density.

The data transmission procedure according to the proposed routing scheme includes five steps. Firstly, a source node S prepares to send a message; secondly, node S determines which groups to receive the message within the range of communication; thirdly, the nodes which belong to the receiving groups are activated; fourthly, the message of source node S is sent to the nodes are activated successfully; fifthly, the nodes that having received the message may send the message to the following-up nodes which belong to the same group but beyond the range of communication of S.

The proposed MSGR strategy has better purposiveness and adaptability for actual traffic environment at intersections in urban cities, we will prove the effectiveness of this strategy through the network simulation results.

4.2   Simulation

The simulation is performed by MATLAB and NS-2 based on the Manhattan style grids, the source and the destination nodes are selected randomly between 2000m and 2000m. The performance of the proposed routing strategy is evaluated, compared to DSR and GPSR routing protocols. The simulation parameters are shown in Table 1.

Table 1. Simulation Parameters

Parameter	Value
Simulation area	2000m×2000m
Simulation time	1000s
Number of Intersections	9
Number of Vehicles	40~160
Vehicle Speed	5~20m/s
Maximum Transmission Range	250m
Data Packet Size	512bytes
Data Rate	11Mbps
MAC Protocol	802.11DCF
Wireless Propagation Model	Two Ray Ground Reflection

Our performance evaluations include the following metrics:

1) *The data packet delivery ratio* is the ratio of the number of data packets received by the destination to the number of data packets sent by the source;

2) *The average end-to-end delay* characterizes the average time that a packet experiences in the network from the source to the destination;

3) *The routing overhead* represents the ratio of the size of controlling packets to the size of total packets, including controlling packets and data packets.

Fig.5 and Fig.6 shows that the normalized packet delivery rate and the average end-to-end delay versus the number of vehicles, as the vehicles increases, the packet delivery rate increases and the average end-to-end delay decreases monotonically. Obviously, our MSGR protocol is better than other two protocols. The improvement is attributed to the consideration of the vehicle grouping strategy and multiple attribute routing forward mechanism. Consequently, it increases the success delivery ratio and avoids the routing void.

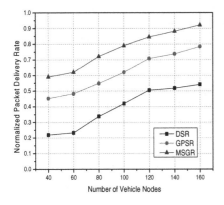

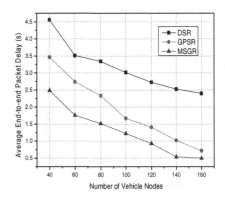

Fig. 5. Data Packet Delivery Ratio vs. Number of Vehicles

Fig. 6. Average end-to-end Delay vs. Number of Vehicles

The routing protocol overheads is also related to the density of vechiles, as shown in Fig.7. Among three protocols, since DSR does not need to periodically send Hello packets, its overhead is least. Compared to the GPSR, our MSGR reduces unnecessary information transmission by vehicles grouping, therefore the routing overhead is significantly reduced relatively. Although Hello packet increases some overhead in MSGR, considering the network performances of delivery ratio and end-to-end delay are significantly improved, it can be acceptable.

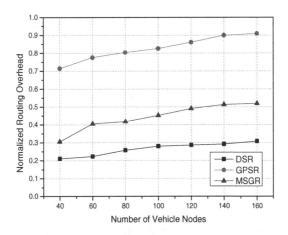

Fig. 7. Routing Overhead vs. Number of Vehicles

5   Conclusion

In this paper, we present a specific scenario model at intersection in urban environment for IOV, and then analysis the mobility model and validate the rationality. According to the realistic issues of traffic flow at intersections, we proposed a novel group routing protocol based on mobile temporary social relationship between vehicles, the simulation results show that our MSGR outperformed the DSR and GPSR. In the future, we would explore a more realistic joint system to improve the multiple attributes routing forward mechanism.

Acknowledgment. This paper is supported by the Natural Science Foundation of China (Grant No.: U1334202) and the NCET-13-0657. This paper is also partially supported by the Fundamental Research Funds for the Central Universities under Grant 2012JBM030.

References

1. Papadimitratos, P., La Fortelle, A., Evenssen, K., Brignolo, R., Cosenza, S.: Vehicular Communication Systems: Enabling Technologies, Applications, and Future Outlook on Intelligent Transportation. IEEE Communications Magazine 47(11), 84–95 (2009)
2. Sharef, B.T., Alsaqour, R.A., Ismail, M.: Vehicular Communication Ad Hoc Routing Protocols: A Survey. Journal of Network and Computer Applications 40(1), 363–396 (2014)
3. Kang, G.D., Diaz, M., Perennou, T., Senac, P., Xu, J.D.: Mobility Model Based on Social Community Detection Scheme. In: 2011 Cross Strait Quad-Regional Radio Science and Wireless Technology Conference (CSQRWC), pp. 769–773. IEEE Press, Piscataway (2011)
4. Harri, J., Filali, F., Bonnet, C.: Mobility Models for Vehicular Ad Hoc Networks: A Survey and Taxonomy. IEEE Communications Surveys & Tutorials 11(4), 19–41 (2009)
5. Baumann, R., Heimlicher, S., May, M.: Towards Realistic Mobility Models for Vehicular Ad-Hoc Networks. In: 2007 Mobile Networking for Vehicular Environments, pp. 73–78. IEEE Press, Piscataway (2007)
6. Tayal, S., Tripathy, M.R.: VANET-Challenges in Selection of Vehicular Mobility Model. In: 2012 Second International Conference on Advanced Computing & Communication Technologies (ACCT 2012), pp. 231–235. IEEE Press, Los Alamitos (2012)
7. Liu, J.C., Chen, F., Xu, J.K.: The Study of Routing Strategies in Vehicular Ad-Hoc Networks. In: 2010 International Conference on Wireless Communications and Signal Processing (WCSP), pp. 1–5. IEEE Press, Piscataway (2010)
8. Li, F., Wang, Y.: Routing in Vehicular Ad Hoc Networks: A Survey. IEEE Vehicular Technology Magazine 2(2), 12–22 (2007)
9. Zhao, J., Cao, G.H.: VADD: Vehicle-assisted Data Delivery In Vehicular Ad Hoc Networks. IEEE Transactions on Vehicular Technology 57(3), 1910–1922 (2008)
10. Yang, Q., et al.: ACAR: Adaptive Connectivity Aware Routing Protocol for Vehicular Ad Hoc Networks. In: Proceedings of 17th International Conference on Computer Communications and Networks (ICCCN), pp. 535–540. IEEE Press, Piscataway (2008)
11. Naumov, V., Gross, T.R.: Connectivity-Aware Routing(Car) in Vehicular Ad Hoc Networks. In: Proceedings of IEEE INFOCOM 2007, pp. 1918–1926. IEEE Press, Piscataway (2007)
12. Rak, J.: LLA: A New Anypath Routing Scheme Providing Long Path Lifetime in VANETs. IEEE Communications Letters 18(2), 281–284 (2014)

A Link State Aware Hierarchical Road Routing Protocol for 3D Scenario in VANETs

Ying He, Changle Li, Xiaolei Han, and Qin Lin

State Key Laboratory of Integrated Services Networks, Xidian University,
Xi'an, Shaanxi 710071, China
clli@mail.xidian.edu.cn

Abstract. In urban VANETs, nodes on the road appear three-dimensional (3D) distribution. However, the existing protocols only consider the case of planar distribution. It may cause problems in 3D scenarios, like hop count increase and packet delivery ratio decrease. Moreover, most of plane-based protocols determine the road connectivity by collecting the node density information, but it does not accurately reflect the road connectivity. Hence, we propose a novel protocol named Link State aware Hierarchical Road routing (LSHR). LSHR selects the next intersection based on the distance and the road connectivity. Meanwhile, LSHR represents the road connectivity more accurately. In addition, considering the problems of hop count increase and packet delivery ratio decrease, LSHR prior selects the neighbor has the largest transmission range of two hops as the forwarder. Comparing with classic protocols, LSHR is shown to increase the packet delivery ratio and decrease the end-to-end delay and hop count in simulation.

Keywords: VANETs, 3D, link state, hierarchical road.

1 Introduction

Routing protocol is important to determine the performance of Vehicular Ad hoc NETworks (VANETs) [1]. Quite a lot of routing protocols have been proposed, which can be classified into two types [2]: topology-based and geographic routing. Topology-based routing [3-5] always suffers from routing breaks and does not suitable for VANETs. In geographic routing [6-15], routing decision is made hop by hop and nodes unnecessary to maintain topology map or exchange link state information. Therefore, this type of routing can better adapt to VANETs.

All of these routing protocols in VANETs are designed and applicable to the ideal plane scenarios. Nowadays, a large number of overpasses and viaducts are build up on roads and highways in order to make full use of urban space. These overpasses and viaducts make the urban network from planar to three-dimensional (3D), and the 3D of urban network leading to the vehicle distribution appears layered phenomenon. Fig. 1 is an example of 3D realistic scenario. Hence, applying existing plane-based routing protocols in 3D scenarios is inappropriate. Although there have been some works for 3D scenarios in MANETs [16-18], it can't be directly applied in VANETs,

R.C.-H. Hsu and W. Shangguang (Eds.): IOV 2014, LNCS 8662, pp. 11–20, 2014.

Fig. 1. An example of realistic three-dimensional scenario

because VANETs have some own features that are different from MANETs. To address this issue, we present a new geographic routing named Link State aware Hierarchical Road routing (LSHR). LSHR aims to reduce routing hop count and the transmission delay, while increasing packet delivery ratio and enhancing the overall performance of the routing. It contains intersection judgment strategy and data transmission strategy on 3D sections. LSHR selects the next intersection based on the distance factor and the road connectivity. Meanwhile, LSHR represents the road connectivity more accurately. In addition, considering the problems of hop count increase and packet delivery ratio decrease, LSHR prior selects the neighbor that has the largest transmission range of two hops as the forwarding node.

The rest of the paper is organized as follows: In Section 2, we will analyze issues of the existing plane-based routing protocols. Section 3 will present the details in the proposed LSHR scheme. The performance evaluations of the proposed scheme are presented in Section 4. The last section is the conclusion.

2   Issues and Analysis

In this section, we will analyze the issues of the existing protocols.

2.1   Analysis about the Determination of Road Connectivity

There is a kind of geographic routing protocol which based on road topology [19, 20] for the urban scenario. In Geographic Source Routing (GSR) [19], the source node first selected the shortest path to the destination. However, GSR does not consider whether there are sufficient forwarding nodes on the selected streets, and the packet transmission disruptions may occur. Greedy Traffic Aware Routing protocol (Gy-TAR) [20] is a classic intersection based geographic routing. Different from GSR, GyTAR dynamically determine its intermediate intersection. The process is determined according to the real-time node density information. The node density refers to the average number of vehicles on the candidate road, not the actual distribution of vehicles. GyTAR thinks the greater the density, the better the quality of links, which

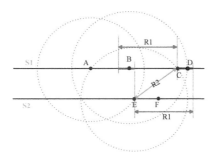

Fig. 2. An auxiliary abstract scenario graph

in fact is unreasonable. There are many routing protocols that use the density information for routing judgment and have the same problem with GyTAR, i.e. the collected
density information can't accurately reflect the actual road connectivity.

2.2   Analysis about Plane-based Routing Protocols Applied in 3D Scenarios

In this section, we use GPSR [6] as the research object. We consider a simple 3D
scenario which composed of two or more than two parallel but with different height
roads. Fig. 2 shows an auxiliary abstract scenario. S1 and S2 are two parallel road
segments which have different layers. R1 and R2 represent the transmission ranges of
the same layer and the inter-layer. The inter-layer transmission occurs between nodes
A and E. Packets can be transmitted to the farthest position of the location of node C.
But if there are some nodes in the red region, through the layer transmission, packets
can be transmitted to the blue region. It indicates that when the source and destination
on the road settled, the number of hop count between inter-layer transmissions is bigger than that of layer transmission. When node E reaches a local maximum, GPSR
uses the perimeter mode. However, if the node E forwards packets to node B instead
of switching into the perimeter mode, packets can avoid entering the local maximum
area. It could reduce the risk of packet delivery ratio dropping.

Similar with GPSR, the existing protocols that use greedy forwarding can't show
the best performance because of the inevitable inter-layer transmissions. So, it is need
to propose a routing protocol for 3D scenarios.

3   Link State aware Hierarchical Routing Protocol

Based on the above analysis, we put forward a geographic routing protocol called
Link State aware Hierarchical Road routing (LSHR), which aims to address the increase of routing hop count and transmission delay. LSHR contains intersection
judgment strategy and data transmission strategy on 3D sections. Firstly, when LSHR
selects the next temporary objective intersection, besides considering a general distance factor, it focus on the effect of road connectivity which expressed by the unit of
communication delay. Therefore, the selected path not only has shortest possible

transmission distance, but also has stable network connectivity to ensure rapidly and effectively packet transmission. Secondly, during the transmission of a packet, the agreement combines the 3D characteristics of the actual scenarios and the 3D distribution of nodes, and prior selects the neighbor who has the largest transmission range of two hops as the forwarding node.

Table 1. The format of Hello packet

Node ID	Node position	Road segment ID	Intersection ID	d_f	d_b

In VANETs, each node periodically broadcasts a Hello packet for its neighbors and creates or updates its neighbor list information based on received Hello packets. The format of Hello packet in LSHR is shown in Table 1. The node position is the 3D coordinates which provided by GPS. If the node is located at an intersection, the road segment ID is marked as null. If the node is not located at an intersection, the intersection ID is marked as null. The d_f refers to the distance between the current node and the node that is nearest to the front port of the road segment (i.e. front intersection). The d_b represents the distance between the current node and the node that is nearest to the back port of the road segment (i.e. back intersection).

3.1   Intersection Judgment Strategy

Assume that road topology is known. In LSHR, the current node determines the destination intersection according to its location. There are two destination intersection determination mode, i.e. road mode and intersection mode.

If the current node is located on the road segments, then it chooses the road mode, i.e. selects the port that nearest to the destination as the destination intersection from two ports of the road segment which the node is located on. Record the ID of the port in the dynamic address field of the packet. Here, we use (x_F, y_F, z_F), (x_B, y_B, z_B) and (x_D, y_D, z_D) express the locations of the road segment's front port, back port and the destination respectively. The distance between the destination and the front port is

$$d_F = \sqrt{\left(x_F - x_D\right)^2 + \left(y_F - y_D\right)^2 + \left(z_F - z_D\right)^2} , \tag{1}$$

and the distance between the destination node and the back port is calculated by

$$d_B = \sqrt{\left(x_B - x_D\right)^2 + \left(y_B - y_D\right)^2 + \left(z_B - z_D\right)^2} . \tag{2}$$

Compare d_F and d_B, and the smaller one is the temporary destination intersection.

Table 2. The format of a data collect packet

I_i	t_1	t_2

If the current node is located at an intersection, then it chooses the intersection mode. This node checks its cache to see whether there is a sort table which reflects the connectivity of the adjacent road connections. If not exists, the node establishes this sort table. It needs to collect the real-time traffic information and the process is as follows: The node Ns who needs to establish a sort table sends a collect packet (CPi) to each candidate adjacent intersection Ii, and records the time when the CPi is sent in the CPi. The node Nr which is located within the one hop transmission range of the intersection at where the node Ns is located receives the CPi, and records the time when the CPi is received in the CPi. Table 2 is the format of CPi in LSHR. The node who received the CPi calculates the unit of communication delay τ_{ji}, and records the τ_{ji} and the corresponding intersection's ID in a reference packet. Then broadcasts the reference packet to all neighboring nodes, and the τ_{ji} is calculated as:

$$\tau_{ji} = (t_2 - t_1) / l_{ji} .$$

(3)

t_1 and t_2 represent the timestamps when the CP corresponding to the candidate intersection j is sent and received, respectively. l_{ji} is the length of road segment between the candidate intersection whose ID is j and the current intersection i. Then, the node who receives the reference packet extract the intersection's ID and the unit of communication delay in reference packet, and sorts both of them by ascending values of the unit of communication delays. The node stored the sort table in its cache, and then broadcasts the sort table to all neighboring nodes. Finally, calculates a weight value for all candidate adjacent intersections according to the contents of the sort table and the positions of the intersections:

$$W_j = \alpha \cdot \tau_{ji} + \beta \cdot D_j .$$

(4)

W_j in the formula represents the weight value of the candidate adjacent intersection whose ID is j. D_j refers to the distance from the candidate adjacent intersection j to the destination. α and β are constants for two different values, and both of them are greater than 0 and the sum of them is equal to 1. The selecting temporary destination is the intersection that has the minimum weight value, and fills in the packet's dynamic address field with the ID of the corresponding intersection.

3.2   Data Transmission Strategy on 3D Sections

When the current node receives a packet, it first determines the current temporary destination, after that, data transmission starts. From the above description, we can see the intersection that corresponding to the ID which is recorded in the packet's dynamic address field is the destination for packet transmission. The current node checks its neighbor list to see whether there exist some nodes that are closer to destination node than current node.

If there are some neighbors closer to the destination than current node, calculate a virtual distance for all these neighbor nodes. Here, the virtual distance refers to the node forwards the packet through one of its neighbors, the largest two-hop distance the packet can be transmitted to. It equals to the distance between the current node and the neighbor node plus the neighbor node's d_f or d_b. If the temporary destination intersection is the front port of the neighbor node, plus d_f; otherwise, plus d_b. As shown in Equation (5):

$$d = \begin{cases} d_{nc} + d_f, \\ d_{nc} + d_b, \end{cases}$$
(5)

Finally, choose the neighbor has the largest virtual distance as the next hop. The node received the packet checks the ID recorded in the packet's destination address field. If the ID coincides with the node's own ID, the received packets are submitted to the MAC layer and the routing process finish. Otherwise, check the ID recorded in the packet's dynamic address field, if the ID coincides with the intersection ID where the node is located at, the node selects the next temporary destination intersection.

If there are no neighbor nodes that are closer to the destination than current node, then current node will carry the packet for some distance until meeting with other nodes, that is, when a neighbor appears on the direction to approach the destination, forwards the packet to the neighbor node based on the above metric.

4   Performance Evaluation

We study the performance of LSHR via NS2 [21]. GPSR is the most fundamental geographic routing and first propose the most widely used strategy in VANETs, i.e. greedy forwarding. In addition, GPSR is the basis for most of the geographic routings and often used as the comparison protocol. Meanwhile, there is little agreement to consider a 3D scene and we use GPSR as the research object to analyze the issues in the Section 2. So, we evaluate the performance of LSHR with the 2D-GPSR and 3D-GPSR, respectively. The last comparison protocol is another classic routing AODV.

4.1   Simulation Settings

We set the simulation scenario as shown in Fig. 3, which presents a grid layout with 10 intersections, size 2500m*2500m. The intersection ID from the bottom to the top, from the left to the right is in the order of 1 to 10. The road between the intersection 7 and the intersection 8, i.e., on which the vehicle 19 and the vehicle 22 are located at

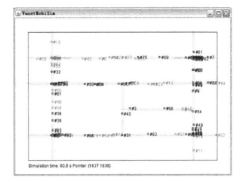

Fig. 3. Simulation scenario

this time, is the overpass. The height of the overpass is 10 meters. The transmission ranges of the same layer and the inter-layer are 250m and 200m, respectively. There are 60 vehicles randomly distributed on the roads and the vehicles velocity ranges from 10m/s to 20m/s. The simulation time is 150s and each simulation running contains 10 random source-destination pairs. A packet size is 512bytes. The values of α and β are both 0.5, it is because that we can get the best performance of the protocol LSHR when α and β are equal to 0.5. The map is generated by the VanetMobiSim. The mobility model in this scenario we used is Intelligent Driver Model (IDM). The mobile model makes the motion state of each vehicle in the scene such as velocity, acceleration by the surrounding vehicle restrictions to keep a safe distance. At the same time, this model also supports the simulation of lane change and overtaking behavior. We repeat the simulation process 20 times for a given scenario.

4.2 Simulation Results

As shown in Fig. 4, we compare the packet delivery ratio of four protocols. The average packet delivery ratio of LSHR is about 81.4%, while that of 2D-GPSR and 3D-GPSR are about 70.4% and 63.5%. Since LSHR can obtain the road connectivity

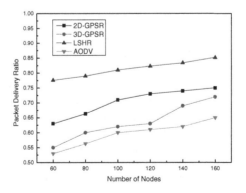

Fig. 4. Packet Delivery Ratio vs. Number of Nodes

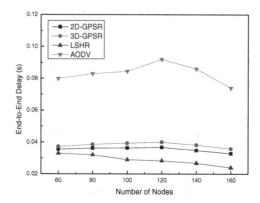

Fig. 5. End-to-End Delay vs. Number of Nodes

more accurately, it selects the sections that in good conditions to transmit packets, increasing the packet delivery ratio. However, GPSR uses perimeter mode when the greedy forwarding fails that will increase the probability of packet dropping. So, the packet delivery ratio of LSHR is higher than that of GPSR. Meanwhile, the packet delivery ratios of geographic routings are higher than that of AODV, it is because AODV uses the information about links to perform packet forwarding. Due to the highly dynamic topology changes, AODV suffers from routing breaks.

Fig. 5 illustrates the variation of end-to-end delay with the number of nodes. The end-to-end delay of 2D-GPSR ranges from 0.033s to 0.036s, while that of 3D-GPSR increases from 0.036s to 0.037s. However, we find that the end-to-end delay of LSHR is always lower than that of both 2D-GPSR and 3D-GPSR. For one reason, during the transmission of a packet, LSHR prior selects the neighbor who has the largest transmission range of two hops as the forwarding node. For the other reason, LSHR selects the sections that in good conditions to transmit packets, and the selected path not only has shortest possible transmission distance, but also has stable network connectivity. It increases the probability of successful transmission of a packet, and reduces retransmission. So, the end-to-end delay of LSHR is reduced. Moreover, the end-to-end delay of AODV is much higher than that of other three protocols. It is because AODV is not suitable for highly dynamic networks, and suffers from frequently routing breaks. It needs to often re-establish the route, and it will take a long time.

Fig. 6 shows the performance of the hop count. The hop count of LSHR is nearly 5.6. For 2D-GPSR, the hop count ranges from 6.6 to 7.4, while that of 3D-GPSR ranges from 6.8 to 7.9. The hop count of LSHR achieves 1.2 and 1.6 average gain compared with 2D-GPSR and 3D-GPSR, respectively. It is because LSHR selects the node that has the largest value of virtual distance as the next hop. When packets were transmitted to the same distance, LSHR needs fewer hop count than GPSR. Since AODV selects route hop by hop, while GPSR based protocols take greedy forwarding which always chooses the farthest neighbor in the current node's communication range. The hop count of AODV is higher than that of GPSR based scheme.

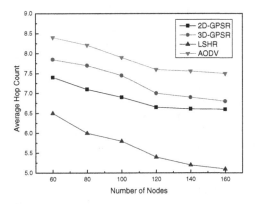

Fig. 6. Average Hop Count vs. Number of Nodes

5   Conclusion

In this paper, we propose a Link State aware Hierarchical Road routing (LSHR) which contains intersection judgment strategy and data transmission strategy on the 3D sections. Moreover, LSHR can represent the roads connectivity more accurately. To verify the performance of the protocol, we compare it with 2D-GPSR, 3D-GPSR, and AODV in a simple 3D scenario. The simulation results show that when the number of nodes changes, LSHR's packet delivery ratio is increased, and the end-to-end delay and the hop count is reduced. It indicates that in such a hierarchical 3D scenario, LSHR could reduce routing hop count and the end-to-end delay, while increasing packet delivery ratio and enhancing the overall performance of the routing.

Acknowledgment. This work was supported by the National Natural Science Foundation of China under Grant No. 61271176 and No. 61231008, the National Science and Technology Major Project under Grant No. 2011ZX03001-007-01 and No. 2013ZX03004007-003, the Fundamental Research Funds for the Central Universities, and the 111 Project (B08038).

References

1. Sun, X., Li, X.: Study of the feasibility of VANET and its routing protocols. In: Proceedings of the 4th International Conference on Wireless Communications, Networking and Mobile Computing (WiCOM 2008), DaLian, pp. 1–4 (October 2008)
2. Lin, Y., Chen, Y., Lee, S.: Routing protocols in vehicular ad hoc networks: a survey and future perspectives. J. Inf. Sci. Eng. 26(3), 913–932 (2010)
3. Park, V.D., Corson, M.S.: A highly adaptive distributed routing algorithm for mobile wireless networks. In: Proceedings of the 16th Annual Joint Conference of the IEEE Computer and Communications Societies (INFOCOM 1997), Kobe, pp. 1405–1413 (April 1997)

4. Perkins, C.E., Royer, E.M.: Ad-hoc on-demand distance vector routing. In: Proceedings of the 2nd IEEE Workshop on Mobile Computing Systems and Applications (WMCSA 1999), New Orleans, pp. 90–100 (February 1999)

5. Naumov, V., Baumann, R., Gross, T.: An evaluation of inter-vehicle ad hoc networks based on realistic vehicular traces. In: Proceedings of the ACM MobiHoc 2006 Conference, Florence, pp. 108–119 (May 2006)

6. Karp, B., Kung, H.T.: GPSR: greedy perimeter stateless routing for wireless networks. In: Proceedings of Mobile Computing and Networking, Boston, pp. 243–254 (August 2000)

7. Lee, K.C., Haerri, J., Lee, U., Gerla, M.: Enhanced perimeter routing for geographic forwarding protocols in urban vehicular scenarios. In: Proceedings of the IEEE 2007 Globecom Workshops, Washington, DC, pp. 1–10 (November 2007)

8. Naumov, V., Gross, T.R.: Connectivity-aware routing (CAR) in vehicular ad-hoc networks. In: Proceedings of the 26th IEEE International Conference on Computer Communications (INFOCOM 2007), Anchorage, pp. 1919–1927 (May 2007)

9. Nzouonta, J., Rajgure, N., Wang, G., Borcea, C.: VANET routing on city roads using real-time vehicular traffic information. IEEE Trans. Veh. Technol. 58(7), 3609–3626 (2009)

10. Saleet, H., Langar, R., Naik, K., Boutaba, R., Nayak, A., Goel, N.: Intersection-based geographical routing protocol for VANETs: a proposal and analysis. IEEE Trans. Veh. Technol. 60(9), 4560–4574 (2011)

11. Al-Rabayah, M., Malaney, R.: A new scalable hybrid routing protocol for VANETs. IEEE Trans. Veh. Technol. 61(6), 2625–2635 (2012)

12. Wu, T., Wang, Y., Lee, W.: Mixing greedy and predictive approaches to improve geographic routing for VANET. Wirel. Commun. and Mob. Comput. 12(4), 367–378 (2012)

13. Cha, S.H., Lee, K.W., Cho, H.S.: Grid-based predictive geographical routing for inter-vehicle communication in urban areas. Int. J. Distributed Sensor Networks 2012 (2012)

14. Xiang, Y., Liu, Z., Liu, R., Sun, W., Wang, W.: GeoSVR: A map-based stateless VANET routing. Ad Hoc Networks 11(7), 2125–2135 (2013)

15. Wang, S., Fan, C., Hsu, C.H., Sun, Q., Yang, F.: A vertical handoff method via self-selection decision tree for internet of vehicles. IEEE System Journal, 1–10 (article in press, March 2014)

16. Liu, C., Wu, J.: Efficient geometric routing in three dimensional ad hoc networks. In: Proceedings of the 28th IEEE International Conference on Computer Communications (INFOCOM 2009), Rio de Janeiro, pp. 2751–2755 (April 2009)

17. Abdallah, A.E., Fevens, T., Opatrny, J.: High delivery rate position-based routing algorithms for 3D ad hoc networks. Computer Communications 31(4), 807–817 (2008)

18. Su, H., Wang, Y., Fang, D.: An efficient geographic surface routing algorithm in 3D ad hoc networks. In: Proceedings of the 5th International Conference on Pervasive Computing and Applications (ICPCA 2010), Maribor, pp. 138–144 (December 2010)

19. Lochert, C., Hartenstein, H., Tian, J., Fussler, H., Hermann, D., Mauve, M.: A routing strategy for vehicular ad hoc networks in city environments. In: Proceedings of the IEEE Intelligent Vehicles Symposium (IVS 2003), Columbus, pp. 156–161 (June 2003)

20. Jerbi, M., Senouci, S.M., Ghamri-Doudane, Y., Rasheed, T.: Towards efficient geographic routing in urban vehicular networks. IEEE Trans. Veh. Technol. 58(9), 5048–5059 (2009)

21. The Network Simulator - ns-2, http://www.isi.edu/nsnam/ns/

Efficient Profile Routing for Electric Vehicles

René Schönfelder, Martin Leucker, and Sebastian Walther

Institute for Software Engineering and Programming Languages,
University of Lübeck, Germany
{schoenfr,leucker}@isp.uni-luebeck.de, sebastian.walther@web.de

Abstract. This paper introduces a powerful, efficient and generic framework for optimal routing of electric vehicles in the setting of flexible edge cost functions and arbitrary initial states.

More precisely, the introduced state-based routing problem is a consolidated model covering energy-efficiency and time-dependency. Given two vertices and an initial state the routing problem is to find optimal paths yielding minimal final states, while the profile routing problem is to find optimal paths for all initial states. A universal method for applying shortest path techniques to profile routing is developed. To show the genericity and efficiency of this approach it is instantiated for two typical shortest path algorithms, namely for A* and Contraction Hierarchies. Especially using the latter, a highly efficient solution for energy-efficient profile routing is obtained.

Keywords: State-based, energy-efficient, time-dependent, flexible routing, profile search, electric vehicles.

1 Introduction

Computing energy-efficient paths for electric vehicles is of particular interest because of their limited range and long recharge periods. Shortest path algorithms can be used to provide a user with optimal driving directions, but the question is how to adapt efficient algorithms to respect the requirements of an accurate model of the vehicle and its environment.

Dijkstra's algorithm [4] is probably the most known shortest path algorithm, with A* being a natural extension using a heuristic lower bound on shortest path distances [9]. There are numerous extensions to the simple shortest path problem, two prominent examples of interest here are time-dependent routing described e.g. by Delling and Wagner [3] and energy-efficient routing described by Sachenbacher et al. [11]. Both of these problems are based on the idea of having an initial state, i.e. the departure time or the initial battery charge, and functions mapping the current state to edge costs, but they do not explicitly consider finding paths for all initial states.

Many different shortest path techniques were developed reducing the query time in a trade for preprocessing time and space requirements, a thorough review classifying those techniques is given by Bast et al. [1]. A prominent example of such an algorithm is Contraction Hierarchies (CHs) introduced by Geisberger [7].

R.C.-H. Hsu and W. Shangguang (Eds.): IOV 2014, LNCS 8662, pp. 21–30, 2014.

The problem is, that those techniques cannot be directly applied to solve state-based routing problems or profile queries. While the concept of CHs was adapted to time-dependent routing by Batz et al. [2] and to energy-efficient routing by Eisner et al. [5], this was done using a clever trick, which is applicable in these two specific settings: One can use backwards reachability to label all relevant edges and then run a simple routing algorithm such as Dijkstra's on the labeled edges. However, no general solution is given by these two approaches.

The routing problem considering all initial states is called *profile query* or *profile search* and was mentioned in the context of time-dependent routing [3]. It is a particularly interesting problem, because the initial state is often not known precisely, maybe due to inexact measurements of an electric vehicle's battery, or because it is configurable – for instance by charging the battery a little more before starting. Another reason for searching profiles might be the dependency on other problems, for example when routing is done in the context of vehicle scheduling problems, where different initial states are of interest. We expect this to be of particular interest for intermodal mobility, i.e. the combination of different modes of transportation, with Masuch et al. describing a promising example [10].

This paper introduces a powerful framework by adapting efficient state-of-the-art shortest path algorithms to find profiles describing optimal solutions for all initial states in a generic network with flexible edge weight functions. It is organized as follows. Section 2 introduces the state-based routing problem and the theory of profiles. Energy-efficient routing is shown to be one instance of this model. The profile routing problem is introduced and a theorem connects the routing problem to profile queries. Section 3 covers the generic approach to adapting shortest path algorithms to the profile routing problem. This approach is presented for a typical algorithm, namely A^*. For the evaluation in Section 4, we also implemented Contraction Hierarchies and adapted them in the same way. Section 5 concludes with an interpretation and a discussion of open problems.

There are various approaches to introduce and combine different kinds of optimization criteria. The bicriteria search is probably the most known approach for finding Pareto-optimal paths, described for example by Skriver and Andersen [13]. It is similar to the profile search, because both problems use partially ordered values, but the state-based approach is more general and shortest path techniques can still be applied.

Another approach is to melt multiple criteria into a single criterion, for example by a linear function as described by Geisberger et al. [6]. The coefficients are meant to be dynamic, such that the precomputation of shortest path techniques must be valid for all coefficients. We consider a more general approach, where the coefficients of linear cost functions might be incorporated in the state, but probably losing the possibility of exploiting the special nature of linear functions – that is, handling flexible edge cost functions which are known to be linear is probably easier than handling non-linear functions.

2   Modelling

We define state-based routing and show energy-efficient routing to be an instance interesting for electric mobility. A formal definition of the profile routing problem is then based on defining routing profiles and profile preorders.

2.1   State-Based Routing

Instead of weighting edges with fixed and totally preordered costs, we use *monotone* $(s_1 \leq_S s_2 \to f(s_1) \leq_S f(s_2))$ and *extensive* $(s \leq_S f(s))$ state functions $S \to S$ on an arbitrary set of states S partially preordered by $\leq_S$ ensuring reflexivity and transitivity. If an edge's function $f : S \to S$ is undefined for some $s \in S$, written $f(s) = \bot$, it is not traversable for that state. We define $\bot \leq_S s$ for all states $s \in S$. Notice, that these functions are not necessarily commutative with respect to functional composition. We use the composition order $(f \circ g)(x) = g(f(x))$ to reflect how edges are concatenated to form a walk. A walk is a sequence of vertices, while a path is a cycle-free walk.

Definition 1. *The tuple* $(G, S, \leq_S, \mathcal{W})$ *is called a* state-based network, *if*

- *$G = (V, E)$ is a directed graph,*
- *$(S, \leq_S)$ is a partially preordered set of states,*
- *$\mathcal{W} : E \to (S \to S)$ is a weighting of monotone and extensive state functions.*

We extend $\mathcal{W}$ to walks by edge-wise functional composition $\mathcal{W}(\gamma) = \mathcal{W}(v_0, v_1) \circ \dots \circ \mathcal{W}(v_{k-1}, v_k)$ for all walks $\gamma = (v_0, \dots, v_k)$ of G. For the initial state $s \in S$, *we call $\mathcal{W}(\gamma)(s) \in S$ a* final state *with respect to walk γ and state s.*

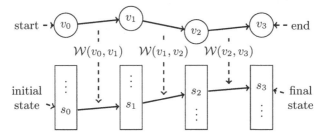

Fig. 1. A walk of four vertices (v_0, v_1, v_2, v_3) is shown as part of a state-based network. Every edge (v_i, v_{i+1}) is labeled with a state function $\mathcal{W}(v_i, v_{i+1}) : S \to S$. The state changes as we move along the walk: $s_{i+1} = \mathcal{W}(v_i, v_{i+1})(s_i) = \mathcal{W}(v_0, \dots, v_{i+1})(s_0)$.

The following definition of the state-based routing problem requires two things to notice: Both monotonicity and extensivity is preserved under composition and for all walks there is at least one path (without cycles) yielding equivalent or better final states.

Definition 2. *Given a state-based network $(G, S, \leq_S, \mathcal{W})$, a start $x \in V$, a destination $y \in V$ and an initial state $s \in S$, the* state-based routing problem *is to find corresponding paths π from x to y for each minimal final state $\mathcal{W}(\pi)(s)$ except for equivalence.*

2.2 Energy-Efficient Routing

Finding energy-efficient routes is interesting for reasons of saving fossil fuels and anthropogenic carbon dioxide, but it is also of particular interest for users of electric vehicles which have a short cruising range and slow recharge rates. We want to determine if the battery charge is sufficient to reach the destination and which route we should take in order to retain most of the battery's energy. There is an algorithmic approach to this problem adapting A^* using vertex potentials naturally given by their altitudes [11]. This example is used for evaluating our approach.

Energy-efficiency comprises various aspects, but we focus on battery constraints for electric vehicles. Given a battery capacity $K > 0$, we describe battery charges with $J \in [0, K]$. Energy is consumed as we travel along the edges of the road network, but by recuperation the battery status may also increase while losing potential energy. We consider recuperation from driving downhill, so we incorporate the altitude map in the form of potential energy levels. Battery constraints play a role whenever recuperation reaches the battery's capacity and whenever the battery is exhausted.

We can model this problem using a state-based network in the following way. The energy state is a pair of battery charges and potential energy levels $S = [0, K] \times \mathbb{R}$. The preorder $\leq_S$ is given by comparing the sums, i.e. $(J, h) \leq_S (J', h')$ if and only if $J + h \geq J' + h'$ (the sum of both values could also be used, but we want to keep the battery's state unbiased). Notice, that the comparison is inverted because of maximizing the remaining energy (instead of minimizing costs). Using potential energy as vertex potentials originates from [11]. We denote the potential energy by h_v for vertex $v \in V$.

We define a battery constraint $\mathcal{B}_{a,b}$ as a soft upper bound $b \in \mathbb{R}$ to represent fully charged batteries and a hard lower bound $a \in \mathbb{R}$ to represent empty batteries:

$$\mathcal{B}_{a,b}(x) = \begin{cases} b & \text{if } x > b, \\ x & \text{if } a \leq x \leq b, \text{and} \\ \bot & \text{if } x < a. \end{cases}$$

We can now define battery functions $S \to S$ from a vertex v to a vertex w with potentials h_v and h_w by

$$(J, h_v) \mapsto (\mathcal{B}_{a,b}(J - c - \Delta), h_w),$$

where $0 \leq a \leq b \leq K$ describe battery constraints, $c \in [0, K]$ describes the costs and $\Delta = h_w - h_v$ describes the difference of potentials. The function is undefined, if the second parameter is not equal to the potential h_v of v. Notice, that these functions are extensive, because $\mathcal{B}_{a,b}(J - c - \Delta) + h_w \leq J - c - \Delta + h_w = J - c + h_v \leq J + h_v$. The functions are also monotone due to the monotonicity of the battery constraint $\mathcal{B}_{a,b}$.

2.3   Profiles

While state-based routing problems ask for optimal paths given an initial state, we might also ask for a minimal set of optimal paths covering all initial states. This idea is adapted from time-dependent routing, where it is called a profile query [3]. The motivation behind profile routing is twofold: providing the user with more information and enabling bidirectional searches.

A profile shall be described by a set of walks sharing common end vertices, i.e. the same start and end vertex. At the same time, those profiles shall represent partially preordered values. The reason for that distinction is, that there may be values not representing any walks. This corresponds to the concept of heuristics in A* and in ALT using landmarks [8].

Two operations, namely concatenation $\circ$ and combination $\cup$, are essential. The former means to connect two consecutive profiles to form a new profile containing all pair-wise composed walks. The latter means to join both sets of walks to form a combined profile.

We define a partial preorder on profiles with the intended meaning that a profile may consist of more valuable walks than another profile. The imposed requirements are essential for proving the correctness of algorithms, but they also follow directly from the specification of state-based networks.

Definition 3. *Let $G = (V, E)$ be a graph, let $(M, \leq_M)$ be a partially preordered set of* profile values *and let $\circ, \cup : M \times M \to M$ be two operations on M, such that we can identify start and destination vertex of each profile $M \to V \times V$. We write $m_{x,y}$ in short to say that a profile m has start vertex x and destination vertex y. The partial preorder $\leq_M$ is called a* profile preorder *if all of the following conditions (for all resp. profiles) are satisfied:*

$$m_{x,y} \cup m'_{x,y} \leq_M m_{x,y} \tag{1}$$

$$m_{x,y}, \ m_{y,z} \leq_M m_{x,y} \circ m_{y,z} \tag{2}$$

$$m_{x,y} \leq_M m'_{x,y} \to m_{x,y} \cup m''_{x,y} \leq_M m'_{x,y} \cup m''_{x,y} \tag{3}$$

$$m_{y,z} \leq_M m_{y,z'} \to m_{x,y} \circ m_{y,z} \leq_M m_{x,y} \circ m_{y,z'} \tag{4}$$

$$m_{x,y} \leq_M m_{x',y} \to m_{x,y} \circ m_{y,z} \leq_M m_{x',y} \circ m_{y,z} \tag{5}$$

$$m_{x,y} \leq_M m_{x',y'}, m'_{x',y'} \to m_{x,y} \leq_M m_{x',y'} \cup m'_{x',y'} \tag{6}$$

When talking about profiles as sets of walks, the following definition helps understanding and handling profiles.

Definition 4. *Given a graph $G = (V, E)$, a* profile *$m_{x,y} \subseteq \text{walks}_{x,y}$ is a set of walks from x to y in G. The set of all profiles from x to y is denoted by $M_{x,y}$ (the power set of all walks from x to y) and the union of all profiles is denoted by $M := \bigcup_{x,y \in V} M_{x,y}$. Let $\leq_M$ be a profile preorder on M.*

- *The* combination *$m_{x,y} \cup m'_{x,y}$ of profiles $m_{x,y}, m'_{x,y}$ is the union of both sets.*
- *The* concatenation *$m_{x,y} \circ m_{y,z}$ of consecutive profiles $m_{x,y}, m_{y,z}$ is the set of element-wise concatenations $\{\gamma_1 \circ \gamma_2 \mid \gamma_1 \in m_{x,y}, \gamma_2 \in m_{y,z}\}$.*

- *A walk γ from x to y is said to* improve *(or is* not dominated by*) a profile $m_{x,y}$, if and only if $m_{x,y} \not\leq_M m_{x,y} \cup \{\gamma\}$. A profile $m'_{x,y}$ improves $m_{x,y}$ if there is a walk $\gamma \in m'_{x,y}$ improving $m_{x,y}$.*
- *A profile $m_{x,y}$ is said to be* complete*, if and only if there is no walk γ from x to y improving $m_{x,y}$.*
- *A profile $m_{x,y}$ is said to be* minimal*, if and only if all walks $\gamma \in m_{x,y}$ improve $m_{x,y} \setminus \{\gamma\}$.*
- *A method* reduce *finds minimal subprofiles $m'_{x,y}$ of $m_{x,y}$, i.e. $m'_{x,y} \equiv_M m_{x,y}$ and $m'_{x,y}$ is minimal (not uniquely determined).*

In order to connect state-based routing and profiles the following definition introduces an induced profile preorder. Intuitively, a profile m_{x_1,y_1} is better than another profile m_{x_2,y_2}, if the walks in m_{x_1,y_1} yield better final states than all walks in m_{x_2,y_2} for all comparable initial states. We define that comparison formally as follows.

Definition 5. *Let $(G, S, \leq_S, \mathcal{W})$ be a state-based network and let M be the set of profiles, then $\leq_M$ is an induced profile preorder on M, where $m_{x_1,y_1} \leq_M m_{x_2,y_2}$ if and only if for all $s_2 \in S$ we have*

$$\forall \gamma_2 \in m_{x_2,y_2} : \mathcal{W}(\gamma_2)(s_2) = \bot$$

or else there is an $s_1 \in S$ with $s_2 \leq_S s_1$ and

$$\forall \gamma_2 \in m_{x_2,y_2} \; \exists \gamma_1 \in m_{x_1,y_1} : \mathcal{W}(\gamma_1)(s_1) \leq_S \mathcal{W}(\gamma_2)(s_2).$$

One of the main theoretical results of the paper is this relation and the following theorem. It is essential for connecting profile searches with the problem of finding optimal paths. It states, that routing problems in a state-based network always have an induced profile problem, which can be solved efficiently as described in the next section. The proof makes use of the state preorder $\leq_S$ and of the monotonicity and extensivity of weight functions, but must thoroughly account for the partiality of the weight functions and the genericity of states.

Theorem 1. *The induced profile preorder $\leq_M$ of a state-based network is a preorder and satisfies all conditions from Definition 3.*

After introducing profiles, which are the sets of paths contributing to optimal final states, we define a routing problem looking for minimal and complete profiles as follows.

Definition 6. *Given a state-based network $(G, S, \leq_S, \mathcal{W})$ and two vertices $x, y \in V$ the* state-based profile routing problem *is to find a minimal and complete profile $m_{x,y}$ with respect to the induced profile preorder $\leq_M$.*

For the sake of completeness, a solution to a state-based routing problem can be determined from the minimal and complete profile:

Lemma 1. *Given a solution $\pi \in \text{paths}_{x,y}$ of a state-based routing problem for a given initial state $s \in S$ and a solution $m \subseteq \text{paths}_{x,y}$ of a profile routing problem, then there is a path $\pi' \in m$ such that $\mathcal{W}(\pi)(s)$ is equivalent to $\mathcal{W}(\pi')(s)$.*

3   Algorithms

Shortest path algorithms explore the graph step by step labeling vertices with intermediate results. Because usually multiple queries need to be processed on the same graph, preprocessing the graph while preserving shortest paths is the key to improve query times.

The general idea for applying shortest path techniques to the profile routing problem is to replace comparison of values, addition of values and labeling of predecessors by their respective definitions on profiles, i.e. comparison, concatenation and combination of profiles.

In our experiments we use unbalanced binary trees, in which elements are inserted to the right subtree, if it is greater than the subtree's root, and to the left subtree otherwise.

As an example, the A* variant for profile searches is presented in Algorithm 1. The variables $m_{x,v} \in M_{x,v}$ are profiles for reaching vertex v from start x (similar to the predecessor variables of the original algorithm). In A* we additionally use heuristic lower bound values on the remaining distance denoted by $h_{v,y}$. We require $m_{x,v} \circ h_{v,y} \leq_M m_{x,y}$ for all $m_{x,v} \leq_M m_{x,y}$ representing a lower bound. In the case of a simple Dijkstra's algorithm, the heuristic profile values would be left out in line 4 and 5.

Algorithm 1. A* for Profile Routing

---

1   $m_{x,v} \leftarrow \emptyset$ for all $v \in V$
2   $m_{x,x} \leftarrow \{(x)\}$
3   queue $q \leftarrow \{x\}$
4   **while** $m_{x,y} \not\leq_M m_{x,v} \circ h_{v,y}$ *for some* $v \in q$ **do**
5   $\quad$ remove v from q with minimal $m_{x,v} \circ h_{v,y}$
6   $\quad$ **for** *every successor* w *of* v **do**
7   $\quad\quad$ **if** $m_{x,v} \circ \{(v,w)\}$ *improves* $m_{x,w}$ **then**
8   $\quad\quad\quad$ $m_{x,w} \leftarrow \text{reduce}(m_{x,w} \cup (m_{x,v} \circ \{(v,w)\}))$
9   $\quad\quad\quad$ add w to q

10   **return** $m_{x,y}$

Notice, that because of building solutions step by step only paths (walks without cycles) are constructed by this algorithm. This is important for the following theorem, an essential result of this paper:

Theorem 2. *Algorithm 1 computes a minimal and complete profile $m_{x,y}$ from x to y consisting only of paths (no cycles).*

This theorem can be proven by establishing a loop invariant and showing its initialization, its maintenance and its termination. Let π^v denote the prefix of a path π up to a certain vertex $v \in V$ (including v) and let π_v denote the suffix of a path π starting from a certain vertex $v \in V$ (including v). The loop invariant is: For each path π improving a (non-complete) profile $m_{x,y}$ or $m_{x,u}$ with $m_{x,y} \not\leq_M m_{x,u}$ there is a vertex v in π also contained in q, such that $\pi^v \in m_{x,v}$ and π^w improves $m_{x,w}$ for all consecutive successors w of v on π.

4   Evaluation

We evaluate our approach within the prototypic framework of Green Navigation, a tool for providing energy-efficient driving directions and for computing the range of electric vehicles. The project was initialized at the Technische Universität München and is continued at the University of Lübeck.

The energy-efficient routing problem and its profile variant is implemented based on the geospatial data taken from the collaborative OpenStreetMap (OSM) project and the altitude values taken from the NASA Shuttle Radar Topographic Mission (SRTM). A section representing Bavaria, a state of Germany with an interesting relief, is used in the experiments. A full charge allows a cruising range of about 150 km. For 1000 test cases the start and destination are chosen randomly (uniformly distributed among vertices) within reach. The experiments were carried out by the Java SE Runtime Environment on a single core of an Intel(R) Core(TM) i7-3520M CPU at 2.90GHz provided with 4 GB RAM.

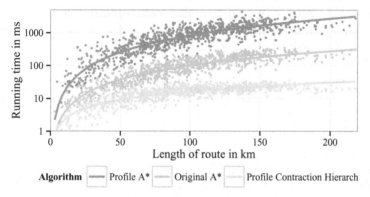

Fig. 2. The running times of different algorithms are shown on a logarithmic scale together with linear regressions of a logarithmic model

Figure 2 shows the running times for 1000 in-range test cases. The road graph contains 975,806 vertices and 1,885,037 edges. The original algorithm refers to the specialized A^* version for energy-efficient routing [11] yielding an average running time of 281 ms. Profile searches are more complex, the adapted A^* for profile searches is therefore slower with an average running time of 1106 ms.

Contraction Hierarchies were adapted in a similar way. The preprocessing of CHs takes approximately 15 minutes and contains 1,970,615 additional edges. The maximum profile size of the contracted graph is 6. Despite of solving a more difficult problem, the queries are much faster with an average running time of about 19 ms.

While A^* performs reasonably good for profile routing, the CHs drastically improve the query time. This makes profile queries highly efficient for the energy-efficient routing problem. We are convinced, that these results can be significantly improved by using specialized data structures and sophisticated heuristics for the node ordering of CHs.

5   Conclusions

The essential idea of many routing problems is to maintain accumulated costs while traversing the network. The state-based routing problem is a generalization of the simple shortest path problem comprising a set of states and edge weight functions. The problem of finding solutions for all initial states is the profile routing problem. One interesting instance is energy-efficiency, but in the future we will show, that also time-dependent routing and even some variants of stochastic routing are instances.

One important aspect when considering instances of state-based routing is the descriptive complexity of the profiles. In case of the simple shortest path problem, profiles would be trivial and operations would be constant in time and space. In case of energy-efficient routing, concatenation does not add complexity while combination increases the complexity linearly.

We distinguish between profile values and profile walks in order to be able to use heuristics. In A^* a lower bound on the remaining path costs is computed usually using the straight-line distance, which does not represent an actual path. In the same way we use a profile value not representing an actual set of walks.

Many practical shortest path techniques trade preprocessing time and space for faster queries. However, it is not in general possible to apply those techniques to other routing problems. This paper defines the profile routing problem as a general class of routing problems that has a similar nature to the simple shortest path problem, such that shortest path techniques can be applied relatively easy, yet solving a more complex problem.

As a proof of concept, we instantiated our profile routing with A^* and contraction hierarchies and have shown its efficiency in the context of energy-efficient routing. Using Contraction Hierarchies we have now, to the best of our knowledge, obtained the currently most efficient profile routing system for the energy-efficient routing problem.

In the future, we want to analyze other aspects for state-based routing such as dynamic data, intermodality, fleet routing, congestion and also combinations of these. Furthermore, we want to integrate certain stochastic aspects, as described in our previous work [12] which is based on Uludag et al. [14]. We will show, that this can be done by using distribution functions of random variables as states and convolutions as state functions, which results also in interesting numerical challenges.

Acknowledgements. This work was supported by Gesellschaft für Energie und Klimaschutz Schleswig-Holstein (EKSH) GmbH and by the Graduate School for Computing in Medicine and Life Sciences at the University of Lübeck. We would like to thank our colleagues Christofer Krüger and Anne Reichart for their contributions.

References

1. Bast, H., Delling, D., Goldberg, A., Müller-Hannemann, M., Pajor, T., Sanders, P., Wagner, D., Werneck, R.: Route planning in transportation networks. Tech. rep., Microsoft Research (2014)
2. Batz, G.V., Delling, D., Sanders, P., Vetter, C.: Time-dependent contraction hierarchies. In: Proceedings of the 11th Workshop on Algorithm Engineering and Experiments (ALENEX 2009), pp. 97–105 (2009)
3. Delling, D., Wagner, D.: Time-dependent route planning. In: Ahuja, R.K., Möhring, R.H., Zaroliagis, C.D. (eds.) Robust and Online Large-Scale Optimization. LNCS, vol. 5868, pp. 207–230. Springer, Heidelberg (2009)
4. Dijkstra, E.W.: A note on two problems in connexion with graphs. Numerische Mathematik 1, 269–271 (1959)
5. Eisner, J., Funke, S., Storandt, S.: Optimal route planning for electric vehicles in large networks. In: Twenty-Fifth AAAI Conference on Artificial Intelligence, vol. 25, pp. 1108–1113 (2011)
6. Geisberger, R., Kobitzsch, M., Sanders, P.: Route planning with flexible objective functions. In: ALENEX, pp. 124–137. SIAM (2010)
7. Geisberger, R., Sanders, P., Schultes, D., Delling, D.: Contraction hierarchies: Faster and simpler hierarchical routing in road networks. In: McGeoch, C.C. (ed.) WEA 2008. LNCS, vol. 5038, pp. 319–333. Springer, Heidelberg (2008)
8. Goldberg, A.V., Harrelson, C.: Computing the shortest path: A search meets graph theory. In: Proceedings of the Sixteenth Annual ACM-SIAM Symposium on Discrete Algorithms, pp. 156–165. Society for Industrial and Applied Mathematics (2005)
9. Hart, P., Nilsson, N., Raphael, B.: A formal basis for the heuristic determination of minimum cost paths. IEEE Transactions on Systems Science and Cybernetics 4(2), 100–107 (1968)
10. Masuch, N., Lützenberger, M., Keiser, J.: An Open Extensible Platform for Intermodal Mobility Assistance. Procedia Computer Science 19, 396–403 (2013), http://www.sciencedirect.com/science/article/pii/S1877050913006625, the 4th International Conference on Ambient Systems, Networks and Technologies (ANT 2013), the 3rd International Conference on Sustainable Energy Information Technology, SEIT 2013
11. Sachenbacher, M., Leucker, M., Artmeier, A., Haselmayr, J.: Efficient energyoptimal routing for electric vehicles. In: AAAI Publications, Twenty-Fifth AAAI Conference on Artificial Intelligence, vol. 25, pp. 1402–1407 (2011)
12. Schönfelder, R., Leucker, M.: Stochastisches Routen für Elektrofahrzeuge. Energieinformatik (2011)
13. Skriver, A., Andersen, K.: A label correcting approach for solving bicriterion shortest-path problems. Computers & Operations Research 27(6), 507–524 (2000), http://www.sciencedirect.com/science/article/pii/S0305054899000374
14. Uludag, S., Uludag, Z., Nahrstedt, K., Lui, K.S., Baker, F.: A laplace transform-based method to stochastic path finding. In: IEEE International Conference on Communications, ICC 2009, pp. 1–5 (2009)

A Message Efficient Intersection Control Algorithm Based on VANETs

Wei Ni and Weigang Wu

Department of Computer Science, Sun Yat-sen University,
Guangzhou 510006, China
wuweig@mail.sysu.edu.cn

Abstract. Intelligent traffic management via V2V communications in VANETs is attracting more and more attentions from researchers. In this paper, we design a new algorithm to realize intersection control based on coordination among vehicles via VANETs. We basically adopt the concept of mutual exclusion originally proposed for resource management in computer systems. Vehicles at an intersection compete for the privilege of passing by message exchange. The core of such an approach is the algorithms to coordinate vehicles and control the privilege granting. Following our previously proposed intersection control algorithm in [16], we design a new algorithm that can realize intersection control with much less communication cost. The advantage of our new algorithm is validated by simulations using ns-3.

Keywords: VENETs, distributed mutual excision, traffic control, message cost.

1   Introduction

Traffic control at intersections has been always a key issue in the research and development of ITS [1]. Traditional intelligent intersection control focuses on how to optimize the scheduling of green signal [2][3][4]. Recent efforts on traffic light control focus on adaptive and smart traffic light scheduling, mainly by making use of computational intelligence approaches [5]. Unfortunately, due to the dynamics of traffic load, traffic control systems are large complex nonlinear stochastic systems, so determining the optimal time of green light is very hard even if not impossible [5][6]. Moreover, the complexity of computational intelligence algorithms makes them usually not applicable to real-time traffic light control.

Intelligent intersection control has also be realized via advanced sensing and communication technologies [7] have enabled real-time traffic-response green light control [8][9]. The traffic light is scheduled under a certain control strategy according to real-time traffic data and predefined logic rules. Such approaches rely on the deployment of sensors at the road, which is usually very costly.

Recently, with the fast development of VANETs [10], intersection control via VANETs has become a noteworthy advance. In [11][12], a controller node is placed at the intersection to collect queue length information and compute proper cycle time of traffic signal via the Webster formula. In addition to queue length information,

R.C.-H. Hsu and W. Shangguang (Eds.): IOV 2014, LNCS 8662, pp. 31–41, 2014.

priority of vehicles is considered in [13], and traffic signal is scheduled with quality-of-service provisioning. The concept of "Virtual Traffic Light" is proposed in [14][15], where a vehicle among all the vehicles waiting at intersection is elected as virtual traffic light, which is responsible to schedule all the vehicles in the intersection by sending passing permission to them through V2V communication. These algorithms use VANET mainly as a source of traffic information, and vehicles are controlled in a centralized way.

In our previous work [16], we have proposed a totally different approach, where, vehicles at an intersection can negotiate about the time and order of passing, via V2V communications. More precisely, vehicles need to compete for the privilege of passing via message exchange. Vehicles with conflicting direction need to wait until the winners have passed. A vehicle sends request to others. Then others may reject its request, or permit its preemption. When permissions from others are collected, it can pass the intersection. Since no traffic light facility is necessary, and no optimization of green signal is calculated, such an intersection control approach has two major advantages. 1) It is simple and with low cost because no optimal problem is involved and no centralized facility is necessary. 2) It is efficient and flexible, because the vehicles are directly controlled with real-time information and resources are fully used.

However, how to realize the privilege control in VANET based intersection control is not trivial. The core part is the algorithm to coordinate vehicles. In our previous work [16], we model the problem of VANET based intersection control as the Vehicle Mutual Exclusion for Intersections (VMEI) problem, a variant of the classic mutual exclusion (MUTEX) problem [17], and propose an algorithm to solve the VMEI problem. For the simplicity of presentation, the algorithm proposed in [16] is called MEV, i.e. the mutual excision algorithm for VMEI.

In this paper, we extend our previous work by reducing communication cost. In MEV, each vehicle plays exactly the same role, and participants in the privilege negotiation simply for itself. On the other hand, usually vehicles at the same lane can pass the intersection together upon the grant of one privilege. That is, vehicles may follow its predecessor at the same lane. In such a situation, the following vehicles may not need to fully participant in the privilege competition. Such an observation motivates us to pursue a new design of intersection control algorithm with reduced coordination operations.

In our new design, vehicles are grouped virtually. One group of vehicles will be granted privilege of passing as a whole. Then, only the head vehicle in the group needs to participant in the competition with vehicles at other lanes. The key issue in such a design lies in how to determine and recognize the head of a group. By addressing this issue and others, we design a new algorithm to realize intersection control with low communication cost. The new algorithm is called R-MEV, i.e. MEV with reduced communication cost.

Simulations are conducted to evaluate the performance of our new algorithm. The MEV algorithm is also simulated for comparison purpose. The simulation results show that our new design can significantly reduce communication cost, which confirms the advantage of our work.

The rest of the paper is organized as follows. In Section 2, we describe the system model and preliminaries of our work. Especially, we briefly introduce the VMEI problem and related definitions. Our new algorithm is presented in Section 3, including message types and detailed operations. Simulation via ns-3 is reported in Section 4, with various performance metrics are measured and analyzed. Finally, Section 5 concludes the paper. Please notice that, the formal proof of our new algorithm is omitted to save space.

2   System Model and Preliminaries

Since this work is based on the algorithm in [16], we adopt the same system model and assumptions. The following definitions are originally proposed in [16].

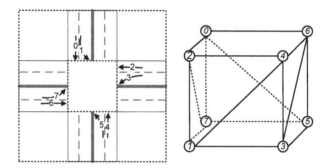

Fig. 1. The Illustration of an Intersection   **Fig. 2.** The Conflict Graph

2.1   System Model and Definitions

1) The Road and Intersection
As shown in Figure 1, we consider an individual intersection with four directions, i.e. north, south, east, and west. In each direction, there are two lanes, for going forward and turning left respectively. For the simplicity of presentation, the lanes are numbered from 0 to 7, and denoted by l_0 to l_7 respectively.

The small dashed rectangle represents the core area of the intersection. A vehicle in this area is called to be "passing" the intersection. The large dashed rectangle represents the queue area. A vehicle in this area is viewed as in the queue to pass the intersection.

Definition 1. *The concurrency/conflict relationship.* According to road rules, vehicles at some pair of lanes may pass the intersection simultaneously. We call such a pair of lanes "concurrent" lanes. On the other hand, if vehicles at two different lanes cannot pass simultaneously, we say they are "conflicting" lanes.

Accordingly, the vehicles at concurrent/conflicting lanes are called concurrent/ conflicting vehicles. The concurrency and conflict relationship is denoted by " $\approx$ " and " $\propto$ " respectively. For example, we have $l_0 \approx l_4$.

Definition 2. *The conflict graph of lanes, GL.* The relationship among eight lanes can be clearly represented by a conflict graph GL (Fig. 2). The vertices represent the lanes at an intersection and the edges (dashed and real lines) represent the "conflicts" between lanes. Two lanes without connecting edge are concurrent lanes. GL is exactly a cube with one diagonal line at each side face, as shown in Fig. 2.

Definition 3. *The strong concurrency relationship.* A pair of lanes represented by the two vertices of the same face in the conflict graph is called strong concurrent lanes. The strong concurrency relationship is denoted by "$\cong$". For example, we have $l_2 \cong l_3$.

2) The Vehicle and Wireless Network

Each vehicle has a unique id, which can be the license plate number. The vehicles are AVs driven by autopilots. Also, we assume there are sensors and other necessary devices for collision avoidance and navigation. A vehicle can get the knowledge of its lane number based on the digital map or other methods.

The vehicle is assumed to be able to detect the boundary of the queue/core area when it crosses the boundary. (This can be realized by deploying sensors at the boundary or making use of positioning system like GPS.)

Please notice that we do not assume a vehicle can recognize other vehicles queuing at the intersection by sensing because this is costly and not always feasible.

Wireless communication devices onboard enable vehicles to communicate with each other by sending and receiving messages. The *id* of the vehicle can be used as the address for communication.

We assume that the transmission range of the communicating device is larger than the length of the queue area. That is, the vehicles inside the queue area constitute a one-hop ad hoc network and the each vehicle pair can communicate directly. We assume the wireless channel is FIFO channel. Same as in [16], we do not consider message loss because our work focuses on coordination operations rather than communication protocols.

The procedure of a vehicle passing the intersection can be described by an automaton with three states.

- IDLE: A vehicle is in the idle state if it is out of the queue area. That is, when a vehicle has not entered queue area its state is set to be idle. Also, after a vehicle has passed the intersection (exited the core area), it also becomes "idle".
- WAITING: The state that a vehicle waits for the permit to pass the intersection (i.e. to enter the core area).
- PASSING: The state that a vehicle is moving to pass the intersection. A vehicle is in the passing sate during the time interval between receiving the permit and exiting the core area.

2.2   The VMEI Problem

In the classical mutual exclusion (MUTEX) problem, at most on process can be in the critical section at any moment. All the processes have to compete with each other to get the privilege to access the critical section. This is similar to the traffic control at the intersection, where the vehicles cannot pass the intersection at the same time and they have to compete to obtain the privilege to access the core area.

On the other hand, the traffic control problem is different from the MUTEX problem because, at the intersection, some lanes can be used simultaneously. That is, not all the vehicles are "competitors" of each other. For example, vehicles at the lane 0 and lane 4 can pass the intersection at the same time.

By considering the new requirements of traffic control, we define a variant of MUTEX, i.e. the problem of Vehicle Mutual Exclusion for Intersections (VMEI).

Definition 4. *The VMEI problem.* Each vehicle at the intersection requests to pass the intersection along the direction as it wants. Accordingly, vehicles queue up at the correct lane when they enter the queue area. To avoid collision or congestion, vehicles can pass the intersection simultaneously if and only if they are in concurrent lanes.

The VMEI problem can be formally defined by correctness properties, which can guarantee that all the vehicles can eventually pass the intersection successfully.

- Safety (*mutual exclusion*): At any moment, if there is more than one vehicle in the core area, they must be concurrent with each other.
- Liveness (*deadlock free*): If there are no vehicles in the core area, some vehicle must be able to enter the core area in a finite time.
- Fairness (*starvation free*): Each vehicle must be able to pass the intersection after a finite number of vehicles do so.

2.3   The MEV Algorithm

To help understanding our new algorithm, we briefly introduce the basic idea of the MEV algorithm in [16]. Please refer to the original paper for details.

Vehicles have different priorities to pass, which is generally determined by the arrival time. A vehicle broadcasts request message and the receivers with higher priority will prevent the sender via response message. If no receivers prevent the sender, it can pass the intersection. We have also designed mechanism to achieve high efficiency by allowing vehicles at concurrent lanes pass simultaneously.

3   The Proposed Algorithm, R-MEV

3.1   Notations and Message Types

Like in MEV, a vehicle undergoes three phases to pass the intersection and correspondingly, there are three states: IDLE, WAITING and PASSING. Each vehicle i maintains the following notations or data structures to execute the distributed algorithm.

- HL_i: High list, the list of vehicles that have a higher priority than i to pass the intersection. The priority is generally, but not always, determined by the arrival time of vehicles.
- LL_i: Low list, the list of vehicles that have a lower priority than i to pass the intersection.

- *CntPmp*: This is a counter to record the number of preemptions occurred at i. A preemption means a vehicle allow another with low priority to pass first at some special situation.

Different from MEV, in R-MEV, vehicles play different roles, which is different from MEV. Basically, there are three roles: HEAD, INT, TAIL.

- *HEAD*: The first vehicle of a group, the vehicle that sends REJECT message and FOLLOW message when its group is waiting for passing. If there are no other vehicles in its group, it will also send RELEASE message when it has passed the intersection.
- *TAIL*: The last vehicle of a group, the vehicle that sends REJECT message when its group is passing intersection and RELEASE message when its group has several vehicles.
- *INT*: Vehicles between HEAD and TAIL.

3.2   Algorithm Operations

The pseudo code of the R-MEV is listed below. It basically follows the operations in MEV. The major new operations designed for R-MEV are presented with border.

1)   Operations of Request

When vehicle i enters the queue area, it switches from IDLE to WAITING and broadcasts a request message REQUEST(i, lid_i). Its default role is tail. Then, i waits for REJECT messages from others after setting a timeout *tmt*.

Base operations inherited from MEV. When a vehicle j, in the WAITING or PASSING state, receives the request message from i, a vehicle at some conflicting lane, if some vehicle k in j's high list is strong concurrent with i, j will give way to i, i.e. it puts i in its high list and will not send REJECT; otherwise, j puts i in its low list and sends REJECT(j, i) to i. A counter *CntPmp* is used to record how many times a vehicle has been preempted. If the value reaches the threshold *TH*, the vehicle will not give way anymore. The preemption may also cause deadlock if two strong concurrent or conflict vehicles take different actions on the preemption of another vehicle. To avoid such problem, mechanism are designed to coordinate the grant of preemption. When some REJECT(j, k) is received and i has put k to its high list due to preemption, i will cancel the preemption of k,   if a) j is a conflicting vehicle and not in *HLi*,   b) j is strongly concurrent with i. (if j is in PASSING and it has switched to PASSING by a FOLLOW(x, *flt*) message and j is not the TAIL in *flt*, or j is in WAITING and j is not the HEAD, j will not send the REJECT message.) On receiving the REJECT(j, i) message from j, i puts j in its high list HL_i.

New operations specifically for R-MEV. In operations above, all vehicles at conflicting lanes with response to a REQUEST message, which is in fact not necessary. To avoid such a problem, we divide vehicles into groups and let only the head vehicle of a group handle competitions for privilege of passing the intersection. Other vehicles just need to follow the head and do not need to reply requests. Then, the new algorithm for handling REQUEST is changed as follows.

CoBegin //for a vehicle i
On entering the monitoring area:
   st_i =WAITING; $\boxed{\textbf{role = TAIL;}}$
   broadcast REQUEST(i, lid_i);
   wait for REJECT from others;
On Receiving REQUEST(j, lid) from j
if$((st_i$ = WAITING|PASSING) and $(lid_i = lid_j \vee lid_i \propto lid_j))$\{

  $\boxed{\textbf{if}(lid_i = lid_j \wedge role = TAIL\ )\{}$

   $\boxed{\textbf{if}(\exists k, k \in HL_i \ \wedge \ lid_i = lid_k)}$

     $\boxed{\textbf{role = INT;}}$
    $\boxed{\textbf{else role = HEAD}}$

  $\boxed{\ \}}$

  if$((\exists k, k \in HL_i \wedge j \cong k)$ and $CntPmp<TH)\{$
   add j to HL_i;
   $CntPmp$ ++;
  \}**else**\{
   add j to LL_i;
   $\boxed{\textbf{if(role = HEAD} \wedge \textbf{\ } st_i \textbf{=WAITING) or}}$
    $\boxed{\textbf{(role = TAIL} \wedge \textbf{\ } st_i \textbf{=PASSING)}}$
   $\boxed{\text{broadcast REJECT}(i, j);}$
  \}
\}
On Receiving REJECT(j, k) from j
if$(st_i$=WAITING)\{
  if $(i=k)$ add j to HL_i;
  if$(i \neq k$ and$(k \in HL_i$ with preemption$)$ and

    $(((\ j \propto i \wedge \ j \notin HL_i)\vee \ j \cong i)\ ))\{$

   $\boxed{\text{delete } k \text{ from } HL_i;}$
   $\boxed{\text{broadcast REJECT}(i, k);}$
  \}
\}
On Receiving PERMIT(j) or timeout tmt occurs (no JECECTs received)
delete j from HL_i;
if$(HL_i$ is empty)\{
  st_i=PASSING;
  construct the follow list flt;
  $(\ flt = \{v \mid lid_v = lid_i \wedge v \in LL_i \wedge flt's\ length < NF\}\ )$
  broadcast FOLLOW(flt);
\}
move and pass the core area;
On Receiving FOLLOW(j, flt) from j
if$(i \in flt\ )\{$
  st_i =PASSING;
  move and pass the core area;
\}**else if** $(i \propto j)$ \{
  delete j from HL_i;
  delete vehicles in flt from HL_i or LL_i;
  add the last one in flt to HL_i;
\}
On exiting the intersection
if(the passing is triggered by a FOLLOW(x, flt) and i is the last in flt)
  broadcast PERMIT(i);
 CoEnd

When vehicles i and j are in the same or conflicting lanes and j is the TAIL, if there exists vehicle k which is in the same lanes as j and k is in j's high list, then j's role turns into INT; otherwise, j's role turns into HEAD. Once roles of vehicles have been identified, our work for reducing reject messages becomes possible and easier. Then if vehicle k in j's high list has a strong concurrency relationship with i, j puts i in its high list; otherwise, j puts i in its low list. And especially when j is the HEAD of waiting group or the TAIL of passing group, j will send REJECT(j, i) to i.

The new operation divides vehicles into groups, and different vehicles deal with received messages with different responses on the basis of their states and roles. That means when a waiting HEAD vehicle receives the request message from a coming vehicle, it will performance differently from an INT vehicle or a TAIL vehicle. A vehicle can only possess a role at one time and the role can change from time to time as position changes. On the other hand, the correctness of roles' changes ensures the passing of vehicles. To be specific, once TAIL vehicles are in the lanes as coming vehicles, changes of roles occur.

2) Operations of Passing

If no REJECT messages are received before the timeout tmt occurs, or the high list becomes empty upon receiving PERMIT messages, i's role should be HEAD, and then i switches to be PASSING and starts to pass the core area. If there are other waiting vehicles in the same group (they must be in low list), i will add these vehicle to the follow list flt and broadcasts FOLLOW(i, flt).

To avoid starvation, the length of flt should be bounded by a threshold NF. The value of NF can be a static value determined based on the historic data, or a value adaptive to the real time traffic volume. In addition, NF means the maximal length of group.

On receiving a FOLLOW(i, flt) message at j, if j is included in flt, j will empty its high list, switch to PASSING and starts to pass the core area of the intersection.

Please notice that, in this case, j will not further construct and send FOLLOW message. Such a design is to avoid starvation at other lanes.

If the receiver of FOLLOW(i, flt), say w, is conflicting with i, w deletes i and vehicles in flt from its high list or low list, and then puts the last vehicle in flt into its high list.

3) Operations of Release

After i passes the core area (crosses the exit boundary), i will empty its low list. It will also broadcast the PERMIT(i) message UNLESS its passing has been triggered by a FOLLOW(x, flt) message and i is not the last in the flt.

On receiving the PERMIT(i) message at j, if i is in the high list of j, j deletes i from its high list. If the high list becomes empty, it will switch to PASSING.

4   Performance Evaluation

Simulations are conducted using ns-3. Besides R-MEV, we also simulated two other algorithms for comparison. MEV is the most similar one, and C-MEV is the centralized version of MEV proposed in [16]. We basically follow the system settings in [16]. The area of intersection is 100m×100m. IEEE 802.11 is adopted as the communication protocol, with a transmission range of 200m. The time for a vehicle to pass the intersection is set to be 3s (for going straight), and 4s (for turning left).

Same as in [16], we use four metrics to measure the performance of intersection control algorithms. Basically, R-MEV achieves similar waiting time, queue length, and system throughput as MEV, while R-MEV costs much fewer messages than MEV does. Due to page limit, we report here only the results of message cost and results of other metrics are omitted.

As shown in Fig. 3, the message costs of the three intersection algorithms differ a lot. With the centralized algorithm, a vehicle needs roughly three messages per passing. On the other hand, the distributed algorithms cost more messages. Such message costs are reasonable and the difference is expected. In the centralized algorithm, one vehicle needs communicate with only the central node and at most three messages (one REQUEST, one PERMIT and one RELEASE) are sent for each pass of a vehicle. However, the distributed algorithm needs to send more messages, especially REJECT messages, due to the lack of a centralized control node.

Compared with MEV, R-MEV can significantly reduce message cost, in various traffic cases. In MEV, upon receiving a REQUEST message, almost all waiting vehicles in conflicting lanes will send REJECT messages. In R-MEV, with the new design, only head vehicles need to send REJECT. Since REJECT messages account for a large part of message cost, R-MEV can save a lot of communication. Fig. 3 shows that the reduction can be as much as 50%. This definitely confirms our objective to design R-MEV is well achieved.

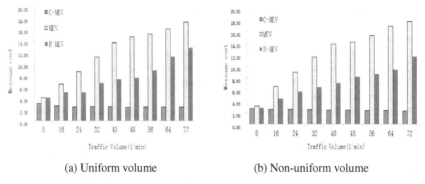

(a) Uniform volume   (b) Non-uniform volume

Fig. 3. Message cost of intersection control algorithms

5   Conclusions

In this paper, we propose a new algorithm for intersection control via V2V communications. Vehicles at an intersection obtain the privilege of passing by competing with other vehicles. Such an approach is more efficient than traditional ones based on traffic light signals. Compared with our previous work in [16], this paper focuses on reducing communication cost. By letting only the head vehicle in a group handle reply passing requests, the new algorithm can save message cost as much as 50%.

Acknowledgments. This research is partially supported by National Natural Science Foundation of China (No. 61379157), Guangdong Natural Science Foundation (No. S2012010010670), and Pearl River Nova Program of Guangzhou (No. 2011J2200088).

References

1. Day, I.: Scoot-split, cycle and offset optimization technique. TRB committee AHB25 adaptive traffic control (1998)
2. Bingham, E.: Reinforcement learning in neurofuzzy traffic signal control. Eur. J. Operat. Res. 131, 232–241 (2001)
3. Chen, X., Shi, Z.: Real-coded genetic algorithm for signal timings optimization of a signal intersection. In: Proceedings of International Conference on Machine Learning and Cybernetics, vol. 3, pp. 1245–1248. IEEE Press, Beijing (2002)
4. Gokulan, B.P., Srinivasan, D.: Distributed geometric fuzzy multiagent urban traffic signal control. In: 13th International IEEE Conference on Intelligent Transportation Systems, vol. 11(3), pp. 714–727. IEEE Press, Madeira Island (2010)
5. Zhao, D., Dai, Y., Zhang, Z.: Computational Intelligence in Urban Traffic Signal Control: A Survey. IEEE Transactions on Systems, Man, and Cybernetics, Part C: Applications and Reviews 42(4), 485–494 (2012)
6. Zhao, L., Peng, X., Li, L., Li, Z.: A fast signal timing algorithm for individual oversaturated intersections. In: 14th International IEEE Conference on Intelligent Transportation Systems, vol. 12(1), pp. 280–283. IEEE Press, Washington (2011)
7. Tubaishat, M., Zhuang, P., Qi, Q., Shang, Y.: Wireless sensor networks in intelligent transportation systems. Wirel. Commun. Mob. Comput. 9, 287–302 (2009)
8. Lee, J., Park, B.: Development and Evaluation of a Cooperative Vehicle Intersection Control Algorithm Under the Connected Vehicles Environment. In: 15th International IEEE Conference on Intelligent Transportation Systems, vol. 13(1), pp. 81–90. IEEE Press, Anchorage (2012)
9. Zhou, B., Cao, J., Zeng, X., Wu, H.: Adaptive Traffic Light Control in Wireless Sensor Network-Based Intelligent Transportation System. In: IEEE 72nd Vehi. Tech. Conf. Fall, pp. 1–5. IEEE Press, Ottawa (2010)
10. Hartenstein, H., Laberteaux, K.P.: A tutorial survey on vehicular ad hoc networks. IEEE Comm. Mag. 46(6), 164–171 (2008)
11. Gradinescu, V., Gorgorin, C., Diaconescu, R., et al.: Adaptive traffic lights using car-to-car communication. In: IEEE 65th Vehi. Tech. Conf. Spring, pp. 21–25. IEEE Press, Dublin (2007)
12. Prashanth, L.A., Bhatnagar, S.: Reinforcement learning with function approximation for traffic signal control. In: 14th International IEEE Conference on Intelligent Transportation Systems, vol. 12(2), pp. 412–421. IEEE Press, Madeira Island (2011)
13. Wunderlich, R., Liu, C., Elhanany, I., et al.: A novel signal-scheduling algorithm with quality-of-service provisioning for an isolated intersection. In: 13th International IEEE Conference on Intelligent Transportation Systems, vol. 9(3), pp. 536–547. IEEE Press, Beijing (2008)

14. Ferreira, M., Fernandes, R., Conceicao, H., et al.: Self-organized traffic control. In: Proceedings of the Seventh ACM International Workshop on VehiculAr InterNETworking, pp. 85–90. ACM Press, New York (2010)
15. Ferreira, M., d'Orey, P.M.: On the impact of virtual traffic lights on carbon emissions mitigation. In: 15th International IEEE Conference on Intelligent Transportation Systems, vol. 13(1), pp. 284–295. IEEE Press, Anchorage (2012)
16. Wu, W.G., Zhang, J.B., Luo, A.X., Cao, J.N.: Distributed Mutual Exclusion Algorithms for Intersection Traffic Control. IEEE Transactions on Parallel and Distributed Systems. Preprint, online version (2014)
17. Lamport, L.: A Fast Mutual Exclusion Algorithm. ACM Trans. Comput. Syst. 5(1), 1–11 (1987)

A Histogram-Based Model for Road Traffic Characterization in VANET

Hesham El-Sayed[1], Liren Zhang[1], Yasser Hawas[2], and Hadeel El Kassabi[1]

[1] College of Information Technology, United Arab Emirates University, Al-Ain, UAE
{helsayed,lzhang,HtalaaT}@uaeu.ac.ae
[2] College of Engineering, United Arab Emirates University, Al-Ain, UAE
y.hawas@uaeu.ac.ae

Abstract. This paper presents a new route guidance algorithm and a compact road traffic model that can be easily obtained and transmitted in real-time by individual vehicles while they are travelling on streets or queuing in road cross junctions. The proposed algorithm uses histograms as the network traffic model that captures the arrival rate distribution in VANET. In addition, the paper presents an analysis method that works directly with the histogram model to obtain the queue occupancy distribution at cross-junctions or traffic signals using a finite queue model. A microscopic simulation model is utilized to assess the effectiveness of the traffic model in detecting traffic congestion and directing vehicles to choose better paths. Results show that the proposed road traffic model provides a good prediction of road traffic status, and can be used in conjunction with any standard shortest path algorithms to provide an efficient mechanism for selecting fastest road path.

Keywords: VANET, Traffic Modeling, Histograms, Route Guidance.

1 Introduction

Vehicular ad hoc networks (VANETs) are expected to support a large spectrum of distributed applications such as route guidance and navigation, traffic alert dissemination, context-aware advertisement and file sharing. All these applications require an efficient mechanism for selecting shortest road path.

In general, the travel time changes dynamically as the result of interactions between demand, capacity, weather conditions, accidents, work zones and traffic composition [1]. Therefore, the correctness of the fastest or best route plan depends heavily upon the correctness of the cost model of the route. Typical route cost model based on static information cannot entirely be appropriate for determining fastest route, because real-time conditions of routes such as the severity of congestion and the ratio of traffic density on the different streets play an important role. Provision of traffic information to motorists has the potential to influence traffic patterns and thereby reduce congestion and improve network efficiency while also benefiting users in less tangible ways by decreasing uncertainty and reducing stress. Consequently, the

R.C.-H. Hsu and W. Shangguang (Eds.): IOV 2014, LNCS 8662, pp. 42–55, 2014.

provision of traffic information to motorists via roadside or in-vehicle systems has become a priority for many road authorities. Moreover, systems for gathering and disseminating traffic data are required to provide drivers with effective fastest route services reflecting on the real-time traffic conditions.

In general, the best predictions of road traffic status can be made using road traffic traces. However, considering the large number of nodes participating in VANET and their high mobility, collecting full traces is not always possible. In addition, the analysis of these road traffic traces may need the support of huge amount of computing power and memories that is impossible in vehicle-to-vehicle network environment. Therefore, there is a pressing need for an efficient mechanism for modeling the real-time traffic information and disseminate it through the transport network to satisfy the throughput and delay requirements of such applications.

Many researches have been proposed in literature to gather traffic information and disseminate it to users, so they can make better-informed decisions regarding their route and improve the quality of driving experience [2-4]. Much work has also been done on the Data Harvesting and Information Dissemination schemes needed to support these types of applications [5]. The problem of efficient data delivery in VANETs has also been studied in literature [6-7]. Furthermore, the design of routing protocols and the computation of shortest or best paths in vehicular networks have been the subject of extensive research for many years. Lee et al. [8] and Lin [9] provided a comprehensive survey of VANET routing protocols and summarized their main characteristics.

In this paper, we do not attempt to propose yet another system for traffic management or another variation of the shortest path problem. We propose a compact road traffic model that can be easily obtained and transmitted in real-time by individual vehicles while they are travelling on streets or queuing in road cross-junctions. The proposed model uses histograms as the network traffic model that captures the arrival rate distribution in VANET. We also present an analysis method that works directly with the histogram models and obtains the queue occupancy distribution at cross-junctions or traffic signals using a finite queue model. With this queue occupancy distribution, we obtain the waiting time delay and congestion probabilities. Furthermore, we have developed a simulation model to study the effectiveness of the traffic model in detecting traffic congestion and directing vehicles to choose better paths. The results showed that the proposed road traffic model provides a good prediction of road traffic status, and can be used in conjunction with of one of the existing shortest path algorithms to provide an efficient mechanism for selecting shortest road path

This paper is structured as follows. Section 2 describes the proposed histogram traffic model. Section 3 describes the queuing models for vehicular road traffic in inter-connected streets. Analysis of the proposed model is presented in Section 4. Section 5 discusses the usage of the proposed models for selecting the best road path. Performance evaluation and simulation results are discussed in Section 6. Conclusion and future work are presented in section 7.

2   Histogram Traffic Model

In this paper, we use traffic histograms to model the road traffic (number of vehicles) on the street during a pre-established equal time periods, called the Observation period O (e.g. 10 minutes per observation period during rush hour on city urban street). During each observation period, we count number of cars entering the road over equal time intervals, called Sampling periods T (e.g. 15 seconds per sampling period during rush hour on city urban street). Therefore, the number of sampling periods N within an observation period is equal to O/T.

Let $V(t)$ be a discrete random variable representing the number of vehicles entering the street during the tth sampling period. Hence, the total number of vehicles entering the street during an observation period $V(t) | t \in \{1, 2, ..., N\}$ can be described as a discrete random process with a state space, denoted as I, which is a set of integers between 0 and the maximum number K of vehicles held in the street, that is, $I = \{0, 1, ..., K\}$.

As the statistical variable $V(t)$ can, in general, varies over a big range of values [0, K]. We divide this range into a limited number of equal width classes and compute the grouped probability distribution (gpd) over each class. For example, Table 1 shows the statistics of number of vehicles on road that has been analyzed using a sampling period of T = 10 seconds by a vehicle to-vehicle network over a total observation period of N = 1000 sampling windows. The range of the number of vehicles during the observation period is [0, 60], which is divided into Nc = 6 classes, with a class length Lc = 10 vehicles, as shown in Table 1. Hence, the statistical histogram based on the observations is given in a grouped probability distribution format as shown in Figure 1.

Table 1. No. of vehicles in road during the observation period

Class number I	Class Interval $\{C_i^-, C_i^+\}$	Midpoint C_i	Probability $P(C_i)$
0	{0, 10}	5	0.2
1	{10,20}	15	0.4
2	{20,30}	25	0.15
3	{30,40}	35	0.15
4	{40,50}	45	0.1
5	{50,60}	55	0

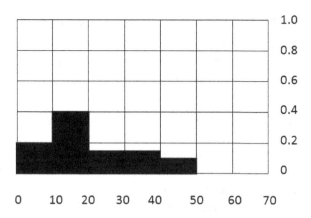

Fig. 1. Statistical histogram of the workload shown in Table 1

In order to ensure that the statistical model of histogram is suitable for practical use, the histogram used in the following analysis is defined as follows. All sampling periods has equal width T. The number of vehicles in a sampling period is stationary and independent from each other. Let C_i^-, C_i^+ and C_i be the lower limit, the upper limit and the middle point of number of vehicles in class i, respectively. The probability p (C_i) is defined as follows:

$$P\ (C_i) = \frac{\text{No. of windows with an observation of} \left(C_i^- \le C_t \le C_i^+ \right)}{\text{Total No. of windows}} \tag{1}$$

In general, a statistical histogram, denoted as C, is presented by two attributes: (1) the set of class midpoints or mean values C_i averaged by $\{C_i^-, C_i^+\}$, denoted as $\overline{C}$ and (2) the set of class probabilities P, also referred as probability mass function (pmf). Hence, a statistical histogram is defined as

$$C = \left(\overline{C}, P \right) = \begin{cases} \overline{C} = [C_i : i = 0, 1, ..., N_c - 1] \\ P = [p(C_i) : i = 0, 1, ..., N_c - 1] \end{cases} \tag{2}$$

Where N_c is the number of classes

In fact, the histogram defined in this paper is a form of a bar graph representation of a grouped probability distribution (GPD), which is a table representing the number of vehicles in an observation window basis against their corresponding probabilities (or frequencies). This is important, since $C = (\overline{C}, P)$ can be easily obtained by vehicles moving on the road and these statistical information are able to be shared by all other vehicles through an ad hoc based vehicle-to-vehicle network. Here, we note that the arrival process of vehicles into the queuing system is stationary at a uniform rate in a sampling period, and the number of vehicles $V(t) \mid t \in \{1, 2, ..., N\}$ arriving in an observation period is independent and has a distribution modeled by a histogram $C = (\overline{C}, P)$. Therefore, $V(t) \mid t \in \{1, 2, ..., N\}$ is a stochastic process used to characterize variable number of vehicles input into the queue under investigation, which is not a function of time, but it is a discrete statistics of distribution, called histogram, for modeling the number of vehicles on observation window basis.

3   Queuing Models for Vehicular Road Traffic

Figure 2 shows two adjacent road cross-junctions, which are inter-connected by a two-way street of length W. Let $d(t) \mid t \in \{1, 2, ..., N\}$ be the required minimum distance for road safety between consecutive vehicles on the street during a sampling period $t \in \{1, 2, ..., N\}$. According to the 2-second rule for road safety, $d(t) \mid t \in \{1, 2, ..., N\}$ is given by $d(t) = \frac{r(t) \times 1000 \times 2}{3600}$ meter, where $r(t)$ is the vehicle speed during a sampling period t in terms of kilometer per hour. Furthermore, vehicles from the street move into the road cross-junction at a rate of $D(t) = \frac{r(t)}{d(t) + \overline{V}} \times \frac{1000}{3600}$ vehicles per second, where $\overline{V}$ is the average length of vehicle in meters. Hence, the maximum number of vehicles that can be held by the street during a sampling period is given by $K(t) = \frac{W}{d(t) + \overline{V}}$ vehicles, where W is the road length between adjacent road junctions.

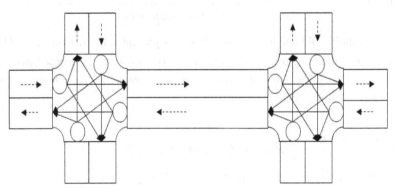

Fig. 2. Streets inter-connected by road junctions

The vehicles entering to the inter-section from the street are controlled by red and green traffic signals (in this case, yellow signal is not taken into account). This process is modeled as a Markov modulated Bernoulli process (MMBP) consisting of ON state and OFF state as shown in Figure 3. The ON state represents the Green signal and the OFF state represents the Red signal. The transition rate from ON state to OFF state is α and the transition rate from OFF state to ON state is β. If vehicles from different directions are equally accessing to the road cross junction, in this case,

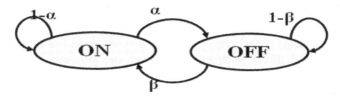

Fig. 3. Markov modulated Bernoulli process model

the transition rate α should to be equal to β. Then vehicles from one direction moves into the inter-section at a rate of D(t)/2 vehicle units per second.

Hence, the process of vehicles entering the inter-section from street is called as MMBP modulated deterministic process. The vehicles traveling on the street and moving to the cross junctions is modeled as finite buffer HD/D/1/K queue as shown in Figure 4. Where HD stands for the Histogram Deterministic Inter-arrival Distribution, which represents vehicle flow in the queue, D represents the deterministic process of vehicles moving from the street into the cross junction at a rate of D(t)/2 and K(t) represents the maximum number of vehicles can be held by the street during a sampling period $t \in \{1, 2, ..., N\}$.

Fig. 4. HD/D/1/K queuing model

Likewise, a road junction with round-about of radius x is modeled as a slotted ring. A road junction with fly-over can be modelled as free-access buffer without traffic control mechanism. Therefore, a roadway in urban city can be modelled as a tandem chain of HD/D/1/K queues, as shown in Figure 5.

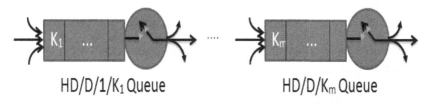

Fig. 5. Urban Roadway Model – A Tandem Queuing Chain

4   Analysis of HD/D/1/K Queuing Chain System

The following analysis of statistics of real-time road traffic histogram is based on the following procedures. Let $v(t)| t \in \{1, 2, ..., N\}$ represents the vehicle input flow in the tth sampling period, i.e. the number of vehicles entering the street during the tth sampling period. Let $\tau[t]$ is the number of vehicles that have moved out from the queue during the same period. The vehicle input flow is supplied through buffer of finite capacity. The buffer accumulates pending vehicles $Q[t]$ that cannot move from the street and enter the road inter-section during the observation period. The system is assumed to be in stationary if the pending traffic convergences to a finite value. The server discipline is first come first served. Let $Q[t]$ represents the queue length in sampling period $t \in \{1,2,...,N\}$. Then $Q[t]$ can be expressed as follows:

$$Q[t] = \int_0^t \phi_0^K(V(t) - \tau[t]) \, dt \tag{3}$$

Where, Operator ϕ limits the buffer lengths so that they cannot be either underflow or overflow based on the vehicle speed $\tau[t]$ and the road safety distance d(t) in the tth sampling period. The operator ϕ is defined as

$$\phi_a^b(x) = \begin{cases} 0, & \text{for } x < a \\ x - a & \text{for } a \le x < b + a \\ b & \text{for } x \ge b + a \end{cases} \tag{4}$$

Expression (3) can be rewritten using a recurrence equation (known as Lindley's equation [11]) assuming a discrete time space T=t0, t1, t2, etc. Where tn = n * T is a multiple of the sampling period. This way, functions $Q[t]$, $V(t)$ and $\tau[t]$ can be represented by the discrete time functions as follows:

$$Q[n] = \phi_0^K(Q[n-1] + V[n] - \tau[n]) \qquad n \in \{1,2,...,N\} \tag{5}$$

Since the number of vehicles moving from the street into the cross junction during the nth sampling window is given by $\tau(n) = \dfrac{D(n)}{2} \times T$, where T is the duration of the sampling period. Likewise, if the cross junction is a round-about, then $\tau(n) = \dfrac{D(n)}{4} \times T$. When $V[n] \le \tau(n)$, the buffer size is not increased. However, when $V[n] > \tau(n)$, the buffer occupancy increases until queuing buffer is full. Therefore, equation (5) can be expressed as

$$Q[n] = \phi_0^K(Q[n-1] + V[n] - \tau) = \phi_\tau^K(Q[n-1] + V[n]) \tag{7}$$

The foundation of the histogram method basically consists of eliminating the time dependence of V[n] in the previous expression and replacing it by a discrete random variable that describes the arrival process. As our traffic model assumes that traffic is stationary, i.e. $C = V(n) \; \forall n \in N$, the previous equation can be transformed into the statistical equation (7):

$$Q[n] = \phi_\tau^K (Q[n-1] \otimes C) \tag{7}$$

Where C is a statistical histogram defined in Equation (2). The operator $\otimes$ stands for the standard statistical convolution, which is described as follows. If X and Y are two independent random variables with n and m intervals respectively, the convolution $X \otimes Y$ is a new random variable Z with n+m-1 intervals and

$$P_Z[i] = \sum_{k=0}^{i} P_X(i-k) \times P_Y(k)$$

The bound operator ϕ_τ^K is defined as the statistical generalization of the previously defined ϕ_a^b operator. If X is a random variable with n intervals then $Y = \phi_\tau^K(X)$ is a random variable with K+1 intervals where

$$\phi_\tau^K(X) = [\sum_{i=0}^{\tau} P_X(i), P_X(\tau+1), P_X(\tau+2), .., P_X(\tau+K-1), \sum_{i=\tau+K}^{n-1} P_X(i)] \tag{8}$$

Combining of equation (7) and (8), the buffer length Q[n] is now a discrete time stochastic process whose steady state probability can be calculated through an iterative process as described in [10-11]. The algorithm for calculating the steady state probability of the buffer length is shown below and will be referenced as HBSP (Histogram Based Stochastic Process) algorithm.

```
Algorithm HBSP (C, τ , K ) {
   Q (0) = 1;
   j = 0;

   Do {
        j = j + 1;
        Q ( j ) = φ_τ^K (Q ( j − 1) ⊗ C )
   } While  E [Q ( j )] − E [Q ( j − 1)] > ξ

   Return  Q ( j )
}
```

Where,
  C: the arrival process (Histogram),

$$C = (\overline{C}, P) = \begin{cases} \overline{C} = [C_i : i = 0, 1, ..., N_c - 1] \\ P = [p(C_i) : i = 0, 1, ..., N_c - 1] \end{cases}$$

D: Rate of vehicles moving into the inter-section. $D = \dfrac{r}{d + \overline{V}} \times \dfrac{1000}{3600}$, where r is the vehicle speed in terms of kilometer per hour, $\overline{V}$ is the average length of a vehicle

(5 meters), and d the required minimum distance for road safety between consecutive vehicles on the street. According to the 2-second rule for road safety, d is given by $d = \dfrac{r \times 1000 \times 2}{3600}$ meter

τ : The service rate, or the rate of vehicle moving out of the road junction at an observation period, $\tau = \dfrac{D}{2} \times T$, where T is the sampling period (10 seconds in our example).

$\bar{\tau}$: The service rate class of τ , $\bar{\tau} = \left\lfloor \dfrac{\tau}{L_C} \right\rfloor$ where L_C is the class length

K: the maximum buffer length, or the maximum number of vehicles that can be held in the queue. If W is the street length in meters, then $K = \dfrac{W}{d + \bar{V}}$

$\bar{K}$: The maximum buffer length class, $\bar{K} = \left\lfloor \dfrac{K}{L_C} \right\rfloor$ where L_C is the class length

$E(X)$: The mean value (or expectation) of gpd X is defined as: $E(X) = \sum_{i=0}^{n-1} P(x_i) * x_i$. Analogously, the mean value of a probability mass function pmf X is defined as $E(X) = \sum_{i=0}^{n-1} P(x_i) * i$

Once the steady state probabilities of the buffer length are calculated, the expected buffer length can be calculated as follows:

$$E(Q) = \sum_{i=0}^{K} P(q_i) * i \qquad (9)$$

The queuing delay is the time spent by the car waiting for previous buffered cars to be leave the street and enter the cross junction. In the case of a cross-junction with a output rate of τ , and a buffer length characterized by a gpd Q, the queuing delay W is proportional to Q and has the same pmf. $W = \dfrac{1}{\tau} \times Q$ Therefore, the expected queuing delay at each intersection can be calculated as follows:

$$E(W) = \dfrac{1}{\tau} \times E[Q] \qquad (10)$$

5   Statistical Histogram Model Usage for Selecting Best Road Path

Figure 6 shows an example of how the statistical histogram model can be used in vehicular network environment. It shows a road map for all possible routes from ingress junction to egress junction with statistical histograms, which are obtained from vehicular network. Based on the information provided by histograms, combined with shortest path algorithm, a driver is able select a best route between the ingress node and egress node and relevant speed and end-to-end delay. Note that since the histograms are updated periodically via vehicle-to-vehicle network, the driver is also able to dynamically change his driving route according to the road traffic conditions obtained from histogram statistics.

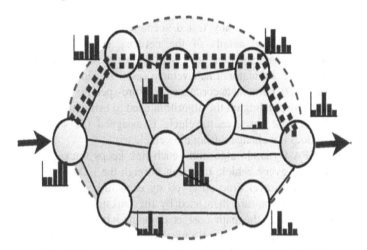

Fig. 6. An example of using the histogram model in VANET

6   Performance Evaluation

In this paper, we compare the performance of the proposed Histogram-Based Algorithm (HBA), with two variations of the standard shortest path algorithm; (i) the shortest path algorithm with static link cost (SPA-Static) and (ii) the optimal shortest path algorithm with dynamic link cost (SPA-Dynamic). The optimal SPA-Dynamic algorithm and the SPA-Static were already embedded in the TSIM microscopic simulator developed by Hawas [12]. However, the HBA algorithm was developed and then embedded in the TSIM microscopic.

The comparative assessment of the three algorithms (HBA, SPA_Static and SPA_Dynamic) is done by comparing various performance measures; namely, number of vehicles entered the network, number of vehicles exited the network and network average travel time (in mins). These attributes are measured under various traffic conditions, such as source volumes, speed, and link length.

Figure 7 shows a grid network of 12 nodes which was used for testing. A summary of the simulation parameters is given below.

- Duration of simulation is 60 minutes
- Maximum vehicle speed along all links is set to 80 km/hour
- Number of source nodes is 6. Each node generates vehicles at a certain rate (ranging from 50 vehicles per hour until 2000 vehicles per hour). The generated vehicles are uniformly distributed in time.

- Number of destination nodes is 14
- Number of intersections is 12 intersections. The length of the links between any two intersections is either 300 m or 150 m long
- Class length of the histogram $L_C = 2$. In other words, the class intervals are $\{\{1,2\}, \{3,4\}, \{5,6\}, etc.\}$

The total simulation time for any tested scenario is set as 60 minutes. At the beginning of the simulation, details of the network structure, connectivity and characteristics, signal characteristics and settings over the analysis period are provided as input to the simulator. Each vehicle (as it is generated) is assigned an Origin-Destination (OD) pair, in accordance to a pre-specified OD matrix for the entire network. Then, depending on the algorithm used to estimate the expected travel time on the links or link costs, each vehicle is assigned the shortest path to its destination, which does not change during the vehicle trip.

In the optimal SPA-Dynamic algorithm, each link keeps tracks of the maximum travel time reported by every vehicle traveling through the link. Then, the algorithm considers the maximum travel time observed by each link as the link cost. These measured travel times (costs) are then used by the Dijkstra's algorithm to find the shortest path. In this case, the path cost is computed by summing the measured "Maximum Travel Time" per link for all links along the path. The path with the least cost is then chosen as the best path. However, in the SPA-Static algorithm, the travel time along the link, and consequently the cost of the link, does not depend on traffic conditions. The travel time (or link cost) is estimated as the link length divided by the maximum speed along that link. Path cost is also measured by summing the cost of all links along the path.

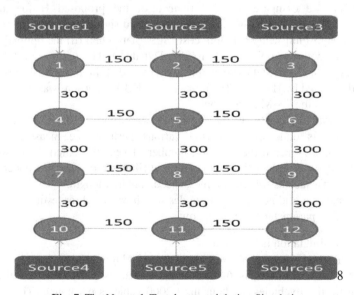

Fig. 7. The Network Topology used during Simulation

In the HBA algorithm, the expected travel time on any link is estimated by adding the expected queuing delay to enter the link (as calculated by Equation 9 and the HSBSP algorithm discussed in Section 4) and the average travel time through the link (link length/ speed limit on the link). The expected travel times computed on every link is then considered as the link cost and used by a Dijkstra's algorithm to find the shortest path. Each generated vehicle is then assigned this shortest path as a pre-specified path.

During simulation, traffic jam is introduced in some routes to trigger the vehicles to change their route to a less crowded route. This is simulated in our experiments by reducing the green-light period at certain intersections to generate a traffic jam at this intersection. In particular, we simulate a traffic jam along the path between node 5 and node 8 by reducing the green light period at this intersection from 30 seconds to 4 seconds.

6.1   Full Network Monitoring

In this experiment, we use the total travel time metric to compare the performance of the proposed HBA algorithm against the optimal SPA-Dynamic algorithm and the SPA-Static algorithm. We computed the travel time for each vehicle entered the network, which represents the time spent by the vehicle in the network, by calculating the vehicle exit time – the vehicle entry time. The total travel time in the experiment is then computed by summing up the travel times of all vehicles entered the network. Figure 8 shows a summary of the simulation results. We did not see much difference in the performance of the three algorithms. That is because the average of all vehicle travel times across the network conceals the excessive delays along any traffic jams. Please note that in this experiment, we only show the results of the HBA algorithm with a class length $L_C = 2$. The results of the other version of the algorithm (when $L_C = 5$) is omitted for clarity as it shows similar performance.

6.2   Critical Path Monitoring

In this experiment, instead of monitoring all vehicles and compute the total travel time across the network, we monitored only the vehicles which pass through the bottleneck path (i.e. the link between node 5 and node 8), where we introduced the traffic jam. Figure 9 shows a summary of the simulation results. In this experiment, each point in the graph represents the total travel time of all vehicles passed through the bottleneck link between node 5 and node 8. It is clear from Figure 8 that the proposed HBA algorithm adopts well with network conditions and guides vehicles for better routes when some links get congested. It outperforms the performance of the SPA-Static algorithm even when the network was not crowded (i.e. when the source rate = 50 vehicles per hour). Furthermore, the performance of the HBA algorithm is very comparable with that of the optimal SPA-Dynamic algorithm, which assumes that the travel times of each vehicle across all the links are available and known to all other vehicles in the network.

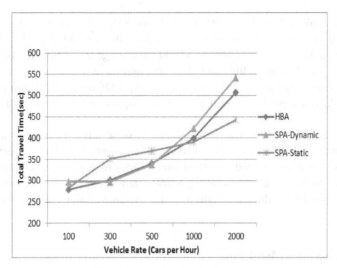

Fig. 8. Full Network Monitoring

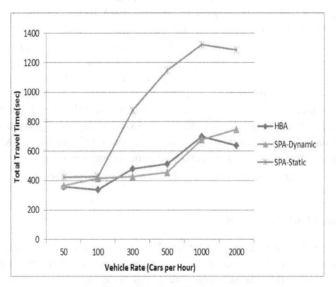

Fig. 9. One Path Monitoring

7   Conclusion

This paper presented a novel histogram-based route guidance algorithm for selecting shortest road path and alerting drivers to potential traffic jams. A microscopic simulation model was developed to assess the effectiveness of the route guidance algorithm against the benchmark shortest path algorithm. Simulation results showed that the proposed road traffic model provides a good prediction of road traffic status, and can be used in conjunction with any standard shortest path algorithms to provide an efficient mechanism for selecting fastest road path.

References

1. Mehran, B., Nakamura, H.: Implementing travel time reliability for evaluation of congestion relief schemes on expressways. J. Applied Sci. 2124, 137–147 (2008)
2. Chen, W., Zhu, S., Li, D.: VAN: Vehicle-Assisted Shortest-Time Path Navigation. In: IEEE 7th International Conference on Mobile Adhoc and Sensor Systems, MASS (2010)
3. Collins, K., Muntean, G.-M.: A vehicle route management solution enabled by Wireless Vehicular Networks. In: IEEE INFOCOM (April 2008)
4. Soua, A., Afifi, H.: Adaptive Data Collection Protocol using Reinforcement Learning for VANETs. In: IEEE International Wireless Communications and Mobile Computing Conference (IWCMC), pp. 1040–1045 (July 2013)
5. Byun, T.-Y.: ICSW^{2}AN: An inter-vehicle communication system using mobile access point over wireless wide area networks. In: Kim, T.-H., Stoica, A., Chang, R.-S. (eds.) SUComS 2010. CCIS, vol. 78, pp. 355–366. Springer, Heidelberg (2010)
6. Zhao, J., Cao, G.: VADD: Vehicle-Assisted Data Delivery in Vehicular Ad Hoc Networks. IEEE Transactions on Vehicular Technology 57(3) (May 2008)
7. Nzouonta, J., Rajgure, N., Wang, G., Borcea, C.: VANET Routing on City Roads using Real-Time Vehicular Traffic Information. IEEE Transactions on Vehicular Technology 58(7) (2009)
8. Lee, K.C., Lee, U., Gerla, M.: Survey of Routing Protocols in Vehicular Ad Hoc Networks. In: Advances in Vehicular Ad-Hoc Networks: Developments and Challenges, pp. 149–170. IGI Global (October 2009)
9. Lin, Y.: Routing Protocols in Vehicular Ad Hoc Networks: A Survey and Future Perspectives. Science 932, 913–932 (2010)
10. Orallo, E., Carbó, J.V.: A Stochastic Analysis of Network Traffic Based on Histogram Workload Modeling, Technical Report, Universidad Politécnica de Valencia (2009), http://www.disca.upv.es/enheror/pdf/TR_DISCA_06_09.pdf
11. Hernández-Orallo, E., Vila-Carbó, J.: Network queue and loss analysis using histogram-based traffic models. Elsevier Computer Communications 33, 190–201 (2010)
12. Hawas, Y.E.: A Microscopic Simulation Model for Incident Modeling in Urban Networks. Transportation Planning and Technology 30(2), 289–309

Understanding Human Driving Behavior
through Computational Cognitive Modeling

Ajay Kumar[1], Jai Prakash[1], and Varun Dutt[1,2]

[1] School of Computing and Electrical Engineering
{ajay.iitmandi,jaiiitmandi}@gmail.com
[2] School of Humanities and Social Sciences,
Indian Institute of Technology, Mandi, India
varun@iitmandi.ac.in

Abstract. As per an article in *The Economist*, someone, somewhere, dies in a road crash every 30 seconds, and about 10 people are seriously injured. Currently, there are about 1.3 million global deaths per year due to road accidents. Most of these deaths and injuries are caused by either factors that are internal to the driver (e.g., driving experience), or due to factors that are external to the driver (e.g., track complexity). However, currently little is known on how these factors influence human driving behavior. In this research, we investigate the role of an external factor (track complexity) on human driving behavior through computational cognitive modeling. Eighteen human participants were asked to drive on two tracks of the same length: simple (4 curves; N=9) and complex (20 curves; N=9). Later, we used two computational models to fit the human steering control data: an existing near-far-point model and a new heuristic model involving tangent and car-axis angles and a position-correction term. Our modeling results show that the fit of the heuristic model to human data on the simple and complex tracks was superior compared to that by the near-far-point model. We highlight the implications of our model results on human driving behavior.

Keywords: Road accidents, external factors, heuristics, human driving, computational cognitive modeling.

1 Introduction

According to *The Economist*, every 30 seconds someone, somewhere, dies in a road accident, and about 10 people are seriously injured [1]. World Health Organization (WHO) estimates that currently 1.24 million people die due to road accidents world over and this number is expected to increase to 2 million by 2030 (WHO, 2014). More worrisome is the fact that 91% of the world's deaths on the roads occur in low- and middle- income countries (like India), even though these countries have approximately half of the world's vehicles [7]. Young adults aged between 15 and 44 years account for 59% of global road traffic deaths and it is very likely that a number of these road accidents are due to external factors (like track complexity and prevailing weather conditions) [7]. Thus, it is important to investigate the role of these factors on the driving behavior of young adults in the low- and middle- income countries.

R.C.-H. Hsu and W. Shangguang (Eds.): IOV 2014, LNCS 8662, pp. 56–65, 2014.

However, up to now, only little research has taken place that investigates the role of external factors on the decision making of a driver in a vehicle. Cognitive Science is concerned with understanding the processes that the brain uses to accomplish complex tasks like learning, thinking, problem solving and decision making. The goal of a cognitive model is to scientifically explain one or more of these basic cognitive processes or interaction between them [9]. In this regard, driving is one of the complex tasks for which researchers have developed variety of models to simulate human driving behavior. Some researchers have used Hidden Markov Models (HMMs) to characterize and detect driving maneuvers [10]. Beyond HMMs, rule-based models have been proposed as a promising approach towards modeling human driving behavior [11].

Among the rule-based models developed more recently, Dario Salvucci has presented a model for human driving using a popular cognitive architecture [2]. This model has been used for studying driving behavior and distraction during driving [2]. In this paper, we consider a Near-Far-Point model (section 3.1) and this model is the same model as presented by [2].

Beyond the Near-Far-Point model, research has shown that simple heuristic rules seem to perform very well to account for human decision making in a wide variety of decisions tasks [3]. Although heuristic models have been tested in a large number of decision tasks, yet there is less evaluation of such models in complex decision tasks like driving. Thus, we develop a heuristic model (section 3.2) involving tangent and car-axis angles and a position-correction term. The steering-control equation used in this model tries to minimize the car deviation from the center of the track and the model tries to drive the car parallel to the track axis.

In this paper, we investigate the role of track complexity on a person's driving and further model the human driving behavior computationally. We model track complexity in terms of the number of curves on the driving track. Specifically, we take two tracks, simple (with 4 curves) and complex (with 20 curves) and collect human driving data on these tracks. Given that a high 59% of road accidents involve younger population, participants in our study were young people with age ranging from 21 to 24. Furthermore, given the lack of studies in low- and middle- income groups in developing countries, we took participants from the hill state of Himachal Pradesh (in Northern India). The Himachal's terrain is also complex as people drive on roads with a number of mountain curves and steep slopes. For the purpose of modeling human driving, we use the Near-Far-Point model and the heuristic model on a simple and a complex track. Here, we evaluate the ability of these models to steer vehicles in ways similar to those done by humans. We close the paper by highlighting the implications of our models and their mechanisms for human driving behavior on simple and complex tracks.

2   Methods

2.1   Experimental Design

Participants were randomly divided to perform on one of the two driving scenarios: a track having 20 curves (complex; N = 9 participants; see fig. 1.a) and a track having 4 curves (simple; N = 9 participants; see fig. 1.b). Both the tracks were of equal length and width (length = 2,200 meters; width = 10 meters). The average time taken by participants to complete the simple and complex tracks was 1.5 and 2.5 minutes, respectively. In both the track conditions, the goal for participants was to drive in a way that their car remains at the centre of their track as much as possible.

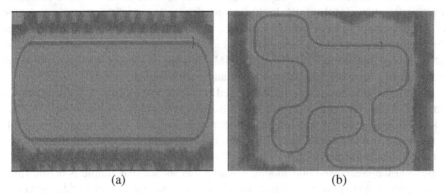

(a)   (b)

Fig. 1. (a) Simple Track Map (4 curves) (b) Complex Track Map (20 curves)

2.2   Simulation Environment

We used The Open Racing Car Simulator (TORCS) [4], an open-source driving simulation program written in the C++ language, for running the study with human and model participants (see fig. 2). The tracks were created using the TORCS's *track editor* program. The track editor allows designing of the track (i.e., a track's shape, length, and elevation). Additional features like track's slope, background and coefficient of friction were added using the trackgen utility of TORCS.

Fig. 2. TORCS Simulation Environment

2.3   Participants

Eighteen undergraduate students from various disciplines at Indian Institute of Technology Mandi participated in this experiment. Ages ranged from 21 to 24 years (average = 21.5 years; st. dev. = 0.61 years). Around 70% of the participants possessed a valid driving license. The average driving experience of the participants was around 1.5 years. All participants received a base pay of INR 10 for their participation.

2.4   Procedure

Participants were given full instructions about the car controls buttons and the tracks before the experiment. Before the actual driving began, participants were given some training in which they played on a demo track. The purpose of the training was to make participants familiar with the simulation environment and the car controls. Once the participants acknowledged that they had fully understood the car controls and task goals, they were allowed to drive on the complex or simple tracks. The assignment of participants to simple and complex tracks was done randomly. Finally, participants were reminded that they have to drive in a way that their car remains at the centre of their track as much as possible.

3   Implementation and Execution of the Models

Both the Near-Far-Point model and the Heuristic model were implemented in Visual C++, i.e., within the TORCS environment as driving bots.

3.1   Near-Far-Point Model

The steering control in this model centers on a new steering model [8] that utilizes "two-level" control based on the perception of two salient visual points ([5], [6]). First, the *near point* represents the vehicle's current lane position, used to judge how close the vehicle is to the center of the roadway (see fig. 3). The near point is characterized as a point in the center of the near lane visible in front of the vehicle, set at a distance of 10 m from the vehicle's center. Second, the *far point* (see fig. 3) indicates the curvature of the upcoming roadway, used to judge what the driver should execute to anticipate the upcoming curvature. The far point is characterized as one of two targets: (a) the vanishing point (up to a maximum distance equivalent to 3 seconds of time headway) of a straight roadway; or, (b) the tangent point of an upcoming curve.

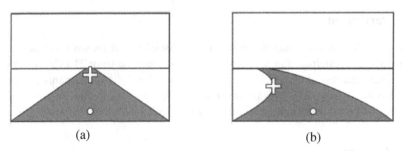

(a)   (b)

Fig. 3. Near and far point on (a) straight track (b) curve   (" ○" represents near point and "+" represents far point) [2]

The model used the following equation for steering control:

$$\Delta\Phi = k_{far}\Delta\theta_{far} + k_{near}\Delta\theta_{near} + k_I\theta_{near}\Delta t$$

Where,

$$\Delta\Phi = change\ in\ steering\ angle$$
$$\theta_{near} = current\ near\ angle\ (see\ fig.\ 4)$$
$$\theta_{far} = current\ far\ angle\ (see\ fig.\ 4)$$
$$\Delta\theta_{near} = change\ in\ near\ angle\ (see\ fig.\ 4)$$
$$\Delta\theta_{far} = change\ in\ far\ angle\ (see\ fig.\ 4)$$

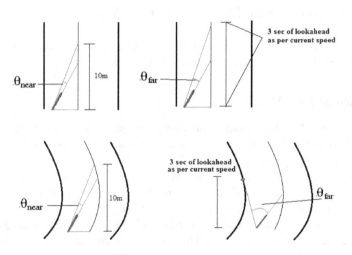

Fig. 4. θ_{near} and θ_{far} angle on a straight track and on a curve (red/bold line represents car axis)

3.2   Heuristic Model

The second model we have implemented follows a heuristic rule, where the goal is to keep the car at the center of the track. In the Heuristic model we calculate the angle that car axis makes with the tangent to the track axis and uses this information along with a position correction term to control steering.

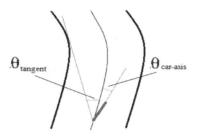

Fig. 5. θ_{tangent} and $\theta_{\text{car-axis}}$ angle on a sample track

The model used the following equation for steering control:

$$\Phi = \theta_{tangent} + \theta_{car-axis} + pos\_correc$$

Where, $\Phi = new\ steering\ angle$

$\theta_{tangent} = angle\ that\ tangent\ to\ the\ track$
$makes\ with\ the\ track\ axis$
$\theta_{car-axis} = angle\ that\ tangent\ to\ the\ track$
$makes\ with\ the\ car\ axis$
$pos\_correc = \dfrac{car\ distance\ from\ the\ center\ of\ the\ track}{width\ of\ the\ track}$

3.3   Acceleration and Braking Control

Our main focus in this paper is on steering control. We made a number of simplifications for acceleration and braking control in the models. Both the model and humans try to drive the car with the maximum possible speed. On a straight track, the car uses full acceleration. On a curve we use following equation to get the allowed speed:

$$\frac{mv^2}{r} = mg\mu$$
$$v = \sqrt{\mu r g}$$

Where,

$$m = car\ mass$$

$v = allowed\ speed\ on\ the\ approaching\ curve$
$r = radius\ of\ approaching\ curve$
$\mu = coefficient\ of\ friction$

3.4   Model Execution

Both the Heuristic and Near-Far-Point model were made to run on the simple and complex track once. The driving data was collected for each of the model on both the track. The models were not given any training but the parameter values for the Near-Far-Point model were set to 8, 8 and 3 for k_{far}, k_{near} and k_I respectively. The model parameters values were determined experimentally by a trial-and-error procedure till the models drove the car like humans did. There were no parameters in the heuristic model.

3.5   Human and Model Data

We recorded the car steering angle for each meter of the track covered by both model and human participants. Therefore, for each participant, we had a vector v of length 2,200 where v_i is the steering angle of the car at a distance of ith meter from the start of the track. We had 9 such vectors for each of the track (simple and complex). We calculated average steering control for each track by taking the average of the 9 participant's data for that track.

The steering angle values ranged from $-\pi$ to $+\pi$ which was normalized to the range -1 to +1. The negative value for steering angle means steering towards the right side of the track and the positive value means steering towards the left side of the track.

4   Results

The models' steering control was compared with average human steering control on both the tracks. We used Mean Square Deviation (MSD) and Correlation coefficient (r) as the two measures to compare model performance with respect to human steering control.

4.1   Comparison of Steering Control on Simple Track

Fig. 6 shows that Heuristic model correlates slightly better with human steering control than Near-Far-Point model on simple track. Since there were two major right curves on this track, we find more negative steering control values in the graph (negative steering control value means steering to the right side of the track while driving clockwise). The two models do not differ much in MSD values with respect to human steering control.

4.2   Comparison of Steering Control on Complex Track

Fig. 7 shows that the Heuristic model correlates significantly better to human steering control as compared to Near-Far-Point model. The MSD value for Heuristic model is also slightly better than the Near-Far-Point model.

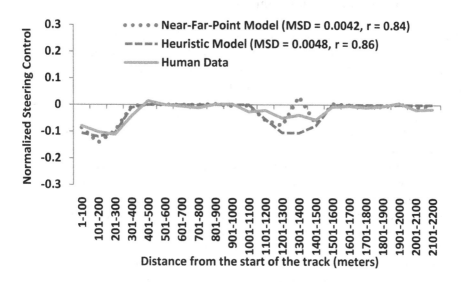

Fig. 6. Steering Control on Simple Track

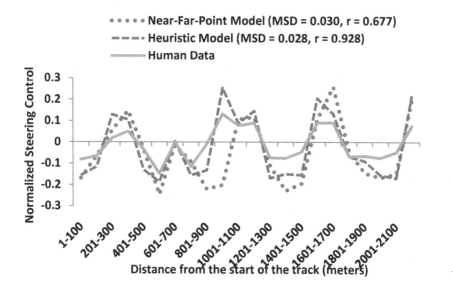

Fig. 7. Steering Control on Complex Track

5   Discussion and Conclusion

Global death rate due to road accidents is very high and is expected to increase in the coming future [7]. Most of these accidents are likely due to the effect of external factors like track complexity or climatic condition on human driving. However, currently, not much research has been carried out in studying the effect of such external factors on human driving behavior. In this paper, we have tried to bring into consideration track complexity as an external factor effecting human driving.

As expected, the performance of human participants was poor in complex track condition compared to simple track condition. That is because human participants were able to drive more smoothly in case of simple track. The steering control of both the models was almost equally close to human steering control in case of simple track; however, their performance varied in case of complex track.

The Near-Far-Point model controls the steering using two perceived visual points namely the near point and the far point. The model steering control graphs show that the model was late in negotiating curves as compared to human participants. This delay is much more visible in case of complex track and that is, perhaps, the reason for poor performance of the model (the complex track have significantly more curves).

The heuristic model basically tries to follow the track axis by steering along the tangent to the track. The role of the position correction term becomes more important when the model tries to steer along a curve. During curve negotiation, the car position shifts from the center of the track towards the edge of the track (right edge in case of left turn and left edge in case of right turn). Further, the better correlation of heuristic model data with human data can be because of the fact that similar shift in car position is also seen for human participants on curves. By varying the weight of the position correction term we can control this shift of the car. This opens some scope for improving the heuristic model by giving weights to the position correction and angle correction terms, which is the focus of our present and future research.

In this research, we used TORCS to simulate the driving scenarios. TORCS has a 2-D visual display and the output is shown on a standard desktop PC monitor. With this simulation environment participants cannot actually feel the ups and downs of the track as they are not physically present in a car; but, they can see it on the monitor. Although up to what extent such hardware limitation affect the presented results is hard to quantify but none of the models presented in this paper take into account any parameter which is directly affected with such limitations of the simulation environment.

Most human drivers drive on some fixed tracks and hence are used to those driving scenarios. We can broadly classify such driving scenarios as simple or complex based on the driving complexity of those tracks. Since drivers occasionally drive on some not-common tracks, it can be helpful to study the effect of such changes in driving scenarios on human driving. In our ongoing research, we are trying to study the effect of such changes by making the model calibrated on simple track to run on complex track and vice versa. These and other interventions form the next steps in this ongoing research program.

Acknowledgements. The students are very thankful for the guidance provided by Prof. Varun Dutt on this project. Also, we are grateful to the computational resources provided by the Indian Institute of Technology, Mandi, India for this project.

References

1. Road deaths-Driving to an early grave. The Economist (2014)
2. Salvucci, D.D.: Modeling Driver Behavior in a Cognitive Architecture. Human Factors 48(2), 362–380 (2006)
3. Todd, P.M., Gigerenzer, G., ABC Research Group: Simple Heuristic That Make Us Smart. Oxford University Press (1999)
4. Wymann, B., Espié, E., Guionneau, C., Dimitrakakis, C., Coulom, R., Sumner, A.: TORCS: The Open Racing Car Simulator, v1.3.5 (2013)
5. Donges, E.: A two-level model of driver steering behavior. Human Factors 20, 691–707 (1978)
6. Land, M.F., Horwood, J.: Which parts of the road guide steering? Nature 377, 339–340 (1995)
7. World Health Organization, http://www.who.int/mediacentre/factsheets/fs358/en/#content
8. Salvucci, D.D., Gray, R.: A two-point visual control model of steering. Perception 33, 1233–1248 (2004)
9. Busemeyer, J.R., Diederich, A.: Cognitive Modeling. SAGE Publications, Inc., USA (2009)
10. Kuge, N., Yamamura, T., Shimoyama, O., Liu, A.: A Driver Behavior Recognition Method Based on a Driver Model Framework. SAE Technical Paper 2000-01-0349 (2000), doi:10.4271/2000-01-0349
11. Michon, J.A.: Explanatory pitfalls and rule-based driver models. Accident Analysis & Prevention 21(4), 341–353 (1989)

Vehicular Network Enabling Large-Scale and Real-Time Immersive Participation

Theo Kanter, Rahim Rahmani, Yuhong Li, and Bin Xiao

Department of Computer and Systems Sciences
Stockholm University
{Rahim,kanter,yuhongli,xbin}@dsv.su.se

Abstract. This paper presents a system and mechanisms enabling real-time awareness and interaction among vehicles connected via heterogeneous mobile networks. Information obtained by vehicles is considered as the centre in our system. Vehicles are organized dynamically in overlaid clusters. In each cluster, vehicle-related information is pushed in time. As a network node, each vehicle has the function of content abstraction and distribution. Through processing and abstracting the sensed data, various vehicle-related information are organized and denoted in hierarchical names at each node. The data are transmitted and forwarded using protocols accordant with the characteristics of the content. In this way, large-scale and real-time information exchanges among vehicles are realized. Part of our system has been implemented and tested. An open source platform providing standard sensor and actuator API can be provided.

Keywords: Internet of Vehicle, Information-centric networking, MediaSense.

1 Introduction

Internet of Vehicles (IoV) has been acknowledged as an important part of people' daily life. It has been identified as a key technology for increasing road safety and transport efficiency, and providing infotainment in the wireless and mobile environment. By connecting people with vehicles, vehicles with vehicles, and vehicles with environments, various information and services can be obtained.

At a high level, the goal of the IoV is to enable the efficient exchange of information among the vehicles, which can act as both information producers and consumers. However, due to the highly dynamic topology and non-uniform distribution of vehicles as well as the large amount of information in IoV, exchanging diverse information efficiently among the vehicles is a great challenge.

First, with the development of IoV and the increasing number of vehicles, more information needs to be sensed and transmitted. For example, for safe driving on the road, various types of information are needed, as shown in Figure 1. The safety data and other road conditions need to be exchanged among the vehicles in the similar situation. The vast number of vehicles may exacerbate the amount of information by orders of magnitude. All the information data need to be processed, organized and

R.C.-H. Hsu and W. Shangguang (Eds.): IOV 2014, LNCS 8662, pp. 66–75, 2014.

Fig. 1. Information for road safety

abstracted in each vehicle in order to be cached and transmitted among the vehicles efficiently and economically.

Secondly, the information related to vehicles has time and spatial constraint. The data transmission mechanism should consider the characteristics of the information.

Thirdly, real-time awareness is more important in IoV. Local experiences and interaction include sources and sinks globally. All of which may require instant responses. In addition, infotainment becomes more and more important for people, for example, for those having long journey on buses. In this case, on-line games with friends at home maybe interesting for them. Thus, large amount of video and audio data needs to be transmitted in time.

Fourthly, the IoV has highly dynamic topology and non-uniform distribution of nodes. Therefore, a scalable data dissemination mechanism, which can adapt to frequent topology changes with variable vehicle density, and can satisfy certain real time requirement is necessary.

Current research on IoV has concentrated on routing, service performance, security and mobility management in heterogeneous wireless networking environment etc. [1]. Various results have been obtained regarding establishing physical communication links among the vehicles using ad-hoc technique [2][3]. Compared with these work, we concentrate on vehicle-related information distribution. Work [4] [5] has introduced the idea of Information-centric Networking (ICN) to disseminate data in vehicular networks. However, how to organize and store the large amount of data sensed by vehicles efficiently and disseminate the data in real-time and through the large-scale vehicular network has not been discussed in detail.

In this paper, we concentrate on how to provide a real-time IoV from the point of view of information distribution in large-scale. We propose to use ICN and ontology techniques to disseminate efficiently information in the context of IoV. A new method for constructing the IoV and a new architecture of end-device are proposed. Using this architecture, the sensed data by each vehicle are abstracted and organized in named contents. Through the publication and subscription mechanisms, vehicles can obtain their interested content in less delay. The rest of the text is organized as follows. First, the vehicle network system enabling large-scale immersive participation is introduced and the architecture of end-devices is presented in section 2.Following this in section 3, mechanisms for information abstraction and organization, as well exchanges among vehicles are also addressed. Then the implementation and tests of the system are depicted in section 4, and conclusions are made in section 5.

2   Vehicular Network System Enabling Large-Scale Immersive Participation

2.1   System Architecture

The whole IoV system is consist of logical clusters, as shown in Figure 2. A logical cluster implies that vehicles might reside remotely physically but clustered logically based on the same or similar contexts. This allows resources (data, services) to be shared among different physically distributed vehicles more easily. Each cluster is identified by a context.

A cluster is constructed when a vehicle publishes a new context. Any vehicle can join a cluster dynamically depending on whether it is interested in the context. A vehicle can join different clusters simultaneously according to the contexts it is interested. Several contexts can be shared in one cluster.

Contexts are keys for forming the various clusters. In our system, a context is defined as a certain category of vehicle-related information. The contexts have life period, so clusters can dissolve dynamically.

Each cluster is maintained autonomically. According to the characteristics of a context, a context is published periodically by the vehicle that creates it. Vehicles interested in this context will record the context name in their own Subscribed Table. Afterwards, when the vehicle receives data with the same context, the data will be delivered to the corresponding consumer part of the vehicle. If a vehicle does not interest in the context anymore, it will delete the corresponding entry in the Subscribed Table. Then the data packets will be forwarded or discarded instead of delivering to the consumer part. The context entry in the Subscribed Table will also be deleted after it expires.

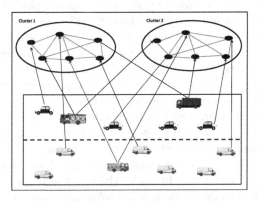

Fig. 2. System architecture

In order to be able to exchange information among the vehicles in real-time, contents are pushed in every cluster. In other words, no procedure of content requirement from a vehicle is needed. But physically, the data packets can be forwarded by any vehicles within the wireless radio connection, no matter if the vehicles belonging to the same cluster or not. Through this way, the logical clusters increase the scalability of the IoV and reduce the complexity for distributing the contents.

2.2   Functions of Vehicle Nodes

In order to achieve the above goal, the following design principles are followed:

- Flexible construction and adaption of the overlay clusters. Self-adaptation with little or no human intervention in the dynamic environment is needed. Moreover, the adaptation should be based on the contexts.
- Efficient management and distribution of contexts. Contexts should be well organized. The underlying network infrastructure should not be overloaded due to the exchanges of context data in time during the operation of the vehicles.

Hence, a modular architecture comprising four blocks is suggested for each vehicle device to allow for flexibility and extensibility while additionally supporting a clear separation of concern. Figure 3illustrates the architecture of a vehicle as a networking node.

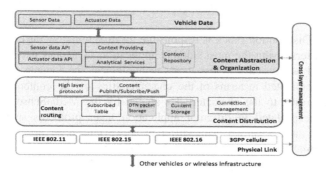

Fig. 3. Architecture of a vehicle node

The architecture consists of four blocks, namely Vehicle Data, Content Abstraction&Organization, Content Distribution and Physical Link.

Figure 4 illustrates the Vehicle Data block. It has mainly two functions. One is data sensing. Various data can be obtained through the event sensing and monitoring functions integrated in the vehicles, such as the current position and status of the vehicles, the geographical environment etc. The other is to receive information from other vehicles. The information can be used to configure the vehicle or provide for the people in the vehicle as infotainment. We call this part of data actuating. Both sensor data and actuator data contact with Content Abstraction & Organization block through the standard API provided by the Content Abstraction & Organization block.

Content Abstraction & Organization block is responsible for processing, abstracting and organizing the sensed data. It is the core of the system. In this block, Media-Sense platform [6] provides access to all types of sensors and actuators via gateway, by translating communication protocols or methods used by sensors or actuators, or which is connected into the MediaSense through the API interface. The data is analyzed and abstracted by MediaSense using data mining and machine learning techniques. New information can also be created according to the contexts based on the ontology technique, such as traffic jam indication or danger warning, which can be passed to the Vehicle Data block to further conduct the vehicle. All the information are named by MediaSense, and stored in the content repository.

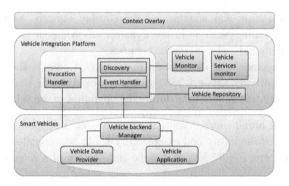

Fig. 4. Integration platform providing vehicle-related data

The Content Distribution block is responsible for disseminating the content data in the overlay clusters, using the most suitable application layer and networking layer protocols as well as physical wireless access technologies. The contents stored in each vehicle are disseminated in terms of the characteristics of the contents using ICN technique. According to the characteristics signed by the MediaSense, the content data can be encapsulated in different application layer protocols such as DTN, P2PSIP, XMPP, and forwarded using different networking layer protocols, such as immediate flooding or opportunistic forwarding (DTN mode).

A vehicle may have several physical interfaces supporting different wireless access technologies, such as WiFi, 3GPP cellular or Bluetooth. The link status of different physical interfaces, such as the signal strength etc. are collected by the cross-layer management module, which will be used by the Connection Management module in order to transfer data in the most suitable link.

3   Content Organization and Distribution

3.1   Content Organization and Abstraction

The information at each vehicle is organized hierarchically. At the top level, two types of contexts are defined, namely network condition context and content context. A network condition context is generated periodically, including the physical network interfaces available, a list of known connected nodes, a list of out-of-contact nodes, by overhearing network traffic and detecting the retransmission failure towards known destination. The network condition contexts are used for the efficient information distribution. Content contexts in our system mean the contexts for organizing a certain category of vehicle-related information. For example, /toSundsvall means the aggregation of all the information for vehicles driving to the city Sundsvall; whereas /toSundsvall/ traffic means the traffic context to Sundsvall.

A specific piece of information is named in a URL- like way hierarchically by using its context name plus the content name. For example, /toSundsvall/traffic/accident_Stockholm is the name of content that an accident happens near Stockholm in the direction to Sundsvall. We support variable context length (i.e., the number of components in a context name). As mentioned below, the longest name prefix matching algorithm is used for matching the context name for content distribution.

Besides the name, some characteristics of the information are also recorded together with the information, including the interval for disseminating the content periodically and the life time of the content etc.

The MediaSense platform is responsible for the context organization and abstraction. MediaSense abstracts data from all sensors into a generalized and standardized format. The ontology technique is used to create and organize the information according to the categories of the information, such as the position of the vehicles, the geographical environment, the status of the vehicles and the general traffic on the road etc. To support the description logic of ontology, OWL-DL [7], a branch of OWL, is used. OWL-DL is an ontology formatting language standardized by W3C [8], which provides rich syntax to annotate the raw content data with description logic. Vehicle-related data, such as the position and the geographical environment and so on are formed as ontology entities using OWL/XML files. Each of the entity is slotted by variables to present the current features within the raw context under certain problem domain.

For example, by utilizing the hierarchical mechanism of ontology, we carry out layered marking to the contents. Thing, as the content context, is the super class for the whole ontology. Taking "/toSundsvall/traffic/accident_Stockholmas" as an example, under the super class "toSundsvall" is defined as a subclass to mark the destination of a certain travel, as shown in Figure 5. The content file is marked accordingly using OWL/XML file. Each hierarchy is annotated as a class in the file system based on object-oriented concept, where ontology based reasoning is supported. The contents are maintained in the content repository.

```
<?xml version="1.0"?>

<!DOCTYPE rdf:RDF [
    <!ENTITY owl "http://www.w3.org/2002/07/owl#" >
    <!ENTITY xsd "http://www.w3.org/2001/XMLSchema#" >
    <!ENTITY rdfs "http://www.w3.org/2000/01/rdf-schema#" >
    <!ENTITY rdf "http://www.w3.org/1999/02/22-rdf-syntax-ns#" >
]>

<rdf:RDF xmlns="http://www.owl-ontologies.com/Ontology1398761667.owl#"
    xml:base="http://www.owl-ontologies.com/Ontology1398761667.owl"
    xmlns:rdfs="http://www.w3.org/2000/01/rdf-schema#"
    xmlns:xsd="http://www.w3.org/2001/XMLSchema#"
    xmlns:owl="http://www.w3.org/2002/07/owl#"
    xmlns:rdf="http://www.w3.org/1999/02/22-rdf-syntax-ns#">
    <owl:Ontology rdf:about=""/>
    <owl:Class rdf:ID="Accident_Stockholm">
        <rdfs:subClassOf rdf:resource="#Traffic"/>
    </owl:Class>
    <owl:Class rdf:ID="toSundsvall"/>
    <owl:Class rdf:ID="Traffic">
        <rdfs:subClassOf rdf:resource="#toSundsvall"/>
    </owl:Class>
</rdf:RDF>
```

▼ Thing
  ▼ toSundsvall
    ▼ traffic
      Accident_Stockholm

Fig. 5. The hierarchy for a piece of message sample

3.2   Content Distribution

A scalable data dissemination mechanism is necessary, which can adapt to frequent topology changes with variable vehicle density and can satisfy certain real time requirement, taking network resources into consideration. Therefore, we use information-centric networking (ICN) technique [9][10] to realize the data dissemination in our architecture. One the one hand, ICN insulates fundamentally the data transmission from dynamic topologies through naming the information and routing/forwarding them according to their identities. On the other hand, the in-networking caching feature of ICN can help to reduce the data response time and data traffic. The receiver-oriented operation solves the mobility issues internally, and the natural support for multicast make the data exchanges more fault tolerance. However, the time and spatial constraint of the information, as well as the highly dynamic topology and non-uniform distribution of nodes must be considered.

In addition, the receiver-oriented chunk based data transmission (i.e., pull-based) designed by ICN, may degrade the performance of IoV. For example, normally the information about an accident needs to be broadcasted to a certain geographical scope immediately. Therefore, we introduce also the push-based data dissemination mechanism in our system.

Hence, three data exchange procedures are used in our system.

- Publishing: when a new content context is created, the corresponding vehicle will broadcast the context. The name of the content together with its life time and publishing interval is included in the message. To be more efficient, the message is broadcasted periodically and storing and forwarding mode is used.
- Subscribing: when a vehicle is interested in a certain category of contents, it will register the context name in the Subscribed Table.
- Pushing: whenever a vehicle has information to be announced, it broadcasts the information in its cluster. According to the features of the context, the broadcast can be done periodically in a certain time.

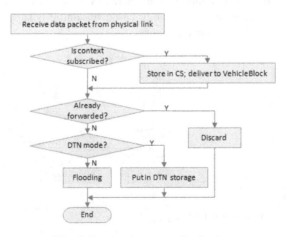

Fig. 6. Routing in content distribution

Figure 6 illustrates how data packets are routed by a physical vehicular node. When a vehicular node receives a data packet from the physical link, according to the content name in the data packet and the subscribed content context, it can decide if the data is that it wants. If yes, the data is delivered to the Vehicle Data block and cached in the Content Storage (CS) in terms of the context name. Otherwise, the node will check if there is any connection available and if the information should be forwarded in DTN mode according to the features of the context, and then flooding the packet through the physical link in terms of the results.

When a vehicle wants to send any data, the Content Publish/Subscribe/Push module will check the characteristics of the content and then encapsulate the data in a certain application and transport layer protocols, select a suitable physical link according to the network condition contexts and send out. For the moment, we support DXCP and DTN at the application layer.

To speed up the data forwarding, the Subscribed context Table (ST) is used, which records all the contexts it has subscribed. When the content name in the data packet matches an entry in the context table, the data packet will be delivered to the Vehicle Data block. Otherwise, it will be forwarded according to the network conditions. The algorithm based on hash table [11] is used in the system to implement the longest name prefix matching.

For the moment, we simply use flooding mechanism to ensure the reliable hop-by-hop data transmission for an ad-hoc ICN.

4   System Implementation and Tests

Part of the system has already been implemented and tested.

The core module–MediaSense [6][12] in the Content Abstraction & Organization block has already been implemented and launched as an open source IoT platform (www.mediasense.se) for scalable distributed context sharing and control. The Sensor and Actuator Data API has been tested by different IoT scenarios, such as energy profiling (for energy awareness), health monitoring (for medical status and alerts) and intelligent home automation. Currently the data sharing in MediaSense is implemented through the application layer overlay (P2P) techniques. We are now implementing the ICN mechanisms in order to disseminate the information more efficiently.

To validate the Content Abstraction & Organization block, we define an ontology as shown in Figure 7. Each white ellipse is a sub context domain, while each arrow shows the entity properties for each entity. Entity property is the way to mark the relations among entities, where each entity can be regarded as a property for its peers. The blue ellipse describes the constructions for the message in each context domain. According to a case scenario abstracted from the system, Position, Vehicle Status, Geo-information, Traffic-information and Infotainment are extracted out as the context domains, where each message can be marked with category under the construction format. A proof-of-concept prototype is written with Jess [13], which helps to establish the entity properties. AOWL/XML file is generated by a short Jess code, as illustrated in Figure 8.

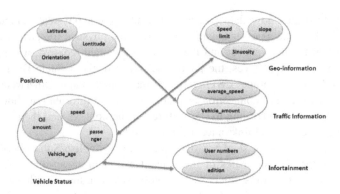

Fig. 7. An example of the created content and ontology

```
<?xml version="1.0"?>

<!DOCTYPE rdf:RDF [
    <!ENTITY owl "http://www.w3.org/2002/07/owl#" >
    <!ENTITY xsd "http://www.w3.org/2001/XMLSchema#" >
    <!ENTITY rdfs "http://www.w3.org/2000/01/rdf-schema#" >
    <!ENTITY rdf "http://www.w3.org/1999/02/22-rdf-syntax-ns#" >
]>

<rdf:RDF xmlns="http://www.owl-ontologies.com/Ontology1398340415.owl#"
    xml:base="http://www.owl-ontologies.com/Ontology1398340415.owl"
    xmlns:rdfs="http://www.w3.org/2000/01/rdf-schema#"
    xmlns:xsd="http://www.w3.org/2001/XMLSchema#"
    xmlns:owl="http://www.w3.org/2002/07/owl#"
    xmlns:rdf="http://www.w3.org/1999/02/22-rdf-syntax-ns#">
    <owl:Ontology rdf:about=""/>
    <owl:DatatypeProperty rdf:ID="active">
        <rdf:type rdf:resource="&owl;FunctionalProperty"/>
        <rdfs:domain rdf:resource="#infotainment"/>
        <rdfs:range rdf:resource="&xsd;boolean"/>
    </owl:DatatypeProperty>
    <owl:DatatypeProperty rdf:ID="average_speed">
        <rdf:type rdf:resource="&owl;FunctionalProperty"/>
        <rdfs:domain rdf:resource="#traffic_inf"/>
        <rdfs:range rdf:resource="&xsd;int"/>
    </owl:DatatypeProperty>
    <owl:DatatypeProperty rdf:ID="edition">
        <rdf:type rdf:resource="&owl;FunctionalProperty"/>
        <rdfs:domain rdf:resource="#infotainment"/>
        <rdfs:range rdf:resource="&xsd;string"/>
    </owl:DatatypeProperty>
    <owl:Class rdf:ID="geoenvironment"/>
    <geoenvironment rdf:ID="geoenvironment_1">
        <speedlimit rdf:datatype="&xsd;int">100</speedlimit>
        <slope rdf:datatype="&xsd;int">10</slope>
        <Sinuosity rdf:datatype="&xsd;int">60</Sinuosity>
    </geoenvironment>
    <geoenvironment rdf:ID="geoenvironment_2">
        <speedlimit rdf:datatype="&xsd;int">105</speedlimit>
        <slope rdf:datatype="&xsd;int">15</slope>
        <Sinuosity rdf:datatype="&xsd;int">10</Sinuosity>
    </geoenvironment>
    <geoenvironment rdf:ID="geoenvironment_3">
        <speedlimit rdf:datatype="&xsd;int">90</speedlimit>
        <slope rdf:datatype="&xsd;int">5</slope>
        <Sinuosity rdf:datatype="&xsd;int">30</Sinuosity>
    </geoenvironment>
```

Fig. 8. The OWL/XML file generated depicting the context

5   Conclusions and Future Work

An IoV system enabling interaction among vehicles in large scale has been presented
in the paper. Each vehicle in the system abstracts and organizes the data it sensed, and
shares them with other vehicles that have the common interests denoted using contexts. The sensed data are abstracted and organized using hierarchical context and
content names. ICN technique is used to distribute the data and push-based data

distribution mode is introduced considering the real-time characteristic of vehicle-related information. Depending on the characteristics of the information, the data can be encapsulated using different application layer protocols and transmitted in the network. At the network layer, the data packet can be forwarded in both opportunistic or storing and forwarding mode according to the network conditions and the abstracted characteristics of the content. The content abstraction and organization block of our system has been implemented and tested. The MediaSense can be provided as an open source platform providing standard sensor and actuator API.Currently we are implementing and testing other modules of the system. Security such as DoS attack is also our consideration of next step work.

Acknowledgements. Research funding from the European (FP7) MobiS Project is deeply appreciated.

References

1. Hossain, E., Chow, G., et al.: Vehicular Telematics over Heterogeneous Wireless Networks: A survey. Journal of Computer Communications 33(7), 775–793 (2010)
2. Yu, Y., Tandiono, C., Li, X., et al.: ICAN: Information-centric Context-aware Ad-hoc Network. In: ICNC 2014, Honolulu, Hawaii (February 2014)
3. Chen, W., Cai, S.: Ad hoc Peer-to-Peer Network Architecture for Vehicle Safety Communications. IEEE Communications Magazine 43(4) (April 2005)
4. Tsilopoulos, C., Xylomenos, G.: Supporting Diverse Traffic Types in Information Centric Networks. In: ACM SIGCOMM Workshop on Information-Centric Networking, Toronto, Canada (August 2011)
5. Leal, M., Röckl, M., Kloiber, B., et al.: Information-centric Opportunistic Data Dissemination in Vehicular Ad-hoc Networks. In: 13th International IEEE Annual Conference on Intelligent Transportation Systems, Madeira Island, Portugal, September 19-22 (2010)
6. Kanter, T., Forsstrom, S., Kardeby, V., et al.: MediaSense– an Internet of Things Platform for Scalable and Decentralized Context Sharing and Control. In: ICDT 2012 (2012)
7. McGuinness, D.L., van Harmelen, F.: OWL web ontology language overview. W3C recommendation 10.2004-03, 10 (2004)
8. Web ontology language, http://www.w3.org/2001/sw/wiki/OWL
9. Ahlgren, B., Dannewitz, C., Imbrenda, C., et al.: A Survey of Information-centric Networking. IEEE Communications Magazine (July 2012)
10. Jacobson, V., Smetters, D.K., et al.: Networking Named Content. In: 5th International Conference on Emerging Networking Experiments and Technologies (December 2009)
11. Li, F., Chen, F., Wu, J.: Fast Longest Prefix Name Lookup for Content-centric Network Forwarding. In: 8th ACM/IEEE Symposium on Architecture for Networking and Communications Systems (2012)
12. MediaSense open source platform, http://www.mediasense.se
13. Chen, H., Finin, T., Joshi, A., Kagal, L.: Intelligent Agents Meet the Semantic Web in Smart Spaces. IEEE Internet Computing 8(6), 69–79 (2004)

Internet of Vehicles Service in Dual Channel Supply Chains: Who Should Provide?

Zhang Rong[1] and Liu Bin[2,*]

[1] Scientific Research Academy, Shanghai Maritime University, Shanghai, China 201306
[2] School of Economics and Management, Shanghai Maritime University,
Shanghai, China 201306
liubin@shmtu.edu.cn

Abstract. Internet of Vehicles is strategic industries in China, which can provide information service for consumer and further increases the market demand for firms. When a manufacturer uses a retailer as a channel for reaching end customers, the IOV strategy takes on an additional dimension: who should provide IOV service to end customers, and what is the equilibrium for providers. We examine the efficacy of IOV service by manufacturer, IOV service by retailer, and overall supply chain in a model of two competing manufacturer-retailer supply chains who sell partially substitutable IOV service that may differ in market size. Findings suggest that that supply chain efficiency is higher with the IOV service by retailer if the service substitutability is low.

Keywords: Internet of Vehicles (IOV), IOV by manufacturer, IOV by retailer, Game theory, Dual channel supply chains.

1   Introduction

The technology of internet of things is strategic and recently emergent industries in China, which is prioritized. IOV (Internet of Vehicles) is an important application field of the technology of internet of things, to which is paid close attention by many fields since 2010.

At present, on the one hand study on IOV is focused on how to realize IOV including relevant important technologies, data handling technology, developing and designing for cloud computing platform, software development for information service, network security etc, and on the other hand the study is focused on the application of IOV including how to enhance safety and economical efficiency with IOV, or how to realize intelligent traffic control with IOV [1-5]. However, the development and realization, and successful general application of IOV involve factors in many ways. The development of IOV depends on not only technologies, but also investment; and the development of IOV depends on not only propaganda and guidance from government, but also enterprise benefit driving. In the IOV industry chain, all enterprises such as suppliers, manufacturers and retailers that lie different places, who is more willing to

---

* Corresponding author.

R.C.-H. Hsu and W. Shangguang (Eds.): IOV 2014, LNCS 8662, pp. 76–86, 2014.

provide IOV service and what is the equilibrium for the providers? However, on the above two questions, now there is no relevant research to reach. So with the game theory, this paper addresses these questions such as the profits of enterprises which stand different position in supply chain from providing IOV and the whole performance of the supply chain.

The remainder of this study is organized as follows. We describe the basic model in section 2. We study IOV service by the manufacturers in section 3 and IOV service by the retailers in section 4. We analyze supply chain efficiency in section 5 and conclude in section 6.

2 The Basic Model

2.1 The Background and Relevant Notations

Based on the characteristic of vehicle industry, and referencing literature [6], we consider a dual exclusive model. The model is also addressed as dual exclusive supply chain, defined as two manufacturer-retailer dyads whose products compete in the end-customer market. In our notations, the index $i(i = 1, 2)$ identifies the channel or supply chain or its product. We list all notations in the paper as follow.

D_i represents the demand for the product produced and sold by supply chain $i.\theta$ captures product substitutability, and need to satisfy $0 \leq \theta \leq 1.p_i$ are retail prices.w_i are wholesale prices.A_i is supply chain i's initial base demand/market, meaning the amount that would be consumed when $p_i = 0$, no developing IOV is performed, and the supply chains do not compete. e_{mi} is the IOV service level by Manufacturer $i.e_{ri}$ denotes the IOV service level by Retailer $i.\alpha_i$ is the new base demand with the impact of IOV service.l_{mi} is the indicator of whether Manufacturer i provides IOV service in supply chain i, and $l_{mi} = 1$ or 0. l_{ri} is the indicator of whether Retailer i provides IOV service in supply chain i, and $l_{ri} = 1$ or $0.C$ represents the cost of IOV effort. In supply chain i, there is the cost of IOV by the Manufacturers $C(e_{mi}) = \lambda_{mi}e_{mi}^2$, or the cost of Retailer's IOV service $C(e_{ri}) = \lambda_{ri}e_{ri}^2$, where λ_{mi} and λ_{ri} are the cost coefficient. We assume $\lambda_{mi} = \lambda_{ri} = 0.5$.

Based on the above notations and literature [6], demand for product i takes the following form,

$$D_i = \frac{\alpha_i - \theta\alpha_{3-i} - p_i + \theta p_{3-i}}{1 - \theta^2}, i = 1, 2, \tag{1}$$

where the new base demand $\alpha_i = A_i + l_{mi}e_{mi} + l_{ri}e_{ri}$, and requires $l_{mi} + l_{ri} \leq 1$.

To communicate the potential asymmetry between the markets faced by the two supply chains, we define $\Omega = \frac{A_1}{A_2}$. We refer to Ω as base demand ratio. If $\Omega > 1$, supply chain 1's initial base demand is larger than supply chain 2's. This parameter will play a prime role in framing the findings of this research. In the dual exclusive supply chain system, Manufacturer i's and Retailer i's profits are respectively as follows,

$$\Pi_{mi} = D_i w_i - l_{mi}C(e_{mi}), \tag{2}$$

$$\Pi_{ri} = D_i(p_i - w_i) - l_{ri}C(e_{ri}). \tag{3}$$

2.2   The Basic Model NN of None Developing IOV

In the dual exclusive supply chain system, Manufacturer developing IOV and retailer developing IOV each proceed as a three-stage game. In the first stage, in the two channels, the potential investors for developing IOV decides whether develop IOV or not; in the second phase, each manufacturer determines his wholesale price and the IOV developing intensity if he has decided to develop IOV in phase 1; in the third phase, each retailer determines his retail price and the IOV developing intensity if he has decided to develop IOV in phase 1. In each sub-game, each party completes his decision by maximizing his profit.

First we study the basic model. The basic model describes the situation that there are no manufacturers and retailers to develop IOV in the two channels and is noted as NN. So in the structure NN, there is $l_{mi} = 0, i = 1, 2$, and $l_{ri} = 0$, $i = 1, 2$.

According to the game process, we use the backstepping method. First Retailer 1 and Retailer 2 determine their retail prices, and then Manufacturer 1 and Manufacturer 2 determine their wholesale prices. For ease of calculation, we assume $A_2 = 1$. So there is $A_1 = \Omega$. And the full text follows the assumption. Finally, by calculating, the retail prices, wholesale prices, manufacturer's profits and retailer's profits are respectively as follows,

$$p_1 = \frac{2(-3+\theta^2)[(8-9\theta^2+2\theta^4)\Omega+\theta(-2+\theta^2)]}{(-4+\theta^2)(16-17\theta^2+4\theta^4)}, \quad p_2 = \frac{2(-3+\theta^2)[\theta(-2+\theta^2)\Omega+(8-9\theta^2+2\theta^4)]}{(-4+\theta^2)(16-17\theta^2+4\theta^4)},$$

$$w_1 = \frac{(8-9\theta^2+2\theta^4)\Omega+\theta(-2+\theta^2)}{16-17\theta^2+4\theta^4}, w_2 = \frac{\theta(-2+\theta^2)\Omega+(8-9\theta^2+2\theta^4)}{16-17\theta^2+4\theta^4},$$

$$\Pi_{m1} = -\frac{(-2+\theta^2)[(8-9\theta^2+2\theta^4)\Omega+\theta(-2+\theta^2)]^2}{(4-5\theta^2+\theta^4)(16-17\theta^2+4\theta^4)^2}, \Pi_{m2} = -\frac{(-2+\theta^2)[\theta(-2+\theta^2)\Omega+(8-9\theta^2+2\theta^4)]^2}{(4-5\theta^2+\theta^4)(16-17\theta^2+4\theta^4)^2},$$

$$\Pi_{r1} = -\frac{(-2+\theta^2)^2[(8-9\theta^2+2\theta^4)\Omega+\theta(-2+\theta^2)]^2}{(-4+\theta^2)^2(-1+\theta^2)(16-17\theta^2+4\theta^4)^2}, \text{ and } \Pi_{r2} = -\frac{(-2+\theta^2)^2[\theta(-2+\theta^2)\Omega+(8-9\theta^2+2\theta^4)]^2}{(-4+\theta^2)^2(-1+\theta^2)(16-17\theta^2+4\theta^4)^2}.$$

From the expressions of wholesale prices and retail prices, we can derive the conditions that Ω should satisfy, when $0 \le \theta \le 1$ and prices and profits are all have actual meanings. This boundary values are noted as Ω_{NN}. So the meaningful district is described as follow $\frac{\theta(2-\theta^2)}{8-9\theta^2+2\theta^4} < \Omega < \frac{8-9\theta^2+2\theta^4}{\theta(2-\theta^2)}$. In figure 1 the left region of Ω_{NN} is the meaningful district of NN.

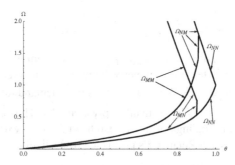

Fig. 1. The boundary of structure NN, MN, NM and MM

3   IOV Service by Manufacturers

IOV service by manufacturers is noted as M, and N means that none provider the IOV service. In our dual exclusive channel, IOV service by manufacturer can manifest in four different ways, both manufacturers develop (MM), only manufacturer 1 develops (MN), only manufacturer 2 develops (NM), or neither manufacturer develops (NN). Specifically, $l_{ri} = 0$ and $l_{mi} = 1$ in Equations (2) and (3) for MM, MN, and NM whenever Manufacturer i would develop IOV for supply chain i; otherwise $l_{mi} = 0$.

Because IOV can provide certain information service and relevant add on service for consumer. So IOV increases the base demand for products, allowing the option to develop IOV would seem to potentially increase the players' profits.

3.1   IOV Service by Only One Manufacturer: MN and NM Model

First we study the structure MN that only manufacturer 1 develops IOV, but manufacturer 2 doesn't. Now $l_{m1} = 1$, and $l_{m2} = 0$.

With the same method as NN, we obtain the retail prices, wholesale prices, manufacturer's profits, retailer's profits and the IOV service level of Manufacturer 1 as follows,

$$p_1 = \frac{2(3-4\theta^2+\theta^4)[(8-9\theta^2+2\theta^4)\Omega+\theta(-2+\theta^2)]}{48-122\theta^2+104\theta^4-35\theta^6+4\theta^8}, \quad p_2 = \frac{2(3-4\theta^2+\theta^4)[\theta(-2+\theta^2)\Omega+2(3-4\theta^2+\theta^4)]}{48-122\theta^2+104\theta^4-35\theta^6+4\theta^8},$$

$$w_1 = \frac{(4-5\theta^2+\theta^4)[(8-9\theta^2+2\theta^4)\Omega+\theta(-2+\theta^2)]}{48-122\theta^2+104\theta^4-35\theta^6+4\theta^8}, \quad w_2 = \frac{(4-5\theta^2+\theta^4)[\theta(-2+\theta^2)\Omega+2(3-4\theta^2+\theta^4)]}{48-122\theta^2+104\theta^4-35\theta^6+4\theta^8},$$

$$\Pi_{m1} = -\frac{(-12+24\theta^2-13\theta^4+2\theta^6)[(8-9\theta^2+2\theta^4)\Omega+\theta(-2+\theta^2)]^2}{2(48-122\theta^2+104\theta^4-35\theta^6+4\theta^8)^2},$$

$$\Pi_{m2} = -\frac{(-4+\theta^2)(2-3\theta^2+\theta^4)[\theta(-2+\theta^2)\Omega+2(3-4\theta^2+\theta^4)]^2}{(48-122\theta^2+104\theta^4-35\theta^6+4\theta^8)^2}.$$

$$\text{and } e_{m1} = -\frac{(-2+\theta^2)[(8-9\theta^2+2\theta^4)\Omega+\theta(-2+\theta^2)]}{48-122\theta^2+104\theta^4-35\theta^6+4\theta^8}.$$

We get the meaningful district of MN is $0 < \theta < 0.9$ and $\frac{\theta(2-\theta^2)}{8-9\theta^2+2\theta^4} < \Omega < \frac{2(3-4\theta^2+\theta^4)}{\theta(2-\theta^2)}$. In figure 1 the left region of Ω_{MN} is the meaningful district of MN.

NM is the symmetrical structure with MN. So the relevant values are as follows,

$$p_1 = \frac{2(3-4\theta^2+\theta^4)[2(3-4\theta^2+\theta^4)\Omega+\theta(-2+\theta^2)]}{48-122\theta^2+104\theta^4-35\theta^6+4\theta^8}, \quad p_2 = \frac{2(3-4\theta^2+\theta^4)[\theta(-2+\theta^2)\Omega+(8-9\theta^2+2\theta^4)]}{48-122\theta^2+104\theta^4-35\theta^6+4\theta^8},$$

$$w_1 = \frac{(4-5\theta^2+\theta^4)[2(3-4\theta^2+\theta^4)\Omega+\theta(-2+\theta^2)]}{48-122\theta^2+104\theta^4-35\theta^6+4\theta^8}, \quad w_2 = \frac{(4-5\theta^2+\theta^4)[\theta(-2+\theta^2)\Omega+(8-9\theta^2+2\theta^4)]}{48-122\theta^2+104\theta^4-35\theta^6+4\theta^8},$$

$$\Pi_{m1} = -\frac{(-4+\theta^2)(2-3\theta^2+\theta^4)[2(3-4\theta^2+\theta^4)\Omega+\theta(-2+\theta^2)]^2}{(48-122\theta^2+104\theta^4-35\theta^6+4\theta^8)^2},$$

$$\Pi_{m2} = -\frac{(-12+24\theta^2-13\theta^4+2\theta^6)[\theta(-2+\theta^2)\Omega+(8-9\theta^2+2\theta^4)]^2}{(48-122\theta^2+104\theta^4-35\theta^6+4\theta^8)^2},$$

$$\text{and } e_{m2} = -\frac{(-2+\theta^2)[\theta(-2+\theta^2)\Omega+(8-9\theta^2+2\theta^4)]}{48-122\theta^2+104\theta^4-35\theta^6+4\theta^8}.$$

We get the meaningful district of NM is $0 < \theta < 0.9$ and $\frac{\theta(2-\theta^2)}{2(3-4\theta^2+\theta^4)} < \Omega < \frac{8-9\theta^2+2\theta^4}{\theta(2-\theta^2)}$. In figure 1 the left region of Ω_{NM} is the meaningful district of NM.

3.2   IOV Service by Both Manufacturers: Model MM

In this structure, $l_{mi} = 1$, $i = 1, 2$. With the same method as NN, we obtain relevant expressions are as follows,

$$p_1 = \frac{2(3-4\theta^2+\theta^4)[2(3-4\theta^2+\theta^4)\Omega+\theta(-2+\theta^2)]}{36-100\theta^2+92\theta^4-33\theta^6+4\theta^8}, \; p_1 = \frac{2(3-4\theta^2+\theta^4)[\theta(-2+\theta^2)\Omega+2(3-4\theta^2+\theta^4)]}{36-100\theta^2+92\theta^4-33\theta^6+4\theta^8},$$

$$w_1 = \frac{(-4+\theta^2)(-1+\theta^2)[2(3-4\theta^2+\theta^4)\Omega+\theta(-2+\theta^2)]}{36-100\theta^2+92\theta^4-33\theta^6+4\theta^8}, \; w_2 = \frac{(-4+\theta^2)(-1+\theta^2)[\theta(-2+\theta^2)\Omega+2(3-4\theta^2+\theta^4)]}{36-100\theta^2+92\theta^4-33\theta^6+4\theta^8},$$

$$\Pi_{m1} = -\frac{(-12+24\theta^2-13\theta^4+2\theta^6)[2(3-4\theta^2+\theta^4)\Omega+\theta(-2+\theta^2)]^2}{2(36-100\theta^2+92\theta^4-33\theta^6+4\theta^8)^2},$$

$$\Pi_{m2} = -\frac{(-12+24\theta^2-13\theta^4+2\theta^6)[\theta(-2+\theta^2)\Omega+2(3-4\theta^2+\theta^4)]^2}{2(36-100\theta^2+92\theta^4-33\theta^6+4\theta^8)^2},$$

$$e_{m1} = -\frac{(-2+\theta^2)[2(3-4\theta^2+\theta^4)\Omega+\theta(-2+\theta^2)]}{36-100\theta^2+92\theta^4-33\theta^6+4\theta^8}, \text{ and } e_{m2} = -\frac{(-2+\theta^2)[\theta(-2+\theta^2)\Omega+2(3-4\theta^2+\theta^4)]}{36-100\theta^2+92\theta^4-33\theta^6+4\theta^8}.$$

For MM is meaningful, Ω must satisfy the following condition $\frac{\theta(2-\theta^2)}{2(3-4\theta^2+\theta^4)} < \Omega < \frac{2(3-4\theta^2+\theta^4)}{\theta(2-\theta^2)}$. So in figure 1 the leftmost two curves consist of the boundary of MM structure.

3.3   Equilibrium Analysis of IOV Service by Manufacturers

Next we compare manufacturers' profits in four models when manufacturers provide the IOV service. First, we compare the manufacturer 1's profit under case MN with NN, and manufacturer 2's profit under case NM with NN The following theorem is the result.

Theorem 1. In the meaningful district of MN, NM, and NN, manufacturer 1's profit in MN always outperforms his profit in NN, and manufacturer 2's profit in NM always outperforms his profit in NN.

Theorem 1 means that in the dual exclusive supply chain system if the manufacturer provides the IOV service, a manufacturer necessarily benefits from its own IOV service when its rival manufacturer doesn't provides the IOV service. Therefore, the manufacturer has the incentive to launch the IOV service.

Then, we compare case MM with NM about manufacturer 1's profit, and case MM with MN about manufacturer 2's profit. The following theorem is the result.

Theorem 2. In the meaningful district of MM, NM, and MN, manufacturer 1's profit in MM always outperforms his profit in NM, and manufacturer 2's profit in MM always outperforms his profit in MN.

The result means that in the dual exclusive supply chain system under manufacturer providing the IOV service, a manufacturer necessarily benefits from its own IOV service when its rival manufacturer provides the IOV service.

At last, we compare MM with NN about two manufacturers' profit, then get theorem 3. As shown in the figure 2, with respect to Manufacturer 2, the boundary values of MM dominating NN is denoted as $\hat{\Omega}_{m2}^{MM-NN}$. Likewise, $\hat{\Omega}_{m1}^{MM-NN}$ shows the boundary values that MM dominates NN with respect to Manufacturer 1.

Theorem 3: Under manufacturer developing IOV, MM is the unique equilibrium strategy. However, the manufacturers can encounter a Prisoner's Dilemma if product substitutability is sufficiently high (e.g., $0.7905 < \theta < 0.8711$ when $\Omega = 1$).

As shown in the figure 2, the left district of boundary value $\hat{\Omega}_{m1}^{MM-NN}$ and $\hat{\Omega}_{m2}^{MM-NN}$ is the dominant region of MM.

Theorem 3 suggests that both manufacturers benefit from providing the IOV service when the service substitutability is low. However, the IOV service could make both manufacturers worse off in MM than in NN if their substitutability is sufficiently intense.

4   IOV Service by Retailers

As with manufacturer provides the IOV service, the IOV by retailers has four possible outcomes: RR, RN, NR, and NN. In all four cases, $l_{mi} = 0$ for $i = 1,2$, while $l_{ri} = 1$ in Equations (2) and (3) whenever Retailer i would develop IOV for supply chain i; otherwise $l_{ri} = 0$.

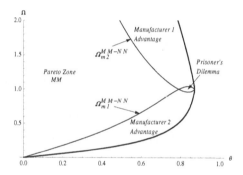

Fig. 2. Manufacturers' profit comparison between MM and NN under manufacturer developing IOV

4.1   IOV by Only One Retailer: Model RN and NR

First we study the case RN that only Retailer 1 provides the IOV service, but Retailer 2 doesn't. With the same method as manufacturer developing IOV, we obtain the relevant values as follows,

$$p_1 = \frac{(4-7\theta^2+2\theta^4)[(4-7\theta^2+2\theta^4)\Omega+\theta(-1+\theta^2)]}{(2-4\theta^2+\theta^4)(8-13\theta^2+4\theta^4)}, \quad p_2 = \frac{(3-6\theta^2+2\theta^4)[\theta(-2+\theta^2)\Omega+(4-7\theta^2+2\theta^4)]}{(2-4\theta^2+\theta^4)(8-13\theta^2+4\theta^4)},$$

$$e_{r1} = -\frac{(-2+\theta^2)((4-7\theta^2+2\theta^4)\Omega+\theta(-1+\theta^2))}{(2-4\theta^2+\theta^4)(8-13\theta^2+4\theta^4)}, \quad w_1 = \frac{(4-7\theta^2+2\theta^4)\Omega+\theta(-1+\theta^2)}{8-13\theta^2+4\theta^4},$$

$$w_2 = \frac{\theta(-2+\theta^2)\Omega+(4-7\theta^2+2\theta^4)}{8-13\theta^2+4\theta^4}, \quad \Pi_{r1} = -\frac{(-2+\theta^2)^2(-1+2\theta^2)[(4-7\theta^2+2\theta^4)\Omega+\theta(-1+\theta^2)]^2}{2(2-4\theta^2+\theta^4)^2(8-13\theta^2+4\theta^4)^2},$$

and $\Pi_{r2} = -\frac{(-1+\theta^2)^3[\theta(-2+\theta^2)\Omega+(4-7\theta^2+2\theta^4)]^2}{(2-4\theta^2+\theta^4)^2(8-13\theta^2+4\theta^4)^2}.$

Derived from the above expressions, the boundary values of all values having actual meanings for Ω are as follows $\frac{\theta(1-\theta^2)}{4-7\theta^2+2\theta^4} < \Omega < \frac{4-7\theta^2+2\theta^4}{\theta(2-\theta^2)}$. In the middle of figure 3 the top curve is the boundary values Ω_{RN} of RN.

Because case NR is symmetrical with RN, we can get relevant values as follow,

$$p_1 = \frac{(3-6\theta^2+2\theta^4)[(4-7\theta^2+2\theta^4)\Omega+\theta(-2+\theta^2)]}{(2-4\theta^2+\theta^4)(8-13\theta^2+4\theta^4)}, \quad p_2 = \frac{(4-7\theta^2+2\theta^4)[\theta(-1+\theta^2)\Omega+(4-7\theta^2+2\theta^4)]}{(2-4\theta^2+\theta^4)(8-13\theta^2+4\theta^4)},$$

$$e_{r2} = -\frac{(-2+\theta^2)[\theta(-1+\theta^2)\Omega+(4-7\theta^2+2\theta^4)]}{(2-4\theta^2+\theta^4)(8-13\theta^2+4\theta^4)}, \quad w_1 = \frac{(4-7\theta^2+2\theta^4)\Omega+\theta(-2+\theta^2)}{8-13\theta^2+4\theta^4},$$

$$w_2 = \frac{\theta(-1+\theta^2)\Omega+(4-7\theta^2+2\theta^4)}{8-13\theta^2+4\theta^4}, \quad \Pi_{r1} = -\frac{(-1+\theta^2)^3[(4-7\theta^2+2\theta^4)\Omega+\theta(-2+\theta^2)]^2}{(2-4\theta^2+\theta^4)^2(8-13\theta^2+4\theta^4)^2}, \text{ and}$$

$$\Pi_{r2} = -\frac{(-2+\theta^2)^2(-1+2\theta^2)[\theta(-1+\theta^2)\Omega+(4-7\theta^2+2\theta^4)]^2}{2(2-4\theta^2+\theta^4)^2(8-13\theta^2+4\theta^4)^2}.$$

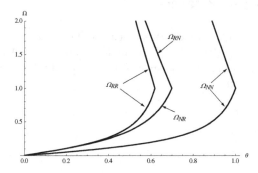

Fig. 3. The boundary values of NN、 RN、 NR and RR

The boundary values for Ω are as follows $\frac{4-7\theta^2+2\theta^4}{\theta(1-\theta^2)} < \Omega < \frac{\theta(2-\theta^2)}{4-7\theta^2+2\theta^4}$. In the middle of figure 3 the below curve is the boundary values Ω_{NR} of case NR.

4.2   IOV by Only Both Retailers: Model RR

In case RR that both retailers develop IOV, so $l_{ri} = 1$, for $i = 1,2$. Relevant values and IOV service level are as follows,

$$p_1 = \frac{(2-5\theta^2+2\theta^4)[(2-5\theta^2+2\theta^4)\Omega+\theta(-1+\theta^2)]}{(1-3\theta^2+\theta^4)(4-9\theta^2+4\theta^4)}, \quad p_2 = \frac{(2-5\theta^2+2\theta^4)[\theta(-1+\theta^2)\Omega+(2-5\theta^2+2\theta^4)]}{(1-3\theta^2+\theta^4)(4-9\theta^2+4\theta^4)},$$

$$w_1 = \frac{(2-5\theta^2+2\theta^4)\Omega+\theta(-1+\theta^2)}{4-9\theta^2+4\theta^4}, \quad w_2 = \frac{\theta(-1+\theta^2)\Omega+(2-5\theta^2+2\theta^4)}{4-9\theta^2+4\theta^4},$$

$$\Pi_{r1} = -\frac{(-1+\theta^2)^2(-1+2\theta^2)[(2-5\theta^2+2\theta^4)\Omega+\theta(-1+\theta^2)]^2}{2(1-3\theta^2+\theta^4)^2(4-9\theta^2+4\theta^4)^2},$$

$$\Pi_{r2} = -\frac{(-1+\theta^2)^2(-1+2\theta^2)[\theta(-1+\theta^2)\Omega+(2-5\theta^2+2\theta^4)]^2}{2(1-3\theta^2+\theta^4)^2(4-9\theta^2+4\theta^4)^2},$$

$$e_{r1} = -\frac{(-1+\theta^2)[(2-5\theta^2+2\theta^4)\Omega+\theta(-1+\theta^2)]}{(1-3\theta^2+\theta^4)(4-9\theta^2+4\theta^4)}, \text{ and } e_{r2} = -\frac{(-1+\theta^2)[\theta(-1+\theta^2)\Omega+(2-5\theta^2+2\theta^4)]}{(1-3\theta^2+\theta^4)(4-9\theta^2+4\theta^4)}.$$

For Ω the boundary values are as $-\frac{\theta(-1+\theta^2)}{2-5\theta^2+2\theta^4} < \Omega < \frac{-(2-5\theta^2+2\theta^4)}{\theta(-1+\theta^2)}$. In the figure 3, the rightmost 2 curves are Ω_{RR}, and their left district is the meaningful region for RR.

4.3   Equilibrium Analysis of IOV Service by Retailers

Now we compare the retailer's profits when they provide IOV service and when they do not in the four cases, RN, NR, RR and NN.

First, we compare case RN with NN about Retailer 1's profit, and case NR with NN about Retailer 2's profit. The following theorem is the result. Regarding Retailer 1, the boundary values of RN dominating NN is denoted as $\hat{\Omega}_{r1}^{RN-NN}$. Likewise, regarding Retailer 2, $\hat{\Omega}_{r2}^{NR-NN}$ show the boundary values of NR dominating NN.

Theorem 4. In the meaningful district of RN, NR, and NN, Retailer 1 benefits from its own developing IOV when its rival does not develop IOV (going from NN to RN) if and only if $\Omega < \hat{\Omega}_{r1}^{RN-NN}$, and Retailer 2 benefits from its own developing IOV when its rival does not develop IOV (going from NN to NR) if and only if $\Omega > \hat{\Omega}_{r2}^{NR-NN}$.

Theorem 4 means that in the dual exclusive supply chain system under retailer providing the IOV service, a retailer can still earn extra profits from its own IOV service when its rival retailer doesn't provide the IOV service.

Then, we compare case RR with NR about Retailer 1's profit, and case RR with RN about Retailer 2's profit. The following theorem is the result.

Theorem 5: In the meaningful district of RR, NR, and RN, Retailer 1 benefits from its own developing IOV when its rival develops IOV (going from NR to RR) if and only if $\Omega > \hat{\Omega}_{r1}^{RR-NR}$, and Retailer 2 benefits from its own developing IOV when its rival develops IOV (going from RN to RR) if and only if $\Omega < \hat{\Omega}_{r2}^{RR-RN}$.

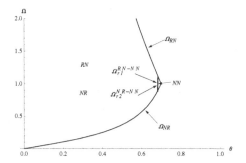

Fig. 4. Retailers' profits comparison in RN, NR, and NN

Theorem 5 shows that in the dual exclusive supply chain system under retailer providing the IOV service, a retailer can still earn extra profits from its own IOV service and is hurt as its rival retailer provides the IOV service.

After comparing case RR with NN about two retailers' profits, and combining with the above analysis, we find that in the four cases under some conditions case RR dominates RN and NR, and RN and NR dominate NN. So we get theorem 6.

Theorem 6: Under retailer providing the IOV service, RR is the equilibrium strategy if and only if $\hat{\Omega}_{r1}^{RR-NR} < \Omega < \hat{\Omega}_{r2}^{RR-RN}$; RN is an equilibrium if and only if $\hat{\Omega}_{r2}^{RR-RN} < \Omega < \overline{\Omega}_{RR}$; NR is an equilibrium if and only if $\underline{\Omega}_{RR} < \Omega < \hat{\Omega}_{r1}^{RR-NR}$.

Theorem 6 indicates that the existence of a specific equilibrium depends on the extent of service substitutability and the base demand disparity between supply chain 1 and 2, as illustrated in Figure 5.

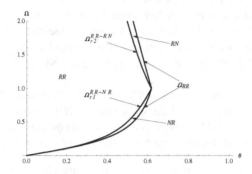

Fig. 5. Retailers' profits comparison in RN, NR, and RR

5   Comparison Analysis of Supply Chain Efficiency

This section studies the profit of whole supply chain profit instead of individual firm profit. We define supply chain efficiency as the sum of all players' profits. To investigate supply chain efficiency for all previously studied developing IOV structures, we divide two cases: one is under the symmetric demand setting, namely, $\Omega = 1$; another is the case of asymmetric channels, namely Ω takes any feasible value.

5.1   The Symmetric Demand

When $\Omega = 1$, by symmetry, MN has the same as NM, and likewise RN and NR are equally efficient. So we analyze RR, MM, RN, MN, and NN. Table 1 shows the rank ordering of the five structures as product substitutability varies.

Table 1. Rank ordering with respect to supply chain efficiency when $\Omega = 1$

	[0, 0.51]	[0.51, 0.52]	[0.52, 0.55]	[0.55, 0.59]	[0.59, 0.62]	[0.62, 0.67]	[0.67, 0.7]	[0.7, 0.76]
RR	1	2	3	4	5	×	×	×
RN	2	1	1	1	1	1	2	×
MM	3	3	2	2	2	2	1	1
MN	4	4	4	3	3	3	3	2
NN	5	5	5	5	4	4	4	3

× shows that the interval fall out of the region of this structure.

Table 1 demonstrates that case RR performs the best when product substitutability is low ($\theta < 0.51$). Table 1 also shows that case NN is not necessarily the worst, and, as product substitutability becomes sufficiently high ($0.59 < \theta < 0.72$), RR becomes the worst because of the intense supply chain competition. The trends n rank ordering confirm that retailer developing IOV worsens supply chain efficiency, more so than does manufacturer developing IOV, if supply chain competition becomes too intense.

5.2   The Asymmetric Demand

We extend to the case of asymmetric channels. Now case RN and NR have different efficiency, so we study respectively. We analyze RR, RN, and MM, the top three structures in symmetric case, and NR together. Figure 6 displays the structure that give the highest supply chain efficiency for each feasible combination of θ and Ω. Case RR dominates most of the time, but gives away to case RN and NR when product substitutability gradually becomes high and the base demand is more asymmetric. Then we compare RR with MM. Likewise. Case RR dominates most of the time, but gives away to MM when product substitutability becomes sufficiently high. At the extremes, case RR takes the lead because the intensifying competition increase total profit in the supply chain with larger base demand more than it takes away from the supply chain with the smaller base demand.

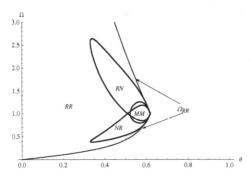

Fig. 6. Comparison regards to supply chain efficiency in RR with in RN and NR, and in RR with in MM

6   Conclusion

This study evaluates the efficacy of the IOV service by the manufacturers and the IOV service by the retailers in a dual exclusive channel model with asymmetric competing supply chains. Our results offer managerial insights to better understand a variety of providing IOV strategies in practice. First, a dominant strategy for both manufacturers is to develop IOV at a positive level in manufacturer developing IOV, although a Prisoner's Dilemma may occur. In retailer developing IOV, asymmetric developing structures can arise as equilibria. Our analysis demonstrates that commitment to not developing IOV service in competitive supply chains is credible. Second, our analysis suggests that supply chain efficiency is higher with retailer's IOV service if the service substitutability is low, but otherwise is higher with manufacturer developing IOV. When service substitutability is pretty high, case NN is not necessarily the worst.

Acknowledgments. The authors gratefully acknowledge support from the National Natural Science Foundation of China through grants 71171074, U1204701 and 71301045.

References

[1] Liu, Y.X., Zhao, J.K., Yang, H.O., et al.: An Intelligent Charging Station Matching Method for Electric Vehicles in Internet of Things. Advanced Materials Research 846-847, 243–257 (2013)

[2] Leng, Y., Zhao, L.: Novel design of intelligent internet-of-vehicles management system based on cloud-computing and Internet-of-Things. In: Proceedings of 2011 International Conference on Electronic and Mechanical Engineering and Information Technology, vol. 6, pp. 3190–3193 (2011)

[3] Wang, J., Liu, Y., Gao, W.: Securing Internet of Vehicles Using TCM. International Journal of Digital Content Technology and its Applications 4(7), 226–233 (2010)

[4] Wang, Q., Yu, Y., Tang, Z.: Architecture design for intelligent vehicle computing platform based on internet of vehicles. Applied Mechanics and Materials 253-255(PART 1), 1423–1426 (2013)

[5] Duan, X., Wang, X.: Design of school bus safety regulation system based on the internet of vehicle technology. Applied Mechanics and Materials 263-266(PART 1), 2911–2914 (2013)

[6] Liu, B., Cai, G., Tsay, A.A.: Advertising in asymmetric competing supply chains. Production and Operations Management Society, 1–14 (2013)

Toward Designing Efficient Service Discovery Protocol in Vehicular Networks

Lamya Albraheem, Mznah AlRodhan, and AbduAllah Aldhlaan

Computer Science departement, Collage of Computer Science and Information,
King Saud University, Riyadh, Saudi Arabia

Abstract. Nowadays, it can be seen that there is an increasing interest in the field of vehicular networks due to its important applications. These applications depend mainly on the service discovery protocols which show the need for giving more work and effort to design an efficient VANET service discovery protocol. In fact, little studies have been conducted in this field. Therefore, this paper attempts to highlight some directions that can be considered for designing service discovery solution for VANETs. To explore these directions, the paper provides a literature review for the earlier studies and presents a qualitative analysis of them in order to provide some recommendations for the best design issues. This is can be considered as a step toward designing efficient protocol and may encourage researchers to contribute more in this field.

1 Introduction

Recently, it can be seen that there is an increasing interest in the Intelligent Transportation Systems (ITS) especially in the vehicular networks. They can be considered as the most important area of ITS and become an active field of research. These networks give the ability to the smart vehicles to communicate and exchange information with each other to represent Vehicular Ad hoc Networks (VANETs). In fact, the essential applications of VANETs present the need for giving this area more interest and research [1]. The VANETs applications can provide several services not only for safety purposes like emergency warning but also for convenience services such as restaurant menus, prices of gas stations and discount sale. These services require a communication between service provider and service requester in order to perform dissemination and discovery processes. This is show that VANETs applications depend mainly on service discovery systems. For this reason, there is a need for giving more work and effort to design an efficient VANET service discovery protocol [2] [3].

In the research community, there are a lot of service discovery protocols (SDPs) that were designed for wired networks, mobile ad hoc networks (MANETs) and mesh networks. In addition, little studies have been conducted in VANETs. Although there are many similarities between MANETs and VANETs, it is hard to apply traditional protocols to vehicular network due to its unique characteristics. These characteristics are the high mobility, rapid changing topology, high probability of disconnecting and limited bandwidth. Therefore, designing a service discovery protocol for vehicular network is a challenging topic [1] [4].

This paper provides a literature review for the earlier studies in the VANETs service discovery protocols. Furthermore, it makes a qualitative analysis between

R.C.-H. Hsu and W. Shangguang (Eds.): IOV 2014, LNCS 8662, pp. 87–98, 2014.
© Springer International Publishing Switzerland 2014

them in order to give attentions to the issues and challenges that require more improving. Since the identifying of these issues can be considered as a step toward designing efficient service discovery protocol. The paper will be organized as follows: Section 2 present background information about vehicular networks. Section 3 provides a review for the service discovery protocols for VANETs, which include its components, architectures, modes and protocols. In addition, section 4 gives a qualitative analysis of the presented service discovery protocols according to different criteria. Finally, section 5 contains the discussion and findings while section 6 present the conclusion and future works that suggested from this research.

2   Background

2.1   Vehicular Networks Characteristics

The vehicular networks share some general characteristics with the Mobile Ad Hoc Network (MANET). Both of them can be defined as a wireless network of mobile nodes without predefined topology. In addition, they have limited bandwidth, need multi-hop communication and move very fast. However, there are significant differences between them that can be discussed according to many aspects such as: mobility pattern, mobility properties and node properties [5, 6].

Mobility pattern: The movement of vehicles is not random since it is restricted by the physical map with highways, roads, traffic lights and junctions which can affect mainly on the nodes mobility pattern. It can be seen also that the network performance can be affected by the density of the region. If the density is high, collisions may occur in the wireless network; on the other hand, network fragmentation may happen in the low density regions [5].

Mobility properties: The vehicles move faster than the nodes in the MANET networks. This high mobility propriety can be considered as a huge challenge since the time in which any two vehicles are connected can be very short which cause frequent disconnection. This can make the maintenance of rout between the vehicles so difficult [5].

Node properties: In VANET networks, vehicles need to communicate with each other, with fixed infrastructure and sometime with any device or sensor insides the vehicles. Therefore, they need communication devices that have to be equipped into their body to give them the ability to perform the required tasks. It is should be mentioned here that these devices does not have the problem of power consumption since it is supplied by vehicles batteries[5] [2] It is obvious that the significant properties of VANET that discussed above clarify the need for developing new protocols and architectures especially for VANET environments.

Table 1. Differences between MANET and VANET

Aspect	MANET	VANET
Mobility pattern	random	Not random , According to physical map
Mobility properties	Slower	Move very fast
Node properties	Limited power	Continuous power

2.2 Overview of Communication Systems in Vehicular Networks

The VANETs communication system architecture can be categorized into three domains: in-vehicle domain, ad hoc domain and infrastructure domain. In-vehicle domain represents the network that consists of On-Board Unit (OBU) and many Application Units (AUs). The OBU contains network devices for wireless communications that based on IEEE 802.11p/a/b radio technology, while the AU is a device that benefit from the OBU communication abilities to execute one or more applications. The AU device can be integrated to OBU or portable like PDA, also it can be connected as a wired and wireless connection [7].

The second domain of VANETs communication system is ad hoc domain or vehicular ad hoc network (VANET). It is networks of vehicles, which attached with OBUs, and fixed infrastructure called road–side units (RSUs). The communication between these nodes is decentralized and performed in peer-to-peer fashion. If the wireless connection is available between vehicles, OBUs can communicate directly. On the other hand, if the direct connection is not available, there is a need for routing protocols to perform multi-hop communication in which the data are sent through multiple OBUs to the destination [7].

In the infrastructure domain, the network is centralized. Therefore the vehicles can communicate with each other through infrastructure. If any road-side unit (RSU) is connected to the infrastructure network, the vehicles can access the infrastructure through the RSU and communicate with any node on the Internet [7]. Actually, different applications of VANETs in safety, monitoring and entertainment require a lot of information that available outside their network and can be accessed through infrastructure units. Then the vehicles can share this information between them in the ad hoc domain. Therefore, using hybrid architecture of ad hoc and infrastructure domain can give the ability to access more contents make the network more flexible [8].

3   Service Discovery System for VANET

There are a lot of useful services that can be provided by vehicular networks. These services can be classified into two categories: safety services and convenience services. The safety services are related to traffic safety and emergency situations. On the other hand, the convenience services are related to entertainment services or informative services such as providing information about parking, advertisement, local gas prices and restaurant menus [1]. In order to locate these services, there is a need for efficient service discovery protocol. In this section, the information that required for understanding the service discovery system will be provided. This information will be about the architectures, service discovery modes and protocols.

3.1 Service Discovery Architectures for VANET

The service discovery protocols can be designed based on different architectures which are Directory-based architecture, Directory-less architecture and hybrid architecture [10]. The definitions for each of them with their drawbacks will be discussed below.

3.1.1 Directory-Based Architecture
In this architecture, there is a need for a service directory to coordinate the service

discovery process. There are two types of service directories: centralized and distributed or decentralize. The centralized service directories are implemented in a single node that can be vehicle or roadside units, while the distributed directories are implemented in many nodes [10]. The centralized directory is not recommended solution for mobile ad hoc network since the single node directory is not reachable by all nodes. In addition, the vehicular network will be affected if there is a failure in the single point. Another obvious problem is the scalability; single point cannot handle all service requests for large number of nodes. For these reasons, distributed directories are more recommended for designing mobile ad hoc network [11].

The distributed directories can be implemented in mobile ad hoc network using different approaches. In the backbone-based approach, the directories nodes are formed to represent a backbone that responsible about handle the requests and advertising the services to the members of the backbone. The directories that included in the backbone can be selected using a Minimum Dominating Set algorithm [11]. Another approach for implementing distributed directories is clustered-based approach. In this technique, each cluster that contain a group of node has a cluster head that represent the service directory and responsible about answering the discovery requests [11]. In the Distributed Hash Table based techniques (DHT-based), the network is divided into many regions based on the geographical position. In each region, a few nodes will be elected to represent the directories. These directories store a set of keys that represent the services and can be mapped to regions using the hash-table[11]. The service directories can be implemented over an infrastructure or over a vehicle. In the first case, the service providers register their services in the infrastructure that provide lists of all available services descriptions. The services requesters search for the required service descriptions through the infrastructure and after finding the intended information, a connection will be established between the requester and provider. In case of service discovery over a vehicle, if there is a group of vehicles provides a specific service, one of them will be selected to be the service directory [12].

The drawback of directory-based architecture is that the directories need frequent update and maintenance of the services information due to the high mobility of vehicles. If the number of update queries is high, traffic overhead and congestion will be happen in the network. Moreover, information inconsistency will be resulted in case that the number of updating is low [12].

3.1.2 Directory-Less Architecture

In Directory-less architecture, there is no need for service directory which can avoid the problem of frequent update. The service discovery process will be performed as following: the service providers advertise in the network about their services while the service requester broadcast their queries about the intended services waiting for a response from any providers [12]. The most significant issue in this architecture is the way of selecting the advertisement frequency and range of service providers. This is due to the bandwidth consumption that can be increased by the advertisement transmission [12].

3.1.3 Hybrid Architecture

The hybrid architecture combines between the directory-based and directory-less architecture. The service discovery process is performed as following: the service providers register their service descriptions in the service directory in case that exists in the surrounding area. However, if the directory not exists, they will advertise their services in the network. On the other hand, the service requesters send the queries to the service directory in the surrounding area, or they broadcast their request waiting for a reply from any service providers [12].

3.2   Service Discovery Modes for VANET

3.2.1   Reactive

In this mode, which is called also pull-based mode, service requesters send their requests in the vehicular network. Also, the service providers does not advertise about their services, however, they are waiting for receiving a request to reply with the required information [11]. The communication model that based on reactive mode is request-reply model. It is a simple way to exchange information through message passing. The sender/requester sends a specific request to the receiver who should send a reply with the required information. This model is used by different communication protocols such as HTTP. It is based on one to one Interaction and it has a limited support to the space, time and flow/synchronization decoupling which make this mode not appropriate for a network with high mobility[13].

3.2.2   Proactive

In this mode, which is called also push-based mode, the service providers advertise about their services in the vehicle network. There are two main parameters that should considered which are advertisement range and advertisement frequency. In fact, these parameters depend greatly on the mobility rate, the type application (safety, traffic monitoring and driving comfort), level congestions and failure. Furthermore, this mode is affected obviously by the way of aggregation and dissemination of advertised information [1]. The problem of push mode is that the network overhead is too high. In addition, the scalability is limited unless if the aggregation method is efficient. However, this mode is suitable for safety application [1].

3.2.3   Hybrid

The hybrid mode combine both proactive and reactive mode. The service providers advertise their services to the services directories and the service requesters may issue their requesters to the directories only reactively (on demand). There are different strategies for hybrid mode according to the way of advertising and requesting; it could be greedy, conservative or adaptive. In the greedy mode, the service directories advertise their services to all nodes and also the requesters send their requests to all nodes. In the conservative mode, the advertising and requesting will be sending to a random set of nodes. In adaptive mode, the advertisement and request propagation ranges depend on different factors such as level of mobility, network congestion and etc [11].

The hybrid service discovery mode can be classified also according to its structure into clustered-based structure and flat-based structure. The clustered-based structure the vehicles will be organized in clusters. For each cluster, the cluster-head will receive the service requests from its node then aggregate the required information from the nodes if its clusters or from the neighboring cluster-heads and then send the response to the service requester. On the other hand, the vehicles in the flat structure communicate with each other without level of information aggregation [1].

The publish/subscribe communication model use both push and pull modes. The idea of this model can be described as following: the services providers/publishers advertise their services through the network while the service requesters/subscribers express their interest in certain services [13]. The publishers send a publication messages to the directories, these messages contain information about the services. On the other hand, the subscribers send a subscription message that contains the required services. When the directory receives a publication, it will distribute the publication to all subscribers. The features of publish/subscribe model is the highly supported to space, time, and flow decoupling which make it appropriate for network with high mobility [14].

3.3   VANET Service Discovery Protocols

In vehicular network, the service discovery protocols can be classified into two main classes which are: Address-based protocols and Geographical based protocols. The address-based protocols use the IP address information to locate the services while the geographical positions are used in the second type of protocols, assuming that each vehicle have knowledge about its position.

3.3.1   Address-Based Protocols

In 2008, Mohandas, et al. proposed a new protocol for service discovery which called Address Based Service Resolution Protocol (ABSRP). This protocol is designed to discover location-based services such as information about gas station or restaurant menus. Moreover, it is independent of the network layer. This protocol works as following: the roadside units within the same area share their service information, which are service type and IP address of service providers, through the Internet. Each roadside unit broadcast hello_packets periodically to the around vehicles and they rebroadcast the packet if the number of hops is less than pre-defined maximum hops. Each vehicle associates itself with the closest roadside unit to be its leader. At any time a vehicle need a service, it will send a request which contains the service type and the desired area to its leader. The roadside unit will take one of these actions: if the roadside unit has information about the requested service, it will forward the request to the target service provider. Otherwise, it will broadcast the request over the vehicular network or internet to reach the target service provider. When the service provider receives the request, it will send a response to the service requester. It should be mentioned also that this protocol use the routing protocol to check if the roadside unit is reachable, if not the backbone network (internet) will be used.

The performance of this protocol was evaluated using the Qualnet Simulation tool. The test was performed with 50 vehicles and five roadside units that exist in area of (5000m*1000m) terrain. In addition, the routing protocol that used for the test is AODV routing protocol (Ad hoc On Demand Distance Vector), which is considered as the best address based routing protocol that can be used for vehicular network. The metrics that used to evaluate the performance is the success rate, which are average number of successful requests, and the time that taken to service request. The results of testing this protocol showed that 70% to 80% of service requests were resolved in less than 270 milliseconds [2].

In 2011, Abrougui provided a protocol that designed for large-scale vehicular network which called Vehicular Service Discovery Protocol: VSDP. It is infrastructure-based protocol which makes the communication between vehicles more efficient through the roadside backbone. Moreover, it is dependent on the network layer which means that the service discovery protocol is integrated with routing protocol. Therefore, when a specific request finds a service, the routing information is piggybacking in the service replay message. This is can make the protocol lightweight and decrease the overhead that may happen from flooding the network. This protocol works as following: the service providers advertise their services to their roadside units, the range of advertizing is called advertisement zone. On the other hand; the service requesters send their requests to their roadside units that propagate them with the vehicles until they reach to the proactive advertisement zone (PAZ). After that, the service providers will adjust the size of their PAZ for future requests, this adjustment called PAZ adaptation. Therefore, the propagation zone will be reduced for future request after the adaptation process. Finally, the service providers will send the reply messages to the requesters from the roadside units that exist on the boundary of PAZ [1]. The main feature of this protocol is the adaptation of the advertisement zone which depend on different factors such as network congestion, mobility rate and the density of the service providers. This feature can enhance the performance metrics that include service availability, network overhead or discovery latency. In addition, VSDP use hybrid approach that combine the proactive and reactive strategies in which the vehicles that exist in the advertisement zone will disseminate their service information, while the vehicles that outside this zone will send their service requests. This makes the protocol more efficient than simple protocol that based on proactive or reactive strategies. Furthermore, since the protocol is hybrid, it is integrated with hybrid routing protocol which are SHARP [1].

The performance of VSDP was evaluated using two different mobility models city scenario and highway. In addition, it compared to the performance of Service Location Protocol SLP. The comparison was performed between SLP, hybrid multichannel VSDP, hybrid single channel VSDP, multichannel Reactive VSDP and multichannel Proactive VSDP. The metrics that used for evaluation are success rate, response time and total bandwidth usage. The results showed that VSPP have higher success rate and low response time than SLP. In addition, it has lower bandwidth usage than SLP which support the scalability [1].

3.3.2   Geographical-Based Protocols

The Vehicular Information Transfer Protocol (VITP) has been introduced in 2007 by Dikaiakos, et al. This protocol was developed to locate location-aware services which related to traffic conditions, traffic alerts and roadside facilities. The architecture of VITP, which is an application-layer communication protocol, was designed to be distributed directory-based over vehicle ad hoc network. The service discovery modes that used for this protocol are both reactive and proactive modes. The reactive mode used for request the infotainment types of services while the proactive mode used for disseminate information that related to safety services. The main design concepts of this protocol can be presented as following: software components, which called VITP peers, are installed on modern vehicles to communicate and collect useful information from vehicles' on-board sensors. Moreover, the services requesters have to send their queries to particular geographical area, which routed to destination through VANET infrastructure or other available network such as Internet. The query is forwarded through intermediate nodes until it reach to the target area. After that, the VITP peers in the target location will establish a virtual ad-hoc server (VAHS) that responsible about resolving the query. The query will be transported between VAHS peers until it reach the required peer, which means that the return condition is detected or satisfied. Then the replay will be broadcasted to reach the originated VITP peer. The intermediate nodes in this protocol support cashing which allow them to initiate replay to VITP query. Moreover, each query has identifier to avoid multiple processing to the same query and to match the replies with its queries [15].

The performance of this protocol was evaluated using simulation experiment. Two traffic model was used which are highway and city pattern. They generated by highway generator and SUMO (Simulation of Urban Mobility). The wireless-network and VITP traffic was simulated using NS-2 simulator. The metrics that used to describe the performance are: response time, which are the time between initiating the query and receiving the replay, dropping rate, which represents the percentage of unsuccessful quires, accuracy and efficiency. Different results have been shown to prove the protocol effectiveness. However, it should be mentioned that the response time will be affected linearly with the query distance in the highway mode. Also, the dropping rate will increase with the gaps that related to vehicle density [15].

In 2009, Abrougui presented Location-aware Service Discovery Protocols (LocVSDPs) for a large scale VANETs. They are clustered infrastructure-based protocols. They are based on network layer and integrated with a modified version of the Connectionless Approach for Streets CLA-S routing protocol. Furthermore, the roadside routers are support multiple interface and channel diversity [1].

The Election-Based LocVSDP protocol has four phases: the first phase is the service advertisement phase in which the providers send messages or location-based proactive discovery packet to the neighboring roadside routers. This packet contains routing information and service information. When the message received to the roadside router, the integrated module, which contains the service module and routing module, will split the discovery information from the routing information to make the required processing. The service module will add or update the service information in the table while the routing information will be added or updated in the routing table. In the second phase, the service requesters propagate a location-based reactive discovery packet. This packet contains information about the location of intended service, which represents the region of interest RI. This region is a disc area that described by the coordinate of the origin and the radius. The sent packet also contains both routing information and service information. As the same way in service advertisement, the roadside routers will separate the routing information from the service information. Each roadside router will forward the request or not based on location-based request propagation mechanism. If the roadside router not in the region of interest, it will compare its distance to the center of the RI to the received distance that separate the source vehicle from the center of RI. If it's shorter, the packet will be forwarded. If the roadside router inside the region of interest, it will forward the request and start the election process to select a leader roadside router for the region [16].

In the election process, the leader will be responsible about collecting the services responses from other service providers and sending accurate service reply to the service requester. The benefit of having a leader is to prevent sending many responses to the service requester. The leader that selected is the roadside router that has the minimum distance to the center of the region of interest. At the end of this process, a spanning tree of roadside units for the region is generated, and the root of this tree is the elected leader. When the leader propagates the service reply, each integrated module in the roadside units that exist on the way will use the routing information for determine the next step and cashes the service information [16].

The performance of this protocol is compared to the VITP, the result showed that Election-Based LocVSDP outperforms VITP in message and time complexities. The message complexity includes the number of advertisements, the number of location-based requests, the number of election messages, the number of local-replies and the number of reply messages. On the other hand, the time of complexity represent the average time that required for processing a discovery process [16].

Little studies in service discovery protocol integrate the fault tolerance and Qos features in their protocol. For this reason, in 2011, a new enhancement for the LocVSDP is provided, which is FTQosLocVSDP. It includes efficient fault tolerance, load balancing and Qos features [17].

4   Qualitative Analysis

In this section, we qualitatively analyze the service discovery protocols that described above in order to get the best features that can be considered to design efficient service discovery protocol. The analysis was performed according to different criteria that get from these studies [1, 18].(See Table 1).

5   Discussion and Finding

According to the architecture of service discovery protocols, it is proven in the literature studies that the centralized directory-based architecture is not a good choice for these protocols which can be returned to the single node failure and the problem of scalability. For these reasons, the distributed architecture can be considered in designing efficient SD protocol [11]. Furthermore, the directory-based is usually preferred than directory-less for many reasons which include: efficient communication in large scale network that increase the number of successful discovery request, reducing the network traffic, maintaining a level of stability which support the high mobility and increase the bandwidth usage [1]. In addition, according to Kleanthis et al, designing a protocol with hybrid architecture is still an open issue [12].

Regarding the service discovery mode, the proactive mode outperform the reactive mode in the latency and overhead if the number of server providers is less than the number of service requesters. On the other hand, if the number of server providers is more than the number of service requesters, the reactive mode will be better. Therefore, it is recommended to use the hybrid mode for better performance. However, the main issue in hybrid mode is determining the range and frequency of service providers advertisement. The best solution to this issue is using adaptive mechanism for determining these two parameters according to different network characteristics [1] [11]. It should be mentioned also that the results in previous studies show that the service discovery protocol that integrated with network layer is outperform application layer based protocol. The piggybacking of service information onto routing message will resulted in lightweight protocol and avoids redundant transmission of service discovery packets. Therefore, the network resources will be saved and the scalability will supported more[1] [11].

According to the two main types of SDPs which are addressed-based and geographical-based protocols, it is recommended to design SDP that based on the geographical information. It will be more efficient since the position information will participate in having less delay and decreased the overhead problems comparing with other types of protocols [19]. Finally, to design efficient SDP, it is recommended to take into account the mechanisms that can be used for fault tolerance, load balancing and quality of services.

Properties	EB-LocVSDP	FTQosLocVSDP	VITP	ABSRP	VSDP
Network layer	Network layer	Network layer	Application layer	application layer	Network layer
Traffic model	City model	City model	highway + city	random waypoint	highway + city
SD mode	Hybrid (proactive+ Reactive)	Hybrid (proactive+ Reactive)	Reactive: Request Replay in the service discovery. Proactive: disseminate safety information.	Reactive : Request/Replay	Hybrid (proactive+ Reactive)
Architecture	Directory-based (Distributed)	Directory-based (Distributed)	Directory-based (Distributed)	Directory-based (Distributed)	Directory-based (Distributed)
Routing algorithm	CLA-S (Geographical protocol)	CLA-S (Geographical protocol)	Geographical + Broadcast	AODV	SHARP
Type of services	time-sensitive and location-based services	time-sensitive and location-based services	Safety + Convenience	Convenience services	convenience services (fixed + mobile)
Performance 1-Scalability	Yes Clusteredbased Integrated w/ network layer	Yes Clusteredbased Integrated w/ network layer	Yes	No	Yes Integrated w/ network layer
1.1 load balancing	Cashing	Yes	Cashing , Service Grouping	-	-
1.2 Query efficiency	Yes (channel diversity)	Yes	-	-	Yes (adaptation) (channel diversity)
2- Fault tolerance	No	Yes	No	No	No
3-Mobility support	-	-	-	Not determined	Yes Adaptation
Privacy	No	No	No	No	No

6   Conclusion

In conclusion, this paper presents the background information that required for understanding the vehicular network. Moreover, it provides a comprehensive study for the service discovery protocols that designed for VANETs. As a result of this study, different recommendations for designing efficient service discovery protocol are highlighted which can be considered for designing efficient protocol as future work.

References

1. Abrougui, K.: Design and Performance Evaluation of Service Discovery Protocols for Vehicular Networks, p. 207. University of Ottawa, Ottawa (2011)
2. Mohandas, B.K., et al.: ABSRP- A Service Discovery Approach for Vehicular Ad Hoc Networks. In: Asia-Pacific Services Computing Conference, APSCC 2008. IEEE (2008)
3. Abrougui, K., Boukerche, A.: Secure service discovery protocol for intelligent transport systems: proof of correctness. In: Proceedings of the First ACM International Symposium on Design and Analysis of Intelligent Vehicular Networks and Applications, pp. 101–108. ACM, Miami (2011)
4. Yue, L., Jun, B., Ju, Y.: Research on Vehicular Ad Hoc Networks. In: Control and Decision Conference, CCDC 2009, Chinese (2009)
5. Fonseca, A., Vazão, T.: Applicability of position-based routing for VANET in highways and urban environment. Journal of Network and Computer Applications (2012)
6. Zhang, G., et al.: A survey on the routing schemes of urban Vehicular Ad Hoc Networks. In: Proceedings of the 27th Chinese Control Conference (2008)
7. Grilli, G.: Data dissemination in vehicular ad-hoc networks. Department of Computer Science, Systems and Production 2010, University of Rome "Tor Vergata" (2010)
8. Duddalwar, P., Deshmukh, A., Dorle, S.S.: A Comparitve Study of Routing Protocol in Vehicular Ad Hoc Network. International Journal of Emerging Technology and Advanced Engineering 2(3), 71–76 (2012)
9. Popescu-Zeletin, R., Radusch, I., Rigani, M.A.: Vehicular-2-X communication state-of-the-art and research in mobile vehicular ad hoc networks. Springer, Heidelberg (2010)
10. Pazzi, R.W., Abrougui, K., De Rezende, C., Boukerche, A.: Service Discovery Protocols for VANET Based Emergency Preparedness Class of Applications: A Necessity Public Safety and Security. In: Prasad, S.K., Vin, H.M., Sahni, S., Jaiswal, M.P., Thipakorn, B. (eds.) ICISTM 2010. CCIS, vol. 54, pp. 1–7. Springer, Heidelberg (2010)
11. Ververidis, C.N., Polyzos, G.C.: Service discovery for mobile Ad Hoc networks: a survey of issues and techniques. IEEE Communications Surveys & Tutorials 10(3), 30–45 (2008)
12. Kleanthis, D., Aristeidis, C., Despoina, P.: Transforming vehicles into e-government 'Cloud computing' nodes. In: Georgiadis, C.K., Jahankhani, H., Pimenidis, E., Bashroush, R., Al-Nemrat, A. (eds.) ICGS3/e-Democracy 2012. LNICST, vol. 99, pp. 1–8. Springer, Heidelberg (2012)
13. Rodríguez-Domínguez, C., Benghazi, K., Noguera, M., Garrido, J.L., Rodríguez, M.L., Ruiz-López, T.: A Communication Model to Integrate the Request-Response and the Publish-Subscribe Paradigms into Ubiquitous Systems. Sensor 12(6), 7648–7668 (2012)

14. Noguchi, S., Matsuura, S., Fujikawa, K.: Performance Analysis of Mobile Publish-Subscribe Service Discovery on IPv6 over GeoNetworking. In: 2012 Sixth International Conference on Innovative Mobile and Internet Services in Ubiquitous Computing, IMIS (2012)
15. Dikaiakos, M.D., et al.: Location-Aware Services over Vehicular Ad-Hoc Networks using Car-to-Car Communication. IEEE J. Sel. A. Commun. 25(8), 1590–1602 (2007)
16. Boukerche, A., Abrougui, K., Pazzi, R.W.N.: Context-aware and location-based service discovery protocol for vehicular networks. In: Proceedings of the 6th ACM Symposium on Performance Evaluation of Wireless Ad Hoc, Sensor, and Ubiquitous Networks, pp. 93–100. ACM, Tenerife (2009)
17. Abrougui, K., Pazzi, R.W.N., Boukerche, A.: Towards a balanced and reliable localization of services in heterogeneous vehicular ad hoc networks. In: Proceedings of the 7th ACM Symposium on QoS and Security for Wireless and Mobile Networks, pp. 63–70. ACM, Miami (2011)
18. Marin-perianu, R., Hartel, P., Scholten, H.: A Classification of Service Discovery Protocols (2005)
19. Ghafoor, H., Aziz, K.: Position-based and geocast routing protocols in VANETs. In: 2011 7th International Conference on Emerging Technologies, ICET (2011)

Vehicles Congestion Control in Transport Networks Using an Adaptive Weight Model

Bin Jiang[1,2], Xiao Xu[1], Chao Yang[1,2], Renfa Li[1], and Takao Terano[2]

[1] College of Computer Science and Electronic Engineering, Hunan University, China
{jiangbin,yangchaoedu,lirenfa}@hnu.edu.cn,
tearxuxiao@gmail.com
[2] Department of Computational Intelligence and Systems Science,
Interdisciplinary Graduate School of Science and Engineering,
Tokyo Institute of Technology, Japan
terano@dis.titech.ac.jp

Abstract. This paper proposed an adaptive weight congestion control model in a vehicle transport network. Our focus was to construct a quantitative index series to describe the network congestion distribution, and to shunt vehicles on seriously congested links based on such index sequence. We achieved this goal by combing both feedback and iteration strategy in the congestion control field. First, we developed an agent based model which captured the nonlinear feedback mechanism between the vehicle routing behavior and the road congestion state. Then, the model implemented an adaptive intersection weight adjustment mechanism based on the evolutionary congestion degree of the nearby links, through which to achieve congestion distribution evaluation and network congestion control at the same time. The simulation results verified the validity of our model for congestion control under predefined networks, and proved an applicability of the intersection weight sequence as a measurement for the congestion degree and distribution of road networks.

Keywords: Road-Network Congestion Control, Adaptive Weight Model, Feedback Strategy, Iterate Strategy.

1 Introduction

Intelligent Transportation System (ITS) finds applications in almost every transportation domain, infrastructure planning and management, route planning, vehicle navigation during incidences management, pedestrian safety and congestion management. Congestion management is one of the key application of ITS. Effective management of traffic congestion will result in even distribution of traffic on arterial roads, thus reducing travel times, vehicle emissions and probability of road hazards [1].

Current congestion control strategies can be divided into two categories: (1) feedback strategy, which employs the feedback information of real-time road status and equalizes the travel time of alternative routes through control measures, the ultimate goal of this kind of strategy is to pursuit the system-level or user-level optimal. For

R.C.-H. Hsu and W. Shangguang (Eds.): IOV 2014, LNCS 8662, pp. 99–109, 2014.
© Springer International Publishing Switzerland 2014

example, Pavlis et al. compared various feedback route guidance strategies, such distributed feedback control strategies as Bang-bang, P or PI type. The results showed that feedback strategies could effectively balance the travel time between alternative routes of the same start and destination, meanwhile compared with the non-strategic situation, the travel delays had been greatly improved [2]. Wang proposed a predictive feedback routing control strategy that combined the advantages of iterative strategy and feedback strategy, which could meet the needs of the path well than other strategies [3]. Furthermore, the simulation experiments on macroscopic traffic simulation modeling tools *METANET* proved that Wang's real-time feedback route guidance method could effectively reduce the congestion to achieve the user equilibrium [4]. (2) iterative strategy, which operates the traffic flow model   repeatedly based on the measured data of road requirement and O-D (Original-Destination) matrix, and obtains the prediction of the traffic conditions over a future time horizon, through which to provide route guidance to reduce the occurrence of congestion. Messmer et al. used iterative modification of splitting rates of road junctions to reach a balance of the travel times over alternative routes, so as to reduce the total system time [5]. Wedde proposed a distributed adaptive vehicle guidance system based on the swarm intelligence of colony system, and the experiments on the agent-based simulation system obtained better results than the shortest routing method with congestion avoidance and average travel time [6]. Zhou presented a prediction controlling methodology to provide reasonable path of vehicles, which included simulation prediction, rolling optimization and feedback adjustment. The iterative feedback correction based on simulation prediction could be used to prevent congestion when it occurs [7]. M. Battarra proposed an iterative solution to handle minimum multiple trips vehicle routing problem, and the adaptive guidance mechanism was proved effective and could reduce the total number of vehicles required in a limited time [8]. Besides, adaptive route guidance method is a key part of the congestion control. Park et al. proposed a route guidance system based on user's personal behavior, which could adaptively update routing rules when a predicted path was different from what a user chose [9]. Pang et al. proposed a fuzzy-neural approach used to recommend or rank paths for drivers, and the link selection function could adaptively provide decisions for users based on their historical selections [10]. Li proposed a system methodology of real-time traffic information, which achieved vehicle guidance by adaptive link selection between the predefined route and real-time route [11].

Based on the above literature review, feedback strategies have a good performance on real-time congestion control, but they lack an accurate description of the congestion distribution from a global perspective. Iterative strategies are able to predict congestion within a short time range but the effect of real-time control is poor. Moreover, most feedback and iterative strategies focused on the macroscopic traffic flows, lacking user behaviors to guide the routing selection. In this sense, we proposed an adaptive weight model which combined both iterative and feedback strategies: a real-time feedback mechanism between users routing behavior and intersection's congestion status; and an iterative mechanism of adjusting the weight of intersections according to the feedback information. The adaptive weight sequence would construct a quantitative index to evaluate the network congestion distribution, and shunt vehicles on those seriously congested links based on the value of index.

The rest of this paper is arranged as follows: Section 2 describes the designed concept and components of our model; Section 3 presents the simulation settings and results, and Section 4 discusses the results. In the last section, we conclude our work and give an outlook of future work.

2   Model Description

2.1   Purpose

This paper aims to design a model which considers both feedback and iteration strategies to ease the vehicles congestion in transport networks. For this purpose, we propose an adaptive weight model which captures the nonlinear feedback mechanism between the vehicle routing behavior and the road congestion status through agent-based approach, and it executes iteration strategy by repeatedly adjusting the weights of intersections based on the dynamic congestion degree of the nearby links, through which to achieve congestion distribution evaluation and network congestion control at the same time.

2.2   Model Description

There are two types of entities in our model: 1) transport network entity, which consists of intersection nodes and road links; 2) vehicle agent entity, which refers to the vehicle individuals which perform the route selection behaviors. The vehicle agent will automatically move through the network until they arrive at the destination.

2.2.1   Transport Network
We preset the composition of transport network in Table.1.

Table 1. Transport Network Composition

Definition	Description	Identification
Intersection Nodes	The nodes which connect links	$Node\_Id$
Links	Road links in the network topology	$(Node\_a, Node\_b)$

Table 2 describes several key variables of nodes and links.

Table 2. Description of Intersection Nodes and Links

Variable	Description	Identification
Intersection Weight	The weight of each node; adaptively update according to the congestion degree nearby.	N_Weight (NW)
Link Length	The physical length of the link.	$L\_Length(LL)$
Link Situation	The current status of the link, either Congested or un-congested.	$L\_Situation$ (LS)
Link Congestion Index	The congestion degree of different links.	$LinkCon$ (LCI)

Each intersection node in the road network has an independent weight N_Weight, which indicates the current congestion degree of this node. When the vehicle arrives at the end of a fork, it would make its routing decision based on the weights of adjacent intersections. The physical length of link L_Lenght is calculated by the direct distance. $L\_Situation$ describes the current status of the link, either congested or uncongested, and $LinkCon$ gives the quantitatively values of the congestion degree of links, calculated by Equation (1) and (2) respectively.

$$LS_{(a,b)} = \begin{cases} Congested & n_{(a,b)} < e_{max} \\ Uncongested & n_{(a,b)} >= e_{max} \end{cases}, \tag{1}$$

$$LCI^t_{(a,b)} = \frac{n^t_{(a,b)}}{e_{max}} \quad (LS_{(a,b)} = Congested), \tag{2}$$

Where e_{max} is the largest traffic capacity of a link, and n is the current number of vehicles on this link.

2.2.2   The Adaptive Updating Rules for Intersection Weight

The design principles of adaptive updating rules for intersection weight come from P or PI regulator [2][5]. The main idea of P regulator is to balance the travel time of different ways which connects the same start and destination. When a vehicle agent moves to the node a of link (a, b), and link (a, b) is along the shortest routing of current agent path, then the weight of node a would be updated by equation (3) and (4).

$$NW^t_a = NW^{t-1}_a - K\Delta T_{(a,b)}, \quad NW_a \in (0,1], \tag{3}$$

$$\Delta T_{(a,b)} = \frac{T^t_{(a,b)} - T^{t-1}_{(a,b)}}{T^t_{(a,b)}}, \tag{4}$$

In the above equations, $T^t_{(a,b)}$ is the travel time of link (a,b) at time step t, $T^{t-1}_{(a,b)}$ is the travel time of link (a,b) at time step $t-1$. NW^t_a is the weight of node a at time step t, NW^{t-1}_a is the weight of node a at time step $t-1$. K is the model parameter. According to the equation, the intersection weight NW will be modified at each time step when a vehicle passes by, and the travel time of link (a, b) would directly affect the self-updating process.

During the simulation process, vehicle agents dynamically make their routing decisions based on the intersection weight. The emergent agent aggregation on some links would change the situation of such links to be congested, thus the travel time of congested link would increase. Meanwhile, the intersection weight of these links would increase. It consequently affect other agents routing behaviors, and vice versa. In the simulation results, we define those intersections with their weights not equal to 1 as congestion feedback nodes.

2.2.3   Agent Definition

We defined two types of agents: Floyd agents with shortest routing strategy and autonomous agents make their routing decisions based on a two-objective utility function depending on intersection weights, as described in Table 3.

Table 3. Agent Definition

Agent Type	Description	Routing Decision
Floyd Agent	This type of agent travels along the shortest route, and ignores the link's congestion status.	The shortest routing
Autonomous Agent	This type of agent makes a routing decision based on a multi-objective utility function, depending on the intersection weight.	A multi-objective decision function based on the intersection weights.

The travel time T of located link is measured by equation (5), where T_{uncon} is the travel time of link (a, b) with the link status uncongested, and T_{con} is the travel time of link (a, b) with the link status congested, LL is the physical length of link (a, b), V is the velocity of the moving agent. The model parameter α and β are set to 0.15 and 4, respectively [11].

$$T = \begin{cases} T_{uncon} = \dfrac{LL_{(a,b)}}{V}, & LS_{(a,b)} = Uncongested , \\ T_{con} = T_{uncon}(1 + \alpha(LCI_{(a,b)}^{t})^{\beta}), & LS_{(a,b)} = Congested \end{cases} \quad (5)$$

During the link selection process, the first type-Floyd agent would choose the link on its shortest routing. But the second type-Autonomous agent would make its link selection based on equation (6).

$$U_{(a,b)}^{t} = NW_a * g_{(a,b)} + f_{(a,b)}^{t} * (1 - NW_a) + Guass , \quad (6)$$

Where $U_{(a,b)}^{t}$ is the utility value of link (a,b) at time step t and NW_a is the weight of intersection a. In equation (6), the first term $g_{(a,b)}$ represents the strength which attracts the agent moving towards its destination intersection; the second term $f_{(a,b)}^{t}$ reflects the congested degree of the link. Furthermore, in order to reflect a certain randomness of the agent motion, we add Gaussian stochastic disturbance as the third term of the utility function.

If the shortest routing of autonomous agent is not congested, then the target link is the shortest link; otherwise we would compare the utility values of each nearby link through equation (6), and choose the target link with a minimum value.

2.3 Congestion Evaluation Criteria

In order to analyze the simulation results, we defined two evaluation criteria: LCI and LCT in Table 4.

Table 4. The Definition of Evaluation Criteria

Criteria	Description	Name
Link Congestion Index	The congested degree of different links	LCI
Link Congestion Time	The regulated link congestion time	LCT

Where LCI reflects the congested degree at different time steps, calculated by equation (1). *LCT* is a quantitative indicator which describes the average congestion time of a link during the simulation process, given in equation (7).

$$LCT_{(a,b)} = \frac{\sum_{t=0}^{t=st} LCI^{t}_{(a,b)}}{st} * ct \tag{7}$$

Where *st* is the total simulation time step and *ct* is the sum of congestion time of link (a, b).

3   Experiment and Result

3.1   Experimental Setup

We designed three simulation experiments to validate an applicability of our model in congestion control; the details were presented in Table 5.

Table 5. The Description of Simulation Experiments

Id	Purpose	Evaluation Criteria
Experiment 1	Validation of the model on congestion evaluation and control.	LCI , LCT
Experiment 2	Sensitivity analysis of the parameter K on congestion control.	Congestion feedback nodes statistical analysis
Experiment 3	Fitness analysis with the composition of different vehicles/agents.	Node weight distribution analysis

Experiment 1 examined the applicability of our proposed adaptive weight model on congestion control. Meanwhile, we analyzed the effectiveness as a quantitative weight sequence to measure the network congestion. Experiment 2 analyzed the parameter sensitivity of the adaptive weight model. Experiment 3 compared the weight distribution of intersections with the composition of different agents. Table 6 presented the different agent composition of the three experiments.

At the beginning of the simulation, the model initialized the values of weights of all the intersections to one. The start and destination intersections of the two types of

Table 6. Agent composition in different experiments

Id	Agent Composition	
	Trial 1	Trial 2
Experiment 1	3000 Floyd	1500 Floyd and 1500 Autonomous
Experiment 2	1500 Floyd and 1500 Autonomous	
Experiment 3	1500 Floyd and 1500 Autonomous agents with different starts and destinations	Agents scaled in {1500,2000,2500,3000, 3500, 4000, 4500}. Floyd and Autonomous agents occupied 50%, respectively.

agents are randomly generated. At the initial stage, the two types of agents would travel along the shortest routing according to the equation (6). When the simulation forwarded, some roads would become congested, and the intersections nearby would adjust their weights based on equation (3). Then the model could adaptively shunts vehicles according to the index. The adaptive weight model constructed a dynamic evaluation index of congested degree of transport network, thus achieving congestion control based on the index.

3.2   Experiment Result

3.2.1   Validation of the Model on Congestion Evaluation and Control
The first experiment aimed to validate the applicability of the model on congestion evaluation and control. We executed the adaptive weight model on a simulated transport system and compared the evaluation criteria as *LCI* and *LCT* of congested links in the network. The predefined road network topology was given in Fig.1, consisting of 39 intersection nodes.

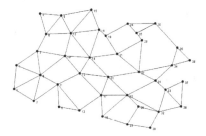

Fig. 1. The predefined network topology

Fig.2 gave the experimental results of *LCI* and *LCT* with congested links in the network, respectively.

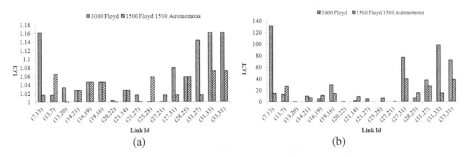

(a)   (b)

Fig. 2. The LCI and LCT Distribution of Congested Links

As shown in Fig.2 (a), most congested links, like link (7, 13) and link (31, 27), their values of *LCI* were decreased from 1.16, 1.15 to 1.02. Some links' *LCI* appeared slight increased, like link (13, 7) and link (25, 28). In Fig.2 (b), the values of LCT of link (7, 13), (33, 31) were decreased from 130,110 to 18. Further, Fig.3 presented the weight distribution of congestion feedback nodes by applying the adaptive model.

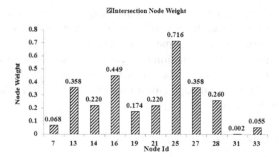

Fig. 3. The weight distribution of congestion feedback nodes

It was interesting that we found the *Ids* of congestion feedback nodes just corresponding to the nodes of congested links in Fig.2. Especially, the seriously congested links like (7, 13), (31, 33) and (33, 31), their connected intersection nodes 7, 31 and 33 with their weights much smaller than other nodes as 0.068, 0.002 and 0.055.

3.2.2 Sensitivity Analysis of Parameter K on Congestion Control

The second experiment conducted sensitivity analysis of parameter K on congestion control. The network topology was set to the same structure as in the first experiment. We tested the adaptive model under different K values, ranging from 0.2 to 2. The number of congestion feedback nodes was counted as presented in Fig.4.

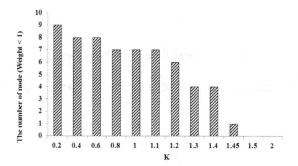

Fig. 4. The count of congestion feedback nodes under different *K*

With an increasing K, the count of congestion feedback nodes was getting smaller. It was decreased from 9 (K=0.2) to 1 (K=1.45). There was no more congestion feedback nodes in the network when K was bigger than 1.45.

3.3.3 Fitness Analysis with the Composition of Different Vehicles

The third experiment tested the fitness value of the model under different compositions of vehicles/agents. First, we examined the distribution of congestion feedback nodes with a constant agent number for several times. The agents groups were randomly initialized with different start and destination intersections. The result was given in Fig.5, which was the count of congestion feedback nodes over the 39 nodes in the network of Fig.1.

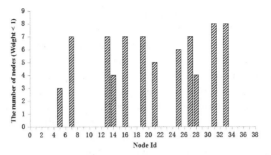

Fig. 5. The count distribution of congestion feedback nodes under different agent composition

Even though, the start and destination intersections of agent composition were different, congestion feedback nodes were located on some specific intersections like nodes 7, 13, 27, 31 and 33. The count of these nodes reached 6~8 times. Besides, these nodes also corresponded to the nodes of congested links in Fig.2. In the trial 2, we tried to test the fitness of models under different agent scale. Table.7 gave the count of the congestion feedback nodes after simulation.

Table 7. The count of congestion feedback nodes under different agent scale

Agent Scale	1000	1500	2000	2500	3000	3500	4000	4500
Average Number of Nodes（Weight < 1）	1	2	4	7	10	12	16	17

The count of congestion feedback nodes of the 39 nodes was given in Fig.6. As shown in Fig.6, the count of average congestion feedback nodes increased with the agent scale. We observed the similar results that the congested intersection node was still concentrated in certain nodes, such as node 7, node 31, 33 and so on.

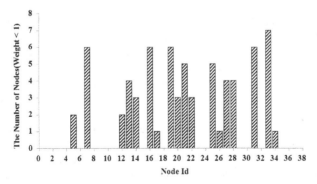

Fig. 6. The count distribution of congestion feedback nodes under different agent scale

4　Discussion

The results obtained in experiment one indicated that our proposed adaptive weight model could obviously improve congestion status of a network, like the seriously congested links (7, 13) and (33, 31); which had a high value of *LCI* and *LCT*. During the simulation, *LCI* of some links would have a slight increase, which exactly explained the model effect on vehicle shunting and congestion equilibrating. The achieved adaptive weight sequence confirmed that the value of node weight could reflect the intersection congestion degree in a quantitative way. An extremely small weight of nodes meant a seriously congested link while those nodes with higher values of weights approximating to one meant less congestion or never congested. The adaptive weight sequence would construct a new quantitative description index to evaluate the congestion distribution of the network.

Experiment 1 proved that weight sequence could be used to evaluate congestion distribution. Further, experiment 2 discovered that the number of congestion feedback nodes was reduced with a growing value of parameter K of the model; meaning that the congested nodes and links were also decreased and the network congestion was greatly improved. On the contrary, the adaptive weight model as an evaluation index of congestion, with a bigger model parameter K would lead to an over-modification and a coarsness of the evaluation. In this case our model was unable to accurately measure congestion distribution in the network.

In experiment 3, the result obtained from the first trial indicated that transport network congestion mainly depended on the network topology. Under the different initial agents' group, the congestion feedback nodes were mainly located on specific nodes, just like the transportation junction and the intersection of the arterial. In the second trial of simulation, the number of congestion feedback nodes would increase with a growing number of agents' scale. This demonstrated that the intersection weight was affected by the agent scale to a certain degree. The distribution of congestion feedback nodes under different agents' scale also proved the congestion mainly depended on the network topology.

5   Conclusion

In this paper, we proposed an adaptive weight model consisting of feedback and iteration strategies to handle the congestion control problem of road network. Most studies with feedback and iteration strategies on vehicle transport network congestion control rarely considered the dynamic evaluation of congestion status; meanwhile iteration strategies was not suitable for real time control. Our model combined the advantages of two kinds of strategies. First, we developed an agent based model which captured the nonlinear feedback mechanism between the vehicle routing behavior and the road congestion state. Then, the model implemented an adaptive intersection weight adjustment mechanism based on the evolutionary congestion degree of the nearby links. The model built on such concepts could adaptively modify the intersection weight based on the real-time congestion degree to evaluate the congestion distribution, and dynamically change the routing behavior as a feedback to the congestion degree, through which to achieve congestion distribution evaluation and network congestion control at the same time.

Three simulation experiments validated the model effectiveness, tested the parameter sensitivity and analyzed the fitness of the model under different agents groups. The simulation results showed that the model realized a real-time road congestion control, thus improved the road congestion and promoted network capacity. The adaptive weight model could successfully construct a new quantitative index to describe the network congestion distribution, and shunt vehicles on seriously congested links based on that index.

In the future work, we plan to test model effectiveness and accuracy based on a real traffic map and exact traffic flow data. We also consider the implementation of this idea to a real world traffic environment.

Acknowledgments. This work was supported by the Natural Science Foundation of Hunan Province, China, grant no. 13JJ3049, the Science and Technology Research Plan of Hunan Province, China, grant no. 2012FJ4131 and the Fundamental Research Funds for the Central Universities.

References

1. Desai, P., Loke, S.W., Desai, A., Singh, J.: Multi-agent based vehicular congestion management. In: 2011 IEEE Intelligent Vehicles Symposium (IV), pp. 1031–1036. IEEE (June 2011)
2. Pavlis, Y., Papageorgiou, M.: Simple decentralized feedback strategies for route guidance in traffic networks. Transportation Science 33(3), 264–278 (1999)
3. Wang, Y., Papageorgiou, M., Messmer, A.: Predictive feedback routing control strategy for freeway network traffic. Transportation Research Record: Journal of the Transportation Research Board 1856(1), 62–73 (2003)
4. Wang, Y., Papageorgiou, M., Sarros, G., Knibbe, W.J.: Feedback route guidance applied to a large-scale express ring road. Transportation Research Record: Journal of the Transportation Research Board 1965(1), 79–88 (2006)
5. Messmer, A., Papageorgiou, M.: Automatic control methods applied to freeway network traffic. Automatica 30(4), 691–702 (1994)
6. Wedde, H.F., Senge, S.: BeeJamA: A Distributed, Self-Adaptive Vehicle Routing Guidance Approach (2013)
7. Zhou, Y., Yang, X., Mi, C.: Dynamic Route Guidance Based on Model Predictive Control. CMES: Computer Modeling in Engineering & Sciences 92(5), 477–491 (2013)
8. Battarra, M., Monaci, M., Vigo, D.: An adaptive guidance approach for the heuristic solution of a minimum multiple trip vehicle routing problem. Computers & Operations Research 36(11), 3041–3050 (2009)
9. Park, K., Bell, M., Kaparias, I., Bogenberger, K.: Learning user preferences of route choice behaviour for adaptive route guidance. IET Intelligent Transport Systems 1(2), 159–166 (2007)
10. Pang, G.K., Takabashi, K., Yokota, T., Takenaga, H.: Adaptive route selection for dynamic route guidance system based on fuzzy-neural approaches. IEEE Transactions on Vehicular Technology 48(6), 2028–2041 (1999)
11. Li, C., Anavatti, S.G., Ray, T.: Adaptive route guidance system with real-time traffic information. In: 2012 15th International IEEE Conference on Intelligent Transportation Systems (ITSC), pp. 367–372. IEEE (September 2012)
12. Bureau of Public Roads, Traffic assignment manual. U.S. Department of Commerce, Urban Planning Division, Washington, DC (1964)

Enhancing GNSS-Based Vehicle Positioning Using DSRC and a Nonlinear Robust Filter under the Connected Vehicles Environment

Liu Jiang[*], Cai Bai-gen, and Wang Jian

School of Electronic and Information Engineering, Beijing Jiaotong University,
Beijing 100044, China
Beijing Key Laboratory for Cooperative Vehicle Infrastructure Systems and Safety Control,
Beijing 100191, China
jiangliu@bjtu.edu.cn

Abstract. The concept of IOV (Internet of Vehicles) is capable of ensuring the safety and efficiency in road transportation by using wireless communication among the vehicles and the infrastructure facilities. Precise and real-time positioning of vehicles in the road net is of great significance for many intelligent functions and applications. In this paper, we expand the capability of Dedicated Short Range Communication (DSRC) devices to enhance the GNSS (Global Navigation Satellite System) for vehicle positioning. By utilizing the Huber-based M-estimation technique, an improved robust cubature filter is proposed with a novel approach for real-timely updating the measurement covariance, and a strategy for tuning the filter parameter is designed to improve the adaptability. Simulation results with specific tools show that the robustness and estimation precision of information fusion for positioning can be improved under the uncertain measurement and operating conditions.

1 Introduction

Due to the developing requirements for transportation in nowadays, the mobility, sustainability and safety of road transportation systems have been critical topics of interests all over the world [1]. The concept of Internet of Vehicles (IOV) has been an important part of future intelligent transportation and the realization of the wisdom city, which envisages the vehicles and the objects of the transportation infrastructure are all connected as an internet-based system that is capable of exchanging information for achieving a more efficient, safe and green world of transportation [2]. For lots of IOV applications, vehicle positioning is of great significance for providing fundamental information to support decision-making and further functions.

Traditionally, using the satellite navigation has been a common approach to solve the vehicle location detection issues with a relatively low cost, where the rapid developing GNSSs (Global Navigation Satellite Systems), including GPS, GLONASS

---

[*] Corresponding author.

R.C.-H. Hsu and W. Shangguang (Eds.): IOV 2014, LNCS 8662, pp. 110–119, 2014.

and BDS (BeiDou Navigation Satellite System), are strengthening the belief of the users. In order to compensate the drawbacks of GNSS positioning, especially the service unavailability and performance consistency in complex urban environments, many solutions and strategies have been proposed [3~5]. Compared with the sensor-assisted solutions, the wireless communication promotes a novel information resource for enhancing the satellite-based vehicle positioning. DSRC (Dedicated Short Range Communication) based inter-vehicle communication is also involved in the vehicle positioning solution, which uses the Carrier Frequency Offset (CFO) measurements to extend the information used for position computation and is with great potential for assisting the GNSS [6]. In order to make good use of the advantages of GNSS/DSRC integration, the position information processing logic employed in the integrated system has to deal with the problems of nonlinearity in system and measurement model, and uncertain interference in practical operation conditions. The conventional nonlinear filters mainly focus on the nonlinearity approximation capability. However, the deviation between the assumed posterior density and the practical features may result in failures of the connected vehicles services and even greatly rein the availability for some vehicle safety critical applications.

In this paper, we focus on the improvement of the nonlinear filter using the M-estimation technique [7]. A novel nonlinear filtering-based solution is proposed and applied to enhance the performance of GNSS/DSRC positioning, and simulations are carried out to illustrate the performance of the proposed method.

2   Improved Huber-Based Robust Filtering

As many other Bayesian filters, the CKF consists of time update and the measurement update equations. By using the cubature rule, a set of cubature points is involved to solve the nonlinearity in system and measurement models. Consider the discrete-time nonlinear dynamic process:

$$
\begin{cases}
x_{k+1} = f_k(x_k, v_k) \\
z_k = h_k(x_k, w_k)
\end{cases}
\tag{1}
$$

where x_k is the n-dimensional state vector, z_k is the p-dimensional measurement vector, $f_k(*)$ and $h_k(*)$ are system and measurement functions, v_k and w_k are the system process and the measurement noise vectors, which are assumed fulfilling

$$
\mathrm{E}[v_i v_j^{\mathrm{T}}] = \delta_{ij} Q_i, \mathrm{E}[w_i w_j^{\mathrm{T}}] = \delta_{ij} R_i, \mathrm{E}[v_i w_j^{\mathrm{T}}] = 0, \quad \forall i, j
\tag{2}
$$

According to standard CKF [8], the cubature point set $\{\xi_i, \omega_i\}$ is designed as:

$$
\xi_i = \sqrt{m/2}[1]_i, \omega_i = 1/m, m = 1, 2, \cdots, m = 2n
\tag{3}
$$

The state is estimated and the corresponding error covariance is derived as:

$$\hat{x}_k = \hat{x}_{k|k-1} + K_k(z_k - \hat{z}_{k|k-1}) \tag{4}$$

$$P_k = P_{k|k-1} - K_k P_{zz,k|k-1} K_k^{\mathrm{T}} \tag{5}$$

where $\hat{x}_{k|k-1}$ is the state prediction, K_k is the filtering gain, z_k is the measurement vector with its estimation $\hat{z}_{k|k-1}$, $P_{k|k-1}$ is the covariance of prediction, and $P_{zz,k|k-1}$ denotes the innovation covariance matrix.

In the design of the original CKF algorithm, the nonlinearity is highly concerned to achieve an effective solution for the Bayesian filtering scheme. However, since the posterior density is assumed with a fixed form, there are limitations for its nonlinearity approximation capability, especially when the deviations from the assumption exist and the property of interferences is uncertain and complicated due to the operation environments. Therefore, the improvement of robustness is of great necessity in many applications with certain critical performance requirements. By applying the Huber technique, the measurement process of a Bayesian filter can be modified for realizing a Huber-based robust cubature Kalman filter (HRCKF).

With the consideration of the process-based HRCKF approach, the measurement equation can be approximated by integrating the measurement prediction result and the transformed prediction error, which is expressed as:

$$z_k \simeq \hat{z}_{k|k-1} + H_k r_k = \hat{z}_{k|k-1} + H_k(x_k - \hat{x}_{k|k-1}) \tag{6}$$

Thus, the measurement update can be changed to a linear regression problem:

$$\begin{aligned}
y_k &= \Phi_k x_k + \xi_k \\
&\to M_k^{-\frac{1}{2}} \begin{bmatrix} z_k - \hat{z}_{k|k-1} + H_k \hat{x}_{k|k-1} \\ \hat{x}_{k|k-1} \end{bmatrix} = M_k^{-\frac{1}{2}} \begin{bmatrix} H_k \\ I \end{bmatrix} x_k + M_k^{-\frac{1}{2}} \begin{bmatrix} w_k \\ -r_k \end{bmatrix}
\end{aligned} \tag{7}$$

where $M_k = diag\{R_k, P_{k|k-1}\}$.

According to the principle of the robust M-estimation, the measurement update is enhanced with a minimization target for a cost function [9]:

$$J(x_k) = \sum_{i=1}^{n} \rho(\Delta_i) \tag{8}$$

where Δ_i represents the i th component of the vector as $(\Phi_k x_k - y_k)_i$, and $\rho(*)$ depicts the Huber's score function that is defined with an adjusting parameter γ [10]

$$\rho(\Delta_i) = \begin{cases} \dfrac{1}{2}\Delta_i^2, & |\Delta_i| < \gamma \\ \gamma|\Delta_i| - \dfrac{1}{2}\gamma^2, & |\Delta_i| \geq \gamma \end{cases} \tag{9}$$

In order to obtain a direct solution of the modified filtering with the cost function, it is expected that $J'(x_k) = 0$, and the solution for $\hat{x}_k$ is achieved using the matrix $\boldsymbol{\Theta} = \text{diag}[\psi(\Delta_i)]$, $\psi(\Delta_i) = \rho'(\Delta_i) / \Delta_i$, which means the estimation is solved by

$$\hat{x}_k^{(j+1)} = (\boldsymbol{\Phi}_k^{\mathrm{T}}\boldsymbol{\Theta}^{(j)}\boldsymbol{\Phi}_k)^{-1}\boldsymbol{\Phi}_k^{\mathrm{T}}\boldsymbol{\Theta}^{(j)}y_k, P_k = (\boldsymbol{\Phi}_k^{\mathrm{T}}\boldsymbol{\Theta}\boldsymbol{\Phi}_k)^{-1} \tag{10}$$

where j represents the number of iteration step, and the initial value $x_k^{(0)}$ is derived as $\hat{x}_k^{(0)} = (\boldsymbol{\Phi}_k^{\mathrm{T}}\boldsymbol{\Phi}_k)^{-1}\boldsymbol{\Phi}_k^{\mathrm{T}}y_k$.

With a proper parameter γ, the measurement update process of standard CKF can be replaced, and the Huber function can contribute the robustness capability with its segmentation features. It can be found that the matrix $\boldsymbol{\Theta}$ is actually an integration of two components corresponding to the measurement prediction residual and the state prediction error. If we transform $\boldsymbol{\Theta}$ to be an integration of four parts as:

$$\boldsymbol{\Theta} = \begin{bmatrix} \boldsymbol{\Theta}_z & \boldsymbol{0} \\ {\scriptstyle p\times p} & {\scriptstyle p\times n} \\ \boldsymbol{0} & \boldsymbol{\Theta}_x \\ {\scriptstyle n\times p} & {\scriptstyle n\times n} \end{bmatrix} \tag{11}$$

Since the true state is unknown in practical problems, the prediction error is set to zero and thus $\boldsymbol{\Theta}_x = \boldsymbol{0}$. If we introduce Eq. (11) into Eq. (10), it can be derived that the state estimation returns to a standard Kalman filtering form [11]. When we substitute $\boldsymbol{\Theta}_x = \boldsymbol{0}$ into the expressions, the filtering process is given as:

$$P_k = [I - \tilde{K}_k H_k]\tilde{P}_{k|k-1} = [I - \tilde{K}_k H_k]P_{k|k-1} \tag{12}$$

where $\tilde{P}_{k|k-1} = P_{k|k-1}^{1/2}\boldsymbol{\Theta}_x^{-1}(P_{k|k-1}^{1/2})^{\mathrm{T}} = P_{k|k-1}$, and hence $\tilde{K}_k$ is the reweighted Kalman gain that is written as $\tilde{K}_k = P_{k|k-1}H_k^{\mathrm{T}}[H_k P_{k|k-1}H_k^{\mathrm{T}} + R_k^{1/2}\boldsymbol{\Theta}_x^{-1}(R_k^{1/2})^{\mathrm{T}}]^{-1}$. And the state vector will be estimated as:

$$\hat{x}_k = \hat{x}_{k|k-1} + \tilde{K}_k[z_k - h_k(\hat{x}_{k|k-1})] \tag{13}$$

From the results, it is obvious that the matrix $\boldsymbol{\Theta}$ used in the Huber-based filtering just affects the measurement component, where the conventional measurement error covariance is modified to be $R_k^{1/2}\boldsymbol{\Theta}_x^{-1}(R_k^{1/2})^{\mathrm{T}}$. Therefore, it is naturally considered that the enhancement of robustness can be realized by improving only the measurement related component. The covariance M_k will be further enhanced with $\boldsymbol{\Theta}$ as

$$\tilde{M}_k = M_k^{1/2}\boldsymbol{\Theta}^{-1}(M_k^{1/2})^{\mathrm{T}} \tag{14}$$

According to the same reason that mentioned in Eq. (11), the state prediction error is assumed zero so that the improved measurement error covariance $\tilde{\boldsymbol{R}}_k$ is updated by extracting the corresponding components from $\tilde{\boldsymbol{M}}_k$. Based on that, the robustness can be improved by a novel strategy that updates the measurement covariance in standard CKF, rather than the reweighted least-square solution as Eq. (10).

Since the statistical features of the errors cannot accurately described by a certain known distribution, the value of γ will directly affect the performance of nonlinear estimation. In the improved RCKF approach, with an initial γ_0, a simple adjusting strategy is involved to increase the adaptability of the filter. We define a time-varying parameter η_k referring to the discrepancy status of the state prediction and the final estimation, which is described as

$$\eta_k = \chi_k - \chi_{k-1}$$
$$\chi_k = (\hat{\boldsymbol{x}}_k - \hat{\boldsymbol{x}}_{k|k-1})^{\mathrm{T}} (\hat{\boldsymbol{x}}_k - \hat{\boldsymbol{x}}_{k|k-1}) \tag{15}$$

where $\eta_k > 0$ illustrates the strong effect of calibration to the model-based prediction compared to the previous iteration, which requires an enhanced concentration to the filtering performance of the robust method. Therefore, we consider employing a large γ_k in the case of $\eta_k > 0$. An adaptive logic for selecting γ_k is proposed as

$$\gamma_k = \gamma_{k-1} + \omega_0 \eta_k \tag{16}$$

where ω_0 is a fixed scale factor for tuning the adjusting capability of η_k.

3   Application in GNSS/DSRC Vehicle Positioning

In GNSS/DSRC integrated vehicle positioning system, the measurement information from the on-board sensors can be collected and used for the data fusion logic. The architecture of sensor collecting and information fusion is described as Fig.1.

The on-board GNSS receiver obtains the pseudo range from the available satellites. With a different information awareness method, the range (also range rate) between a DSRC transmitter in a neighborhood vehicle and a DSRC receiver within an objective vehicle can be measured based on the Doppler Effect.

According to the principle of sensor measuring for GNSS and DSRC, the proposed filtering-based sensor information fusion will be performed, for which the most decisive step is to set up the system and measurement model as the form in Eq. (1). The three-dimensional position and the related components are involved to make the definition for state vector as $\boldsymbol{x}_k = (x_k, \dot{x}_k, \ddot{x}_k, y_k, \dot{y}_k, \ddot{y}_k, z_k, \dot{z}_k, \ddot{z}_k)^{\mathrm{T}}$.

For the generation of the system kinematical model, with the consideration of implementing a robust estimator, the simple conventional constant acceleration model is sufficient to describe the short-term state transition from instant $(k-1)$ to k.

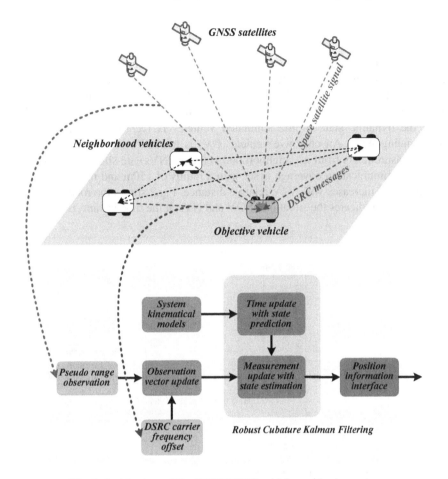

Fig. 1. Architecture of the GNSS/DSRC vehicle positioning system

By this approach, the nonlinear system function $f_k = (*)$ is replaced by a linear state transition process $x_k = F_{k,k-1}x_k + v_k$ with the state transition matrix $F_{k,k-1}$.

For the measurement process, at a certain time instant k, the observations from n_s GNSS satellites and n_d neighborhood vehicle nodes are combined to update the measurement vector z_k. It can be seen that the measurements from two positioning systems are integrated with a tightly coupled architecture, where the observations are combined to achieve a complete calculation solution for vehicle position estimation. With the definitions of the system model $F_{k,k-1}$ and measurement model $h_k(*)$, the integration of GNSS and DSRC can be performed according to the proposed robust filtering algorithm, and the performance of vehicle positioning will be improved than the conventional filters, especially the capabilities under uncertain conditions.

4   Simulation Analysis and Discussion

We present our simulation results to validate the proposed improved robust cubature Kalman filter for the GNSS/DSRC vehicle positioning problem. We generate a traffic simulation scenario, where a local road network is built covering totally 9 signalized intersections. The traffic flow is generated according to a pre-defined OD condition, where the dynamic state of the simulated vehicles is recorded real-timely using corresponding APIs. An objective vehicle (OV) is tracked based on its ID and the DSRC measurements from its neighborhood vehicles (NVs) are simulated, where the effective communication coverage is set with a radius of 150m and the measurement error of DSRC increases with V2V relative distance. Fig.2 shows the road network in simulation and indicates the situation of OV and NVs at the time instant $t = 66s$.

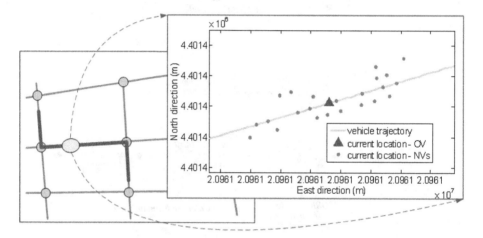

Fig. 2. Vehicle trajectory and the distribution of neighborhood vehicles as t=66s

As presented in the Fig.2, there are 23 neighborhood vehicles travelling within the DSRC coverage of the OV. In positioning calculation for the OV, we use four neighborhood vehicle nodes to update measurement vector in an iteration, according to the relative distance and the space distribution of the NVs, which may influence the communication quality and the dilution of precision for locating the vehicle.

With the extracted trajectory of the OV, the satellite receiver measurement is simulated with a GNSS Simulator. The pseudo-ranges of the BDS satellites are generated according to specific observation models. In order to validate the vehicle positioning performance in the practical environment, the ionospheric delay and tropospheric delay can be coupled in the original observation simulation process, which provides effective conditions for validating the filtering performance.

When using the BDS simulation results under normal conditions, three positioning modes are involved in the comparison to illustrate the performance of IHRCKF, including (1) BDS-based positioning, (2) BDS/DSRC with standard CKF, and (3) BDS/DSRC with the improved IHRCKF method. With the real state of the OV, the positioning errors in both the east and north direction under a Gauss plane coordinate can be calculated. We use RMSE (Root Mean Square Error) to evaluate the filtering precision. Fig.3 and Fig.4 depict the RMSE in east and north directions.

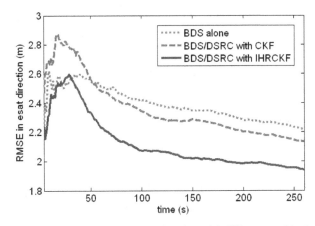

Fig. 3. Comparison of RMSE in east direction with different positioning modes

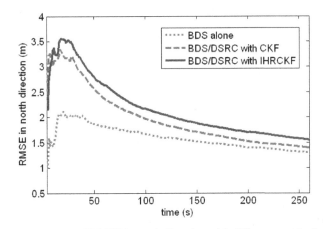

Fig. 4. Comparison of RMSE in north direction with different positioning modes

From the figures, it can be found that, compared to the BDS alone mode and the CKF-based integration mode, the IHRCKF solution contributes certain improvement in positioning precision. However, the performance of the IHRCKF is not enhanced greatly where the BDS is simulated with normal conditions.

In order to validate the effectiveness of the proposed approach, both the CKF and the IHRCKF solutions are involved in simulation with GNSS measurements under the challenging conditions. Different values for diagonal elements of $\boldsymbol{R}_k$ are compared. We use σ_{G} and σ_{D} to indicate the predefined measurement covariance of each satellite and the on-board DSRC device of those related neighborhood vehicles, which means $R_k = diag(\sigma_G^2, \cdots, \sigma_G^2, \sigma_D^2, \cdots, \sigma_D^2)$. A wide range of covariances (from 2.0 to 100.0) for both σ_G and σ_D are tested.

The results of CKF and IHRCKF are summarized in Table 1 and Table 2, where the deviation between the maximum and minimum RMSE with different σ_G values for a certain σ_D is calculated and recorded as $\Delta D_{max-min}$ in the tables. The meaning of $\Delta G_{max-min}$ can be described with a similar approach. Both the $\Delta D_{max-min}$ and $\Delta G_{max-min}$ provide obvious descriptions for evaluating the sensitivity to the different covariance assumption conditions.

Table 1. RMSE and its max-min deviation of CKF with different measurement covariances

σ_G	2.0	5.0	10.0	50.0	100.0
$\Delta G_{max-min}$	1.0169	0.9601	1.6082	7.2037	14.3639
σ_D	2.0	5.0	10.0	50.0	100.0
$\Delta D_{max-min}$	4.7672	10.2799	13.1983	1.7245	1.6937

Table 2. RMSE and its max-min deviation of IHRCKF with different measurement covariances

σ_G	2.0	5.0	10.0	50.0	100.0
$\Delta G_{max-min}$	1.4958	1.1279	1.4836	1.4227	1.6358
σ_D	2.0	5.0	10.0	50.0	100.0
$\Delta D_{max-min}$	0.9858	0.7852	0.6315	1.7163	2.3167

It can be found that a better robustness performance of state estimation of vehicle positioning is obtained by the proposed IHRCKF. Compared to the results from CKF, the response of IHRCKF to the variety of covariance assumptions is insensitive and relatively stable, while the deviation of CKF is with distinct diversity in a wide range from 1.0169 to 14.3639. It is illustrated that the modification of the measurement covariance in IHRCKF and the adaptive γ strategy greatly enhance the robustness of GNSS/DSRC integration to deal with the unknown error characteristics and operation conditions, while the conventional filtering method that uses a fixed R_k is lack of adaptability and cannot cope with the uncertainties with the specific assumptions.

5   Conclusions

In this paper, we proposed an improved robust cubature Kalman filter to fuse the sensor data for locating the vehicles, using the GNSS/ DSRC positioning scheme. The proposed approach solves the issues of nonlinearity and robustness, and poses problem for the conventional filtering techniques like the cubature Kalman filter and other related solutions. By modifying the measurement process of the standard CKF using an adaptive strategy for measurement covariance matrix and the key parameter γ, the sensitivity of the estimation precision to the covariance assumptions and the operating conditions is effectively constrained. Simulation results demonstrate the capability of the proposed filter approach, and show its potential for implementation in practical connected vehicles environment.

Acknowledgement. This research was supported by the International Science & Technology Cooperation Program of China (2014DFA80260), Fundamental Research Funds for the Central Universities (2014JBM003), Beijing Natural Science Foundation (4144081), National Natural Science Foundation of China (U1334211, 61273089).

References

1. Lee, J., Park, B.: Development and evaluation of a cooperative vehicle intersection control algorithm under the connected vehicles environment. IEEE Transactions on Intelligent Transportation Systems 13(1), 81–90 (2012)
2. Dimitrakopoulos, G.: Intelligent transportation systems based on internet-connected vehicles: Fundamental research areas and challenges. In: The 11th International Conference on ITS Telecommunications, St. Petersburg, pp. 145–151 (2011)
3. Liu, J., Cui, X., Lu, M., Feng, Z.: Direct position tracking loop based on linearised signal model for global navigation satellite system receivers. IET Radar, Sonar and Navigation 7(7), 789–799 (2013)
4. Sazdovski, V., Silson, P.: Inertial navigation aided by vision-based simultaneous localization and mapping. IEEE Sensor Journal 11(8), 1646–1656 (2011)
5. Wei, L., Cappelle, C., Ruichek, Y.: Camera/laser/GPS fusion method for vehicle positioning under extended NIS-based sensor validation. IEEE Transactions on Instrumentation and Measurement 62(11), 3110–3122 (2013)
6. Alam, N., Balaei, A., Dempster, A.: An instantaneous lane-level positioning using DSRC carrier frequency offset. IEEE Transactions on Intelligent Transportation Systems 13(4), 1566–1575 (2012)
7. Chang, L., Hua, B., Chang, G., Li, A.: Robust derivative-free Kalman filter based on Huber's M-estimation methodology. Journal of Process Control 23(10), 1555–1561 (2013)
8. Arasaratnam, I., Haykin, S.: Cubature Kalman filters. IEEE Transactions on Automatic Control 54(6), 1254–1269 (2009)
9. Wang, X., Cui, N., Guo, J.: Huber-based unscented filtering and its application to vision-based relative navigation. IET Radar, Sonar and Navigation 4(1), 134–141 (2009)
10. Karlgaard, C., Schaub, H.: Huber-based divided difference filtering. Journal of Guidance, Navigation and Control 30(3), 885–891 (2007)
11. Chang, L., Hu, B., Chang, G., Li, A.: Huber-based novel robust unscented Kalman filter. IET Science, Measurement and Technology 6(6), 502–509 (2011)

OPUVRE: Overall Performance
for Urban Vehicle Routing Environments

Mengchao Song and Wenbin Yao

Beijing University of Posts and Telecommunications, Beijing, China
ft6515594@gmail.com, yaowenbin_cdc@163.com

Abstract. In recent years, with the great development in assisted driving, traffic monitoring and vehicle entertainment applications, vehicle networking (VANET) attracted a large number of academic research. Because of the vehicle mobility, wireless transmission ranges limit and the loss of wireless channel characteristics in VANET, providing a reliable multi-hop routing protocol in VANET is a significant challenge. This paper proposed a VANET routing protocol OPUVRE (Overall Performance for Urban Vehicular Routing Environments). OPUVRE is an overlay link state routing protocol .It uses traffic density, distribution uniformity and road length to calculate the score of each road, then uses the Dijkstra algorithm to select the best routing path. We evaluate OPUVRE against the traditional geographic routing protocols GSR and LOUVRE. The result shows that OPUVRE provides a higher performance in average packet delivery radio (PDR) and average latency.

Keywords: overlay link state routing protocol, traffic density, distribution uniformity, road length.

1 Introduction

Intermittent VANET should rely on the effective Ad hoc network routing strategies to ensure the successful transmission. According to AODV (Ad hoc on-demand) [1] distance vector routing protocol, when a mobile node needs to deliver a packet, the continuous connected path will be established on demand. But the constringency period can't meet the VANET requirements because of frequent topology, high mobility and link breakages.

GPSR (Greedy perimeter stateless routing) [2] is the first geographical protocol, it use greedy and perimeter mode together to forward packets. But it often has a bad performance in the intersections. GSR(Geographic Source Routing) [3] protocol, which improved from GPSR, use RLS(Reactive Location Service) to get destination position, and then use electronic map and Dijkstra algorithm to calculate the shortest path to the destination node. The disadvantage is that whether there are sufficient vehicles to support the road connectivity is uncertain. In other words, the shortest path is not the best path. GPCR (Greedy Perimeter Coordinator Routing) protocol [4] improved from GPSR utilizes restricted greedy mode at the intersections of streets. It

R.C.-H. Hsu and W. Shangguang (Eds.): IOV 2014, LNCS 8662, pp. 120–129, 2014.
© Springer International Publishing Switzerland 2014

does not depend on any additional equipment, such as electronic maps, location-based services. However its performance depends on correct determination of forwarding direction node at the intersections. In areas of poor connectivity, GPCR protocol has extremely high dependency on intersection node. One advantage of CAR (Connectivity Aware Routing) [5] is that the connected path between source node and destination node could be found when the source node is positioning the location of destination node. The connected path has adaptability, when link breakage appears, it needn't to re-search process. But the routing overhead is still high. LOUVRE (Landmark Overlays for Urban Vehicle Routing Environments) [6] assumes every car is equipped with GPS (Global Positioning System) to get its current location and electric map to get road information and density of vehicles. But its density threshold are always too low because it don't consider the distribution uniformity. GyTAR(Geographic Routing in Urban Vehicular Networks) [7] is an intersection-based geographical routing protocol that is capable of finding robust and optimal routes with urban environments, The main principle behind GyTAR is the dynamic and in-sequence selection of intersections through which data packets are forwarded to the destinations. The intersections are chose considering parameters such as the remaining distance, vehicle density and distribution uniformity. But GyTAR can only guarantee the next street have a good performance. It may be not the best candidate street in routing path from the view as a whole.

2   OPUVRE

OPUVRE propose a geo-proactive overlay routing solution that uses traffic density, distribution uniformity and road length as the metric for route creation. We discuss our assumptions and describe our routing protocol in this section.

2.1   Definitions and Assumptions

OPUVRE define a junction as one where more than one road segment meets. A road segment is a road which cars are on and is only up to the junction. In other words, the road segment before a junction is different from the road segment after the junction. Finally, a junction node is a node at a junction.

OPUVRE make the following assumptions when designing our routing protocol:

- All nodes constantly know their position and global time thanks to a NAV/GPS system, possibly enhanced with kinematic models when GPS signal is lost. Moreover, the NAV/GPS can provide the road topology information of any node given its location;
- Local time across nodes is synchronized with GPS;
- Location service allows finding the location of a node;

- Non-junction nodes on a road can only transmit to one other and not to other non-junction nodes in adjacent roads unless these non-junction nodes are on road segments that are extensions of each other. This is due to road side obstacles such as buildings and trees;
- Junction nodes, these nodes located at junctions, are the only nodes that can transmit to neighboring nodes on a different road segment since they are the only types of nodes at a junction.

2.2   OPUVRE Routing

OPUVRE is an overlay link state routing protocol whose link state table contains information for routing between overlay nodes represented by junctions. We rely on the on-board NAV system to provide the map of the area. This map is used to construct a road topology graph with roads as vertices and edges between the two roads. We creating the overlay link state table, we use the well-known Dijkstra's forward search algorithm to pick the route whose sum of road scores is minimal. The minimal sum gives us the small number of hops and high deliver ratio to the destination.

OPUVRE use the cellular mechanisms similar to GYTAR to collect the information of the road. In addition, we need an information collection unit on each junction. These units have two functions. On the one hand, they collect the road information around the junction and broadcast the existing road information to the nearby vehicles, then the vehicle broadcast these information to other vehicles. On the other hand, they update their road information through interaction with other information collection units. In order to improve the speed of interaction in units, they can use some other special communication mode.

Although each overlay link state routing table entry is a road instead of a node to preserve scalability, the number of roads can increase when the map become too big. We keep the full overlay link states up to a predefined grid area. The boundary points of the grid will keep overlay link states of adjacent grids. To forward to another node B outside of its grid, node A would simply route to the boundary point closest to B and have the boundary point route to B.

To formally estimate the score of an intersection, we define the following notations:

X : the current road;

$Score(X)$: $Score(X)$ must bigger than 0 or road X will have no connectivity

N_{avg}: average number of vehicles per cell

L : road length

N_{ideal} : constant that represents the ideal connectivity degree we can have within a cell;

σ : standard deviation of cell density

k : constant that can adjust cell density threshold $\frac{k-1}{k}(1+\sigma)\,N_{ideal}$

Hence

$$Score(X) = \frac{L}{1 - kmax\left(1 - \frac{N_{avg}}{N_{ideal}} \cdot \frac{1}{1+\sigma}, 0\right)} \quad (Score(X) > 0) \tag{1}$$

As we can see, this equation is based on two factors:

The shorter the road length X is and the smaller the average number of vehicles per cell N_{avg} is, the lower the Score(X) is. So the low Score(X) (S>0) represents that road X is a good candidate road. Hence, it ensures that we can use Dijkstra's algorithm to select the best routing path.

If N_{avg} is lower than the cell density threshold $\frac{k-1}{k}(1+\sigma)N_{ideal}$, Score(X) is lower than zero, it represents that road X have no connectivity and X can't be a candidate road in any case. If N_{avg} is bigger than $(1+\sigma)N_{ideal}$, Score(X) is equals to L. it represents that road X have a well connectivity and road X can be a perfect candidate road.

We distinguish between two types of routing in OPUVRE: inter-road routing or overlay routing, and intra-road routing or underlay routing. Inter-road routing is used to route packets between roads on the overlay network, and intra-road routing is used to forward packets between vehicles within a road on the underlay network. Both inter-road and intra-road routing require consulting the overlay link state table to determine to which road to forward next. Inter-road routing uses this information to correctly locate a forwarding neighbor on the new road. Intra-road routing uses the next road information from the overlay network to determine the best intersection to forward packets to. Then, it would choose the neighbor that makes the furthest progress to the intersection on the underlay network.

Packets are always routed by using inter-road routing, the overlay network providing routing directions, while the underlay network providing a guaranteed greedy forwarding. Unless a node cannot find any neighbors that are on the next forwarding road, it switches to intra-road routing in order to find a neighbor closer to the intersection where it might have nodes that have neighbors on the next forwarding road. Neighbor discovery is done with periodic beacons.

2.3   Recovery Strategy

Despite the road we choose have well connectivity, it can't guarantee that every vehicle always have a next hop node and encounter a local maximum. Then, depending on the application requirements, two recovery strategies have been designed. If applications are time-sensitive, packets can be routed back to the previous road where the second best road (the sum of road scores is second minimal) to the destination can be chosen. Packets are only dropped if an alternative road is not alternative road is not available. If the application are delay-tolerant, packets can be stored, carried, and the forwarded until the node meets another vehicle on the next road in the routing table.

3   Performance Evaluation

In this section, we evaluate the performance of OPUVRE. Experiment in this paper consists of two parts: In the first part of the experiment, we optimize our routing scheme by comparing its performance with different constant k. In the second part of the experiment, we evaluate our routing scheme by comparing its performance with GSR and LOUVRE, two well-known geographic routing protocols that have been previously applied in VANET environments. In particular, we are interested in two types of metrics: 1) packet delivery ratio (PDR), 2) average latency.

The open source tool NS2 (Network Simulator 2) [8] is used to simulate the wireless data transmission. The OPUVRE is implemented in NS2, and the programming language used is C++ and Tcl/OTcl. The key simulation parameters are summarized in Table 1:

Table 1. Simulation Parameters

Simulation time	300 sec.
Topology Size	3000mX3000m
Mobility Model	VanetMobisim[9]
Number of intersections	11
Number of roads	31
Number of Vehicles	250~500
Average vehicles velocity	50km/h
Source/destination	Random (50 connections)
Propagation model	Two-ray ground
Media Access Control	802.11b
Transmission range	250m
Data packet type	CBR(Constant Bit Rate)
Data pack size	512 B
Packet sending rate	0.1~1sec

Due to static obstacles (such as building), we assumed that nodes on different roads cannot communicate to one another, unless two roads share the same extension in either the horizontal or vertical direction.

3.1   Fine-Tuning Constant K in OPUVRE

Constant K can adjust cell density threshold $\frac{k-1}{k}(1 + \sigma)N_{ideal}$. When k is small, the road of low road density of vehicles will be taken into account as a candidate routing road. We define the lowest continuous connectivity probability that can be accepted is 80%. Previous studies have shown that the continuous connectivity probability under conditions (1.5km, 6/cell), (1.5km, 8/cell) (2.75km, 8/cell) and (4km, 8/cell) are 77.5%, 91.2%,83.2% and 75.6%. So the average number of vehicles per cell should be bigger than 8. Hypothesis $\frac{k-1}{k}(1+\sigma)N_{ideal} = 8$, $\sigma = 0$, $N_{ideal} = 14$, we can calculate K=2.33.

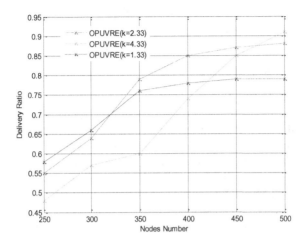

Fig. 1. Sending Rates=0.5

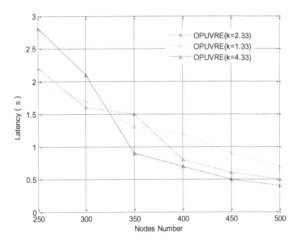

Fig. 2. Sending Rates=0.5

To study the effect of K in routing performance, we simulated OPUVRE in three cases: k = 1.33, k = 2.33, k = 4.33. The results in Figure 1 and Figure2 showed that when the node number is small, k =1.33 can get the best performance in PDR and average latency. When the node number is big, k=4.33 can get the best performance. The reason may be that the smaller K is, the smaller cell density threshold $\frac{k-1}{k}(1+\sigma)N_{ideal}$ is. When the node density is low, the small threshold can ensure there are enough candidate roads and select a relatively well routing path. When the node density is high, there are enough candidate roads which have good connectivity, In this case, the big K can ensure that the roads in routing path all have good connectivity because of the big cell density threshold $\frac{k-1}{k}(1 + \sigma)N_{ideal}$. In order to obtain a stable performance in OPUVRE, we set k=2.33.

3.2   Compare with GSR and LOUVRE

Packet Sending Radio(PDR)

Figure 3 and Figure 4 show the performance of the average PDR in OPUVRE are better than the others. This is mainly because that all the calculate roads in OPUVRE have a high continuous connectivity probability because of the high vehicle density and high uniformity. On the other hand, some calculate roads in GSR have a low continuous connectivity probability because of the high vehicle density. It leads to a frequent interruption in forwarding packets. Although LOUVRE considering the effect of road vehicle density on connectivity, it don't consider the effect of road vehicle distribute or distinguish between the roads of which vehicles density are higher than threshold.

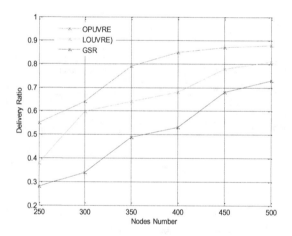

Fig. 3. Sending Rates=0.5

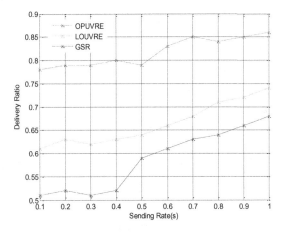

Fig. 4. Nodes Number=400

At the same time, we noted that PDR performance in OPUVRE is better than GSR and LOUVRE, but the difference in low density are more obvious. OPUVRE are higher than GSR by 27% and higher than LOUVRE by 18%.When the node number increased to 500,OPUVRE are only higher than GSR by 15% and higher than LOUVRE by 7%.

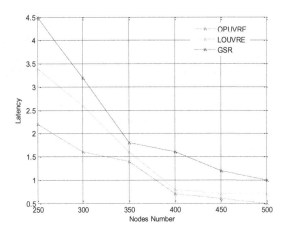

Fig. 5. Sending Rates=0.5

Average Latency

Figure 5 show the performance of the average latency in OPUVRE are better than the others. This is mainly because the candidate roads in OPUVRE have a high ve-hicle density, so there are more candidate vehicles in forwarding packets in road

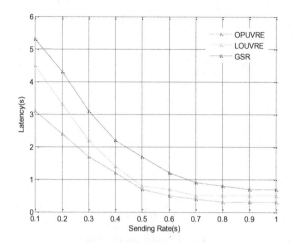

Fig. 6. Nodes Number=400

and more likely to choose a next vehicle which is nearer to the destination, then the average hop count become less. At last, the average latency become less because of the less hop count.

4   Conclusion

This paper presented OPUVRE, a density and uniformity based landmark overlay routing protocol for urban vehicular environments. We described the concept and the protocol as well as a novel road score estimation scheme. We implemented the protocol in NS2 and find the suitable k in OPUVRE, then compare it with GSR and LOUVRE protocols using realistic road information. Results showed that due to the smart calculate of road score, OPUVRE provide a better pack delivery ratio and latency than the other protocols. Future work includes verifying the necessity of recovery mode and how to reduce the communication overhead in traffic information interaction.

References

1. Liu, Y., Han, L.: The research on an AODV-BRL to increase reliability and reduce routing overhead in MANET. In: International Conference on Computer Application and System Modeling, ICCASM (2010)
2. Karp, B., Kung, H.T.: GPSR: Greedy Perimeter Stateless Routing for Wireless Networks. In: Proceedings of the 6th Annual International Conference on Mobile Computing and Networking (2000)
3. Lochert, C., Hartenstein, H., Tian, J., Fussler, H., Hermann, D., Mauve, M.: A Routing Strategy for Vehicular Ad Hoc Networks in City Environments. In: IEEE Intelligent Vehicles Symposium (2003)

4. Christian, L., Martin, M., Füßler, H., Hartenstein, H.: Geographic Routing in City Scenarios. Proceedings of ACM SIGMOBILE Mobile Computing and Communications Review (January 2005)
5. Naumov, V., Gross, T.R.: Connectivity-Aware Routing (CAR) in vehicular Ad-hoc Networks. In: Proceedings of 26th IEEE International Conference on Computer Communications, INFOCOM 2007, Anchorage, Alaska, USA (May 2007)
6. Lee, K., Le, M., Haerri, J., Gerla, M.: Louvre: Landmark Overlays for Urban Vehicular Routing Environments. In: Proc. IEEE 68th Vehicular Technology Conf., VTC (2008)
7. Rasheed, T., Jerbi, M., Senouci, S.M., GhamriDoudane, Y.: Towards efficient geographic routing in urban vehicular networks. IEEE Transactions on Vehicular Technology (November 2009)
8. NS2, http://www.isi.edu/nsnam/ns/
9. Ko, Y., Vaidya, N.: Location aided routing (LAR) in mobile ad hoc networks. In: Proc. 4th ACM/IEEE Int. Annu. Conf. MOBICOM, Dallas, TX (August 1998)

Implementation and Demonstration of WAVE Networking Services for Intelligent Transportation Systems*

Minpeng Miao, Qiang Zheng, Kan Zheng, and Zhiwei Zeng

Wireless Signal Processing and Network Lab,
Key Laboratory of Universal Wireless Communication, Ministry of Education,
Beijing University of Posts and Telecommunications, Beijing 100876, China
miaominpeng@bupt.edu.cn

Abstract. Intelligent Transportation System has been a hot topic during the past decades. The Wireless Access in Vehicular Environments (WAVE) system is a radio communication system which is capable of providing safety, efficiency and sustainability. Major researches have been done to evaluate the performance of IEEE 802.11p which concerns PHY and MAC layer. However, the networking services provided by IEEE 1609.3 are essential contributors to the low-latency and low-overhead characteristics, which deserves its attentions. In this paper, after a detailed description of both Data Plane and Management Plane functions of the IEEE 1609.3, we implement this particular standard based on Linux system and develop a GUI program to demonstrate three safety related application scenarios.

Keywords: ITS, V2V, DSRC, WAVE, IEEE 1609.3, Safety-related applications.

1 Introduction

According to statistics, traffic accidents accounted for $230 billion in damaged property, 2889000 nonfatal injuries and 42643 deaths in 2003 in USA alone [6]. World Health Organization (WHO) reported that more than 100 million people died in traffic accidents worldwide and financial loss caused by traffic accidents reach up to $ 500 billion one year [7]. Most of those accidents can be avoided through vital safety and emergency information exchange between vehicles. Wireless communication technologies have the potential to enable a host of safety related applications in vehicular environment to prevent collisions and save thousands of lives. It was reported that over 50% of interviewed consumers are interested in the idea of connected cars and 22% of them are willing to

* The work was supported in part by the China Natural Science Funding (61331009), Program for New Century Excellent Talents in University (NCET-11-0600),National Key Technology R&D Program of China (2013ZX03001003), and the Chinese Universities Scientific Fund under Grant 2013RC0116.

R.C.-H. Hsu and W. Shangguang (Eds.): IOV 2014, LNCS 8662, pp. 130–139, 2014.

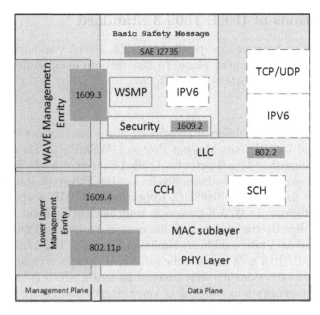

Fig. 1. WAVE stack

pay $30 to $65 per month for value-added connectivity services while on the road [12]. The U.S. Federal Communications Commission allocated 75 MHz of licensed spectrum in the 5.9 GHz (from 5.850 GHz to 5.925 GHz) for Dedicated Short-Range Communication (DSRC). The primary goal for deploying DSRC is to enable collision prevention applications[10]. The US Department of Transportation and several automakers in the United States have teamed up to study DSRC-based collision avoidance [8]. IEEE series of standards for Wireless Access in Vehicular Environment (WAVE) is currently considered as the most promising technology for vehicle-to-vehicle (V2V) and vehicle-to-infrastructure (V2I) communication.

Fig. 1 illustrates the protocol stack for DSRC communications: IEEE 802.11p for PHY and MAC layers, IEEE 1609.4 for channel switching, IEEE 1609.2 for security services, IEEE 1609.3 for networking services and SAE J2735 message set dictionary standard for application layer [2][3][4][5].

The IEEE 1609.3 which provides networking services is the core of the WAVE protocol stack. Industrial, governmental and university research efforts have been made in projects around the world, such as Vehicle Infrastructure Integration (VII) and Vehicle Safety Communication(VSC) in USA, Smartway and ITS-Safety 2010 in Japan and CVIS in Europe. In early 2014, the Department of Transportation in USA announced plans for a regulatory proposal that would require V2V communication devices, which uses the WAVE protocol stack, in the next year. Detailed descriptions and implementation of IEEE 1609.3, application scenarios design and demonstrations are given in the following sections.

2   Descriptions of IEEE 1609.3 Standard

WAVE Networking Services are specified in IEEE 1609.3 standard and consist of data plane and management plane. In this section, detailed descriptions of the IEEE 1609.3 standard are be given [3].

2.1   Data Plane

The data plane defines two different networking protocols: Internet Protocol Version 6 (IPv6) and WAVE Short Message Protocol (WSMP) [1]. These two protocols can be distinguished by a 2-octet field called Ethertype in the LLC (Logical Link Control) header. The hexadecimal values of the Ethertype indicating IPv6 and WSMP are 0x86DD and 0x88DC, respectively. WSMP is specifically designed for the efficiency of WAVE devices in vehicular environment which allows applications to directly control physical parameters i.e., channel number, transmitter power and data rate used in transmitting messages. The minimum packet overhead for UDP/IPv6 is 48 bytes, while for WSMP 5 bytes is enough, and even with options and extensions it rarely exceeed 20 bytes, which is quite valuable for vehicular communications concerning lower latency and higher reliability.

Fig. 2 below illustrates the Wave Short Message (WSM) exchange flow between the sender and receiver. When a higher layer entity wants WSMs to be sent on its behalf, it sends a WSM-WaveShortMessage.request to WSMP. On receipt of the request, WSMP calculates the length of the WSM data and compare with a predefined parameter WsmMaxLengh. Upon successful verification, the data is delivered to lower layers for subsequent transmission operations.

The lower layers of receiving side deliver the received WSMs to WSMP. Then WSMP shall pass the received information to the destination higher layer entity if the ProviderServiceIdentifier (PSID) from WSMP header exists in WsmServiceRequestTable in Management Information Base (MIB), otherwise the messages are to be abandoned.

2.2   Management Plane

Management functions are performed by the WAVE Management Entity (WME). Two WAVE device roles are defined. Devices transmitting WAVE Service Advertisements (WSAs) which indicate the availability for data exchange assume

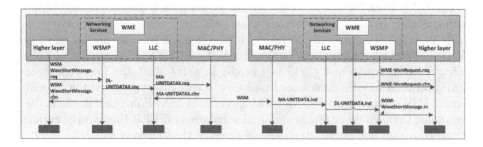

Fig. 2. WSM flow

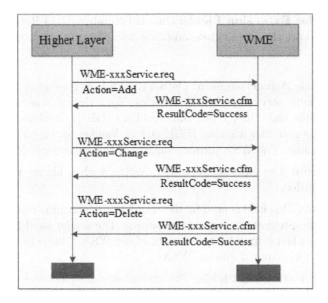

Fig. 3. Service request information flow

the provider role while those can receive WSAs and have the potential to participate in data exchanges perform the user role. A WAVE device may assume one, both or neither role. One of the main functions of the WME is accepting service requests from higher layers which may cause management messages to be transmitted periodically or provide Service Channel (SCH) access. Fig. 3 shows the service request primitives defined in the standard.

WAVE devices may monitor WSA to collect currently available services nearby. The WME maintains information about requested and available services for use in the MIB. The main informations in MIB are listed in four tables: Provider-ServiceRequestTable, UserServiceRequestTable, WsmServiceRequestTable and CchServiceRequestTable. The WME may exchange management data with other entities such as higher layer entities, MAC Layer Management and Security Management Entity. Meanwhile, the WME controls the data exchange parameters like data rate and transmit power in the data plane.

2.3   Information Format

Wave Short Message (WSM). The WSM format consists of variable-length header and corresponding payload.

WSMP Version: One octet contains 4-bit WSMP version number and 4 reserved bits for future use. A device that receives a WSMP packet with a higher version number should discard the packet.

Provider Service Identifier: This field determines the appropriate higher layer destination of the WSM. For bandwidth efficiency, PSID is defined in a variable-length format from 1 octet to 4 octets.

WSMP Header Extension Fields: Channel Number, Data Rate and Transmit Power Used are the three extension fields defined in current version of IEEE 1609.3.

WAVE Service Advertisement (WSA). WSA is generated by WME to broadcast available services to nearby vehicles. Normally most services are provided by Roadside Unit (RSU), but Onboard Unit (OBU) could also send WSA. WSA should be carried within an IEEE 802.11 Vendor Specific Action (VSA) management frame. The WSA format consists of the following fields:

WAVE Version: The current value is 1, WSAs with a higher version value should be discarded.

Change Count: This field is used by the recipient to determine whether a WSA is a repeat of the previous from the same source. The sender shall increment its value modulo-4 when it updates the content of the WSA. This is an efficient way for a receiver to filter out duplicate WSAs.

WSA Header Extension Fields: The current standard includes 6 extensions: Repeat Rate, Transmit Power Used, 2DLocation, 3DLocationAndConfidence, Advertiser Identifier and Country String.

Service Info: This field may include 0 to 32 instances of a Service Info unit. Each unit contains a detailed description of a service, such as PSID, Service Priority, Channel Index and so on.

Channel Info: 0 to 32 instances Channel Info unit composes this field. Each unit provides key parameters of the channel such as Channel Number, Data Rate and Transmit Power Level. A Service Info unit is linked to a Channel Info unit by the Channel Index.

WAVE Routing Advertisement: WRA is an optional field of the WSA. It is present only if a services utilizes the IPv6 protocol. The WRA provides information about how to connect to the Internet, indicating receiving devices how to configure to participate in the advertised IPv6 network. Each WSA contains at most one WRA.

3   Implementation of IEEE 1609.3

3.1   Data Plane Development

Different from UDP/IPv6 protocols, WSMP allows applications to directly control physical parameters which can be encapsulated into WSM header extension fields. WSM header is more efficient and flexible than UDP/IPv6 header in case of vehicular communication. The main task in the data plane is encapsulation and decapsulation of WSM frame. To facilitate the process, a dedicated data structure called struct wsmp_buff is designed, along with four operation functions (wbf_put, wbf_push, wbf_pull and wbf_reserve). Fig. 4 describes a detailed WSM flow from the sender's application layer to the receiver's application layer.

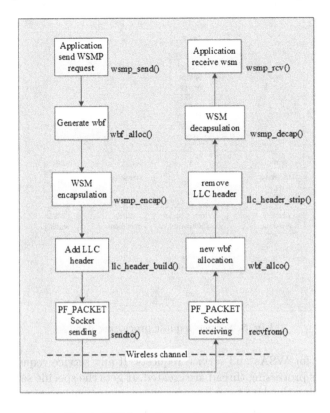

Fig. 4. WSM sending and receiving flow

The application layer of the sender calls wsmp_send to request WSMs to be sent on its behalf. After encapsulating WSM and adding LLC header, the data is transmitted through PF_PACKET socket which calls the actual transmitting function of network card. On the receiver side, the received data goes through the process of decapsulation corresponding to the encapsulation on the sender's side. Finally, the application layer obtains the actual data it needs.

3.2   Management Plane Development

Compared to the data plane, Management plane components are the core of the IEEE 1609.3 protocol. The main three functions performed by WME are:

1. Processing service requests from higher layers
2. Monitoring WSA
3. Maintaining Management Information Base

To accomplish these three functions, four main components are proposed: Main process, Service requests processing thread, WSA sending thread and WSA processing thread. The main process initiates the values in MIB, then

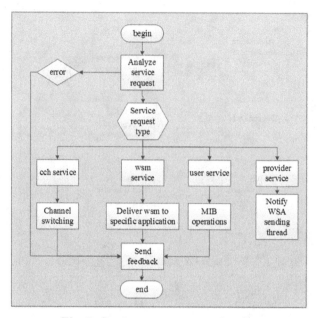

Fig. 5. Service request processing flow

keeps listening for WSAs and service requests. If any service requests arrive, a service requests processing thread are created. It gets the specific service request through analyzing the data from inter-process communication. Fig. 5 illustrates corresponding actions against different service requests. In particular, if provider service request arrives, a WSA is generated and broadcasted periodically based on key parameters from the request. Monitoring and processing WSA is a vital function. After resolving the received WSA, available services are added to UserAvailableServiceTable in MIB and if these services match those in UserServiceRequestTable, one service is selected as per service priorities.

4   Application Scenarios Design and Demonstrations

Vehicular networking applications can be divided into three categories [9]: road safety applications, traffic efficiency and management applications and infotainment applications. Road safety applications are primarily to largely decrease the probability of traffic accidents and the loss of life while improving traffic flow and coordination is the focus of traffic efficiency and management applications. Examples of infotainment applications include point of interest, local electronic media downloading and parking zone management. Despite various applications, the most important use case for a WAVE system is still communications between vehicles for the purpose of enabling collision avoidance applications, i.e., road safety applications. In this section, we focus on three use cases: Vulnerable Road User Warning (VRUW), Emergency Vehicle Warning (EVW) and Emergency Brake Warning (EBW). The main message type vehicles use is Basic Safety

Table 1. Use cases requirements

Application scenar-ios	Reliability requirements	Minimum broadcast frequency	Maximum laten-cy time
Vulnerable Road User Warning	High	1 Hz	100 ms
Emergency Vehicle Warning	High	10 Hz	100 ms
Emergency Brake Warning	High	10 Hz	100 ms

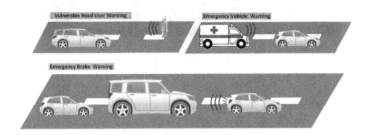

Fig. 6. Use cases

Message (BSM) which refers to SAE J2735. Table 1 gives the requirements of these three use cases.

As shown in Fig. 6, for the first use case, vulnerable road users, like pedestrians and cyclists, broadcast their presence with BSMs periodically, and vehicles equipped with WAVE devices can get information about their presence, trajectory and speed through decoding the BSMs. If vehicles are too close to the vulnerable users, a warning is then given to the drivers. In this way, potential accidents may be avoided to a large extent.

Emergency vehicles have a much higher risk of being involved in accidents than normal vehicles during emergency response trips. The probability of traffic accidents of emergency vehicle is higher than normal vehicles [11]. One of the explanation of this phenomenon is that drivers nearby can not determine the location and trajectory of the emergency vehicle. Therefore, it is necessary and effective to broadcast the vehicles' BSMs to nearby vehicles which would perform a better maneuver.

In the last use case, vehicles provide the emergency brake warning information when they have to brake emergently. This information lasts for several seconds to make vehicles behind to be aware. Vehicles which have the potential to get a crush send a warning to the drivers preventing accidents from happening.

A GUI program is developed with Qt4 in Linux to support these three use cases simultaneously for both sender and receiver. Users can choose the sender role to broadcast BSMs in different scenarios. As depicted in Fig. 7, those who choose receiver can see the display of relative distance and location on a simple

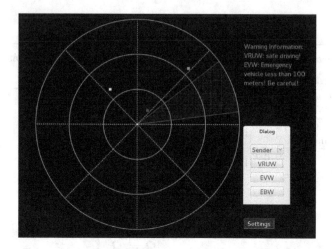

Fig. 7. Receiver side program

map and different warning messages are shown under the radar view for each scenarios chosen. We tested that the network delay of V2V communications is around $1ms$ while the delay of cellular networks is mostly more than 100 ms, which means with WAVE, the display of nearby drivers is real-time. This visualized program is effective and intuitive for drivers equipped with WAVE devices to use while driving.

5   Conclusions

Vehicles are evolving into a stage where information can be shared to improve road safety and traffic efficiency. The development of IEEE 1609.3 and demonstration of application scenarios in this paper makes efficient and reliable communications in vehicular networks visible and applicable. Drivers with the aid of V2V communications are aware of the traffic conditions nearby and can be informed of potential danger in advance. However, there are still several areas for further improvements. Privacy of drivers is a basic right, so the tradeoff between the authentication, privacy and liability becomes a challenge. Under the constrains of vehicular speeds, unreliable connectivity and fast topological changes, how to provide excellent delay performance still needs more research efforts.

References

[1] Guide for Wireless Access in Vehicular Environments (WAVE) - Architecture, 1–77 (2014)
[2] Standard for Wireless Access in Vehicular Environments Security Services for Applications and Management Messages, 1–289 (2013)
[3] Standard for Wireless Access in Vehicular Environments (WAVE) - Networking Services, 1–212 (2010)

[4] IEEE Standard for Wireless Access in Vehicular Environments (WAVE)–Multi-channel Operation, 1–89 (2011)

[5] Standard for Information technology–Local and metropolitan area networks–Specific requirements–Part 11: Wireless LAN Medium Access Control (MAC) and Physical Layer (PHY) Specifications Amendment 6: Wireless Access in Vehicular Environments, 1–51 (2010)

[6] Morgan, Y.L.: Notes on DSRC & WAVE Standards Suite: Its Architecture, Design, and Characteristics. IEEE Communications Surveys & Tutorials, 504–518 (2010)

[7] Martinez, F.J., Chai-Keong, T.: Emergency Services in Future Intelligent Transportation Systems Based on Vehicular Communication Networks. IEEE Intelligent Transportation Systems Magazine, 6–20 (2010)

[8] Kenney, J.B.: Dedicated Short-Range Communications (DSRC) Standards in the United States. Proceedings of the IEEE, 1162–1182 (2011)

[9] Karagiannis, Altintas, Ekici: Vehicular Networking: A Survey and Tutorial on Requirements, Architectures, Challenges, Standards and Solutions. IEEE Communications Surveys & Tutorials, 584–616 (2011)

[10] Wang, S., Fan, C., Hsu, C.-H., Sun, Q., Yang, F.: A Vertical Handoff Method via Self-Selection Decision Tree for Internet of Vehicles. IEEE Systems Journal (2014)

[11] Buchenscheit, Schaub, Kargl.: A VANET-based emergency vehicle warning system. In: IEEE Vehicular Networking Conference, pp. 1–8 (2009)

[12] Araniti, Campolo, Condoluci.: LTE for vehicular networking: a survey. IEEE Communications Magazine, 148–157 (2013)

A Receiver-Based Routing Algorithm Using Competing Parameter for VANET in Urban Scenarios

Lujie Wang, Yiming Wang[*], and Cheng Wu

School of Urban Rail Transportation, Soochow University,
Suzhou 215131, P.R. China
ymwang@suda.edu.cn

Abstract. This paper proposes an AODV-based routing algorithm for Vehicular Ad Hoc Network (VANET).This routing algorithm uses a routing metric, which includes the length of each hop as well as the link remaining lifetime. In addition, it can effectively reduce routing overhead by the use of receiver-based method. Furthermore, we design a new urban road scenario and a new mobility model for vehicles to describe the movement of cars. The simulation results we provide confirm the superiority of the proposed algorithm. These simulation comparisons of different ratios between both link-length and link stability also show improvements.

Keywords: VANET, routing algorithm, competing parameter, remaining lifetime.

1   Introduction

With the rapid development of urban modernization, automobile ownership surges at an average rate of 20%. Unfortunately, this leads to congestions, accidents and other traffic problems that impair urban development. Intelligent transportation system (ITS) can analyze traffic problems accurately and help travelers deal with them with the help of its powerful information processing and transmitting technology [1]. Vehicular Ad Hoc Network (VANET), as a special kind of ad-hoc network particularly designed for transport sector, plays an important part in ITS. Compared with the universal ad-hoc network, the biggest challenge posed to the VANET is the frequently changing topology resulting from the fast movement of vehicles. In spite of this, the special application still brings many advantages, such as a regular pattern of mobility model since cars always move along roads and a convenient availability of geographic information by a great deal of accessory equipment on the car [2].

Ad hoc on-demand distance vector routing (AODV) possesses the strengths of low network overhead, adaptability to dynamic routes and quick route establishment. However, fast-moving vehicles spoil its performance. A series of studies [1][3] indicate that the AODV protocol simulated in the traffic scenarios displays reducing

---

[*] Corresponding author.

R.C.-H. Hsu and W. Shangguang (Eds.): IOV 2014, LNCS 8662, pp. 140–149, 2014.
© Springer International Publishing Switzerland 2014

routing coverage, and a serious decline of information throughput. The study [4] works out a new protocol called double-forwarding AODV considering only remaining route lifetime when selecting best path. Also,it use directional and dynamically probabilistic forwarding to restrict the propagation range of Routing Request(RREQ). In addition, to relieve the negative effects caused by flooding approach for broadcasting, some papers give several solutions as follows. 1. Choose a forwarding area [5]. Only the nodes located farther than a certain distance away from the previous node are entitled to forward route request packet (RREQ).The result shows the number of RREQs can reduce 50%. 2. Set forwarding intervals [1]. Give higher priority to the node that has a longer distance from previous one. 3. Send RREQs to the specific area using directional antennas [6].

Due to the real-time control of traffic lights, traffic on the city roads is often divided into different sections. Vehicles between two intersections move as a whole group. It can be said that vehicle groups segment by segment form the whole traffic on the road. We focus our research on one segment of them and propose a routing algorithm receiver-based AODV. For the sake of reducing network overhead, we use receiver-based forwarding method, combining the strategies of forwarding area and forwarding intervals [7]. On the other hand, both link-length and link stability are taken into account to improve link stability. The rest of paper is organized as follows. Section 2 describes how to implement receiver-based approach , and the algorithm to select optimal route with competing parameter ω. Section 3 addresses the scenario considered in the simulations. Section 4 presents experimental results achieved with the proposed receiver-based routing algorithm. Finally, some concluding remarks are given in Section 5.

2   Receiver-Based AODV Routing Protocol

2.1   Receiver-Based Route Establishments

Although the approach of flooding is simple,it introduces a large number of duplicate messages that may cause network congestion. On the other side, many routing protocols applied for VANET use sender-based method, such as: GPSR (greedy perimeter stateless routing), GSR (geographic source routing). The sender of RREQ determines one or several nodes as the next forwarders. This method needs geographic information from neighboring nodes beforehand. On the contrary, in the receiver-based method, it is the receiver who determines whether to forward RREQs according to its own status. All the nodes that decide to forward RREQs compete for this right [8]. This method can keep routing overhead under control and there is no need to exchange geographic information ahead of route discovery.

Forwarding Area. Forwarding area refers to the specific region designated by the previous node within its communication range. Nodes in this region have the right to forward RREQs, while the nodes outside have to drop them directly. In Figure 1, the shaded area indicates the forwarding area of the source S or the previous node N_i. As nodes A and B are in the forward area, they are entitled to forward RREQs directed to the destination N_d. Node C, however, has to discard RREQ as it is outside. In the receiver-based protocol, the forwarding area is designed as a circle field with the radium of R/2 (R is the radium of communication range), taking the P-D line (from the previous node to the destination node) as the centerline. In that case, the maximum distance between any two nodes in the forwarding area is no more than R. So other nodes can monitor the message and respond accordingly.

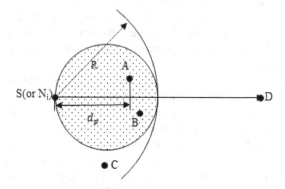

Fig. 1. Forwarding Area

Dynamic Forwarding Delay. Any node in the forwarding area that hopes to forward RREQs has to compete with others. Each one of these competitors calculates its own forwarding delay t_d according to the equation shown as (1).

$$t_d = \max \_delay \times (1 - \omega) \tag{1}$$

Where ω is the competing parameter calculated on the basis of the routing metric hereinafter mentioned in 2.2. Max_delay is equal to node transmission time, that is, an estimate of the one-hop traversal time for a packet. It includes queuing delays, interrupt processing times and transfer times. If one node has the maximum ω among all the competitors in the forwarding area, the path between this node and the previous one is believed to be the most suitable link and is able to limit the spread of the routing control messages effectively. So this node deserves the minimum forwarding delay and finally forwards the RREQs first. When other nodes in the same forwarding area overhear the packet from this node, they cancel the scheduled timing for forwarding.

2.2   Competing Parameter ω

As mentioned above, the competing parameter ω depends on routing metric which is the key for routing establishment. In our algorithm, the best route is judged not only by its hops but also by its stability. It is a straightforward and intuitive method to assess the stability by measuring the lifetime of this route from its connection to breakage, called link remaining lifetime. The route is thought to be more stable if it has a long link remaining lifetime. We consider the interleaving affection of both link remaining lifetime and the least number of hops in the routing metric.

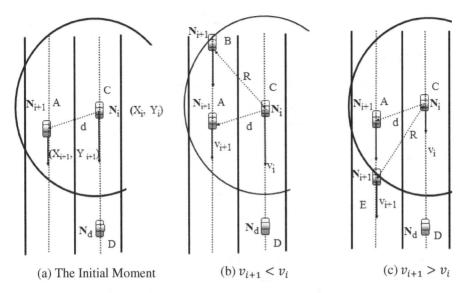

(a) The Initial Moment   (b) $v_{i+1} < v_i$ (c) $v_{i+1} > v_i$

Fig. 2. The Calculation of Link Remaining Lifetime

Calculation of Link Remaining Lifetime. We assume that all vehicular routing nodes can obtains its own geographical information such as location, speed and direction, with the help of global positioning system (GPS). And the movement of any node is regarded to be same in a short period of time. Then the link remaining lifetime of the path between two nodes is calculated as follows. Because the designated forwarding area points to the destination node, thus all nodes that qualified are located in the area between the previous node and the destination one. In figure 2, assume that node N_i located in position C with the coordinates of (X_i, Y_i) is the previous node and node N_{i+1} at the position A is the receiver of RREQs from N_i. Its coordinates are (X_{i+1}, Y_{i+1}). Destination node N_d is located in front of them. R denotes the communication range. As the Figure 2(a) shows, at the initial moment t, N_{i+1} is ahead of N_i on the right. During the short period of Δt, assuming that N_i is static, then the relative movement of N_{i+1} to N_i is divided into two types. Each type is characterized by different speed conditions. In figure 2(b), N_i has a higher speed v_i than N_{i+1}'s speed, v_{i+1}. At the time $t + \Delta t$, N_i moves from the location A to B relative to N_i. In this process, N_{i+1} first moves closer to N_i. Then goes far from it. On the contrary, in Figure 2 (c), the speed v_i is less than v_{i+1}, during the period Δt, N_{i+1} gradually moves far away from N_i from location A to E. Both location B and E are at the boundary of N_i's communication area. If N_{i+1} moves beyond this boundary, the established link between two nodes breaks. So the distance between A and B (or A and E) is just the remainder distance that N_i can move before link breakage. Furthermore, T_P represents the link remaining lifetime, namely the remainder time that the communication between two nodes can maintain. The calculation is shown as (2) to (7):

$$T_P = \frac{D(A,B)}{|\Delta v|} \left(\text{or} \frac{D(A,E)}{|\Delta v|} \right) \tag{2}$$

When $v_{i+1} < v_i$,

$$D(A,B) = \sqrt{R^2 - (X_i - X_{i+1})^2} + (Y_{i+1} - Y_i) \tag{3}$$

$$T_P = \frac{\sqrt{R^2 - (X_i - X_{i+1})^2} + (Y_{i+1} - Y_i)}{v_i - v_{i+1}} \tag{4}$$

When $v_{i+1} > v_i$,

$$D(A,E) = \sqrt{R^2 - (X_i - X_{i+1})^2} - (Y_{i+1} - Y_i) \tag{5}$$

$$T_P = \frac{\sqrt{R^2 - (X_i - X_{i+1})^2} - (Y_{i+1} - Y_i)}{v_{i+1} - v_i} \tag{6}$$

Combine (4) with (2), we can get the link remaining lifetime:

$$T_P = \frac{\sqrt{(v_i - v_{i+1})^2 [R^2 - (X_i - X_{i+1})^2]} + (v_i - v_{i+1})(Y_{i+1} - Y_i)}{(v_i - v_{i+1})^2} \tag{7}$$

The Routing Metric. Our routing metric takes both link stability and hops into account. Except for link remaining lifetime, another parameter is also considered for the sake of the number of hops. That is the projection distance of the link between the node and its previous node to the P-D line. As shown in Figure 1, d_p represents the projection distance of node A and the source S (or intermediate node Ni) to the P-D line, Select a forwarding node that is further away from the source (or intermediate node) as the next-hop node N_{i+1}. Routing metric integrates these two parameters and gets the competing parameter ω, with a weight α to measure the effects of these two parameters to ω, as equation (8) shows.

$$\omega = (1 - \alpha)\frac{T_P}{T_{max}} + \alpha\frac{d_p}{R} (\text{T} <= Tmax) \tag{8}$$

Where T_P is the remaining lifetime and T_{max} is the designed maximum value of remaining lifetime. R is the radius of communication range. If the value of α is set properly, an optimal route, with relatively few hops and greater stability, can be discovered. And the competing parameter ω of this link should be the maximum value.

3   Simulation Scenario and Mobility Model

One of the most common scenarios during our daily commutes looks like this: you are at the intersection. When the traffic light turns green, all waiting vehicles start to move forward, and stop at the next intersection (if the traffic light is red). Between these two intersections, all vehicles move to the same direction but at different speeds on different lanes. This constitutes a temporary mobile ad-hoc network. Each vehicle can be source or forwarder of data. We describe the scenario above on the OPNET simulation platform.

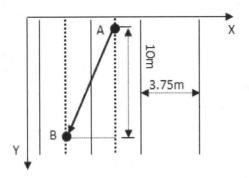

Fig. 3. Changing Lanes

In order to describe the movement of vehicles, this paper presents a new type of mobility model especially for vehicles. The detailed movement is explained as follows: before the simulation, all nodes wait at the first intersection, that is, the zero point of the y-axis. When simulation starts, every node figures out whether or not its own location is along the centerline of any lanes. If not, the nodes quickly and randomly select an alternative lane and move to its centerline. After the initialization, each one picks a goal from "go straight" and "change to another lane" randomly. If "go straight" is selected, the node needs to choose a target location alone the same lane and moves to it at a speed selected from a uniformly distributed interval. If the node chooses to "changing lanes", it then selects a changing direction (left or right), and moves as Figure 3 shows: assuming that this car changes to the right lane from point A to point B. Once this goal is achieved, the node then sets another target with another direction to move again. The movement state changes through cycles until the node reach the second intersection. Specifically, it is 2000 meters on the y-axis.

4   Simulation Analysis

The simulation is carried out on the OPNET simulation platform. All nodes use the vehicular mobility model. Five pairs are communication nodes. The sources start to generate data packets 30 seconds after the start of the simulation, considering all the nodes at that time have left the first intersection and scattered on the road. As soon as the couple communication nodes reach the second intersection, communication between them stops. When all the 5 pairs arrive at the second intersection, the whole simulation ends. Simulation parameters are given in Table 1. T_{max} is set as 80. Because according to the simulation in [9], the probability of the link that lives up to 80s is close to 0. So the remaining lifetime is meaningless if its value is larger than 80s.

Table 1. Simulation Parameters

Parameter	Value
Simulation area	37.5m×2000m
Number of lanes	10
Number of nodes	40,60,80,100,150,200
Traffic type	CBR(Constant Bit Rate)
Packet rate	5 packets/sec
Data Packet Size	512 bytes
Node speed	10km/h~80 km/h
Communication range(R)	250m
T_{max}	80sec
Max_delay	0.04sec
MAC	802.11b

4.1   Comparisons

Three performance indexes, packet delivery rate, the average end-to-end delay, normalized routing overhead, are collected to compare the function of receiver-based AODV with that of double-forwarding AODV and AODV. Here the parameter α is set to be 0.5 to obtain better performance. To improve the simulation accuracy, the results are obtained by averaging all the values simulated with 50 different seeds.

Packet Delivery Ratio. This is obtained by dividing the total number of data packets received to that sent by the source. It reflects the transmission quality of the network. Figure 4 illustrates that the packet delivery ratio of AODV,double-forwarding AODV and receiver-based AODV protocols are gradually increasing as the node group expands. This is because network connectivity is strengthen due to the growth in number of nodes, reducing the possibility of packet loss caused by inexistence of any route from source node to destination. The packet delivery ratio of receiver-based AODV is larger than that of double-forwarding AODV in the case of different number of nodes and furthermore the superiority is more evident when the number of nodes is larger. This can be explained by the added prediction of route lifetime in receiver-based AODV that help avoid frequent link breaks and improve packet delivery ratio.

Average End-to-End Delay. It means the average time that one data packet takes to reach the application layer of destination node, characterizing smoothness level of the network. It includes all possible delays as route discovery latency, queuing time and propagation delay. Figure 5 shows the relationship between the average end-to-end delay and the number of nodes. It is clearly that they are gradually decreasing with the rise in node density. Because each node can have more neighbors and has more choice to find an appropriate route if total number is large. Hence both route establishment time and route rediscovery frequency declines, resulting in lower average end-to-end delay. Double-forwarding AODV protocol simply use route remaining time in the route maintaining process instead of choosing a more stable link in the route discovery process. While receiver-based AODV considers not only the hops of route but also the stability, selecting the node located relatively farther but longer link lifetime. Thus its delay is shorter as compared to that of AODV, which is really helpful in VANET environment where topology change and packet retransmission occur frequently.

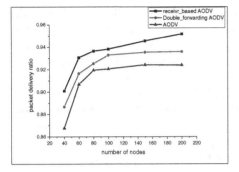
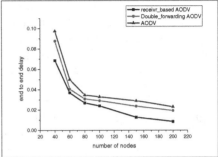

Fig. 4. Packet Delivery Ratio (α=0.5)   **Fig. 5.** Average End-to-End Delay (α=0.5)

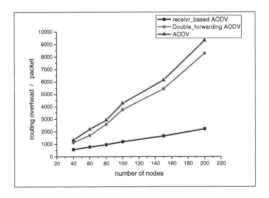

Fig. 6. Normalized Routing Overhead (α=0.5)

Normalized Routing Overhead. It denotes the ratio of the number of routing packets propagated by all nodes and the number of data packets received by the application layer of destination, indicating the congestion degree of the network. A Routing packet forwarded between intermediate nodes once is considered as a new one. It is clearly concluded in Figure 6 that as the number of nodes increases, RREQs can be received by more neighboring nodes and hence be further disseminated, leading to the constant rise in routing overhead. However, the growth of receiver-based AODV protocols routing overhead is significantly slower than the double-forwarding AODV and AODV protocol. This can be attributed to two reasons: on the one hand, the forwarding method based on receivers is able to effectively control the widespread of RREQs during route discovery process. On the other hand, the receiver-based AODV protocol builds a more stable route than double-forwarding AODV, thus needing less routing packets in the route maintenance process. As a whole, receiver-based AODV has greater efficiency as it cost less when transmitting equal number of data packets.

4.2   Effect of Weight α

This optimized routing metric includes two parts, the projection distance of the link between a node and its previous node to the P-D line, as well as the link remaining lifetime. Add these two parameters together in different proportion and then get the competing parameters ω and corresponding forwarding delay d_p. Similarly, every other node within the forwarding area calculates its own competing parameter and forwarding delay. Of all these nodes, the one with the maximum competing parameter enjoys higher priority to forward. The different proportion here is denoted by the weight α. Different α means the different proportion occupied by two factors in the competing parameter. Figure 7 and Figure 8 respectively depict the effect of weight α from 0 to 1 to the network with different number of nodes by two different perfor-mance indexes, route discovery times and routing overhead. As the curves show, both of them decrease first then increase with the minimum value existing at around α=0.5.This is due to the consideration of both the link remaining lifetime and the pro-jection distance that help find a relatively stable route hence ,leading to less route discoveries and further lower routing overhead.

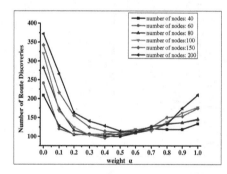
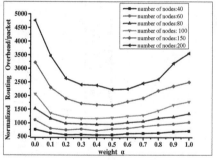

Fig. 7. Number of Route Discoveries   **Fig. 8.** Normalized Routing Overhead

If two nodes in the forwarding area move with the same speed and direction, then the one located close to the previous node can retain longer connection time with previous one. When α is 0, which means the competing parameter ω depends entirely on the link remaining lifetime, the node with maximum link remaining lifetime for-ward RREQ first in every hop, finally constituting the route from source to destina-tion with numerous nodes. In that case, any one of them that changes its speed or direction can break the link. So the route established here is more fragile. When α = 1, that is to say, only the projection distance to P-D line is considered. The node located in the farther site from the previous one has a greater competing parameter ω and takes precedence to forward packets. Consequently, the route is linked by small number of nodes, with long distance between each two, even close to the bonder of communication area. So the tiny movement of any nodes can lead to link break, increasing the route discovery times and hence routing overhead.

5   Conclusion

This paper can be summarized into two parts: one is the proposal of a receiver-based routing algorithm in which the routing metric considers the link stability as well as the number of hops. The decision-maker changes from sender to receiver when establishing a new route. All these can effectively reduce the generation and dissemination of broadcasting packets and also improve the stability of the route. The other one is the design of a new mobility model and a road simulation scenario on OPNET simulation platform in terms of urban traffic characteristics. The simulation results confirm that receiver-based AODV is more suitable for VANET in urban traffic environment. When the ratio of link remaining lifetime and projection distance in the routing metric is around half to half, receiver-based AODV can achieve best performance.

Acknowledgments. The work was supported by National Natural Science Foundation of China (No.61172056), (No.61201215), and Doctoral Fund of Ministry of Education of China (20093201110005) from Soochow University.

References

1. Li, F., Wang, Y.: Routing in Vehicular Ad Hoc Networks: A Survey. IEEE Vehicular Technology Magazine 2(2), 12–22 (2007)
2. Yang, Q., Shen, L.: System Architecture and Communication Protocols in Vehicular Ad Hoc Networks. ZTE Technology Journal (2011)
3. Haerri, J., Filali, F., Bonnet, C.: Performance Comparison of AODV and OLSR in VANETs Urban Environments under Realistic Mobility Patterns. Department of Mobile Communication BP 193, 06904 (2006)
4. Xia, R., Liu, C., Zhao, Z., Shu, Y.: Routing Algorithm for Vehicular Ad Hoc Network Based on Double Forwarding Mechanism. Computer Engineering 39(06), 124–128 (2013)
5. Sun, Y., Chen, Y., Xu, Y.: A GPS Enhanced Routing Protocol for Vehicular Ad-hoc Network. In: 2011 IEEE International Conference on Robotics and Biomimetics (ROBIO), pp. 2096–2101 (2011)
6. Wang, W., Xie, F., Chatterjee, M.: Small-Scale and Large-Scale Routing in Vehicular Ad Hoc Networks. IEEE Transactions on Vehicular Technology 58(9), 5200–5213 (2009)
7. Taysi, Z., Yavuz, A.: Routing Protocols for GeoNet: A Survey. IEEE Transactions on Intelligent Transportation Systems 13(2), 939–954 (2012)
8. Heissenbüttel, M., Braun, T., Bernoulli, T., Wälchli, M.: BLR: Beacon-Less Routing Algorithm for Mobile Ad Hoc Networks. Computer Communications 27(11), 1076–1086 (2004)
9. Wu, Y., Liao, W., Tsao, C., Lin, T.: Impact of Node Mobility on Link Duration in Multihop Mobile Networks. IEEE Transactions on Vehicular Technology 58(5), 2435–2442 (2009)

Path Accumulation Extensions for the LOADng Routing Protocol in Sensor Networks

Thomas Clausen and Jiazi Yi

Laboratoire d'Informatique (LIX), Ecole Polytechnique, France

Abstract. The "Light-weight On-demand Ad-hoc Distance-vector Routing Protocol – Next Generation" (LOADng) is a simple, yet efficient and flexible routing protocol, specifically designed for use in lossy networks with constrained devices. A reactive protocol, LOADng – as a basic mode of operation – offers discovery and maintenance of hop-by-hop routes and imposes a state in intermediate routers proportional to the number of traffic paths served by that intermediate router.

This paper offers an extension to LOADng, denoted LOADng-PA (Path Accumulation). LOADng-PA is designed with the motivation of requiring even less state in each intermediate router, and with that state being independent on the number of concurrent traffic flows carried. Another motivation the design of LOADng-PA is one of monitoring and managing networks: providing more detailed topological visibility of traffic paths through the network, for either traffic or network engineering purposes.

1 Introduction

Since the late 90s, the Internet Engineering Task Force (IETF)[1] has embarked upon a path of developing routing protocols for networks with increasingly more fragile and low-capacity links, with less pre-determined connectivity properties and with increasingly constrained router resources. In '97, by chartering the MANET (Mobile Ad hoc Networks) working group, then subsequently in 2006 and 2008 by chartering the 6LoWPAN (IPv6 over Low power WPAN) and ROLL (Routing Over Low power and Lossy networks) working groups.

The MANET working group converged on the development of two protocol families: reactive protocols, including AODV (Ad hoc On-demand Distance Vector routing [1]), and proactive protocols, including Optimized Link State Routing (OLSR) [2,3]. A distance vector protocol, AODV operates in an *on-demand* fashion, acquiring and maintaining paths only while needed for carrying data, by way of a Route Request/Route Reply exchange. A link state protocol, OLSR is based on periodic control messages exchanges, and each router proactively maintaining a routing table with entries for all destinations in the network, which provides low delays but constant control overhead.

LOAD [4] is a protocol derived from AODV [1], simplified for LLNs, and standardised by the ITU-T as part of the G3-PLC standard [5] for mesh-under

---

[1] http://www.ietf.org

R.C.-H. Hsu and W. Shangguang (Eds.): IOV 2014, LNCS 8662, pp. 150–159, 2014.
© Springer International Publishing Switzerland 2014

routing for utility (electricity) metering networks. The emergence of LLNs thus triggered a renewed interest in AODV-derived protocols for specific scenarios, resulting in continued work within the IETF [6] and [7] for the purpose of standardisation of a successor to LOAD – denoted LOADng (the Lightweight On-demand Ad hoc Distance-vector Routing Protocol – Next Generation). LOADng incorporates the experiences from deploying LOAD – including, but not only, in LLNs – and has been accepted as part of an update to the G3-PLC ITU-T standard for communication in the "smart grid" [8].

1.1 The Lightweight On-demand Ad Hoc Distance Vector Routing Protocol - Next Generation (LOADng) Overview

A reactive protocol, the basic operations of LOADng [15,6] include generation of Route Requests (RREQs) by a LOADng Router (originator) and flooded through the network when discovering a route to a destination, and Route Replies (RREPs) generated by the sought destination ad transmitted to the originator by way of unicasts. When an intermediate router forwards a RREQ, it installs temporary routing table information towards the originator of the RREQs – the "reverse route" from the destination to the originator. When the sought destination receives a RREQ, it will respond by an unicast RREP, which is forwarded along this installed reverse route – and the forwarding of which will serve to install a "forward route" from the originator to the destination. Thus, for each bidirectional path through a LOADng router, four entries are thus maintained in the routing table: for directions, an entry is recorded for the "next hop" and for the "destination" via that "next hop".

One of the key features of LOADng is, that it combines simplicity with extensibility: the core protocol provides mechanisms for discovering and maintaining bi-directional routes between pairs of routers, but offers the ability to develop functional extensions, optimising its behaviour and performance for specific deployments, topologies and traffic patterns.

LOADng provides the information required for hop-by-hop routing of data packets: a router will know the next hop towards the destination, for a data packet, but not the full path that the packet will take. To this end, the header of a data packet contains only the destination address, relying on intermediate routers to be able to make forwarding decisions based on their local knowledge of the routing topology. This provides agility for each router to make a local decision (*e.g.*, if local connectivity changes more frequently than routing updates can be propagated globally through the network) and, *e.g.*, enables "fast re-routing" mechanisms to engage and improve data packet delivery when a data packet arrives at a router without, or with outdated, topological information [12,13].

The LOADng Collection Tree Protocol (LOADng-CTP) is of the protocol extensions, developed for LOADng [9]. This extension permits efficient construction of a bi-directional collection tree, rooted in one router and covering the entire network. LOADng-CTP permits reducing the number of RREQ flooding operations from (n-1) to 2 in order to construct bi-directional paths between the root and all other routers in the network, but otherwise incurs the same state requirements as described above. This extension is applicable for deployments where a central controller, or monitoring entity is present and operating the network, *e.g.*, as is the case in a smart grid management, or for home/building/factory automation.

1.2   The Case for Source Routing and Path Accumulation

There are, however, potential downsides to hop-by-hop routing combined with a reactive protocol: by their very nature, reactive protocols acquires and maintains only topological information about actively used paths – and, at that – at their basic form only "next hops" along those paths. Thus, no router has access to a "global view" of the network topology, or even of which destinations are reachable through which paths. This may be unfortunate in some scenarios, *e.g.*, for management purposes: paths from a central unit (*e.g.*, a monitoring station) to a set of devices (*e.g.*, sensor devices) may, all pass through a faulty intermediate router rendering the network inoperative – and absence of a topological view of the paths actually used, this faulty router may be difficult to identify. Also, lack of such global information renders establishing path-diversity, *i.e.*, that data packets (as far as possible) are not concentrated across a few unfortunate routers (which may, if battery-driven, see their energy depleted prematurely, or experience congestion) or across a few unfortunate links (which may incur higher media contention and losses) hard to accomplish.

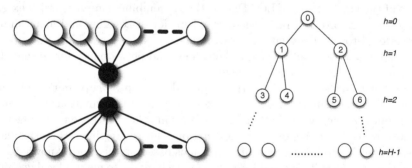

(a) Simple network topology with choke-point.

(b) Bi-directional traffic in a collection tree network.

Fig. 1. Example network topologies

A final downside is, and probably the most critical issue for memory-constrained devices, of hop-by-hop routing is, that with hop-by-hop routing and a reactive protocol, the state required in each router is proportional to the number of active paths passing through that router. Thus, any individual device in the network may, worst case, be required to maintain a routing table with entries to many (or all) destinations, as illustrated in figure 1(a): each of the white routers on top establishes a (bi-directional) path to each of the white routers in the bottom, requiring the two intermediate black routers to, each, maintain entries for each of the white routers in the network (plus, for each other, of course). In large networks with a topology in which a router finds itself an intermediary of a large number of active paths, this may put undue requirements on some routers. Figure 1(b) shows an example of such a network topology: if the root (0) is a network controller or monitoring station, and as such needs establishing bi-directional paths to all destinations in the network for command-and-control, then the two routers immediately below it (1 and 2), each, will need to maintain routing table entries for all destinations in their respective sub-trees. While, in such a case, the root (0) typically can be provisioned with sufficient resources, in an unplanned network, or a network evolving over time, it may not be possible to determine which non-root routers will thus become "choke-points" and therefore will also need to be provisioned to be able to maintain this much routing state.

The alternative to hop-by-hop routing is source-routing: the router, by which a data packet enters a routing domain, inserts the complete path information (for transversing that routing domain — which may be the complete path, up to and including the destination) into the data packet header. Consequently, intermediate routers need only inspect this information when making forwarding decisions. In order for a router to be able to insert complete path information into data packet headers, sufficient topological information must be available to construct the complete path – the task of acquiring this topological information is denoted *path accumulation.*

Literature contains a few examples of such path accumulation mechanism for reactive protocols: Dynamic Source Routing [14] and AODV-PA [16], both, use aggressive caching mechanisms to reduce the cost of route discovery. Because the routers need not only keep the routing tuples to the destinations of the route discovery, but also the routing tuples of the intermediate routers, those protocols requires maintaining more state in all routers, possibly exceeding the memory capacity of devices in a sensor network.

1.3   Paper Outline

This paper explores path accumulation extensions to LOADng, intended to – in topologies and with traffic patterns where it is appropriate – alleviate these difficulties, and (i) eliminate the requirements of routers in a strangulation point, (ii) provide visibility of the paths used and (iii) enable traffic engineering, *e.g.,* for path diversity. Consequently, the remainder of this paper is organised as follows: section 2 specifies the the path accumulation extension. The performance of LOADng with this path accumulation is, then, studied, and compared with core LOADng, by way of network simulations, and results are presented in section 3. This paper is concluded in section 4.

2   LOADng Path Accumulation

Each of the two message types used for route discovery by LOADng – RREQ and RREP – provide an option for doing path accumulation, by way of inclusion of appropriate TLVs and addresses, as the message is forwarded. While doing path accumulation in either message will result in the source learning the full path used, and while the same TLVs and general mechanism can be applied to either RREQ or RREP, the two approaches are not equivalent, and are therefore discussed independently in sections 2.1 and 2.2 below. Either way, once a path is established by way of Path Accumulation, user data is forwarded by way of source routing, carrying the complete path in each data packet: essentially, trading off router state for channel occupation.

2.1   RREQ Path Accumulation (RREQ-PA)

As indicated in section 1.1, a router seeking a path to a destination initiates Route Discovery by generating an RREQ, flooded through the network. Augmenting the RREQ so as to support Path Accumulation (RREQ-PA) requires including a flag, requesting that intermediate routers include path information when receiving the RREQ and prior to either forwarding or replying (by way of an RREP).

The regular LOADng processing of RREQs, specified in [6], can be modified slightly, so as to reduce the amount to state is required in each intermediate router: LOADng [6] stipulates that while forwarding RREQs, temporary "reverse path information" towards the source is installed in each intermediate router so as to facilitate forwarding of RREPs. The destination for an RREQ extend with RREQ-PA, will know the exact path that the RREQ took, and will be able to use this path for source-routing the RREP back to the initiator of the Route Discovery process. Figure 2(a) gives an example of RREQ-PA route discovery from A to D.

If the initiator of the Route Discovery process conveys additional requests – such as multiple disjoint paths, or paths avoiding/passing specific routers, the destination for a RREQ extended with RREQ Path Accumulation will be able to make intelligent decisions as to which RREQs to respond to.

The benefits of this operation are that (i) either end of the path will know the full path, all intermediaries – although only the initiator of the Route Discovery process will know if the path is actually bi-directional; (ii) traffic engineering is possible – the destination router can wait and receive multiple RREQs, and elect to send RREPs in response to multiple RREQs, for example so as to ensure that multiple non-overlapping paths are made available for carrying traffic, and (iii) no intermediate routers are required to maintain any state.

The downside to RREQ-PA is, that the over-the-channel overhead can get large: RREQs are flooded through the network, and each additional octet added is amplified by the number of routers which are participating in the network, consuming channel capacity and energy, both.

Either way, once a path is established by way of RREQ-PA, user data is forwarded by way of source routing, carrying the complete path in each data packet: essentially, trading off router state for channel occupation.

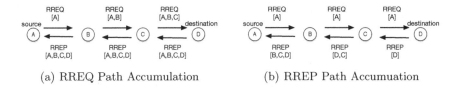

(a) RREQ Path Accumulation   (b) RREP Path Accumuation

Fig. 2. RREQ-PA and RREP-PA examples. *A* is the source and *D* is the destination.

2.2   RREP Path Accumulation (RREP-PA)

An alternative, somewhat lighter, approach is to do path accumulation by way of RREPs: a router, seeing a path to a destination generates an RREQ, which is augmented by way of a flag requesting only the destination router to process the RREQ differently: The regular LOADng processing of RREQs, specified in [6], is maintained, reverse paths installed, etc., by all intermediate routers.

When the destination router receives an RREQ indicating "path accumulation requested", it will generate an RREP – which, also, will contain that "path accumulation requested" flag – and send it in unicast along the reverse path installed when forwarding the RREQ. Then all the intermediate routers are accumulated in RREP messages. Figure 2(b) depicts an example of RREP-PA from *A* to *D*. Processing of an RREP in intermediate routers is changed, in a fashion similar to that of RREQ processing in section 2.1: on receiving a RREP, add the address of the router, and a distance to the source of the RREP. When the router, which initiated the Route Discovery process, receives this RREP, it will have acquired the complete path traveled between itself and the destination.

The benefits results of this operation are that (i) the source – but not the destination – acquires a full path, (ii) intermediate routers need only one entry towards the source – which, in case of path accumulation being used for providing a topological view of the network to a root means, that each intermediate router will maintain exactly one entry for the "upwards route" towards that root, and (iii) the size of RREQs, which are flooded through the network, does not change as compared to LOADng – which was otherwise the case for RREQ-PA.

The potential downside to RREP-PA is, that neither traffic engineering nor path diversity is enabled: (i) the destination router, responding to an RREQ, is not able to, in any meaningful way, select to respond to one RREQ over another (except for, that is, the metrics contained in the RREQ [6], since the RREQs do not carry any detailed path information, and (ii) when generating the RREP, this is forwarded in unicast and by way of the (unique) "reverse path" installed as part of RREQ processing.

3   Performance Evaluation

In order to understand the performance impact of the path accumulation extension to LOADng, this section presents a set of ns2 simulations, comparing LOADng with and without path accumulation. Of particular interest is, of course, the size of routing table required, as well as the increase in control message size.

3.1   Simulation Settings

Simulations were made with static scenarios of 63 to 500 routers, randomly placed in a square field, but maintaining a constant density of routers. From among the routers, one is designated as "root" and the network is subject to traffic between the root and each other router in the network: sensor-to-root traffic, emulating a smart meeter sending its reading to a "controller", and SCADA-like bidirectional data exchange every 5 seconds, lasting for 80 seconds each. The simulations were undertaken using the TwoRayGround propagation model and the IEEE 802.11 MAC[2].

As discussed in section 1.2, path accumulation is proposed, in part, to reduce memory requirements in intermediate routers, and in part to provide a topological view of the network to a central management station in the network. As a consequence, the performance LOADng-CTP alone, as described in section 1.1, is compared with LOADng-CTP combined with RREQ-PA and RREP-PA.

3.2   Simulation Results and Discussions

For packet delivery ratio and end-to-end delay, all three protocols combinations exhibit similar performance, depicted in [9].

Figure 3(a) shows the average number of routing table entries required for the three protocol combinations. As expected, with path accumulation, the average number of routing table entries is (almost) constant – opposed to LOADng-CTP, where each router maintains state for its entire sub-tree. For the same reason, LOADng-CTP exhibits significant variance on the number of routing table entries, as shown in figure 3(b).

The overhead of RREQ messages (each RREQ retransmission is counted) is presented in figure 4. The number of RREQs retransmitted is generally the same, however as expected, RREQ-PA incurs larger RREQ messages, with as consequence up to twice as many bytes sent across the network as the LOADng-CTP and RREP-PA.

The overhead of RREP message transmission is given in figure 5, with RREQ-PA as expected exhibiting larger RREP messages and, thus, the most bytes sent across the network.

Based on the simulation results and the discussion in section 1, the characteristics of three protocol settings are summarised qualitatively in Table 1.

---

[2] IEEE 802.11b is, of course, not suggested as a viable interface for LLNs, but serves to illustrate general protocol behaviours.

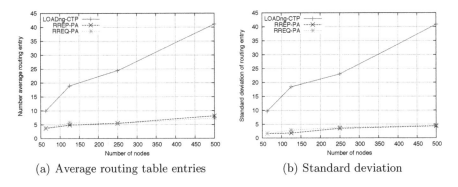

(a) Average routing table entries   (b) Standard deviation

Fig. 3. Routing table information

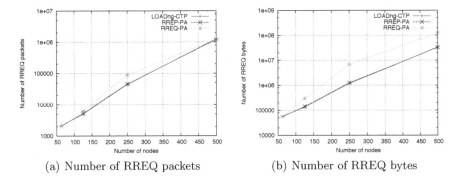

(a) Number of RREQ packets   (b) Number of RREQ bytes

Fig. 4. RREQ overhead

Table 1. Characteristics of LOADng path accumulation

	LOADng-CTP	RREQ-PA	RREP-PA
Source routing	no	yes	yes
Network topology at the root	no	yes	yes
Traffic engineering	no	yes	yes
Path diversity	no	yes	no
RREQ overhead	low	high	low
RREP overhead	low	high	medium
Sensor memory requirement	high	low	low

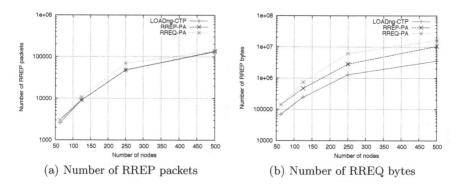

(a) Number of RREP packets   (b) Number of RREQ bytes

Fig. 5. RREP overhead

4   Conclusion

Hop-by-hop routing requires each intermediate router to maintain routing entries
– for a protocol such as LOADng, the worst case becomes four entries per active
traffic flow it carries. In certain topologies, such as where there are "bottlenecks"
or where all traffic originates/terminates in a single location in the network, the
memory requirements that come from maintaining these entries by intermediate
routers may be non-trivial to satisfy: in sensor networks, smart grid deployments,
etc., devices typically measure their memory in KB (so as to keep the price,
energy consumption, down), and "adding memory" to devices in such networks,
once deployed, is impossible.

Furthermore certain network deployments may require either control over
which paths are used for data traffic, so as to enable traffic engineering, or
information as to which paths have been used, e.g., for debugging. A reactive
protocol, a core optimisation of LOADng is, that it not provides any devices with
a complete topology map, but only provisions relevant "next-hop" information
in intermediate routers on active paths.

This paper proposes a path accumulation extensions for LOADng (LOAng-
PA), which addresses these issues. Using LOADng-PA path information is accumulated when an intermediate router forwards an RREQ or RREP message, and
carried within that message towards the sought destination or to the originator
of the route discovery process. Consequently, path diversity, traffic engineering,
and path/topology visibility can be provided – and source routing used, eliminating the requirement of (worst case) recording four entries per active traffic
flow carried across an intermediate router.

This paper has explored two different path accumulation extensions to
LOADng, has enumerated their advantages and inconveniences, and has provided a performance study, by way of network simulations, quantifying their
respective benefits. A key result is, that LOADng-PA effectively is able to reduce the size of routing tables in intermediate routers – with the cost of slightly
increasing the routing overhead, which is also quantified in this paper.

References

1. Perkins, C., Belding-Royer, E., Das, S.: Ad hoc On-Demand Distance Vector (AODV) Routing, Experimental RFC 3561 (July 2003)
2. Clausen, T., Jacquet, P.: Optimized Link State Routing Protocol (OLSR). RFC 3626, IETF (October 2003)
3. Clausen, T., Dearlove, C., Jacquet, P.: Optimized Link State Routing Protocol (OLSR) Version 2. Standard Track RFC 7181 (April 2014)
4. Kim, K., Park, S.D., Montenegro, G., Yoo, S., Kushalnagar, N.: 6LoWPAN Ad Hoc On-Demand Distance Vector Routing, Internet Draft, work in progress, draft-daniel-6lowpan-load-adhoc-routing-03 (June 2007)
5. ITU-T G.9956: Narrow-Band OFDM power line communication transceivers - Data link layer specification (November 2011)
6. Clausen, T., de Verdiere, A.C., Yi, J., Niktash, A., Igarashi, Y., Satoh, H., Herberg, U.: The lln on-demand ad hoc distance-vector routing protocol - next generation. The Internet Engineering Task Force, internet Draft, work in progress, draft-clausen-lln-loadng (October 2011)
7. Clausen, T., Camacho, A., Yi, J., de Verdiere, A.C., Igarashi, Y., Satoh, H., Morii, Y.: Experience with the loadng routing protocol for llns. The Internet Engineering Task Force, internet Draft, work in progress, draft-lavenu-lln-loadng-interoperability-report (October 2011)
8. ITU, ITU-T G.9903: Narrow-band orthogonal frequency division multiplexing power line communication transceivers for G3-PLC networks: Amendment 1 (May 2013)
9. Yi, J., Clausen, T., de Verdiere, A.C.: Collection Tree Extension of Reactive Routing Protocol for Low-Power and Lossy Networks. In: International Journal of Distributed Sensor Networks (2014)
10. Yi, J., Clausen, T., Bas, A.: Smart Route Request for On-demand Route Discovery in Constrained Environments. In: Proceedings of the IEEE International Conference on Wireless Information Technology and Systems (September 2012)
11. Bas, A., Yi, J., Clausen, T.: Expanding Ring Search for Route Discovery in LOADng Routing Protocol. In: Proceedings of the 1st International Workshop on Smart Technologies for Energy (September 2012)
12. Clausen, T., Yi, J., Bas, A., Herberg, U.: A depth first forwarding (dff) extension for the loadng routing protocol. In: ASON 2013 Sixth International Workshop on Autonomous Self-Organizing Networks (December 2013)
13. Yi, J., Clausen, T., Herberg, U.: Depth first forwarding for low power and lossy networks: Application and extension. In: Proceedings of IEEE World Forum on Internet of Things, WF-IoT (March 2014)
14. Johnson, D., Hu, Y., Maltz, D.: The Dynamic Source Routing Protocol for Mobile Ad Hoc Networks for IPv4. IETF Std. RFC 4728 (February 2007)
15. Clausen, T., Yi, J., de Verdiere, A.C.: LOADng: Towards AODV Version 2. In: VTC Fall, pp. 1–5. IEEE (2012)
16. Gwalani, S., Belding-Royer, E., Perkins, C.: Aodv-pa: Aodv with path accumulation. In: IEEE International Conference on Communications, ICC 2003, vol. 1, pp. 527–531 (May 2003)
17. Clausen, T., Dearlove, C., Dean, J., Adjih, C.: Generalized MANET Packet/Message Format, Std. Track RFC 5444 (February 2009)

Fusion of Decisions in Multi-hop Wireless Sensor Networks with Three-Level Censoring Scheme

Shoujun Liu[1], Kezhong Liu[2], and Wei Chen[1]

[1] Wuhan University of Technology, School of Information Engineering, 430070, Wuhan, China
{lsj,greatchen}@whut.edu.cn
[2] Wuhan University of Technology, School of Navigation, 430070, Wuhan, China
kzliu@whut.edu.cn

Abstract. This paper examines the impact of the three-level censoring scheme on the performance of decision fusion in multi-hop wireless sensor networks (WSNs). In performing the decision fusion process, an optimal fusion rule is derived for the model of the Rayleigh fading channel. However, the optimal fusion rule requires the instantaneous channel state information which may be too costly for resource constrained sensor networks. Hence, considering the approximation of the optimal fusion rule, a sub-optimal alternative with the knowledge of channel statistics is proposed. Simulation results show that the optimal fusion performance can be obtained via adjusting the censoring probability. It implies that with the three-level censoring scheme, the goal of energy saving and performance improvement can be achieved. In addition, the sub-optimal fusion rule exhibits only slight performance degradation compared with the optimal fusion rule which needs much more system resource.

Keywords. decision fusion, censoring, multi-hop transmission, Rayleigh fading, wireless sensor networks.

1 Introduction

A typical wireless sensor network (WSN) is made up of a large number of simple sensors which are inexpensive and low-power. Due to resource constraints and rugged surroundings, the observation collected by a single sensor may not be reliable. In order to avoid the damage from unreliability, data fusion has become an effective solution which can improve the system detection performance significantly [1]. Considering the transmission of raw data may consume more energy, sensors only transmit local decisions to the fusion center in the distributed detection system. After receiving the local decisions, the fusion center thus makes a global decision according to a certain fusion rule. Based on the Bayesian rule, an optimal fusion rule has been proposed in [2]. Chen et al. and Niu et al. have further discussed the problem of the decision fusion using the channel information in parallel WSNs with limited bandwidth [3, 4]. Li et al. and Rong et al. [5, 6] have proposed several sub-optimal fusion rules which need less computation and information cost. Meanwhile, a tradeoff can be achieved among performance, resource cost and computation complexity. Furthermore, the problem of channel-aware

R.C.-H. Hsu and W. Shangguang (Eds.): IOV 2014, LNCS 8662, pp. 160–169, 2014.

decision fusion with unknown sensor performance has been studied in [7, 8]. To reduce the energy consumption on transmission, Rago et al. [9] introduced a "yes/no" censoring scheme into the decision fusion system in single-hop WSNs. In [10], decision fusion issues in multi-hop censored WSNs have been investigated. To increase the amount of information made available to the fusion center, Cheng et al. [11] have proposed a three-level censoring scheme in WSNs, with which an energy-efficient detection can be achieved by appropriately choosing the censoring probability. Furthermore, Wang et al. [12] considered the impact of censoring scheme on the decision fusion performance of WSNs in which the number of sensors is unknown to the fusion center. It has been shown that the use of the three-level censoring scheme can improve the global fusion performance by overcoming the negative effects of erroneous local decisions. However, in [11, 12], the research is made without consideration of the multi-hop transmission in a large-scale WSN. In view of this, we will further investigate the problem of fusing decisions in multi-hop WSNs with the three-level censoring scheme.

2   System Model

We consider a network scenario where N sensors observe a common phenomenon whose status is defined as H_0 and H_1 under two hypotheses, where H_0 means that no event occurs and H_1 means that an event occurs. The prior probabilities of H_0 and H_1 are assumed to be equally likely. As depicted in Fig.1, a typical decision fusion system in the multi-hop censored WSN is composed of local sensors, wireless channels and a fusion center.

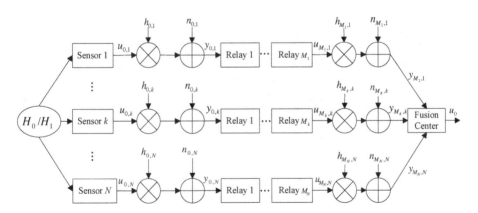

Fig. 1. Block diagram of a decision fusion system in multi-hop censored WSNs

2.1   Local Sensors

The observed signal under two hypotheses at sensor k can be expressed as

$$H_0 : z_k = -\alpha + \delta_k \tag{1}$$

$$H_1 : z_k = \alpha + \delta_k \tag{2}$$

where α is the signal strength of the phenomenon and δ_k, $k=1, 2,..., N$, are independent and identically distributed Gaussian random variables with zero means and unit variances.

After receiving its own observation z_k, each sensor makes a ternary local decision $u_{0,k}$:

$$u_{0,k} = \begin{cases} 1 & if \ z_k > \eta_k \\ -1 & if \ z_k < -\eta_k \\ 0 & otherwise \end{cases} \tag{3}$$

where η_k is a nonnegative censoring threshold of sensor k. Here, $u_{0,k}=1$ and $u_{0,k}=-1$ correspond to the decisions on H_1 and H_0, respectively, $u_{0,k}=0$ corresponds to a decision that is censored. When the value of z_k falls into the censoring region $(-\eta_k, \eta_k)$, sensor k will fail to choose between H_0 and H_1, and then, no transmission is made to the fusion center.

The local detection performance of each sensor can be characterized by false alarm and detection probabilities, denoted by p_{fk} and p_{dk}, i.e., $p_{fk} = p(u_{0,k}=1|H_0)$ and $p_{dk} = p(u_{0,k}=1|H_1)$.

Let the censoring probability of local sensor k be defined as $p^c_{0,k} = (q_{1k}+q_{0k})/2$, where $q_{1k} = p(u_{0,k}=0|H_1)$ and $q_{0k} = p(u_{0,k}=0|H_0)$.

Some local sensors not only directly observe the phenomenon, but they also act as relay points for others in the multi-hop transmission network. Original decisions of local sensors can be transmitted to the fusion center through several relay nodes. Each relay node tries to retrieve the original decision from its observation impaired by fading and noise. Supposing that there are M_k relay nodes between local sensor k and the fusion center, then, relay decisions $u_{m+1,k}$, $m=0, 1,..., M_k -1$, where $m+1$ is the relay index, can be made as follows

$$u_{m+1,k} = \begin{cases} 1 & if \ y_{m,k} > \eta_{m,k} \\ -1 & if \ y_{m,k} < -\eta_{m,k} \\ 0 & otherwise \end{cases} \tag{4}$$

Here, $\eta_{m,k}$ denote the relay threshold and $y_{m,k}$ denote the signal received by the relay node. Let the censoring probability of the relay node be defined as

$$p^c_{m+1,k} = [\int_{-\eta_{m,k}}^{\eta_{m,k}} p(y_{m,k}|u_{m,k}=1)dy_{m,k} + \int_{-\eta_{m,k}}^{\eta_{m,k}} p(y_{m,k}|u_{m,k}=-1)dy_{m,k}]/2. \tag{5}$$

2.2   Wireless Channels

In this paper, wireless channels are assumed to undergo independent fading and phase coherent reception is adopted, thus the effect of a fading channel is further simplified as a real scalar multiplication. We further assume that the channel noise is additive white Gaussian and uncorrelated between channels. Then, the channel output of sensor k can be expressed as

$$y_{m,k} = h_{m,k} \cdot u_{m,k} + n_{m,k} \tag{6}$$

where $m=0, 1,..., M_k - 1$, $n_{m,k}$ is a zero-mean Gaussian random variable with variance $\sigma_{m,k}^2$, and $h_{m,k}$ is the fading channel gain which follows Rayleigh distribution with unit power.

2.3   Fusion Center

Based on the received data $y_{M_1,1}, y_{M_2,2},..., y_{M_N,N}$ and the employed fusion rule, the fusion center decides which hypothesis is more likely to be true. Then, the global decision u_0 is derived.

Let probabilities of system-level detection and false alarm be denoted by p_d and p_f, respectively, i.e., $p_d = p(u_0 = 1|H_1)$ and $p_f = p(u_0 = 1|H_0)$.

Let the probability of the fusion error be denoted as

$$p_e = [p(u_0 = 0|H_1) + p(u_0 = 1|H_0)]/2. \tag{7}$$

Once the signal strength α is given and the channel signal-to-noise ratio (SNR) is known to the fusion center, the goal of the censoring scheme is to minimize the fusion errors via adjusting the threshold of each sensor.

3   Fusion Rule

Under the assumption of the independence of $y_{M_1,1}, y_{M_2,2},..., y_{M_N,N}$, the likelihood ratio fusion rule is given as follows

$$\Lambda = \log \frac{p(y_{M_1,1}, y_{M_2,2}, \cdots y_{M_N,N}|H_1)}{p(y_{M_1,1}, y_{M_2,2}, \cdots y_{M_N,N}|H_0)} = \sum_{k=1}^{N} \log \frac{p(y_{M_k,k}|H_1)}{p(y_{M_k,k}|H_0)} \tag{8}$$

where the likelihood function $p(y_{M_k,k}|H_1)$ and $p(y_{M_k,k}|H_0)$ can be derived by the total probability formula:

$$p(y_{M_k,k}|H_0) = p(y_{M_k,k}|u_{M_k,k} = 1)p_{fk}^m + p(y_{M_k,k}|u_{M_k,k} = 0)q_{0k}^m + p(y_{M_k,k}|u_{M_k,k} = -1)(1 - p_{fk}^m - q_{0k}^m) \tag{9}$$

$$p(y_{M_k,k}|H_1) = p(y_{M_k,k}|u_{M_k,k}=1) p_{dk}^m + p(y_{M_k,k}|u_{M_k,k}=0) q_{1k}^m + p(y_{M_k,k}|u_{M_k,k}=-1)(1-p_{dk}^m-q_{1k}^m) \quad (10)$$

where $p_{fk}^m = p(u_{M_k,k}=1|H_0)$, $p_{dk}^m = p(u_{M_k,k}=1|H_1)$, $q_{0k}^m = p(u_{M_k,k}=0|H_0)$ and $q_{1k}^m = p(u_{M_k,k}=0|H_1)$.

We can obtain p_{fk}^m , p_{dk}^m , q_{0k}^m and q_{1k}^m using the total probability formula as follows

$$p_{fk}^m = p(u_{M_k,k}=1|u_{0,k}=1) p_{fk} + p(u_{M_k,k}=1|u_{0,k}=0) q_{0k} + p(u_{M_k,k}=1|u_{0,k}=-1)(1-p_{fk}-q_{0k}) \quad (11)$$

$$p_{dk}^m = p(u_{M_k,k}=1|u_{0,k}=1) p_{dk} + p(u_{M_k,k}=1|u_{0,k}=0) q_{1k} + p(u_{M_k,k}=1|u_{0,k}=-1)(1-p_{dk}-q_{1k}) \quad (12)$$

$$q_{0k}^m = p(u_{M_k,k}=0|u_{0,k}=1) p_{fk} + p(u_{M_k,k}=0|u_{0,k}=0) q_{0k} + p(u_{M_k,k}=0|u_{0,k}=-1)(1-p_{fk}-q_{0k}) \quad (13)$$

$$q_{1k}^m = p(u_{M_k,k}=0|u_{0,k}=1) p_{dk} + p(u_{M_k,k}=0|u_{0,k}=0) q_{1k} + p(u_{M_k,k}=0|u_{0,k}=-1)(1-p_{dk}-q_{1k}) \quad (14)$$

Here, the multi-step transition probabilities such as $p(u_{M_k,k}=1|u_{0,k}=1)$ can be derived by recursions. For example,

$$\begin{aligned}
p(u_{M_k,k}=1|u_{0,k}=1) &= p(u_{M_k,k}=1|u_{M_k-1,k}=1) p(u_{M_k-1,k}=1|u_{0,k}=1) \\
&+ p(u_{M_k,k}=1|u_{M_k-1,k}=0) p(u_{M_k-1,k}=0|u_{0,k}=1) \\
&+ p(u_{M_k,k}=1|u_{M_k-1,k}=-1)[1-p(u_{M_k-1,k}=1|u_{0,k}=1)-p(u_{M_k-1,k}=0|u_{0,k}=1)].
\end{aligned} \quad (15)$$

3.1 Decision Fusion Rule Based on Instantaneous Channel State Information

Given the instantaneous channel state information (CSI), we can get the likelihood ratio fusion rule based on the channel state information (LR-CCSI)

$$\Lambda_{LR-CCSI} = \sum_{k=1}^{N} \log \frac{e^{-\frac{(y_{M_k,k}-h_{M_k,k})^2}{2\sigma_{M_k,k}^2}} p_{dk}^m + e^{-\frac{y_{M_k,k}^2}{2\sigma_{M_k,k}^2}} q_{1k}^m + e^{-\frac{(y_{M_k,k}+h_{M_k,k})^2}{2\sigma_{M_k,k}^2}} (1-p_{dk}^m-q_{1k}^m)}{e^{-\frac{(y_{M_k,k}-h_{M_k,k})^2}{2\sigma_{M_k,k}^2}} p_{fk}^m + e^{-\frac{y_{M_k,k}^2}{2\sigma_{M_k,k}^2}} q_{0k}^m + e^{-\frac{(y_{M_k,k}+h_{M_k,k})^2}{2\sigma_{M_k,k}^2}} (1-p_{fk}^m-q_{0k}^m)} \quad (16)$$

The performance of the LR-CCSI fusion rule is optimal. However, it requires instantaneous CSI which is unavailable for a resource-constrained WSN. Considering the statistics of fading channel can be estimated in advance, we will develop an alternative fusion rule with only the prior knowledge regarding the channel statistics instead of the instantaneous CSI.

3.2 Decision Fusion Rule Based on Channel Statistics

With the assumption of Rayleigh fading channels with unit power and zero-mean Gaussian random noises, it is easy to get [4]

$$p(y_{m,k}|u_{m,k}=1)=\frac{2\sigma_{m,k}}{\sqrt{2\pi}(1+2\sigma_{m,k}^{2})}e^{-\frac{y_{m,k}^{2}}{2\sigma_{m,k}^{2}}}\left[1+\sqrt{2\pi}a_{m,k}y_{m,k}e^{\frac{a_{m,k}^{2}y_{m,k}^{2}}{2}}Q(-a_{m,k}y_{m,k})\right] \quad (17)$$

$$p(y_{m,k}|u_{m,k}=0)=\frac{1}{\sqrt{2\pi}\sigma_{m,k}}e^{-\frac{y_{m,k}^{2}}{2\sigma_{m,k}^{2}}} \quad (18)$$

$$p(y_{m,k}|u_{m,k}=-1)=\frac{2\sigma_{m,k}}{\sqrt{2\pi}(1+2\sigma_{m,k}^{2})}e^{-\frac{y_{m,k}^{2}}{2\sigma_{m,k}^{2}}}\left[1-\sqrt{2\pi}a_{m,k}y_{m,k}e^{\frac{a_{m,k}^{2}y_{m,k}^{2}}{2}}Q(a_{m,k}y_{m,k})\right] \quad (19)$$

where $a_{m,k}=\dfrac{1}{\sigma_{m,k}\sqrt{1+2\sigma_{m,k}^{2}}}$ and $Q(x)$ is the standard normal complementary cumula-

tive distribution function, i.e., $Q(x)=\dfrac{1}{\sqrt{2\pi}}\int_{x}^{+\infty}e^{-\frac{t^{2}}{2}}dt$.

Next, we can obtain

$$p(u_{m+1,k}=1|u_{m,k}=1)=Q(\frac{\eta_{m,k}}{\sigma_{m,k}})+\frac{e^{-\frac{\eta_{m,k}^{2}}{1+2\sigma_{m,k}^{2}}}}{\sqrt{1+2\sigma_{m,k}^{2}}}Q(-a_{m,k}\eta_{m,k}) \quad (20)$$

$$p(u_{m+1,k}=-1|u_{m,k}=1)=Q(\frac{\eta_{m,k}}{\sigma_{m,k}})-\frac{e^{-\frac{\eta_{m,k}^{2}}{1+2\sigma_{m,k}^{2}}}}{\sqrt{1+2\sigma_{m,k}^{2}}}Q(a_{m,k}\eta_{m,k}) \quad (21)$$

$$p(u_{m+1,k}=1|u_{m,k}=-1)=Q(\frac{\eta_{m,k}}{\sigma_{m,k}})-\frac{e^{-\frac{\eta_{m,k}^{2}}{1+2\sigma_{m,k}^{2}}}}{\sqrt{1+2\sigma_{m,k}^{2}}}Q(a_{m,k}\eta_{m,k}) \quad (22)$$

$$p(u_{m+1,k}=-1|u_{m,k}=-1)=Q(\frac{\eta_{m,k}}{\sigma_{m,k}})+\frac{e^{-\frac{\eta_{m,k}^{2}}{1+2\sigma_{m,k}^{2}}}}{\sqrt{1+2\sigma_{m,k}^{2}}}Q(-a_{m,k}\eta_{m,k}) \quad (23)$$

Here, the threshold $\eta_{m,k}$ is calculated by (5) with a given relay censoring probability.

The derivation for (20) is given in Appendix A. Following a similar procedure, it is easy to obtain (21)-(23). Further, we can get the likelihood ratio fusion rule based on the channel statistics (LR-CCS)

Λ_{LR-CCS}

$$= \sum_{k=1}^{N} \log \frac{q_{1k}^m + \dfrac{2\sigma_{M_k,k}^2}{(1+2\sigma_{M_k,k}^2)} \left\{ 1 - q_{1k}^m + \sqrt{2\pi} a_{M_k,k} y_{M_k,k} e^{\frac{a_{M_k,k}^2 y_{M_k,k}^2}{2}} \left[p_{dk}^m - (1-q_{1k}^m)Q(a_{M_k,k} y_{M_k,k}) \right] \right\}}{q_{0k}^m + \dfrac{2\sigma_{M_k,k}^2}{(1+2\sigma_{M_k,k}^2)} \left\{ 1 - q_{0k}^m + \sqrt{2\pi} a_{M_k,k} y_{M_k,k} e^{\frac{a_{M_k,k}^2 y_{M_k,k}^2}{2}} \left[p_{fk}^m - (1-q_{0k}^m)Q(a_{M_k,k} y_{M_k,k}) \right] \right\}} \quad (24)$$

4   Performance Evaluation

In evaluating the performance, we assume that all the wireless channels have the same SNR, i.e., $\sigma_{m,k}^2 = \sigma^2$, for all m and k. In addition, $\alpha = 0.5$, $p_{m+1,k}^c = p_{0,k}^c = p^c$. The number of hops between sensor k and the fusion center is set to {2, 1, 2, 2, 1, 3, 2, 1}, for $k=1, 2, \ldots, 8$, respectively.

Fig. 2 gives the probability of fusion error for the LR-CCSI fusion rule, while the channel SNR is set to 0dB, 10dB and 20dB, respectively. Simulation results are obtained using 10^6 Monte Carlo runs. As illustrated in this figure, the error probability varies as a convex function of the censoring probability. There exists a non-zero censoring probability which offers the optimum fusion performance (i.e., the minimum error probability). It implies that the goal of energy saving and performance improvement can be achieved. In addition, it can be seen that the optimal censoring probabilities corresponding to the minimum error probabilities increase accordingly with the increase of the channel SNR.

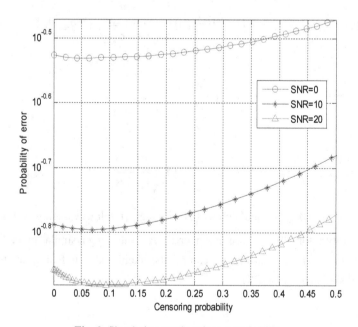

Fig. 2. Simulation results of error probability

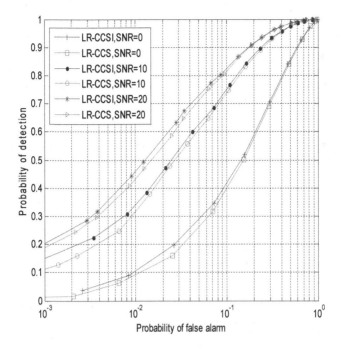

Fig. 3. ROC curves for different rules

Fig. 3 plots the ROC curves corresponding to different fusion rules at the channel SNR of 0dB, 10dB and 20dB, respectively, while the censoring probability is set to 0.1. Simulation results are obtained using 10^4 Monte Carlo runs. The LR-CCSI fusion rule provides the optimal performance, however it requires instantaneous CSI. On the other hand, its performance can be approached closely by the LR-CCS fusion rule.

5   Conclusions

The three-level censoring scheme is introduced into multi-hop WSNs under Rayleigh fading channels. We presented the optimal LR-CCSI fusion rule which requires the instantaneous CSI and the sub-optimal LR-CCS fusion rule which requires only the prior statistics of wireless channels. Simulation results show that with the three-level censoring scheme, the minimum fusion error can be obtained via adjusting the censoring probability. The LR-CCS fusion rule exhibits only slight performance degradation compared with the LR-CCSI fusion rule which needs much more system resource. Therefore, the LR-CCS fusion rule is suitable to be adopted in multi-hop WSNs with the three-level censoring scheme.

Acknowledgment. This work was supported in part by the National Natural Science Foundation of China under Grant 51279151.

References

1. Tenncy, R.R., Sandell, N.R.: Detection with distributed sensors. IEEE Trans. on Aerospace and Electronic Systems 17, 501–509 (1981)
2. Chair, Z., Varshney, P.K.: Optimal data fusion in multiple sensor detection systems. IEEE Trans. on Aerospace and Electronic Systems 22, 98–101 (1986)
3. Chen, B., Jiang, R., Kasetkasem, T., Varshney, P.K.: Channel aware decision fusion in wireless sensor networks. IEEE Trans. on Signal Processing 52, 3454–3458 (2004)
4. Niu, R., Chen, B., Varshney, P.K.: Fusion of decisions transmitted over Rayleigh fading channels in wireless sensor networks. IEEE Trans. on Signal Processing 54, 1018–1027 (2006)
5. Li, Y.-J., Wang, Z., Sun, Y.-X.: Decision fusion under fading channel in re-source-constrained wireless sensor networks (in Chinese). Journal of Software 18, 1130–1137 (2007)
6. Rong, Z., Wang, S.: Sub-optimal decision fusion under fading channels in wireless sensor networks (in Chinese). Chinese Journal of Scientific Instrument 31, 2622–2628 (2010)
7. Ciuonzo, D., Romano, G., Salvo Rossi, P.: Optimality of received energy in decision fusion over Rayleigh fading diversity MAC with non-identical sensors. IEEE Trans. on Signal Process. 61, 22–27 (2013)
8. Ciuonzo, D., Salvo Rossi, P.: Decision fusion with unknown sensor detection probability. IEEE Signal Processing Letters 21, 208–212 (2014)
9. Rago, C., Willett, P.K., Bar-Shalom, Y.: Censoring sensors: a low-communication-rate scheme for distributed detection. IEEE Trans. on Aerospace and Electronic Systems 32, 554–568 (1996)
10. Yuan, X.-G., Yang, W.-H., Shi, L.: Fusion decisions in censored wireless sensor networks with multi-hop transmission strategy (in Chinese). System Engineering and Electronics 32, 1780–1784 (2010)
11. Cheng, V.W., Wang, T.-Y.: Performance analysis of distributed decision fusion using a censoring scheme in wireless sensor networks. IEEE Trans. on Vehicular Technology 59, 2845–2851 (2010)
12. Wang, T.-Y., Wu, J.-Y.: Does more transmitting sensors always mean better decision fusion in censoring sensor networks with an unknown size? IEEE Trans. on Communications 60, 2313–2324 (2012)

Appendix A

Derivation for equation (15):

$$p(u_{m+1,k} = 1 | u_{m,k} = 1) = \int_{\eta_{m,k}}^{+\infty} P(y_{m,k} | u_{m,k} = 1) dy_{m,k}$$

$$= \int_{\eta_{m,k}}^{+\infty} \frac{2\sigma_{m,k}}{\sqrt{2\pi}(1+2\sigma_{m,k}^2)} e^{-\frac{y_{m,k}^2}{2\sigma_{m,k}^2}} [1 + \sqrt{2\pi} a_{m,k} y_{m,k} e^{-\frac{a_{m,k}^2 y_{m,k}^2}{2}} Q(-a_{m,k} y_{m,k})] dy_{m,k}$$

$$= \frac{2\sigma_{m,k}}{\sqrt{2\pi}(1+2\sigma_{m,k}^2)} \{ \int_{\eta_{m,k}}^{+\infty} e^{-\frac{y_{m,k}^2}{2\sigma_{m,k}^2}} dy_{m,k} + \int_{\eta_{m,k}}^{+\infty} \sqrt{2\pi} a_{m,k} y_{m,k} e^{-\frac{y_{m,k}^2}{1+2\sigma_{m,k}^2}} dy_{m,k} - \int_{\eta_{m,k}}^{+\infty} \sqrt{2\pi} a_{m,k} y_{m,k} e^{-\frac{y_{m,k}^2}{1+2\sigma_{m,k}^2}} Q(a_{m,k} y_{m,k}) dy_{m,k}$$

$$= \frac{2\sigma_{m,k}}{1+2\sigma_{m,k}^2} \{ \sigma_{m,k} Q(\frac{\eta_{m,k}}{\sigma_{m,k}}) + \frac{\sqrt{1+2\sigma_{m,k}^2}}{2\sigma_{m,k}} e^{-\frac{\eta_{m,k}^2}{1+2\sigma_{m,k}^2}} + \frac{1}{2\sigma_{m,k}} [Q(\frac{\eta_{m,k}}{\sigma_{m,k}}) - \sqrt{1+2\sigma_{m,k}^2} e^{-\frac{\eta_{m,k}^2}{1+2\sigma_{m,k}^2}} Q(a_{m,k} \eta_{m,k})] \}$$

$$= Q(\frac{\eta_{m,k}}{\sigma_{m,k}}) + \frac{e^{-\frac{\eta_{m,k}^2}{1+2\sigma_{m,k}^2}}}{\sqrt{1+2\sigma_{m,k}^2}} Q(-a_{m,k} \eta_{m,k})$$

A Multi-Channel Frame-Slot Assignment Algorithm for Real-Time MACs in Wireless Sensor Networks[*]

Van Vinh Phan and Hoon Oh[**]

Ubicom Lab, School of Computer Engineering and Information Technology,
University of Ulsan, Ulsan, Korea
pvvinhbk@gmail.com, hoonoh@ulsan.ac.kr

Abstract. In this paper, we propose a multi-channel frame-slot assignment algorithm to reduce the total number of slots required for data packet transmissions and enable a slot reuse against the irregular interference caused by the gradual signal fading. This becomes possible thanks to the efficient scheduling scheme of multiple channels. In our approach, each node determines a sending channel and a receiving channel based on the channel selection rule in a totally distributed manner. The channels are scheduled to the nodes at different depths such that any vertically two-hop away nodes can use the same slot without causing any inference. We evaluate the performance of the proposed algorithm by resorting to simulation. The simulation results show that our proposed approach significantly improves network throughput, packet latency and superframe size.

Keywords: Sensor node, scheduling, data channel, frames/slots, superframe.

1 Introduction

Wireless Sensor Networks (WSNs) can be used for building a Safety Monitoring and Control System (SMOCS) that monitors the safety of the workers who have to work long in the closed and dangerous working environments and warns them of any hazardous situation. The SMOCS server stores, manages, and analyses data or context information that were sent periodically by every node, and judges whether the target field is safe or not based on the collected context information. If a dangerous situation is perceived, the server sends a request to the workers so that they can take some measures against the danger.

In this paper, we propose a new frame-slot scheduling algorithm for a real-time MAC protocol in WSNs. The existing MAC protocols in WSNs can be classified into the contention-based ones and the Time Division Multiple Access (TDMA) based ones. A contention-based MAC protocol, based on the Carrier Sense Multiple Access

---

[*] This research was supported by Basic Science Research Program through the National Research Foundation of Korea (NRF) funded by the Ministry of Education (2013R1A1A2013396).
[**] Corresponding author.

R.C.-H. Hsu and W. Shangguang (Eds.): IOV 2014, LNCS 8662, pp. 170–179, 2014.

(CSMA) scheme, is widely employed in wireless networks due to its simplicity, flexibility, and robustness. Because of energy constraint, most of the early contention-based MAC protocols focused on achieving a low-duty cycle. For example, S-MAC [1] with an active-sleep cycle puts nodes to sleep periodically in idle listening period to conserve energy. However, a static active-sleep cycle of S-MAC can cause packet delay and low throughput in case of variable traffic loads. T-MAC [2] can mitigate the drawbacks of S-MAC by using an adaptive active-sleep cycle. B-MAC [3] employs Clear Channel Assessment (CCA) to enhance the utilization of channel and uses Low Power Listening (LPL) scheme to minimize the energy consumption. However, because of using the long preamble mechanism, the latency is gradually accumulated when packet travels through multi-hop path and energy is wasted at both sender and receiver after the receiver has woken up. In general, most of early MAC protocols for low duty applications try to improve energy efficiency, but increase latency as well since they use an active-sleep cycle. In addition, they usually suffer from low transmission reliability because of interference or collision problem. This phenomenon will become worse in the network with higher traffic. On the other hand, the TDMA technique can mitigate the interference and collision problem, and reduce packet latency. Several TDMA-based MAC protocols have been proposed for wireless ad hoc networks [4-6] and wireless sensor networks [7]. TreeMAC [7] suggests a frame-slot pair slot assignment (FSA) algorithm in which every node is allocated a frame-slot pair such that a node is assigned a number of frames in proportion to the number of its descendants. FSA allows a slot reuse for any two nodes that are three-hop away vertically. However, this suffers from the lack of data packet aggregation and filtering and irregular interference because of the gradual fading of a radio signal. It also suffers from the waste of slots due to the characteristic of the slot scheduling. To resolve these problems, DSA [6] does not allow a slot reuse and schedule the slots to each node in the form of a sequence of receiving slots and then a sequence of sending slots. However, DSA tends to increase a superframe size as the network size increases due to the inherent refusal of the slot reuse. Generally, the MAC protocols proposed so far mostly operate on a single channel. However, the above problems can be well addressed if multiple channels are used. Some multi-channel approaches have been proposed recently. TMCP [8] partitions the network into multiple sub-trees, each sub-tree is assigned one unique channel and uses the CSMA technique within the same channel. This is simply to reduce the contention scope of each node. In TFMAC [9], each node is assigned transmission slots during a control contention slot, each transmission slot is assigned a different channel that is used for data transmission. However, it may not be easy that two-hop away nodes make conflict-free channel selection.

In this paper, we propose a new multi-channel frame-slot assignment algorithm to reduce the total number of slots for data transmissions and enable a slot reuse against the irregular interference by the gradual signal fading. In our approach, each node is assigned a number of frames (each frame has two slots) that corresponds to the number of its descendants. Then, each node determines a sending channel and a receiving channel based on its depth according to the channel selection rule which works in a totally distributed manner. The channel selection rule guarantees that any vertically two-hop neighbors do not interfere with each other in either sending or receiving. Our experimental results indicate that the proposed approach improves network performance significantly.

In what follows, the network model is described in Section 2. We present the formal description of the proposed approach in Section 3. Section 4 covers performance evaluation. Finally, we make concluding remarks in Section 5.

2   Network Model

In this study, we consider a wireless sensor network that consists of one server (sink) and several sensor devices integrated with various sensor modules such as a thermal sensor module, a gas sensor module, an oxygen sensor module, a smoke sensor module, etc., which can be used for building a Safety Monitoring and Control System (SMOCS) to monitor the safety of the workers who have to work long in the closed and dangerous working environments. The SMOCS server is wall-powered, while sensor nodes are battery-powered. A sensor node senses data from environment periodically and sends it toward the server in multi-hop fashion. The server collects data from sensor nodes in the target environment, and analyses these data to judge whether a dangerous situation has occurred or not. Sometimes, a link between nodes can be broken because of node failure, battery depletion, or the intervention of some communication obstacles.

3   Multi-Channel Frame-Slot Scheduling

3.1   Reliable Tree Construction

At the initialization, all nodes co-operate to build a tree which is rooted at the sink. A link (x, y) is said to be *reliable* if node x can transmit packet to node y successfully when there is no interference. Then, we can construct a robust tree such that every tree-link is bi-directionally reliable (*B-reliable*) as follows [10].

Tree construction is initiated by an *advertisement* (*ADV*) message issued by the sink which is the only tree member at the initialization stage. Upon receiving the *ADV* message, an orphan that has a *reliable link* joins the sink by sending a *join request* (*JREQ*) message. A sending node includes a set of its neighbors with a reliable link in the *ADV* or *JREQ* message so that the receiver can determine whether it has a B-reliable link to the sender or not. Upon receiving *JREQ*, the member sends a *join response* (*JRES*) message and takes the orphan as its child if the corresponding link between them is *B-reliable*. When the orphan receives *JRES*, it takes the member as its parent. Another orphan who has overheard *JREQ* can take the same procedure to become a member if its link is *B-reliable*. If an orphan overhears *JREQs* from multiple members with *B-reliable* links, it pairs with a member that has the shortest distance to the sink. During the operation time, if a certain node detects the failure of the link to its parent, it tries to find one neighbor that can provide the *B-reliable* link and shortest distance to the sink and then joins that node by sending *JREQ*.

3.2   Frame-Slot Assignment

After the tree construction period, the frame-slot assignment process that consists of a frame demand calculation (FDC) function and a frame start-time assignment (FSA) function is performed. Each data frame consists of two slots, *sending slot* and *receiving slot*. A node uses the sending slot to send one data packet to its parent while it uses the receiving slot to receive one data packet from one of its children. Then an intermediate node needs a number of data frames to receive and transmit all the packets generated by its descendants plus some data frames to transmit data packets generated by its own node. The total number of data frames that a node needs to process (i.e., receive and send) data packets is referred to as a *frame demand*.

In the FDC function, starting with leaf nodes, every node calculates its frame demand, and then sends the frame demand to its parent. If an intermediate node receives all frame demands from its children, it calculates its frame demand and then forwards it to its parent. In this way, a sink can know total frame demand for the whole network. Thus, each node *i* sends a *frame demand calculation message, FDCM = (nFs(i), sysTime())*, to its parent, where *sysTime()* is the current time of system and *nFs(i)* as a frame demand of node *i* is given as follows:

$$nFs(i) = \sum_{x \in C(i)} nFs(x) + \eta_i = \sum_{x \in T(i)} \eta_x \qquad (1)$$

where $C(i)$ is a set of children of node i and $T(i) = D(i) \cup \{i\}$, $D(i)$ is the set of node i's descendants, and η_x is the number of packets that node x has to send for one round of data transmission.

Fig. 1 shows an example of the frame demand calculation when $\eta_i = 1$ for every node i, except for a sink.

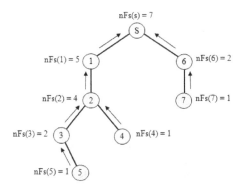

Fig. 1. An example of the frame demand calculation

As soon as the FDC function is finished, starting with a sink, the FSA function tries to assign the start frame number to each node based on the start time of the whole data frame demand (i.e., nFs(s)). For convenience, suppose that *startFrame(i)* indicates the start frame position of node *i* and also node *i* has *k* children represented as $(c_{i1}, c_{i2}, ..., c_{ik})$, $k \geq 0$. Each node *i* assigns data frames to its children by sending the *frame start-time assignment* message, *FSAM = (schedFrame(i),sysTime())* where *schedFrame(i) = (startFrame(c_{i1}),startFrame(c_{i2}), ..., startFrame(c_{ik}))*, and *startFrame(c_{ij}), $1 \leq j \leq k$,* indicates the start frame position of the jth child of node *i*. Then, *startFrame(c_{ij})* is calculated as follows:

$$startFrame(c_{ij}) = startFrame(i) + \sum_{x=1}^{j-1} nFs(c_{ix}), j \le k \qquad (2)$$

According to Eq. 2, a node i appoints the start frame to each child c_{ij} since it knows the frame demand of each of its children. Then, the remaining data frames are used for sending its own data packets.

Now, it is necessary to perform a *slot scheduling* that determines the usage of the slots in each frame as either sending slot or receiving slot. Basically, each node either sends data packet to its parent after receiving it from its child, or only sends data packet to its parent if it is a leaf. Thus, for a node at depth i, receiving and sending have to alternate for its frames, and sending or receiving for its child at depth $i+1$ has to alternate in each allocated frame.

Furthermore, to make parallelism (slot reuse) in data transmission possible, for each slot in the same frame, the same slot scheduling has to be repeated every other depth. For example, suppose that two slots of any frame are numbered as 0 and 1. If a node at depth 1 is scheduled as (Rx, Tx), a node at depth 2 should be scheduled as (Tx, Rx) where Rx indicates the receiving slot and Tx does the sending slot. For next pairs of depths, 3 and 4, 5 and 6, and so on, the same slot scheduling is repeated, so that these transmissions can be performed simultaneously. Then, the sending slot (S_d^{TX}) and the receiving slot (S_d^{RX}) of a frame of depth d can be determined as follows:

$$\begin{cases} S_d^{TX} = d \bmod 2 \\ S_d^{RX} = (d+1) \bmod 2 \end{cases} \in \{0, 1\} \qquad (3)$$

where d is the depth of a node in a tree. Especially, for a sink (with depth 0), $S_0^{TX} = 0$. The sending slot of the sink is slot 0. However, since the sink does not have to send, the 0th slot of a sink becomes *sleeping slot*.

3.3   Channel Scheduling

Even though the slots are scheduled as discussed in the previous section, the parallel transmissions may not be made because of channel interference. For example, if a node at depth 2 and a node at depth 4 use the same slot for a data transmission, a node at depth 3 that receives data packets from the node at depth 4 is interfered by over-hearing the data packet that the node at depth 2 sends to the node at depth 1. Thus, we try to avoid channel interference by allocating different channels every pair of depths such that if a node at depth 1 is a receiving slot, the nodes at a pair of depths (1+4k, 2+4k) gets channel *1* and those at depths (3+4k, 4+4k) gets channel *2*, and if a node at depth 1 is a sending slot, the nodes at a pair of depths (0+4k, 1+4k) gets channel *1* and those at depths (2+4k, 3+4k) gets channel *2*. In this way, a slot using the same channel is reused every four depths vertically. Thus, a sending node at depth 1 can be interfered with a sending node at depth 5. Even though signal attenuation makes interference, the possibility of collision is significantly lowered or negligible. This is compared with the irregular interference of the vertical three hops in TreeMAC [7].

For channel scheduling, each node at depth d determines the sending channel (Ch_d^{TX}) for a sending slot and the receiving channel (Ch_d^{RX}) for a receiving slot according to the following formulae:

$$\begin{cases} Ch_d^{TX} = \left\lceil \dfrac{\left((d-1)\bmod 4\right)+3}{4} \right\rceil \\ Ch_d^{RX} = \left\lceil \dfrac{(d \bmod 4)+3}{4} \right\rceil \end{cases} \in \{1,2\} \tag{4}$$

Accordingly, *our approach needs two data channels only* such that the same channel is reused by the nodes every other depth.

Fig. 2 shows an example of the execution of the frame-slot assignment for the simple tree shown in Fig. 1 where each frame consists of two slots, sending slot or sleeping slot (if there is not data to send) and receiving slot and the small number in each data slot indicates the channel number that the corresponding node uses. A sink node S distributes 7 data frames to nodes 1 and 6 according to their demands. Then *startFrame(1)* = frame #1 and *startFrame(6)* = frame #6. In turn, node 1 distributes 4 data frames to its only child 2 and reserves one data frame for its own data transmission. The curly upward arrow indicates the movement of the data packet generated by node 5.

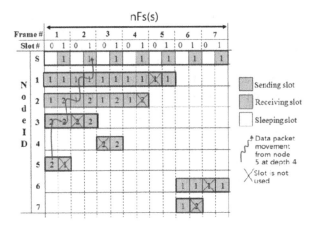

Fig. 2. An example of frame-slot assignment for the scenario in Fig. 1

4   Performance Evaluation

4.1   Simulation Setup

For evaluation of the proposed approach, we used the QualNet 5.0.2 simulator which is commercially used. We compared our proposed approach (abbreviated as MC-FSA) and the DSA approach [6] which showed the good performance over the existing protocols. In the experiments, sensor nodes are static and are randomly distributed in a square terrain 100 x 100 (m^2). Three different scenarios, S1, S2 and S3, which have the sink locations at the center, the top center and the corner of the simulation area, respectively, are used to reflect the variation of tree size in the experiments. Every node generates one data packet of 100 bytes, and then sends the data packet to the sink. The number of sensor nodes (*nNodes*) is varied from 25 to 100. Some key simulation parameters and values in the experiments are shown in Table 1.

Table 1. Simulation parameters and values

Parameter	Value
Default transmission power	−25 dBm (power level 3)
Sensor energy model	MicaZ
Path loss model	2-ray
Noise factor	10 dB
Slot size	6 ms
Dimensions	100×100 (m^2)
Simulation time	600 s
Number of nodes	1 sink; 25 sensor nodes
Data packet length	100 bytes

In the simulations, each sensor node uses one transceiver for its operation. Therefore, a node can operate in receiving mode or transmitting mode, but cannot do both at the same time. DSA uses the channel frequency of 2.405 MHz in the IEEE 802.15.4 band while MC-FSA uses two channels: channel 1 with the frequency of 2.405 MHz and channel 2 with the frequency of 2.430 MHz. We compare the proposed MC-FSA approach and the DSA approach by using the following performance metrics:

- Network throughput: The rate of successful data packet delivery measured at the sink per second (*bps* or *kbps*).
- Average packet latency: The average elapsed time that a data packet is delivered from a sensor node to the sink.
- Superframe size: The number of data slots required by all nodes in the network for data packet delivery in one cycle.

4.2   Simulation Results

(a) Network Throughput

One primary goal of the protocol design is to achieve higher network throughput. In this work, we evaluated the network throughput by measuring the number of data packets that are successfully delivered from all nodes to the sink in one second in the three different scenarios (S1, S2 and S3) with the network size of 25 nodes.

As shown in Fig. 3, our proposed approach MC-FSA can achieve the network throughput of 67 kbps, outperforms the DSA approach by more than 30%. Indeed, it can be seen that, the network throughput is affected by the superframe size (SF). The SF of MC-FSA depends on the number of nodes in the network, but not the network topology. However, the SF of DSA increases as the scenario changes (the tree size increases), resulting in a decrease of the network throughput.

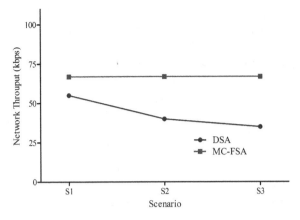

Fig. 3. Network throughput

(b) Average Packet Delay

In order to measure the average packet delay, we measure the average elapsed time that a packet is delivered from the source node to the sink. Fig. 4 compares the two protocols in terms of average packet delay with the network size of 50 nodes and the three different deployment scenarios (S1, S2 and S3).

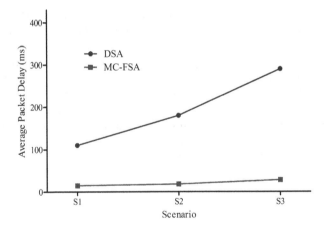

Fig. 4. Average packet delay

The three deployment scenarios have the same number of nodes, but have the different tree sizes (the scenario S3 has the longest tree size with the maximum depth of 9). Fig. 4 also shows that MC-FSA achieves the better performance in terms of the average packet delay while the packet delay of DSA is much more than the other. This is because in DSA, the data slots are allocated to a node in the form of a sequence of receiving slots and then a sequence of sending slots. Hence, before forwarding to the next hop, the packet is buffered at the receiving node until that node receives all packets from its children.

(c) Superframe Size

In the slot scheduling-based algorithms, the superframe (SF) size is directly related to the average packet latency. Thus, in this work, we compare the SF size between the two protocols by using the S1 scenario and changing the number of nodes (*nNodes*) in the network.

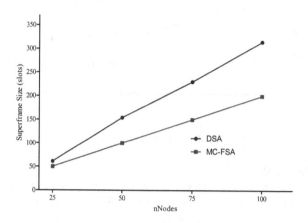

Fig. 5. Superframe size

As shown in Fig. 5, the SF sizes of the two approaches have the increasing curves as *nNodes* increases. It is obvious since the SF size is proportional to the number of sensor nodes. However, Fig. 5 also shows that the SF size of MC-FSA is smaller than that of DSA. The reason is that our proposed approach uses the spatial reuse technique, which allows multiple parallel packet transmissions. On the other hand, DSA does not use the slot reuse technique; therefore the SF size of DSA increases proportionally to the tree size and depth. In general, MC-FSA can reduce the SF size by more than 30% comparing with DSA, resulting in a decrease of the packet latency significantly.

5   Concluding Remarks

In this paper, we proposed a new frame-slot assignment algorithm for real-time applications to deliver data packets timely and reliably. Our proposed approach uses the spatial reuse technique, thus it can achieve higher network throughput, reduce packet latency significantly and satisfy the tight time constraint of real-time applications. The simulation results show that our proposed approach outperforms the other protocol in terms of network throughput, packet latency and superframe size. Therefore, our approach can be potentially used for real-time applications which require the high bandwidth and tight time constraint in the medium-sized to large-sized monitoring and control sensor networks.

References

1. Ye, W., Heidemann, J., Estrin, D.: Medium access control with coordinated adaptive sleeping for wireless sensor networks. IEEE/ACM Trans. Netw. 12, 493–506 (2004)
2. van Dam, T., Langendoen, K.: An adaptive energy-efficient MAC protocol for wireless sensor networks. In: Proceedings of the 1st International Conference on Embedded Networked Sensor Systems, pp. 171–180. ACM, Los Angeles (2003)
3. Polastre, J., Hill, J., Culler, D.: Versatile low power media access for wireless sensor networks. In: Proceedings of the 2nd International Conference on Embedded Networked Sensor Systems, pp. 95–107. ACM, Baltimore (2004)
4. Han, T.-D., Oh, H.: A Topology Management Routing Protocol for Mobile IP Support of Mobile Ad Hoc Networks. In: Ruiz, P.M., Garcia-Luna-Aceves, J.J. (eds.) ADHOC-NOW 2009. LNCS, vol. 5793, pp. 341–346. Springer, Heidelberg (2009)
5. Oh, H.: A tree-based approach for the Internet connectivity of mobile ad hoc networks. Journal of Communications and Networks 5793, 523–534 (2009)
6. Oh, H., Han, T.-D.: A demand-based slot assignment algorithm for energy-aware reliable data transmission in wireless sensor networks. Wirel. Netw. 18, 523–534 (2012)
7. Wen-Zhan, S., Renjie, H., Shirazi, B., LaHusen, R.: TreeMAC: Localized TDMA MAC protocol for real-time high-data-rate sensor networks. In: Proceedings of IEEE International Conference on Pervasive Computing and Communications (PerCom 2009), pp. 1–10 (2009)
8. Yafeng, W., Stankovic, J.A., Tian, H., Shan, L.: Realistic and Efficient Multi-Channel Communications in Wireless Sensor Networks. In: Proceedings of the 27th Conference on Computer Communications (INFOCOM 2008), pp. 1193–1201 (2008)
9. Jovanovic, M.D., Djordjevic, G.L.: TFMAC: Multi-channel MAC Protocol for Wireless Sensor Networks. In: Proceedings of the 8th International Conference on Telecommunications in Modern Satellite, Cable and Broadcasting Services, TELSIKS 2007, Serbia, pp. 23–26 (2007)
10. Oh, H., Van Vinh, P.: Design and Implementation of a MAC Protocol for Timely and Reliable Delivery of Command and Data in Dynamic Wireless Sensor Networks. Sensors 13, 13228–13257 (2013)

Maximizing Lifetime Data Aggregation in Multi-sink Wireless Sensor Networks with Unreliable Vehicle Communications

Zhihuang Su[1], Yongzao Chen[1], Hongju Cheng[1], and Naixue Xiong[2,*]

[1] College of Mathematics and Computer Science, Fuzhou University,
Fuzhou, FJ 350108, China
zhihuangsu@126.com, chenyongzao178@163.com, cscheng@fzu.edu.cn
[2] Department of Computer Science, Colorado Technical University,
CO 80907, USA
nxiong@coloradotech.edu

Abstract. In this paper, we study the problem of maximizing lifetime data aggregation in multi-sink wireless sensor networks with unreliable vehicle communication environment. Firstly, we analyze the communication between adjacent nodes, and present the optimal emission radius that can guarantee the minimum expected energy consumption. Secondly, we discuss the problem that how sensor nodes choose the sink node to send message. Thirdly, we propose the Tree-based topology Data Aggregation algorithm (TDA) based on the energy consumption balancing and the Directed Acyclic Graph based Data Aggregation algorithm (DAGDA) to improve the data acceptance probability. The simulation results show that our algorithms can extend network lifetime effectively.

Keywords: Wireless Sensor Network, Maximizing Lifetime, Data Aggregation, Unreliable Vehicle Communication Environment.

1 Introduction

Wireless sensor network is consisting of numerous micro-sensor nodes which are inexpensive and low energy consumption [1]. Sink nodes in network are responsible for accepting and processing data collected by sensor nodes. But, with the increasing network size, deploying a single sink node in network results in some nodes transmitting data to the sink node over a longer distance, which shorts network lifetime. In this case, deploying multiple sink nodes in network can be considered [2-4].

The in-network data aggregation [5-6] has been proposed and has become an important technology. The data collection operations from all nodes in network can be performed with the data aggregation tree, where sink node is a root node. A problem faced by the construction of data aggregation tree is how to construct the tree in an energy efficient way.

---

* Corresponding author.

R.C.-H. Hsu and W. Shangguang (Eds.): IOV 2014, LNCS 8662, pp. 180–189, 2014.

In this paper, we study the problem of maximizing lifetime data aggregation problem in multi-sink wireless sensor network with unreliable vehicle communication environment. To resolve the problem, we firstly propose a Tree-based topology Data Aggregation algorithm (TDA) to extend network lifetime, then propose the Directed Acyclic Graph based Data Aggregation algorithm (DAGDA) to improve the data acceptance probability.

2   System Model and Preliminary Work

2.1   Probability Model and Energy Cost Model of Accepted Signal

Stojmenovic et al. [7] apply the log-normal shadow fading model to derive the probability $p(d)$ for accepting a packet successfully as a function of distance d.

$$P(d) = \begin{cases} 1 - 0.5(d/R)^{qa}, & d < R \\ 0.5(2 - d/R)^{qa}, & R \leq d < 2R \\ 0, & d \geq 2R \end{cases} \tag{1}$$

where qa is the power attenuation factor, the value of q associated with the size of a data packet.

n this paper, we also adopt the model to quantify the acceptance probability [7], where $q = 2$ and $a \in [2, 6]$.

The energy of a node mainly consumed in the wireless communication during data aggregation, and we analyze the energy cost model for the aggregation operation of a node as follows:

$$\begin{aligned} E'_{Tx}(k,R) &= k * E_{amp} * R^a + m \\ E_{Rx}(k) &= k * Eelec \end{aligned} \tag{2}$$

where k denotes the size of a data packet, $E_{amp} = 100pJ/bit/m^2$, $E_{elec} = 50nJ/bit$, R is the emission radius, a is the path loss exponent, m denotes the energy consumed in signal processing, $E_{Tx}(k,R)$ and $E_{Rx}(k)$ respectively denote the energy consumed in sending and accepting data packet. The energy cost model for the aggregation operation of a node can be simplified as follows:

$$\begin{aligned} E_{Tx}(k,R) &= k * E_{amp} * R^a \\ E_{Rx}(k) &= k * Eelec \end{aligned} \tag{3}$$

2.2   Analysis of Energy Cost in Point to Point Communication

We use the average number of transmissions to quantify the number of a data packet need to be retransmitted, which can efficiently indicate the degree of randomness in a real network [8 - 9]. For a link (u, v) with reliability P ($P \neq 0$), node u need to transmit a data $1/P$ times to ensure that node v can accept the data. Assuming that the emission radius radio is $\delta = R/d$, $q = 2$ and combing formula (1) and formula (3), it was found that the average energy cost of a data packet is

$$E_{Tx} = \begin{cases} kE_{amp}\delta^a d^a / (1 - 0.5\delta^{-2a}), & \delta > 1 \\ 2kE_{amp}\delta^a d^a / (2 - \delta^{-1})^{2a}, & 0.5 < \delta \leq 1 \end{cases}. \tag{4}$$

For the two cases of $\delta > 1$ and $\delta \leq 1$ as show in formula (5), according to the function monotonic, the minimal average transmission cost can be described in formula (6)

$$\delta = \begin{cases} (3/2)^{1/(2a)}, & \delta > 1 \\ 1, & 0.5 < \delta \leq 1 \end{cases}. \tag{5}$$

$$E_{\min Tx} = \begin{cases} (3/2)^{3/2} kE_{amp} d^a, & \delta > 1 \\ 2kE_{amp} d^a, & 0.5 < \delta \leq 1 \end{cases}. \tag{6}$$

From formula (5) and formula (6), we can see that the minimal average transmission cost between any two node is $(3/2)^{3/2} k E_{amp} d^a$ when the emission radius is $(3/2)^{1/(2a)} d$. The minimal average transmission cost can be described in formula (7).

$$E_{\min Tx}(k,d) = (3/2)^{3/2} kE_{amp} d^a, \quad \overline{R} = (3/2)^{1/(2a)} d. \tag{7}$$

From the above analysis, we can know that there always exits a minimal average transmission cost between any two nodes in network. Without confusion, in this paper we use the transmission cost to represent the minimal average transmission cost.

2.3   Problem Formulation

We consider a wireless sensor network with sensor nodes equipped with an omnidirectional radio transmission device. Each node in network can receive data from any direction and send data to any direction. The emission radius of nodes is adjustable. The position of nodes and sink nodes are stationary and each node can obtain its own position information. In this paper, we use V to denote the set of all nodes which consists of the set of sink nodes and the set of sensor nodes $V - S$.

The wireless sensor network collects data in a periodical manner. Each node has a finite initial energy and Sink nodes are powered nodes. A node dead when its energy is depleted. Each node in network should be assigned a corresponding receiving node and this process is called aggregation scheduling. An aggregation scheduling scheme may contains more than one scheduling. In this paper, we study the problem of how to optimize the data scheduling scheme to maximize network lifetime. The network lifetime defined in this paper is the round of aggregations during which the fraction of survived nodes c remains above a given threshold [10 - 11].

2.4   Sink Node Selecting Problem

For the minimum-time aggregation scheduling problem in multi-sink sensor networks, each node just cares the correctly received of data by sink nodes. The node that communicates directly with the sink node should send data to the nearest sink node to ensure the minimal transmission cost. For those nodes that need to transmit data via multi-hop sensor to the sink node, the data may not be sent to the nearest sink node which can increase the choice of the receiving node.

3   Tree-Based Topology Data Aggregation Algorithm (TDA)

This section firstly describes the steps of constructing data aggregation trees and the reconstructing procedures, and then introduces the complete process of TDA algorithm.

3.1   Construction of Data Aggregation Trees

The process of constructing data aggregation trees is to select nodes from N_2 and add them into N_1. We can enable a node in N_2 selects a nearest node in N_1 as parent node to ensure the minimal transmission cost, calculate the value of residual aggregation rounds r_{ij} according to formula (8), and let the nodes with large r_{ij} have a priority to join the data aggregation trees, which is contributed to the nodes with low residual energy and large transmission cost become leaf nodes, thus perform more aggregation rounds.

$$r_{ij} = e_i \ / \ E_{Txij}. \tag{8}$$

The main idea of constructing a data aggregation trees is as follows: the initial T is empty and the initial N_1 is the set of sink nodes S, we search the parent node and calculate the residual aggregation rounds of each node in N_2 during current round; each time we select a node with maximum aggregation rounds from N_2 and its corresponding parent node to join the data aggregation trees, while updating the maximum aggregation rounds of nodes in N_2 and their corresponding parent node, repeat this process until the set N_2 is empty. The detail process is as follows.

Process 1. Construction of data aggregation trees T.

```
T = ∅, N₁ = S, N₂ = V - S;
Selecting a parent node pᵢ for each i in N₂, the resi-
dual aggregation rounds of i is rᵢ = rᵢₚᵢ;
while (N₂ ≠ ∅) do
   Selecting a node i ∈ N₂ with maximum rᵢ;
   T = T ∪ (i, pᵢ), N₂ = N₂ - {i}, N₁ = N₁ + {i};
   for (j₁ = 1 to | N₂|)
        The j₁-th node is node j;
     if (dⱼᵢ < dⱼₚⱼ) then pⱼ = i, rⱼ = rⱼᵢ;
   end for
end while
```

3.2   Reconstruction of Data Aggregation Trees

To let the nodes that are easy to die have enough residual energy in later data aggregations and avoid the frequent of reconstructing data aggregation trees, the constructed data aggregation trees calculate the stage aggregation rounds according to formula (9).

$$F(T) = \max\{freq * \min(e_i / (E_{Txi} + cn_i * E_{Rxi})), LR\} , \tag{9}$$

where $freq$ is the coefficient of the stage aggregation rounds which in the range of $(0,1]$, cn_i is the number of child node of node i, $E_{Txi} + cn_i E_{Rxi}$ is the energy cost E_i of node i. LR denotes the minimum stage aggregation rounds. In addition, it also needs to reconstruct the data aggregation trees if there are nodes dead.

The information, such as residual energy of nodes, should be updated before performs the reconstruction of data aggregation trees.

Process 2. Updating Information before Reconstruction.

```
Calculate the stage aggregation rounds F(T) of T;
for (each sending node i in T)
    ar_i = ar_i + F(T), e_i = e_i - F(T) * E_i;
    if (node i dead), then V = V - {i}, dn = dn + 1, set
    the state of i as dead;
end for
```

3.3   Algorithm Process

The TDA algorithm performs the aggregation operation through data aggregation trees, and reconstructs the data aggregation trees after a certain aggregation rounds. The process will continue until the network dead, i.e. the fraction of dead nodes c larger than a given threshold. The algorithm is described as follows.

Algorithm 1. Data Aggregation algorithm (TDA).

```
Input: V, S, The position information of sensor nodes
Output: Scheduling scheme and network lifetime
    dn = 0, e_i = E_0, for i ∈ V - S, j ∈ V, calculate the
    E_ij with formula (7), all nodes' state is Un-dead;
    while (dn < n * c) do
        Construct trees T by calling the Process 1;
        Calling the Process 2 and the network perform F(T)
        rounds data aggregation according to T;
    end while
    Obtain the scheduling scheme and network lifetime.
end
```

4   Directed Acyclic Graph Based Data Aggregation Algorithm (DAGDA)

We can improve the acceptance probability by the way that multiple nodes simultaneously receiving the data. Based on this, we propose the Directed Acyclic Graph based Data Aggregation algorithm (DAGDA) to improve the data acceptance probability.

4.1   Analysis of Data Transmission Probability in Directed Acyclic Graph

For a node i, the probability of the currently transmitting data be accepted is P_i. We can update the accept probability by formula (10) when assigning a new node j to receive the data sent by node i.

$$P_i = 1 - (1 - P_i)(1 - P(d_{ij}) \tag{10}$$

4.2   Strategies to Avoid Loops

In order to avoid the presence of loops, we use the strategy in opportunistic routing: nodes in network send forward the data they received [12 - 13]. Specifically as follows: we establish a transmission link for each node in network according to a certain rules in sequence; the corresponding graph G' corresponding to the established links is no loop; in order to judge whether link (i, j) is a viable link, we can firstly assume that join the link into G' and the new graph can be denoted as G'', then start from j, depth-first search in G'', and   the link (i, j) is not a viable link if we can traversal node i which means that there is a loop in G'', otherwise we establish a new link (i, j) and update G' into G''. The time complexity of the operation that judge whether there is a loop for a given node is $O(n)$.

4.3   Strategies to Avoid Loops

DAGDA starts from the point of balancing the energy consumption: we let these nodes die easily when they communicate directly with the sink node have a priority to establish scheduling thus extend the network lifetime. The DAGDA includes two processes: the establishment of aggregation scheduling and the reconstruction of aggregation scheduling.

(1) Establishment of aggregation scheduling. This paper select the node which nearest to the given node and its join would not result in the new graph G'' containing loops as one of the receiving nodes and determining the optimal emission radius. Then, we make the node that is equipped with two times of emission radius and would not form loop to become receiving nodes of sending nodes. We sort nodes in network with increasing order of the distance to the sending node, and select the receiving node that does not form a loop by a first adaptation method. In addition, we let the nodes die easily when communicate directly with the sink node have a priority to be selected as receiving node to die soon. The specific process is as follows:

Process 3. Process of constructing the aggregation scheduling S on the basis of directed acyclic graph.

```
S = ∅;
for (i₁ = 1 to |V|)
    for the i₁-th node i, calculate the distance between i
        and sink node d_is' = min d_ij(j ∈ S) and corresponding
        E_is';
end for
Sort nodes in V with increasing order of aggregation
rounds;
for (i₁ = 1 to |V|)
    The i₁-th node i, search j which nearest to i and
        without loop, S = S ∪ (i, j);
    Calculating R_ij;
    Sort nodes whose distance to node i is smaller than
2R_ij;
```

```
for (k₁ = 1 to |Nh_i|)
    The k₁-th node is k;
    if join (i, k) and there is no loop in S, then S =
    S ∪ (i, k) and Update i's acceptance probability;
end for
end for
```

(2) Reconstruction of aggregation scheduling. We also consider the reconstruction of aggregation scheduling in DAGDA, where the stage aggregation rounds can be determined by formula (9). The DAGDA executed the two steps that establishment of aggregation scheduling and reconstruction of aggregation scheduling repeatedly, until the network dead. The algorithm is described as follows:

Algorithm 2. Directed Acyclic Graph based Data Aggregation algorithm (DAGDA).

```
Input: V, S, Position information of all nodes
Output: Scheduling scheme, network lifetime
    dn = 0, e_i = E₀, for i ∈ V - S, j ∈ V, calculate the
    E_ij according to formula (7); set the state of all
    nodes as Un-dead;
    while (dn < n * c) do
        Calling the Process 3 to establish the scheduling;
        Calling the Process 3 to update the node information
        and the network perform F(T) rounds data aggregation
        according to the established scheduling;
    end while
    Obtain the network lifetime
end
```

5   Simulation Results and Analysis

We adopt MATLAB as the platform tool and demonstrate detailed simulation experiments to evaluate the performance of the above algorithms. In this paper, we assume that the distance between nodes is far away and the energy mainly consumed in communication. The target area size is 1000m × 1000m. The Size of data packet is 100bits. The value of c is E_0. The value of a is 2. All experimental results are obtained by 10 different network topologies and calculated with the average value.

5.1   Analysis of the Value of *freq*

The value of *freq* determines when to reconstruct an aggregation scheduling. Its value affect the network lifetime and we analysis the value by experiments.

Figure 1 study the impact of network size on network lifetime and we respectively give the experiment results of TDA and DAGDA. In simulation environment setup, the number of sink nodes is 3, the value of c is 0.2, the value of *freq* is select from [0.1, 1]. Experiment results show that, as *freq* increases, both the network lifetime of

TDA and DAGDA will first increase and then decrease, and the network lifetime is large while the *freq* is small.

Fig. 2 study the impact of the number of sink nodes on network lifetime, where the number of nodes in network is 60, the value of *c* is 0.2. It is easy to know that, the trends of network lifetime in Fig. 2 are the same as Fig. 1. The network lifetime is large when the value of *freq* is 0.2, thus we set *freq* as 0.2 in the follow experiments.

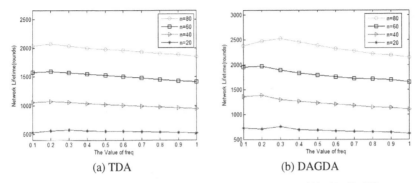

(a) TDA   (b) DAGDA

Fig. 1. Impaction of *freq* on network lifetime, where $n \in \{20, 40, 60, 80\}$

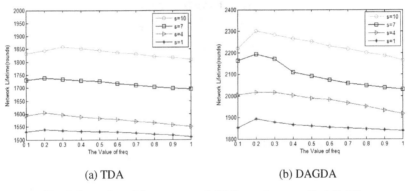

(a) TDA   (b) DAGDA

Fig. 2. Impaction of *freq* on network lifetime, where $s \in \{1, 4, 7, 10\}$

5.2   Algorithms Performance Analysis

In this paper, to applied these two strategies in [12 - 13] to our problem, we modify them as follows: The VDA apply the way of our construction and reconstruction data aggregation tree; DDA uses the acceptance probability model of our proposed to designate the nodes within two times of emission radius, and to receive data sent by sending node after the emission radius of nearest node is determined.

The first set of experiment compare the network lifetime through the following parameters: the number of sensor nodes is 60, the number of sink node is 3 and the value of *c* varies from 0.05 to 0.5. As we can see from Fig. 3, the network lifetime increased with the value of *c* increasing. The performance of DAGDA and DDA are better than the tree-based topology algorithms and the performance of DAGDA is better than DDA regardless of the value of c varies. In those tree-based topology algorithms, the performance of TDA is better than the VDA.

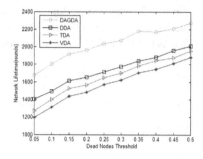
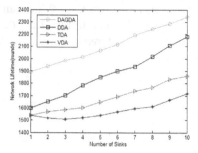

Fig. 3. Impact of c on network lifetime   **Fig. 4.** Impact of number of sink nodes

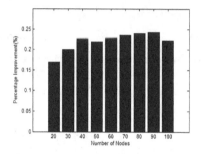

Fig. 5. Improvement of average acceptance probability with DAGDA

The third set of experiment compare the network lifetime through the following parameters: the number of nodes is 60, the value of c is 0.2 and the number of sink nodes in network varies from 1 to 10 and the result is shown in Fig. 4. We can see that, the network lifetime increased with the increasing of sink nodes in network, but the incensement of network lifetime of VDA is small.

Compared with TDA algorithm, the DAGDA can extend the network lifetime. Thus, we compare the average data acceptance probability between DAGDA and TDA through the following parameters: the number of sink nodes is 3, the number of sensor nodes varies from 20 to 100, the results as are shown in Fig. 5. We can see that, the average data acceptance probability of DAGDA better than TDA.

6   Conclusion

In this paper, we study the problem of maximizing network lifetime data aggregation in multi-sink wireless sensor networks with unreliable vehicle communication environment. We propose the Tree-based topology Data Aggregation algorithm (TDA) and the Directed Acyclic Graph based Data Aggregation algorithm (DAGDA) to extend network lifetime. Experimental results on synthesized data sets show that our proposed algorithms can significantly extend the network lifetime compared with related works.

Acknowledgement. This work is supported by the National Science Foundation of China under Grand No. 61370210 and the Development Foundation of Educational Committee of Fujian Province under Grand No. 2012JA12027.

References

1. Akyildiz, I.F., Su, W., Sankarasubramaniam, Y., Cayirci, Y.: A survey on sensor networks. IEEE Communications Magazine 40(8), 102–114 (2002)
2. Xue, Y., Cui, Y., Nahrstedt, K.: Maximizing lifetime for data aggregation in wireless sensor networks. Mobile Networks and Applications 10(6), 853–864 (2005)
3. Wu, Y., Mao, Z., Fahmy, S., Shroff, N.: Constructing maximum-lifetime data gathering forests in sensor networks. IEEE/ACM Transactions on Networking (TON) 18(5), 1571–1584 (2010)
4. Liu, S.Y., Huang, C.C., Huang, J.L., Hu, C.L.: Distributed and localized maximum-lifetime data aggregation forest construction in wireless sensor networks. In: IEEE International Conference on Pervasive Computing and Communications Workshops (PERCOM Workshops), pp. 655–660. IEEE (2012)
5. Rajagopalan, R., Varshney, P.K.: Data aggregation techniques in sensor networks: A survey. IEEE Communications Surveys 6(4), 48–63 (2006)
6. Krishnamachari, L., Estrin, D., Wicker, S.: The impact of data aggregation in wireless sensor networks. In: Proceedings of 22nd International Conference on Distributed Computing Systems Workshops, pp. 575–578. IEEE (2002)
7. Tan, H.O., Korpeoglu, I., Stojmenovic, I.: Computing localized power-efficient data aggregation trees for sensor networks. IEEE Transactions on Parallel and Distributed Systems 22(3), 489–500 (2011)
8. Shi, L., Fapojuwo, A.O.: TDMA scheduling with optimized energy efficiency and minimum delay in clustered wireless sensor networks. IEEE Transactions on Mobile Computing 9(7), 927–940 (2010)
9. Xiong, N., Huang, X., Cheng, H., Zheng, W.: Energy-Efficient algorithm for broadcasting in Ad Hoc wireless sensor networks. Sensors 13(14), 4922–4946 (2013)
10. Aziz, A., Sekercioglu, Y.A., Fitzpatrick, P., Ivanovich, M.: A survey on distributed topology control techniques for extending the lifetime of battery powered wireless sensor networks. IEEE Communications Surveys and Tutorials 15(1), 121–144 (2013)
11. Cheng, H., Su, Z., Zhang, D., Lloret, J., Yu, Z.: Energy-Efficient Node Selection Algorithms with Correlation Optimization in Wireless Sensor Networks. International Journal of Distributed Sensor Networks 2014, Article ID 576573, 1–14 (2014)
12. Chachulski, S., Jennings, M., Katti, S., Katabi, D.: Trading structure for randomness in wireless opportunistic routing. In: Proceedings of the 2007 Conference on Applications, Technologies, Architectures, and Protocols for Computer Communications, pp. 169–180 (2007)
13. Zeng, K., Yang, J., Lou, W.: On energy efficiency of geographic opportunistic routing in lossy multihop wireless networks. Wireless Networks 18(8), 967–983 (2012)

The Study of OFDM Synchronization
Based on the Particle Swarm Optimization Algorithm[*]

Guihua Kang, Hongbo Kang, and Jingbo Meng

College of Internet of Things Engineering, Hohai University, Changzhou 213022
kanggh@hhuc.edu.cn

Abstract. The OFDM technology has been widely applied for the effective information transmission in the Internet of Vehicles. In order to solve the problem that synchronization process is complex and the amount of calculation is very large by using the current synchronization algorithm of OFDM system, we propose a synchronization method based on the particle swarm optimization algorithm in the paper. Through being taken the symbol timing and frequency offset of the OFDM system as a two-dimensional particle, the estimations of the symbol timing and frequency offset value are implemented simultaneously by the particle swarm optimization algorithm. Thus the synchronization of OFDM system is achieved by compensating the time and frequency. The computer simulation results show that the proposed algorithm has the better performance, the simpler implementation, and the lower complexity than the existing synchronization algorithms.

Keywords: OFDM, PSO, synchronization, CAZAC.

1 Introduction

The orthogonal frequency division multiplexing (OFDM) technology divides a broadband channel into many orthogonal sub-channels. The spectrum of sub-channels is overlapped each other. So the rate of spectrum utilization is efficiently improved. The parallel transmission of low rate data and the addition of cyclic prefix greatly expand the width of data symbol. Therefore the multi-path interference can be effectively combated. The OFDM technology has been widely applied for the dedicated short-range communications (DSRC) in vehicular environments due to its advantages [1]. But the OFDM system also has some obvious shortcomings, such as very sensitive to the symbol timing error and frequency offset. The timing errors will cause the phase rotation of OFDM signal in the frequency domain. Instabilities caused by the Doppler shift and the local oscillator frequency offset are easy to destroy the orthogonality between the sub-channels. Therefore the timing errors and frequency offsets have severely impact on the performance of the OFDM system.

With relation to the synchronization methods of OFDM system, there presently are a number of synchronization algorithms being proposed [2-4], which is mainly summarized the two categories of blind synchronization algorithms and data-aided synchronization algorithms. The former is synchronized by the characteristics of the

---

[*] This project is supported by research program of Changzhou applied foundation.

R.C.-H. Hsu and W. Shangguang (Eds.): IOV 2014, LNCS 8662, pp. 190–200, 2014.
© Springer International Publishing Switzerland 2014

OFDM signal itself and the performance of synchronization is not very good [2], this paper focuses on the latter. For the most of these current algorithms [3, 4], the training sequence received is correlated with the known training sequence at the receiving end. After the consideration of all possible symbol timing position, the location corresponding to a maximum correlation value is chosen the position of the coarse symbol timing synchronization, and the fractional frequency offset is obtained at same time. Then through the corresponding compensation operation, the signals received are correlated again with the known training sequence, the frequency offset corresponding to a maximum correlation value is the integer frequency offset. Then the compensation operation of the integer frequency offset is accomplished. The process of the synchronization is complex and the amount of calculation is very large.

In order to simplify the above synchronization process, the OFDM synchronization algorithm based on the particle swarm optimization (PSO) is put forward in the paper. By using the related properties of PSO algorithm, the estimation value of the symbol timing position and frequency offset for OFDM system can be obtained simultaneously. Thus the OFDM synchronization is achieved. The PSO algorithm was first proposed by the Eberhart and Kennedy in 1995[5]. The ideological background was inspired by the mathematical modeling and Simulation of the social behavior of the birds. Similar to the genetic algorithm, the PSO algorithm is starting from a stochastic solution, iterative search for the optimal solution, using the fitness to evaluate the solutions and no "crossover" and "mutation" operation of the genetic algorithm. The global optimum is found by following the optimal value of the current search. The PSO algorithm is, simple and easy to implement, high precision, fast convergence rate, does not need to adjust multiple parameters, has been widely applied in the function optimization, neural network training, fuzzy system control and etc. The computer simulation results show that the proposed OFDM synchronization method based on PSO algorithm in the paper has the better performance, the simpler implementation, and the lower complexity than the existing synchronization algorithms.

2   The OFDM System Model

In the transmitter, the OFDM signal after the IFFT operation and the sampling process can be expressed as [3]

$$x(k) = \frac{1}{\sqrt{N}} \sum_{n=0}^{N-1} x_n e^{j2\pi kn/N} \tag{1}$$

where x_n is the transmitting signal sequence over the nth sub-carrier, $x(k)$ is the signal sequence after the IFFT operation, N is the total number of sub-carriers of system. The OFDM symbol sequence can be expressed as: [x $(N-G)$, x $(N-G+1)$, ... , x (0), x (1),... , x $(N-1)$], where the data before the x (0) position are the cyclic prefix, which is used to eliminate the inter symbol interference (ISI), G is the length of the cyclic prefix.

In the receiver, the signal received after the sampling process can be expressed as:

$$r(k) = y(k - \delta)e^{j2\pi\varepsilon k/N} + \omega(k) \tag{2}$$

Where δ represents the symbol timing error, ε represents the frequency offset, $\omega(k)$ is the additive white Gaussian noise. While

$$y(k) = \sum_{l=0}^{L-1} h(l)x(k-l) \tag{3}$$

where $x(k)$ is the transmitting OFDM signal, $h(l)$ is the impulse response of the lth multi-path channel, L is the number of multi-path channel.

3   The OFDM Synchronization Algorithm Based on PSO

3.1   The Basic Particle Swarm Optimization Algorithm

In the basic particle swarm algorithm, the position of each particle represents a potential solution. The good and bad degree of each solution depends on the fitness value of the objective function relative to the particle's position. The objective function is designed according to the practical optimization problems. Each particle position is determined by the velocity vector, which includes the flight direction and speed value of the particles.

Assuming the particle swarm is composed of L particles, which L is also called as the scale of colony. The oversize colony will affect the convergence speed of PSO algorithm. In the D dimension of the search space, the position of the ith particle ($1 \leq i \leq L$) in the k iteration can be expressed as $\mathbf{z}_i^k = [z_{i1}^k, \ldots, z_{id}^k, \cdots, z_{iD}^k]$, d is expressed as the dth dimension of particle ($1 \leq d \leq D$), the same below. According to the setting of objective function in advance, the current fitness value of the $\mathbf{z}_i$ is calculated, which can measure the particle position on the merits. The flight velocity is expressed as $\mathbf{v}_i^k = [v_{i1}^k, \cdots, v_{id}^k, \cdots, v_{iD}^k]$, which is the moving distance of particle in a unit of time. The optimal position of a particle to search hitherto is represented as $\mathbf{p}_i^k = [p_{i1}^k, \ldots, p_{id}^k, \cdots, p_{iD}^k]$. The best position of whole particle swarm so far to search is expressed as $\mathbf{p}_g^k = [p_{g1}^k, \ldots, p_{gd}^k, \cdots, p_{gD}^k]$. According to the following formula, the velocity and position of particles are updated for each of iteration [6]:

$$v_{id}^{k+1} = w v_{id}^k + c_1 r_1 (p_{id}^k - z_{id}^k) + c_2 r_2 (p_{gd}^k - z_{id}^k) \tag{4}$$

$$z_{id}^{k+1} = z_{id}^k + v_{id}^{k+1} \tag{5}$$

$$w = w_{max} - \frac{w_{max} - w_{min}}{N_m} k \tag{6}$$

In the formula (4), w is the inertia weight of the algorithm. r_1, r_2 is the random parameter which is uniformly distributed between the interval [0, 1]. The two parameters are used to represent the diversity of the colony. c_1, c_2 is the learning factor, which is also called as the acceleration factor. The two factors make the particles with ability of the self-summary and learning from the excellent individuals in the group. Thereby the particles can approach to the historical optimal position themselves and the best position of the group in the history. The right of the formula (4) is composed of the three parts. The first part is the previous velocity of a particle, which can be understood as the inertia of previous speed of a particle. The second part is the cognitive action of a particle, which is on behalf of the learning from a particle itself. According to the learning result, the next search location is updated. The third part is the social action of a particle, which represents the collaboration between the particles and indicates that the particles improve the next search position through the group learning. The formula (4) means that the particles update their velocities according to the speed of the previous iteration, the distance between the current position and the individual optimal position, the group best position respectively. Then the particle gets to a new location according to the formula (5). In the formula (6), w_{max} is the initial weight of the algorithm, w_{min} is the final weight of the algorithm, and N_m is the maximum iteration number of the algorithms. Being set the inertia weight according to the formula (6), the performance of PSO algorithm can be improved greatly.

Due to no real mechanism to control the change range of the particle speed for the PSO algorithm, so it is necessary to limit the maximum speed. Assuming the maximum speed is the V_{max}, the range of speed is the $[-V_{max}, +V_{max}]$. This parameter is very important, the reason is that if the speed value is too bigger, the particles may skip the best solution, otherwise if the speed value is too small, it will be caused that search of the search space is not sufficient.

3.2   The Structure and Properties of the CAZAC Sequence

The training sequence of synchronization algorithm for OFDM system in this paper consists of the constant amplitude zero correlation (CAZAC) sequence, which has the character of constant amplitude. The peak is sharp and the sidelobe is zero for the correlation function of the CAZAC sequence. Assuming $\mu(k)$ is the CAZAC sequence of length N, which is satisfied with the following conditions:

① For any value of k, $/\mu(k)/=C$, (7)

$$② \quad c_\mu(m) = \sum_{k=0}^{N-1} \mu(m+k)\mu(k) = \begin{cases} N, m=0; \\ 0, \ m=1,2,\cdots,N-1. \end{cases} \quad (8)$$

In addition, the DFT and IDFT of the CAZAC sequence are still the CAZAC sequence. Therefore, after the OFDM modulation and demodulation, the training sequence designed by using the CAZAC sequence is still the CAZAC sequence. Make full use of this nature can design the better estimation algorithm of timing error and frequency offset.

Let S be a training sequence of OFDM system. According to the literature [7], S can be expressed as:

$$S(k) = e^{j\pi k^2 M/N}, k=0, 1, 2, \cdots, N\text{-}1. \tag{9}$$

where j is the imaginary unit, M and N are prime numbers. N is the length of the training sequence. When M takes a great value, the large frequency offset can lead to the cycle shift generation of the CAZAC sequence, so the M should be as large as possible. M generally takes $N\text{-}1$[8], which can effectively reduce the frequency offset on the impact of the timing error estimation.

3.3   The Algorithm of the Timing and Frequency Estimation Based on the PSO

The synchronization scheme of OFDM system based on the training sequence is used. According to the principles and implementation steps of the PSO algorithm, the fitness function of PSO algorithm is constructed by the correlating the received training sequence with a known training sequence. Because the CAZAC sequence has the good properties of autocorrelation, which the peak is sharp and the sidelobe is zero, the maximum decision of the fitness function becomes very easy. Two dimension component of the particle position will represent the symbol timing value and carrier frequency offset. By searching the particle position corresponding to the maximum of the fitness function, we can estimate the symbol timing and carrier offset value, and then on the basis of the estimated value, the time and frequency compensation is respectively performed on the training sequence received. Then the fitness function value is calculated from the received training sequence after the compensation, and the particle position corresponding to the maximum of the fitness function is estimated again. Repeat the above process, the accurate symbol timing value and frequency offset can be finally found.

3.3.1   The Design of the Fitness Function

Let S be the transmitting training sequence, and the received training sequence is r_s.

$\hat{d}$ is the estimate value of the symbol timing, and $\hat{\varepsilon}$ is the estimation value of frequency offset. The above correlation operation can be expressed as

$$R(\hat{d},\hat{\varepsilon}) = \sum_{k=0}^{N-1} [r_s(\hat{d}+k)e^{-j2\pi\hat{\varepsilon}k/N}]S^*(k), \quad k = 0,1,2\cdots N-1 \tag{10}$$

In order to reduce the time spending of the synchronization process and the computational complexity, the threshold R_{th} can be set for the PSO algorithm according to the nature of the known OFDM channel and the properties of the training sequence. When the iterative number of the algorithm reaches the k (k=0, 1,2,..., N_m), the value of fitness function of the best position of particle group in the history exceeds this threshold, it indicates the location of particles at present can meet the synchronous requirements of OFDM system, then the process of iteration is stopped. If no value of the fitness function exceeds this threshold in the iteration, the process of iteration is not stopped until a maximum number of iteration is reached.

3.3.2   The Parameter Settings of the PSO Algorithm

In accordance with the requirements of the PSO algorithm, let L be the total number of particles of the colony, and the position of the ith particle is denoted as the $\mathbf{z}_i$. According to the requirement of time and frequency synchronization algorithm for OFDM system, $\mathbf{z}_i$ should be set to a two-dimensional variables, which includes the estimation value (z_{i1}) of the symbol timing and the estimation value (z_{i2}) of the frequency offset, that is $\mathbf{z}_i = [z_{i1}, z_{i2}]$. Similarly, the velocity of a particle movement is two-dimensional variables, which contains the motion velocity (v_{i1}) of the timing position and the motion velocity (v_{i2}) of the frequency offset, that is $\mathbf{v}_i = [v_{i1}, v_{i2}]$. p_i is the position of the maximum value that the fitness function of the formula (10) reaches in the iteration process of the ith particles, which is the best position of the particle in the history. p_g is the position of the maximum value that the fitness function reaches for the entire group of the particle, which is the best position of the particle group in the history. The two parameters are two dimensional variables.

Let N_L be the maximum iteration number of the PSO algorithm. After the $k(k=0,1,2,..., N_L)$ iterations, the historical best position of the particle group in the PSO algorithm for OFDM system contain the p_{g1} and p_{g2}, where p_{g1} is the estimation value of symbol timing position, and p_{g2} is the estimation value of frequency offset.

Because the position of OFDM symbol timing should be integers(which is represented by samples), and the obtained values according to the formula (5) may be a decimal fraction, so the rounding operation should be done for the $\mathbf{z}_i$ (i=1, 2,3,...) in the iterative process, and the integer vector of the closest to $\mathbf{z}_i$ is taken in the paper.

3.3.3   The Steps of Achieving Synchronization Algorithm

The steps of realizing synchronization algorithm based on PSO theory for the OFDM system are as follows:

(1) The initial parameter setting. Let N_L be the maximum iteration number of the PSO algorithm. The position of two-dimensional particle represents a symbol timing and frequency offset. The position and velocity of particle are the two-dimensional components respectively. The ranges of the initial position of the

ith particle are the $[z_{i1\min}, z_{i1\max}]$ and $[z_{i2\min}, z_{i2\max}]$. The ranges of the velocities of the ith particle are the $[v_{i1\min}, v_{i1\max}]$ and $[v_{i2\min}, v_{i2\max}]$.

(2) According to the above settings of the parameters, the particle position is initialized. The initial values of symbol timing and frequency offset are set to the random number, which corresponds to the range of position of the particle.

(3) According to the formula (10) to calculate the fitness value of each particle, which is expressed as R_i^0. The optimal value of the ith particle represents as $p_i^0 = z_i^0$. After comparison of the fitness values of all particles, the particle position of corresponding to the maximal fitness value is selected as the best position of the swarm.

(4) According to the formula (4), (5) and (6), update the position and velocity of particles, and calculate and compare the fitness value of corresponding to each particle position again. In accordance with the result of the comparison, the optimal position of particle p_i^k and the best position of the swarm p_g^k are updated respectively.

(5) If the fitness value of the best position of the swarm meets the threshold of the OFDM synchronization algorithm, then the process of iteration is stopped. The best position of swarm is also obtained. If not, the process of iteration is not stopped until the requirement of the threshold is satisfied in certain iterations or the maximum number of iterations is reached.

4 The Computer Simulation and Synchronization Performance Analysis

4.1 The Design of Simulation Experiment

The performance of the proposed algorithms in Rayleigh fading channel is verified by using of computer simulation experiment. The settings of simulation parameters are as follows: IFFT/FFT points are 1024, the guard interval is 128 samples, the carrier frequency is 5GHz, the channel bandwidth is 10MHz, the sampling frequency is 20.48M samples per second. The total number of the transmission paths is $L=6$ ($l=0,1,2,\ldots,5$), each of path is independent Rayleigh fading channel, the delay of each of path is $10l$, which is respectively represented by the samples and less than the cyclic prefix length of the OFDM symbol. The training sequence is constituted by the CAZAC sequence of the length 1024. The value of the normalized frequency offset is 25.7.

Let the size of particle swarm be 20, the range $[z_{i1\min}, z_{i1\max}]$ of the initial value of the timing position be the interval [60, 160] and the range $[z_{i2\min}, z_{i2\max}]$ of the initial value of the frequency offset be the interval [10, 60]. Similarly, the velocity range $[v_{i1\min}, v_{i1\max}]$ of timing position is set to the interval [1, 10] and the velocity range $[v_{i2\min}, v_{i2\max}]$ of the frequency offset is set to the interval [1, 3].

4.2   The Simulation Results and Analysis

The distribution of two-dimensional particles at the beginning and end of the process of iteration are shown in the Fig. 1 and Fig. 2 respectively. As can be seen from the Fig. 1, two-dimensional particles at the start of the iteration are randomly distributed in the intervals [60,160] and [10, 60]. At the end of the process of iteration, two-dimensional particles converge towards the synchronous position of the timing and frequency from the Fig. 2.

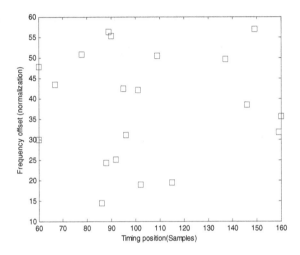

Fig. 1. The distribution of two-dimensional particles at the beginning of the iteration

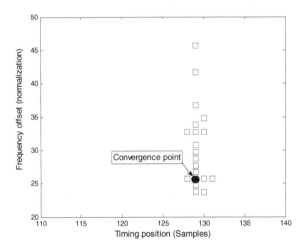

Fig. 2. The distribution of two-dimensional particles at the end of the iteration

Assuming the maximum number of iterations of the PSO algorithm is set to 30, 40 and 50 respectively. The synchronization performance of the PSO algorithm for OFDM system is represented by the MSE (mean square error) of the estimation of timing position and frequency offset. The computer simulation results are shown in the Fig. 3 and Fig. 4 respectively.

As shown in the Fig. 3 in addition to the smaller deviation of timing estimation in the low SNR(S/N), the MSE of estimation of other timing position are minimal. The Fig. 4 exhibits the good performance in the estimation of frequency offset. Moreover, as can be seen from the Fig. 3 and Fig. 4, with the increase of the number of iterations, the synchronization performance of the proposed algorithm is gradually enhanced.

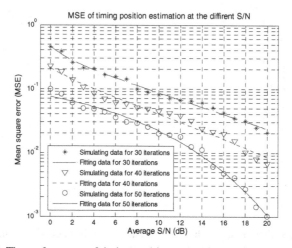

Fig. 3. The performance of timing position estimation by the PSO algorithm

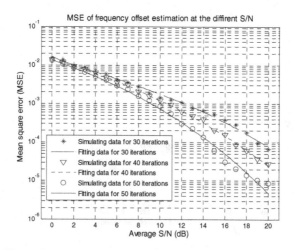

Fig. 4. The performance of frequency offset estimation by the PSO algorithm

4.3   The Analysis and Comparison of Algorithm's Complexity

According to the design of the same simulation parameters in the paper, the traditional synchronization algorithm is used. Take Ren algorithm [4] as an example, which uses also the CAZAC sequence as the training sequence to estimate the OFDM symbol timing and frequency offset. There are a total of 2177 operations for correlating the known training sequence with the training sequence received, where each operation can be divided as two parts of multiplication and addition operation. A total of 2177*2048 multiplication and addition operations are need. As for the proposed synchronization algorithm in the paper, even in the maximum number of the 30 and 40 iterations, there are only 1200*2048, 1600*2048 multiplication and addition operations respectively. A total of 2000*2048 operations are only need for 50 iterations. Compared with the traditional algorithm, the complexity of calculation is significantly lower.

According to the characteristics of the PSO algorithm, at the stage of particle swarm initialization, if we can follow the statistical law, summarize the possible values of symbol timing position and frequency offset, narrow the range of initial position of the algorithm, adjust the inertia weight and speed of the algorithm and the other related parameters, then the convergence rate of the algorithm to the optimal location will be greatly accelerated, the computational complexity will further be reduced and the performance of the algorithm will be significantly improved.

5   Conclusions

A new synchronization algorithm based on the principle of the PSO algorithm and combined with the properties of the CAZAC sequence for OFDM system is put forward in the paper. It can simultaneously estimate the symbol timing position and frequency offset, and simplifies the traditional synchronization algorithm for OFDM system. Moreover, the synchronization process is simple and the computational complexity is low. The simulation results show that the performance of proposed algorithm is good and even better than the one of the existing synchronization algorithms for OFDM system.

References

1. Kenney, J.B.: Dedicated Short-Range Communications (DSRC) Standards in the United States. Proceedings of the IEEE 99(7), 1162–1182 (2011)
2. Schmidl, T.M., Cox, D.C.: Robust frequency and timing synchronization for OFDM. IEEE Transaction on Communications 45(12), 1613–1621 (1997)
3. Awoseyila, A.B., Kasparis, C., Evans, B.G.: Improved Preamble-Aided Timing Estimation for OFDM Systems. IEEE Communication Letters 12(11), 825–827 (2008)
4. Ren, G., Chang, Y., Zhang, H., et al.: Synchronization Method Based on a New Constant Envelop Preamble for OFDM Systems. IEEE Transactions on Broadcasting 51(1), 139–143 (2008)

5. Kennedy, J., Eberhart, R.: Particle swarm optimization. In: Proceedings of the 4th IEEE International Conference on Neural Networks, Perth, Australia, pp.1942–1948 (November 1995)

6. Clerc, M., Kennedy, J.: The particle swarm - explosion, stability, and convergence in a multidimensional complex space. IEEE Transactions on Evolutionary Computation 6(1), 58–73 (2002)

7. Chu, D.C.: Polyphase codes with good periodic correlation properties. IEEE Trans. on Information Theory 45(7), 531–532 (1972)

8. Yan, C.-L., Li, S.-Q., Tang, Y.-X., et al.: New frequency offset estimation methods for OFDM systems by using CAZAC sequence. Journal of Electronics & Information Technology 28(1), 139–142 (2006)

Crossroads Optimal Geographic Routing
for Vehicular Ad Hoc Networks in City Scenario[*]

Zhipeng Gao[1], Kan Chen[1], Jingchen Zheng[2], Yuwen Hao[2,**],
Yang Yang[1], and Xuesong Qiu[1]

[1] State Key Laboratory of Networking and Switching Technology,
Beijing University of Posts and Telecommunication, P.R. China
{gaozhipeng,yyang,xsqiu}@bupt.edu.cn
[2] General Hospital of Chinese People's Armed Police Forces, P.R. China
how_yuwen@163.com

Abstract. As it is a big challenge to adapt routing protocol to different applications and dynamic network topology in Mobile Ad Hoc Networks, geographic routing protocols such as Greedy Perimeter Stateless Routing protocol (GPSR) have attracted significant attention. However, unintelligent routing path selecting strategy and outdated neighbor information lead to unwanted performance decline. In this paper, we propose a routing protocol called Crossroads Optimal Geographic Routing protocol (COGR) for vehicular ad hoc networks (VANET) in city scenario, which features on intelligent routing path planning, efficient recovery strategy from dead holes and feasible neighbor position distribution protocol without map information ahead. Through simulation experiments, we prove that COGR does substantially improve performance such as packet delivery ratio, delay and throughput in highly dynamic network environment as VANET in city scenario.

1   Introduction

As far as we know, Greedy Perimeter Stateless Routing protocol (GPSR) is generally accepted as a responsive routing protocol for mobile ad hoc networks. It takes advantage of position information and denotes routing as two modes: greedy and perimeter. GPSR does routing real time but recover from perimeter slowly and get large redundant hops. In city scenario, improved protocols as Greedy Perimeter Coordinator Routing protocol (GPCR) have been proposed featuring on road pattern. However, outdated neighbor information causes non-optimal packet forwarding which consequently results in performance reduction. Moreover, GPCR brings serious results when falsely planning path in big probability. We also notice that GPSR and GPCR both

---

[*] This work was partly supported byNSFC (61272515, 61372108, 61121061), Ph.D Programs Foundation of Ministry of Education of China (No. 20110005110011), Fundamental Research Funds for the Central Universities (No. 2014RC1102), and Beijing Higher Education Young Elite Teacher Project (YETP0474).
[**] Corresponding author.

R.C.-H. Hsu and W. Shangguang (Eds.): IOV 2014, LNCS 8662, pp. 201–210, 2014.

choose the path unintelligently in city scenario, thus may result in packet losing and poor routing performance. For city scenario, VADD [14] is proposed as a map-reliant routing protocol. In the premise of obtaining map information, routing protocols as VADD do outperform existing geographic routing protocol in delay. However as we see many cars on roads nowadays don't have built-in maps or devices of that kind. Meanwhile, since different traffic density is distributed in different roads, the nearest geographic path isn't equals to best routing path in most cases, achieving dynamic real time traffic information does cost a lot power. Moreover, cases as city rebuilding, natural disasters will make maps not referable. Thus the problems come up as how could routing protocols which are fully depend on maps work enduringly stable?

2   Related Works

A considerable amount of people have paid their attention on geographic routing protocols and proved them powerful.

Brad Kar [10] proposes GPSR and provides the basis of geographic routing metrics. GPSR makes greedy forwarding using only neighbor information and adopts perimeter forwarding to recover from a local optimal using left hand rule. Christian Lochert[3] puts forward GPCR which is designed for city scenario. While GPCR takes advantages of characteristics of roads and tries its best to route adaptively to city scenario without storage of global roads information. This approach is able to improve performance such as hops in city scenario. T. Guoming[5] proposes a metric combined left and right-hand rule in GPSR's perimeter mode. We take it for reference when meet crossroads. M. Xiaoli[9] present an effective path pruning strategy to reduce the excessive number of hops, and H. Liansheng[4] takes similar angle of view with [9] and presents an improved metric when facing MAC failure. X. Xiaojing[2] focuses on negative effects of outdated neighbor and proposes different distribution schemes to obtain local topology on demand. S. Funke[1] and Biao Zhou[11] both feature on avoiding and recovering from holes. VADD[14] adopts the idea of carry and forward and make use of predicable vehicle mobility by traffic pattern, they propose several vehicle-assisted data delivery aiming at lower delay. Vincent.L[15] introduces density-based anycast route protocol using the model that allows for pure proximity-based, pure density-based and hybrid routing strategies and simulation results shows importance of node's connectedness in routing.

3   Crossroads Optimized Geographic Routing

Before describing the COGR process, we show the primary problem of redundant hops of GPSR in city scenario in Fig 1

Assume that A is a source node. While in GPSR the packet will forward as A→B→C→D in greedy mode and go D→E→F→G→H→B→I→J→K in perimeter mode, which at last may lose for TTL expire. But we obviously hope packet to be routed by taking farthest forwarding to the crossing and turn left, hence GPSR should be improved in city scenario.

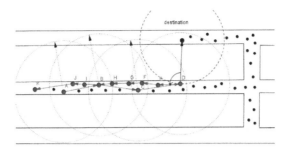

Fig. 1. Case of GPSR in city scenario

Hence we further study GPCR as reference to make protocol more adaptive to VANET. In GPCR, it raises the idea of taking farthest forwarding strategy in straight line road in the proceeding range. We learn from this idea and make it clear. First we propose an algorithm in Section III-B(1) to judge whether it is in a straight line road, then we define proceeding range for farthest choosing metric here as Fig.2 shows. Taking tangency in current black node as forwarding direction and rotate a range between 0 （0.5+α）π and （1.5-α）π 2π in anticlockwise, we get the red curve range as proceeding range, all the red nodes are covered in it.

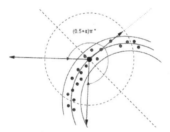

Fig. 2. Forwarding direction range definition

3.1 Improvements of COGR

1) Crossroads identification

Before giving our algorithm to judge crossroad nodes, we analyze drawbacks of GPCR's metrics. GPCR[3] proposes two metrics. One is GPCR-NT which broadcast so large beacons that is not practical in wireless network for limited bandwidth. Another way is called GPCR-CC, it calculate correlation value with neighbor information to check if it approaches a definite limit 1, namely node is in linear road, otherwise is at crossroads.

However, GPCR-CC makes errors in big probability in crossroads judging, two common examples are given as Fig 3 As we see in (a) nodes of current node and neighbors form a curve. In (b) we place neighbor nodes in an up-down-up linear and set the total node number less than 10. We get both correlations less than 0.5 which means make error crossroads judgment. (Serious results caused by error judging in GPCR will be depicted in Fig 6. Hence we develop a novel algorithm for crossroads judging.

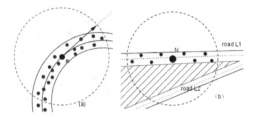

Fig. 3. Cases of GPCR in error judging a node to be crossroads

First we take polynomial regression to imitate the road, we take univariate cubic equation as imitation result. Then we determine whether a node is at crossroads by two criteria: (1) judge whether minimum distance of the point to road line is less than road width, namely check whether all points are in the line. We get minimum distance according to Newton Iteration metric[7]. Function denoted as NewtonIteration() judges if the point is verified to be on the road, return true, otherwise return false. (2) Whether coefficient of determination of the curve is close to 1. Coefficient of determination is calculated as below:

$$R^2 = 1 - \frac{\sum (y - \hat{y})^2}{\sum (y - \bar{y})^2} \tag{1}$$

We carry out many cases and prove it a better metric compared with *GPCR-CC* without any extra overheads. And algorithmic complexity is well accepted.

2)   Path Selecting Strategy for Crossroads in repair mode

Firstly we show the way GPCR takes for crossroads to route in repair mode before introducing our strategy. In Fig.4 we assume that packet is previously forwarded as G N O L and two destination node as des1 above and des2 in bottom. We see for either destination when packets reach L in repair mode, GPCR select the north direction using right hand rule as the red arrow shows(reference to [3]'s figure). However, we obviously want the packet to be routed to the green direction for des2. This situation is common in VANET, hence we work out a more intelligent forwarding strategy as Fig.5 shows, and there are two improvements to ensure a robust routing.

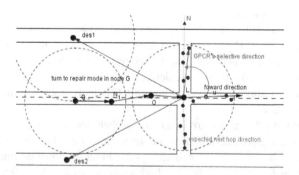

Fig. 4. Case of GPCR forwarding strategy at crossroads in repair mode

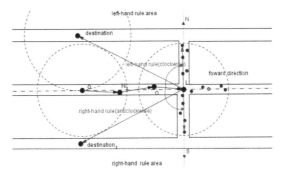

Fig. 5. Case of COGR forwarding strategy at crossroads in repair mode

In Fig.5, we firstly get the idea of left-hand rule as rotate in clockwise accordingly to right-hand rule[1]. Then we define left and right hand areas by the position of destination node bounded by forwarding direction. As Fig.5 shows, node 'des1' is in left-hand area and node 'des2' is in right-hand area. We define the strategy taken by crossroad node in repair mode as: (1) destination node is in the left-hand area, we take left-hand rule. As in Fig.5 in L we choose north direction L N as next routing direction. (2) Accorddingly, we take right-hand rule to select south direction L S for des2 in right-hand area.

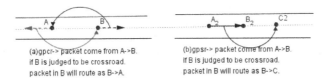

(a)gpcr-> packet come from A->B.
if B is judged to be crossroad.
packet in B will route as B->A.

(b)gpsr-> packet come from A->B.
If B is judged to be crossroad.
packet in B will route as B->C.

Fig. 6. Case of right hand rule used in GPCR and GPSR

We highlight that we take the rotating axis as O L as GPSR showed in Figure.6(b) for the sake of making packet detour around exterior face, but not the detour method GPCR as Fig.6(a), which will result to a infinite loop of packet from A->B and from B->A if node is falsely judged to be crossroads.

To sum up two metrics we present above, we first take bothleft and right-hand rule for crossroad routing in repair mode, and we take *GPSR's* hand-rule detouring in crossroad in case of false judging. Both of them contribute to a robust routing.

3)   COGR-Neighbor Distribution Protocol

Geographic routing protocols as GPCR broadcast with a fix beacon period, outdated neighbor information may lead to a false routing as Fig.7 shows. The problem is also presented in [2] for GPSR, while here we focus on city scenario for COGR.

We define COGR-Neighbor-Distribution-Protocol (COGR-NDP) on demand to adapt to VANET, in consideration of not having to listen and analyze all the packets transmitting in wireless channel. We take mobility and data demand factors to consideration on the basis of periodic distribution mechanism.

COGR-NDP defines four types of packet format as RS (router solicitation), RA (router advertisement), NS (neighbor Solicitation), NA (neighbor advertisement). RS is triggered to be sent just when there comes a packet to be sent and   . RA for a node

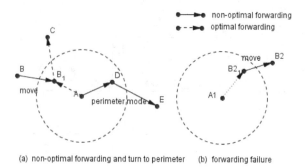

(a) non-optimal forwarding and turn to perimeter   (b) forwarding failure

Fig. 7. Case of general problems for GPSR and GPCR

to broadcast carries the content of . We set trigger condition of RA as . Among them, $\alpha>1$, refers to the latest time of sending RS, refers to the latest time of sending RA. is set as:

$$T_{int\,erval} = \begin{cases} \alpha \times T = T_{int\,erval}^{max} & if\ v < \dfrac{V_{max}}{\alpha} \\[2ex] \dfrac{V_{max}}{v} \times T & if\ \dfrac{V_{max}}{\alpha} \leq v \leq V_{max} \\[2ex] T = T_{int\,erval}^{min} & if\ v > V_{max} \end{cases} \tag{2}$$

We set as shows in order to make interval inversely proportional to speed, for the higher the speed is, the bigger probability the neighbor table is outdated. Node continues to broadcast beacon RA to all neighbors cyclically when . refers to the latest time of receiving a RS. Otherwise RA will not go on be broadcasted. If there is no RS comes, that means there is no data demand and the node can stop broadcast its position. Moreover, if the routing mode is about to change from greedy to repair, COGR-NDP is triggered to broadcast a NS to ask whether there is any node arriving in neighbor range to best avoid repair mode. Nodes received NS and satisfied condition of nearer than the NS-asking node will send a NA of to it as a reply. Finally we introduce MP rule [6] to calculate position of a neighbor node currently more accurately.

4   Simulation

4.1   Simulation Parameters Setting

We deploy a traffic model in OPNET to simulate vehicular ad hoc network according to one area in Beijing. All parameters are set as Table 1 shows.

4.2   Simulation Results – Delivery Ratio

In the first set of experiments, we investigate the delivery ratio of COGR under various speeds and different node density in VANET compared to other routing protocols. The default speed is set to be 10m/s and nodes number 250.

Table 1. Network setting parametersD

Parameter	value
Simulation area	2km × 3km
Of crossroads	15
default transmitting power(communication range)	0.000516w(400m)
Default Number of vehicles	250
Of packet senders	10
Of packet receivers	20
default vehicle velocity/speed	10 m/s
average packet size	512 byte
Bacon interval parameter a	2

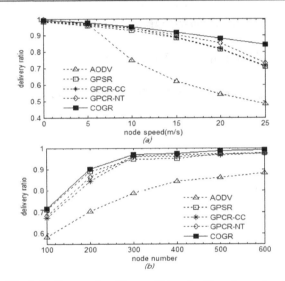

Fig. 8. Delivery ratio with speed(a) and with node numbers(b)

As Fig.8 (a) depicts, higher efficiency of COGR in packet delivery ratio is found because it makes corresponding improvement for path strategy and NDP, so it gets a lower probability of packet dropping either caused by TTL limit or forwarding failure than GPCR, as the merit gets more obvious under high dynamic. GPSR behaves inferior to GPCR in default 250 nodes for not considering traffic pattern and needs more forwarding. While in Fig.8 (b) we find that delivery ratio raises for all protocols as a trend, mostly contribute to trapping in less holes in bigger nodes density. When density is lower in first several cases, GPCR gets lower delivery ratio for wasting hops in straight roads when recognize crossroads wrongly compared to GPSR, as we analyze in section III-B-(2), GPCR may loop transmitting but GPSR will rotate around exterior face to recovery from holes sooner or later unless TTL expire. Hence a conclusion can be driven as GPCR is not suitable in sparse network. As in a whole, COGR gets an overall superiority over others, by fixing GPCR's drawbacks in recognizing crossroads and enhancing turning strategy in crossroads to ensure robust routing by considering where the destination node is.

Specifically, we track the number of packets loss for GPSR, GPCR in contrast to COGR in OPNET debug mode in scenario of 250 nodes and average 10m/s speed. As Fig.9 shows, it turns out that more than 90% of packet loss rate (denote as not yellow block) goes to TTL expire caused by redundant hops for all three protocols. We find GPCR is obviously complicated by the fact that vehicular networks are highly mobile and somewhere sparse in 18% packet loss rate, the tangible causes found in Fig 9 goes to 0.035 in error crossroads judging (denoted as green block), while 0.03(denoted as the blue block) in crossroads direction unintelligent selecting. We see the COGR's 11.3% nearly equals to COGR's (0.18-0.035-0.03) and prove measures raised in Section III-B are effective.

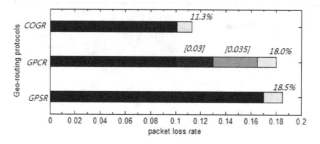

Fig. 9. Causes of Geo-routing protocol in data delivery loss

4.3   Simulation Results –Routing Control Overheads

Routing control overheads are collected and concrete statistics are shown in Fig10.

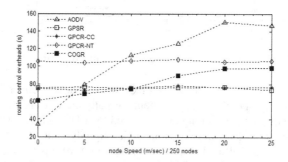

Fig. 10. Routing control overheads with speed

We collect bits that neighbor beacon totally cost while routing. We find that GPCR-CC and GPSR get stable line since both of them adopt fix period mechanism. While GPCR-NT produces high overheads for delivering neighbor information through beacon. And AODV gives the worst performance since it generates more routing overhead to recover link failures. COGR gets stable increase with speed in beaconing overheads for we have defined NDP distribution interval to adapt itself to dynamic network such as vehicular ad hoc network. In other words, we choose to sacrifice tolerant routing control overheads with speed to exchange for better delivery ratio and delay.

4.4   Simulation Results –End to End Delay

In this part of experiments, we further investigate the stabilization of protocols in VANET by collecting delay under varying speed, nodes amount and communication range.

In Fig.11 (a), AODV are seen to have a longer end-to-end delay as a table-driven protocol, due to the time required to build the whole path before packet forwarding in traditional on-demand routing protocols, and its delay climbs drastically with speed, for the reason that end-to-end paths obtained during route discovery phases easily broken and needs to be reconstructed. GPSR's delay increases faster with increased mobility due to its more rerouting and non-optimal routing paths.

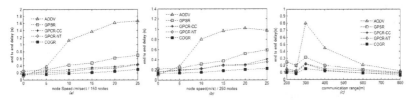

Fig. 11. Delay and average hops with node numbers 150(a) and 250(b) and communication range(c)

As expected in Fig.11(b), a global reduction in delay is shown for the bigger node density is, the bigger probability Geo-routing takes Greedy forwarding that will save a lot hops in perimeter recovery mode.

In Fig.11(c), we set different communication range and find that all protocols be-haves well before abscissa value 300 meters, but it is not meaningful simply because the delivery ratio is low in such a node density. Look at value after 300, we find routing protocols delay get closer and closer, as when connectedness of nodes gets bigger, they conducts routing mostly in greedy mode and takes less hops to reach destination. When range increased to 800m, all of them take nearly same delay for nearly no invalid hop and no perimeter transmissions. Combined with diagram (a), (b) and (c), we evaluated the delay performance and finding out that average delay of COGR is reduced by 49% over GPSR and 19.7% over GPCR, as delay value is pro-portional to routing hops, which means COGR does save the network energy a lot.

5   Conclusion

In this paper, we propose Crossroads Optimized Geographic Routing Protocol for VANET in city scenario and prove it to be efficient. COGR focus on intelligent path planning and feasible neighbor position distribution protocol according to the characteristics of city scenario, so as to realize a robust routing protocol without extra storage taken. Theories as polynomial regression and Newton iteration method are introduced in our paper to better complete the protocol.

References

1. Funke, S., Milsavljevic, N.: Guaranteed-delivery Geographic Routing under uncertain node locations. In: 26th IEEE International Conference on Computer Communications, pp. 1244–1252 (May 2007)
2. Xiaojing, X., Zehua, Z., Xin, W.: Self-Adaptive On Demand Geographic Routing Protocols for Mobile Ad Hoc Networks. In: IEEE International Conference on Computer Communications, pp. 2296–2300. IEEE (2007)
3. Lochert, C., Mauve, M., Füßler, H.: Geographic Routing in City Scenarios. ACM SIGMOBILE Mobile Computing and Communications 9(1), 69–72 (2005)
4. Liansheng, H., Weibing, L., Nanxiang, L.: Research and improvement of greedy geographical routing protocol. Computer Engineering and Applications 43, 160–162 (2007)
5. Guoming, T., Yi, X., Jiuyang, T., Weidong, X.: Regional perimeter routing for GPSR based on left & right-hand rules. Application Research of Computers 38(3), 1109–1101 (2011)
6. Quan, J.C., Kanhere, S.S., Mahbub, H., Kun, C.L.: Adaptive Position Update in Geographic Routing. In: IEEE International Conference, vol. 9, pp. 4046–4051 (June 2006)
7. Zhenyuan, W., Musheng, T.: Nonlinear equations of the Newton iteration. Electric Information and Control Engineering (ICEICE), 3380–3383 (April 2011)
8. Caizzone, G., Erangoli, W., Giacomazzi, P., Verticale, G.: An enhanced GPSR Routing Algorithm for TDMA-based Ad-Hoc Networks. In: IEEE Global Telecommunication Conference, pp. 2616–2621 (January 2005)
9. Ma, X., Sun, M.-T., Liu, X., Zhao, G.: Improving Geographical Routing for Wireless Networks with an Efficient Path Pruning Algorithm. Sensor and Ad Hoc Communications and Networks 1, 246–255 (2007)
10. Kar, B., Kung, H.T.: GPSR Greedy Perimeter Stateless Routing for Wireless Networks. In: Proc. the ACM/IEEE International Conf. on Mobile Computing and Networking (MobiCom), pp. 243–254 (August 2000)
11. Biao, Z., YengZhong, L., Gerla, M.: 'Direction' assisted Geographic Routing for mobile ad hoc networks. In: Military Communication Conference IEEE, pp. 1–7 (January 2009)
12. Bose, P., Morin, P., Stojmenovic, I., Urrutia, J.: Routing with guaranteed delivery in ad hoc wireless networks. In: ACM DIALM Wordkshop, pp. 48–55. ACM Press, Seattle (1999)
13. Kunhn, F., Wattenhofer, R., Zhang, Y., Zollinger, A.: Gemetric ad hoc routing: of theory and practice. In: Proceedings of PODC 2003, pp. 63–72. ACM Press, Boston (2003)
14. Jing, Z., Guohong, C.: VADD: Vehicle-Assisted Data Delivery in Vehicular Ad Hoc Networks. IEEE Transactions on Vehicular Technology 57(3), 1910–1922 (2008)
15. Lenders, V., May, M., Plattner, B.: Density-Based Anycast: A Robust Routing Strategy for Wireless Ad Hoc Networks. IEEE/ACM Transactions on Networking 16(4), 852–863 (2008)

Indoor Coverage Performance Comparison between IEEE 802.11g and IEEE 802.11 ah of Wireless Nodes in M2M Network

Mingming Li[1] and Dongxu Wang[2]

[1] State Radio Monitoring Centre, Beijing, China
mili-i@163.com
[2] China Unicom, Beijing, China
limingyue-i@163.com

Abstract. This paper mainly presents the indoor coverage performance and time delay comparison between IEEE 802.11g and IEEE 802.11 ah of wireless sensor node in Machine to Machine（M2M）network. Firstly, three key problems about the development of M2M network are proposed in order to bring out why IEEE chooses to release IEEE 802.11ah standard and its current situation and tendency. And also, we simply introduce the standard of IEEE 802.11g. Secondly, the paper illustrates the indoor coverage performance and time delay comparison of wireless sensor nodes according to different indoor path loss models respectively for Sub 1GHz and 2.4GHz ISM band. And numeral simulation results and simulation results are respectively offered to depict sensor nodes' coverage and the time delay.

Keywords: M2M network, IEEE 802.11x, Coverage performance, Time delay.

1 Introduction

The Machine to Machine network has presents huge growth opportunities and revenue-generating possibilities. Thanks to numerous sensors' easily deployed and low cost, their wide utilization has become a critical factor to accelerate economic growth. In the M2M network, there are a lot of Industry application such as the power industry, the medical field, vehicles service, even including intelligent home furnishing. Though ETSI's M2M market report [1] recently analyze three key problems about the development of M2M network:

1) Lack of global unitive frequency resource allocation;
2) Highly fragmented M2M technical solutions are usually dedicated to a single application;
3) Multitude of technical solutions and dispersed standardization activities result in the slow development of the M2M market.

Upon the upper questions, we find out the main techniques used in different production field are WLAN technology, RFID, Zigbee etc. Global standardization of wireless

R.C.-H. Hsu and W. Shangguang (Eds.): IOV 2014, LNCS 8662, pp. 211–217, 2014.
© Springer International Publishing Switzerland 2014

communication technology for M2M network is a key enabler to remove the technical barriers and ensure interoperable M2M services and networks.

IEEE Std. 802.11 working group has triggered a new sub-group called TGah, which attempts to release a new project, named IEEE 802.11ah, attracting extensive attention from the year 2011. 802.11ah standard uses sub 1 GHz unlicensed bands for cost-effective and large scale wireless networks. The time schedule of TGah is: 1) in April of 2010, TGah was founded to discuss the new ideas about 802.11ah; 2) in the middle of 2013, approval of the draft by the working group; 3) at the final of 2016, the draft will be ratified by the IEEE Standards Association board. Considering the ISM (Industrial, Scientific, and Medical) spectrum bands allocation below 1GHz, global unitive frequency resource allocation may be in 900MHz. Lower frequency for 802.11ah, is an opportunity for its data rates and broad coverage targets with low power consumption. IEEE 802.11ah standard insists on its physical Layer (PHY) using OFDM and MAC layer using carrier sense multiple access with collision avoidance (CSMA/CA) as key techniques[2].

IEEE 802.11g standard is one most-widely used in M2M network as its high speed and proven techniques currently. This technology operates in the 2.4GHz ISM (Industrial, Scientific, and Medical) radio spectrum with signal bandwidth 20MHz. IEEE Std. 802.11g-2003[3], part 11 gives the specifications about 802.11g's MAC layer and physical Layer (PHY). Extended Rate PHY is the proprietary vocabulary for 802.11g standard. ERP-CCK, ERP-DSSS, ERP-OFDM, ERP-PBCC and DSSS-OFDM are all key techniques used in the physical layer for the compatibility for Std. 802.11g [3]. And also carrier sense multiple access with collision avoidance (CSMA/CA) is used as key techniques in WLAN Medium Access Control (MAC) layer, supporting data rates from 1 to 54Mbps.

In order to draw out its current details, the rest of this document is structured as follows: In Section 2, we give the performance learn of wireless node including its indoor coverage performance of wireless sensor nodes according to its indoor path loss models in 900MHz bands. Section 3 quantifies a numeral simulation results are offered to depict sensor nodes' coverage simulation for a dense wireless sensor network based on 802.11ah. At the end, some proposals are mentioned to M2M sensor network operators and conclude our study.

2   Indoor Coverage Performance Comparison

2.1   Coverage Calculation

Wide coverage of wireless signal is one consideration of M2M network deployment. The follow formula is normally used to obtain coverage when doing network planning.

$$P_r = P_t - L_d + G_r + G_t - L_s \tag{1}$$

In formula 1, P_r and P_t are the receiver power and the transmitting power, L_d and L_s are the path loss and feeder loss respectively, G_r and G_t are the gains of the receiver antenna and the transmitting antenna. For calculating the maximum coverage radius of one node, a threshold of the lowest received power is supposed as -75dBm in more than 95% area. ITU-R Std. P.1238-7 [4] and Std. P.1411-7 [5] generally represent how to calculate the path loss from 30MHz to 100GHz bands of indoor scenario and outdoor scenario separately. To obtain the indoor path loss models in 900MHz for 802.11ah and in 2.4GHz for 802.11g. The authors studied the proposal 3GPP. TR 36.814 [6] and finally choose the follow formulas as its indoor path loss model:

$$L(d) = L_{FS}(d) = 20log_{10}\left(\frac{4\pi d f_c}{c}\right) \quad for \ d \le d_{BP} \tag{2}$$

$$L(d) = L_{FS}(d) + 35log_{10}\left(\frac{d}{d_{BP}}\right) \quad for \ d > d_{BP} \tag{3}$$

The path loss can be worked out with formula 2 and 3where d is the distance with the units coming out in meter, d_{BP} is the distance of breakpoint with the units being meter, fc and C are the centre carrier frequency set to 900MHz/2.4GHz and speed of light. Moreover shadow fading should be considered as:

$$p(x) = \frac{1}{\sqrt{2\pi}\sigma} \exp^{\left(-\frac{x^2}{2\sigma^2}\right)} \tag{4}$$

Table 1. Indoor path loss model parameters for single floor scenario

Model	A	B	C	D	E	F
d_{BP} (m)	5	5	5	10	20	30
Slope before d_{BP}	2	2	2	2	2	2
Slope after d_{BP}	3.5	3.5	3.5	3.5	3.5	3.5
Shadow fading std. dev. (dB) before d_{BP} (LOS) (900MHz)	2	2	2	2	2	2
Shadow fading std. dev. (dB) after d_{BP} (NLOS) (900MHz)	3	3	4	4	5	5
Shadow fading std. dev. (dB) before d_{BP} (LOS) (2.4GHz)	3	3	3	3	3	3
Shadow fading std. dev. (dB) after d_{BP} (NLOS) (2.4GHz)	4	4	5	5	6	6

In the table, the standard deviations of log-normal shadow fading is included. A to F six scenarios includes Flat fading (no multipath), Residential, Residential / Small Office, Typical Office, Large Office and Large Space (indoors / outdoors) respectively.

2.2   Numerical Simulationf on different Sensor Nodes' Coverage Performance

We learned the typical sensor nodes by suggestion [7]. In term of industrial process case, Industrial Process Sensors (Leaf Sensors) and Backhaul aggregation of sensors (Backhaul Sensors) are typical sensor nodes in use. The following parameters are set up in numerical simulation as shown in Table 2.

Table 2. Parameters for numerical simulation

Parameters	Unit	Value
EIRP (Backhaul)	dBm	23
EIRP (Sensor Leaf)		13
Gr	dBi	3
Gt	dBi	8

In table 2, EIRP (equivalent isotropic radiated power) which represents the total effective transmit power of the radio, including gains that the antenna provides and losses from the antenna cable is often used to describe the power limitations for M2M network.

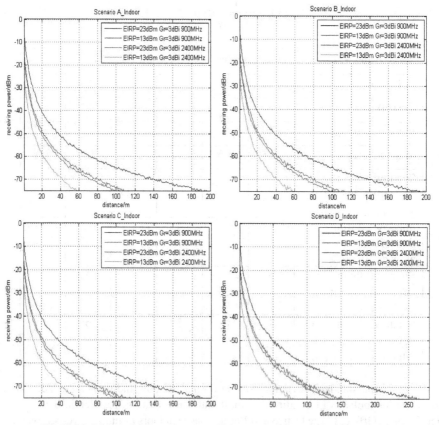

Fig. 1. Node's maximum coverage radius contrast under different scenarios

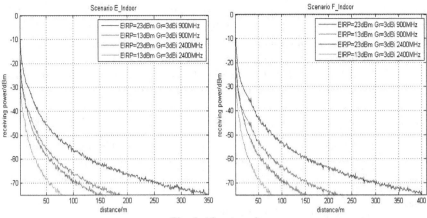

Fig. 1. (*Continued*)

Figure 1 shows different sensor nodes' maximum coverage radius under the upper scenarios. Leaf Sensor nodes' maximum coverage radius can be manifested in the following table 3 according with the scenarios.

Table 3. One AP's maximum coverage radius

Model	A	B	C	D	E	F
Scenarios description	Flat fading (no multi-path)	Residential	Residential/Small Office	Typical Office	Large Office	Large Space (indoors)
900MHz, Leaf	100m	100m	100m	140m	180m	220m
900MHz, Backhaul	190m	190m	190m	270m	350m	410m
2.4GHz, Leaf	60m	60m	60m	70m	70m	75m
2.4GHz, Backhaul	110m	110m	110m	150m	150m	152m

As shown in table 3, nodes using IEEE 802.11ah in 900MHz cover much large radius than nodes using IEEE 802.11g in 2.4GHz with the same power transmission and antenna gains. That is to say, sensor nodes in 900MHz can consume much little power than nodes in 2.4GHz under the same radius.

3   Simulation on Leaf Sensor Nodes' Time Delay

The data transmitting in M2M service for leaf sensors is usually not so huge. Then Channelization for IEEE 802.11ah in 900MHz is proposed for 1 MHz, 2 MHz, and 4 MHz or 8 MHz channels. As the standards draft will be ratified by the IEEE in 2016, here we only take OFDM as an example to demonstrate the problem of time delay comparison with 802.11g, also using 1MHz channel with other parameters shown in table 4. Then we ping the other leaf node from the current leaf node simultaneously in the same M2M network, we can obtain the total time delay of network is nearly the same between IEEE 802.11ah and IEEE 802.11g in figure 2. The result in simulation scene can encourage the production developing fast recently.

Table 4. Parameters configuration in the scene of time delay under 802.11ah & 802.11g

Parameters	Nodes Number	service	Protocol	Channel condition
Values	2	MAC Ping	802.11g & 802.11ah respectively	802.11g & 802.11ah same
Parameters	DATA Length	Access Mechanism		
Values	1500B	CTS_self		

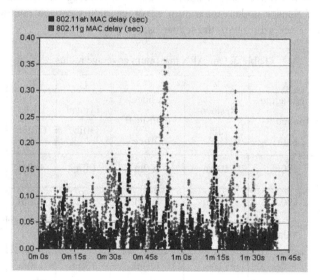

Fig. 2. Node's time delay contrast under 1500B Ping

4   Conclusion

In this paper we have proposed indoor path loss models, simulation cases to illustrate the coverage performance and time delay comparison of 802.11ah in 900MHz and 802.11g in 2.4GHz. From the upper contrast, we can obtain that sensor nodes using IEEE 802.11ah in 900MHz can consume much little power than nodes using IEEE 802.11g in 2.4GHz under the same radius. But the time delay is a little smaller than the value in the IEEE 802.11g M2M network, which also shows the IEEE 802.11ah is much better than IEEE 802.11g in the large radius M2M network. But IEEE 802.11ah standards has a long way to be better than IEEE 802.11g in industry chain. Let us recall here that our final goal is to suggest the details which should be paid attention to in deploying M2M network services. Different sensor nodes' maximum coverage radius should be considered in different scenarios. With the constraint of power, proper coverage can be obtained with different channel condition in real circumstance.

Acknowledgements. This work is supported by Important National Science and Technology Specific Projects NO.2013ZX03003016.

References

1. ETSI. Machine 2 Machine: When the machines start talking (May 2010)
2. IEEE. Status of Project IEEE 802.11ah (May 1, 2014), http://www.ieee802.org/11/Reports/tgah_update.htm
3. IEEE Computer Society, Wireless LAN Medium Access Control (MAC) and Physical Layer (PHY) Specifications, IEEE Std.802.11-2003
4. ITU-R. P.1238-7: Propagation data and prediction methods for the planning of indoor radiocommunication systems and radio local area networks in the frequency range 900 MHz to 100 GHz (February 2012)
5. ITU-R. P.1411-7: Propagation data and prediction methods for the planning of short-range outdoor radiocommunication systems and radio local area networks in the frequency range 300 MHz to 100 GHz (September 2013)
6. 3GPP. TR 36.814 - Further advancements for E-UTRA physical layer aspects, Annex A.2-system simulation scenario (March 2010)
7. IEEE TGah. 11-11-0568-02-00ah-industrial channels of usecases (May 2011)

SCHAP: The Aggregate SignCryption Based Hybrid Authentication Protocol for VANET[*]

Yiliang Han[1,2], Dingyi Fang[1], Zelun Yue[2], and Jian Zhang[2]

[1] School of Information Science and Technology, Northwest University,
Xi'an 710069, China
yilianghan@hotmail.com, dyf@nwu.edu.cn
[2] Department of Electronic Technology, Engineering University of Armed Police Force,
Xi'an 710086, China
yuezelun@gmail.com, jianzhang9599@163.com

Abstract. To secure the message transmission in vehicular ad hoc networks (VANET), the hybrid authentication protocol was proposed. The aggregated signcryption scheme was used to authenticate the private vehicular while protect them from being leak the identities. The aggregated signature was used to authenticate the public vehicular. And the batch-verification was employed to reduce the overheads also. Compared with the existed schemes, the proposal reduced the message overhead 15% at least, and speedup 50% in signing operation. Besides, the simulation experiment also shows that it has the lower communication delay and smaller message loss ratio than others.

Keywords: Vehicular Communication, Aggregate Signcryption, Aggregate Signature.

1 Introduction

With the rapid development of the wireless and mobile networks, vehicles can be equipped with intelligent processing equipment and communicate with each other. The onboard units (OBUs), as well as the fixed infrastructure usually named roadside units (RSUs), form a self-organized network, Vehicular Ad Hoc Network (VANET) and provide information services. VANET is the wireless network that does not rely on any central administration for providing communication among the OBUs on a cluster of vehicles, and between OBUs and nearby RSUs. Thus, VANET combines Vehicle TO Vehicle (V2V) also known as Inter-Vehicle Communication (IVC) with Vehicle TO Infrastructure (V2I) and Infrastructure TO Vehicle (I2V) communications.

Some technology was emerged to standardize the vehicular communication. The IEEE 802.11p [1] (WAVE, Wireless Access in the Vehicular Environments) task

---

[*] This work is supported by Natural Science Foundation of China (61103231, 61272492), the Project funded by China Postdoctoral Science Foundation, and the Natural Science Basic Research Plan in Shaanxi Province of China (2014JQ8358, 2014JQ8307).

R.C.-H. Hsu and W. Shangguang (Eds.): IOV 2014, LNCS 8662, pp. 218–226, 2014.

group is the most famous one, which working on the Dedicated Short Range Communication (DSRC). Besides the MAC layer and routing protocol in VANET, its information security and privacy issues are crucial also. Only if the messages are trust-worthy, can VANET improve traffic management. It will cause serious harm to other vehicle to send false or altered traffic information. It will also leak privacy information of the drivers and cars without encryption in some cases. So, digital signature is required all of the time, while encryption is required sometimes. Once someone deliberately sends fake traffic information, he will be severely punished. Furthermore, when the accident reconstruction and accountability happens, the sender of relevant information is also needed to be found. In addition, as VANET is very flexible and short-lived, furthermore the messages about life and death must be processed very fast, so the protocol must be efficient and dynamic aware.

To solve the problem, a number of schemes have been proposed so far. The proposals in [2] and [3] used regular digital signatures, but privacy can't be preserved. In [4], authors proposed the scheme with a set of anonymous keys that frequently change, but it incurred huge overhead costs. In [5], a novel group-signature based secure framework was proposed, but they provided no concrete scheme. In [6], authors proposed a secure and privacy-preserving protocol by using group signature and identity-based signatures, however the signature's length and computational overhead is big. In [8], authors gave a better scheme by integrating a posteriori and a priori countermeasures, but they didn't distinguish the vehicular, and the threshold is difficult to determine.

In this paper, we divide the vehicles into two classes: private vehicles and public vehicles. An efficient and secure scheme is proposed for VANET messages authentication. Aggregate signcryption is used for the messages from private vehicles. Aggregate signature is used for public vehicles and RSU. Furthermore, it employs batch message-processing techniques to accelerate the verification. Its efficiency has been improved, which was at least 50% higher than the scheme in [8]. The reminder of this paper is organized as follows. Preliminary is presented in Section 2. The proposed protocol is detailed in Section 3. Performance and security are analyzed in Section 4. Simulations are given in Section 4 to evaluate the performance of the proposal. A conclusion is given in the last section.

2   Preliminaries

2.1   Computational Assumption

– **Bilinear Map.** Let G_1, G_2 and G_T, be three cyclic groups of the same prime order q, and $a, b \in Z_q^*$. Bilinear map e: $G_1 \times G_2 \to G_T$ satisfies the follows.

(1) Bilinary. $\forall P \in G_1$, $Q \in G_2$, $e(P^a, Q^b) = e(P, Q)^{ab}$.

(2) Non-degeneracy. $\exists P \in G_1$, $Q \in G_2$, satisfies $e(P, Q) \neq 1$.

(3) Computability. $\forall P \in G_1$, $Q \in G_2$, there exists an efficient algorithm to compute $e(P, Q)$.

- **CDH Problem.** (Computational Diffie-Hellman Problem) For unknown $a,b \in Z_q^*$, given $P^a \in G_1$, $P^b \in G_1$, to compute for $P^{ab} \in G_1$.
- **DDH Problem.** (Decisional Diffie-Hellman Problem) For unknown $a,b \in Z_q^*$ and $c \in Z_q^*$, given $P^a \in G_1$, P, P^a, P^b, $P^c \in G_1$, to determin whether $c \equiv ab \in \bmod q$.
- **GDH Assumption.** (Gap Diffie-Hellman Problem). For any probabilistic polynomial-time adversary, the probability of resolving the CDH problem is negligibly away from 1/2 with the help of the resolved DDH problem.

2.2   Signcryption

Signcryption is a new cryptographic primitive that perform the signature and encryption in a single logical step. Thus, it could achieve the confidentiality and authenticity simultaneously.

- **Signcryption.** A signcryption scheme SC = (Gen, SC, DSC) consists of three algorithms. $(SDK_U, VEK_U) \leftarrow Gen(U, 1^k)$ is a randomized keys generation algorithm, takes a secure parameter k and generates a pair of keys for user U. SDK is a private key. VEK is a public key. $\omega \leftarrow SC(m, SDK_S, VEK_R)$ is a probabilistic signcryption algorithm. For any m, a sender S and a receiver R, it outputs a cipher text ω. $m \cup \{\bot\} \leftarrow DSC(\omega, SDK_R, VEK_S)$ is a deterministic designcryption algorithm. For cipher text ω, a sender S and a receiver R, it returns the message or a symbol $\bot$.

3   Proposed Protocol

3.1   System Setup

Every entity in VANET is equipped with reliable positioning system (e.g. GPS), and receives accurate synchronic information. The authentication system includes vehicles, RSU, registration manager (RM). The local RM is responsible for vehicle registration and revocation management, issues digital certificate for private vehicle, issues identity certificate for public vehicles and RSUs. To improve the authentication efficiency, we divide vehicles into two classes: one is private vehicles, they need privacy-preservation; the other one is public vehicles such as police cars, ambulances, buses, fire engines, etc. They do not need privacy-preservation. So the authentication is also divided into two kinds.

OBUs must be initialized by RM before the protocol running. OBUs initialization could be finished when the vehicular is registered. RM performs the following operation.

1. It inputs the secure parameter k and the Identities of the vehicles.   Then it initialized the parameters for the system.

2. For each of the vehicle S_i ($i = 1, ..., n$), $(x_{Si}, Y_{Si}) \leftarrow Gen(S_i, 1^k)$ is the key pair, where $x_{Si} \leftarrow_R Z_q^*$, and $Y_{Si} = x_{Si} P \in G_1$. RM issues the secret keys to each OBUs privately, and publishes the public keys to all.

3. For the RSU R, $(x_R, Y_R) \leftarrow Gen(R, 1^k)$ is the key pair, where $x_R \leftarrow_R Z_q^*$ and $Y_R = x_R P \in G_1$. RM stores the secret key in the RUS privately, and publishes the public key to all.

3.2 Private Vehicles' Messages Authentication

Private vehicles' messages authentication must be very fast and correct, as well as it satisfies conditional anonymous.

A bilinear map based aggregate signcryption scheme is proposed for the private vehicles' messages authentication, it can meet the security requirements.

— Signcryption

For the message m_i, each of the senders S_i performs the following operation.
1. Selects the randomness $r_i \leftarrow_R Z_q^*$, computes $U_i = r_i P$.
2. Computes $V_i = x_{Si} H_1(m_i, Y_{Si})$.
3. Computes $Z_i = m_i \oplus H_2(U_i, Y_R, r_i Y_R)$.
4. Returns $w_i = (U_i, V_i, Z_i)$.
The triple w_i is the signcryption text produced by the sender S_i.

— Aggregate

The RSU perform the aggregate operation as the follows.

$$V = \sum_{i=1}^{n} V_i ,$$

The $W = (U_1, ..., U_n, V, Z_1, ..., Z_n)$ is the aggregate signcryption text.

— Designcryption and Verification

Receiving the message $W = (U_1, ..., U_n, V, Z_1, ..., Z_n)$, the receiver R performs as follows.

1. For $i=1, ..., n$
   a. Computes $H_2 (U_i, Y_R, x_R U_i)$.
   b. Computes $m_i = Z \oplus H_2(U_i, Y_R, x_R U_i)$.
   c. Computes $h_i = H_1(m_i, Y_{Si})$.
   EndFor
2. If the following equation holds, accepts the verification, otherwise rejects it.

$$\prod_{i=1}^{n} e(Y_{si}, h_i) = e(P, V) \tag{1}$$

3.3 Public Vehicles and RSUs' Messages Authentication

Public vehicles and RSUs needn't privacy preservation, but also the messages sent from them are very trust-worthy, so we use a provably secure aggregate signature scheme [9], it is also one of the most efficient schemes, furthermore the length of the signature is very short due to the use of bilinear pairing.

— **Signing**

For the message m_i, each of the sender S_i performs the following operation.
1. Computes $V_i = x_{Si}H_1(m_i, Y_{Si})$.
3. Returns (m_i, V_i).
The V_i is the signature produced by the sender S_i on message m_i.

— **Aggregate**
The RSU perform the aggregate operation as the follows.

$$V = \sum_{i=1}^{n} V_i,$$

The resulted V is the aggregate signature.

— **Verification**

Receiving the message and aggregate signature $(m_1, ..., m_n, V)$, the receiver R performs as follows.

1. For $i=1,..., n$, Computes $h_i = H_1(m_i, Y_{Si})$.
2. Checks whether the following equation holds. Accepts the verification if the equation holds, otherwise rejects it.

$$\prod_{i=1}^{n} e(Y_{si}, h_i) = e(P, V) \tag{2}$$

4   Security and Performance Analysis

4.1   Performance Analysis.

According to [1], the format of the secure messages sent from private vehicles consists of six fields: message ID (message type), group ID, Timestamp (message sent time), TTL (time to live), payload (vehicle's speed, position, direction, and so on), and signature. It is presented in table 1. From Section 3.2, To achieve the security level of 2^{80}, the length of p must be 170-bits, each element in G_1 must be 171-bits long. In the private authentication scheme, the payload is the encrypted message. In the public authentication scheme, the payload is the plain message. In both of the schemes, the signatures are aggregated. So the aggregated signature has the same length as the plain signature, i.e. 171-bits≈22-bytes. Under the same security level, the message size is shorter than that in [6] and [8], respectively $192n$ -bytes and $128n$ - bytes.

Table 1. Format of the messages from vehicles

Type-ID	Grou-pID	Timestamp	TTL	Payload	Signature
2bytes	2 bytes	4 bytes	1bytes	100bytes	22bytes

From table 2, we can see the comparison between our scheme and those in [6] and [8], the signature's length and computational complexity are both better than the schemes in [6] and [8]. The message overhead is reduced 15% at least. The signing operational speed is 50% faster at least. The verification speed is faster also.

Table 2. Comparison summary

	Message size	Signing	Verification
Ours	109 n +22 bytes	3 nExps	n Pairing+2n Exps
		or nExps	or n Pairing
[8]	128 n –bytes	6 n Exps	n Pairing+6n Exps
[6]	192n –bytes	n Pairing+9n Exps	n Pairing+6n Exps

4.2   Security Analysis

The security of the scheme for private authentication lies in the IND-CCA2 (indistinguishable against adaptive chosen ciphertext attacks) and UF-CMA (Unforgeable against adaptive chosen message attacks).

Theorem 1. In the random oracle model with secure parameter k, if an adversary **A** (t, q_{SC}, q_{ADSC}, q_{H1}, q_{H2}, ε) has the non-negligible advantage ε against the IND-CCA2 security of the proposed scheme. **A** runs in time t and performs q_{SC} signcryption queries, q_{ADSC} designcryption queries and q_{Hi} queries to oracles H_i ($i = 1, 2$), then it exits an algorithm **B** that solves the GDH problem in G_1 with the probability $\varepsilon' \geq \varepsilon$ - n $q_{ADSC}(q_{H1} / 2^k + q_{H2} / 2^z)$ - n $q_{SC} q_{H1} / 2^k$ within time $t' = t + (2q_{SC} + q_{SC} q_{H1})$ t_e + (4n q_{DSC} +2$q_{SC} q_{H2})$ t_b. Where t_b denotes the time required for one pairing evaluation, t_e denotes the time required for one exponention.

Theorem 2. In the random oracle model with secure parameter k, if a forger **F** has the non-negligible advantage ρ to forge a valid signcryption text of the proposed scheme. **F** runs in time t and performs q_{SC} signcryption queries and q_{Hi} queries to oracles H_i, ($i = 1, 2$), then it exists an algorithm **E** that solves the GDH problem in G_1 with the probability $\varepsilon \geq e(q_{SC} + n + 1)\varepsilon'$ within time $t \leq t' - t_{exp} (2q_{H1} + 4 q_{SC} + 3n + 1)$ - t_e ($2q_{H2}$). Where t_b denotes the time required for one pairing evaluation, t_e denotes the time required for one exponention.

The security of the scheme for public authentication is presented in [9].

5   Simulation

The simulation used the simulator NS-2[11]. The VANET scenario was built using the scenario generator presented in [12]. Urban traffic environment as figure 1 and highway environment is a straight bidirectional six-lane highway. Vehicles are randomly generated, the average speed in urban scenario is 55km/h or so, the average speed in the highway scenario is 100km/h or so, the communication range is 10-300m.In both scenarios, an RSU is allocated every 500m along each road, which sends messages every 300ms,The channel bandwidth bound is 6Mb/s, the package size is 216 bytes and 180 bytes, the TTL is 20s, the urban scenario covers 1000m×1000m, the highway scenario covers 2000m × 30 m, RSU and OBU send a message every 300ms,the average message delay $avgD$ and the average message loss ratio $avgLR$ are defined as follow[6].

$$avgD = \frac{1}{N_D \cdot M_n \cdot K_n} \sum_{n \in D} \sum_{m=1}^{M_n} \sum_{k=1}^{K_n} \left(T_{sig}^{n\_m} + T_{tra}^{n\_m\_k} + T_{ver}^{n\_m\_k} \left(L_{n\_m\_k} + 1 \right) \right) \qquad (3)$$

$$avgLR = \frac{1}{N_D} \sum_{n=1}^{N_D} \left(M_{nc} / \sum_{k=1}^{K_n} M_{na} \right) \qquad (4)$$

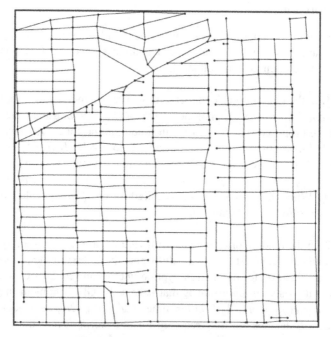

Fig. 1. Road scenario in simulation

Where D is the sample district in the simulation, N_D is the number of vehicles in D, M_n is the number of the messages that sent from the vehicle n. K_n is the number of the vehicles in the one-hop communication range of the vehicle n. $T_{sig}^{n\_m}$ is the time that it takes for the vehicle n to signing message m. The notation n_m_k is the message m sent from the vehicle n and received by the vehicle k. $T_{tras}^{n\_m\_k}$ and $T_{ver}^{n\_m\_k}$ represent transfer time and verification time, and $L_{n\_m\_k}$ is the length of message that sent by vehicle n to vehicle k. M_{nc} is the number of messages consumed by vehicle n in application layer. M_{na} is the number of messages that are received by vehicle n in MAC layer. Here we only consider the message loss caused by the security protocol rather than the wireless transmission channel. In addition, the message will be lost if the queue is full when the message arrival rate is higher than the message verification. In the NS-2 simulation, we adopted the measurement of cryptographic library MIRACL [13], we considered the delay induced by some cryptographic operation. One paring operation takes 3.6ms. The following table 3 and table 4 indicate the impact of traffic load on the message end-to-end delay and loss ratio under urban and highway. The two tables show that with the increase of the number of vehicles in the communication, the message end-to-end delay does not vary a lot, around 20ms, which is far smaller than the maximum allowable message end-to-end transmission latency of 100ms defined in [4]. But the message loss ratio increases when the traffic load is increased. When the traffic load is up to 150, the loss ratio reaches 54%. However, such a traffic load can only be experienced when there is a severe traffic jam. Normal traffic load happens when traffic load is below 50, and the message loss ratio is below 10%.

Table 3. Impact of traffic load on the message delay (ms)

Vehicles	10	30	60	90	120	150
Urban	6.1	9.3	11.3	12.7	14.0	15.1
Highway	5.9	9.2	12.4	18.5	16.2	16.4

Table 4. Impact of traffic load on the message loss ratio(%)

Vehicles	10	30	60	90	120	150
Urban	1.3	3.4	23.6	32.4	43.5	53.7
Highway	1.2	3.4	17.3	29.3	40.1	53.8

6   Conclusions

A novel and efficient authentication protocol has been proposed for public and private vehicle authentication in VANETs. The aggregate signature and aggregate signcryption are employed to speedup the many-to-one communication. In the same time, batch-verification enable the RSU to authenticate the vehicles and verify the message in the efficient way, which enhances the reliability and efficiency dramatically. The analysis and simulation results show the protocol has the lower communication delay and smaller message loss ratio than others.

226   Y. Han et al.

References

1. Status of Project IEEE 802.11 Task Group p: Wireless Access in Vehicular Environments.
   IEEE 2004-2010, `http://grouper.ieee.org/groups/802/11/Reports/`
   `tgp_update.htm` (retrieved August 10, 2011)
2. Armknecht, F., Festag, A., Westhoff, D., Zeng, K.: Cross-layer privacy enhancement and
   non-repudiation in vehicular communication. In: Proc. 4th WMAN, Bern, Switzerland
   (March 2007)
3. Raya, M., Hubaux, J.P.: Securing vehicular ad hoc networks. Comput. Secur. Special Issue
   Security Ad Hoc Sensor Networks 15(1), 39–68 (2007)
4. Raya, M., Papadimitratos, P., Aad, I., Jungels, D., Hubaux, J.-P.: Eviction of misbehaving
   and faulty nodes in vehicular networks. IEEE J. Sel. Areas Commun. 25(8), 1557–1568
   (2007)
5. Guo, J., Baugh, J.P., Wang, S.: A group signature based secure and privacy-preserving vehicular communication framework. In: Proc. Mobile Netw. Veh. Environ., pp. 103–108
   (2007)
6. Lin, X., Sun, X., Ho, P.-H., Shen, X.: GSIS:A secure and privacy Preserving protocol for
   vehicular communications. IEEE Trans. Veh. Technol. 56(6), 3442–3456 (2007)
7. Daza, V., Domingo-Ferrer, J., Sebe, F., Viejo, A.: Trustworthy privacy-Preserving car-
   generated announcements in vehicular ad hoc networks. IEEE Trans. Veh. Technol. 58(4),
   1876–1886 (2009)
8. Wu, Q., Domingo-Ferrer, J.: Balanced Trustworthiness, Safety, and Privacy in Vehicle-to-
   Vehicle Communications. IEEE Trans. Veh. Technol. 59(2), 559–573 (2010)
9. Bellare, M., Namprempre, C., Neven, G.: Unrestricted aggregate signatures. In: Arge, L.,
   Cachin, C., Jurdziński, T., Tarlecki, A. (eds.) ICALP 2007. LNCS, vol. 4596, pp. 411–422.
   Springer, Heidelberg (2007)
10. Galbraith, S.D., Paterson, K.G., Smart, N.P.: Pairings for cryptographers, `http://`
    `eprint.iacr.org/2006/165.pdf`
11. The Network Simulator-ns-2, `http://nsnam.isi.edu/nsnam/index.php/`
    `Main_Page`
12. Saha, A.K., Johnson, D.B.: Modeling mobility for vehicular ad hoc networks. In: Proc. 1st
    VANET, pp. 91–92 (2004)
13. Multiprecision Integer and Rational Arithmetic C/C++ Library (MIRACL),
    `http://indigo.ie/mscott`

tNote: A Social Network of Vehicles under Internet of Things

Kazi Masudul Alam*, Mukesh Saini,
and Abdulmotaleb El Saddik, *Fellow, IEEE*

Multimedia Communications Research Laboratory
University of Ottawa, Ottawa, ON, Canada
{mkazi078,msain2,elsaddik}@uottawa.ca
http://www.discover.uottawa.ca/

Abstract. The main vision of Internet of Things (IoT) is to equip real life physical objects with computing and communication power so that they can interact with each other for social good. As one of the important members of Internet of Things (IoT), vehicles have seen steep advancement in communication technology. In this paper we instantiate IoT to define a social network of vehicles, *tNote*, where vehicles can share transport related safety, efficiency, and comfort notes with each other. We leverage the infrastructure laid down by Vehicular Ad-Hoc Networks (VANETs) to propose an architecture for social network of vehicles in the paradigm of Social Internet of Things (SIoT). We have identified the social structures of vehicles, their relationship types, interactions and the components to manage the system. We also define the *tNote* message structure following the Dedicated Short Range Communication (DSRC) standard. The paper ends with prototype implementation details of the *tNote* message and the proposed system architecture along with experimental results.

1 Introduction

The number of vehicles has increased dramatically in recent times causing high speed roads jam packed during peak hours [15]. A small road maintenance task, or accident, can result in huge traffic jam and further accidents. This situation could be improved by sharing vehicular experience. Fortunately, in recent years, the vehicular technology has made tremendous advancements [12]. Nowadays, state-of-the-art sensing devices built into the vehicles and intelligent machine learning algorithms can actively assist the driver [3]. Emerging wireless technologies allow vehicles to form ad-hoc networks (VANETs) and connect with each other through wireless channels [11]. VANETs is effective for social sharing of sensory information among vehicles on the roadway, which is helpful to make safety and efficiency related decisions more effectively.

Smaldone et al. first used vehicular social network (VSN) terminology in Road-Speak [13] where they used the vehicular network for human socialization from

---

* Corresponding Author.

R.C.-H. Hsu and W. Shangguang (Eds.): IOV 2014, LNCS 8662, pp. 227–236, 2014.
© Springer International Publishing Switzerland 2014

entertainment, utility, and emergency messaging perspectives. Hu et al. introduced *Social Drive* system which promotes driver awareness about fuel economy [7]. Guinard et al. [5] discussed how *Web-of-Things* can share their functionality interfaces using available human social network infrastructure such as Facebook, Linkedin, and Twitter. *Smart-Its Friends* [6] looked into how qualitative wireless connections can be established between *smart-artifacts*. In recent times, there has been a growing interest in building Social Internet of Things (SIoT) [1] [2]. SIoT focuses on establishing and exploiting social relationships (e.g. Parental Object Relationship, Co-location Object Relationship, etc.) among *things* rather than their owners. It is found in SIoT research that the structure of human social networks is not adequate for *things* social network due to specific nature of different *things* [2].

Though the simulation results show SIoT to be a viable approach, current research does not address domain specific requirements for an operational SIoT. In our research, we place vehicular social network on SIoT philosophy and provide necessary details to establish a Social Internet of Vehicles (SIoV). Our proposed system, *tNote*, is an architecture for SIoV as well as an infrastructure to retain sensory data in the VANETs. *tNote* is a platform to support real-time safety, efficiency, and infotainment applications for vehicular users, as well as data mining applications for transport authorities. The rest of the paper is organized as follows. Section 2 describes the vehicular social network, more specifically Section 2.1 provides the vehicular social network structure, relation types, interactions and Section 2.2 details the system architecture. Later Section 3 presents prototype implementation details and experimental results. Finally, Section 4 concludes the paper with possible future works.

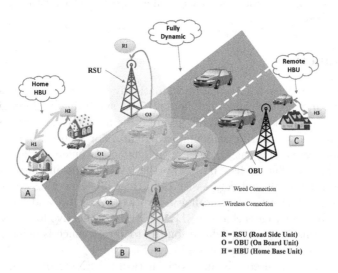

Fig. 1. Social network structures: A) Vehicle's home based static social network, B)Fully dynamic social network, C)Visiting vehicle's dynamic social network

2   Social Network of Vehicles

We describe *tNote* system using already established acronyms in the VANETs model such as OBU (On-Board Unit) and RSU (Road Side Unit) [8]. OBUs, along with RSUs, form an ad-hoc network and exchange safety and non-safety messages with each other. *tNote* is a virtual overlay application on top of the physical vehicular network of WAVE (IEEE 802.11p) [8] communication model. In the *tNote* social graph, every vehicle represents a node and any relationships between two vehicles are represented using a link representing the DSRC[1] message exchange. Every vehicle belongs to a household and there is a Home Base Unit (HBU) to which all the vehicles and household devices are connected to form the Internet of Vehicles (IoV).

2.1   *tNote* Relations and Interactions

In the *tNote* infrastructure we have different classes of social structures with various types of social relationships and interactions. We will first discuss relationship types for given network structure and then social interactions among main entities.

Network Structure and Relationship Types. *tNote* consists of both dynamic nodes (OBU) and static (RSU and HBU) nodes. We have identified three main scenarios for *tNote*. In the first scenario vehicles (OBUs) are parked at owner's residence and form a social network with HBU. As both OBU and HBU are static in this scenario, we consider a static *tNote* which extends to its neighbouring OBUs and HBUs as shown in Figure 1A. For example, all the cars parked in an apartment's basement or in the parking lot can form *static tNote* with HBUs of the building. In the second scenario, one OBU leaves its resident HBU and after a travel arrives at a remote HBU. The visiting OBU and remote HBU are in a temporary dynamic relationship. Example: a car comes in contact with its mechanic's HBU (Figure 1C). The most dynamic temporary connections are created in third scenario when a vehicle is on the move on a roadway. In this scenario, *tNote* consists of moving OBUs on roadway and static RSUs on road side as shown in Figure 1B.

We have adopted the social relationships described in SIoT [1] where Parental Object Relationship (POR) means relationship between an object (i.e. vehicle) and its manufacturer. Co-Location Object Relationship (CLOR) and Co-Work Object Relationship (CWOR) apply to *tNote* OBU-OBU communications where *things* are working to achieve a common goal placed in geo-neighbouring locations. Ownership Object Relationship (OOR) represents the OBU-HBU(resident) relationship where owner has the authority to configure the vehicle's *tNote* settings. And Social Object Relationship (SOR) applies to OBU-HBU(remote) when vehicle's owner shares *protected* information with friends (e.g. car mechanic). We also have defined an additional relationship named Guardian Object

---

[1] http://www.sae.org/standardsdev/dsrc/

Relationship (GOR) in order to define the communication between OBU-RSU. Here OBU is a child node of an RSU super node where RSU changes over time on the path. All these relationships govern the behaviour of the participating *things* in an SIoV.

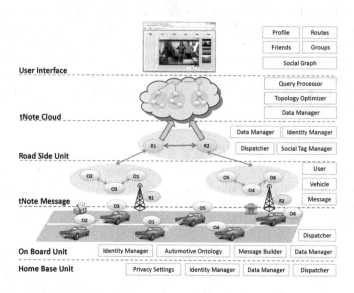

Fig. 2. Architecture of *tNote*: Vehicular Social Network

Interactions. *OBU-OBU*: When one vehicle (i.e. OBU) with a GPS comes in contact with another vehicle, then, based on DSRC social message exchange, a virtual link of type CLOR-CWOR is created between the communicating vehicles. This virtual connection and corresponding physical message is stored in the OBU's storage. Every time a new vehicle comes in contact with another vehicle, they exchange so far gathered messages of other vehicles and update their social graph links. This OBU-OBU social network grows until an OBU comes in contact of an RSU.

OBU-RSU: When an RSU receives OBU-OBU graph data along with interaction messages, the GOR transaction is completed. At this level of physical communication a new virtual social link is created between the participating OBU and RSU. After this step, the network takes a shape where a group of OBU nodes form a small social network with a super node RSU. Every RSU, based on its wireless technology and GPS location, maintains a radius of geo-social space.

RSU-RSU: Geo-locally neighbour RSUs generally have direct wired connection which is a CLOR-CWOR relationship and is mimicked with a virtual link in the *tNote*. If an OBU fails to complete the GOR transaction to the RSU then the rest of the transaction is completed in the next RSU and the neighbouring RSUs exchange the parts to complete the transaction.

OBU-HBU: A vehicle placed in its residence creates OOR type relation with the home HBU. This allows the owner of the vehicle to change OBU settings. When an OBU is travelling and connected to a remote HBU, it creates SOR relationship which enables the OBU to share *private* information with the remote HBU.

HBU-HBU: Each HBU knows its geographical coordinates in the SIoV map and is connected with other HBUs through the Internet. HBUs engage in interactions following CLOR-CWOR relationship to achieve any common task. Static OBUs placed in their residence can communicate with other static geo-neighbour OBUs through HBU-HBU communication.

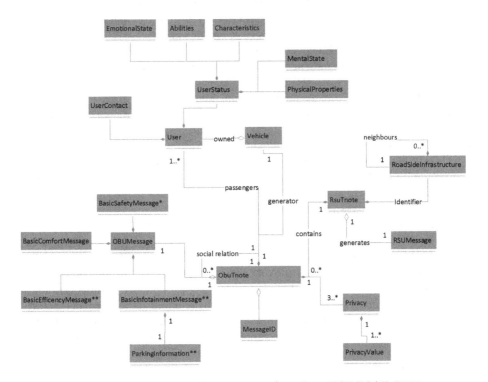

Fig. 3. Information model of the tNote message. * are from DSRC SAE J2735 message set. ** are from Advanced Traveler Information System (ATIS) schema

2.2 tNote System Architecture

The overall architecture of *tNote* system is found in Figure 2. It consists of six components: *tNote* Message, On Board Unit (OBU), Road Side Unit (RSU), Home Base Unit(HBU), *tNote* Cloud, and User Interface. Following is the detailed description of all the given components.

***tNote* Message:** The *tNote* message structure is built following an automotive ontology [4], SAE J2735 Dedicated Short Range Communications (DSRC[2])

---
[2] http://www.sae.org/standardsdev/dsrc/DSRC_R36_Source.ASN

message set, and `ITISEventType`[3] of Advanced Traveler Information System (ATIS) schema (Figure 3). *tNote* is a metadata which consists of `User` for user details (e.g. physiological state, mental state), `Vehicle` for vehicular details (e.g. identity, physical attributes), `OBUMessage` for different types (e.g. safety, efficiency) of messages (e.g. `BasicSafetyMessage`). OBU-OBU interactions are represented using `ObuTnote` which maintains social interactions in recursive collection of children `ObuTnotes`, and `Privacy` in three levels (*public, private* and *protected*). On the other hand, OBU-RSU and RSU-RSU interactions are corresponded using `RsuTnote` message which contains social information as a collection of `ObuTnote` messages, RSU command-control messages, and RSU neighbour details. *Public* data is always visible to every participating node in the *tNote* system. Whereas, *private* data is only visible to vehicle's owner who can decide to share it with his friends (e.g. car mechanic).

On Board Unit (OBU): OBU plays the key role in sensing and building the vehicular interaction messages. Every vehicle has a unique registration number for the vehicle such as IPV6, Universal Product Code (UPC), Electronic Product Code (EPC), etc. A similar virtual identifier is required for the OBU in the online vehicular social network. *Identity Manager* is responsible for the ID update management of OBU. *Automotive Ontology* dictates the structure of the *tNote* data. *Message Builder* manages the *tNote* message structure building part. *Data Manager* keeps OBU-OBU social graph up-to-date by ruling out stale data generated in OBU-OBU communication. Once one carrier OBU reaches into the range of an RSU, *Dispatcher* pushes the OBU based *tNote* data (i.e. OBU message + friends message) to the RSU.

Road Side Unit (RSU): Whenever a travelling OBU comes in contact with an RSU, either the RSU pulls or the OBU pushes the *tNote* messages to the RSU. *Identity Manager* maintains the virtual ID of the RSU. At any specific time, one RSU can receive several *tNote* bulk messages from various approaching OBUs. RSU collects the *tNote* bulks and *Social Tag Manager* assigns ontology defined appropriate tags to the data in order to enhance data discovery before sending them to the cloud. *Data Manager* enhances the topology of the OBU-OBU connections where RSU is the super node by reducing the redundancy due to omnidirectional communication. After a predetermined period, the RSU-OBU network is synced to the *tNote* data cloud by the *Dispatcher*.

Home Base Unit (HBU): HBU plays an important role in the static network building of the *tNote*. The home or remote area networks are built based on the data sent from the HBU. Every HBU has an *Identity Manager* to maintain the virtual ID in the *tNote* social graph where static OBUs are connected to the super node HBU. HBU-HBU relationship and corresponding *tNote* data are managed by the *Data Manager*. *Privacy Settings* helps in privacy management of devices connected to HBU other than the vehicles.

tNote **Cloud:** This is the final infrastructure that retains all the vehicular interactions (e.g. OBU-OBU, OBU-RSU) and their related data along with

---

[3] http://www.itsware.net/ITSschemas/ATIS/ATIS-03-00-79/0xDocs/
ITISAdopted-03-00-02.xsd.html

corresponding timestamps which allows various time related roll-up, drill-down, and mining operations offline. *Topology Optimizer* operates on this offline data structure to remove unnecessary redundancies. *Query Processor* is the interface to the cloud data to receive queries and *Data Manager* retains the query results.

User Interface: There are five different types of users of the entire *tNote* system: drivers, passengers, social web users, transport authorities and intelligent vehicle agents. Safety messages are useful for the vehicle drivers as an input to automated early warning systems. The interface for social web user can further be divided into *Profile, Routes, Friends, Groups,* and *Social Graph.* The *Profile* of the *tNote* presents all the up-to-date vehicle related *public, private* information. Important traffic incidents are reported as status in the vehicle's social page. All the public information about the vehicle is easily accessible through its social graph. But, private information is only available for the owner of the vehicle. *Social Graph* is the node-link relationship among RSU, HBU, and OBU of a particular vehicle. Vehicular friends represent the neighbours which participated in the *tNote* message exchange at a certain time in a specific geographical region which is visible in the social graph. *Routes* collects all the frequently travelled routes. *Groups* collect different interest groups which can be based on owner's interest, manufacturer, vendor, travel interest, etc. Transport authority can use the social graph to extract patterns for transport related analysis. Passengers can use the efficiency and infotainment messages for entertainment, parking, etc.

3   Implementation Details and Experimental Results

The objective of the prototype implementation is to verify the proof of concept of the entire system. For this purpose, we have developed the *tNote* message structure using Abstract Syntax Notation One (ASN.1)[14] and have mocked the *tNote* VANET system infrastructure. At present we are working on mobility and network simulators to measure the scalability of the proposed system which would be reported in future articles.

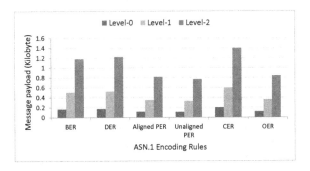

Fig. 4. Safety message size comparison of encoding types for *tNote* friends population at different levels

3.1   tNote Message

We have used OSS Nokalva ASN.1/java[4] Studio to build the *tNote* message. For any value instance of a *tNote* message, the corresponding hexadecimal data dump has been analysed using the mentioned tool. In Figure 4, we find the data size comparison of byte type encoding formats at different level of friend population size for safety type messages. The figure denotes that with the increase of depth level of a friend's population the size of *tNote* grows. In our experiment, we have considered that each vehicle has seen two friends and further disseminated their status messages. In real life settings, the number of visible friends at any time depends on the speed and communication range of OBU. OBU settings should consider the VANET service channel (SCH) bandwidth availability for acceptable level of friend size and depth. So far the analysis denotes that current standard for SCH bandwidth [10] should be able to allocate discontinuous population messages.

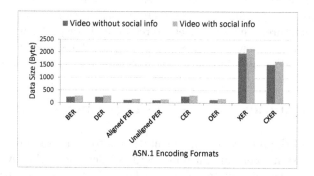

Fig. 5. Video comfort message size comparison for different ASN.1 data encoding types

In Figure 5, we present a comparative data size of various X.690 encoding formats for *tNote* video comfort messages. In this analysis, we compare the data size of video comfort messages with or without the social information (e.g. view count, like, dislike and related comments) for metadata based video sharing application built on *tNote*. Here we see that PER type encoding ensures the smallest data size and XML representations XER-CXER encodings result in the largest data size. BER-DER-CER are preferable for their Type-Length-Value (T-L-V) type structure over data heavy XML representations XER-CXER. XML representations are not suitable for *tNote* friends related messages for their heavy size and VANET bandwidth limitation. As DER is recommended [9] in the VANET type communication, so the data size of DER encoding from both Figure 4 and Figure 5 ensure that friends population and friends social information can be supported using VANET communication infrastructure. Overall analysis shows that the *tNote* system is a viable option for SIoV.

---

[4] http://www.oss.com/asn1/products/asn1-java/asn1-java.html

3.2 tNote System Infrastructure

In our mock setup, we represent OBUs as Samsung Galaxy Tab 10.1 and Google Nexus 7 tablets, and RSU as Windows Acer Aspire V5 laptop, and *tNote* cloud as Dell desktop server. Acer laptop and Dell desktop are connected using Ethernet LAN. Tablets use Wi-Fi Direct technology to communicate with each other and with the laptop. Tablets participate in OBU-OBU and OBU-RSU communication. The messaging platform is implemented using Android technology. We have used the *WifiP2pManager*[5] class for device discovery and peer-to-peer connection. When an OBU comes inside the wireless range of another OBU they establish a TCP socket connection to exchange the `BasicSafetyMessage`. The scenario of vehicles dynamically joining and leaving the network is mocked by taking the tablets away from peers range and bringing them close again. For simplicity, we implemented messages in XER encoding. RSU laptop runs JAVA application developed in JDK1.7.0. In the RSU laptop, Wi-Fi network interface manages the tablet communication, and the Ethernet network interface manages the *tNote* cloud server and laptop communication. RSU laptop runs Windows 7 operating system. We have used the *Software Network Bridging* method built-in to Windows 7 to connect the wireless and the wired network interfaces. Safety messages from OBU Tablets are tunnelled through the TCP data sockets to the *tNote* cloud. Web interfaces for social user is created using JSP and the underline database is built using MySQL.

In our experiments, we have seen that social links between tablets get lost when a DSRC message is not consumed by neighbouring connected peers since they have moved away from communication range. The physical system test is cumbersome since the Tablets face quick battery drainage due to working as network access points. Another difficulty is the lack of Wi-Fi emulators for Android which forces all the tests to the physical devices which requires certain human resources to be physically available to carry tablets and log observations.

4 Conclusion and Future Works

The paper describes an architecture of social network of vehicles, *tNote*, as a compelling use case of Internet of Things. The proposed architecture defines important components, their interactions, and interrelations, which are inspired from the structure of SIoT. A structure of interaction message is provided which adopts DSRC standards that can support various applications such as safety, efficiency, and infotainment. We also provide implementation approach of the message structure and the proposed *tNote* system architecture along with experimental results and observations. In our future works we want to focus on scalability analysis and optimization factors. Designing a non-intrusive *tNote* interface is one of the main challenges to present safety messages to the driver. Other important issues include data redundancy, and synchronization.

---

[5] http://developer.android.com/reference/android/net/wifi/
p2p/WifiP2pManager.html

References

1. Atzori, L., Iera, A., Morabito, G.: Siot: Giving a social structure to the internet of things. IEEE Communications Letters 15(11), 1193–1195 (2011)
2. Atzori, L., Iera, A., Morabito, G., Nitti, M.: The social internet of things (siot)–when social networks meet the internet of things: Concept, architecture and network characterization. In: Computer Networks (2012)
3. Dong, Y., Hu, Z., Uchimura, K., Murayama, N.: Driver inattention monitoring system for intelligent vehicles: A review. IEEE Transactions on Intelligent Transportation Systems 12(2), 596–614 (2011)
4. Feld, M., Müller, C.: The automotive ontology: managing knowledge inside the vehicle and sharing it between cars. In: Proceedings of the 3rd International Conference on Automotive User Interfaces and Interactive Vehicular Applications, pp. 79–86. ACM (2011)
5. Guinard, D., Fischer, M., Trifa, V.: Sharing using social networks in a composable web of things. In: 2010 8th IEEE International Conference on Pervasive Computing and Communications Workshops (PERCOM Workshops), pp. 702–707 (March 2010)
6. Holmquist, L.E., Mattern, F., Schiele, B., Alahuhta, P., Beigl, M., Gellersen, H.-W.: Smart-its friends: A technique for users to easily establish connections between smart artefacts. In: Abowd, G.D., Brumitt, B., Shafer, S. (eds.) UbiComp 2001. LNCS, vol. 2201, pp. 116–122. Springer, Heidelberg (2001)
7. Hu, X., Leung, V., Li, K.G., Kong, E., Zhang, H., Surendrakumar, N.S., TalebiFard, P.: Social drive: a crowdsourcing-based vehicular social networking system for green transportation. In: Proceedings of the Third ACM International Symposium on Design and Analysis of Intelligent Vehicular Networks and Applications, pp. 85–92. ACM (2013)
8. Karagiannis, G., Altintas, O., Ekici, E., Heijenk, G., Jarupan, B., Lin, K., Weil, T.: Vehicular networking: A survey and tutorial on requirements, architectures, challenges, standards and solutions. IEEE Communications Surveys & Tutorials 13(4), 584–616 (2011)
9. Kenney, J.B.: Dedicated short-range communications (dsrc) standards in the united states. Proceedings of the IEEE 99(7), 1162–1182 (2011)
10. Morgan, Y.L.: Managing dsrc and wave standards operations in a v2v scenario. International Journal of Vehicular Technology (2010)
11. Morgan, Y.L.: Notes on dsrc & wave standards suite: Its architecture, design, and characteristics. IEEE Communications Surveys & Tutorials 12(4), 504–518 (2010)
12. Plotkin, S., Stephens, T., McManus, W.: Vehicle technology deployment pathways: An examination of timing and investment constraints. Technical report, Transportation Energy Futures Series, Department of Energy (2013)
13. Smaldone, S., Han, L., Shankar, P., Iftode, L.: Roadspeak: enabling voice chat on roadways using vehicular social networks. In: Proceedings of the 1st Workshop on Social Network Systems, pp. 43–48. ACM (2008)
14. Steedman, D.: Abstract syntax notation one (ASN. 1): the tutorial and reference. Technology appraisals (1993)
15. Warner, M.: General motors sales up in december (2013)

Impervious Surface Detection from Multispectral Images Using Surf

Anu Paulose, Sreeraj M., and Harikrishnan V.

Department of Computer Science,
Federal Institute of Science And Technology,
Cochin, India
anupaulose1990@gmail.com,
sreerajtkzy@gmail.com,
harikrishnan.vadakkath@outlook.com

Abstract. Detection of different regions like impervious surfaces, vegetation and water from a multispectral satellite image is a complex task. This paper introduces a novel idea for impervious surface detection from multispectral images using SURF descriptors. To determine the efficiency of the proposed system, a comparative evaluation is done with other two techniques, namely histogram based and spectral-value-based technique. The result shows that the proposed system outperforms the other two techniques in detecting impervious surfaces like buildings and vehicles with an accuracy of 80.48%. The histogram-based technique and spectral-value-based clustering obtained an accuracy of 61.89% and 68.29% respectively. However, in classifying vegetation the other two techniques outperforms SURF descriptors. The histogram based technique gives an accuracy of 86.46% and an accuracy of 94.35% is obtained by using the spectral-value-based clustering. Whereas SURF based technique gives only an accuracy of 50.71%.

Keywords: Clustering, Histogram, Impervious surface detection, Multispectral, Surf.

1 Introduction

Satellite image processing is a complex task. It is mainly because of the huge amount of data present even in a single image. Object detection is an important research area in satellite image processing. During the past decade, many methodologies have been proposed for automatic identification of objects from multispectral images. It is in fact a type of image classification, where the given image is classified into different object classes like vegetation, water and impervious surfaces (buildings, vehicles etc.,). The recent availability of high-resolution satellite imaging sensors such as IKONOS and QuickBird provide a new data source for impervious surface extraction. In such images the visibility of terrestrial features, especially urban objects, has been increased drastically, which helps in easy detection of small objects like vehicles. Detection of vehicles from

R.C.-H. Hsu and W. Shangguang (Eds.): IOV 2014, LNCS 8662, pp. 237–246, 2014.

satellite images can be used effectively in various fields such as military and surveillance applications to find unauthorzed vehicle entry to a particular area.

In this paper, SURF descriptors are being used for detecting objects, mainly impervious surfaces, from multispectral images. Detection of In order to analyze the efficiency of proposed technique, the detection is also done using Histogram-based method and Spectral-value-based Clustering

This paper is organized as follows: section 2 gives a brief description about the state-of-the-art, section 3 explains the architecture of proposed method, section 4 describes the results and discussions and conclusion is given in section 5.

2   State-of-the-Art

During last four decades, a number of satellite image processing techniques were developed. Based on the literature survey done, a topology of image processing techniques being used was created as shown in Figure 1. The image processing techniques can be grouped into per-pixel, sub-pixel, per-field and object-based approaches. Traditional techniques were on a per-pixel basis, in which, information is extracted from each of the pixels. The spectra of all the pixels are combined to get a spectral signature in such methods. The spectral signature will be having information from all the materials in the pixel which is then used for further processing [1, 2]. However, these methods suffer from mixed pixel problem in which the same pixel may belong to different classes. This will in turn reduce the efficiency of remotely sensed data in per-pixel classifications [3, 4].

The sub-pixel based methods were introduced to avoid the mixed pixel problem in the per-pixel techniques. In these methods, pixels are divided into sub-pixels and features are then extracted from each of the sub-pixels. A fuzzy representation

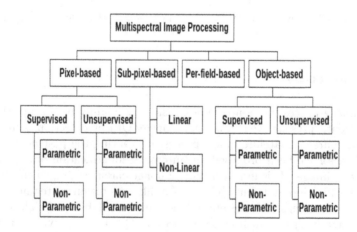

Fig. 1. Topology of Image Classification Techniques

is being used, in which each location contains many partial membership degrees belonging to each of the classes. Sub-pixel classification approaches have been developed to provide a more efficient classification than per-pixel approaches, especially when coarse spatial resolution data are used [3], [5]. Many methods have been introduced for developing a soft classifier such as fuzzy-set theory, softening the output of a hard classification from maximum likelihood, certainty factor [6] and neural networks [7].

Since pixel-based approaches group each of the pixels into a specific class, increase in the spatial frequency may lead to incorrect results. The per-field classifier was developed so as to avoid problems with heterogeneous environments. Many researches have proved the increased classification accuracy of per-field approaches [8–10]. The per-field classifier reduces the noise by using individual units of land called fields [8, 9] . Per-field classification is implemented by integrating both vector and raster data [2] . The vector data are used to subdivide an image into fields, and classification is then conducted based on the fields, thus avoiding intraclass spectral variations. However, per-field classifications are often affected by such factors as the spectral and spatial properties of remotely sensed data, the size and shape of the fields, the definition of field boundaries, and the land cover classes chosen [11] . The per-field classification approach is not very common due to the difficulty in handling both vector and raster data.

An alternate approach is to use an object-based classification [12] , which does not require the use of GIS vector data. Mainly there are two stages in an object-based classification: image segmentation and classification. Using image segmentation pixels are merged into objects, and then a classification is carried out based on objects, instead of individual pixels. This approach has proven to be better when compared to pixel-based approach especially for fine spatial resolution data. The eCognition method is so far the most commonly used object-oriented classification [12].

3   System Architecture

An object based technique is being proposed for identifying different classes in a multispectral image using SURF descriptors. Figure 2 illustrates the generic system architecture. The input images are initially segmented into objects and features are extracted from them. The extracted features are then grouped using clustering algorithm which represents the detected classes. Each of these phases are explained in the following sections.

3.1   Image Segmentation

Segmentation is the process of partitioning an image into regions based on a discontinuity or a similarity criterion. The proposed technique uses Canny Edge Detector for segmenting the images. The working of Canny operator involves multiple stages. Initially, the image is smoothed by Gaussian convolution. Then a simple 2-D first order derivative is applied to highlight the regions of the image

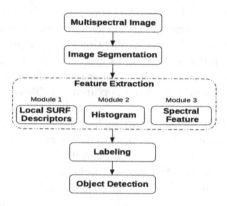

Fig. 2. System Architecture

with high first spatial derivatives. Edges will result in ridges in the gradient magnitude image. The algorithm will then moves along the top of these ridges and all pixels that are not actually on the ridge top are set to zero so as to give a thin line in the output. The tracking process carries out hysteresis with two thresholds: T1 and T2, where T1 < T2. Tracking begins only at a point on the ridge which is higher than T1. Tracking is then continued in both directions until the height of the ridge becomes less than T2. By using this hysteresis, it can be ensured that the noisy edges are not broken up into small edge fragments.

3.2 Feature Extraction

Feature extraction is a special form of dimensionality reduction. It transforms the huge amount of data present in a multispectral image into a reduced representation set of features. Feature extraction is done from each of the segments obtained from the previous phase. The features used in this paper are described in the following subsections.

Speeded-Up Robust Features (SURF). Even though there are many state-of-the-art techniques, most of them uses global features for image classification. Two most popular local feature descriptors in computer vision are SIFT(Scale Invariant Feature Transform) and SURF(Speeded Up Robust Features). They are often used for performing tasks like object recognition. These descriptors are stable under viewpoint and lighting changes, so they are able to cope with significant amounts of image variability. At the same time, discriminative power is achieved by representing feature points as high-dimensional vectors. The technique proposed in [13] extracts SIFT descriptors from the satellite image and uses a graph-cut method for object classification. However, the standard version of SURF is much faster than SIFT. Hence the SURF descriptors are used for classifying the image in this paper. In SURF, the interest points are detected by using Hessian matrix approximation. The use of integral images have drastically reduced the computational complexity. A distribution-based descriptor is used, which makes use of 2D Haar wavelet responses ([14]).

Histogram. The histogram of an image graphically represents the tonal distribution of an image. It plots the number of pixels for each tonal value. The vertical and horizontal axes in the graph represents the tonal variations and number of pixels in that particular tone respectively. The black and dark areas are plotted in left side of the horizontal axis, medium grey in the middle and light and pure white areas towards the right side. Thus, a very dark image creates a histogram having majority of its data points on the left side and center of the graph. Conversely, for a very bright image with few dark areas and/or shadows, the histogram will have most of its data points on the right side and center of the graph.

3.3 Object Detection

In both SURF-based and spectral-value-based techniques, the extracted features are to be grouped using any clustering algorithms. There are many clustering methods available for classification of a wide variety of data. K-means algorithm is useful for determining the natural spectral regions present in the satellite data. K-means is an unsupervised clustering technique. The user will initiate the algorithm by explicitly specifying the number of clusters to be segmented from the image. In other way, the algorithm can be started in the feature space, each with some pixel clusters defined by its center. By associating each of the pixels to the given nearest centroid, the initial cluster can be created. The mean values of the cluster elements are then computed which replaces the existing centroids. These steps are done repetitively until no more new clusters can be formed.

Whereas in the case of histogram-based technique, the pixels will be automatically grouped into different classes based on their intensity values. Different colors are assigned for the pixels in each class. The impervious surfaces normally appear bright in color. The green colored vegetation areas are seen as red color in a satellite image. Similarly water bodies will be black in color. Keeping these in mind, a rule-based approach was incorporated. For example, green color was assigned to the class which corresponds to red colored pixels.

4 Results and Discussion

4.1 Experimental Setup

Multispectral images of both urban and rural (vegetated) areas were used for the experiments. The dataset used in this paper consists of multispectral images of both urban and rural areas. Two input images used are shown in Figure 4(a) and Figure 5(a). For comparing the performance of image segmentation two edge detectors, namely Sobel and Canny filters, were applied. Results of applying both the filters are given in Figure 3. The result shows that the Canny filter produces better and thin edges compared to the Sobel filter. The Canny edge detector was therefore selected for image segmentation as it outperformed the Sobel filter.

(a) Canny Filter   (b) Sobel Filter

Fig. 3. Canny Edge Filter vs. Sobel Edge Filter

The image segmentation was done using the Canny edge detector for various thresholds (both T1 & T2). When T1 = 1, T2 = 5 the result obtained was very poor, since too many edges in the figure was identified. By increasing the T1 to 10 and the higher threshold to 20, better results were obtained. A more optimal classification was obtained while keeping T1 = 20 & T2 = 40 and the objects were easily detected from the results. When T1 = 30 & T2 = 60, many of the useful edges were eliminated which resulted in poor classification results.

The segmented image is then used as the input to second phase ie., feature extraction. Initially SURF local descriptors are extracted which are to be labelled in the next phase. The second feature being used is the image histogram. The histogram was computed for different number of bins and optimal results were obtained when the number of bins equal to 20. When the histogram was calculated for lesser or higher number of bins, the rate of misclassification increased. Next, the spectral value of each of the pixels is extracted and passed to the next phase.

In the object detection phase, all the extracted features are labelled inorder to detect the various classes present in the image. K-means clustering algorithm is used to group the extracted SURF and spectral features. The spectral-value-based clustering was implemented with the number of clusters being 4, as it gave more accurate results compared to lower or higher number of clusters. The result of object detection using the three techniques for urban area is given in Figure 4 and for rural area is given in Figure 5.

4.2 Performance Evaluation

The proposed technique for object detection, using SURF, proved to be efficient in detecting impervious surfaces, like buildings and vehicles. It outperforms the other two techniques in impervious surface detection. The performance of the proposed system is evaluated using following statistical measures.

(a) Input Urban Image   (b) SURF based Object Detection   (c) Histogram based Object Detection   (d) Spectral value based Clustering

Fig. 4. Object Detection in urban areas

(a) Input Rural Image   (b) SURF based Object Detection   (c) Histogram based Object Detection   (d) Spectral value based Clustering

Fig. 5. Object Detection in rural areas

- Accuracy $= \dfrac{\text{detected number of objects}}{\text{total number of objects}}$
- Sensitivity or True Positive Rate $= \frac{tp}{tp+fn}$
- Specificity or True Negative Rate $= \frac{tn}{tn+fp}$
- Precision or Positive Predictive Value $= \frac{tp}{tp+fp}$
- False Positive Rate $= \frac{fp}{fp+tn}$
- False Discovery Rate $= \frac{fp}{fp+tp}$

where tp = true positive, tn =true negative, fp = false positive and fn = false negative. The confusion matrix developed for Figure 4(a) is shown in Table 1. The image consists of 328 buildings, 475 vehicles, 23 vegetated regions and 10 bare land regions. The confusion matrix for each of the classes is shown in Table 2 which is used for performance evaluation.

After implementing the proposed system using SURF for Figure 4(a), the results obtained are shown in Table 2. Out of the 328 buildings 264 were identified using SURF, which resulted in an accuracy of 80.48%. By using histogram-based technique, only 203 buildings were detected which gave 61.89% accuracy. The spectral-value-based technique produced an accuracy of 68.29%, in which only 224 building were detected. Hence, it is clear that the SURF descriptors outperforms the other three techniques in building detection.

However, other impervious surfaces like vehicles present in the image were not easily identified using the proposed technique. Among the 475 vehicles, only 56 were detected. This is mainly because of the low resolution of images being used in this paper. This problem can be rectified by using high resolution images such as IKONOS. In the case of vegetations, both histogram-based and spectral-value-based techniques outperformed the proposed technique. An accuracy of 94.35% is obtained using the spectral-value-based technique. Histogram-based technique gave an accuracy of 86.46%. Whereas SURF-based technique produced only an accuracy of 50.71%.

Table 1. Generic Confusion Matrix

	Buildings	Vehicles	Trees	Bare Land
Buildings	264	56	7	1
Vehicles	56	419	0	0
Trees	7	0	16	0
Bare Land	1	0	0	9

Table 2. Confusion Matrix For Each Class

	Buildings	Others
Buildings	264	64
Others	64	444
Sensitivity = 80.48%, Specificity = 87.40% Precision = 80.48%, FPR = 12.59%, FDR = 19.51%		

	Vehicles	Others
Vehicles	56	419
Others	272	289
Sensitivity = 17.07%, Specificity = 40.81% Precision = 11.78%, FPR = 59.18%, FDR = 88.21%		

	Trees	Others
Trees	7	16
Others	321	692
Sensitivity = 2.13%, Specificity = 97.74% Precision = 30.43%, FPR = 2.25%, FDR = 69.56%		

5   Conclusion

An impervious surface detection technique from multispectral images was presented. The proposed technique, which uses local SURF descriptors, extracts impervious surfaces with an accuracy of 80.48%. After comparison with two other techniques, namely histogram-based technique and spectral-value-based clustering, results show that our technique was more accurate in detecting impervious surfaces. Among the different impervious surfaces, buildings were more easily identified using the proposed technique than the smaller surfaces like vehicles due to low resolution of images being used. The performance can be improved by the use of high resolution images. However, in rural vegetated areas, SURF descriptors failed to efficiently classify the vegetations. Whereas, both histogram-based and spectral-value-based techniques produced better results in classifying vegetations.

References

1. Lu, D., Weng, Q.: A survey of image classification methods and techniques for improving classification performance. International Journal of Remote Sensing 28(5), 823–870 (2007)
2. Dean, A.M., Smith, G.M.: An evaluation of per-parcel land cover mapping using maximum likelihood class probabilities. International Journal of Remote Sensing 24, 2905–2920 (2003)
3. Aplin, P., Atkinson, P.M., Curran, P.J.: Fine spatial resolution simulated satellite sensor imagery for land cover mapping in the United Kingdom. Remote Sensing of Environment 68, 206–216 (1999)
4. Schowengerdt, R.A.: On the estimation of spatial-spectral mixing with classifier likelihood functions. Pattern Recognition Letters 17, 1379–1387 (1996)
5. Cracknell, A.P.: Synergy in remote sensing – what's in a pixel. International Journal of Remote Sensing 19, 2025–2047 (1998)
6. Binaghi, E., Brivio, P.A., Ghezzi, P., Rampini, A.: A fuzzy set accuracy assessment of soft classification. Pattern Recognition Letters 20, 935–948 (1999)
7. Janssen, L.F., Molenaar, M.: Terrain objects, their dynamics and their monitoring by integration of GIS and remote sensing. IEEE Transactions on Geoscience and Remote Sensing 33, 749–758 (1995)
8. Foody, G.M., Cox, D.P.: Sub-pixel land cover composition estimation using a linear mixture model and fuzzy membership functions. International Journal of Remote Sensing 15, 619–631 (1994)
9. Foody, G.M.: Image classification with a neural network: from completely-crisp to fully-fuzzy situation. In: Atkinson, P.M., Tate, N.J. (eds.) Advances in Remote Sensing and GIS Analysis, pp. 17–37. John Wiley and Sons, New York (1999)
10. Paola, J.D., Schowengerdt, R.A.: A review and analysis of back propagation neural networks for classification of remotely sensed multispectral imagery. International Journal of Remote Sensing 16, 3033–3058 (1995)
11. Wang, L., Sousa, W.P., Gong, P., Biging, G.S.: Comparison of IKONOS and Quick-Bird images for mapping mangrove species on the Caribbean coast of panama. Remote Sensing of Environment 91, 432–440 (2004)
12. Fisher, P.: The pixel: a snare and a delusion. International Journal of Remote Sensing 18, 679–685 (1997)
13. Schmitt, D., Mccoy, N.: Object Classification and Localization Using SURF Descriptors. CS 229 Final Project (2011)
14. Bay, H., Ess, A., Tuytelaars, T., Van Gool, L.: SURF: Speeded Up Robust Features. Computer Vision and Image Understanding (CVIU) 110(3), 346–359 (2008)
15. Aplin, P., Atkinson, P.M., Curran, P.J.: Per-field classification of land use using the forthcoming very fine spatial resolution satellite sensors: problems and potential solutions. In: Atkinson, P.M., Tate, N.J. (eds.) Advances in Remote Sensing and GIS Analysis, pp. 219–239. John Wiley and Sons, New York (1999)

16. Benz, U.C., Hofmann, P., Willhauck, G., Lingenfelder, I., Heynen, M.: Multiresolution, object-oriented fuzzy analysis of remote sensing data for GIS-ready information. ISPRS Journal of Photogrammetry & Remote Sensing 58, 239–258 (2004)
17. Bloch, I.: Information combination operators for data fusion: a comparative review with classification. IEEE Transactions on Systems, Man, and Cybernetics 26, 52–67 (1996)
18. Foody, G.M.: Status of land cover classification accuracy assessment. Remote Sensing of Environment 80, 185–201 (2002)
19. Sarma, T.H., Viswanath, P., Reddy, B.E.: Single pass kernel k-means clustering method. Sadhan 38, Part 3, 407–419 (2013)
20. Thomas, N., Hendrix, C., Congalton, R.G.: A comparison of urban mapping methods using high-resolution digital imagery. Photogrammetric Engineering and Remote Sensing 69, 963–972 (2003)
21. Walter, V.: Object-based classification of remote sensing data for change detection. ISPRS Journal of Photogrammetry & Remote Sensing 58, 225–238 (2004)

The Paradigm of Big Data for Augmenting Internet of Vehicle into the Intelligent Cloud Computing Systems

Gebeyehu Belay Gebremeskel, Yi Chai, and Zhimin Yang

Chongqing University, College of Automations, Postcode 400044, Main Building 1911,
Chongqing, China
{gebeyehu,chaiyi,yangzhimin}@cqu.edu.cn

Abstract. Big Data for IoV development is about turning imperfect, complex, often unstructured data into actionable information, which implies leveraging advanced computational tools to visualize trends and correlations within and across large IoV data sets that would otherwise remain undiscovered. The current research on IoV and cloud system is focusing on data in terms of its complexity and the connections to share it, in consideration of costs and efficiency. However, in few years after, there will be IoV populated and heterogeneous networked embedded devices, which are generating large-scale data in an explosion fashion. The intelligent IoV system should be also capable of learn, think and understand the physical systems by themselves. Therefore, in this paper, we investigate and introduced a paradigm augmenting big data for IoV intelligent system to optimize massive data exploration in the field. The paradigm of big data augmentation is a systematic approach to development raises great expectations and concern to the analytical value of large-scale data that address IoV in the natural progression of intelligent IoV and cloud computing. The intelligent IoV technology is transforming to cloud system to satisfy a variety of IoV applications and user needs, which provide analytic and access of massive data.

Keywords: Big data, IoV, intelligent system, cloud computing, data, data mining.

1   Introduction

Technology is transferring our lives, which brings enormous benefits that the beginnings of our connected future, such as cars are computers with wheels, and sensor and/or wearable devices notify the objects' movement and its current conditions. The signal or sensor and mobile experiences collectively yield of data are pertinent to vehicular system safety and service optimizations in regardless of the demand of advanced and more capable analysis tools. That is the emergent of big data [1] technology that provides a big opportunities vehicular intelligent system and its future generation research tendencies. It is a multi-dimensional approaching to handle and analysis the ever increasing of collecting data from various agents in unlike formats, from independent or connected appliances of the Internet of Vehicle (IoV). Furthermore, the mobile technologies and the transportation intelligent systems to get

R.C.-H. Hsu and W. Shangguang (Eds.): IOV 2014, LNCS 8662, pp. 247–261, 2014.
© Springer International Publishing Switzerland 2014

real-time data on cars and people from different aspects are other additional and the vast amount of data that can potentially process to optimize the service and safety [2]. However, the challenges are also coming together on the data deluge.

The advanced and more complex road network systems are the agglomerations of many objects and systems, including cars that generate large-scale spatial data, which catalyze the emergence of increasingly powerful technologies to enable more sophisticated data management and analytics [3]. The vehicles and roadside's sensors and moveable agents generating data, including mobile, time series and other sensor devices, which required to process in an integrated way that to extract the hidden data value for proper decision-making process and outcomes [4, 5]. Therefore, it is the issue of how to handle, transforming and analyzing such a data deluge? How the transport industry is cost-effective and efficient in their performance and safety? What type of technology should capable and scalable to the analytics of ever increasing vehicular data, and how to analyze in an integrate way? Even more than that, how big is the global IoV ecosystem now and how will it be in the future? These and other related challenges are the focus of this paper, what we motivated to investigate and introduce a novel approach and techniques in the field of IoV intelligent systems. To ensure that the advances of Big Data Mining (BDM) research and technology will effectively benefit the progress of vehicular intelligent systems, which is important to examine the challenges on DM, posed in data-intensive domains. BDM is an advanced approach to explore complex and large-scale data to gain valuable information and knowledge, and also capable of predict systems forthcoming. Moreover, augmenting big data is the fundamental of IoV intelligent cloud revolutions that create economic opportunity and performance optimizations [6] by having the knowledge-based decision-making process.

In this paper, we discussed the promising and also periling of big data for vehicular intelligent systems, data handling and analyzing based on agent integrated DM techniques to optimize IoV performance and safety. The main focus of the techniques is to augment and enhance advanced and scientific application of big data towards IoV incorporating intelligent Cloud Computing (CC) systems, which provides capable and scalable analytics to optimize automated, reliable, and efficient information retrieval [7]. The approach is inherently developed in mining algorithm's contents, which evaluate the science of big data to scale well on high-performance computing infrastructures and intelligent systems.

The paper is organized as section 2 the technology of IoV systems data deluge, big data promising and periling. Section 3 an augmenting application of big data for IoV, which include massive data structure, cloud system, virtualization and others. Section 4 related works, section and section 5 summarize the main ideas of the paper followed by the acknowledgements and cited reference, which are cited in this research work.

2   The Technology of IoV

These days, technology is evolving so rapidly it has become an integral component of everyday life. This dramatic convergence of technology in the car is quickly making it a key device in the Internet of Things (IoT) [7-9] with the ability to both receive data and feed it to the cloud, to the traffic infrastructure, to other vehicles and more.

Therefore, the Internet of Vehicle (IoV) is an emerging technology for data communication between moving vehicles and fixed sensor equipment, which are integrated the agents and technologies in a definite protocols to facilitate data transfer between cars, roadside equipment, wearable devices and traffic data management centers. The standards needs of vehicular links are unique that communications occur in a constantly fluctuating environment, which the signal must accommodate multiple signal and traffic densities and work in both urban and rural environments. The technology of IoV system is also the interface of intelligent vehicular connectives via the Internet (Wide Local Area Network –WLAN) that objects have the inter-connected vehicle to Sensor devices (V-to-S), Vehicle to Mobile V-to-M), Vehicle to Vehicle (V-to-V), Mobile to Sensors (M-to-S), and others in the roadside infrastructure. These interactions between the interconnected equipment, including cars are pertinent not only keep track of the objects, but also many other agents' sensors that interacted in their surrounding and report it to other machines such as traffic data management centers, the radar, … [4] to varying purposes as the human need. The equipment to cars and vice versa communications involves various technologies and applications, wherein people interact with software agents, including remote access to objects by users that continuously report the records, where about and sensor data that V-to-V communications encompass everyday objects and infrastructure interact each other's and with the users (fig.1) [3].

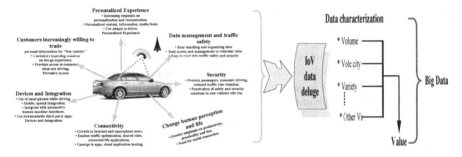

Fig. 1. Cars connectivity and its fertility for new and advanced data management and exploration

The IoV is the next technological revolution, which integrated intelligent systems to support Intelligent Transportation Systems (ITS) applications [10] that includes sensor networks, camera [7], mobile communication [11], real-time localization [12], ubiquitous computing and other technologies [13]. It is the age of smart objects of sensor inputs, actuators, etc. that able to communicate via the Internet based on the paradigm standards and/or protocols of ICT. Therefore, advanced techniques are necessary to consider how to manage data of IoV effectively and how to implement online analytical query and processing conveniently [2]. The data exchange between high-speed vehicles and the roadside infrastructure in dedicated ITS systems and a complementary standardized set of services and interfaces that together enable to secure V-to-V and V-to-infrastructure connectives. Thereby, the big data analysis outcomes are pertinent to the transportation benefits, include cost efficiency, time utilization, ITS service and safety, traffic management and automated tolling. Based on these facts big data is a paradigm and promising technology for IoV intelligent systems as (i) handling and integrating IoV audio, video and sensors produce massive data streams [4]. (ii) Spatial data of IoV objects in the context of the environments is describing as time series and location based. (iii) Integration of federated IoV smart objects' data are tended to have its own implicit semantics to recognize the inferred justifications. (iv) The capability and scalability of big data analytics and future predictions for IoV data management, exploration and exploitations in a dynamic and scalable technological fact, which includes:

- It is vitally significant to identifying and addressing of IoV smart objects in order to query or interact with various objects to realize each other's and addressing effectively.
- Data abstraction and compression for effective methods should be developed for filtering redundant data.
- Data archive, index, scalability and access control for IoV data.
- Data warehouse and its query language for multi-dimensional analysis, interoperability and semantic intelligibility for heterogeneous data of IoV,
- Time-series and event level data aggregation,
- It is essential to privacy and protection problem in data management of IoV.

2.1   The Current and Future Vehicular Data Systems Data Deluge

The existing data processing and analysis technologies are still far from being able to scale to demands of global and, in case of large industry and service, intelligent systems even of local data, which makes up the core of the data exploratory and management. With regard to this, the current data analysis algorithm requires to be reconsidered business dynamisms and the ever growing technologies, which is pertinent to overcome the challenge of the data deluge. That is the emerging and need to augment the paradigm of big data analytics is paramount. The advantage is multi-aspects. (i) The need of the solid design of current algorithms makes the integration with other techniques that would help increase the analysis quality of impossible or challenging issues. (ii) Sequential design of the algorithms prevents porting them to parallel computing infrastructures for which those do not fulfil high performance and do have other requirements. (iii) It is the future technological development intent, such as intelligent CC systems. Therefore, not only in the future, even now IoV data sets inquiry generic and dynamic tools, i.e. the big data analytics as of integrated and agent integrated DM to optimize large-scale data computation performance and mining algorithm, which is the process of inspecting data in order to extract useful information and predictions too [12].

The need of exploring IoV information/data is the concern to argument big data roles that lead to the cloud intelligent systems (data cloud), which provide computing and the networks to connect users and thing's access and services become more efficient and effective everywhere and anytime as-use-go. The paradigm of BDM is an iterative and multi process that involves various steps, which includes the DM-KDD work flows, future predictions, optimization of object's performance and safety incorporation of IoV prior knowledge and the network ecosystems with computational algorithms and/or visual approaches, interpretation and evaluation of the results' formulation or modification of intelligent system architecture, and others. BDM is therefore, exploratory in nature, more inductive than traditional statistical methods. It naturally fits in the initial stage of an IoV infrastructure deductive discovery process, where researchers develop and modify theories based on such nugget information from IoV observation data [9].

2.2   Promising and Periling of Big Data for Vehicular Intelligent System

How big data is promising and periling for vehicular intelligent systems data, is interesting even a controversial research issue. The tool seems designed for other businesses or corporate, but not. It is a computing technology of large-scale data exploration and exploitation techniques. Therefore, big data is for all and it not just about the data itself, even not the data infrastructure. It can be foreseen that the Internet of things (IoT) and IoV applications that will raise the scale of data to an unprecedented level, which is a big potential and promising tool [13, 14]. Big data for IoV also encompasses a scientific and dynamic way to process huge data as the domain contexts and derive patterns for the given data. It is a tactical approach of complex event processing by event-driven of IoV intelligence systems, which uses algorithms and rules to process streams of event data that it receives from multiple devices (fixed and/or wearable) including cars as of the meaningful insight of the events, contents and bandwidth [15]   as showed fig.2a.

IoV intelligent system data sets and events are essential to identify threat and opportunity of car's situations. This information is then used to guide the response in sense-and-respond the service's effectiveness and efficiency that triggered by the receipt of vehicular data interface (fig.2a). The systems store large-scale data that aggregate events from multiple sources and executing highly complex analyses for the upcoming processes and applications.

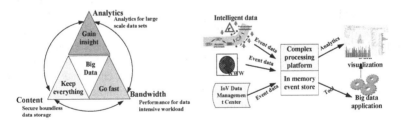

a.   Big data analytic contexts   b. IoV data set processing flow

Fig. 2. Big data opportunities and vehicular intelligent system data processing

3   Augmenting Application of Big Data for IoV

The augmenting of big data is a systematic approach to optimize the applications in how to manage and explore intelligent transport large-scale data, which is a fundamental paradigm to fostering, varies fields, including transportations industry. The approach is for comprehensive theory and technology that blend a set of hardware and software solutions to allow organizations to obtain the value from the ever increasing data sets [16]. Therefore, the paradigm of big data for IoV is more than connectivity, which concatenate the techniques of simulations, analytical visualization, ontological and data driven into one form or picture called the dashboard. An augmenting of complex data analysis in the context of agents and the network or infrastructure that needs to be capable of learn, sense and understand both the real world by themselves, which is fundamental to the intelligent cloud system that would be generating massive data in an explosive fashion as showed on fig.3. The IoV technological revolution is passing to a new ubiquitous connectivity, computing, and communication era that depend on dynamic technical innovations in a number of fields, from wireless sensors to nanotechnology [4].

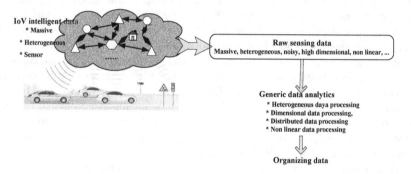

Fig. 3. The model of IoV massive data analytics framework

As it is shown in Fig. 3, the algorithms of big data for IoV data set analysis can be grouped in many forms, which include heterogeneous, nonlinear, high-dimensional and distributed and data processing [17]. The systems (vehicular data sets) are much complex, including spatial, time series, and multimedia type data modes, which are challenging to analysis and visualize by conventional data exploration. Decision on traffic jam, safety, and other events need to visualize different events at a time as showed on fig.4. It is the outcome of Chongqing City 6GB traffic data analysis, which is pertinent to minimize or tackling the traffic jam challenge in the city. The need of big data is essential to analyze such massive and complex data for the solution of the current traffic situations and its future predictions. It is a capable and scalable technology to large-scale data. In a nutshell, it is a system of spoon feed to decision-makers and experts as of their level of understanding.

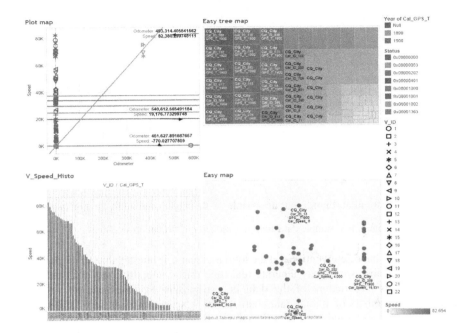

Fig. 4. Illustrative visualization of IoV massive data by big data applications

It is an advanced and systematic way of massive data handling and visualizing its hidden value in terms of color, image, time and location, including other factors or data such as multimedia and sensor analysis. Big data analytics is an integrated and foremost technology to gain a solution and visualize on a single dashboard of the exploration results to make proper decision and tasks [14]. Integration not only to reveal the outcomes in an interactively and advancing the exploratory tools but also important to contextual analysis and prediction in consideration of map services as of the vehicular ecosystems such as weather and landscapes that describe as spatial, and spatio temporal data sets [9, 18] in the system.

We can merely visualize how big data much visualize than the traditional way of analysis of a given sample data set on fig.5a & b. Decision-makers and experts or simply the traffic officer how could come up the right decision by looking fig.5b type of analysis, just having car attributes without having the spatial data description. Whereas on fig.5a, he/she can find the details as long as the image is visible, and they can arrive the proper decision on their traffic or some other problem in relation to the vehicular system data analytics. Furthermore, on big data the analytic results, they can also predict the better time and direction for the specified location or destination of the car [7]. Deploying big data is the proper approach to generate and distinguish the required data for investigation and further predictions. In the analytic process, the discovery of interesting and previously unknown, but potentially useful patterns are also sophisticated as compared to numeric and categorical data that empower the role of big data analysis.

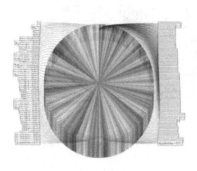 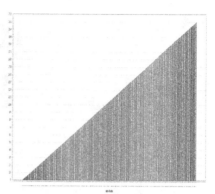

a. Multidimensional and nonlinear approach   b. Traditional analytic approach

Fig. 5. IoV sample data analytics model in different approaches

On the other hand, conventional data source center did not capable to record such garner object's observations to generate real-time traffic situation map and statistical traffic data sets. The nature of the data in terms of its volumes, verity, velocity, variability, and others of spatial data characteristics, spatial relationships, and spatial auto correlation are varied [13], which augmented the dynamic tools' applications and performances. For example, the prediction of events at particular node's locations or car speed or other factors would collect from different sources, which need to be an analysis in an integrated and generic level that foster the analysts and decision-makers to come up the most proper ends. Time series in IoV data set is also other major components, which represent the sequences of recorded values; appear naturally in almost all fields of applications, including bioinformatics and others [2].

Moreover, agent integrated BDM is essential to point out the pivot (data similarity) in different formats as the context of the system by including attribute's descriptions. Some agents in the roadside perform many tasks such as by having sound sense taking car image and recording other spatial data, which help to classify the images based on their contents, extracting pattern clusters, categorizing attributes and recognizing and tracking objects that need to be gained proper data models [20] as it is shown on fig.6.

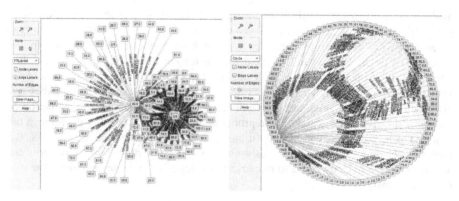

Fig. 6. Agent based bi data mining massive pivot visualization

Agent integrated DM technique in big data is a big potential analytic tool and pertinent for optimize big data analytics purpose due to the following reasons:

- To enabling and routing nodes and ages of the complex analysis that allow to visualize the pivot of data similarities for guaranteed 1 of N delivery or more complicated multi-mode or high fan-out delivery of data.
- It needs to guarantee the sequential delivery of data elements across many downstream storage nodes and applications.
- To handling the real-time de-duplication of data through the use of last value queues, sequence number generation and content-based selectors.
- To captured data, elements need to be routed to the right storage location, and subsequent updates need to have an affinity to that location, which uses dynamic address space and internode routing protocols to make sure every data element is routed appropriately.
- For incoming data can spike to rates that exceed the average inbound rate. Solace appliances act as a big data "shock absorber" to smooth out the peaks without losing information.
- To avoid replications and data recovery, i.e. capturing data in a single location can expose your business to continuity problems. Solace's appliances can efficiently replicate data streams across the WAN to provide failsafe delivery to remote data centers.

3.1   Big Data and the Technology of Data Structure

Big data analytics is the technology of designing and structuring massive and complex data (both structured and unstructured) to extract value and knowledge implicit through high-velocity capture, discovery and analysis. It is the modern approach to analyze the large volumes of bytes associated with big data in a cost-efficient manner and also a shift in the common approach to computer architecture. By moving from costly hardware to commodity computing, operators will be able to meet the resource requirements for huge amounts of data storage and heavy server-processing power [13, 19]. The paradigm sequential and procedural pattern is shown on fig.7. The integrated tools, such the infrastructures (network safety), semantic intelligent (cloud system) and analytics applications are big potential to data structure to a proper data representation and its associated operations. Moreover, the approach is capable of visualize an integer or floating point number stored in the computer that can be viewed as a simple data structure for which to mean a structuring of collected or generated data.

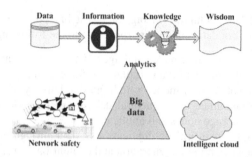

Fig. 7. Big potential of big data for massive data structure

Furthermore, properly structured and stored data is a pre-hand solution of the issue what researchers exploring on their subject matter and the domain too. It gives a chance to a performer an integrated analytics; optimize disk spacing and processing time. It is fundamental to simplify searching process for specified items within the collection, print or otherwise process the data items in any desired order, or modify the value of any particular data item.

3.2   Big Data for the Verge of IoV Intelligent Cloud System

Big data for IoV is pertinent to drive a wide range of important decisions and activities, which include designing more dynamic, and efficient system infrastructures, cost optimizations, future predictions to a profound of intelligent cloud systems. All these and other activities enable improved system performance, system and/or service safety, and also to create smarter networks, and extended network functionality to facilitate progress toward the networked systems. Therefore, big data is a big potential to create business opportunities in new areas for IoVs with dynamic real-time connectivity and manageable data center to establish easy access and secured data sets, readily available for analysis and machine learning [17, 21].

In the history of transportation industry, there is a dynamic and incremental contribution in the world economies. The data sets in terms of its volume, velocity, variability, variety, veracity, values, even venerability (i.e. V_i –where i = 1, 2, ..., n) – of big data characteristics were simply overwhelming. Those data-handling challenges have now largely been met by a variety of easily obtained tools, which includes Hadoop, Alteryx, distributed databases, complex event-processing frameworks, analytics libraries and so on.

3.3   Big Data for Virtualization of IoV Data

Data virtualization is a promising process that federates disparate systems of relational databases, legacy applications, files repositories, website data sources and others into a single data access layer integrating data services for consuming applications and users. However, big data applications often require a cluster of nodes that communicate in some protocols, which pertinent to solve the problem that typically a large volume of data transferred through network connections [13]. For a large-scale data storage facility is a big challenging, which demand federated storage that can be kept in a virtual machine. An Integrated and dynamic application is a solution to virtual connection for further analysis. The process is demonstrated by concerned or delegated agent or machine to operate in distributed systems [15], such as data replication, when using Virtual Machine (VM) since the performance of various steps could drastically alter the performance of the overall system depending on the frequency of data loading, replication, backups, etc. [22]. Therefore, virtualization in big data environment is typical processes that implement to utilize complex storage systems that are not physically a part of the servers containing virtualizes nodes. These storage systems are often accessed through network connections. For example, Hadoop and Alteryx tableau analytics tools in which using data by connectivity rather than transforming or importing itself as showed on fig.8.

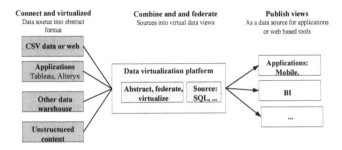

Fig. 8. Big data approach IoV data virtualization

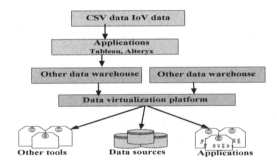

Fig. 9. Practical setup for IoV data virtualization focusing on data warehouse and big data

Big data for IoV data virtualization passed various steps, including to connect and virtualizes data sources into an abstract format, combine and federate sources into virtual data and deploy the data service for web-based application, via the networks as it showed on fig.8 and actual work on fig.4 IoV data analytics dashboard results. The role of big data approaches virtualization is just to combine federated data as of their sources, which showed on fig.9 and fig.3 of IoV massive data modeling platform.

3.4 Big Data Inside and Outside the IoV Datacenter

Collecting, storing and managing IoV intelligent systems activity's data from inside and outside sources to a data center with connected data servers can easily exceed the capability of most systems to capture reliably [23]. Storing information generated from millions of concurrently linked agents (sensor nodes) and users require enormous numbers of servers when done in agent software. The most effective way to handle this volume of data is with a data movement layer that takes care of message delivery so the sensors can send data without worrying about where it needs to go or how it needs to get there [22]. This entails the establishment and management of queues and topics, application of subsequent routing rules; intelligent handling of fault conditions such as applications or network links being down or slow, etc. [17].

Table 1. IOV big data categorical descriptions

Inside	Outside
IoV inside a datacenter is coming from applications and systems connected directly via the transport infrastructure include: ▪ Click streams ▪ Application events ▪ Transaction records ▪ IoVlog/Monitoring data ▪ Cloud Computing Virtual Machine (VM) Infrastructure monitoring	The outside datacenter, data sources include phones, distributed sensors, and partners. The massive number of endpoints and connections becomes the main challenge, include: • Road side and remote Telemetry • Sensors devices and nets • Smart Phone and wearable devices • RFID and barcode scanners • GPS Position Tracking • Point-of-Sale Terminals

4 Related Works

There is a massive increase in the amount of IoV data that is generated globally, which sourced by different and autonomous devices that interfacing by IoV to communicate without human intervention [3]. It is the emerge of the need of big data and its potential comes from the identification of novel patterns in activity and the development of predictive models that would have been hard or impossible with smaller samples or fewer variables [1, 17]. As the matter of facts, the transportation industry networks and communications are dynamic and complex in the context of time, location and other environmental and natural factors, which is fertile to big data analytics [24]. However, the network density which is related to traffic density is challenging to define in terms of location and time, which demanding big data analytics to overcome the problems. Big data technology is capable of integrate GPS technology to detect car's moments, speed, and other events [10].

Big Data could help reveal key insights into the drivers, triggers, and early signs of large-scale transport services and safety to the better of human life. It is fundamental and imprecise technology that refers to the use of large data sets in data science and predictive analytics, which emphasis on aspects of data magnification and manipulation. In [18] big data refers to technology that maximizes computational power and algorithmic accuracy, whereas [14] described big data as of a type of analytics that draw on a range of tools to clean and compare data [20] and also discussed about big data promotes the belief that large data sets generate results with greater truth, objectivity, and accuracy. Therefore, the promise of big data's ability to analyze data and provide novel insights has led to profound IoV investment in consideration of and excitement about big data's power to solve problems in numerous disciplines and business arenas.

IoV is a multidisciplinary field, which generates a growing supply of objects from which data can be collected for further analysis using big data tools. Mobile and other sensors, including wearable objects are always activated as the users demanding in the context of location aware with multiple road side cameras, microphones, movement sensors, GPS, and Wi-Fi capabilities–have revolutionized the collection of data in the public sphere and enabled innovative data harvesting and use [5]. For example, traffic loop detection data consists of measurements of traffic intensity, which counts the number of vehicles per minute that pass at that location, and measure speed and length, including sensor device's other recording data. Such data are interesting for IoV and other transport statistics and potentially for other economic phenomena related to the field [21, 25].

5   Conclusions

Big data refers to the exponential increase in the volume and speed of data/information being created every day in our digital, hyper-connected world. Therefore, big data for IoV is best characterized by its potential rather than by its track record. IoV intelligent systems technological innovation has become a fertile land for such dynamic and complex analysis and a fundamental profound to the intelligent cloud system. In this paper, we investigate and introduced An augmenting a paradigm big data for IoV intelligent system how to manage and handling the large-scale data, optimize the infrastructure performance, road safety, gaining a clear insight that the agents how to connect – end-to-end – data from multiple sources to yield an enriched set of information sources. This is what ultimately enables a range of service and user-centric applications to be created. Big data for IoV data sets modeling, data structure and virtualizations and others were a major and main focused in this research, while big data storage and processing techniques are discussed in depth to visualize its applications in the field. Furthermore, the big data tools and technologies' key role for future predictions are well discussed. In most big data literatures, it characterized as three Vs, however, on our works, the Vs are more than that need focus as long as researchers doing on this technology. IoV as the fundamental of cloud intelligent system explored as BDM models and framework to realize the future generation computing technology. Big data analytics from multi-technology integration perspective describes the corresponding framework for the forthcoming Internet.

Acknowledgements. We are very thanks to the anonymous reviewers for their useful comments, and the works is supported by National Natural Science Foundation (NNSF) of China under Grant 61203321.

References

[1] Fan, W., Bifet, A.: Mining Big Data: Current Status, and Forecast to the Future. SIGKDD Explorations 14(2), 1–5 (2013)

[2] Bifet, A.: Mining Big Data in Real Time. Informatica 37, 15–20 (2013)

[3] Verma, N., Kumar, R.: A Method for Improving Data Delivery Efficiency in Vehicular Ad hoc Networks. International Journal of Advanced Science and Technology 44, 11–24 (2012)

[4] Dlodlo, N., et al.: The State of Affairs in Internet of Things Research. The Electronic Journal Information Systems Evaluation 15(3), 244–258 (2012)

[5] Zhang, Y., et al.: On Scheduling Vehicle-Road side Data Access. In: VANET 2007, Canada (2007), ACM, 978-1-59593-739-1/07/0009...$5.00

[6] Saboowala, H., et al.: Designing Networks and Services for the Cloud. Cisco Systems, Inc. (2013) ISBN-10:1-58714-294-5

[7] Wu, B.: Internet-of-Vehicles based on Technologies of Internet-of-Things. In: ICLEM, pp. 348–356 (2012)

[8] Vermesan, O., Friess, P.: Internet of Things: Converging Technologies for Smart Environments and Integrated Ecosystems. River Publishers (2013) ISBN: 978-87-92982-96-4

[9] Bin, S., et al.: Research on Data Mining Models for the Internet of Things. IEEE, 978-1-4244-5555-3/10/$26.00 (2010)

[10] Leng, Y., Zhao, L.S.: Novel Design of Intelligent Internet-of- vehicles Management System Based on Cloud Computing and internet-of-things. In: IEEE, International Conference on Electronic & Mechanical Engineering and Information Technology, pp. 3190–3195 (2011) 978-1-61284-088-8/11/$26.00

[11] Goggin, G.: Driving the Internet: Mobile Internets, Cars, and the Social. Future Internet 4, 306–321 (2012), doi:10.3390/fi4010306

[12] Guo, D., Mennis, J.: Spatial data mining and geographic knowledge discovery: An introduction. Elsevier, Computers, Environment and Urban Systems 33, 403–408 (2009)

[13] Crawford, K., Schultz, J.: Big Data and Due Process: Toward a Framework to Redress Predictive Privacy Harms, 55 B. C. L. Rev. 93 (2014), http://lawdigitalcommons.bc.edu/bclr

[14] Tene, O., Polonetsky, J.: Big Data for All: Privacy and User Control in the Age of Analytics, 11 Nw. J. Tech. & Intell. Prop. 239 (2013), http://scholarlycommons.law.northwestern.edu

[15] Gama, J.: Data Stream Mining: the Bounded Rationality. Informatica 37, 21–25, 21 (2013)

[16] Ceri, S., et al.: Towards Mega Modeling: A Walk through Data Analysis Experiences. SIGMOD Record 42(3), 19–27 (2013)

[17] Diebold, F.X.: Big Data Dynamic Factor Models for Macroeconomic Measurement and Forecasting, pp. 115–122. Cambridge University Press, Cambridge (2003)

[18] Lin, J., Ryaboy, D.: Scaling Big Data Mining Infrastructure: The Twitter Experience. SIGKDD Explorations 14(2), 6–19 (2013)

[19] Zikopoulos, P.C., et al.: Understanding Big Data Analytics for Enterprise Class Hadoop and Streaming Data. The McGraw-Hill Companies, New York (2012)

[20] Gorcitz, R.A., et al.: Vehicular Carriers for Big Data Transfers (Poster). In: IEEE Vehicular Networking Conference (VNC), Korea, Republic, Seoul (2012)

[21] Sharma, T., Banga, V.K.: Efficient and Enhanced Algorithm in Cloud Computing. International Journal of Soft Computing and Engineering (IJSCE) 3(1) (2013) ISSN: 2231-2307

[22] Birke, R., et al.: (Big) Data in a Virtualized World: Volume, Velocity, and Variety in Cloud Datacenters. In: USENIX Association 12th USENIX Conference on File and Storage Technologies, pp. 177–190 (2014)

[23] Agneeswaran, V.S.: Big-Data – Theoretical, Engineering and Analytics Perspective. In: Srinivasa, S., Bhatnagar, V. (eds.) BDA 2012. LNCS, vol. 7678, pp. 8–15. Springer, Heidelberg (2012)

[24] Xi, N., et al.: Decentralized Information Flow Verification Framework for the Service Chain Composition in Mobile Computing Environments. In: IEEE 20th International Conference on Web Services, pp. 563–570 (2013) 978-0-7695-5025-1/13 $26.00, doi:10.1109/ICWS.2013.81

[25] Corcoba Magaña, V., Muñoz Organero, M.: Artemisa: Using an Android device as an Eco-Driving assistant. Cyber Journals: Multidisciplinary Journals in Science and Technology, Journal of Selected Areas in Mechatronics, JMTC (2011)

Crowdsourcing Leakage of Personally Identifiable Information via Sina Microblog*

Chen Fu[1], Zhan Shaobin[2], Shi Guangjun[3], and Guan Mengyuan[1]

[1] Department of Computer, Beijing Foreign Studies University, Beijing, China
[2] Shenzhen Institute of Information & Technology, Shenzhen, China
[3] Computer Network Information Center, Chinese Academy of Science, Beijing, China

Abstract. Since Edward Snowden's leaks about the scale and scope of US electronic surveillance, it has become apparent that security services are just as fascinating as what they might learn from our data exhaust. At the time, cybercrime is becoming a global threat now. Cybercriminals may engage in criminal activities with personal privacy data from microblog. Identity theft is probably an example. In this paper we examine the characteristics of privacy leakage in microblog and its potential threats to the Internet community. Research found that a large number of privacy information in social network space was leaked unintentionally. Users often share too much significant personal information. Our study found that the accumulated privacy information may bring huge spam into Internet space. We examined over 20 million nodes profile information and extracted the name, location, gender, and email from these nodes profiles. After basic analysis and processing, we shown that all these personal information is enough to launch spam storm or other criminal activities. The result suggests that each node in the microblog should protect its privacy information carefully.

Keywords: privacy leakage, microblog personal information, prediction model.

1 Introduction

Cybercrime is one of the fastest growing areas of crime. More and more criminals are exploiting the speed, convenience and anonymity that modern technologies offer in order to commit a diverse range of criminal activities [1]. Personal privacy information plays an important role in the cybercrime activities. After collecting huge privacy information, the third-parties may combine, group, or mix it with other information for ulterior motives. However, with the growing use of mobile communication devices and social networking services, users often disclose their privacy information

---

* Supported by the National Natural Science Foundation of China under Grant No.61170209,61370132; Program for New Century Excellent Talents in University No.NCET-13-0676; Shenzhen strategic emerging industry development funds Grant No.JCYJ20120821162230172; Guangdong Natural Science Foundation Grant No. S2013040012895, Foundation for Distinguished Young Talents in Higher Education of Guangdong, China, Grant No. 2013LYM_0076, the Major Fundamental Research Project in the Science and Technology Plan of Shenzhen Grant No. JCYJ2013032910203205.

R.C.-H. Hsu and W. Shangguang (Eds.): IOV 2014, LNCS 8662, pp. 262–271, 2014.

inadvertently. So privacy information protection in mobile networks has become one of a major concern for everyone nowadays. Information Governance (IG) is emerging as one of the most important issues confronting organizations today, particularly in this age of Big Data and data breaches [2].

Billions of people are on various online social networks, such as Facebook, MySpace, Twitter, LinkedIn, Friendster, Badoo, Netlog, XING, foursquare, and Sina Weibo et al. Many people on these platforms have made huge personal information about themselves available on their social networks. Location, address, emails and even their habits and political beliefs can be got from the profiles and messages published by users. By tracking and aggregating user operations with these online network services for a period, it is very easy to get more personal privacy information. For example, like or comment on some topic, it hints users' tendency, mood, gospel or religion directly without needing large number of data. And even this happen imperceptibly. Such leakage would imply some important trend or demand in some people. Also one can use these data to identify a specific person. Politicians, stars, and even ordinary people dislike their special personal habits to be published. In addition, some information, which may not very important for a person, will bring risks, or to be made improper use by some people if added together. For example, every day we are being plagued by spam. These spam messages sent into the Internet also bring junk traffic. But when we public the email address we will not notice it. Third parties may also build a database of valid email address data to sell.

As mentioned above, some trivial privacy personal information added together may pose risk too. How to avoid and reduce the risk of privacy leakage is a very worthy of attention problem.

There are two problems we should pay more attention to. One is how to avoid personal leakage; the other is how to protect the huge personal information to be gathered. Monitoring network disclosure of privacy information in microblog is this paper's main topic. At first glance, microblog privacy information leakage may be an old and tedious problem. We think, however, there are still several challenges we should pay more attention to:

(1) What can be called privacy in microblog. This is not clearly defined now and the notion is vague to most common people. Even if people know this clearly, can they protect corresponding information actively?
(2) Overall situation about the exposure of personal information should be revealed. For example, how much certain privacy information have users disclosed? That is to say, the extent of disclosure of data in microbolg should be known.
(3) How to protect huge trivial information from being collected by third-parties, the steps that users or social network platforms took to protect those data.
(4) The model of mining the relationship structure, common interests, and gospels. The key question is, for example, how many tweets will reveal one political attitude.

For the purposes of this paper, we aim to acquire the understanding of privacy leakage in microblog and corresponding solutions to protect personal information in microblog. To this end, we collected 20 million users data posted publicly for the analysis.

In summary, the contributions of this paper are as follows:

(1) Measurement of personal information leakage with enough data in Sina weibo space.
(2) Malicious usage of trivial privacy personal information was sum up.
(3) A model of mining the attitude which may be private to users.

The rest of this paper is organized as follows. Section 2 reviews related works and discusses some background materials about the microblog privacy problem; Section 3 introduces measures of personal information leakage; Section 4 gives conclusions and future work.

2   Related Work

Sharing information with one or two sentences less then 140 words is very popular today. More than one-third of China adults on the Internet use Sina Weibo, among which 50 millions are active every day. The same situation in American happens in Facebook, Twitter et al. As a result of this increasing popularity in recent years, social networks analysis is a hot topic to the research community. But privacy protection problems are bound to arise with it. Now privacy protection has become a very serious problem. So many researchers have measured, analyzed and quantified privacy information in the microblog space. Personal identification information is information which can be used to distinguish or trace an individual's identity [3]. The user's social footprint was defined with a set of attributes representing information obtained about a user on social networks [4]. Danesh Irani's work indicates that danger increases substantially with multiple social network profiles. It's critical for users to understand such danger and take defensive measures to prevent personal information from leaking and defend against information misuse [4]. As a result of being enthusiastic about the social network and dependent on it, people prone to post too much privacy information. And safer use of social network services would thus require changes in users' attitude [5]. Specific privacy concerns of online social networking include inadvertent disclosure of personal information, damaged reputation due to rumors and gossip, unwanted contact and harassment or stalking, surveillance-like structures due to backtracking functions, use of personal data by third-parties, and hacking and identity theft [6]. The community needs a clear understanding of the shortcomings of existing privacy protection measures and the new proposals [7]. Balachander Krishnamurthy shown that 56% of the sites directly leak pieces of privacy information with this result growing to 75% if leakage of a site userid is included [7]. Both qualitative and quantitative analysis reveals the characterization of the content and message content varies in the Twitter network [8]. Supporting complex mobile social networking applications with personal information without compromising the anonymity of the users providing the information is a big challenge proposed in [9]. Sometimes one special cue often maps to a particular person even if the user does not directly provide identification information. Aaron Beach et al. pointed out that the indirect anonymity problem exists when a piece of information indirectly compromises a user's identity. So an interesting question is K_N_Anonymity problem occurs when n pieces of information or n sets of related information can be used together to uniquely map back to K particular users. How to determine the constant K or N is a great challenge. By automatically crawling and correlating profiles information about each user, an attacker can launch sophisticated and targeted attacks, or improve the efficiency of spam campaigns [10]. This kind of information is also of great value to entities with potentially malicious intentions. Hence, it is the responsibility of the service provider to ensure that unauthorized access to sensitive profile information is properly restricted [10]. Assessing the privacy is crucial to every user in microblog. Users do should understand the situation of security problems. As the same to the service provider, quantitative measure of the privacy also helps to improve the quality of social network service. A great effort has been devoted to the investigation of privacy metrics, especially in the scenario of statistical disclosure control [11]. Quantitative measures of the privacy of user profiles to assess, compare, improve and optimize privacy-enhancing technologies were approached in [11].

To the best of our knowledge, although there are so many works to the privacy problem in mobile social network, there is no a unified model for measuring the privacy. Besides emotional and political beliefs are also classified as privacy. There is no doubt that information in social network space can also reflect the political belief. People are not fully aware of the serious consequences brought by accumulating trivial personal privacy leakage. And we argue that the situation is worsening and several issues should be explored in depth. A clear definition and uniform metrics about social network personal privacy deserve deep study for its importance. These are just the key elements of the study in this paper.

3   Measures of Personal Information Leakage

In this section we focus on measurement of personal information in microblog network.

To register your account on one social network platform, you need to fill in some personal information, such as name, photo, location, age, gender, email, and QQ et al. Looked at in isolation, these information may not be very important personal privacy. But they may be of great importance in some cases. When parts of the information combined with other relevant information, they may form the critical privacy information. When one kind of information collected with huge volume, some malicious behavior may be implemented. For example if having a large number of email addresses, someone may launch spam or fishing. So we should give a definition about the personal information.

3.1   Crowdsourcing Privacy Leakage

The crowdsourcing privacy leakage (CPL) denotes the overall leakage of privacy information.

$\textbf{CPL}:=\{k_1/n_1, k_2/n_2, \ldots\ldots k_m/n_m\}$, CPL is a M-dimensional vector.

$\textbf{k}_i/\textbf{n}_i$: To define the dynamics of a certain privacy item, that is the distributing law of one privacy with nodes number.

This is because not all nodes will reveal all the privacy information. We want to denote the density of leakage in one element. We denote the rate of trivial personal growth with vector CPL.

Here, we collected the data from Sina Weibo as an example. We collected near 20 million node profiles in Sina Weibo space. After data cleaning, we extracted the gender, self-description, address, career, education, birthday, QQ Number, Email box address, and account creation time from 6 million node profiles. We divided the data into 600 groups, and 10 thousand nodes in a group. Then we computed the ration of $K1/104$, where $K1$ is total number of nodes containing gender information in every group. So the $K1/10^4$ gives the density of gender information leakage, which is shown in Fig.1.

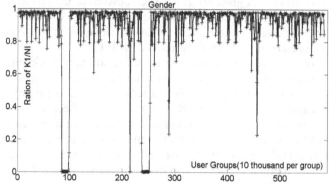

Fig. 1. The gender information in 600 thousand nodes

From Fig.1 we can see that most of nodes have gender information. The average of $K1/N1$ is 0.94. But there are still some group nodes do have no gender information. Even if the user does not provide other information, gender information may be mapped to other identification information in one special domain. So the gender information is not trivial under certain conditions. The fig.2 shows the self-description information vibrating with groups. We can see the $K2/N2$ denotes the density of nodes which have self-description in there profiles. We can get some important information from self-description, such as the professional skill, interest, and even the office. We also notice that most of the $K2/N2$ is between 0.15 and 0.3. We have computed the average and standard deviations of Ki/Ni, which will list in table 1 below. The average of $K2/N2$ is 0.22, and the standard deviation of 0.0226.

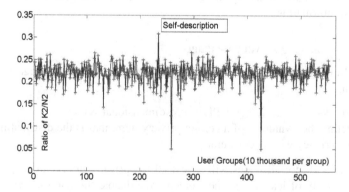

Fig. 2. Self-description information with 10 million users

There are often two common means to use the trivial privacy information. One is to gather huge amount of one type information, such as email spam; the other is to combine different element information to form a complete record. So the relationship among different elements influences the combination. So we compared the fluctuations of gender and self-description, shown in Fig.3. Here we divide the data set into 60 groups to grasp the macro changes. We notice that the two curves have certain similarities from the extreme changes. The change of density with gender and self-description correlated each other, just as shown in Fig.3.

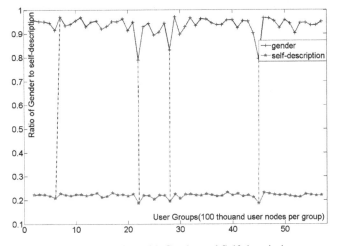

Fig. 3. Comparation with Gender and Self-description

The user's address information may be a little more important. We also extracted the address information from 6 millions node set. Just as done above, one point means 10 thousand nodes. We name it as K3/N3, where N3 is 10^4. The average of address is 0.93. The standard deviation of address is 0.1603. The fluctuations of address leakage with the user's number are shown in Fig.4. Intuitively, the address information is more important than the gender to the user in Weibo. But we can easily notice that the fluctuations of address and gender are so similar both from curve shapes and values.

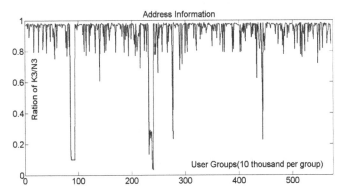

Fig. 4. Address against Users Number

It means if we map the data gender and address with other information, the have even more specific information to identify one user.

And we found that for nodes near 100th and nodes near 250th, fewer users exposure the gender and address information. We'll discuss it later.

We denote the career information density in Sina Weibo space with K4/104. The average of K4/104 is 0.052, and the standard deviation of career is 0.066. The surprise is that the career information exposure fewer than expected. Just at the nodes near 100th group and nodes near 250th group, K4/104 jumps sharply, which is shown in Fig.5. It is just   the reverse of gender and self-description. For many people, compared with gender information, career is not privacy information. The results seem counter-intuitive.

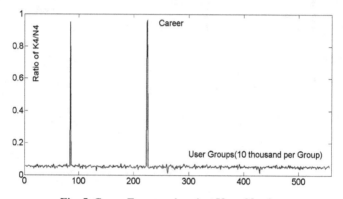

Fig. 5. Career Exposured against Users Number

As for education information for users in Sina Weibo, which we denote it with $K5/10^4$,   the average of $K5/10^5$ is 0.154, and the standard deviation of career is 0.052. Somewhat different with above, the fluctuation curve of education information reaches only one maximum peak value near 240th group, which is shown in Fig.6.

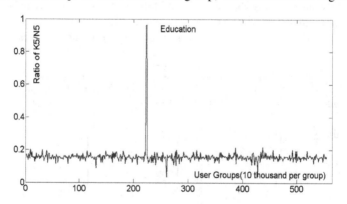

Fig. 6. Education Exposured against Users Number

We denote the birth day information density with K5/10^5. For most people home and abroad, birth date is a private issue. So, intuitively, exact birth date may not be provided to microblog, at least should less than career. But according to our data from Sina Weibo, average around 0.362 of users provides exact date of birth. And the standard deviation of career is 0.0784. Just as career fluctuations above, almost near the same group points, that is 100th group and nodes near 250th group, there are two sharp bulges, shown in Fig.7.

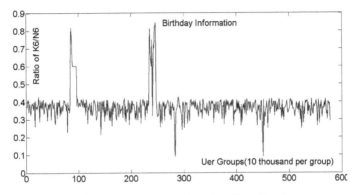

Fig. 7. Birth Day Exposured against Users Number

QQ is the largest social networking and instant messaging platform in China, and it is one of the keys to understanding the shape of the Internet in China today. The numbers revolving around QQ are staggering. QQ is virtually synonymous with online life in China. So the QQ account to one person, of course, is privacy information. According to our data, there are still a considerable number of users whose QQ is available in Sina Weibo personal profile. We denote the QQ information density with K7/10^4. The average of K7/10^4 is 0.0087. And the standard deviation of QQ number is 0.106. Group points near 100th group and 250th, the K7/10^4 nearly reach 0.7, 0.8 respectively. But the shape of peak looks a little different from career above, but it is very similar to that of birth day. The K7/10^4 is shown in Fig.8.

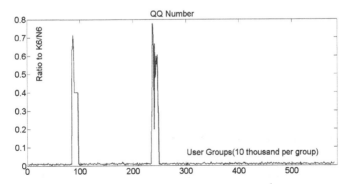

Fig. 8. QQ Leakage Density with K7/10^4

For the majority, Email may be open to the public. However, the evidence shows that it is not the case. We denote the Email information density with $K8/10^4$. And we found that the average of $K8/10^{4 \text{ is}}$ only 0.0013. The standard deviation of $K8/10^4$ is 0.113. Just as done above, group points near 100th group and 250th the density of information is between 0.7 to 0.8.

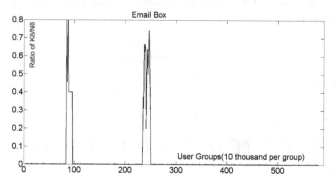

Fig. 9. Email Leakage Density with $K8/10^4$

Last, but certainly not least, we define the creation time leakage density with $K9/10^4$. Creation time early or late is a hint of user's attention to network service. To the surprise of many, intuitively the account creation time is not privacy information. But the account creation time density against user number is very low. The average value of $K9/10^4$ is 0.0098. And the standard deviation of $K9/10^4$ is 0.167. The shape of curve is very similar to that of $K9/10^{4\cdot}$, especially at the point of near 100th group and 250th. The $K9/10^4$ is shown in Fig.10.

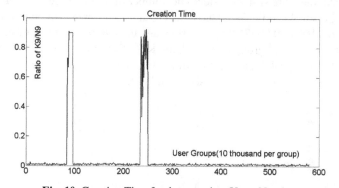

Fig. 10. Creation Time Leakage against Users Number

4   Conclusions and Future Work

We have studied hitherto unexamined huge trivial privacy information leakage problem. 6 million users' information from 20 million users' information is analyzed respectively. The quantitative relations are rendered with Ki/N, P_Ni, and K_N_Anonymity. With our analysis, we think that the trivial information combined with other information should not be neglected, especially for some users who prone to expose personal information. The ratio of fitting data set is computed by the real data from Sina Weibo.

Our plans for future work include continuing investigating the semantic features inferred from user's tweets, such as political beliefs, personal habits, and social relations with outers. We think these also may be exposed by the information in microblog platform. And of course all these are privacy information too.

Acknowledgments. We would like to thank Bai Xue for data collecting. We also give thanks for the National Natural Science Foundation of China Shenzhen strategic emerging industry development funds.

References

[1] http://www.interpol.int/Crime-areas/Cybercrime/Cybercrime

[2] http://www.dataprivacymonitor.com/information-governance-2/the-sedona-conference-hails-the-advent-of-value-based-information-governance/

[3] Johnson III, C.: Protection of Sensitive Agency Information, US Office of Management and Budget (2006), http://www.whitehouse.gov/sites/default/files/omb/assets/omb/memoranda/fy2006/m06-16.pdf

[4] Irani, D., Webb, S., Pu, C., Li, K.: Modeling Unintended Personal-Information Leakage from Multiple Online Social Networks. IEEE Internet Computing 15(3), 13–19 (2011)

[5] Debatin, B., Lovejoy, J.P., Horn, A.-K., Hughes, B.N.: Facebook and Online Privacy: Attitudes, Behaviors, and Unintended Consequences. Journal of Computer-Mediated Communication 15, 83–108 (2009)

[6] Boyd, D.: Facebook's privacy trainwreck: Exposure, invasion, and social convergence. Convergence: The International Journal of Research into Media Technologies 14(1), 13–20 (2008)

[7] Krishnamurthy, B., Naryshkin, K., Wills, C.: Privacy leakage vs. Protection measures: the growing disconnect. Web 2.0 Security and Privacy Workshop (May 2011), Is it really about me message content in social awareness streams

[8] Beach, A., Gartrell, M., Han, R.: Solutions to Security and Privacy Issues in Mobile Social Networking. In: 2009 International Conference on Computational Science and Engineering, CSE, vol. 4, pp. 1036–1042 (2009)

[9] Balduzzi, M., Platzer, C., Holz, T., Kirda, E., Balzarotti, D., Kruegel, C.: Abusing Social Networks for Automated User Profiling. In: Jha, S., Sommer, R., Kreibich, C. (eds.) RAID 2010. LNCS, vol. 6307, pp. 422–441. Springer, Heidelberg (2010)

[10] Parra-Arnau, J., Rebollo-Monedero, D., Forné, J.: Measuring the Privacy of User Profiles in Personalized Information Systems. (Elsevier) Future Gen. Comput. Sys. (FGCS), Special Issue Data Knowl. Eng. 33, 53–63 (2014)

[11] http://www.ft.com/cms/s/2/21a6e7d8-b479-11e3-a09a-00144feabdc0.html#axzz2xifNsxvT

SepStore: Data Storage Accelerator for Distributed File Systems by Separating Small Files from Large Files

Zhenzhao Wang, Kang Chen, Yongwei Wu, and Weimin Zheng

Department of Computer Science and Technology,
Tsinghua National Laboratory for Information Science and Technology (TNLIST),
Tsinghua University, Beijing, China
Research Institute of Tsinghua University in Shenzhen, Shenzhen 518057, China
Technology Innovation Center at Yinzhou,
Yangtze Delta Region Institute of Tsinghua University, ZheJiang
zz-wang11@mails.tsinghua.edu.cn,
{chenkang,wuyw}@tsinghua.edu.cn

Abstract. Distributed file systems often rely on disk file systems for storing data on disks. Disk file systems can do a relative good performance on large files than small files as sequential access patterns often exhibit for large files. This paper improves the performance of data servers for distributed file systems by improving the performance for small files. A LSM structure based *key-value* store is used for storing the data for small files for transforming the random access to sequential access as well as reducing the metadata of disk file systems. The *key-value* store is also used as the index for accessing small files. Experimental results showed that our method could improve the throughput up to 78% as well as 37% improvement on IOPS.

Keywords: Distributed File System, LSM, Small files, IO Accelerator.

1 Introduction

Distributed file systems are usually built on top of traditional local disk file systems as the distributed file systems do not need to deal with disks directly[7,17,4]. The distributed layer of the file system is used for finding the corresponding data blocks in a specific host. The disk file system layer is used to find the specific disk blocks storing data. In this way, each layer will focus on the work they specialised in. There are usually two main components in distributed file systems. One is called as metadata server for storing metadata and the other is called as chunkserver for storing data blocks of files.

Disk file systems usually use multi-index structure to organize the data on disks[14]. For example, in ext series of file systems, one should find the corresponding inode for a specific file before the data can be accessed. Before that, the inode and directory page for parent directories will be first accessed. This is the common procedures called as directory resolution. Such disk access pattern

R.C.-H. Hsu and W. Shangguang (Eds.): IOV 2014, LNCS 8662, pp. 272–281, 2014.

characteristic leads to slow performance of accessing large amount of small files because of random access of disks. For large files, the time spend on the directory resolution can be amortized by the data access time. For small files, the time will be a huge portion of accessing file data. The disk file systems are often reported to have low performance for accessing small files. As the distributed file systems use the disk file systems as the storage backend, they share the same problem[15].

As metadata seemed to be a bottleneck of the distributed file systems, most of the previous works wanted to accelerate small files access focused on how to improve the performance of metadata server[9,16]. We seek the opportunities to improve the performance of data access in chunkserver for small files in distributed file systems. In this paper, we present how to improve the chunkserver performance by combining LSM (Log Structure Merge tree)[10] based *key-value* storage together with traditional disk file systems.

Our method is based on the following observation. The namespace of distributed file systems is usually different from the local one. Thus, the metadata for local files such as data blocks are not needed for distributed file system. For small files, it does not need to create a local file for a file in the distributed file system. Several small files can be packed into a relative large file in the disk file system. There will be only the metadata for this large file i.e. the metadata for all theses small files in disk file system are amortized. The *open/close* interfaces for the distributed file system are different from the *open/close* semantic in disk file system. This means the *open/close* operations of disk file system are actually not needed for distributed file systems. By combining several small files together, the *open/close* operations will be depressed for most of the small files. For the random access issue, the write performance can be improved by using log-structured layout in the large file as the data for those files are often written in total[11,13,12]. Read operation can be improved by keeping indices in memory and simplifying the address resolution.

This paper has made the following contributions:

1. We have analyzed several issues related to small file access in distributed file system. The current design relies on the disk file system has several shortcomings. It will take a long time doing address resolution that makes the performance quite slow.

2. The method on how to improve the performance of chunkserver is proposed. This method combines LSM-based *key-value* store together with traditional file system. LSM-based *key-value* store is used as the storage for small files while traditional file system is used for storing data of relative large files.

3. We have built the storage prototype, SepStore, to provide data service in a distributed file system. This system demonstrates the effectiveness of proposed method. For pure small file access writes, the method can improve the performance by 210%. For mixed workload, experimental results showed that our method could improve the throughput up to 78% as well as 37% improvement on IOPS.

The remainder of the paper is organized as follows. Section 2 will discuss the detail of proposed method. Section 3 studies the implementation of our prototype system. We will give the experimental results in Section 4. Some related work is discussed in Section 5 and we conclude the work in Section 6.

2   Accelerator for Chunkserver

2.1   IO Analysis of Distributed file Systems

The architecture of distribute file system often contains two components. One is used to store the metadata and the other is used to store file data. The former one is usually called as metedata server and the later is called as chunkserver. Many existing distributed file systems such as GFS[7] and MooseFS[3] follow this paradigm.

For accessing the data of a file, the client will first ask the metadata server about the layout of a file. The layout contains the information like where each portion of a file can be found including the host and the local file on the corresponding host. Then the client will send chunkserver requests. The chunkserver will perform the requests on local disk file system. As disk file systems already provide the facilities to manage the data blocks on disks, it is usually not needed for distributed file systems to touch the disks directly.

Relying on the underlying disk file system for distributed file systems will share the same system performance disadvantage for small files. The modern disk file systems can provide the namespace (file tree) operations as well as the file data operations (*open,read,write,close*). For managing the namespace, the disk file systems use multiple level indices to keep the metadata for files. For example, in ext2 (and also in many other disk file systems), the inode for a specific file should be retrieved before the data can be accessed. Thus, all the inodes for parent directories including the root directory have to be accessed. This is so called as the directory resolution. Such procedure is quite time consuming, as it will bring a lot of random access on disks. If we want to access large numbers of small files on disks, the directory resolution will bring a lot of overheads. In addition, accessing large number of small files will also bring random access of disks while reading or writing files. In summary, as the distributed file systems rely on the disk file systems to store data on disks, the performance of accessing large amount of small files will not be good. However, distributed file system and disk file system actually have separate namespaces. The metadata in disk file system should not be needed for distributed file systems.

2.2   SepStore Design

All the metadata on disks for disk file systems are in fact not necessary for distributed file systems. The local file is merely the data block for a specific file in distributed file system namespace. The improvement is similar to Haystack[4]: combine multiple small files into one large file for eliminating the metadata of local file systems. A single file on disk will contain multiple small files. Of course, the metadata for each file will still be maintained for distributed file systems in metadata server. For metadata of disk file systems, only the large file metadata is needed in chunkserver. In addition, we use LSM based *key-value* store for storing these files. This data structure uses log instead of in place modification to store the data as for small files the data of whole file will usually accessed at once.

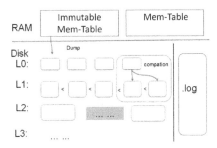

Fig. 1. LevelDB Architecture

Inspired by tablet server in Bigtable[5], LevelDB[2]is an open source embedded *key-value* database featured with Log-structured merge tree (LSM) tree. In LevelDB,every single write is translated to an append of log, then insert into RAM.The data in memory will be flushed to the disk as SSTables that consists of sorted *key-value* pairs asynchronously and periodically. Through this way, the disk seek time can be avoided. As shown in figure 1, SSTables are grouped into different levels with higher level containing more old data and bigger SSTables. SepStore adopts the LevelDB to store data of small files. Thus, the small file storage is separate from the large file storage. This can improve the performance of chunkservers from the following aspects:

1) The first improvement is from the elimination of metadata for large number of small files. Thus, the directory resolution will be simplified. There is no need to find the metadata for each file. The time for directory resolution will be shorten. In addition, this will also reduces the number of system calls. This is especially true for the *open/close* file system calls, as these system calls should be used for each file in disk file systems. When large amount of files are combined together, most of the system calls of *open* or *close* will not be needed. Each system call will cause the hardware to switch the context. Reducing system calls will reduce such costs.

2) Another improvement is from the write pattern of LSM data structure. Small files writes always cause lots of random disk access because of disk fragmentation and data block allocation strategy. By using LSM based *key-value* store, LevelDB can efficiently complete the write of small files by translating random writes into sequential appends to log file. Besides, the LRU cache together with sorted indices on disk avoid the read performance loss of small files.

3   A Prototype System

We have implemented a prototype system based on MooseFS, which uses a GFS-like architecture and exports POSIX interface. In MooseFS, big files are cut into fixed-size chunks and stored across servers while small files are treated as single files on disk file system. As mentioned above, this design could not support small files well.

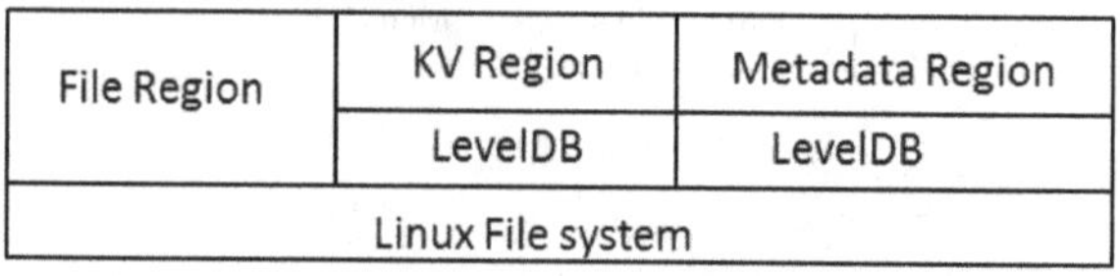

File Region	KV Region	Metadata Region
	LevelDB	LevelDB
Linux File system		

Fig. 2. Chunkserver Structure

As shown in figure 2, LevelDB is embedded in the chunkserver for storing small files as well as the metadata for describing how to find the corresponding data. The chunk server set a size threshold T as the indication for separating big files and small files. T is set to 64KB inferred from our experiments. T can also be adjusted according to real workloads. Files with the size larger than T will be stored in the disk file system directly while smaller files will be put into *key-value* region. Large files might be chunked and consume more than one file in chunkservers according to the rules defined by MooseFS. When the files in *key-value* region reach the size of T, the file will be moved to the disk file system by an asynchronous working thread in the background. Using a dedicated background thread can mitigate the impact of the performance for foreground data serving. Chunkserver supports *read, write* and *delete* operation. Figure 3 shows the steps for processing a write operation.

a) Client will make a write request and ask the location information from the metadata server.
b) The metadata server will decide the corresponding chunkserver for accessing data. If it is a create file operation, the metaserver will allocate a file ID and chunk ID for the file. It replies with the chunk server IPs and ports.
c) The client then send the data to chunkservers. The chunkserver will then try to find the metadata via chunk ID. If a new file has to be created, the chunkserver will decide the location of the file according to the threshold T. The file to be created will be placed in file region when iosize (data size to be written)is bigger than 64KB, otherwise, it will be put into *key-value* region A write job will be generated and put in to the Job Pool.
d) A thread pool is used to perform the jobs in the job pool. The data will either be written to the disk file system or a log appending to the *key-value* store. If this is a write on file region, then the job will be by POSIX API. Otherwise, the thread will finish the job via interfaces provided by LevelDB

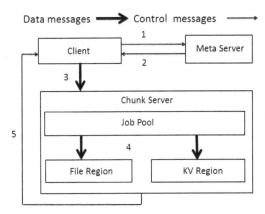

Fig. 3. Write Flow

and a new asynchronous move job will be generated if the chunk is bigger than T after this write.

- Write on File Region. The job will be performed by POSIX API and the CRC will be recalculated.The metadata of the file will be made durable by a background thread.
- Write on the *key-value* Region.The job will be performed by via interfaces provided by LevelDB.If the chunk is larger than T after this write, a new asynchronous move job will be generated.

e) The chunkserver will return the results to the client no matter whether error happens or not. The client implements a retry mechanism and will notify the results to master.

4   Evaluation

4.1   Experiment Setup

We evaluated SepStore on servers with following setup:

Linux   2.6.32-431.5.1.el6.centos.plus.x86_64
CPU   Intel(R) Xeon(R) CPU E5-2609@2.40GHz 4 cores
DRAM   16GB
HARD DISK 24TB (Raid5) 7200 RPM

Three servers are used for the deployment of Moosefs and SepStore. Metadata server and clients are deployed on the same machine while chunkservers are deployed on two other servers. The comparison is between the chunkserver with original ext4 file system and the SepStore accelerated chunkserver. The benchmark used is FileBench[1] and run with cache disabled. Each test result will be the average for 5 runs.

4.2 Write Performance

As SepStore uses LSM like data structure to store data and can performance well under the workload of pure write pattern, we evaluate the write performance using three workloads i.e. small files, big files and small files mixed with big files.

For small write workload, there are about 800,000 files in 500,000 directories. Single thread was used and the iosize was set to the same as file size. Results showed that the improvement was about 210%. For large file write, each test wrote about 400GB of data with iosize set as 1M. As shown in figure 5, the write performances of big files were not degraded in SepStore.

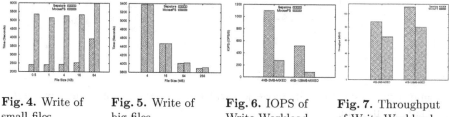

Fig. 4. Write of small files

Fig. 5. Write of big files

Fig. 6. IOPS of Write Workload with mixed size files

Fig. 7. Throughput of Write Workload with mixed size files

In order to evaluate the write performance of mixed file size, we designed a workload that one process for writing small files and another process for writing big files. Each process had 3 threads. The total written size was about 100GB. Figure 6 and figure 7 show the results of different file size. The IOPS of small files were improved by 398% and the throughput was improved by 35% in workloads that consists of 4KB files and 2MB files. The improvement is about 612% and 36.9% for IOPS and throughput respectively when the workload is set to be 4KB writes mixed with 128MB writes.

4.3 Read/Write Performance under Mixed Workloads

We also did the test for mixed workload for *read/write* operations. Figure 8 and Figure 9 shows the results for different configurations. Iosize is set to be 64KB for small files and 1M for big files. For the mixed workloads of 4KB files with 2MB files, IOPS and throughput can be improved by 44% and 79% respectively. For the mixed workloads of 4KB files with 128MB files, the performance will be improved by 37% and 79% for same measurement.

4.4 Application Specific Evaluation

We use varmail and fileserver workloads that are pre-defined in Filebench to evaluate our system for real applications. The file number of varmail was set to be 900000 and the fileserver workload was cofigured with mean-filesize as 16KB

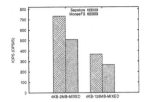
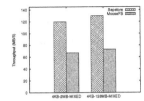
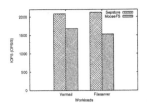
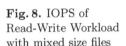

Fig. 8. IOPS of
Read-Write Workload
with mixed size files

Fig. 9. Throughput of
Read-Write Workload
with mixed size files

Fig. 10. Application
Specific Evaluation

and file number as 900000 in our test. As figure 10 shows, the IOPS of varmail
can be improved by 39.7% and the IOPS of fileserver outperforms 24.9%.

4.5 Discussion

As the experiment results show, *key-value* store with LSM structure could improve the performance of small files greatly. It also benefits the workloads mixing
big files access with small files via reducing overall disk seeking. And compared
to the improvement of write performance, the read performance may vary under
different workloads as the read speed of LSM relies heavily on LRU cache.

5   Related Work

Recent distributed file systems have a separate structure for metadata and data
storage[7,17,4],which can greatly improve the system performance and reliability. For improving the performance of distributed file systems, many previous
works focus on the metadata management. In GFS[7], the files are divided into
fixed-size chunks and with the cache in client. Using this schema the number
of interactions of client and metadata server can be greatly reduce. Ceph[17]
does similar work and further separate the decision of how to distribute the data
blocks from the metadata. DHT are also used for load balance among metadata on multiple servers[16,8]. Different from this type of work, SepStore did the
optimization of data storage server (chunkserver) instead of metadata server.

Some of previous works did the work for data access improvement . One way
is to abandon the Posix semantic [7] i.e. release the requirement of consistency.
Haystack[4] optimizes the photo storage for Facebook with only append operations permitted. Other works have done the work of optimization on specific
file types such as optimize the PPT files on HDFS [6]. SepStore is the general
improvement of all types of file systems without losing the Posix semantic.

6   Conclusion

SepStore has used the LSM based *key-value* store, LevelDB, to store the data
for small files in distributed file system. By using such method, SepStore can

avoid the problem of too many *open/close* for in disk file systems as well as the disk seeks for small files. Experiment results show that our method can greatly improve the performance of distributed file systems including the workloads of accessing big files and small files.

Acknowledgments. This work is supported by National Basic Research (973) Program of China(2011CB302505), Natural Science Foundation of China (61373145, 61170210), National High-Tech R&D (863) Program of China (2012AA012600, 2013AA01A213), Chinese Special Project of Science and Technology (2013zx01039-002-002), Ministry of Education-China Mobile Funding (MCM20123021), Ministry of Education-China Mobile Funding: MCM20123021.

References

1. Filebench, http://sourceforge.net/apps/mediawiki/filebench/index.php/
2. Leveldb, https://code.google.com/p/leveldb/
3. Moosefs, http://www.moosefs.org/
4. Beaver, D., Kumar, S., Li, H.C., et al.: Finding a needle in haystack: Facebook's photo storage. In: Proceedings of the 9th Symposium on Operating Systems Design and Implementation (OSDI 2010), vol. 2010, pp. 47–60 (2010)
5. Chang, F., Dean, J., Ghemawat, S., Hsieh, W.C., Wallach, D.A., Burrows, M., Chandra, T., Fikes, A., Gruber, R.E.: Bigtable: A distributed storage system for structured data. ACM Transactions on Computer Systems (TOCS) 26(2), 4 (2008)
6. Dong, B., Qiu, J., Zheng, Q., Zhong, X., Li, J., Li, Y.: A novel approach to improving the efficiency of storing and accessing small files on hadoop: a case study by powerpoint files. In: Proceedings of 7th International Conference on Services Computing (SCC 2010), pp. 65–72. IEEE (2010)
7. Ghemawat, S., Gobioff, H., Leung, S.T.: The google file system. In: Proceedings of the 19th ACM Symposium on Operating Systems Principles (SOSP 2003), pp. 29–43. ACM (2003)
8. Karger, D., Lehman, E., Leighton, T., et al.: Consistent hashing and random trees: Distributed caching protocols for relieving hot spots on the world wide web. In: Proceedings of the 29th Annual ACM Symposium on Theory of Computing (STOC 1997), pp. 654–663. ACM (1997)
9. Mackey, G., Sehrish, S., Wang, J.: Improving metadata management for small files in hdfs. In: IEEE International Conference on Cluster Computing and Workshops, CLUSTER 2009, pp. 1–4. IEEE (2009)
10. O'Neil, P., Cheng, E., Gawlick, D., O'Neil, E.: The log-structured merge-tree (lsm-tree). Acta Informatica 33(4), 351–385 (1996)
11. Ren, K., Gibson, G.: Tablefs: Enhancing metadata efficiency in the local file system. In: Proceedings of 2013 USENIX Annual Technical Conference (2013)
12. Sears, R., Ramakrishnan, R.: blsm: a general purpose log structured merge tree. In: Proceedings of the 2012 ACM SIGMOD International Conference on Management of Data (SIGMOD 2012), pp. 217–228. ACM (2012)
13. Shetty, P., Spillane, R., Malpani, R., et al.: Building workload-independent storage with vt-trees. In: Proccedings of the 11th Conference on File and Storage Technologies, FAST 2013 (2013)

14. Tweedie, S.: Ext3, journaling filesystem. In: Ottawa Linux Symposium (2000)
15. Harter, T., Borthakur, D., Dong, S., et al.: Analysis of hdfs under hbase: A facebook messages case study. In: Proceedings of the 12th USENIX Conference on File and Storage Technologies, FAST 2014 (2014)
16. Weil, S.A., Brandt, S.A., Miller, E.L., Maltzahn, C.: Crush: Controlled, scalable, decentralized placement of replicated data. In: Proceedings of the 2006 ACM/IEEE Conference on Supercomputing (SC 2006), pp. 122–133. ACM (2006)
17. Weil, S.A., Brandt, S.A., et al.: Ceph: A scalable, high-performance distributed file system. In: Proceedings of the 7th Symposium on Operating Systems Design and Implementation (OSDI 2006), pp. 307–320 (2006)

A Mathematic Mobile Cloud Computing System

Tyng-Yeu Liang, You-Jie Li, Ga-Jin He, and Jian-Cheng Liao

Department of Electrical Engineering
National Kaohsiung University of Applied Sciences
Kaohsiung, Taiwan, R.O.C
lty@mail.ee.kuas.edu.tw,
{lyj,hgj,ljc}@hpds.ee.kuas.edu.tw

Abstract. In this paper, we propose a mathematical mobile cloud computing system called M2C. This cloud system allows users to execute MATLAB instructions on their Android-based mobile devices, and take advantage of diverse resources including CPUs and GPUs available in clouds to speed up the execution of their MATLAB applications. On the other hand, M2C supports time sharing on license codes to reduce the waiting time of users, and optimizes resource configurations for maximizing the performance of user applications, and automatically recover system services from faults. Consequently, M2C provides a reliable and efficient service for mobile users to perform data-intensive mathematic computation anytime and anywhere.

Keywords: mobile cloud computing, mobile device, MATLAB, GPU, time-sharing license management, fault tolerance.

1 Introduction

Recently, the kinds of APPs in mobile devices including smart phones and tablets become more and more diverse. Most of PC applications such as Office, Skype and Photoshop have supported a simplified version, i.e., APPs for mobile devices. Consequently, users can do many things in mobile devices as well as in PC by these APPs. Since the mobility of smart phones and tablets is better than that of PCs, mobile devices have become the main equipment for mobile users to handle their daily affairs.

In addition to office APPs, some MATLAB [1]-like APPs such as Addi [2] and Octave [3] recently have appeared in APP store and Android market. Using these APPs, users can perform mathematic computation and simulation of science and engineering in their mobile devices. For mobile scientists and engineers, these APPs enable them to analyze collected data, and make decisions in live to achieve the best time effectiveness. However, it is a pity that these APPs don't support a whole set of MATLAB instructions, and parallel computation like Parallel Computing Toolbox (PCT) [4] of MATLAB. As a result, they cannot completely satisfy user's demands on functions and execution speed. On the other hand, the computational power, memory capability and electricity of mobile devices are relatively smaller than PCs and notebooks. Consequently, they cannot process a large amount of data or compute data for a long time. For this problem, users can take advantage of the APPs of remote

R.C.-H. Hsu and W. Shangguang (Eds.): IOV 2014, LNCS 8662, pp. 282–291, 2014.

desktop to execute MATLAB programs in their office PCs through Internet. However, they must have the license codes of MATLAB and keep their PCs standby. If they want to improve the speed of massive data computation with the PCT of MATLAB, they have to pay additional fee for getting the license of PCT and building a dedicated computing cluster. Obviously, this is not an economic solution for any users.

As previously described, we propose a mathematic mobile cloud computing system called M2C for mobile users in this paper. Users only have to install and execute the APP of M2C on their mobile devices. Then, they can efficiently perform data-intensive mathematic computation and scientific simulation through their mobile devices with exploiting MATLAB software and processors including CPU and GPU [5] in clouds while they need not buy personal software and build their own computing clusters. On the other hand, M2C adopts a time-sharing policy for the management of license codes, and supports the optimization of resource configuration for the execution of user applications. As a result, it can effectively minimize the waiting time of users, achieve fair resource sharing, and enhance the execution performance of user applications without resource wasting. Furthermore, M2C supports automatic system recovery. Therefore, it can deliver a reliable computation service to users.

The rest of this paper is organized as follows. Section 2 discusses related work. Section 3 introduces the framework of M2C. Section 4 discusses the performance evaluation of M2C. Finally, Section 5 gives a brief conclusion for this paper and our future work.

2 Related Work

In recent years, there are several developments in mathematical computing software. For example, MathWorks proposed an APP named as MATLAB Mobile for mobile users. This APP can allow users to submit MATLAB instructions to the data center of MathWorks or user's PCs for execution. No matter where it connects, users have to enter legal license codes, and renew their licenses every year. Although this APP is convenient for MATLAB users, it currently does not support the edition and execution of M-file and parallel computing. Different to MATLAB mobile, Elastic-R [6] provides users with a platform of R and Scilab based on IaaS [7] (infrastructure as a service) such as Amazon EC2 [8] and supports users to create their own working environment by plug-in tools, and to choose proper device combinations and quantities to execute their applications, and release the used resources when they finishes their work. However, Elastic-R is bound to web browsers and have not proposed the APP version.

On the other hand, GPU recently has become an alternative resource for high performance computing. GPU is higher in code density but lower in energy consumption per instruction than CPU. Therefore, more and more researchers change to use GPU clusters for data-intensive computation. According to this trend, some toolkits such as AccelerEyes Jacket [9] and MathWorks GPU-based PCT have been proposed to take advantage of GPU to accelerate the execution of MATLAB. However, these two toolkits are expensive and charged by the number of CPUs and GPUs. Moreover, the maximal number of usable CPUs and GPUs is limited.

Basically, M2C has an interface as same as MATLAB Mobile, and supports the whole instruction set of MATLAB. The difference between M2C and MATLAB Mobile is that the users of M2C need not pay for personal licenses, and they can edit and execute M-file through mobile devices. In addition, the management of license codes in the network version of MATLAB is space sharing. If users don't actively close MATLAB programs, and release the license codes occupied by their programs, other users will not be able to execute their MATLAB programs when no other license code is available. By contrast, M2C uses the way of time sharing to manage license codes. Consequently, it can effectively minimize the time of waiting available license codes for users. On the other hand, Elastic-R let users decide resource configuration by themselves according to their demands. Although it provides users with a flexible way of resource usage, most of users don't have the expertise to decide the best resource configuration for their applications. As a result, users may use too many resources while the performance of their applications is not improved as well as the number of used resources. By contrast, M2C can automatically determine the best of resource configuration for executing MATLAB applications based on the parallelism of instructions and the amount of data. As a consequence, M2C can effectively enhance the execution performance of user MATLAB applications without wasting resources. For parallel computing, M2C have no restriction on the number of used processors while both of PCT and Jacket have this restriction. Finally, M2C supports automatic system recovery from faults while the others either do not consider fault tolerance or rely on the fault recovery of IaaS.

3   Proposed System

Basically, the framework of the proposed system includes M2C APP, MATLAB proxy server, resources manager, license scheduler and server, MATLAB server, and computation server as shown in Fig.1. The user interface of M2C APP is shown in Fig.2. Users can issue instructions in the input field located at the bottom of the window. The top of the window can show the status of users is *offline*, *online* or *running*. The center of the window is used to display the execution result of each instruction. Because the network bandwidth of wireless networks is usually small and not stable, the M2C APP must spend lots of time on receiving the execution results from M2C servers when the size of result data is large. To overcome this problem, the M2C server converts the execution results such as figures or big data arrays into web pages, and returns the hyperlinks connected to the web pages back to the M2C APP. Users can click the hyperlinks appearing in the interface of M2C APP to watch the execution results through web browsers. This display mechanism is specifically designed for mobile devices with low network bandwidths and small LCDs. In addition, the M2C APP currently supports data uploading/downloading, interactive instruction execution, and the editing, saving, loading and executing of M-files.

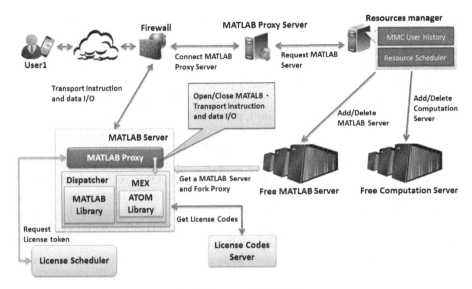

Fig. 1. Framework of M2C

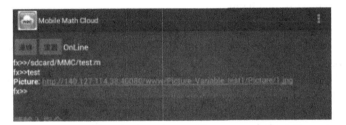

Fig. 2. User interface of M2C

On the other hand, the MATLAB proxy server is responsible to receive the connection requests of users, and ask the resources manager to allocate MATLAB servers for executing MATLAB instructions issued by users. By contrast, the resources manager is aimed at collecting the information and status of resources, and allocating proper MATLAB servers and computation servers for users. Each MATLAB server is used to execute MATLAB proxies and MATLAB programs embedded with the ATOM client for users. The MATLAB proxies are responsible to dispatch the instructions and M-files issued by users into MATLAB programs for execution. The function of ATOM clients is to upload instructions and data onto back-end computational servers for parallel execution. Finally, computation servers are used for massive data computation. Each computation server is hosted by an ATOM server process which is responsible to distribute data over CPUs and GPUs within the computation server for parallel computation. For considering the quality of computation services, each computation servers currently is allowed to serve only one user once.

Basically, the user scenario of M2C is described as follows. When a user intends to make use of M2C services, the user need to execute the APP of M2C on his/her mobile devices to connect with the portal server of M2C. When the portal server receives a connection request from the user, it will ask the resource manager of M2C to select the most lightly-loaded MATLAB server, and will generate a MATLAB proxy dedicated for the user on the allocated MATLAB server. The portal server will return the location information of the created the MATLAB proxy to the M2C APP for connection later. At the same time, the MATLAB proxy will try to get a license token from the license scheduler of M2C, and then fork a MATLAB process on the allocated MATLAB server for executing the instructions of the user. The MATLAB process will wait for executing user instructions after it successfully gets a license code from the license server of MATLAB. By contrast, the MATLAB proxy will start to receive user instructions and dispatch the instructions to the forked MATLAB process for execution. After the instructions are finished, the MATLAB proxy will fetch the execution results from the MATLAB process and then will return the execution results back to the M2C APP. When the user wants to speed up data computation, he/she can make use of M2C instructions to upload data from the MATLAB process to back-end computational servers for parallel computing.

The rest of this section will be focused on license management, fault tolerance and parallel computing in M2C.

3.1   License Management

To prevent idle clients from holding license codes, most of system administrators exploit network monitors to automatically break the connection links between clients and servers if there is no data transmission in the connection links for a given time period. Although this method is useful for minimizing the waiting time of the users who need license codes, it is not effective enough for fair resource sharing. The worse is that users lose their program contexts after their connection links are broken, and they have to re-execute their programs from the beginning.

As previously discussed, M2C uses a time-sharing policy for the management of license codes. This policy is aimed at minimizing the average waiting time of users, and enabling user to fairly share diverse resources including software, hardware and license codes. In order to achieve this goal, we develop a license scheduler which is responsible to distribute license tokens to MATLAB proxies, and let MATLAB proxies maintain the program contexts of users. Before the MATLAB proxy of each user creates a MATLAB process, it asks the license scheduler for getting a license token. The license scheduler checks whether the number of used license codes has reached to the maximal availability. If the answer is yes, the license scheduler appends this token request into a waiting queue, and the MATLAB proxy is blocked until some license code is released. Otherwise, the license scheduler returns a license token with an expiring date for the MATLAB proxy. After receiving the license token, the MATLAB proxy creates a MATLAB process. This MATLAB process will get a license code from the formal license server of MATLAB first, and then start to accept and execute user instructions relayed from the MATLAB proxy.

When the license token expires, the MATLAB proxy will request the license scheduler to extend the expiring date of the token first. The license scheduler will check whether some users are waiting for license codes or not. If there is no waiting user, the license scheduler will accept the request and will return a new license token with extending expiring date. Then, the requesting MATLAB proxy can continue to receive user instructions and dispatch the instructions to the MATLAB process for execution. Otherwise, it will store the program context of the user, and will closes the MATLAB process immediately to release its holding license code for other waiting users. To avoid wasting the utilization of license codes, the MATLAB proxy will not request a new license token from the license scheduler until it receives a new instruction from the user. In order to shorten the time of context recovery, M2C uses an on-demand way for dispatching data into the MATLAB process. That is, a data is not sent into the MATLAB process until it is necessary for the execution of instructions. Since the MATLAB proxy plays an I/O bridge between the client and the MATLAB process, it caches the newest copy of each data accessed by the MATLAB process into a hash table. As a result, the time cost of storing user's program context can be effectively minimized. By the mechanism previously described, M2C can effectively reduce the average waiting time of users, and make users fairly share resources without involving system administrators while it can simultaneously maintains the license contract which limits the number of users who can execute MATLAB at the same time. Moreover, the users can continue the execution of their programs from the breakpoints instead of the beginnings.

Basically, the time of waiting for a license codes is depended on the number of requesting users and the number of available license codes. In fact, it is impossible for M2C to perform context switch without any cost when a time slice is expired. In addition, the instruction scheduling of M2C is non-preemptive. In other words, the MATLAB proxy cannot perform context switch unless the execution of the last instruction issued to MATLAB is finished even when the time slice is expired. However, the cost of context switch and the delay of doing context switch are not a constant. To simplify our work, we omit these factors in estimating the time cost of waiting for license codes. Accordingly, the average time of waiting license codes theoretically can be estimated as follows. Assume k is the number of users, L is the number of license codes, and T is the length of a time slice. For the i-th user, his/her waiting time is $\lfloor \frac{i-1}{L} \rfloor *T$. As a result, the total waiting time of k users is $\sum_{i=1}^{k} \lfloor \frac{i-1}{L} \rfloor * T$, and the average waiting time is shown as follows.

$$\text{Average waiting time} = (\sum_{i=1}^{k} \lfloor \frac{i-1}{L} \rfloor * T)/k. \tag{1}$$

This equation shows that the average waiting time is increased as linearly as k (when k is large enough) and T. The service providers of M2C can make use of this equation to decide if it is necessary to increase the number of license codes for committing the requirement of QoS.

3.2   Fault Tolerance

The fault tolerance of M2C is currently focused on maintaining the contexts of user MATLAB programs, and keeping users be served until they actively close the service connections with their MATLAB proxies. To achieve this purpose, each MATLAB proxy logs the new update of hash table into disks whenever a user instruction is finished. On the other hand, the resource manager monitors the states of all the MATLAB proxies in each server. If it detects the MATLAB server of some user is crashed, it will create a new MATLAB proxy for the user first, and will notify the user's M2C APP of this event with the location information of the new MATLAB proxy as shown in Fig.3. The APP can actively build a connection with the new MATLAB proxy by using the received location information. By contrast, the new MATLAB proxy will rebuild the previous program context of the user in its hash table with the logs, and will generate a new MATLAB process because the old one has been destroyed after the old MATLAB proxy crashed. After building the connection with the user's APP, it can start to accept and dispatch the instructions coming from the user to the new MATLAB process for execution. If MATLAB proxy finds the MATLAB process is dead, it will also create a new one and will resend the last instruction to the new one for execution.

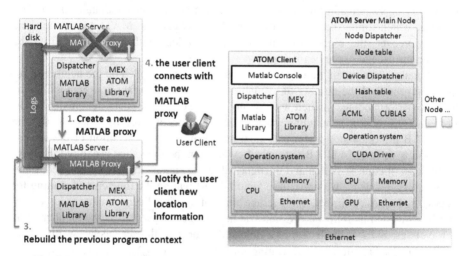

Fig. 3. Process of system recovery   **Fig. 4.** Framework of ATOM

3.3   Parallel Computing

Because of considering cost and scalability, we have developed an acceleration toolkit called ATOM [10] for supporting parallel computation in M2C. This toolkit can support hybrid CPU/GPU cluster computing, and load balance. When users intend to accelerate data computation, they only need to change the type of data to *ksingle* by the ksingle() command of M2C. When MATLAB executes an instruction with *ksingle*-type operands, it automatically calls the ATOM library to offload this instruction and the operands to back-end computation servers for execution. The offloading procedure is described as follow. First, the ATOM client will ask the resource manager to allocate free computation servers. The resource manager will perform a resource-pruning algorithm to obtain the best server configuration and work distribution for the instruction according to the type of instructions and the problem size of the instructions. Next, it will allocate the computation servers which are listed in the server configuration for the MATLAB process. The MATLAB process will upload the instruction and data to the root of the allocated computational servers, and wait for the execution result. The root computation server will relay the instruction to the others, and distribute data over all the allocated servers for parallel computing according to the pattern of work distribution. After all the computation servers finish their jobs, the root computation server will gather the execution results of all the servers, and send the collective result back to the MATLAB process.

Basically, the components of ATOM include Hash table, node dispatcher, and device dispatcher as shown in Fig.4. Hash Table is used to store variable data. Node dispatcher takes care of relaying the instructions and distributing tasks over computational servers. Device dispatcher is responsible to distribute the data received over CPUs and GPUs within each computation server for parallel computing. Because the ability of computational devices is not identical, node dispatcher and device dispatcher distribute data based on the computational power of each server and device for achieving load balance. As to ACML [11] and CUBLAS [12], they are used for implementing the CPU and GPU versions of MATLAB instructions, respectively. Because the development time is too short, ATOM currently supports parallel computation only for the instructions including mtimes, plus, minus, scal, mldivide, polyval, cov, idct, svd, linsolve, rank, gradient, inv, and pinv.

4   Performance Evaluation

Our experimental environment consisted of one mobile device, and one M2C MATLAB server and four computational servers. The mobile device is a Samsung GT-P6810 tablet computer. The MATLAB server is a PC which has one Intel Core 2 CPU 1.86 GHz and 2GB RAM. Each computational server is a PC with one Intel Core2 CPU 1.86 GHz, and 2 GB RAM, and one graphic card of GeForce GTX 550.

As show in Fig.5, Octave calculates data for a long time because the computational power of the mobile device is too small. In contrast, M2C can provide larger computational power than the mobile device. Consequently, M2C can effectively shorten the computation time of MATLAB instructions through either Wi-Fi or 3G. This result proves that M2C indeed can satisfy the demand of large computational power of mobile users, and can resolve the problem of insufficient resource in mobile devices.

On the other hand, the performance of parallel computing in M2C is shown in Fig.6. The resource configurations decided by M2C for these instructions are listed in Table 1. Compared with the MATLAB server, the experimental result shows that offloading data to ATOM for parallel computing is useful for improving the execution performance of high-complexity instructions such as mtimes, mdivide, polyval, svd, rank, inv, pinv, and linsolve because ATOM exploited the GPUs of the computational servers for data computation. By contrast, the resource pruning algorithm predicted using Intel Core 2 CPU is better than using GeFource GTX550 for the low-complexity instructions including plus, minus, scal, cov, gradient, and idct. Although not all the performance of these instructions is improved by ATOM, M2C does not waste the computational power of extra CPUs or GeForce GTX 550. The above experimental result shows that M2C indeed can enhance the performance of user applications while it can simultaneously avoid resource wasting. Moreover, we installed Linux-version Octave on the same machine which plays the MATLAB server for executing these instructions. It can be found that Octave does not support some instructions such as idct and linsolve. Octave is better than MATLAB for mldivide, svd, rank, gradient, and inv while it is worse for mtimes, cov, and pinv. By contrast, ATOM is superior over Octave for all the test instructions.

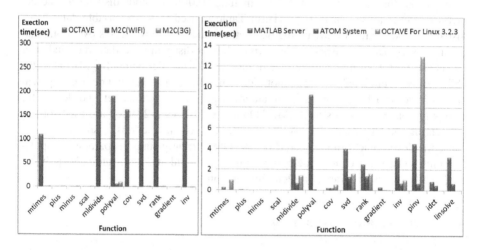

Fig. 5. Performance comparison between M2C and Octave

Fig. 6. Performance of ATOM

Table 1. Resource configuration for tested instructions

instruction	configuration	instruction	configuration
mtimes	1 GPU	svd	1 GPU
plus	1 CPU	rank	1 GPU
minus	1 CPU	gradient	1 CPU
scal	1 CPU	inv	2 GPU
mldivide	2 GPU	pinv	2 GPU
polyval	3 GPU	idct	1 CPU
cov	1CPU	linsolve	1 GPU

5   Conclusions and Future Work

In this paper, we have successfully developed a mathematic mobile cloud computing system called M2C. With the support of M2C, users can take advantage of software and hardware resources in cloud centers for performing mathematical computation and simulation on their mobile devices anywhere and anytime while they invest nothing on buying personal software and constructing dedicated computing clusters. Therefore, M2C provides a convenient, economical and effective solution for users to do a huge size of mathematical data computation on mobile devices. On the other hand, the proxy mechanism and the time-sharing management scheme proposed in this paper can automatically backup and recover the contexts of user's programs, and can make users fairly share cloud resources, and minimize the idle time of resources. Consequently, M2C can effectively provide a reliable working environment and maintain an acceptable QoS for users without involving system managers. The proposed mechanism and scheme also can be applied to other software services in order for increasing the QoS and resource utilization of a whole data center.

In future, we will continue to implement more parallel MATLAB instructions for M2C, and will develop a browser interface for users to use the services of M2C in general computers such as PCs, workstations and notebooks. On the other hand, we will study how to adapt resource provision based on dynamic load states for maintaining the QoS of M2C with the most energy efficiency.

Acknowledgment. This work is supported by National Science Council of Republic of China under the research project numbered as NSC-102-2815-C-151-010-E.

References

1. MathWorks, MATLAB – The language of technical computing, `http://www.mathworks.com/products/matlab`
2. Google Project Hosting, addi–Matlab/Octave clone for Android, `https://code.google.com/p/addi`
3. Eaton, J.W.: GUN Octave, `http://www.gnu.org/software/octave/index.html`
4. MathWork, Parallel Computing Toolbox, `http://www.mathworks.com/products/parallel-computing/?s_cid=sol_compbio_sub2_relprod4_parallel_computing_toolbox`
5. Owens, J.D., Luebke, D., Govindaraju, N., Harris, M., Krüger, J., Lefohn, A.E., Purcell, T.J.: A Survey of General-Purpose Computation on Graphics Hardware. Computer Graphics Forum, 80–113 (2007)
6. Chine, K.: Learning math and statistics on the cloud, towards an EC2-based Google Docs-like portal for teaching/learning collaboratively with R and Scilab. In: 10th IEEE International Conference on Advanced Learning Technologies, pp. 752–753 (2010)
7. Gallagher, P.D.: The NIST definition of cloud computing. National Institute of Standards and Technology, `http://csrc.nist.gov/publications/nistpubs/800-145/SP800-145.pdf`
8. Amazon, Amazon Elastic Compute Cloud, `https://aws.amazon.com/ec2/`
9. AccelerEyes, ArrayFire software library, `http://www.accelereyes.com`
10. Liang, T.-Y., Wu, J.-K., Chen, Y.-C.: An Acceleration Toolkit of MATLAB based on Hybrid CPU/GPU Clusters. In: Proceedings of IEEE 16th Conference on Computer Science and Engineering, pp. 50–57 (2013)
11. AMD Group, Core Math Library (ACML), `http://developer.amd.com/tools/cpu-development/amd-core-math-library-acml`
12. NVIDIA, CUDA toolkit document, `http://docs.nvidia.com/cuda/cublas/index.htm`

SafeBrowsingCloud: Detecting Drive-by-Downloads Attack Using Cloud Computing Environment

Haibo Zhang, Chaoshun Zuo, Shanqing Guo, Lizhen Cui, and Jun Chen

Shandong University,
Shunhua Road, Jinan, P.R. China
{guoshanqing,clz,jchen}@sdu.edu.cn,
gsq_cy@163.com, guosq2002@hotmail.com

Abstract. Drive-by downloads attack has become the primary attack vehicle for malware distribution in recent years. One existing method of detecting drive-by download attacks is using static analysis technique. However, static detection methods are vulnerable to sophisticated obfuscation and cloaking. Dynamic detection methods are proposed to overcome the shortcomings of static analysis techniques and can get a higher detection rate. But dynamic anomaly detection methods are typically resource intensive and introduce high time overhead. To improve performance of dynamic detection techniques, we designed SafeBrowingCloud, a system based on apache S4, a distributed computing platform. And the system is deployed at edge router. SafeBrowingCloud analyzes network traffic, executes webpages in firefox with modified javascript engine, abstracts javascript strings and detects shellcode with three shellcode detection methods to find malicious web pages. Experimental results show efficiency of the proposed system with the high-speed network traffic.

Keywords: Drive-by download, Apache S4, Shellcode, Cloud.

1 Introduction

Drive-by download attack is one of the main vectors used to spread malware. In a drive-by download attack, an attacker first presents a web page including malicious code which tries to exploit a vulnerability in the victim's browser or in a browser plugin. When a web visitor browses the malicious web page, the injected code instructs the victim's computer to download and install malicious software. The installed malware often enables an attacker to control a user's computer and steal sensitive information.

To protect users from drive-by download attack while browsing the Internet, several methods for detecting malicious web pages have been proposed. One existing malicious web page detection technique involves the use of what are known as a static detection technique, which uses data mining and machine learning technique[1,5,7]. The detection time of static detection methods is faster than that of dynamic detection methods but the detection rate is lower due

R.C.-H. Hsu and W. Shangguang (Eds.): IOV 2014, LNCS 8662, pp. 292–303, 2014.

to sophisticated obfuscation and cloaking[3]. To overcome the shortcomings of static detection method, dynamic detection technique is proposed[13], which run the scripts associated with web pages on a virtual machine to detect if the page is malicious. The main idea of these systems is to monitor a computer system for anomalous changes during the rendering of a web page such as changes to the file system, registry information or creation of processes. The dynamic detection method can get a higher detection rate than the static method. [2,9]. Dynamic detection technique can conquer some drawbacks of the static detection and the detection rate is higher than static method. However, most dynamic techniques are typically resource intensive and introduce high time overhead, making these approaches difficult to deploy as online detectors [3].Therefore, dynamic detection is not very applicable to large scale, real time classification[2], especially to complete the analysis of the flow of hundreds of megabytes by intrusion detection equipment[12], not to mention on Gigabit network traffic.

Traditional methods either distribute a security software for users to install or analyze webpages offline. Not every user would like to install a third party software. And offline analysis can't achieve realtime protection for drive-by download attack. To protect hosts from drive-by download attack, we would implement protection at edge router.

To protect from Drive-by downloads attack at edge router, the system should be able to analyze high speed network traffic, get http requests, load the webpages and detect shellcode when javascript executing. The scale of a network can change from several to thousands.One scalable system is necessary to accomplish above jobs, which can adjust its process capacity according to the network's scalability. To detect malious webpage as soon as possible,the system should have good real-time processing capacity. To this end, we implemented our method on Apache S4, a distributed stream processing platform.

Paper Organization. The rest of this paper is organized as follows. Section 2 presents our system design and implementation. Section 3 evaluates SafeBrowsingCloud's performance. Section 4 reviews related works. Section 5 concludes.

2   System

In this section, we proposed SafeBrowsingCloud, a cloud platform used for filtering web-based attack as users visit a web page. We intend the system to act as a first layer of defence against web-based attack.

We show the overall architecture of SafeBrowsingCloud in Figure 1. There are five kinds of nodes in SafeBrowsingCloud:the adapter node, the processing node, the zookeeper node, storage node and idle node. The adapter nodes are responsible for receiving router network traffic and dispatching http packets to processing nodes. The processing nodes hold the PEs to process data. The zookeeper node monitors the status of the system, reports node failures, and records system running statistics. The idle nodes are running as stand-by nodes. Once a node happens to crash, an idle node would take the place of it and take over its function. The storage node stores blacklist, whitelist and third party engine database. Here the third party engine database stores malicious and legitimate URLs provided by third party engine,like google safe browsing service and so on.This database would update periodically.

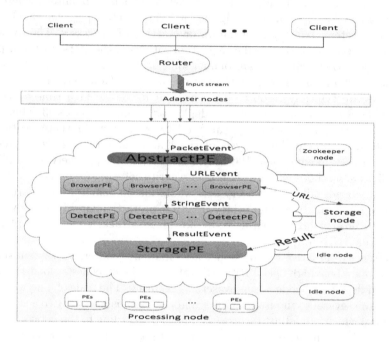

Fig. 1. System Architecture

The processing node processes data by internal PEs. We design four kinds of PE, including AbstractPE, BrowserPE, DetectPE and StoragePE.Every kind of PE is responsible for processing one kind of Event. And the Events are designed as Table 1. The AbstractPE analyzes network data packets, abstracts URL from http request and emits URLEvent which includes the URL. BrowserPE receives a URLEvent, visits each URL by firefox with modified spidermonkey, to collect the strings produced by running the javascript embedded in the web pages, and emit StringEvents. The DetectPE receives a StringEvent, detects if the string is a shellcode and emits ResultEvent. The StoragePE receives a ResultEvent and updates the database in the StoragePE node. SafeBrowsingCloud's final decision is returned to the party that submitted the URL; they can then take appropriate action based on their application, such as displaying a warning that users can click through, or deleting the content that contained the URL entirely. We now give an overview of each PE in this workflow.

2.1   AbstractPE

The AbstractPE is mainly responsible for analyzing network traffic to abstract URLs. We abstract the TCP socket (source IP:source port,destination IP:

Table 1. Events in SafeBrowsingCloud

Event type	Key-Value pair	Event entity
PacketEvent	null	byte array including network data packet
URLEvent	"url",http request url	URL,socket,timestamp
StringEvent	"url",url that produced the string	URL,javascript string
ResultEvent	null	URL,malicious or legitimate,timestamp

destination port), request time and url to record users' http requests history. The url would be submitted to BrowserPE for analyzing the webpage if malicious.

2.2 BrowserPE

For a drive-by attack to succeed, it is important that the shellcode is loaded into memory and interpreted as valid x86 instructions. In javascript,the only way to storing shellcode is by using a string variable.

To detect the shellcode that a malicious script might construct on the heap, we have to keep track of all string variables that the program allocates[2]. To this end, we modified spidermonkey, the JavaScript engine used by Firefox. In javascript, there are mainly three kinds of string operation, including string initialization, string concatenating and string spliting. As strings in JavaScript are immutable, all three kinds of manipulation would lead to string being created in a new memory area. We just need to add code to all points where a new string is created in spidermonkey. To implement string operations, spidermonkey organizes some string classes into a single inheritance hierarchy. For each string in JavaScript, there is a corresponding instance of JSString, the base string class in spidermonkey. Each concrete class corresponds to a particular implementation of JSString. For instance, JSRope is optimized to represent concatenated strings, and JSDependentString to represent substrings. The SpiderMonkey API provides corresponding functions that can be used to create instance of concrete class of JSString. For example, JSNewStringCopyN and JSNewStringCopyZ are used to create instances of JSFixedString. We would track these functions and abstract created strings. Besides, we need to tell which web page produces the string. In spidermonkey, the cx variable of JSContext type contains the html location information.Once a string is created, the string along with the web page url would be both put in a StringEvent.

The BrowserPE first query the database of the storage node if the url has been detected before. If the url has existed in the database, then the BrowserPE does nothing. Otherwise, it would execute the web page with received url, trace the javascript string variables and put them in StringEvent with the url.

2.3 DetectPE

In computer security, a shellcode is a small piece of code used as the payload in the exploitation of a software vulnerability. To evade exploit detection, polymorphic or metamorphic technique is applied to shellcode, which creates a polymorphic shellcode.

Shellcode detection methods can be classified by the shellcode part they detect[4]. There are NOP-sled detection, decryption routine detection, shellcode payload detection and return address zone detection methods.Every detection method has its advantage and disadvantage. NOP-sled detection method has a higher detection speed than other methods. However, NOP-sled may be missing in advanced exploit code and NOP-sled detection method would become invalid. Decryption routine detection method can detect polymorphic shellcode with higher detection rate than other methods. In consideration of decryption routine detection method focusing on decryption routine detection, it would perform badly on typical common shellcode which doesn't have decryption routine.Shellcode payload detection method would have a higher detection rate on detecting typical common shellcode while it's not able to detect polymorphic shellcode well.Given the three methods' feature, we adopt all of them to detect shellcode.

The DetectPE is just a general term of PE that detect shellcode in SafeBrowsingCloud. We designed three kinds of DetectPE, including NOPSledPE, DecryptionPE and PayloadPE to implement above three shellcode detection methods respectively.

The NOPSledPE implements the Racewalk[4] algorithm proposed by Dennis Gamayunov et al. to detect shellcode by NOP-sled. Racewalk proposed a novel approach for NOP-sled detection using IA-32 instruction frequency analysis and SVM-based classification. The method is based on the fact that Intel instructions frequency characteristics for NOP-zones is different from normal data. It first analyzes sequence using cache, pruning techniques and Disassembly prefix tree to reduce computational complexity and then implements SVM classification to reduce the false positives rate.Analysis rate over 600 Mbit/sec using single CPU core allows to use Racewalk algorithm for gigabit network.

The DecryptionPE implements the method proposed by Qinghua Zhang et al. to detect self-decrypting exploit code[14]. The method detects the presence of a decryption routine,which is a characteristic of polymorphic shellcode. It uses static analysis and emulated instruction execution techniques to find the starting location and identify the instructions of the polymorphic exploit code. In addition, it can detect polymorphic exploit code that is self-modifying and that do not have a NOP-sled, which static analysis has previously been unable to detect. Its detection speed is roughly linear to stings' length and amount.The current implementation achieves a speed more than 10M/s.

The PayloadPE implements the SigFree[12], a signature-free buffer overflow attack blocker proposed by Xinran Wang et al.. SigFree first blindly dissembles and extracts instruction sequences from a request. It then applies a novel technique called code abstraction, which uses data flow anomaly to prune useless instructions in an instruction sequence. Finally it compares the number of useful instructions to a threshold to determine if this instruction sequence contains code.SigFree is signature free, thus it can block new and unknown buffer overflow attacks.

In consideration of three DetectPEs' detection speed and shellcode structure, one coming string would be first detected by NOPSledPE. If NOPSledPE determines the string malicious, result would be sent to StoragePE. Otherwise, the string is submitted both to DecryptionPE and PayloadPE to be detected.

There are a large number of DetectPE instances in one processing node to detect shellcode.The DetectPE instances will be automatically removed from the cache once a fixed duration has elapsed after the PEs creation, or last access.

2.4 StoragePE

StoragePE processes the ResultEvent ,which contains the url, malicious or legitimate and the timestamp when the string is detected.The url is default stored in whitelist. Once a malicious ResultEvent is received, the url would be put in blacklist. The StoragePE would detect the blacklist and whitelist periodically. If one record's timestamp exceeds one threshold, the StoragePE would emit an URLEvent with the url to BrowserPE to update the record.

3 Evaluation

This section discusses how we evaluated our prototype as well as the experimental results. The evaluation was carried out in three parts. First we described our experimental setting. Second, we evaluated our system performance, including processing speed and system overhead. Third, we evaluated our system for false positives by accessing a large number of popular benign web pages and we used our system on pages that launch drive-by downloads and evaluated the detection effectiveness.

3.1 Experimental Setting

As shown in figure 1, our datasets come from personal computers' browsing records distributed in our campus. We captured the network packets and then abstracted urls. We make use of firefox to execute one url and modified firefox's javascript engine spidermonkey. Once a string object is produced in spidermoneky, it will be sent to SafeBrowsingCloud for being detected. In our experiment, there is an important parameter, url count that are executed at one time in firefox. We set a threshold of tab count in consideration of local servers' network environment and firefox's procesing capacity. In firefox, we write one extension to monitoring tabs behavior. The extension would notify SafeBrowsingCloud the tab count while tabs count changes and close the tab which has loaded over the url. We implemented the experiment of SafeBrowsingCloud for a small deployment consisting of 5 instances on the infrastructure in our network center. The SafeBrowsingCloud runs on the same infrastructure with four Intel Xeon 3.06 GHz CPU and 2 GB RAM. The computer is connected to a university campus network through 100 Mbps Ethernet;it runs Centos 6.4 Linux with kernel version 2.6.32.

3.2 Processing Performance

In this part, we evaluated the processing capacity of SafeBrowsingCloud. The evaluation was carried out in two parts. First, we tested processing speed. Second, we tested the whole system's overhead.

Processing Speed. To evaluate processing speed of the SafeBrowsingCloud system, we deployed the processing cluster with one to five processing nodes and recorded the maximum number of processed urls per hour respectively. And the result is shown in figure 2. It can be observed that the processing speed of SafeBrowsingCloud is approximately linear to the number of processing nodes, which demonstrated the scalability of SafeBrowsingCloud. To evaluate how many processing nodes are needed at least to process the campus network traffic, we analyzed the http request during one week. After one week analysis, we found at peak time the whole campus produced 11,000 distinct url per hour while it produced less than one thousand per hour when clients are not active. From figure 2, we can see with five processing nodes,the system is able to process the url in time at peak time. If http request speed becomes higher, we just need to add processing nodes. We only detect once for duplicated request. The system would detect one url again once duration between now and last processed time exceeds one threshold at idle time.

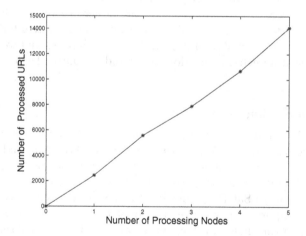

Fig. 2. Processing speed

Experiment Overhead. To evaluate the performance of SafeBrowsingCloud, we also tested its overhead, including cpu, memory and throughout of every processing node. The results are shown in figure 3, figure 4 and figure 5 respectively. It can be observed that the overhead changes of five processing nodes is similar, which demonstrated the SafeBrowsingCloud is decentralized and every processing node is equal. In addition, we periodically dump system running statistics

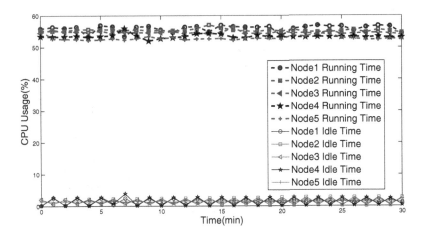

Fig. 3. CPU overhead

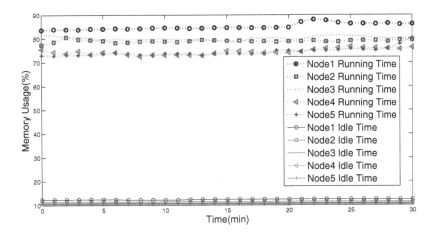

Fig. 4. Memory overhead

to logs using the metrics library, which offers an efficient way to gather such information and relies on statistical techniques to minimize memory consumption. During the running time, we found not events loss, which means all packets get processed and every javascript string is detected in time by our detecting classifiers.Observed from figure 3 and figure 4, memory and CPU is not made full use of. It is the firefoxPE that leads to it. As described before, we set a threshold in firefox to decide whether to request a url. The threshold is determined by network environment and firefox's processing capacity. With better network,the processing node would be able to process more urls per hour and the whole SafeBrowsingCloud would get a higher processing speed.

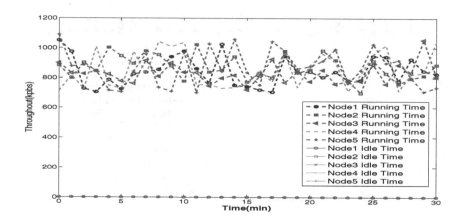

Fig. 5. Network throughout

3.3   Detecting Accuracy

False Positive Evaluation. In the context of our system, a false positive is a page that is detected as malicious without actually loading shellcode to memory. To evaluate the likelihood of false positives, we extended our prototype system to visit a list of k = 1000 known, benign pages. These pages were taken from the Alexa ranking of global top-sites, and simply consisted of the top k pages. We consider this to be a realistic test set that reflects a wide range of web applications and categories of content. For the batch evaluation of URLs, we implemented a Firefox extension that visits all URLs provided in a file. After last URL loaded over, the extension automatically visits the next URL in the list.Our prototype did not produce any false positives for this dataset. This might look suspicious at a first glance: The x86 instruction set is known to be densely packed, thus, almost any sequence of bytes makes up valid instructions. However, one has to consider the fact that JavaScript uses 16-bit Unicode characters to store text. That is, even if a given sequence of ASCII characters results in a valid x86 instruction most of the time, the JavaScript representation of the same characters most likely does not, since every other byte would contain the value 0x0. Of course, an attacker can encode the shellcode appropriately. However, benign pages typically do not contain strings that map to valid instruction sequences.

Detection Effectiveness. In a next step, we evaluated the capabilities of our technique to identify drive-by attacks that rely on shellcode to perform their malicious actions. To this end, we first collected 50 plain malicious shellcodes from the Internet and the Metasploit Framework, a powerful open source framework for the construction and execution of exploits. Based on the plain shellcodes, we generated 1000 polymorphic shellcodes by using Metaspoit Framwork and two off-the-shelf polymorphic engines:ADMmutate and Clet. We then create

1000 javascript codes that generate these malicious shellcodes at runtime. With above malicious javascript codes we created 1000 malicious webpages. We put these malicious webpages on our internal Web server. We used the aforementioned Firefox extension visiting all the URLs provided in a filed. And the our system correctly labeled them as malicious urls.

4 Related Work

Since drive-by download attack came out, several methods have been proposed to mitigate the threat. Efficiency and effectiveness are two main target in detection of drive-by download attack. Given different efficiency, these methods can be used in offline solutions or realtime solutions.

4.1 Off-line Solutions

Webpage content analysis is one technique used in off-line solutions to detect malicious webpages. Seifert et al.[10] proposed high interaction client honeypots to monitor the entire operating system, including a web browser, using a virtual machine. When a malicious page is loaded in browser, unexpected system state changes would happen.

To improve efficiency of off-line solutions, Seifert et al.[11] present an algorithmic approach by batch processing multiple web pages simultaneously. When multiple pages is found in a batch, it would use static analysis to find benign web pages and eliminate them first, thus reducing the number of pages to be detected.

Off-line solutions tend to be resource intensive and introduce long latency. Thus, off-line solutions are not suitable for realtime detection of drive-by download attacks.

4.2 Realtime Solutions

Now realtime solutions are mainly embedded in the web browser.

Lu et al.[8] proposed a BLADE system, that creates a non-executable sandbox to prevent any binary file to execute without explicit user intervention.

Jayasinghe et al.[6] proposed a novel approach to detect drive-by downloads in web browser environment using low resource dynamic analysis. By dynamically monitoring the bytecode stream generated by a web browser during rendering, the approach is able to detect drive-by download attack at runtime.

Ratanaworabhan et al.[9] proposed NOZZLE that detect shellcode in the memory heap using NOP sled detection to detect drive-by download attacks.

Above realtime detection techniques can improve efficiency of detection of drive-by download attacks. Realtime solutions are mainly embedded in the web browser to get realtime information like javascript objects, files, bytecode stream and so on. They make use of the realtime information to detect malicious page. Our solution is similar to NOZZLE, which detects drive-by download attacks by detecting shellcode. Given that not all users would like to accept a third party browser which would introduce latency inevitably, we implemented our solutions at edge router. To process high speed network traffic, we designed our solutions on apache S4, a distributed computing platform.It avoids duplicate detection and detects malicious pages quickly.A page detection database is built that can be used by others like a http proxy to intercept drive-by download attacks.

5 Conclusions

In this paper, we designed SafeBrowsingCloud, a system used to detect drive-by download attack. In doing so, we analyzed network traffic, modified spidermonkey to abstract javascript strings and designed a shellcode detector. SafeBrowsingCloud is implemented based on apache S4, a distributed computing platform. The experiment demonstrates that our system can detect drive-by download attack with high efficiency and provide a safe browsing service at edge router.

References

1. Bannur, S.N., Saul, L.K., Savage, S.: Judging a site by its content: learning the textual, structural, and visual features of malicious web pages. In: Proceedings of the 4th ACM Workshop on Security and Artificial Intelligence, pp. 1–10. ACM (2011)
2. Egele, M., Wurzinger, P., Kruegel, C., Kirda, E.: Defending browsers against drive-by downloads: Mitigating heap-spraying code injection attacks. In: Flegel, U., Bruschi, D. (eds.) DIMVA 2009. LNCS, vol. 5587, pp. 88–106. Springer, Heidelberg (2009)
3. Eshete, B., Villafiorita, A., Weldemariam, K.: Malicious website detection: Effectiveness and efficiency issues. In: 2011 First SysSec Workshop (SysSec), pp. 123–126. IEEE (2011)
4. Gamayunov, D., Quan, N., Sakharov, F., Toroshchin, E.: Racewalk: fast instruction frequency analysis and classification for shellcode detection in network flow. In: 2009 European Conference on Computer Network Defense (EC2ND), pp. 4–12. IEEE (2009)
5. Hou, Y.-T., Chang, Y., Chen, T., Laih, C.-S., Chen, C.-M.: Malicious web content detection by machine learning. Expert Systems with Applications 37(1), 55–60 (2010)
6. Jayasinghe, G.K., Shane Culpepper, J., Bertok, P.: Efficient and effective realtime prediction of drive-by download attacks. Journal of Network and Computer Applications 38, 135–149 (2014)
7. Likarish, P., Jung, E., Jo, I.: Obfuscated malicious javascript detection using classification techniques. In: 2009 4th International Conference on Malicious and Unwanted Software (MALWARE), pp. 47–54. IEEE (2009)
8. Lu, L., Yegneswaran, V., Porras, P., Lee, W.: Blade: an attack-agnostic approach for preventing drive-by malware infections. In: Proceedings of the 17th ACM Conference on Computer and Communications Security, pp. 440–450. ACM (2010)
9. Ratanaworabhan, P., Livshits, V.B., Zorn, B.G.: Nozzle: A defense against heap-spraying code injection attacks. In: USENIX Security Symposium, pp. 169–186 (2009)

10. Seifert, C., Komisarczuk, P., Welch, I.: True positive cost curve: A cost-based evaluation method for high-interaction client honeypots. In: Third International Conference on Emerging Security Information, Systems and Technologies, SECURWARE 2009, pp. 63–69. IEEE (2009)
11. Seifert, C., Welch, I., Komisarczuk, P.: Application of divide-and-conquer algorithm paradigm to improve the detection speed of high interaction client honeypots. In: Proceedings of the 2008 ACM Symposium on Applied Computing, pp. 1426–1432. ACM (2008)
12. Wang, X., Pan, C.-C., Liu, P., Zhu, S.: Sigfree: A signature-free buffer overflow attack blocker. IEEE Transactions on Dependable and Secure Computing 7(1), 65–79 (2010)
13. Wang, Y.-M., Niu, Y., Chen, H., Beck, D., Jiang, X., Roussev, R., Verbowski, C., Chen, S., King, S.: Strider honeymonkeys: Active, client-side honeypots for finding malicious websites (2007), http://research.microsoft.com/users/shuochen/HM.PDF
14. Zhang, Q., Reeves, D.S., Ning, P., Iyer, S.P.: Analyzing network traffic to detect self-decrypting exploit code. In: Proceedings of the 2nd ACM Symposium on Information, Computer and Communications Security, pp. 4–12. ACM (2007)

A Dynamic Requests Scheduling Model
Based on Prediction in Multi-core Web Server

Guohua You, Xuejing Wang, and Ying Zhao

College of Information Science and Technology, Center for Information Technology,
Beijing University of Chemical Technology, Beijing, China
alan_you@163.com, {wxj,zhaoy}@mail.buct.edu.cn

Abstract. Traditional requests scheduling algorithms in multi-core web server couldn't fully exploit the performance of multi-core CPUs. To solve this problem, we proposed the requests scheduling algorithm in the previous paper. But the algorithm couldn't keep load balance between cores in long time period. In this paper, we proposed a new model to solve this problem. Simulation experiments have been done to evaluate the new model. The experiment results show that the proposed model could better keep load balance between processing cores in long time period.

Keywords: multi-core, web server, dynamic requests, load balance.

1   Introduction

With the sharp increase of dynamic and personalized content which are not fully cacheable, the performance of web servers plays an important role in success of many internet corporations because the generation of dynamic web pages is heavy to load on the web servers. The requests scheduling algorithms and the performance of hardware are the two principal factors influencing the processing ability of web servers. Nowadays, web servers with multi-core CPUs are quite common. So it becomes a key issue to fully exploit the performance of multi-core CPUs. Multi-core architecture integrates multiple hardware resources such as ALU, L1 cache, etc on the same die [1][2][3]. All the cores in the same group share L3 cache[4][5]. Multi-core CPUs are deployed widely in web servers, but most traditional web servers, e.g. Apache [6], employ the First-Come-First-Served (FCFS) scheduling strategy and don't consider the characteristics of multi-core web servers. The requests of a web server usually have two types: static requests and dynamic requests. Dynamic requests gain some kind of processing from a server web [7]. Many dynamic requests include some personalized information, so they must be generated dynamically each time and couldn't be fully cached [8]. Generally, some dynamic requests are very simple, but some dynamic requests are very complex. So the service time of the dynamic requests differs greatly. In the paper, we discuss dynamic requests.

FCFS scheduling strategy would lead to ping-pong effect in multi-core web server [9]. So we proposed a WFQ-Based dynamic requests scheduling approach in paper

R.C.-H. Hsu and W. Shangguang (Eds.): IOV 2014, LNCS 8662, pp. 304–312, 2014.
© Springer International Publishing Switzerland 2014

[10]. The previous algorithm could eliminate the ping-pong effect. However, it also has a defect. The assignment solution of threads in the previous algorithm no longer change after it is decided. But the access frequency of requests will change with time, which would lead to the new load imbalance between cores. To solve the new problem, we proposed a new model which not only avoid the ping-pong effect but also dynamically adjust the assignment scheme.

The remainder of the paper is organized as follows: Section 2 introduces the related work. The new dynamic requests scheduling model is described in Section 3. Section 4 presents an evaluation of the performance. And finally, we present our conclusions in Section 5.

2   Related Scheduling Strategy

There have some scheduling strategies in previous studies, such as FCFS, Short-Job First (SJF) etc.

(1) FCFS: In FCFS strategy, requests are handled in the sequence of their arrival time. FCFS is fair, but it takes long time to process the large files that are newly arriving. As a result, the overall average waiting time increases.

(2) SJF: In SJF, requests with the small service time have precedence over requests with the longer service time [12]. In this way, the overall mean waiting time is reduced [11]. Because requests with the longer service time have the lower priority, there will be starvation on long-term heavily loaded web servers.

(3) DRWS: To solve the ping-pong effect in multi-core system, DRWS assigned the threads that serve the same kind of requests to the same core. For more details, see Reference [10]. In this paper, DRWS is the basis of the new scheduling model.

3   Dynamic Request Scheduling Model

3.1   Description of Scheduling Model

To solve the problem of ping-pong effect in multi-core web server, we proposed a dynamic requests scheduling approach in paper [10]. The access frequency and the mean service time of each kind of dynamic requests are gained from log files [13]. Thus, the access frequency is fixed, so the solution of threads assignment in previous algorithm is static. In fact, the access frequency of dynamic requests always changes with time. When the access frequency of dynamic request changes with time, the previous scheduling algorithm couldn't ensure the load balance between cores in a long time period. So we have to adjust the assignment solution of service threads periodically. We therefore propose a new scheduling model in this paper.

In Fig.1, when a dynamic request arrives at the web server, the classifier parses the URL of the dynamic request, and assigns the request to the corresponding requests queue. Thus, multiple request queues are established in the web server. We gain the mean service time of each kind of dynamic requests from log files in web server. The access frequency is predicted by single exponential smoothing with tracking signal. According to the access frequency and the mean service time, we could calculate the weight of each request queue. The weight of the request queue indicates the impact on CPU load. The service threads would be assigned to the processing cores evenly. To avoid ping-pong effect, the same kind of dynamic requests should be scheduled to the same processing core, which may lead to load imbalance between cores. Hence, we obtain the thread allocation solution by HeapSort algorithm. Furthermore, because the access frequency changes with time, the thread assignment solution should be adjusted periodically. In each time period, the weights of dynamic request queues are predicted, and then the request assignment solution is determined based on the weights. The dynamic requests are assigned to the processing cores based on the solution. The procedure is repeated in next time period. After the dynamic request allocation strategy is decided, the dynamic requests are assigned to these threads. Then these threads that have received dynamic requests begin to execute. The results of execution generate the new dynamic pages, which are then sent to I/O buffer, and network scheduled by I/O management, and these are responses.

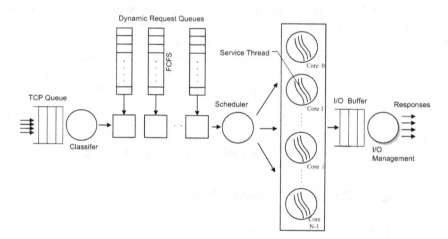

Fig. 1. Description of new scheduling model

3.2   Calculation of Scheduling Parameter

3.2.1 Weight Calculation of Dynamic Request Queue

The same kind of dynamic requests have about the same service time because they have the similar processing procedure. The temporal locality of web traces implies that some contents are more likely frequently accessed in some time period, but they are rarely accessed before and after the time period [14]. So we could predict the access frequency $\tilde{C}_i(t)$ of request queue i in the time period t on basis of the access frequency $C_i(t-1)$ of request queue i in the time period t-1 by means of single exponential smoothing with tracking signal. The algorithm is described as follow:

Let α = the smoothing constant.

$C_i(t-1)$ = the actual access frequency of request queue i for time period t-1.

$\widetilde{C}_i(t-1)$ = the forecast value of access frequency of request queue i for time period t-1, and $e_i(t-1) = \widetilde{C}_i(t-1) - C_i(t-1)$,

$e_i(t-1)$ represents the error between the forecast value and actual value of request queue i for time period t-1.

We define the smoothed error recursively as follows:

$E_i(t-1) = \beta \times e_i(t-1) + (1-\beta) \times E_i(t-2)$ where $0 < \beta < 1$ and β is fixed.

Let $|e_i(t-1)|$ denote the absolute value of the error in time period t. We then define the smoothed absolute error recursively by the following:

$$M_i(t-1) = \beta \times |e_i(t-1)| + (1-\beta) \times M_i(t-2)$$

Let $T(t-1)$ denote the tracking signal for the time period $t-1$. We then define the tracking signal as $T(t-1) = \dfrac{E(t-1)}{M(t-1)}$, obviously, $0 < |T(t-1)| \le 1$.

Let $\alpha(t-1) = |T(t-1)|$, the smoothing forecast for period t is obtained from the following formula:

$$\widetilde{C}_i(t) = \alpha(t-1) \times C_i(t-1) + (1 - \alpha(t-1)) \times \widetilde{C}_i(t-1) \quad \text{where} \quad 0 < \alpha(t-1) < 1.$$

According to the above mentioned algorithm, we could predict the access frequency Ci(t) of request queue i in period t on basis of that in period t-1. So we could gain the access frequency of each kind of dynamic requests.

The access frequency and the mean service time are the two main factors that influence CPU load. Therefore, the predicted weight $\widetilde{w}_{i(t)}$ of the request queue i in period t can be figured out given by

$$\widetilde{W}_i(t) = \widetilde{C}_i(t)T_i \tag{1}$$

where Ti is the service time of request queue i, which could gain from the log files. The weight of the request queues indicates the impact of request queues on CPU load.

3.2.2   Assignment Solution of Dynamic Requests

The weight of each request queue represents the impact of the dynamic requests on processing cores. To keep load balance between cores, we must keep the sum of the weights of all kinds of dynamic requests on each processing core evenly. We can solve the problem with the following algorithm.

If CPU has N cores, and the number of the request queues is M. The weight of each request queue in time period t is $W_1(t)$, $W_2(t)$, ..., $W_M(t)$. We can sort the weights in ascending order by means of HeapSort Algorithm.

We define the array $W_1(t)$, $W_2(t)$, ..., $W_i(t)$, ..., $W_M(t)$ as array A. The heap data structure is an array object that we can view as a nearly complete binary tree. So the array A could represent a heap. Given the index i of a node, we can compute the indices of its parent, left child, and right child:

```
Parent(i){return ⌊i/2⌋;} Left(i){return 2i;}
Right(i){return 2i+1;}
```

In a max-heap, the max-heap property is that for every node i other than the root, $A[Parent(i)] \geq A[i]$. To maintain the max-heap property, we call the *MaxHeapify*. Its inputs are an array A and index i.

```
MaxHeapify(A, i){
  l=LEFT(i); r=RIGHT(i);
  if (l≤A.heap-size and A[l]>A[i])largest=l;  else largest=i;
  if(r≤A.heap-size and A[r]>A[largest]) largest=r;
  if largest≠i exchange A[i] with A[largest];
  MaxHeapify(A, largest);
}
```

We can use the procedure *MaxHeapify* in a bottom-up manner to convert an array $A[1...M]$, where $M=A.length$, into a max-heap. The procedure *BuildMaxHeap* goes through the remaining nodes of the tree and runs *MaxHeapify* on each one.

```
BuildMaxHeap(A){
    A.heap-size=A.length;
    for i=⌊A.length/2⌋ downto 1    MaxHeapify(A, i);
}
```

The array $A[M]$ is sorted in ascending order by *HeapSort* algorithm as follows.

```
HeapSort(A){
BuildMaxHeap(A);
for i=A.length downto 2 { Exchange A[1] with A[i];
A.heapSize=A.heapSize-1; MaxHeapify(A, 1)};
}
```

We could assign the dynamic request queue to the processing cores in the order of the weight of dynamic request queues. The assignment algorithm is described as follows.

```
Assignment(){
for i=M to 1{j=MinWeightCore();
Assign request queue i to core j;}
}
MinWeightCore(){   min=1;
  for i=2 to N {if(weight[i]<weight[min]) min=I;}
  return min;
}
```

Where *weight*[i] represents the sum of weights of dynamic request queues that have been assigned to core i. Since the array A has been sorted in ascending order, the load balance could be kept by the above assignment algorithm.

4   Experiment and Evaluation

4.1   Experiment Setup

We developed a web server simulator, which was called DDRWS. DDRWS is a single-process web server, which incorporates a thread pool. For simplicity, it only handles "GET" dynamic requests. The size of thread pool could be customized. The threads in the thread pool are evenly allocated to every core. The dynamic requests are periodically allocated to the processing core on basis of the new model. We created ten DLL files to simulate the ten dynamic pages, which accomplish different functions. When a request arrives at a core, DDRWS fetches a thread to handle the request. The thread loads and executes a specific DLL file on the basis of the URL and parameters of the request. The execution time of DLL files is different. In every period, the scheduler in DDRWS will predict the weight of every request queue in next period. After DDRWS determine the assignment solution, the requests in the dynamic request queues will be assigned to the service threads that belong to the different cores. The procedure will be repeated periodically. We have also developed the other web server simulators based on SJF, FCFS, and DRWS [10].

4.2   Result Evaluation

4.2.1   The Distribution of Response Time

We measured and analyzed the response time of four dynamic request scheduling algorithms. From Fig.2, most requests' response time of SJF, DRWS, and DDRWS is less than 1000ms, which represents SJF, DRWS, and DDRWS have less mean response time than FCFS. Furthermore, DDRWS has more requests within the first 1000ms and fewer requests over 3000ms than DRWS, which proves that DDRWS could keep the load balancing between cores for a long time period by dynamic adjustment of requests assignment.

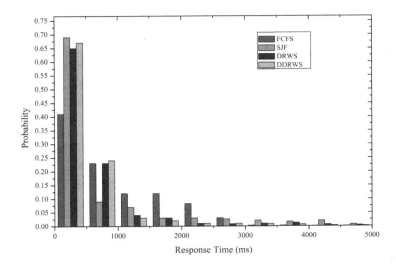

Fig. 2. The distribution of the response times with different scheduling strategies

4.2.2   Changing the Size of Shared Data

To simulate the dynamic web pages with shared data, the DLL files have shared data too. The mean response time for four strategies was measured as the size of the shared data was changed. From Fig.3, when the shared data increases, we can see that the mean response time of FCFS and SJF increases too. But DRWS and DDRWS changes little. That is because that DRWS and DDRWS eliminate the ping-pong effect. So their mean response time was shorter than SJF and FCFS.

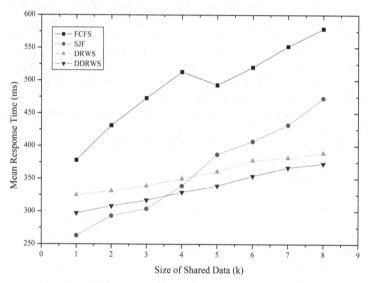

Fig. 3. Mean response time for four scheduling strategies when size of shared data is changed

4.2.3   Comparison between DRWS and DDRWS with Different Adjustment Period

We measured and calculated the mean response time of DRWS and DDRWS with the different adjustment periods. On Fig.4(a), the adjustment period of DDRWS is one minute. DDRWS has the longer mean response time than DRWS. Because the adjustment times of DDRWS in every sampling period is too much. So the overhead of calculating requests' assignment solution is high, which lead to the higher mean response time. On Fig.4(b), the adjustment period of DDRWS is three minutes. We could see that the mean response time of DDRWS is close to that of DRWS in the most of the sampling periods. That is because the overhead of adjusting dynamic requests' assignment solution decreases. When we further increase the adjustment period in Fig.4(c) and (d), DDRWS has the shorter mean response time than DRWS.

4.2.4   Changing the Number of Service Threads

We changed the number of service threads and measured the mean response time of four scheduling strategies. From Fig.5, with the increment of service threads, four scheduling algorithms all drop down. FCFS declines slowly because FCFS has longer overall response time. SJF drops more slowly than DDRWS and DRWS, because SJF may lead to "starvation" and could not avoid ping-pong effect. DDRWS and DRWS could eliminate the ping-pong effect, so their mean response time drops more quickly. DDRWS could keep better load balance than DRWS in long time period, so DDRWS drops more quickly than DRWS.

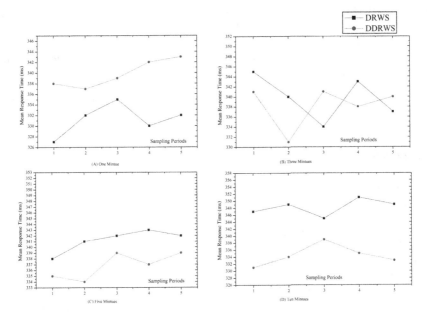

Fig. 4. Comparison between DRWS and DDRWS with different adjustment periods

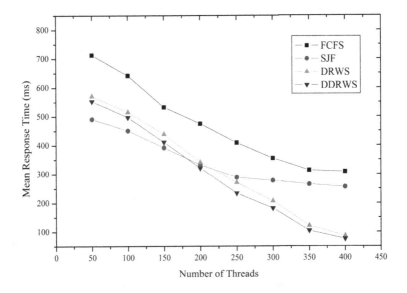

Fig. 5. The mean response time as function of the number of threads

5   Conclusions

To solve the ping-pong effect in multi-core systems and load imbalance between cores in long time period, we proposed the new scheduling model. We describe the principle of the proposed model, and give the calculation formulas of the scheduling model. Furthermore, we developed DDRWS, a simulation program of web server based on the new model, and did the simulation experiment. Experiment results shows that the new model couldn't only keep load balance between cores in long time period but also avoid the problem of ping-pong effect.

Acknowledgments. This paper has been supported by the Fundamental Research Funds for the Central Universities (No.YZ1319).

References

1. Multi-Core from Intel-Products and Platforms, http://www.intel.com/multi-core/products.htm
2. AMD Multi-Core Products, http://multicore.amd.com/en/Products
3. Kongetira, P., Aingaran, K., Olukotun, K.: Niagara: a 32-way multithreaded sparc processor. IEEE Micro 25, 21–29 (2005)
4. Gorder, P.M.: Multicore processors for science and engineering. IEEE CS and the AIP 9, 3–7 (2007)
5. Calandrino, J.M., Anderson, J.H., Baumberger, D.P.: A hybrid real-time scheduling approach for large-scale multicore platforms. In: ECRTS 2007: 19th Euromicro Conference on Real-Time Systems, pp. 247–258. IEEE, Pisa (2007)
6. Apache. The Apache Software Foundation, http://www.apache.org
7. Hernández-Orallo, E., Vila-Carbó, J.: Web server performance analysis using histogram workload models. Computer Networks 53, 2727–2739 (2009)
8. van der Weij, W., Bhulai, S., van der Mei, R.: Dynamic thread assignment in web server performance optimization. Performance Evaluation 66, 301–310 (2009)
9. You, G., Zhao, Y.: Dynamic requests scheduling model in multi-core web server. In: The 9th International Conference on Grid and Cloud Computing (GCC 2010), pp. 201–206 (2010)
10. You, G., Zhao, Y.: A weighted-fair-queuing (WFQ)-based dynamic request scheduling approach in a multi-core system. Future Generation Computer Systems 28(7), 1110–1120 (2012)
11. Cherkasova, L.: Scheduling strategy to improve response time for web applications. In: Bubak, M., Hertzberger, B., Sloot, P.M.A. (eds.) HPCN-Europe 1998. LNCS, vol. 1401, pp. 305–314. Springer, Heidelberg (1998)
12. Harchol-Balter, M., Schroeder, B., Bansal, N., Agrawal, M.: Size-based scheduling to improve web performance. ACM Transactions on Computer Systems 21(2), 207–233 (2003)
13. Sharifian, S., Motamedi, S.A., Akbari, M.K.: A content-based load balancing algorithm with admission control for cluster webservers. Future Generation Computer Systems 24, 775–787 (2008)
14. Lee, D., et al.: LRFU: A Spectrum of Policies that Subsumes the Least Recently Used and Least Frequently Used Policies. IEEE Transactions on Computers 50(12), 1352–1361 (2001)

Cloud Services for Deploying Client-Server Applications to SaaS

Jianbo Zheng and Weichang Du

Faculty of Computer Science, University of New Brunswick, Fredericton, Canada
{jianbo.zheng,wdu}@unb.ca

Abstract. The Software as a Service (SaaS) model of cloud computing is becoming the trend of the new generation of software development due to its low investment, flexibility, and accessibility. Nowadays there are many well used conventional software applications, especially client-server applications. Reuse these application in cloud platforms will benefit both enterprises and the customers. This paper proposes a service framework for easily deploying conventional client-server applications to cloud running as SaaS. The service framework consists of four services: tenant awareness services, tenant management service, application auto-deployment service, and cloud resources management service. The proposed service framework has been implemented and verified on the Amazon AWS cloud engine.

1 Introduction

Software as a Service (SaaS) is an emerging business model in the software industry due to its advantages of flexibility, quick deployment, and scalability. Recently more enterprises have been attracted to build or upgrade their applications or services from local infrastructure to cloud.

In the past decades, the client-server computing model was commonly used in enterprise applications. In this model, software development companies license their software application packages to customers and assist the customers to deploy the software on their own IT infrastructures.

Meanwhile, in SaaS model, software applications usually are adopt by using a multi-tenant architecture, that is, a single application can serve multiple customers or tenants at same time. SaaS based applications can also make enterprises support rapidly onboarding new customers, which is essential to grow user bases of applications. In SaaS model, software developers or venders become service providers which deploy their software applications on cloud and provide deployed applications as services via internet. The customers become tenants of SaaS applications, which no longer need to purchase or install the applications. Instead, customer or tenants subscribe and pay for services on demand via internet.

There have been active research project to investigate migrate conventional client-server applications to cloud environments. Gartner [1] summarizes five general ways to do such migration: re-host on IaaS, refactor for PaaS, revise for IaaS or PaaS,

R.C.-H. Hsu and W. Shangguang (Eds.): IOV 2014, LNCS 8662, pp. 313–324, 2014.

rebuild on PaaS, and replace with SaaS, and gives advice on how to choose the method. Amazon [2] [3] also gives its migration instruction about deploying or moving an existing system to Amazon cloud.

Generally speaking, Enterprises have three options to move their software applications from their local IT infrastructure to the cloud. The first option is to use an existing SaaS application with similar functionality to replace the current local application, such as using the Salesforce CRM to replace the current CRM system. However, it is hard to find out an application which is exactly suited to an enterprise's business. Moreover, an enterprise may have already had their own software which is fit to their current business.

The second option is to re-design and redevelop a current local application based on a PaaS, like Google App Engine, or Windows Azure. However, re-designing and re-developing the application on a new PaaS cloud platform with new technologies will result in high cost and risks to an enterprise.

The third option is to re-deploy or re-host the current local applications to IaaS, like Amazon EC2, or Open Stack. This solution is much more intuitive. With various types of virtual machines, IaaS platform allows enterprises easily to move their current local applications to cloud without many modifications, as shown in Fig. 1. However, this IaaS based solution supports neither resource sharing among tenants nor flexible management of dynamic tenants' subscriptions and usages. As shown in the figure, each tenant keeps an application instance with a running virtual machine on the IaaS cloud. This solution may have a significant resource waste for the software service provider who has more than one tenant to serve.

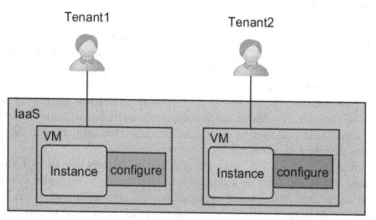

Fig. 1. Simple deployment solution of the application management

To overcome the weak points of the pure IaaS solution, this paper proposes a service framework, named Application to SaaS framework (A2SF), to provide an improved solution and helps software developers deploy their original client-server applications to Cloud, running as SaaS applications. Fig. 2 shows the improved solution for application instance management in A2SF framework. In this improved solution, the original application is divided into two parts, private components and utility components. The private components usually are the customers' data related components, such as the configuration component. For the private components, A2SF wraps them in the multi-tenant awareness layers (service proxy layer in the figure). The utility components usually are the application programs, which will never be changed during application execution. In A2SF, the utility components are considered as shared recourses among tenants. A2SF runs as a service load balancer to share and reuse utility components among tenants.

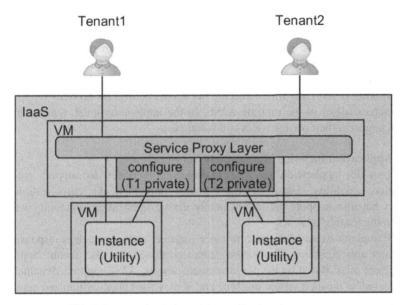

Fig. 2. Improved solution of the application management

The rest of paper is organized as following: Section 2 describes the overview and runtime architecture of A2SF, as well as its components. Section 3 gives a case study on deploying a real web application SugarCRM with A2SF to Amazon AWS cloud, as well as the related experiments' results and analysis. Section 4 briefly describe the related works and compared with our work. Section 5 concludes the paper.

2   A2SF Services

2.1   Overview

A2SF provides multi-tenant awareness services and application instance management services, running as an application container as well as a service load balancer. There are three essential requirements to A2SF services: tenant management and identification, tenant isolation and data security, and automatic service scalability.

2.1.1 Tenant Management and Identification Services

For each tenant, A2SF assigns a unique token to it, which will be carried in each service request from clients. Using the token, the tenant identification service is able to identify which tenant the service request comes from. This tenant identification service, working together with the original application's authentication module, provides identification and authentication functionalities for the deployed application, which is running as a SaaS application in the cloud.

2.1.2 Tenant Isolation and Data Security Services

In A2SF, two approaches of data isolation are applied. One approach is virtualization-based isolation. By this approach, in A2SF, the different tenants' runtime data and configurations of the deployed application will be stored in different virtual machines. The other approach is application-based isolation. A2SF provides two types of multi-tenant awareness services, which execute the access control on services (application) and resources (data) in the runtime A2SF. In the application level, tenants are only allowed to access their own services and resources.

2.1.3 Application Instance Management Services

A2SF provides application instance management services to support automatic application scalability. These services not only implement the virtualization-based isolation but also support the automatically elastic application scalability which is based on the tenants' statuses.

A2SF implements an application instance manager service which is responsible for generating and recycling application instances based on the tenant application management rules. Based on the pre-customized scripts, A2SF supports dynamically to assign an online tenant a virtual machine and deploy the tenant-customized application instance on that virtual machine. The cloud resources management services of A2SF allocate and recycle the cloud resources in the unit of application instance.

2.2 Runtime Services Architecture

A2SF runtime architecture consists of tenant management services, multi-tenant awareness services, and application instance management services, in addition to components or services from the original client-server application.

Fig. 3 shows the runtime architecture of A2SF. The purple parts in the figure are the main services, which includes the service proxy service, tenant manager (including tenant manager interface) service, application instance manager service, data access service, and database service.

Multi-tenant awareness services are implemented by service proxy service and data access service. The tenant manager service provides the tenant information management service and tenant identification service. The application instance manager service is responsible to automatically generate and recycle application instances based on statuses of real-time tenant access. The database service stores the application configuration and tenants' information, such as tenant proxy rules, tenant statuses, and logs.

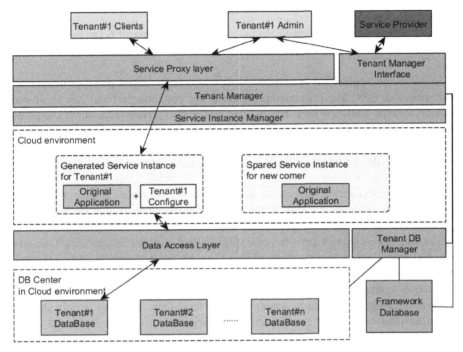

Fig. 3. A2SF runtime architecture

2.3   Services Descriptions

2.3.1 Service Proxy Service

The service proxy service is responsible for service access control. In A2SF, tenants are only allowed to access their own application instances. As shown in Fig. 3, the service proxy service is the single entrance of the deployed application, and all clients or end users' service requests are sent to it, instead of their original local servers.

When the service proxy service starts up, it will load all the tenants' proxy rules. After receiving a client request, the service proxy service first acquires the token of the request and identifies the request's source by invoking the tenant identification service. Once the request is identified, the service proxy service handles the request based on the tenant's proxy rules and forwards the request to the proper application instance. If the request cannot be identified, the service proxy service will deny the service request.

As the original client-server application will be wrapped and deployed to the cloud as a whole package without modification, the original communication protocols as well as the business logic processes between clients and server do not need to be changed between the application deployed in cloud and the original client-side application.

2.3.2 Data Access Service

The data access service is responsible for the data access control between application instances and databases, to assure that tenants are only allowed to access their own data.

In A2SF, an application is considered to have two essential parts, programming code and user data. The programming code is the common part and can be shared with all tenants, while the user data belongs to tenants' private data which should be protected under the access control. Furthermore, the user data can be categorized into local data and remote data. The local data is stored in local files. For instance, the configuration file is a typical example of local data. The remote data is usually stored in a database.

The data access service stores the local data in the database, initializes the local data before the application instance runs, and stores and clears it after the application instance stops.

The data access service provides two ways to deal with the remote data. One way is to implement a data proxy server, which means all data accesses should go through the data proxy server first. This method is for those applications, in which the data connection configurations are hard coded. The other way is to treat the data connection configuration file as tenant's private local data. This way is only suitable for those data connection configurations are separated from the code and easily replaced.

2.3.3 Tenant Manager Service

The tenant manager service consists of the following sub-services: tenant information management service, tenant identification service, and tenant status service.

Through the tenant manager service interface, tenant administrators can manage their information, customize their subscribed services, and review their usage reports. Also, the service provider, namely the vendor of the deployed application, can manage the tenants' subscriptions, set the customization rules for the tenants, and setup the configuration of A2SF runtime.

The tenant identification service is responsible to verify the token, identify the tenant, and return the tenant information including the tenant proxy rules. And the tenant status service is used to obtain the tenants' current statuses. The tenant manager service keeps all the tenants' statuses and updates them regularly, based on the tenants' service requests. The tenant status information includes the tenant application instance status, tenant connection number, tenant live time, and so on. Based on these statuses, the tenant manager service sends the application instance management request to the application instance manager, such as application instance generation request and application instance recycling request.

2.3.4   Application Instance Manager Service

The application instance manager service manages the running application instances in the cloud, including application instance generation and recycle services. This service implements the allocation and recycle of the cloud resources.

The service instance is a server side application, which is composed of a running virtual machine instance and the customized application deployed in it. Each online or live tenant who has clients or end-users to access the deployed application is assigned a customized application instance. Whether or not to generate an application instance is controlled by the tenant manager service. The tenant manager service keeps the tenants' statuses and updates them regularly. When a tenant status matches its rule of generating or recycling the application instance, the tenant manager service will invoke the services, provided by the application instance manager service, to generate or recycle the service instance for the tenant.

When the application instance manager service receives an application instance generation request for a returning tenant, firstly, it obtains an available virtual machine from the IaaS cloud. Secondly the application instance manager service deploys the original application on the virtual machine. Thirdly, the application instance manager service initializes and customizes the original application by loading the tenant's private data to the virtual machine from the data center. Finally, the application instance manager service sends the result and generated application instance information to the tenant manager to update the tenant's statuses.

When the application instance manager service receives a service instance recycling request for an off-line tenant, firstly, the application instance manager service stops the tenant's application instance. Secondly, the application instance manager service collects the tenant's local private data on the virtual machine and saves it to the data center. Finally, the service instance manager service clears the tenant's local private data, returns the virtual machine, and sends the result to the tenant manager to updates the tenant's statuses.

In order to perform the above steps, the application instance manager service wraps the standard operations of the IaaS services (launch, start, stop, and terminate a virtual machine), as well as the remote controlling operations or commands (copy, move, service start, service stop and so on) on the virtual machine, which are usually provided by underlying cloud engine.

Moreover, the virtual instance launching time maybe too long to an application that needs quick responding. So in order to shorten the generation time of application instance, A2SF also implements a virtual pool, managed by the application instance manager service, to always keep a number of spare virtual machines that are waiting to host generated application instances.

3   Experiment

A real-world client-server application SugarCRM has been deployed to Amazon EC2 based on an implemented A2SF prototype. SugarCRM is one of the most popular customer relationship management applications currently, which is implemented in the PHP programming language and supports multiple types of databases including MySQL.

3.1   Deploying SugarCRM on Amazon EC2 with A2SF Services

We classify the components of SugarCRM can be into three types: utility components, local private components, and remote private components, as shown in Table 1.

Table 1. The classification of SugarCRM components

Type	Components
Local private components	Folders: *custom, upload, cache, data, modules;* Files: *.htaccess, sugarcrm.log, config.php, config_override.php*
Remote private components	The database *"sugarcrm"*
Utility components	The rest of components of SugarCRM

The utility components are deployed in the deployable package once for all tenants. The deployable package is a virtual machine image (in the Amazon cloud, it is also called as AMI). The local private components are saved in the bucket of Amazon S3 named by tenant id and tenant name. The remote private components are stored in a MySQL instance in the Amazon RDS.

To integrate the A2SF service and the SugarCRM software together we first configured the Amazon Security Credentials with the list of private components. We then created a customized AMI (Amazon Machine Image) for generating SugarCRM application instances. The AMI ID will be updated later by the tenant management service for dynamic tenant management. Thus when a new or returned tenant comes, the service proxy service can easily and quickly launch a new SugarCRM application instance and customized it for the new tenant based on the AMI. Table 2 shows the contents of the created deployable package for SugarCRM SaaS application.

Table 2. The contents of the deployable package

Component	Description
Service proxy server	This is a runnable jar file, which runs on the portal server as the service entrance.
A2SF management center	This is a war file, which is deployed on a Tomcat server in the portal server.
Data proxy server	This is a runnable jar file. In this migration, it is deployed in the AMI.
A2SF scripts	These scripts are runnable bash files, which can be executed to customize the application instance and save the tenant private local data.
A2SF DB	This is a MySQL database for A2SF framework.
SugarCRM	This is the original application, which is the target of this migration.

Fig. 4 shows the deployed of SugarCRM with A2SF on Amazon AWS Cloud. Firstly, before deploying SugarCRM, A2SF service has already been deployed on Amazon EC2 cloud, and the portal service is the A2SF management service. It will be the entrance of the deployed SugarCRM as well in the cloud. The EC2 AMI is the deployable package of SugarCRM. Secondly, after the portal service is running, we accessed the A2SF management service and registered the SugarCRM deployable package as well as the application information, so that SugarCRM application instances can be generated correctly. Finally, we added several tenants with different IP ranges. We then use several client browsers to access the entrance/portal service on different computers with different IP addresses to simulate multiple tenants' accesses.

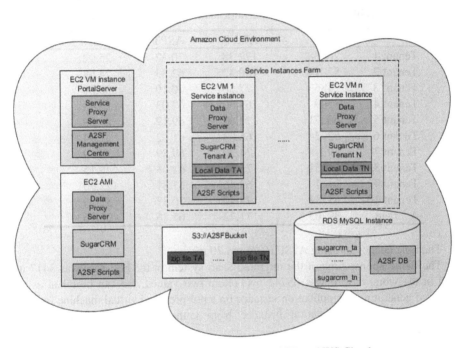

Fig. 4. Deployed of SugarCRM with A2SF on AWS Cloud

3.2   Performance Experiments

For performance evaluation, we also conducted a serial of experiments on the average time latency of A2SF service. In the experiments, 10 computers with different IP address were chosen to simulate 10 tenants. We measured the following four time segments: the first response time, the average time of the normal response, the processing time of the service proxy, and the processing time of the data proxy.

We first recorded the response time of the SugarCRM application deployed on Amazon AWS in IaaS mode without using A2SF. Table 3 shows the performance measurement for a single tenant of the deployed SugarCRM application.

Table 3. Performance of single tenant IaaS SugarCRM

Measure Item	Value (millisecond)
First response time (FRT)	3428
Average stable response time (ASRT)	169.05
Average service proxy time (ASPT)	62.39
The average data proxy time (ADPT)	27.04

We then we used the 10 computers and ran the testing scripts on each computer. Table 4 shows the result measurement.

Table 4. Performance of multi-tenants SugarCRM with A2SF

	FRT	ASRT	ASPT	ADPT
Tenant 1	20438	172.38	70.32	25.92
Tenant 2	52014	180.42	62.83	24.68
Tenant 3	24863	177.50	70.10	30.30
Tenant 4	3509	161.30	62.03	23.43
Tenant 5	60271	172.47	69.19	29.59
Tenant 6	52924	166.03	61.02	21.94
Tenant 7	59248	174.30	69.89	30.59
Tenant 8	54631	175.94	61.08	25.15
Tenant 9	3417	163.46	61.81	22.90
Tenant 10	65741	173.40	70.37	31.05
Average	39705.6	171.72	65.86	26.56

The time latency of using A2SF is around 70 ms.

The first response time of the migrated SaaS system in the best case was 3417 ms and in the worst case it was 65741 ms. These two values also can be taken as the times of generating an application instance on a pre-prepared virtual machine instance and generating an application instance from launching a new virtual machine instance.

The average time of application instance generation is related to the size of the virtual machine pool and the size of target application. Adding a virtual machine pool would improve the efficiency of application instance generation. The experiments show that when the size of virtual machine pool in A2SF was set to 2, the average time of the first response became 39705.6 ms which is significantly lower than the first response time of the worst case.

The experiments also show that the average service proxy processing time is around 65ms, and the average data proxy processing time is around 27 ms. Under the same computing capability, the service proxy processing time and the data proxy processing time are stable. In case of supporting more tenants, we can choose to increase the number of CPU allocate to the service proxy service or add a load balancer service with multiple service proxy service to process service requests.

4   Related Works

Tsai et al. [4] proposes a two-tier SaaS scaling and scheduling architecture that duplicates at both service and application levels along with a resource allocation algorithm that takes different computing power of server nodes into consideration.

Chong et al. [5] proposes a SaaS maturity model, which takes configurability, multi-tenancy efficiency, and scalability as the key attributes of SaaS and classifies SaaS software as four maturity levels. In the model, each level is distinguished from the previous level by addition of one of the three attributes.

Guo et al. [6] proposes a multi-tenancy enabling programming model and framework, consisting of a set of approaches and common services, to support and speed up multi-tenant SaaS application development.

Cai et al. [7] [8] proposes an end-to-end methodology and toolkit for transforming existing web applications into multi-tenant SaaS applications. However, using this migration methodology, developers have to modify the original application software as well as server configurations.

Song et al [9] defines a SaaSify Flow Language (SFL) and proposes a SFL tool which would help convert Java web applications to SaaS applications. However, the SFL tool also has its limitations. First, the SFL tool seems only support Java web applications with JDBC access to databases. Second, since the SFL tool uses memory in threads to keep and share tenant information among layers, it is reasonable to believe that the tool could not support applications whose components deploy on different computers.

The above and other similar research projects have made significant progress in the area of multi-tenant SaaS applications. In our research we more focus on re-deployment of existing client-server applications to cloud, running as SaaS applications, without modification the original code.

5   Concluding Remarks

In this paper, we proposed a cloud services, named A2SF services, for helping deploying conventional client-server applications to cloud, running as multi-tenant SaaS applications. Re-deploying conventional client-server applications, integrated with A2SF services, are relatively easy. The runtime architecture of A2SF services for multi-tenant SaaS are simple and effective, though they are relatively conservative compared to other proposed multi-tenant SaaS systems. The proposed A2SF services have been implemented on Amazon EC2 cloud computing engine with a deployed real-world CRM application. Future work includes performance improvement of A2SF services and implementations of A2SF services on other cloud platforms.

References

1. Gartner. Gartner Identifies Five Ways to Migrate Applications to the Cloud (May 16, 2011), http://www.gartner.com/it/page.jsp?id=1684114
2. Amazon, The total cost of (non) ownership of web applications in the Cloud, Technical report, Amazon Web Services (October 2012)
3. Varia, J.: Migrating your existing applications to the AWS cloud. A Phase-driven Approach to Cloud Migration (2010)
4. Tsai, W.T., Sun, X., Shao, Q., Qi, G.: Two-tier multi-tenancy scaling and load balancing. In: 2010 IEEE 7th International Conference on e-Business Engineering (ICEBE), pp. 484–489. IEEE (November 2010)
5. Chong, F., Carraro, G.: Architecture strategies for catching the long tail. MSDN Library, Microsoft Corporation, pp. 9–10 (2006)
6. Guo, C.J., Sun, W., Huang, Y., Wang, Z.H., Gao, B.: A framework for native multi-tenancy application development and management. In: The 9th IEEE International Conference on E-Commerce Technology and the 4th IEEE International Conference on Enterprise Computing, E-Commerce, and E-Services, CEC/EEE 2007, pp. 551–558. IEEE (2007)
7. Cai, H., Wang, N., Zhou, M.J.: A transparent approach of enabling SaaS multi-tenancy in the cloud. In: 6th World Congress on Services (services-1), pp. 40–47. IEEE (July 2010)
8. Cai, H., Zhang, K., Zhou, M.J., Gong, W., Cai, J.J., Mao, X.: An end-to-end methodology and toolkit for fine granularity SaaS-ization. In: IEEE International Conference on Cloud Computing, CLOUD 2009, pp. 101–108. IEEE (September 2009)
9. Song, J., Han, F., Yan, Z., Liu, G., Zhu, Z.: A SaaSify tool for converting traditional web-based applications to SaaS application. In: 2011 IEEE International Conference on Cloud Computing (CLOUD), pp. 396–403. IEEE (July 2011)

An Event Driven Model for Highly Scalable Clustering for Both on Premise and Cloud Based Systems

P.S. Wickramasinghe[1], L.D.A. Madusanka[1] H.P.M. Tissera[1],
D.C.S. Weerasinghe[1], Shahani Markus Weerawarana[2], and Afkham Azeez[3]

[1] Department of Computer Science and Engineering,
University of Moratuwa, Sri Lanka
pulasthi911@gmail.com
[2] Department of Computer Science and Engineering,
University of Moratuwa, Sri Lanka
[3] Director of Architecture, WSO2 Inc.

Abstract. Computer clustering has emerged as the paradigm of choice in distributed systems and cloud computing. Multicast based approaches are dominant in the computer clustering domain and many clustering systems are built on top of IP multicast based message passing systems. However, most cloud based systems not provide proper support for multicasting because of the dynamic nature of IP's, which complicates the configuration and maintenance of such an approach on the cloud.This paper presents an event driven approach for computer clustering, that can effectively handle dynamic IP's and other issues present in computer clustering and cloud environments. We discuss a clustering implementation based on this event driven approach for an Apache Axis2 cloud deployment. We then compare this event driven clustering implementation with an existing multicast based clustering implementation for a cloud deployed Apache Axis2. The comparisons reveal significantly higher performance in the event driven approach, in addition to solving some of the challenges present in cloud environments.

Keywords: Event Driven, Cloud Computing, Scalable, Clustering.

1 Introduction

Computer clustering has become an vital part in distributed systems to provide better experience and greater flexibility for both service consumers and providers.The ultimate purpose of clustering is to provide high availability, scalability and fault tolerance for enterprise applications. Maintaining a very low downtime, reducing the response time and serving for a large concurrent set of users are some of the basic requirements that enterprise level software systems hope to achieve through clustering. The two main aspects that need to be addressed in a clustering framework is membership discovery and state replication.

R.C.-H. Hsu and W. Shangguang (Eds.): IOV 2014, LNCS 8662, pp. 325–336, 2014.

2   Event Driven Model

2.1   Overview

Event driven systems are not new to the computing world and are used extensively in many areas. Essentially an event driven system consists of event emitters and event consumers. Events are triggered when state changes occur in the system and event emitters publish these events to event consumers through event notifications, and event consumers trigger actions based on the events consumed. This paper introduces an approach to use event driven concepts to develop a clustering framework and explains how each aspect needed to develop a clustering framework can be realized through an event driven model. In this framework cluster nodes (members) act as both event emitters and event consumers to exchange state information and data needed to manage the cluster. The model presented is a high level generic model that can be molded according to the application requirements. The paper presents an implementation based on Apache ZooKeeper as proof of concept.

2.2   Membership Discovery

In order to achieve scalability the framework should be able to efficiently discover new member nodes that belong to the cluster and add them into the system by exchanging state information and updating the new member with up to date state information. Membership discovery aspects also include identification of node (member) failures and handling rejoining events[1]. Node failure identification is generally achieved through heartbeat messages. Since most enterprises would require to deploy their applications both on-premise and in the cloud environment, membership discovery mechanism used for clustering needs to be compatible with both platforms.

Multicast Based Models. Multicast based approaches are dominant in the clustering domain. Two such multicast based approaches are.

Pure Multicast based discovery. In pure multicast based discovery cluster communication is built on top of multicast heartbeats sent using TCP packets to a multicast IP address. Each member sends out a heartbeat with a predefined frequency and this heartbeat is used for dynamic discovery of other nodes in the clustering domain. If a heartbeat has not been received in a time period specified as drop time, a member is considered as failed and the channel and any membership listener will be notified

Well-known address based discovery (WKA). In the WKA discovery each member maintains a predefined set of known members in the initial configuration. When joining to the cluster, members will first register with a well-known member and get the member list of the cluster domain. When new member joins, one of the well-known members will notify others in the group. When a member leaves the cluster, it will be detected using heartbeat mechanism[6].

One of the main drawbacks in multicast based approaches in the post cloud era is that most cloud platforms like Amazon EC2 does not support multicasting thus it can't be used for clustering in cloud environments. Although well known address based discovery can be used for such purposes, cloud related properties can make well-known address based discovery much complex and difficult to configure. As an example, in Amazon EC2 each time an instance is restarted, it gets a new hostname and port and eventually well known address may change. Therefore configuration files will need to be updated resulting in decreased maintainability of the system.

Membership Discovery - Event Driven Model. In order to achieve membership discovery through an event driven model it is vital to identify the correct set of events and actions that are to be taken when such events occur. In the event driven model for membership discovery presented in this paper six events are identified and are as follows.

- *Member join event* – occurs when a new member joins the cluster.
- *Member rejoin event* – occurs when an old member that left the cluster intentionally or due to a failure, rejoins the cluster.
- *Member leave event* – occurs when an existing member leaves the cluster intentionally.
- *Member failure event* – occurs when an existing member leaves the cluster due to a failure. Failures are identified through heartbeats.
- *Member update request event and Member update response event* – occur when a new member requires state information to initialize itself in the cluster member update event is essentially a state replication event and is further discussed in section 3.

The number of events required for membership discovery may vary depending on the application requirements and thus is not bounded by these six events. For example the implementation presented in section 4 for Apache Axis2 considers join and rejoin events as a single event, and leave and failure events as a single event. When event notifications are received each member will update its membership information and trigger actions that are bound the specific event.

Member join and rejoin event. When a member joins or rejoins the cluster event notifications are sent to each member in the cluster with information about the new member.

Member leave event. When a member is about to leave the cluster it acts as an emitter and sends event notifications to all the member of the cluster indicating that it is about to leave the cluster.

Member failure event. Member failures are identified through heartbeats. If a cluster member fails to emit a heartbeat message within a specified time period that particular member is assumed to be lost. When a member is assumed as lost and event notification will be sent to each member of the cluster with information about the failed member.

2.3   State Replication

In distributed systems to improve the reliability and the performance, data is replicated within servers or sometimes in clients. When data is distributed in different geographical locations it will improve scalability of the systems since proximity to the data is reduced when reading and writing is done[1]. Also when replicating, it is an important requirement to synchronize replications instead of reading outdated system state values. This is called as the consistency of the replications.

The level of state replication required and the consistency model that needs to be adapted depends on the application requirements[9][11]. For example one application may require sequential consistency and another may only require causal consistency. The implementation done for Apache Axis2 we adopt a sequential consistency model that guarantees eventual consistency throughout the cluster.

Multicast Based Model. In multicast based models for state replication, state replication information is multicasted to all the members in the multicast group or in this context all the members of the cluster. Upon receiving the state replication message each member will decide whether or not to the state update is applicable to itself. One of the main drawbacks in this model is that it is difficult to define and control who receives each state replication message. Because of this all the members will get all the state replication messages which will clog the network.

Event Driven Model. As in membership discovery it is vital to identify the correct set of events and actions that are to be taken when such events occur. In the event driven model for state replication presented in this paper five events are identified and are as follows.

- *State change event* – When a state change occurs in a member.
- *State update request event* – When a member requests for state update.
- *State update response event* – When a member responds to a state update request.
- *Member update request event* – When a new member requests for state information.
- *Member update response event* – When a member responds to state information request.

The number of events required for state replication may vary depending on the application requirements and thus is not bounded by these five events. In

Apache Axi2 the requirement for state replication is to replicate all or none. Because of this in the implementation presented in section 4 only two events are considered *state change event* and *member update event*.

State change event. When a state change occurs within a member of the cluster it acts as an emitter and sends event notifications to members of the cluster. Depending on the application the event notification for the state change event may or may not include information about the actual state change. If information about the actual state change is included within the notification for state change event the functionality of 'state update request' and 'state update response' events will also be encapsulated within the state change event.

State update request event. Upon receiving an state change if the cluster member requires the state change information it will emit an state update request event specifying that it requires the state information about the changed state.

State update response event. Upon receiving an state update request event the cluster member will respond by emitting an state update response event that will allow the requesting member to gather information about the state change.

Member update request event. When a new member joins the cluster it will need to update all its state information and thus it will emit and Member update request event. The difference between state update request event and member update request event is that the latter request is not for a specific state change rather it request for the complete current state of the receiving member.

Member update response event Upon receiving a member update request event the cluster member will respond by emitting a member update response event that will allow the requesting member to gather information about the current state of the responding member.

3 Implementation

3.1 Overview

The implementation is based on the event driven model introduced in the paper and the generic model was adjusted to meet the requirements of Apache Axis2[2]. For the implementation a centralized approach was taken for Event notification distribution throughout the cluster, this was achieved by developing the framework on top of Apache ZooKeeper.

3.2 Introduction to Apache ZooKeeper

Apache ZooKeeper is a high performance and highly available coordination service.Per client guarantee of FIFO execution of the requests and linearizable writes for all requests ensures the efficient implementations of distributed services and coordination. Ensemble of servers, where state is replicated among, is the key of ZooKeeper service to achieve high availability and performance[3].

ZooKeeper Service. Data objects in a ZooKeeper node are stored as a tree like hierarchy similar to Linux file system. These data objects in the hierarchical name space are referred as znodes and clients can manipulate them through the ZooKeeper client API. Each znode in the tree structure has a name which can be obtained by separating the element names along the path, from node to the required element, by a slash (/).ZooKeeper implements primitives called watchers which can be used to notify about the changes in the data objects. Watchers are one time triggers which are associated with a particular session and once a watcher has been set for a znode, server promises to notify when change happens. ZooKeeper watchers are used as event notifications in the event driven model.Apache ZooKeeper cluster will be running separately from the ApacheAxis2 instances. ZooKeeper server list will be included in the configuration file of each Axis2 server.

3.3   Membership Discovery

The event driven model for membership discovery was adjusted to suit the requirements of Apache Axis2 for the implementation. Thus the six generic events defined in the model were reduced to three events. Apache Axis2 considers join and rejoin events as a single event, and leave and failure events as a single event.

Member join event In the initialization phase, Axis2 server will establish a client connection with one of the ZooKeeper servers. After creating a connection with a ZooKeeper server, it will check whether znode correspond to its own domain is already available (Note: the domain defines the cluster to which the member belongs).If domain is available it will create a unique member znode representing itself under the domain znode. In this scenario it will get the list of children under the domain name and update the members list. If domain is not available, it will first create a domain znode, members' node and then the local member znode of itself.

Once a new member joins with a particular domain, other members will be notified and each member will update their member lists by looking at the member list in the "members" znode. Watchers only notify about the change of the event and it will not provide any information related to the event hence they are essentially event notifications. Since watchers are one time triggers, they need to be set after each notification and this can be done easily at the same time the watch event is processed.

Member failure event. When a member fails or leaves the ZooKeeper Quorum will stop receiving heartbeat messages from that member and when the specified time limit exceeds ZooKeeper will assume that the member was lost and remove the member znode created for that member. When the znode is removed every cluster member will be notified about the change. Once the change event is received each member will update their member lists by looking at the member list in the "members" znode.

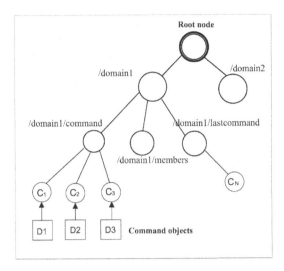

Fig. 1. ZooKeeper znode Hierarchy

Member Update event. Member Update event will be discussed under state replication.

3.4   State Replication

The event driven model for state replication was adjusted to suit the requirements of Apache Axis2 for the implementation. Thus the five generic events defined in the model were reduced to two events

- *State change event*
- *Member update event*

Apache Axi2 defines a mechanism named 'command' which is used within Apache Axis2 to achieve cluster related information sharing. State replication is also handled through commands. Since our implementation did not intend to change the inner functionalities of Apache Axis2, State replication was achieved through commands and the event driven model was applied to distribute commands within the cluster. Below are several of the key commands

- State Clustering Command – All the commands which are responsible for context replication fall under this category.
- Get State Command – Member update event is handled through this command. It encapsulates the whole state of a member

Several more command types exist within Apache Axis2, all commands are treated similarly therefore the implementation supports all type of commands. It is not within the scope of paper to discuss the whole command structure of Apache Axis2.ZooKeeper hierarchical namespace and automatic znode replication capability has been employed in implementing the event driven model for command distribution.

Command Sender. When a command is sent for the first time to the cluster the system creates a znode named "command" under the relevant domain name. In Figure 1, command znode for the domain "domain1" has been created as "/domain1/command". A znode is created for each command sent to the cluster by any member. These nodes are named sequentially starting from "command0000000000". This sequential naming ensures the commands executed in the order they were sent to the cluster "PERSISTENT _SEQUENTIAL" mode has been used for znode creation in which ZooKeeper automatically generate the sequential number of each znode.

In a ZooKeeper znode, a data item is stored as a byte array. To send command objects, it is required to convert the command object to a byte array. This is achieved by using serialization and deserialization. After converting the command object to a byte array, a new znode is created under the command znode and the byte array is stored with the new command znode. ZooKeeper automatically replicates the change across all the ZooKeeper servers in the quorum.

Command Receiver. When a new member initializes,System sets a watcher for the command znode under the relevant domain name. A separate command listener will be set for each member. Each member processes all the commands in the same order. When a new member joins the cluster there can be several commands listed under the command node. New members are only required to execute the commands which were sent to the cluster after that member joined.

Command Handler. When a znode change occurs under the command znode, ZooKeeper fires an event passing the current child list under that znode. Because the current child list contains all the command znodes in the domain, it is required to find the set of unprocessed commands.To make this possible each member stores the last processed command. After finding the list of commands to be processed, the system fetches the data array of the each command node, deserializes it into a command object, finds the category of the command and finally process that command.

Command Accumulation Management. Over time accumulation of unwanted command znodes will decrease the command processing speed. To prevent this drawback it is required to clear the processed command entries regularly. It is also necessary to ensure that unprocessed commands are not removed in the command deletion process.

Each member stores the last processed command under the last command znode in the ZooKeeper namespace.When the command list size exceeds the predefined command update threshold, each member updates its last processed command entry under the last command znode. When the command list length exceeds the command delete threshold, command handler fetches the list of last processed commands, gets the command with minimum sequential number and deletes the command znodes up to the minimum sequential number found in the list.

3.5 Cloud Deployment

The main issue with multicast based systems when working with cloud environments is the need of static IP's. It is possible to obtain static IP's in cloud environments but it is costly. WKA based membership discovery does provide a solution for this issue to some level but it still requires a set of the cluster members to have static IP's. The implementation presented above only requires static IP's for the ZooKeeper Quorum and none of the Axis2 members require static IP's allowing the system to work in cloud environments seamlessly

4 Results

This chapter covers the testing details and provides a comprehensive comparison between the implementation based on the event driven model and the multicast based clustering implementation for Apache Axis2.

4.1 Cloud Sever Test

Cloud tests were done in Amazon EC2. Multiple instances of UNIX servers were used to test both clustering implementations. The Cloud tests were done to determine whether the new system works properly in Cloud environment. Bottlenecks created by the network hindered the ability to use these test results for comparisons. Tests were started through personal computers by connecting via secured shell. JMeter No GUI mode is used to perform the test.Tests were done for 3 and 6 Axis2 servers. Zookeeper servers were deployed on m1.small instances and Axis2 and JMeter servers were deployed on m3.medium instances.

Test Results of Cloud (Amazon EC2) Tests. Table 1:Cloud tests(a) describes the test durations of each scenario in multicast based implementation and event driven model based implementation. Multiple tests were done for each scenario and 3 minimum test durations are shown in the Table 1:Cloud tests.

Clustering implementation comparison. Due to the I/O bottlenecks that were encountered during testing in Amazon EC2, the comparisons between the two implementations using data collected during the cloud tests, does not accurately show a comparison between the two systems. The comparison shows (Figure 2) that the Event driven model based implementation performs slightly better than Multicast based implementation. Although due to the I/O bottleneck encountered in the Cloud environment, this comparison is not as accurate as the local test comparison and does not depict the full performance gains provided by the new event driven model based implementation.

Baseline distribution – Multicast based clustering implementation — Test distribution – Event driven model based clustering implementation.

Table 1. Test Results

Cloud Test (a)			
Axis2	No. of requests	Tribes(s)	ZooKeeper(s)
		25.1	22.6
3 servers	5000	25.1	22.5
		24.6	22.3
		26.0	22.7
6 servers	5000	23.9	22.1
		23.3	21.6
Local tests (b) (Asynchronous tests minimum test duration)			
3 servers	5000	13.3	7.6
	20000	49.2	34.2
4 servers	5000	19.2	18.2
	20000	54.0	42.8
5 servers	5000	18.7	13.8
	20000	58.0	41.6
6 servers	5000	19.6	16.2
	20000	67.2	41.8

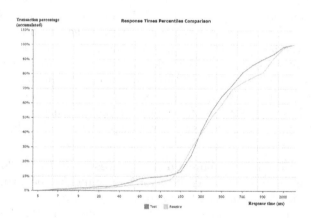

Fig. 2. Comparison Graph of 5000 requests to 3 Servers (Cloud)

4.2   Local Server Test

It was observed that Network bandwidth was creating a bottleneck in the cloud tests. Therefore local servers were started in the personal computers. This would remove network communication which can perform more fast tests.

Test Scenarios. Axis2 servers ranged from 3 to 6. Then 5000 and 20 000 SOAP requests were sent to the two target systems. Each test was done 3 times to get the average value and to avoid single time failures.

Test Results of Local Tests. All the response times of each transaction are recorded to plot the variation of server response according to the load. Apart

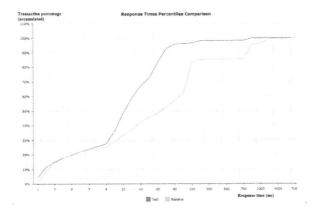

Fig. 3. Comparison Graph of 5000 requests to 3 Servers (Local)

from that, test duration of each scenario is also recorded so that it can compare the performance of two clustering implementations. Asynchronous tests were conducted in the local computers to evaluate the response times by each implementation.

Asynchronous tests. Table 1: Local tests (b)describes the test durations of each scenario in multicast based implementation and Event driven model based implementation. Three or more tests are done for each scenario and minimum test durations are shown.

By comparing duration times it can be concluded that new clustering implementation is more responsive and fast in any scenario. When number of servers increase, test duration is also increased. This is mainly due to sharing CPU time and other limited resources among the servers. The difference of the two systems can be obtained by comparing the response time. Form Figure 3 it can be observed that for the event driven model about 90% of the response times are below 70ms and for the baseline model it is around 55%. By comparing graphs it can be determined that Event driven model based implementation has faster state replication capability than multicast based implementation.

5   Conclusion

Clustered deployments with Multicast based models have been the main medium of achieving scalability, fault-tolerance and high performance for distributed applications. But with the emergence of cloud computing multicast based solutions have become less and less appealing. The event driven model introduced in the paper was not only able to successfully address cloud compatibility issues it also proved to be more efficient than the multicast based model for Apache Axis2. As for our experience the event driven model introduced in the paper is very flexible and easy to implement. It can be easily molded to suit the needs of the application.The goal of this paper was to introduce a novel event driven model for clustering and to test its feasibility, to that extent we believe that the paper was successful based on the test results obtained.

References

1. Tanenbaum, A.S.: Distributed Systems: Principles and Paradigms. Prentice Hall (2006)
2. Jayasinghe, J., Azeez, M.A.: Apache Axis2 Web Services. Packt Publishing Ltd. (2011)
3. Hunt, P., et al.: ZooKeeper: Wait-free Coordination for Internet-scale Systems. In: USENIX Annual Technical Conference, vol. 8 (2010)
4. Vliet, J.V., Paganelli, F.: Programming Amazon EC2. O'Reilly Media, Inc. (2011)
5. Jaatun, M.G., Zhao, G., Rong, C. (eds.): Cloud Computing. LNCS, vol. 5931. Springer, Heidelberg (2009)
6. Azeez, M.A.: Autoscaling web services on amazon ec2. Diss. University of Moratuwa, Sri Lanka (2010)
7. Luo, J., Eugster, P.T., Hubaux, J.P.: Route driven gossip: probabilistic reliable multicast in ad hoc networks. In: Twenty-Second Annual Joint Conference of the IEEE Computer and Communications, INFOCOM 2003, vol. 3, pp. 2229–2239. IEEE Societies (2003)
8. Ganesh, A.J., Kermarrec, A.M., Massoulie, L.: Peer-to-peer membership management for gossip-based protocols. IEEE Transactions on Computers 52(2), 139–149 (2003)
9. Yu, H., Vahdat, A.: Design and evaluation of a conit-based continuous consistency model for replicated services. ACM Trans. Comput. Syst. 20(3), 239–282 (2002)
10. Lamport, L.: Time, clocks, and the ordering of events in a distributed system. Commun. ACM 21(7), 558–565 (1978)
11. Bal, H.E., Kaashoek, M.F., Tanenbaum, A.S., Jansen, J.: Replication Techniques for Speeding up Parallel Applications on Distributed Systems, vol. 4, pp. 337–355 (1992)
12. Zhang, D., et al.: Asynchronous event detection for context inconsistency in pervasive computing. International Journal of Ad Hoc and Ubiquitous Computing 11(4), 195–205 (2012)
13. Dollimore, J., Kindberg, T., Coulouris, G.: Coordination and Agreement in Distributed Systems: Concepts and Design, 4th edn., ch. 12. Pearson Education, Essex (2005)

A BLE-Based Mobile Cloud Architecture
for Longer Smart Mobile Device Battery Life

James Mao and K.H. Yeung

Department of Electronic Engineering City University of Hong Kong, HKSAR, China
eimitmao@gmail.com, eeayeung@cityu.edu.hk

Abstract. Smart mobile devices offer increasingly powerful applications for entertainment and work. Compared with the rapid growth of their computing power, the battery capacity can hardly catch up. One way to address the power consumption problem is to offload some workload to the cloud. Different offloading approaches have been proposed. However, they all have their own limitations. In this paper, we review the proposed approaches and present a BLE-based mobile cloud architecture for workload offloading.

Keywords: Mobile cloud computing, energy model, volunteer computing, pervasive computing, Bluetooth low energy.

1   Introduction

With the rapid advance in mobile technology, smart mobile devices are way beyond simple voice and text exchanging devices. Faster CPUs, more memory and more advanced sensors have been implemented in smart mobile devices today. Resource demanding applications that used to be available only on computers are more common to have their mobile versions. However, one critical part of the smart mobile device is lagging behind compared to the aforementioned hardware advances. It is the battery capacity. According to Robinson et al., the battery capacity grows by 5% yearly [1]. In the computer paradigm where Moore's law dominates most growth rate, 5% is way too slow. To reduce smart mobile device battery consumption without compromising its functionality, offloading energy-demanding workload into the cloud is one possibility.

Roughly, there are three cloud architectures that the workload can be offloaded to. The first type is a remote cloud, for instance the Amazon EC2 [2]. This type of cloud offers elastic resources in an on demand pay-per-use manner. In terms of battery computation, offloading to remote cloud will cost extra energy for data transmission. The tradeoff between offload or not to remote cloud has been studied in [5], [7].

The second type is a cloud formed by P2P connected smart mobile devices in the local vicinity. For instance, Hyrax [3] is a mobile cloud constructed using a cluster of Android mobile devices. The idea of augmenting mobile devices' capabilities by offloading workload to close-by servers is called cyber foraging which first appeared in [8]. A more recent survey about mobile devices cyber foraging can be found in [9]. Sharing workload among P2P connected smart mobile devices is a special case of cyber foraging. Compared to type one, type two cloud is believed to consume less

R.C.-H. Hsu and W. Shangguang (Eds.): IOV 2014, LNCS 8662, pp. 337–344, 2014.
© Springer International Publishing Switzerland 2014

energy in data transmission due to the fact that less energy is needed for short range wireless communication. However, the energy overhead of maintaining a P2P mobile Ad Hoc cloud cannot be oversight [10]. Also, the mobility nature of mobile devices may introduce packet loss due to the possibility that some mobile devices wander off the mobile Ad Hoc network before they finish their assigned tasks.

The third type is introduced in [4], where a cloudlet is used. A cloudlet is placed in the local vicinity to act as an agent for smart mobile devices to communicate with the remote cloud. The advantage of a cloudlet is obvious. Compare to type one, now a mobile device only needs to send its data to the cloudlet that is close to it. Instead of sending it to a remote cloud, energy consumption is surely less. Nevertheless, as mentioned in [4], the incentive of deploying such a cloudlet infrastructure is not clear if not for commercial use. One real life example would be aryaka, a company promises to provide services that can accelerate mobile users' access to cloud-based applications. It is achieved by its "global network of distributed Points of Presence (POPs) that sit close to business users and are connected with a dedicated private core network" [12]. Besides, this type does not make use of vicinity resources, which is a loss considering the rapid growth of pervasive computing devices.

In this paper, we propose a novel mobile cloud architecture to save smart mobile device's energy while addressing drawbacks in the aforementioned architectures. A specific mobility model and a theoretic energy consumption model will be presented. The effectiveness of energy-saving is supported by real life experiment results.

2   Architecture Description

The mobile cloud architecture that we propose makes up of cloud organizers and smart mobile devices in their vicinity. A cloud organizer is a central Bluetooth device. Besides receiving and sending Bluetooth data, it stores information about mobile devices within its vicinity and updates the information periodically. Such a device can easily be incorporated in other more powerful routing and computing devices. It is believed that many routers in the future will have Bluetooth low energy equipped [16]. All we need to do to turn such a router into one of our cloud organizer is to make it capable of storing and updating vicinity mobile device information, which is all software and easy to implement. Hence, we see no incentive of building more costly cloudlets to reduce data transmission cost. As shown in Figure 1, this is the simplest unit of our mobile cloud architecture. Each mobile device is connected to the cloud organizer via Bluetooth low energy (BLE) [6]. The reason of having a centralized cloud organizer instead of forming a mobile Ad Hoc network is to save smart mobile device's energy. Vicinity devices discovery, task decomposition and reconstruction can be done by the centralized cloud organizer, and the energy consumption of routing for mobile devices is less compared to a mobile Ad Hoc network topology. Also, the mobility nature of mobile devices is considered one of the factors that affect the performance of mobile device workload offloading. It is even more so in our case, since the BLE is a short range communication protocol with a maximum theoretical transmission range around 100 meters [17]. Mobility issue will be discussed in the next section.

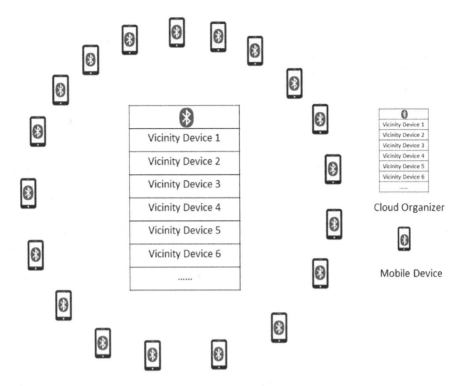

Fig. 1. Mobile cloud with a centralized cloud organizer

Bluetooth low energy was first introduced by Nokia in 2006 and later became part of the Bluetooth standard. The main advantage of Bluetooth low energy technology compared with classic Bluetooth technology is suggested by its name – low energy computation. As shown by other researchers [5], [7], power consumption introduced by data transmission over Wi-Fi or cellular network is one of the major drawbacks of offloading workload to a remote cloud. By employing Bluetooth low energy technology, theoretically our architecture can reduce much data transmission power consumption. We are open to the choice of short range wireless transmission technologies, but for now Bluetooth low energy seems to be the best fit [13].

3   Mobility Model

Understanding human mobility patterns are considered of great importance and different human mobility models have been proposed [13]. However, these mobility models are built to capture the mobility patterns that span over a long period of time, usually in the scale of days. In our case, a typical mobile CPU-bound application workload is most likely to have an upper limit for completion time that under a minute. Hence, we need to construct a specific human mobility model that captures the mobility pattern in the scale of a couple seconds within a radius of 100 meters.

Also, it is reasonable to assume the average mobility speed of each individual is average human walking speed. (For simplicity, we assume each device is moving in a constant speed if it does not offload workload to the cloud organizer.) Because it is not beneficial to install a cloud organizer in an environment that mobile devices are passing by so quickly that cannot stay to form a relatively reliable mobile cloud resource pool. We also assume the mobile device that offload workload to the cloud organizer will stay put or at least not moving out of the cloud organizer's vicinity, since the user is aware that he/she is expecting the result from the cloud organizer.

Given the aforementioned circumstances, our mobility model is much simplified. The cloud organizer will keep track of the distance of mobile devices in its vicinity to itself and their velocity. With the distance and velocity information, the cloud organizer will be able to estimate the minimum time that a mobile device will stay in its vicinity. For instance, a device is 40m away from the cloud organizer and moving at a speed of 2m/s, then the minimum time it will stay in the 100 meter radius vicinity will be $(100-40)/2 = 30s$. Hence, the cloud organizer will know that a workload that can be finished within 30s is ok to offload to this device.

To clarify, this mobility model only considers the scenario of only one cloud organizer in an area. The mobility issue of multiple inter-connected cloud organizers will be further explored in our future work.

4   Profiling

Both at the smart mobile device side and the cloud organizer side, profiling is needed to make offloading decisions. We assume each mobile smart device will monitor its CPU voltage supply, CPU frequency, distance from the cloud organizer and send the information periodically to the cloud organizer via Bluetooth low energy to keep cloud organizers' knowledge of surrounding mobile devices updated. Given a similar CPU condition, the mobile device that closer to the cloud organizer will be preferred to offload to. Other than information about CPU status, the cloud organizer will profile the amount of each mobile device's net offloaded workload. Net offloaded workload equals to the total workload a mobile device has offloaded to other mobile devices minus the total workload a mobile device has been assigned from other mobile devices. As we are focused on CPU-bound applications in this study, the net offloaded workload is measured in CPU instructions. Net offloaded workload is used to prevent selfish users. When a mobile device's net offloaded workload reached preset upper limit, the cloud organizer will no longer assign its workload to other mobile devices. To lower its net offloaded workload under the upper limit, a mobile device will have to undertake other mobile devices' workload. Hence it is a good practice to contribute your idle CPU computing power when a neighboring mobile device is in need to gain offloading quota for future use when the idle and in need situation switches.

5   Energy Consumption Model

Profiling along is not enough to make offloading decisions. An energy consumption model for smart mobile devices' CPU-bound application is needed to put profiled information into calculation and then make offloading decisions. Different from [5], as we have employed the Bluetooth low energy technology, the energy consumption overhead introduced by data transmission is much smaller when compared to the energy consumption of CPU; hence the former can be ignored and this study will focus on the energy consumption caused by CPU.

To extend battery life, dynamic voltage and frequency scaling (DVFS) is commonly used in nowadays smart mobile devices to lower CPU power consumption [11]. The CPU power consumption denoted as P is given as:

$$P = N*C* V^2 *f \tag{1}$$

Where N is the switching activity, C is the load capacitance, V is the CPU supplied voltage and f is the CPU frequency. From equation (1), we can observe that CPU power consumption is proportional to the square of CPU voltage times CPU frequency. To save energy, it is of interest for a mobile device to operate under a relatively lower CPU voltage supply. In this study, we assume the mobile devices have low, median and high three CPU voltage supply levels. Each level has its upper limit of supported CPU frequency.

When a CPU-bound workload is created by a mobile device, its total CPU instructions needed and the maximum time allowed to finish the workload is known. Based on that information, the mobile device can estimate the minimum increment of CPU frequency (total CPU instructions/ maximum time allowed) if this workload is to be performed on the mobile device along. If the required CPU frequency is higher than the maximum CPU frequency the mobile device can support, then the workload will be offloaded to the cloud organizer directly. If the required CPU frequency is higher than the upper limit under current voltage supply but lower than the maximum CPU frequency, the mobile device will send a small packet, transmission time and energy negligible, containing the aforementioned information (total CPU instructions needed and the maximum time allowed) to its cloud organizer. The cloud organizer will then determine based on its record of mobile devices in its vicinity if offloading this workload can save energy and give offload or no-offload order to the mobile device.

The decision of which mobile devices to offload to is made by considering CPU voltage state and idle CPU frequency [1] of all mobile devices within a cloud organizer's vicinity. Lower CPU voltage state and larger idle CPU frequency is preferred. Lower CPU voltage state means less power consumption. Larger idle CPU frequency means less workload decomposition and reconstruction time overhead. We assume the time to decompose and reconstruct a workload is proportional to the number of decomposed parts. For the purpose of this study, we assume enough idle CPU frequency can be found in the cloud organizer's vicinity. The variables related to the offloading decision are shown in Table 1.

---

[1] Idle CPU frequency = maximum supported CPU frequency under current CPU voltage supply – occupied CPU frequency.

Table 1. Offloading decision related variables

Variable	Description
S	Total CPU instructions needed
T	Maximum time allowed
$T_{forward}$	Time to forward a decomposed workload to neighboring cloud organizer
D	Workload packet size
P_b	Bluetooth transmission power
B_b	Bluetooth transmission bandwidth
P_s	CPU power if perform the workload on a single mobile device
P_m	CPU power if perform the workload on a multiple mobile devices
E_s	Energy consumed if does not offload
E_m	Energy consumed if offload

Hence, E_s and E_s can be calculated as shown by equation (2) and (3) respectively.

$$E_s = P_s * T \tag{2}$$

$$E_m = P_m *(T - 2\,D/\,B_b - 2T_{forward}) + P_b *(2*D/\,B_b) \tag{3}$$

If $E_s > E_m$ then the workload will be offloaded.

Below is a summary of the assumptions we made.

a. Workload in this study is generated by elastic CPU-bound applications and can be partitioned freely.

b. Smart mobile devices in this study can run each other's partitioned workload seamlessly.

c. A CPU-bound workload is created with its total CPU instructions needed and time limit specified.

d. Time to decompose and reconstruct a workload is proportional to the number of decomposed parts

e. Sufficient idle CPU frequency at the cloud organizer's vicinity.

6   Experimental Evaluation

We used two Hongmi phones with Android version 4.2.2 to do the energy consumption experiment. Their CPUs are designed to operate under these frequencies: 497MHz, 754MHz, 988MHz, 1209MHz, 1508MHz. We used a simple android app that count prime numbers within user specified range to create CPU intensive workload and we assume the Bluetooth data to be transferred is 50kB, which is fairly large considering the little information it conveys. PowerTutor [14] is used to measure the energy consumption. We did the experiment a couple dozen times and took the average.

The energy to perform the workload in a single Hongmi phone is 1.63J, on two Hongmi phone is 0.59J each, and Bluetooth data transfer 0.13J. Hence, the total energy consumption to offload is 0.59J*2+0.13J = 1.31J and 19.6% energy is saved.

Since the energy consumption is highly device-dependent and application-dependent, there is no fair way to compare our results with other offloading architectures'. However, we will explore the effectiveness of our architecture for different mobile devices and applications as a future work.

7   Conclusion and Future Work

We propose a novel workload offloading architecture for smart mobile devices. The architecture aims to reduce their energy consumption when executing CPU-bound applications. Our experimental results show that such architecture indeed can save mobile devices energy and hence prolong their battery life. We envision such cloud organizer infrastructure is feasible in the very near future. For future work, the effectiveness of our proposed architecture for different mobile devices and applications will be explored. More realistic and robust mobility models will also be included in our study.

References

1. Cui, Y., et al.: A survey of energy efficient wireless transmission and modeling in mobile cloud computing. Mobile Networks and Applications 18(1), 148–155 (2013)
2. http://aws.amazon.com/ec2
3. Marinelli, E.E.: Hyrax: cloud computing on mobile devices using MapReduce. No. CMU-CS-09-164. Carnegie-Mellon Univ. Pittsburgh PA School of Computer Science (2009)
4. Satyanarayanan, M., et al.: The case for vm-based cloudlets in mobile computing. IEEE Pervasive Computing 8(4), 14–23 (2009)
5. Kumar, K., Lu, Y.-H.: Cloud computing for mobile users: Can offloading computation save energy? Computer 43(4), 51–56 (2010)
6. http://www.bluetooth.com/Pages/Bluetooth-Smart.aspx
7. Barbera, M.V., et al.: To offload or not to offload? the bandwidth and energy costs of mobile cloud computing. In: 2013 Proceedings IEEE INFOCOM. IEEE (2013)
8. Balan, R., et al.: The case for cyber foraging. In: Proceedings of the 10th Workshop on ACM SIGOPS European Workshop. ACM (2002)
9. Sharifi, M., Kafaie, S., Kashefi, O.: A survey and taxonomy of cyber foraging of mobile devices. IEEE Communications Surveys & Tutorials 14(4), 1232–1243 (2012)
10. Yu, C., Lee, B., Youn, H.Y.: Energy efficient routing protocols for mobile ad hoc networks. Wireless Communications and Mobile Computing 3(8), 959–973 (2003)

11. Liang, Y., Lai, P., Chiou, C.: An energy conservation DVFS algorithm for the android operating system. Journal of Convergence 1(1) (2010)
12. http://www.aryaka.com/
13. Siekkinen, M., et al.: How low energy is bluetooth low energy? comparative measurements with zigbee/802.15. 4. In: 2012 IEEE Wireless Communications and Networking Conference Workshops (WCNCW). IEEE (2012)
14. http://ziyang.eecs.umich.edu/projects/powertutor/
15. Gonzalez, M.C., Hidalgo, C.A., Barabasi, A.-L.: Understanding individual human mobility patterns. Nature 453(7196), 779–782 (2008)
16. http://www.pcworld.com/article/2148560/cloudsavvy-bluetooth-41-to-reach-devices-by-year-end.html
17. http://www.bluetooth.com/Pages/low-energy-tech-info.aspx

Human Readable Scenario Specification for Automated Creation of Simulations on CloudSim

Manoel C. Silva Filho[1,2,*] and Joel José P. C. Rodrigues[2]

[1] Instituto Federal de Educação do Tocantins (IFTO),
Palmas, Tocantins, 77021-090, Brazil
mcampos@ifto.edu.br
http://www.ifto.edu.br
[2] University of Beira Interior (UBI),
Covilhã, Castelo Branco, Portugal 6201-001
d1365@ubi.pt, joeljr@ieee.org
http://di.ubi.pt

Abstract. Cloud Computing is a widely used computing model which enables customers to deliver services to their end users, with reduced IT management and costs. However, the deployment of applications for the cloud may require the design of the needed environment. CloudSim is a very well-known simulation tool to project these cloud scenarios. However, each scenario creation requires programming efforts that are time-consuming, error prone, not necessarily reusable and commonly only feasible for experienced programmers. This paper presents a tool to define cloud scenarios using YAML files and automates the creation of simulations at CloudSim. The use of human readable YAML data format allows the entire split of the scenario specification and the simulation execution and allows non-programmers to clear and directly define the simulation scenarios, facilitating the scenarios sharing, extension and reuse.

Keywords: CloudSim, Simulation, Automation, YAML, Scenarios, Java.

1 Introduction

Cloud Computing is a consolidated way to provide computing services to customers in a pay-per-use basis. The customers account with virtually unlimited resources which can be used at any time according to the demand of services hosted at the cloud provider. Cloud resources are managed autonomously to enable the multi-tenancy of the hosts, typically using virtualization [1–10].

However, the deployment of applications for the cloud may require tests and experiments prior to the stage where they are turned available for the users. These tests may define the feasibility of the project, but experiments in a real

---

* Scholarship from CAPES - Proc. no 13585/13-4.

R.C.-H. Hsu and W. Shangguang (Eds.): IOV 2014, LNCS 8662, pp. 345–356, 2014.

cloud scenario may not be easy and represent a cost which may be avoided. The use of simulation tools such as CloudSim [11] facilitates the cloud computing research process, avoiding costs and wasting time with other details that are not related to the desired research topic. For customers who want to deploy applications to cloud, the resources required by the application can be measured, demand fluctuations can be tested and costs can be estimated in an easy and predicted way.

The creation of simulation scenarios at CloudSim tool requires programming [11, 12]. So, the researcher will waste time with concerns that are not directly related to the scenario definition and he/she does not have a split between the scenario specification and the code needed to create and execute it. Every change in the scenario may require new changes on the code, so the researcher cannot only focus the attention on the problem that he/she wants to solve, such as creating new algorithms to load balancing, new tasks and virtual machines (VM) scheduling policies, VM placement, resource provisioning, workload prediction, server consolidation, energy efficiency, cost reduction and so on. Besides, the definition of complex simulation scenarios may not be clear to others researches or to customers that will pay for a service that is being developed. This makes difficult the creation of new simulation scenarios, due to the needed programming, and does not give a complete overview of the created scenario.

The current paper presents a solution to solve these problems. It tries to completely avoid the use of programming to define cloud simulation scenarios at CloudSim. The proposed tool allows the specification of simulation scenarios to be defined using a YAML file, that is a pretty human readable data format. The proposed tool was developed using Java 7 and is available under GNU GPLv3 License at http://github.com/manoelcampos/CloudSimAutomation/.

The paper is organised as follows. The related works are reviewed in Section 2. Section 3 presents the available tools used in this work while the proposed approach is described in Section 4. Results are discussed in Section 5. And finally, Section 6 includes the conclusions of this work and proposes several future works.

2   Related Work

There is a restrict set of original and independent cloud computing simulation tools. Some of the most recent ones are presented in the section.

The CloudSched simulation tool is presented in [13]. It is a simulation tool aiming the evaluation of resource scheduling for cloud computing applications. The simulator can be used to experiment different scheduling policies and resource allocation schemes. The tool focuses only in scheduling VMs at the IaaS layer. It has a graphical user interface (GUI) to create the simulation setup and it allows the specification of scenarios using files, but in non-standard and undocumented text file format.

The tool is developed in Java, available for multi-platform and is freely available on the Web (http://cloudsched.sourceforge.net) but it is not open source. So, this limits the tool extension, for instance, forbidding external developers to create and evaluate new scheduling policies.

The GUI allows non-programmers to define simulation scenarios but it is overly simplistic and very limited. In the version available to download, different from the paper, there is only one window where the simulation scenario is specified. At this window, there are only the limited quantity of 3 physical machines (PM) and 8 virtual machine (VM) types. Despite the fact that it is possible to change the configuration using the text files, the number of PM's and VM's is fixed, what severally limits the tool usefulness to simulate real cloud environments. The results are only presented with graphs that are unclear and without the tool source code, they cannot be improved. The scheduling algorithms, despite of many, are pre-defined too.

A survey on cloud-based simulation is presented in [14]. In this kind of simulation the tools run into a real cloud environment instead of the developer local machine. These simulation tools provide new cloud computing service models such as modeling as a service (MaaS), execution as a service (EaaS), analysis as a service (AaaS) and simulation resources as a service (SRaaS). These new service models enable developers to use simulation tools as a service, like software as a service (SaaS) model, but called simulation as a service (SIMaaS).

This work presents an architecture to cloud-based simulation and reports about a prototype which, apparently, is not available on the Web. This kind of simulation is helpful to perform cumbersome simulations directly in the cloud. It releases the developer to configure a simulation environment in his/her local computer and can reduce simulation time using more powerful machines in the cloud. However, the use of simulation as a service (SIMaaS) will represent an additional cost if the developer needs to pay for this service. Not all institutions and research groups can afford this cost, even less develop their own SIMaaS infrastructure. Moreover, depending on the tools available in the SIMaaS provider, to specify and execute the simulation it can require the use of some application programming interfaces (API's), like in the traditional cloud services such as Amazon WS (AWS).

In [15], the design and development of a cloud-based simulation tool is presented, following the simulation service models presented at [14]. However, there is no mentioned a concrete tool or service freely available.

The Stratus cloud computing simulation framework is presented in [16], inside the SciCloud project (http://ds.cs.ut.ee/research/scicloud) [17]. It aims to provide simulations of data processing for scientific applications on the cloud, like the established Hadoop MapReduce framework, but using the bulk synchronous parallel (BSP) computing model. One of the main focus of the framework is to simplify the work for researchers not experts in developing distributed applications. So, the efforts can be concentrated to solve a specific problem, leaving the framework accountable of the parallelization to accomplish the task. The framework uses the elasticity benefits of cloud computing to on-demand provisioning resources for scientific applications. The parallelization task will be realized automatically by the framework using the BSP approach. So, the main goal is to provide a framework for running cumbersome scientific applications on the cloud, not a more general framework to simulate and test different cloud computing features like scheduling algorithms, VM placement and live migration, and so on.

3   Used Simulation Tools

The next sub-sections present the simulation tools used in this work. These tools were chosen because they are open source and widely used tools.

3.1   CloudSim Simulation Tool

CloudSim is an open source tool for modeling and simulation of cloud environments. It was developed on the top of GridSim simulation toolkit, that uses the SimJava discrete event simulation engine [12]. It simplifies the process of asses large cloud environments and the test of algorithms for cloud, such as tasks and VM scheduling, VM placement and migration, load balancing and so on.

However, the creation of cloud environments, and each object on it, is performed programmatically. The tool does not provide a simpler manner to specify the environment and execute the simulation. Each simulation scenario needs to be created by a developer using Java programming language.

3.2   CloudReports Graphical Tool

CloudReports [18] is a front-end to CloudSim [12]. It facilitates the process of creating cloud simulation scenarios using a graphical user interface and avoiding the need of programming. It runs on top of CloudSim, creating and executing the simulation scenarios on it.

It is a ready and easy to use tool which can be used instead of directly programming the cloud scenarios at CloudSim. Nevertheless, the tool does not allow the automation of the process of creating the whole scenario. The scenario is created graphically using the application interface. For larger environments, this can be boring and time-consuming. In addition, the tool does not allow the sharing of specifications among different research teams.

4   Proposal to Automate the Creation of CloudSim Simulation Environments

In this proposed work, cloud simulation scenarios are defined into a YAML file. YAML is the simpler human readable data serialization standard which was found in the literature and it makes easy to define a cloud simulation scenario directly, using any YAML editor or even a simple text editor. It is a non-bureaucratic data format that, different from the XML standard, does not need to close tags (keys). This simplifies and speeds up manual creation of YAML files.

In the YAML simulation scenarios, the YAML keys were defined based on the CloudReports' registries classes, as presented at Figure 1. These classes represent an abstract definition of CloudSim objects for the creation of simulation scenarios. By means of these classes, objects like datacenters, storage area networks (SANs), hosts, virtual machines (VMs), customers and applications (cloudlets) can be defined at a higher level. Using them, the amount of determined objects, like hosts, owning the same configuration, can be specified only one time. So, this speeds up the process of creating the cloud environment's objects. Thus, the creation of, for instance, 1, 2, 10, or even 100000 hosts with the same configuration has the same effort.

At Figure 1 there are the top level registries objects *datacenterRegistries* and *customerRegistries*, that represent, respectively, the abstract information of datacenters and customers in the cloud simulation scenario. These registries are a list of registry objects. The amount key, present in almost all objects which can be specified in the YAML file, defines the amount of the current object to be created during the scenario creation. The scenario is created by the proposed tool and, after this, it is executed on CloudSim. So, for instance, each datacenter in the *datacenterRegistries* list, represents a specific datacenter configuration. For each one in this list, will be created the concrete objects in the amount specified by the amount key.

The YAML snippet, presented at Listing 1.1, shows the creation of 1 datacenter with a specific configuration and the creation of 2 more datacenters that share another configuration. The first datacenter was defined with different costs of the other two ones and has VM migration disabled.

Listing 1.1. Cloud simulation environment 1: YAML sample file

```
1  datacenterRegistries:
2    - !datacenter
3      amount: 1
4      allocationPolicyAlias: Simple
5      vmMigration: false
6      costPerSec: 0.2
7      costPerMem: 0.04
8      costPerStorage: 0.004
9      costPerBw: 0.25
10   - !datacenter
11     amount: 2
12     allocationPolicyAlias: Simple
13     vmMigration: true
14     costPerSec: 0.1
15     ...
```

As can be seen in the Listing 1.2, other cloud objects can be specified. Inside each defined datacenter, a list of storage area networks (SANs) and physical hosts can be specified. Inside each defined customer, a list of virtual machines and cloudlets can be specified.

4.1   Architecture

The tool was developed with Java 7 and runs on top of CloudSim, using some CloudReports' classes presented in the Figure 1. It is a command line application, like CloudSim, that loads a specified YAML file containing the definition(s) of simulation scenario(s). It uses the YamlBeans[1], a very simple and complete YAML parser for Java that can serialize plain old java objects (POJOs) to YAML and deserialize YAML content to POJOs.

---

[1] http://github.com/EsotericSoftware/yamlbeans

The proposed tool parses the YAML file containing the simulation scenario specification, storing the definitions into CloudReports registries objects. These registries are used to autonomously creating the concrete objects that will constitute the cloud environment (datacenters, hosts, VMs, etc). Besides, with all concrete objects created at the desired amount, specified at the YAML file, the tool runs the simulation in CloudSim, organizing and showing the results into appropriated tables.

At Figure 1, this process is drawn. The automation module will parse the YAML file, creating CloudReports' registries objects, and generating the Java code needed to create the cloud environment and run the simulation on CloudSim. This generated code is called "User Code" by CloudSim. After the code generation, the simulation is executed into CloudSim, presenting the results in the terminal.

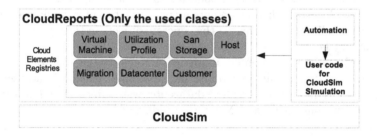

Fig. 1. Architecture for the creation of cloud scenarios (Adapted from [11])

4.2   Demonstration Scenario

To demonstrate the use of the proposed tool, the Listing 1.2 presents a simulation scenario defined into a YAML file. The scenario has 1 datacenter with 4 physical hosts owning the same configuration. Each host has the following configuration: 1 TB of RAM (1000000 MB), 100 Mbps of bandwidth (100000 bps), 40 TB of storage (40000 GB), and a quad-core processor (numOfPes - number of processing elements) with each core having a processing capacity of 50000 million instructions per second (MIPS). The virtual machines placed on each host will be executed using a time shared scheduler, allowing the VMs' execution to be scaled along the time.

Each host will use a simple policy on provisioning RAM (ramProvisioner-Alias), bandwidth (bwProvisionerAlias) and processor's cores (peProvisioner-Alias) to the virtual machines allocated on it. The simple provisioning uses the best effort algorithm to allocate the requested resources. So, if there are enough resources, they will be provisioned, otherwise, the provisioning will fail. These simple provisioners are the only available with CloudSim currently. Whether the developer wants another provisioner policies, he/she needs to implement them, extending the CloudSim classes.

On this scenario 2 customers were defined. In CloudSim they are represented by a broker. A broker is a component on the cloud that works on behalf of the service's users. So, when the users make a request to the service, the broker is responsible for negotiating with the cloud coordinator the provision of the resources needed to meet the application's QoS [12]. Each customer has 2 VMs with the following configuration: 500 MB of image size (size of the entire VM on disk), a dual-core processor (numOfPes) with each core having a processing capacity of 1000 million instructions per second, 2 GB of RAM (2000 MB) and 1 Mbps of bandwidth (1000 bps). The tasks will be executed using a space shared scheduler. This means that when an application starts, it will use the provisioned processor cores until the end of its execution. This can cause a longer wait time for the applications that depend of the busy cores.

For each customer created, 6 cloudlets to be executed were specified. The cloudlets are objects of CloudSim that represent the customer's applications in the simulation scenario. They are abstractions of the real cloud applications. So, one cloudlet only represents the computing requirements of a real application [12].

Each cloudlet was defined with the following requirements: 2 processor cores (cloudletsPesNumber) needed, 100 million of instructions (MI) to be executed, with 50 bytes of input file size (application code + input data) and 70 bytes of output file size (input file size + output data). The cloudlets were defined to use the whole required resources (RAM, bandwidth and CPU) during 100% of its execution time. This is defined by the "Full" value in the *utilizationModelXXX* keys.

Listing 1.2. Cloud simulation environment 2: YAML sample file

```
 1  datacenterRegistries:
 2    - !datacenter
 3      amount: 1
 4      allocationPolicyAlias: Simple
 5      vmMigration: enabled
 6      costPerSec: 0.1
 7      ...
 8      sanList:
 9        - !san
10          capacity: 10000
11          bandwidth: 10000
12          networkLatency: 5
13      hostList:
14        - !host
15          amount: 4
16          ram: 1000000
17          bw: 100000
18          storage: 40000
19          numOfPes: 4
20          mipsPerPe: 50000
21          schedulingPolicyAlias: TimeShared
22          ramProvisionerAlias: Simple
23          ...
24  customerRegistries:
25    - !customer
26      amount: 2
27      vmList:
28        - !vm
29          amount: 10
30          size: 500
```

```
31              pesNumber: 4
32              mips: 1000
33              ram: 2000
34              bw: 1000
35              schedulingPolicyAlias: SpaceShared
36              vmm: Xen
37         utilizationProfile:
38         - !profile
39              numOfCloudlets: 6
40              cloudletsPesNumber: 2
41              length: 100
42              fileSize: 50
43              outputSize: 70
44              utilizationModelCpuAlias: Full
45              ...
```

5   Result Analysis

As can be seen in the scenario presented at Listing 1.2, there are 2 dual-core VMs for each one of the 2 customers. However, for each customer there are 6 cloudlets (applications) requiring 2 processor cores each one. Therefore, there are not enough VMs for each customer to run his/her applications at the same time. So, a space shared scheduler to the VM's tasks was defined and each cloudlet will require all the 2 cores of one customer's VM, only one cloudlet will be executed per time. By this way, the others cloudlets will wait in a queue. This can be seen at the Figure 2.

```
name broker1 id 3 cloudlets executed: 6==============================================================
CloudletID|    STATUS   |    DataCenterID|    VmID|  HostID| ExecTime|    Start Time|    Finish
int        |    string   |    int         |    int |  int   | secs    |    secs      |    secs
1          |    SUCCESS  |    2           |    1   |        | 0,11    |    0,1       |    0,21
2          |    SUCCESS  |    2           |    2   |        | 0,11    |    0,1       |    0,21
3          |    SUCCESS  |    2           |    1   |        | 0,11    |    0,21      |    0,32
4          |    SUCCESS  |    2           |    2   |        | 0,11    |    0,21      |    0,32
5          |    SUCCESS  |    2           |    1   |        | 0,11    |    0,32      |    0,43
6          |    SUCCESS  |    2           |    2   |        | 0,11    |    0,32      |    0,43

name broker2 id 4 cloudlets executed: 6==============================================================
CloudletID|    STATUS   |    DataCenterID|    VmID|  HostID| ExecTime|    Start Time|    Finish
int        |    string   |    int         |    int |  int   | secs    |    secs      |    secs
7          |    SUCCESS  |    2           |    3   |        | 0,11    |    0,1       |    0,21
8          |    SUCCESS  |    2           |    4   |        | 0,11    |    0,1       |    0,21
9          |    SUCCESS  |    2           |    3   |        | 0,11    |    0,21      |    0,32
10         |    SUCCESS  |    2           |    4   |        | 0,11    |    0,21      |    0,32
11         |    SUCCESS  |    2           |    3   |        | 0,11    |    0,32      |    0,43
12         |    SUCCESS  |    2           |    4   |        | 0,11    |    0,32      |    0,43
```

Fig. 2. Execution results of cloud simulation scenario presented at Listing 1.2

At the referred figure, it can be seen 2 brokers representing the customers defined in the simulation scenario. For each customer, 6 cloudlets were executed. The two VMs of each customer were instantiated. The VMs number 1 and 2 were assigned to the customer 1 (represented by broker 1) and the VMs number 3 and 4 were assigned to the customer 2 (represented by broker 2). At the column "ExecTime" it can be seen that all cloudlets took the same time to finish, because all cloudlets and VMs have the same configurations. However, the finish time was variable. According to the VMs and cloudlets configurations and defined restrictions, only one cloudlet can be executed at a VM per time. So, since each customer has two VMs, two customers cloudlets can be executed per time (each one into a separated VM). By this way, the first two cloudlets of each customer have the same finish time. The next two cloudlets have another finish time and the next ones too.

If the processor cores of the VMs are changed to 4, it will be possible to run two cloudlets at the same VM, so the waiting time will be reduced. This can be seen at Figure 3. The cloudlets 1, 2, 3 and 4 had the same finish time due to the fact they started at the same time. Cloudlets 1 and 3 were executed at VM 1 and cloudlets 2 and 4 were executed at VM 2. The cloudlets 5 and 6 had to wait until the end of the other ones, so their start time is exactly the finish time of the previous cloudlets. In this case, the used broker chose to allocate one customer's VM to each cloudlet, even if the two remaining cloudlets would be executed at the same VM. To change this behaviour it is needed to extend the DatacenterBroker CloudSim's class. Only the first customer results were shown because they are identical, once his/her VMs and cloudlets configurations are the same.

```
Broker: name broker1 id 3 cloudlets executed: 6================================================
###|     CloudletID|     STATUS   |     DataCenterID|     VmID|   HostID| ExecTime|      Start Time|     Finish
int|     int        |     string   |     int          |     int |   int    | secs     |      secs       |     secs
  1|     1          |     SUCCESS  |     2            |     1   |          | 0,11     |      0,1         |     0,21
  2|     3          |     SUCCESS  |     2            |     1   |          | 0,11     |      0,1         |     0,21
  3|     2          |     SUCCESS  |     2            |     2   |          | 0,11     |      0,1         |     0,21
  4|     4          |     SUCCESS  |     2            |     2   |          | 0,11     |      0,1         |     0,21
  5|     5          |     SUCCESS  |     2            |     1   |          | 0,11     |      0,21        |     0,32
  6|     6          |     SUCCESS  |     2            |     2   |          | 0,11     |      0,21        |     0,32
```

Fig. 3. Execution's results of cloud simulation scenario with quad-core VMs

The results presented were based on those ones commonly displayed by CloudSim sample applications included with the tool. They were only organized and formatted to be more readable than in the samples. As the developed tool is open source, these results can be easily adapted to the needs of the researcher, because they only summarize the information obtained from the CloudSim objects after running the simulation.

The developed tool, instead of having a limited graphical user interface, like some of the related works, it enables the researcher to use all the features available for CloudSim. This flexibility is feasible due to the fact of the runtime load of the simulation scenario, specified into a external YAML file. The tool also allows the definition of entire and complex cloud environments, without limiting the amount of elements like physical hosts, virtual machines or scheduling algorithms. Considering that it depends of CloudSim, if new scheduling algorithms are included in the tool, there is only the need to recompile the project using the new CloudSim classes to make these new scheduling approaches available to be used in YAML simulation scenarios. Even the *MapReduce* computing model can be simulated by CloudSim applications using works like [19].

Therefore, CloudSim is a very flexible tool that allows a lot of computing paradigms to be implemented and experimented on it, instead of dictating a specific one, like in some presented related works. The proposed tool running on top of CloudSim brings new flexibilities and facilities for cloud simulations.

6   Conclusion and Future Works

This paper proposed a flexible and open source solution to facilitate the process of creating cloud simulation scenarios on CloudSim tool. The tool has been shown easy to use and the specification of simulation scenarios using the human readable YAML data format speeds up this task.

The YAML defined scenarios turn the process easy to overview, understanding, extend and share. They can be created using any simple text file editor. So, the tool can reduce the learning curve in understanding cloud technologies and simulation. Further, it may motivate researches in the cloud computing area due to the easiness of creating any desired cloud simulation scenarios.

As future works it is proposed the implementation of different resource allocation, VM scheduling and placement policies; the creation of random workload; the creation of policies to define elasticity for VM resources; the creation of policies for VM replication to enable load balancing; and the integration with CloudReports graphical user interface.

Acknowledgements. This work has been partially supported by scholarship from the CAPES Brazilian agency; by the Instituto Federal de Educação, Ciência e Tecnologia do Tocantins (Federal Institute of Education, Science and Technology of Tocantins - Brazil); by Instituto de Telecomunicações, Next Generation Networks and Applications Group (NetGNA), Covilhã Delegation; and by National Funding from the FCT – Fundação para a Ciência e a Tecnologia through the Pest-OE/EEI/LA0008/2013 Project.

References

1. Buyya, R., Yeo, C.S., Venugopal, S., Broberg, J., Brandic, I.: Cloud computing and emerging IT platforms: Vision, hype, and reality for delivering computing as the 5th utility. Future Generation Computer Systems 25(6), 599–616 (2009), http://linkinghub.elsevier.com/retrieve/pii/S0167739X08001957
2. Patidar, S., Rane, D., Jain, P.: A Survey Paper on Cloud Computing. In: 2012 Second International Conference on Advanced Computing and Communication Technologies, pp. 394–398 (January 2012), http://ieeexplore.ieee.org/lpdocs/epic03/wrapper.htm?arnumber=6168399
3. Younge, A.J., von Laszewski, G., Wang, L., Lopez-Alarcon, S., Carithers, W.: Efficient resource management for Cloud computing environments. In: International Conference on Green Computing, pp. 357–364 (August 2010), http://ieeexplore.ieee.org/lpdocs/epic03/wrapper.htm?arnumber=5598294

4. Armbrust, B., Griffith, R., Joseph, A.D., Katz, R., Konwinski, A., Lee, G., Patterson, D., Rabkin, A.: A view of cloud computing. Communications of the ACM (2010), http://dl.acm.org/citation.cfm?id=1721672
5. Espadas, J., Molina, A., Jiménez, G., Molina, M., Ramírez, R., Concha, D.: A tenant-based resource allocation model for scaling Software-as-a-Service applications over cloud computing infrastructures. Future Generation Computer Systems 29(1), 273–286 (2013), http://linkinghub.elsevier.com/retrieve/pii/S0167739X1100210X
6. Goyal, A., Dadizadeh, S.: A survey on cloud computing. University of British Columbia, Tech. Rep. (December 2009), http://unbreakablecloud.com/wordpress/wp-content/uploads/2011/02/A-Survey-On-Cloud-Computing.pdf
7. Zhang, Q., Cheng, L., Boutaba, R.: Cloud computing: state-of-the-art and research challenges. Journal of Internet Services and Applications 1(1), 7–18 (2010), http://www.springerlink.com/index/10.1007/s13174-010-0007-6
8. Zhang, Z., Wu, C., Cheung, D.: A survey on cloud interoperability: taxonomies, standards, and practice. ACM SIGMETRICS Performance Evaluation Review 40(4), 13–22 (2013), http://dl.acm.org/citation.cfm?id=2479945
9. Dillon, T., Wu, C., Chang, E.: Cloud Computing: Issues and Challenges. In: 2010 24th IEEE International Conference on Advanced Information Networking and Applications, pp. 27–33 (2010), http://ieeexplore.ieee.org/lpdocs/epic03/wrapper.htm?arnumber=5474674
10. Manvi, S.S., Krishna Shyam, G.: Resource management for Infrastructure as a Service (IaaS) in cloud computing: A survey. Journal of Network and Computer Applications, 1–17 (2013), http://linkinghub.elsevier.com/retrieve/pii/S1084804513002099
11. Calheiros, R.N.R., Ranjan, R., Beloglazov, A., Rose, A.F.D.: CloudSim: a toolkit for modeling and simulation of cloud computing environments and evaluation of resource provisioning algorithms. Software: Practice and Experience 41(1), 23–50 (2011), http://onlinelibrary.wiley.com/doi/10.1002/spe.995/full
12. Buyya, R., Ranjan, R., Calheiros, R.N.: Modeling and simulation of scalable Cloud computing environments and the CloudSim toolkit: Challenges and opportunities. In: 2009 International Conference on High Performance Computing and Simulation, pp. 1–11 (June 2009), http://ieeexplore.ieee.org/lpdocs/epic03/wrapper.htm?arnumber=5192685
13. Tian, W., Zhao, Y., Xu, M., Zhong, Y., Sun, X.: A Toolkit for Modeling and Simulation of Real-Time Virtual Machine Allocation in a Cloud Data Center. IEEE Transactions on Automation Science and Engineering, 1–9 (2013), http://ieeexplore.ieee.org/lpdocs/epic03/wrapper.htm?arnumber=6558510
14. Liu, X., Qiu, X., Chen, B., Huang, K.: Cloud-Based Simulation: The State-of-the-Art Computer Simulation Paradigm. In: 2012 ACM/IEEE/SCS 26th Workshop on Principles of Advanced and Distributed Simulation, pp. 71–74 (July 2012), http://ieeexplore.ieee.org/lpdocs/epic03/wrapper.htm?arnumber=6305887
15. Pan, Q., Pan, J., Wang, C.: Simulation in Cloud Computing Envrionment. In: 2013 International Conference on Service Sciences (ICSS), pp. 107–112 (April 2013), http://ieeexplore.ieee.org/lpdocs/epic03/wrapper.htm?arnumber=6519772

16. Jakovits, P., Srirama, S.N., Kromonov, I.: Stratus: A Distributed Computing Framework for Scientific Simulations on the Cloud. In: 2012 IEEE 14th International Conference on High Performance Computing and Communication & 2012 IEEE 9th International Conference on Embedded Software and Systems, pp. 1053–1059 (June 2012), http://ieeexplore.ieee.org/lpdocs/epic03/wrapper.htm?arnumber=6332290
17. Srirama, S., Batrashev, O., Vainikko, E.: SciCloud: Scientific Computing on the Cloud. In: 2010 10th IEEE/ACM International Conference on Cluster, Cloud and Grid Computing, pp. 579–580 (2010), http://ieeexplore.ieee.org/lpdocs/epic03/wrapper.htm?arnumber=5493427
18. Teixeira Sá, T.: CloudReports: uma ferramenta gráfica para a simulação de ambientes computacionais em nuvem baseada no framework CloudSim. In: Simpósio Brasileiro de Sistemas Distribuídos e Redes de Computadores (SBRC), pp. 103–116 (2011), http://sbrc2011.facom.ufms.br/files/workshops/wcga/ST03_2.pdf
19. Jung, J., Kim, H.: MR-CloudSim: Designing and implementing MapReduce computing model on CloudSim. In: 2012 International Conference on ICT Convergence (ICTC), pp. 504–509 (2012), http://ieeexplore.ieee.org/xpls/abs_all.jsp?arnumber=6387186

A Cloud Computing Framework
for On-Demand Forecasting Services

Kwa-Sur Tam and Rakesh Sehgal

Department of Electrical & Computer Engineering,
Virginia Tech,
Blacksburg, VA 24061, U.S.A.
ktam@vt.edu

Abstract. This paper presents the Forecast-as-a-Service (FaaS) framework, a cloud-based framework that provides on-demand customer-defined forecasting services. Based on the principles of service-oriented architecture (SOA), the FaaS enables the use of different types of data from different sources to generate different kinds of forecasts at different levels of detail for different prices. The FaaS framework has been developed to provide on-demand forecasts of solar or wind power. Forecasts can be long-term forecasts useful for prospecting or planning by potential investors, or short-term forecasts suitable for operational decision making by operators of existing facilities. FaaS provides a more flexible and affordable alternative to the subscription model provided by current forecast service vendors. By improving the flexibility and economics of renewable energy forecasting services with SOA and cloud computing, FaaS achieves the goal of Services Computing.

Keywords: Services Computing, Service-Oriented Architecture, Service Prices.

1   Introduction

Accurate forecasting of resource availability to meet future demand is essential for the success of any business endeavor. Forecasting methods may be classified as quantitative or qualitative [1, 2, 3]. Requiring a lot of data for model formulation and validation, quantitative forecasting is inherently data intensive and computational intensive. Providing almost unlimited computing resources on a pay-as-you-go basis, Cloud Computing can provide new options for the development and deliverance of quantitative forecasts. Cloud Computing is especially meaningful to individuals and small to medium companies that lack the computing resources to obtain and process information that are important for their specific forecasting applications.

This paper presents the Forecast-as-a-Service (FaaS) framework, a cloud-based framework that provides on-demand customer-defined forecasting services. Based on the principles of service-oriented architecture (SOA) [4], FaaS enables the use of different types of data from different sources to generate different kinds of forecasts at different levels of details for different prices. The FaaS framework has been

R.C.-H. Hsu and W. Shangguang (Eds.): IOV 2014, LNCS 8662, pp. 357–366, 2014.
© Springer International Publishing Switzerland 2014

developed to provide on-demand forecasts of solar or wind power at locations specified by the customers. Forecasts can be long-term forecasts useful for prospecting or
planning by potential investors, or short-term forecasts suitable for operational decision making by operators of existing facilities. Results of this project indicate that
the costs of prospecting forecasts are in the range of US$ 60-80 while the costs for
operational forecasts are in the range of US$ 10-20. Additional services such as un-
certainty quantification can be rendered for additional prices in the order of a
few dollars. A major contribution of the FaaS framework is that it provides a more
flexible and affordable alternative to the costly monthly/annual subscription model
provided by current forecast service vendors. In addition, the FaaS framework may be
viewed as a preliminary version of a cloud pattern for forecasting applications.

The underlying concepts for the FaaS framework are discussed in Section 2.
Implementation of the FaaS framework is presented in Section 3. Results are shown
in Section 4. Related work is discussed in Section 5. Conclusions are presented in
Section 6.

2   Concepts

2.1   Quantitative Forecasting Process

Procedures of quantitative forecasting processes may be grouped into four major steps
as shown in Figure 1.

1. Problem Definition: specify the purpose and the level of details. This is the
   most important step and it affects all other steps.
2. Data Collection: collect data relevant to solving the defined problem.
3. Analysis and Model Formulation: analyze the collected data to extract useful
   information to form the forecasting models.
4. Forecasting: generate forecast results by using the forecasting model.

2.2   Service-Oriented Architecture

The service-oriented architecture (SOA) approach in software development offers the
benefits of modularity, reusability, composability, abstraction, standardization, modularity, loose coupling and discoverability [4]. Services and composite services can be
combined into workflows that represent the behavior of business models. The major
steps of a quantitative forecasting process may be viewed as activities in a workflow.
Different types of forecasts, implemented by different workflows, can be formulated by
orchestrating different combinations of services and composite services.

Fig. 1 shows the layered organization of the services, composite services and
workflows in the FaaS framework. Services in the Service Layer consist of the fundamental and agnostic services that are not coupled to any specific application. They
perform tasks such as data transfer over the Internet (Transfer Tools services), statistical analysis (Statistical Tools services), forecasting (Forecast Tools services), etc.

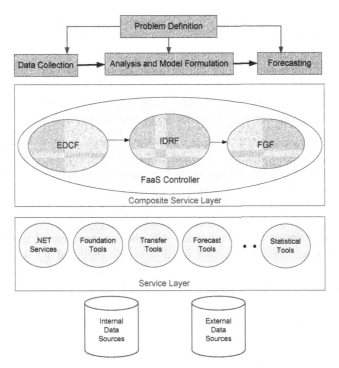

Fig. 1. Service-oriented architecture for the quantitative forecasting process

On top of the Service Layer is the Composite Service and Workflow Layer. The FaaS framework consists of the coordinated operation of the Forecast Generation Framework (FGF), the Internal Data Retrieval Framework (IDRF), the External Data Collection Framework (EDCF), and the FaaS controller. The EDCF, IRDF, FGF and the FaaS controller are all composite services designed by applying SOA principles [4, 5]. They are developed by using the Windows Communication Foundation (WCF) [6], Microsoft Azure and .NET technologies [7]. Each major step of the quantitative forecasting process is performed by a composite service: EDCF for external Data Collection, IDRF for data processing to support Analysis and Model Formulation, and FGF for Forecasting. Based on customer specification, the FaaS controller defines the forecast problem and orchestrates different services to implement the workflow needed to solve the problem.

Due to the complexity of SOA, the costs of SOA-based projects are difficult to estimate although there have been attempts to do so [8, 9]. This project attempts to develop a method to price services so that a customer has the option to decide whether to proceed with the forecast request after viewing the estimated cost. The approach taken by the FaaS adopts the divide-and-conquer concept and product pricing concepts [10]. Instead of estimating the ex-ante costs, the prices of the FaaS services are based on the ex-post costs. The price of each service is computed by using a 3-step process.

Step 1:   Calculate the total cost by combining the cost of manpower for software development, the cost of resources utilized, etc., and imposing an overhead rate and indirect costs.

Step 2:   Estimate the expected number of usage of this service over a time horizon before the next major update.

Step 3:   Divide the total cost computed in step 1 by the expected number of usages in step 2 to obtain the service price per usage.

When services are combined to form composite services, the prices of constituent services are included in the cost of resources utilized (in step 1). All the costs and prices are updated periodically after more usage information becomes available.

To implement this pricing method, each service is equipped with two endpoints – one endpoint is used for technical functionalities and the second endpoint is used for pricing purposes. When a service is consumed because of its technical functionalities, the pricing endpoint of the same service will also be incorporated into the overall pricing workflow. When a certain mission is accomplished by a sequence (or workflow) of services, not only the technical requirement is met but the associated price of accomplishing the mission is also calculated.

2.3   Cloud Computing

While SOA is for service development and building applications, cloud computing provides the infrastructure for the deployment of these services. SOA and cloud computing are complementary to each other and together they provide agile software solutions to many problems.

There is a number of cloud computing service providers such as Amazon, Google, Microsoft, Rackspace, etc. The Microsoft Azure cloud computing platform has been chosen for this project for the following reasons. Azure, as well as compatible software such as the Windows Communication Foundation [6] and the .NET technologies, supports the design principles and implementation of SOA in the cloud [7]. The development environment for Azure is integrated into Visual Studio and provides a simulated runtime for Azure for local desktop-based development and unit testing. Azure has a "staging" environment where an application can be deployed to the cloud, but will not be made live until the developer is happy with how it works. All these features are useful for software development in a university environment.

3   Implementation

The FaaS framework has been developed to provide on-demand forecasts of solar or wind power at locations specified by the customers. Figure 2 shows the FaaS framework for on-demand wind power forecasting. The FaaS framework for solar power forecasting is similar so many services developed for wind can be reused for solar. Figure 3 shows the architecture of the FaaS framework implemented by using Azure.

As shown in Figure 2, the services provided by FaaS can be useful to different kinds of customers. On the other side of the FaaS system is the large volume of data pertinent to renewable energy forecasting. These data are available from a variety of sources: federal agencies (such as several national labs under the U.S. Department of Energy, different agencies under National Oceanic and Atmospheric Administration including the National Weather Services, NASA, etc.), national databases and archives, private organizations, universities, international institutions and vendors that sell data. These sources provide a variety of data types and formats: satellite images, sensor measurement data, computer model data, vendor product data, etc. Part of the FaaS system, the External Data Collection Framework (EDCF), is designed to obtain external data over the Internet and store them in the Azure Blob storage.

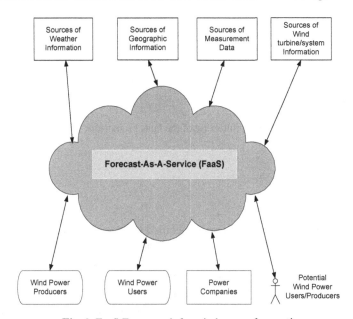

Fig. 2. FaaS Framework for wind power forecasting

IDRF transforms the data stored in the Azure Blob storage into the standardized formats that the analysis services and the forecasting models are designed for. Data in standardized format are then stored in the Azure Table storage.

Different services have been developed to implement various models for renewable energy forecasting. For example, a new characterization and classification method for daily sky condition has been developed so that both the quantity and the quality of solar irradiance can be quantified [11]. These services have been used in the FGF to meet a variety of forecast needs. Upon receiving a customer-specified request, the FaaS controller decides which forecast service to use.

Because of the variety of information involved in the FaaS framework, it is important to have a well-organized Meta Data Repository (MDR) and an effective Meta Data Repository Management System (MDRMS) [12]. EDCF, IDRF, FGF and the FaaS controller all interact with the MDR through the MDRMS.

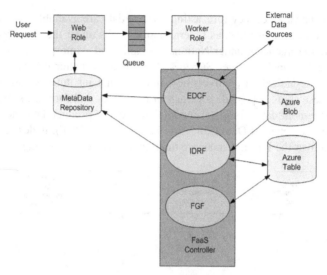

Fig. 3. Architecture of the Faas Framework

4   Results

4.1   Forecast Request

Figure 4 shows an example of a customer-specified forecast request. The customer can specify the renewable energy source (solar or wind), the location (latitude and longitude), the kind of forecasting services (prospecting or operational), uncertainty quantification (with or without), and whether characteristics of energy conversion equipment (such as a particular model of a solar panel or a wind turbine, from a list of manufacturers) should be included in the computation to make the forecast more realistic.

Based on the customer-specified forecast request, the FaaS controller formulates a workflow consisting of all the tasks that need to be performed. Using the economic endpoints of all services involved, the FaaS controller estimates the cost for the request and send the cost estimate to the customer. If the customer accepts the estimated cost, the customer will provide the email address to which the forecast results should be sent. The FaaS system will then perform the required tasks in the cloud and deliver the forecast results over the Internet after the work is complete.

4.2   Service Costs

Table 1 shows an example of the overall costs of the prospecting and operational solar forecasting and the costs of the respective constituent services. The prices for prospecting forecasts are usually higher than those of the operational forecasts because they involve data over longer time horizon and need more work and more computational resources. Results of this project indicate that the costs of prospecting forecasts are in the range of US$ 60-80 per request while the costs for operational forecasts are in the range of US$ 10-20 per request. Additional services, such as uncertainty quantification, can be requested for additional prices in the order of a few dollars. These costs are much lower than the monthly or annual subscription fees charged by current renewable energy forecast service vendors.

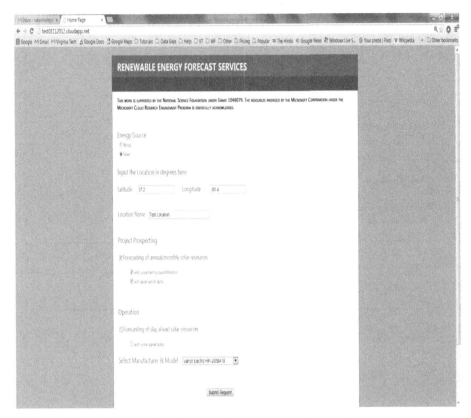

Fig. 4. Example of a solar power forecast request for project prospecting

Table 1. Example of overall costs of solar forecasting services and constituent services

Forecast Type	Service	Cost (US $)	Overall Cost (US $)
Project Prospecting	EDCF	10.55	62.89
	IDRF	32.02	
	FGF	20.32	
	FGF (with uncertainty quantification)	22.87	65.44
Operational	EDCF	3.84	13.92
	IDRF	3.06	
	FGF	7.02	

```
You requested Project Prospecting data with uncertainty quantification.
Time of Report Delivery        4/29/2013 6:09:59 PM GMT

Time of Request                4/29/2013 6:08:56 PM GMT

Cost                           72.43 dollars

Location:    Name              GUAM WFO

             Latitude          13.483      Latitude you entered    13.4

             Longitude         144.8       Longitude you entered   144

             State Code        GU

Source of Renwable Energy      Solar

Solar Panel:  Vendor           Sun Power

              Model            SPR-200-WHT-U

              Efficiency       16.08 %

Distance between the requested co-ordinate and actual location   57.64 Km
```

Annual Energy Production(kWh/m^2)	Average	P95	P90	P75	P50
	282.35	280.59	280.98	281.63	282.35

Monthly Energy Production(kWh/m^2)	Average	P95	P90	P75	P50
January	19.89	19.53	19.61	19.74	19.89
February	18.51	18.15	18.23	18.36	18.51
March	27.58	27.11	27.21	27.39	27.58
April	27.36	26.84	26.96	27.15	27.36
May	29.07	28.59	28.69	28.87	29.07
June	28.49	28.01	28.11	28.29	28.49
July	24.99	24.56	24.66	24.81	24.99
August	22.73	22.34	22.43	22.57	22.73
September	21.64	21.21	21.31	21.47	21.64
October	22.14	21.71	21.81	21.96	22.14
November	21.9	21.51	21.6	21.74	21.9
December	18.06	17.28	17.45	17.74	18.06

Fig. 5. Example of results for solar power forecasts for project prospecting

4.3   Forecast Results

Fig. 5 shows an example of the solar power forecasting results sent to the customer for project prospecting with uncertainty quantification and with the inclusion of the characteristics of solar panel SPR-200-WHT-U made by the SunPower Corporation. The column under P75 indicates the levels of solar energy production that are expected to be reached or exceeded with a probability of 75% for the associated time period. P75 and P90, etc., quantify uncertainties and are widely used by banks in making financing decisions. Forecast accuracy of the FaaS system is in the range of 85% to 94%. Forecasting results are archived to be reused. Depending on whether similar forecast request has previously been made, the time that a new customer will receive forecast results ranges from 1 minute to 45 minutes after the request is made.

5   Related Work

Although both the FaaS and the CloudCast [13] are concerned with forecasting, FaaS is very different from CloudCast not only in terms of the services provided but also in terms of the underlying design. Efforts to bring together SOA and cloud computing have been reported in the literature [14, 15]. FaaS is different from these efforts in that FaaS also addresses service pricing issues. The approach used in pricing the services in FaaS is similar in principle but different in implementation to the concept of work breakdown structure presented in [8] and the concept presented in [9]. There are patterns for object-oriented software design [16] and patterns for SOA service design [5]. The FaaS Framework may be viewed as the preliminary version of a cloud computing pattern for on-demand quantitative forecasting processes. By improving the flexibility and economics of renewable energy forecasting services with SOA and cloud computing, FaaS achieves the goal of Services Computing [17].

6   Conclusions

Concepts and implementation of the Forecast-as-a-Service (FaaS) system, a cloud-based framework that provides on-demand customer-defined forecasting services, are presented. FaaS provides different kinds of renewable energy forecasts at different levels of details for different prices at locations specified by the customers. FaaS provides a more flexible and affordable alternative to the subscription model provided by current renewable energy forecast service vendors. By improving the flexibility and economics of renewable energy forecasting services with SOA and cloud computing, FaaS achieves the goal of Services Computing.

Acknowledgment. This work is supported by the National Science Foundation under grant 1048079.

References

1. Makridakis, S., Wheelwright, S., Hyndman, R.: Forecasting Methods and Applications, 3rd edn. John Wiley & Sons (1998)
2. Montgomery, D., Johnson, L., Gardiner, J.: Forecasting & Time Series Analysis, 2nd edn. McGraw-Hill (1990)
3. Box, G., Jenkins, G., Reinsel, G.: Time Series Analysis Forecasting and Control, 4th edn. John Wiley & Sons (2008)
4. Erl, T.: SOA Principles of Service Design. Prentice Hall (2008)
5. Erl, T.: SOA Design Patterns. Prentice Hall (2009)

6. Lowy, J.: Programming WCF Services, 3rd edn. O'Reilly (2010)
7. Chou, D., deVadoss, J., Erl, T., Gandhi, N., Kommapalati, H., Loesgen, B., Shittko, C., Wilhelmsen, H., Williams, M.: SOA with .NET & Windows Azure. Prentice Hall (2010)
8. Yusuf, L., Olusegun, F., Akinwale, A., Adejumobi, A.: A Framework for Costing Service-Oriented Architecture (SOA) Projects Using Work Breakdown Structure (WBS) Approach. Global Journal of Computer Science and Technology 11(15) (2011)
9. Li, Z., Keung, J.: Software Cost Estimation Framework for Service-Oriented Architecture Systems using Divide-and-Conquer Approach. In: Proc. Fifth IEEE International Symposium on Service Oriented System Engineering, pp. 47–54 (2010)
10. Snyder, H., Davenport, E.: Costing and Pricing in the Digital Age. Library Association Publishing (1997)
11. Kang, B., Tam, K.-S.: A New Characterization and Classification Method for Daily Sky Conditions Based on Ground-Based Solar Irradiance Measurement Data. Solar Energy 94, 102–118 (2013)
12. Marco, D., Jennings, M.: Universal Meta Data Models. Wiley Publishing Inc. (2004)
13. Krishnappa, D., Irwin, D., Lyons, E., Zink, M.: CloudCast: Cloud Computing for Short-Term Weather Forecasts. Computing in Science & Engineering, 30–37 (2013)
14. Wei, Y., Sukumar, K., Vecchiola, C., Karunamoorthy, D., Buyya, R.: Aneka Cloud Application Platform and its Integration with Windows Azure. In: Cloud Computing: Methodology, Systems, and Applications, ch. 27. CRC Press (2011)
15. Tsai, W., Sun, X., Balasooriya, J.: Service-Oriented Cloud Computing Architecture. In: Seventh International Conference on Information Technology (2010)
16. Gamma, E., Helm, R., Johnson, R., Vlissides, J.: Design Patterns Elements of Reusable Object-Oriented Software. Addison-Wesley (1995)
17. Zhao, J., Tanniru, M., Zhang, L.: Services computing as the foundation of enterprise agility: Overview of recent advances and introduction to the special issue. Inf. Syst. Front. 9, 1–8 (2007)

Security and Efficiency Analysis on a Simple Keyword Search Scheme over Encrypted Data in Cloud Storage Services

Chun-Ta Li[1], Jau-Ji Shen[2,*], and Chin-Wen Lee[2]

[1] Department of Information Management, Tainan University of Technology,
529 Zhongzheng Road, Tainan City 71002, Taiwan (R.O.C.)
th0040@mail.tut.edu.tw
[2] Department of Management Information Systems,
National Chung Hsing University,
250 Guoguang Road, Taichung City 40227, Taiwan (R.O.C.)
jjshen@nchu.edu.tw

Abstract. With the growing popularity of cloud computing, cloud storage service becomes an essential part of cloud services and numerous researches have been widely studied in recent years. Recently, Hsu et al. proposed an ElGamal-based simple keyword search scheme over encrypted data in cloud storage services. They claimed that a secure cloud storage service needs to achieve five security requirements, including: consistency, ciphertext indistinguishability, trapdoor indistinguishability, outside keyword guessing attack and inside keyword guessing attacks. However, in this paper, we observe that Hsu et al.'s scheme not only cannot prevent inside keyword guessing attack but also cannot prevent denial of service attack and has low efficiency problem in computing algorithms.

Keywords: Cloud storage service, ElGamal system, Inside keyword guessing attack, Keyword search.

1 Introduction

The more network technologies and communication technologies are being developed [15, 18], many cloud services [2, 6, 10, 11, 16, 17] have been proposed such as cloud storage service, hardware infrastructure facilities and a variety of application software etc. People began to use the cloud storage service to replace the physical hardware device for storing personal data or sensitive data. Users can obtain the important information in anytime and anywhere. On the other hand, enterprises can use the big cyberspace to store huge data and it can reduce operating costs of enterprises. However, there are some security threats when cloud users transmit data via public channel. Therefore, it is important to provide a secure cloud services.

---

* Corresponding author.

R.C.-H. Hsu and W. Shangguang (Eds.): IOV 2014, LNCS 8662, pp. 367–375, 2014.
© Springer International Publishing Switzerland 2014

For enhancing the privacy of cloud data [13, 14, 19–21], cloud users will encrypt data before uploading them to the cloud storage space [1, 3–5, 7, 9, 12, 22]. When the data is encrypted, it will become an unrecognizable ciphertext and even the data owner or an authorized user cannot recognize its contents. Therefore, in 2013, Hsu et al. proposed a simple keyword search scheme [8] based on ElGamal system. Hsu et al.'s scheme has three participants, including: data sender, cloud server and data receiver. Moreover, Hsu et al.'s scheme has three phases, including: setup phase, $KeyGen_{Server}$ phase and $KeyGen_{Receiver}$ phase; and three algorithms, including: $dPEKS$ algorithm, $dTrapdoor$ algorithm and $dTest$ algorithm in Hsu et al.'s research scope. Finally, Hsu et al.'s scheme can achieve four security requirements, including: consistency, ciphertext indistinguishability, trapdoor indistinguishability and outside keyword guessing attacks. The research scope of Hsu et al.'s scheme is shown in Figure 1.

However, in this paper, we found that Hsu et al.'s scheme has low efficiency problem in computing algorithms and it cannot resist denial of service and inside keyword guessing attacks. Unfortunately, to the best of our knowledge, none of researches (including Hsu et al.'s scheme) can against inside keyword guessing attacks in cloud storage services.

The remainder of the paper is organized as follows. Section 2 is a brief review of Hsu et al.'s simple keyword search scheme, and the denial of service and inside keyword guessing attacks are given in Section 3 and Section 4, respectively. Moreover, in Section 5, Hsu et al.'s scheme has low efficiency problem in computing algorithms. We concludes this paper in Section 6.

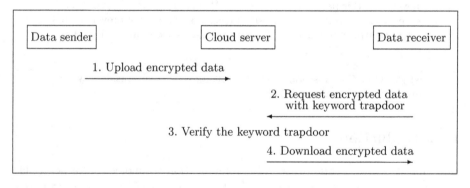

Fig. 1. Research scope of Hsu et al.'s scheme [8]

2 Review of Hsu et al.'s Scheme

In this section, we will review the Hsu et al.'s simple keyword search scheme [8]. Some notations used in [8] are defined in Table 1. Three roles participate in this scheme: the data sender, the cloud server, and the receiver. Data sender can use the cloud storage service to store personal data and download the data.

Data sender also can authorize other users (receiver) to have the permission to download the data. For enhancing the privacy of cloud data, data sender will encrypt data with the keyword w before uploading to the cloud storage space. The authorized receiver can use the keyword w' to generate a request and send it to the cloud server when he/she wants to download the specific cloud data. When the cloud server receives the request which is sent by the receiver, cloud server will search the corresponding keyword ciphertexts from its database and response the specific data to the authorized receiver. Hsu et al.'s scheme is divided into three phases: setup phase, $KeyGen_{Server}(gp)$ phase, and $KeyGen_{Receiver}(gp)$ phase, three algorithms: $dPEKS(gp, pk_S, pk_R, w)$ algorithm, $dTrapdoor(gp, pk_S, sk_R, w')$ algorithm, and $dTest(gp, C, T_{w'}, sk_S)$ algorithm. The flowchart of Hsu et al.'s scheme is depicted in Figure 2.

Table 1. Notations used throughout this paper

Symbol	Description
G	A cyclic group of prime order p with generator g
Z_p^*	The field of integers modulo p
pk_S, sk_S	Cloud server's public/private key pairs
pk_R, sk_R	Data receiver's public/private key pairs
w	A keyword that the data sender sets for the encrypted data
w'	A keyword that the data receiver wants to search
C	A keyword ciphertext
$T_{w'}$	A keyword trapdoor which contains w'
$H(\cdot)$	A secure one-way hashing function
KS_w	The keyword space

Setup phase: Select a cyclic group G with prime order p and a primitive root g. Choose a secure one-way hash function $H : \{0,1\}^* \to Z_p^*$. Let KS_w denotes the keyword space. The global parameter $gp = (G, p, g, H, KS_w)$.

$KeyGen_{Server}(gp)$ **phase:** Choose a random value $\alpha \in Z_p^*$ and compute $pk_S = g^\alpha$. Output the cloud server's public/ private key pairs $(pk_S, sk_S) = (g^\alpha, \alpha)$.

$KeyGen_{Receiver}(gp)$ **phase:** Choose a random value $\beta \in Z_p^*$ and compute $pk_R = g^\beta$. Output the receiver's public/ privat key pairs $(pk_R, sk_R) = (g^\beta, \beta)$.

$dPEKS(gp, pk_S, pk_R, w)$ **algorithm:** In this algorithm, the data sender will encrypt the keyword w with the cloud server's public key pk_S. First, the data sender selects two random values $r, \theta \in Z_p^*$ and compute $C_1 = g^r$, $C_2 = \theta H(w) \cdot pk_S^r$ and $C_3 = \theta pk_R$. It outputs the keyword ciphertext $C = [C_1, C_2, C_3]$ and sends ciphertext C to the cloud server.

$dTrapdoor(gp, pk_S, sk_R, w')$ **algorithm:** In this algorithm, the authorized receiver will generate a trapdoor with the keyword w' that he/she wants to search and will create a signature with sk_R. First, the authorized receiver selects two random values $r', k \in Z_p^*$ and computes $T_1 = g^{r'}$, $T_2 = H(w') \cdot (pk_S)^{r'}$, $T_3 = g^k$ and $T_4 = k^{-1}(H(T_1 \| T_2) - sk_R \cdot T_3) \bmod (p - 1)$. Then he/she outputs trapdoor $T_{w'} = [T_1, T_2, T_3, T_4]$ and sends trapdoor $T_{w'}$ to the cloud server.

$dTest(gp, C, T_{w'}, sk_S)$ **algorithm:** After receiving the ciphertext C from the data sender and trapdoor $T_{w'}$ from the authorized receiver, the cloud server starts to search the corresponding keyword ciphertext. First, this algorithm computes $v = C_2 \cdot (C_1^{sk_S})^{-1} = \theta H(w)$ and $u = T_2 \cdot (T_1^{sk_S})^{-1} = H(w')$. Then, it computes $Z = C_3^{T_3} \cdot T_3^{T_4} = \theta^{T_3} g^{H(T_1 \| T_2)}$. Finally, the cloud server checks if $v^{T_3} \cdot g^{H(T_1 \| T_2)} = u^{T_3} \cdot Z$. If it holds, it means $w = w'$.

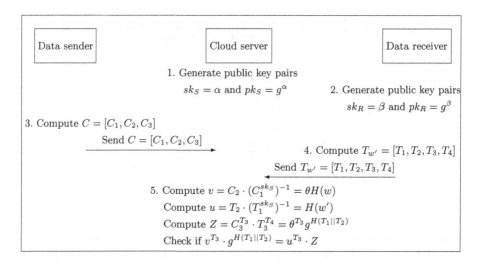

Fig. 2. The flowchart of Hsu et al.'s scheme [8]

3   Denial of Service Attack on Hsu et al.'s Scheme

In Hsu et al.'s scheme, we found that the malicious attacker can perform the denial of service attack on their scheme. Let us consider the following scenario. During $dPEKS$ algorithm, the data sender uploads the encrypted data with ciphertext C via public channel and we suppose that the attacker has the ability to change the ciphertext C into the attacker's ciphertext C_A. Moreover, during the $dTrapdoor$ and $dTest$ algorithms, the authorized receiver sends download request $T_{w'}$ to the cloud server and he/she will not pass the authentication by the cloud server due to the legal sender's ciphertext C has been changed into attacker's C_A. Thus the authorized receiver has no permission to download the corresponding encrypted data anymore. Finally, only malicious attacker has the ability to download the encrypted data and the denial of service attack is described by the following steps:

Step 1. In $dPEKS$ algorithm, the malicious attacker can intercept data sender's ciphertext C and replace it into the attacker's fake ciphertext C_A due to the data sender uploads the encrypted data with ciphertext C via public channel. In the end, the attacker sends the encrypted data with ciphertext C_A to the cloud server.

Step 2. In $dTrapdoor$ algorithm, when the receiver wants to search the corresponding encrypted data which is sent by the data sender, he/she needs to generate the trapdoor request $T_{w'}$ and sends it to the cloud server.

Step 3. In $dTest$ algorithm, when the cloud server receives the download request from the data receiver, the data receiver cannot pass the $dTest$ algorithm authentication by the cloud server. Finally, the data receiver is rejected to download specify encrypted data.

Step 4. On the other hand, due to the data sender's ciphertext C has been changed into the attacker's ciphertext C_A during $dPEKS$ algorithm. Therefore, the unauthorized attacker can generate the fake trapdoor $T_{w'_A}$ to the cloud server in $dTrapdoor$ algorithm and the malicious attacker can still pass cloud server's verification and obtain the encrypted data in $dTest$ algorithm.

From above-mentioned steps show, the attacker can successfully perform the denial of service attack and the legal data receiver has no permission to download specify encrypted data. Instead, only malicious attacker has ability to download the encrypted data and the cloud server is not aware of having caused weakness in cloud storage service.

4 Inside Keyword Guessing Attack on Hsu et al.'s Scheme

For enhancing the security of the cloud computing environments, a secure cloud storage service must resist not only outside keyword guessing attacks but also inside keyword guessing attacks. However, to the best of our knowledge, none of the existing schemes can prevent the inside keyword guessing attack from a malicious cloud server due to the cloud server has plentiful information to perform the $dTest$ algorithm. In this section, we show inside keyword guessing attacks on Hsu et al.'s scheme.

Step 1. In $dPEKS(gp, pk_S, pk_R, w)$ algorithm, data sender computes $C_1 = g^r$, $C_2 = \theta H(w) \cdot pk_S^r$ and $C_3 = \theta pk_R$ and sends $C = [C_1, C_2, C_3]$ to the malicious cloud server.

Step 2. In $dTrapdoor(gp, pk_S, sk_R, w')$ algorithm, authorized receiver computes $T_1 = g^{r'}$, $T_2 = H(w') \cdot (pk_S)^{r'}$, $T_3 = g^k$ and $T_4 = k^{-1}(H(T_1||T_2) - sk_R \cdot T_3) \bmod (p-1)$ and sends $T_{w'} = [T_1, T_2, T_3, T_4]$ to the malicious cloud server.

Step 3. Due to the values C and $T_{w'}$ have been collected from Step 1 and Step 2, the malicious cloud server can use them to derive $v = C_2 \cdot (C_1^{sks})^{-1} = \theta H(w)$, $u = T_2 \cdot (T_1^{sks})^{-1} = H(w')$ and $Z = C_3^{T_3} \cdot T_3^{T_4} = \theta^{T_3} g^{H(T_1 || T_2)}$ by performing $dTest(gp, C, T_{w'}, sk_S)$ algorithm.

Step 4. In this step, the malicious cloud server can execute the $dTest$ algorithm to derive the keyword $w = w'$ and the details of $dTest$ algorithm execution are shown in Figure 3.

Finally, the malicious cloud insider succeeds to derive the low-entropy keyword $w = w'$ and Hsu et al.'s scheme is vulnerable to inside keyword guessing attack.

$$v^{T_3} \cdot g^{H(T_1 || T_2)} = u^{T_3} \cdot Z$$

$$\Rightarrow (\theta H(w))^{T_3} \cdot g^{H(T_1 || T_2)} = H(w')^{T_3} \cdot \theta^{T_3} \cdot g^{H(T_1 || T_2)}$$

$$\Rightarrow H(w)^{T_3} \cdot \theta^{T_3} \cdot g^{H(T_1 || T_2)} = H(w')^{T_3} \cdot \theta^{T_3} \cdot g^{H(T_1 || T_2)}$$

$$\Rightarrow H(w)^{T_3} = H(w')^{T_3}$$

$$\Rightarrow H(w) = H(w')$$

Fig. 3. The $dTest$ algorithm is performed by the attackers

5   Low Efficiency Problem on Hsu et al.'s Scheme

In Hsu et al.'s protocol, their scheme has low efficiency problem in computing $dPEKS$ algorithm, $dTrapdoor$ algorithm and $dTest$ algorithm. Let us consider the following scenario. We assume the data sender uploads encrypted data to cloud storage server with multiple keywords and authorizes uploaded data to multiple receivers in $dPEKS$ algorithm. Moreover, we assume there are many authorized receivers sending download request to cloud server simultaneously in $dTrapdoor$ algorithm. Finally, the cloud server will take such long time in $dTest$ algorithm. The low efficiency problem in computing algorithms is described by the following steps:

Step 1. In $dPEKS$ algorithm, we assume the data sender uploads the encrypted data with j keywords and authorizes uploaded data to k receivers for having the permission to download the encrypted data, the data sender needs to take j times calculations to compute C_2 and needs to take k times calculations to compute C_3.

Step 2. In $dTrapdoor$ algorithm, we assume that there are n receivers use m keywords to generate the download requests to the cloud server simultaneously, where $m \le j$ and $n \le k$. Thus, it takes $(2 \times m \times n)$ times calculations to generate T_2 and T_4 for all receivers.

Step 3. Due to the values C and $T_{w'}$ have been collected from Step 1 and Step 2, the cloud server can use them to compute (v, u, Z). Therefore, the cloud server must take j times calculations to derive v and take $(2 \times m \times n)$ times calculations to derive u and Z.

Step 4. In $dTtest$ algorithm, the cloud server takes $j \times m \times n$ times calculations to compute $v^{T_3} \cdot g^{H(T_1 || T_2)}$ and takes $(2 \times m \times n)$ times calculations to compute $u^{T_3} \cdot Z$.

From above-mentioned steps show, Hsu et al.'s scheme requires enormous computation overheads to execute $dPEKS$ algorithm, $dTrapdoor$ algorithm and $dTest$ algorithm. However, in practice, it exhibits a low efficiency and in application their scheme becomes infeasible for cloud participants to wait for the respondent results for such long time in cloud storage services.

6 Conclusions

Supporting data privacy has become an important topic in the field of cloud storage services, and keyword search over encrypted data has received a great deal of attention in recent years. The cloud server provides the storage spaces for data senders to upload encrypted data and it performs the specific algorithms to search the corresponding encrypted data that data receivers want to query. In this paper, we showed that Hsu et al.'s simple keyword search scheme based on ElGamal system is insecure due to a malicious cloud server may launch the denial of service and off-line inside keyword guessing attacks in cloud storage services. Moreover, we have also found that their scheme has low efficiency problem in computing algorithms due to it is not practical for cloud participants to wait for the respondent results for such long time in the keyword search processes of Hsu et al.'s scheme. In the future work, we plan to propose an improvement on their scheme and we also encourage readers can propose their improvement to remedy security and efficiency flaws of Hsu et al.'s scheme.

Acknowledgements. The authors would like to thank the anonymous reviewers for their valuable suggestions and comments. In addition, this research was partially supported by the National Science Council, Taiwan, R.O.C., under contract no.: NSC 102-3114-C-165-001-ES and NSC 102-2221-E-005-039.

References

1. Baek, J., Safavi-Naini, R., Susilo, W.: Public key encryption with keyword search revisited. In: Gervasi, O., Murgante, B., Laganà, A., Taniar, D., Mun, Y., Gavrilova, M.L. (eds.) ICCSA 2008, Part I. LNCS, vol. 5072, pp. 1249–1259. Springer, Heidelberg (2008)
2. Baliga, J., Ayre, R.W.A., Hinton, K., Tucker, R.S.: Green cloud computing: Balancing energy in processing, storage, and transport. Proc. of the IEEE 99, 149–167 (2011)

3. Boneh, D., Di Crescenzo, G., Ostrovsky, R., Persiano, G.: Public key encryption with keyword search. In: Cachin, C., Camenisch, J.L. (eds.) EUROCRYPT 2004. LNCS, vol. 3027, pp. 506–522. Springer, Heidelberg (2004)
4. Byun, J.W., Rhee, H.S., Park, H.-A., Lee, D.H.: Off-line keyword guessing attacks on recent keyword search schemes over encrypted data. In: Jonker, W., Petković, M. (eds.) SDM 2006. LNCS, vol. 4165, pp. 75–83. Springer, Heidelberg (2006)
5. Cao, N., Yang, Z., Wang, C., Ren, K., Lou, W.: Privacy-preserving query over encrypted graph-structured data in cloud computing. In: IEEE International Conference on Distributed Computing Systems, pp. 393-402 (2011)
6. Cheng, Z.Y., Liu, Y., Chang, C.C., Chang, S.C.: A smart card based authentication scheme for remote user login and verification. International Journal of Innovative Computing, Information and Control 8(8), 5499–5511 (2012)
7. Hsu, S.T., Yang, C.C., Hwang, M.S.: A study of public key encryption with keyword search. International Journal of Network Security 15(2), 71–79 (2013)
8. Hsu, S.T., Hwang, M.S., Yang, C.C.: A study of keyword search over encrypted data in cloud storage service. Master Thesis of National Chung Hsing University, Department of Management Information System (2013)
9. Hu, C., Liu, P.: A secure searchable public key encryption scheme with a designated tester against keyword guessing attacks and its extension. In: Lin, S., Huang, X. (eds.) CSEE 2011, Part II. CCIS, vol. 215, pp. 131–136. Springer, Heidelberg (2011)
10. Iosup, A., Ostermann, S., Yigitbasi, M.N., Prodan, R., Fahringer, T., Epema, D.H.J.: Performance analysis of cloud computing services for many-tasks scientific computing. IEEE Transactions on Parallel and Distributed Systems 22(6), 931–945 (2011)
11. Lee, C.C., Chung, P.S., Hwang, M.S.: A survey on attribute-based encryption schemes of access control in cloud environments. International Journal of Network Security 15(4), 231–240 (2013)
12. Li, X., Qiu, W., Zheng, D., Chen, K., Li, J.: Anonymity enhancement on robust and efficient password-authenticated key agreement using smart cards. IEEE Transactions on Industrial Electronics 57(2), 793–800 (2010)
13. Rhee, H.S., Park, J.H., Susilo, W., Lee, D.H.: Improved searchable public key encryption with designated tester. In: Proceedings of the 4th International Symposium on Information, Computer, and Communications Security, Sydney, Australia, pp. 376–379 (2009)
14. Rhee, H.S., Park, J.H., Susilo, W., Kee, D.H.: Trapdoor security in a searchable public-key encryption scheme with a designated tester. The Journal of Systems and Software 83(5), 763–771 (2010)
15. Rajkumar, B., Yeo, C., Venugopal, S., Malpani, S.: Cloud computing and emerging IT platforms: Vision, hype, and reality for delivering computing as the 5th utility. Future Generation Computer Systems 25(6), 599–616 (2009)
16. Ranchal, R., Othmane, L.B., Kim, A., Kang, M., Linderman, M.: Protection of identity information in cloud computing without trusted third party. In: IEEE International Symposium on Reliable Distributed Systems, pp. 368–372 (2010)
17. Tserpes, K., Aisopos, F., Kyriazis, D., Varvarigou, T.: Service selection decision support in the Internet of services. In: Altmann, J., Rana, O.F. (eds.) GECON 2010. LNCS, vol. 6296, pp. 16–33. Springer, Heidelberg (2010)

18. Wang, Q., Wang, C., Ren, K., Lou, W., Li, J.: Enabling public auditability and data dynamics for storage security in cloud computing. IEEE Transactions on Parallel and Distributed Systems 22(5), 847–859 (2011)
19. Yoon, E.J., Kim, S.H., Yoo, K.Y.: A security enhanced remote user authentication scheme using smart cards. International Journal of Innovative Computing, Information and Control 8(5(B)), 3661–3675 (2012)
20. Yoon, E.J., Choi, S.B., Yoo, K.Y.: A secure and efficiency ID-based authenticated key agreement scheme based on elliptic curve cryptosystem for mobile devices. International Journal of Innovative Computing, Information and Control 8(4), 2637–2653 (2012)
21. Yoon, E.J., Yoo, K.Y.: Improving the Lee-Lee's password based authenticated key agreement protocol. International Journal of Innovative Computing, Information and Control 8(8), 5657–5675 (2012)
22. Zhao, Y., Chen, X., Ma, H., Tang, Q., Zhu, H.: A new trapdoor-indistinguishable public key encryption with keyword search. Journal of Wireless Mobile Networks, Ubiquitous Computing, and Dependable Applications 3(1/2), 72–81 (2012)

A Cloud Server Selection System – Recommendation, Modeling and Evaluation

Yao-Chung Chang[1], Sheng-Lung Peng[2], Ruay-Shiung Chang[3], and Hery Hermanto[2]

[1] Department of Computer Science and Information Engineering,
National Taitung Unviersity, Taitung, Taiwan, R.O.C.
ycc@nttu.edu.tw
[2] Department of Computer Science and Information Engineering,
National Dong Hwa University, Hualien, Taiwan, R.O.C.
slpeng@mail.ndhu.edu.tw, 610021075@ems.ndhu.edu.tw
[3] National Taipei University of Business, Taipei, Taiwan, R.O.C.
rschang@ntub.edu.tw

Abstract. The popularity of cloud computing has increasing rapidly across various sectors. The model that cloud computing offered has drawn attention of the enterprise such as pay as you go model, auto scaling, etc. With those kinds of advantages, it will help enterprise to save their cost while running their business. The benefit of cloud computing leads lots of cloud server providers offering their cloud server for rent in the internet. Each cloud server provider has his advantages and disadvantages. Enterprise needs more time to find a suitable could server provider and it also might not know the differences among cloud server providers. This research presents a search model for searching cloud server providers, and uses enterprise location (context aware method) for recommending the cloud server providers which are nearby the enterprise in order to improve bandwidth and reduce latency problem. Furthermore, this paper implements the search model, recommendation system, and evaluation standard in the system for users using their requirements and locations. Implementation result shows that cloud server which is near to enterprise will improve bandwidth and reduce the latency.

Keywords: Cloud Computing, Context Aware, Cloud Server Evaluation, Enterprise Cloud.

1 Introduction

The cloud computing has become very popular nowadays since it's first introduced. There are three significant points that cloud computing provides such as service, ease of use (setup, maintenance, backup, easy to scale, reliable, and easy to monitor), and low cost (pay as you go). Because of those three points, cloud computing has become an important concern for users to migrate their system into cloud [1] [2] [3].

Recently cloud computing becomes a booming topic in many aspects of people's live. Cloud computing provides a service to the users based on their demands. Uncertainty of

R.C.-H. Hsu and W. Shangguang (Eds.): IOV 2014, LNCS 8662, pp. 376–385, 2014.
© Springer International Publishing Switzerland 2014

computing resources utilization leads many of enterprise to move their service to the cloud. With scalability and elasticity, computing resources can be scaled up and scaled down according to the users' demands. Cloud computing cost is calculated from the resources that have been used by an enterprise. In other way, it can be said pay as we use model. This calculation system can reduce enterprise expense compared to set up a new IT infrastructure for their business. Besides, network connection plays an important role in cloud computing where network connection becomes an intermediary between enterprise and providers. Poor network connection will cause latency problem which become an obstacle for enterprises to move their data to the cloud. In three referred papers below, we discuss how to select a suitable cloud server.

With a huge cloud market nowadays, there are many cloud servers out there for an enterprise to choose. Thus, there is a need for standardizing the evaluation system to help the enterprises find the most suitable cloud server provider. Different enterprises will have different necessities. To define the model, this study determines the basic factor of an enterprise cloud. From the basic factor, this research extends it into more detailed evaluation model. After that, this study builds a web based cloud server selection system to test the accuracy and reliability of the model. This paper is organized as following: background information and related works are introduced in section 2. Section 3 proposes the system framework. Section 4 shows the implementation and evaluation model with the web based cloud server selection system. Finally, section 5 concludes this paper and presents future work.

2   Related Works

2.1   Recommendation System

Many of recommendation systems have been proposed to solve this problem such as content based filtering, collaborative filtering and hybrid system. As shown in Figure 1, most of the recommendation systems have a user interface. User interface becomes an intermediary between user and the system. User will input the request and send the request to the records collection system. In records collection system, user's request will be delivered according to user's behavior and data records in the database. Recommendation system will collect the data from database based on the user request and analyzed data. After finished, recommendation system will generate results (most of the results are presented in a list) and be sent back to the user through user interface.

2.2   Cloud Server Selection

With network connectivity, thousands of cloud computing resources are available to rent for enterprises. It is not easy for an enterprise to choose the right provider among thousands of them. Many of researchers have proposed lots of recommendation system to solve this problem. B.P. Rimal et al. [10] proposed an architectural requirement for cloud computing. Their purpose is to present a model for providers, users, and enterprises to understand clearly their requirements respectively. Provider's perspective provides a high efficient architecture to support services and infrastructure needed. Enterprises or users would not rent any services from providers who have a low level efficiency for their service. From enterprise's perspective, providing a business management service with QoS, secure and scalable system is needed. Moreover, from the end-user's perspective, a simplified interface will make user easier to understand the service that is provided by the provider, and simplified interface should address transparent pricing mechanism and service level agreements (SLAs).

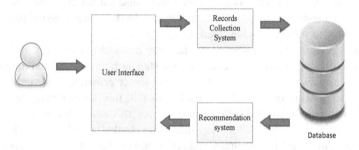

Fig. 1. Interaction between User and Recommendation System

In [11], this paper proposed a "Cloud Evaluation Value" for the enterprise. CEV (Cloud Evaluation Value) is a value to evaluate enterprise cloud model. These factors are calculated differently depend on their characteristics. Each provider's evaluation value is calculated from the total number of sub factors and is divided by business necessities. Finally, Enterprises' needs can be matched with the database and return the results that have high CEV. The advantage of the research is the enterprise could find the cloud server provider very quickly and know the differences between each other's. Shortage of the research is that the research put IaaS factor for cloud server selection but did not show the hardware classification result for the enterprise. With hardware specification it will help enterprise to select the cloud server based on their hardware needs.

In [12], this paper proposed a hybrid method for recommending cloud service providers and evaluated them using CSEC value. In recommendation component, it proposed hybrid method where this method is the combination from user similarity reasoning and item preference reasoning. In evaluation component, the authors defined two models as each of the model contains the essential factors for choosing cloud server providers. These factors are calculated separately depending on their characteristics. Each cloud service providers will be calculated based on the sub factors and divided by the number of available factor for each provider. Finally, users' needs can be matched with the database records and CSEC value will be listed in the web interface. With these advantages it can help user to find the cloud service providers based on their similarity and return the providers list on the website based on the enterprise necessities (search function). The shortcoming of the research is the result of the hardware specification is not listed on the website. With the hardware specification, it would help enterprise easier to know the cloud server that they want to rent.

S.M Han et al. [13] proposed "Cloud Resource Recommendation System" that can help a user to select the cloud providers based on QoS and service rank analysis of resources that is provided by cloud providers. For QoS analysis, it is divided into SaaS and HaaS, QoS of HaaS [10] is given by:

$$QoS_{[Haas]} = \sum[QoS_{network}] + \sum_n SP[Sn, Cn, Mn] \tag{1}$$

Most of the cloud services are web based service, and QoS network becomes an important factor in cloud computing. The researchers can determine QoSnetwork using variety of variables such as response time, execution time, etc. Service quality of HaaS is calculated by QoS network and SP (service performance) like storage, CPU and memory. This approach can help users to select best services from different cloud providers. However, except the network connection and computation factor, other factors that can help enterprise know more about cloud providers such as the security, pricing mechanism, accessibility, and so on are needed. This research proposes recommendation system that recommends cloud server based on enterprise location in order to solve latency problem. The result of the recommendation system will be evaluated using CSEV score.

3   System Framework

Nowadays, various cloud server providers that offer their services for rent in the internet. It is difficult to find a cloud server which has different information about the service. Different cloud providers have different advantages and disadvantages. In order to solve this problem, the CSEV (Cloud Server Evaluation Value) is proposed to evaluate each service provider based on an enterprise's necessities and the enterprise can give its weight value to each factor. CSEV can provide a value for each service provider and use the value to compare with other service providers. The CSEV is included in the search component. The search component is divided into basic model and feature model. In basic model, enterprise can quickly review the important factors in the cloud (e.g. price, cloud deployment, operating system, etc.). In feature model, the enterprises can select the feature based on their necessities (e.g. customer service, security option, accessibility, etc.). Those models will save lots of time for searching cloud service providers. The proposed system architecture is shown as figure 2. The system architecture consists of several components. These components are storage component, search component, recommendation component, and evaluation component.

- Storage component: Storage component contains all information of the cloud server providers. The information of the cloud server providers include the factor that the providers offer for the enterprises. Storage component will be represented as a database.

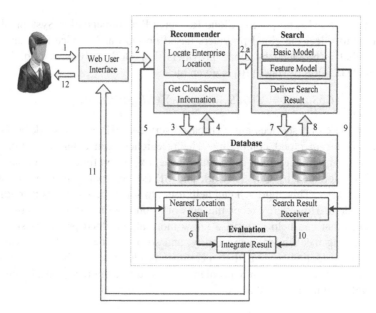

Fig. 2. System Architecture

- Search component: Search component contains the Basic Model, Feature Model, and Deliver Search Result.

— Basic Model is a model that contains basic factor selection of the cloud server providers. Enterprises can search and match the basic model with the database collection. Basic model includes the essential factors in the cloud server providers such as price, cloud deployment, control interface, and so on.
— Feature Model is a model that contains feature factor selection of the cloud server providers. Enterprises can select the feature model that they want and feature model will match with the database for searching the service providers.
— Deliver Search Result will send or deliver search result that has been selected by the enterprise through the two models, namely, Basic Model, and Feature Model.

- Recommender Component: Recommender component is responsible for calculating and recommending the cloud server provider based on the nearest location to the enterprise. Generally, Cloud server itself will be hosted in the data center. In this recommendation component, we use spherical law of cosines algorithm to count cloud server location which is near to the enterprise. The information of the nearest cloud server will be calculated based on the longitudes and the latitudes of the cloud server and the enterprise.
- Evaluation Component: Evaluation component contains Nearest Location Result and Search Result Receiver.

— Nearest Location Result handling the result that is sent from the recommendation component. The result should contain the nearest location of cloud server to the enterprise.

— Search Result Receiver is responsible for receiving and evaluating the result of the cloud server service providers. The evaluation will use Cloud Server Evaluation Value (CSEV). The evaluation will be explained in the next section.
— Integrate Result is responsible for combining and integrating the nearest location result search and result receiver.

4   Cloud Server Evaluation

This study proposes Cloud Server Evaluation Value (CSEV) to solve the cloud server selection problem. CSEV can help the enterprise to distinguish the differences among cloud server providers. CSEV uses the basic model and feature model as characteristic factors to evaluate the cloud server providers. These factors are including control interface, price, license, operating system, cloud deployment, and feature model which will be calculated separately and categorize according to the factors. License factor is not included in the CSEV because license factor cannot show the differences between the factors. The enterprise can put weight for the factors according to their needs. Figure 3 is the flow chart of system process. This process is divided into two parts from the entire system process. Left hand side is the recommendation component while the right hand side is the search component.

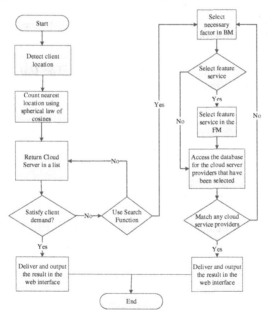

Fig. 3. Flowchart of System Process

Formula 2 represents the CSEV formula. Each parameter listed in table 1 is important issue for evaluation. Therefore, the parameters are treated equally. Those parameters are classified into basic model and feature model. In the CSEV formula, $CSEV_i$ means cloud server evaluation value for provider i. UsD_i means the user weight for the provider i. user User weight must be a number from one to five according to Likert scale where one is strongly unimportant, two is unimportant, three is neutral, four is important and five is the strongly important. This study uses the normalized technique to normalize the value of CSEV. The highest value of CSEV is 1 and the lowest value is 0. Take an example where an enterprise considers about the cloud deployment they can increase the cloud deployment weight. CSEV will return the result from 0 to 1 for each cloud server providers. The CSEV result will be listed on the web interface.

$$CSEV_i = \frac{CI_i \times CI_\gamma + P_i \times P_\gamma + OS_i \times OS_\gamma + CD_i \times CD_\gamma + S_i \times S_\gamma + Sup_i \times Sup_\gamma + A_i \times A_\gamma + F_i \times F_\gamma + Ac_i \times Ac_\gamma}{CI_\gamma + P_\gamma + OS_\gamma + CD_\gamma + S_\gamma + sup_\gamma + A_\gamma + F_\gamma + Ac_\gamma}$$

(2)

$$UsD_i = \{CI_\gamma, P_\gamma, OS_\gamma, CD_\gamma, S_\gamma, Sup_\gamma, A_\gamma, F_\gamma, Ac_\gamma\} \in \mathbb{N}$$

Formula 4 is the formula for calculating the control interface CI_i value. Control interface has four types or sub factors such as, web portal, API, command line, and GUI. CI_i value which will be normalized by dividing the summation of sub factors CI_i with the NEF_{CI_i}. In Formula 5, we use it to calculate the price P_i. Price is divided into three sub factors. They are average basic price, average short term price, and average long term price. We use maximum average price to compare with each sub factor of price. Higher price will produce lower value and the lower price will produce the highest value. P_i value will be normalized by dividing sub factor P_i with the NEF_{P_i}. Formula 6 will explain the operating system OS_i value that is supported by the providers. OS_i contains three sub factors. They are Windows operating system, Mac operating system and Linux operating system. The OS_i value will be normalized by dividing the summation of sub factors OS_i with the NEF_{OS_i}.

$$CI_i = \frac{WP_i + API_i + CL_i + GUI_i}{NEF_{CI_i}}$$

(4)

$$P_i = \frac{\frac{BP_{max} - BP_i}{BP_{max}} + \frac{STP_{max} - STP_i}{STP_{max}} + \frac{LTP_{max} - LTP_i}{LTP_{max}}}{NEF_{P_i}}$$

(5)

$$OS_i = \frac{Win_i + Mac_i + Linux_i}{NEF_{OS_i}}$$

(6)

Formula 7 is applied to calculate the cloud deployment CD_i value. CD_i contains four sub factors. These cloud deployments are public cloud, private cloud, community cloud, and hybrid cloud. CD_i value will be normalized by dividing the summation of sub factors CD_i with NEF_{CD_i}. In Formula 8, we discuss the security S_i value. Factor S_i is composed by snapshot, automatic failover, advance firewall, data protection, and threat and application security. S_i value will be normalized by dividing the summation of sub factors S_i with the NEF_{S_i}. Formula 9 is the formula for calculating the Sup_i value. Sup_i contains six sub factors. These sub factors are auto scaling, load balancing, monitoring, data recovery, advance reporting, backup and restore management. Sup_i value will be normalized by dividing the summation of sub factors Sup_i with NEF_{Sup_i}.

$$CD_i = \frac{Pub_i + Pri_i + Com_i + Hyb_i}{NEF_{CD_i}} \tag{7}$$

$$S_i = \frac{Snap_i + AF_i + Adf_i + DP_i + TAS_i}{NEF_{S_i}} \tag{8}$$

$$Sup_i = \frac{AS_i + LB_i + M_i + DR_i + AR_i + BRM_i}{NEF_{Sup_i}} \tag{9}$$

Formula 10 is the formula for calculating the agreement A_i value. A_i contains two sub factors. These sub factors are round clock services and Service Level Agreement (SLA). SLA will be compared with maximum SLA percentage, so SLA with higher percentage will get higher result and SLA with lower percentage will get lower result. A_i value will be normalized by dividing the summation of sub factors A_i with NEF_{A_i}. Facility F_i is composed of three sub factors. These are fire protection, cooling equipment, and disaster recovery. Formula 11 is the formula for calculate F_i value for each provider. F_i will be normalized by dividing the summation of sub factors F_i with NEF_{F_i}. Formula 12 is applied to calculate the accessibility Ac_i value. Ac_i factor can be divided into two sub factors. These are remote access and secure shell. Ac_i will be normalized by dividing the summation of sub factors Ac_i with NEF_{Ac_i}.

$$A_i = \frac{RCS_i + \frac{SLA_i}{SLA_{max}}}{NEF_{A_i}} \tag{10}$$

$$F_i = \frac{FP_i + CE_i + PDR_i}{NEF_{F_i}} \tag{11}$$

$$Ac_i = \frac{RA_i + SS_i}{NEF_{Ac_i}} \tag{12}$$

In order to present the research and give better understanding of the system for the enterprise, this study implements a web-based cloud server provider's search system. Simple web interface can help enterprise to search cloud server providers according to their necessities. Finally, the result of the request will be returned in the web interface. The system includes how to recommend a cloud service provider based on the enterprise location, and evaluates the cloud server providers.

The latency comparison listed in table 2 shows that the cloud server provider whose location near to the enterprise has small latency. The enterprise conducted the test in Taiwan. The result of table 2 shows that the location indeed can affect latency. The location of the cloud server provider which is located very far from the enterprise (in this case like India, and Australia) has larger latency than the near one. Beside latency problem, nearest cloud server location can improve bandwidth too. Average bandwidth is counted by bandwidth min plus bandwidth max and divided by two. Furthermore, table 2 shows that both Elastic Hosts Cloud Server (Hong Kong) and VPS.NET Cloud Server (Hong Kong) are located near to the enterprise. Thus, they have greater bandwidth compared to other cloud server providers (e.g., Singapore, India and Australia).

Table 1. Definitions of Parameters

Parameter	Definition
$CSEV_i$	Cloud server evaluation value for provider i
UsD_i	User weight for provider i
CI_i	Control interface value for provider i
P_i	Price value for provider i
OS_i	Operating System value for provider i
CD_i	Cloud Deployment value for provider i
S_i	Security value for provider i
Sup_i	Support value for provider i
A_i	Agreement for provider i
F_i	Facility for provider i

Table 2. Latency Comparison between Cloud Server Providers

Cloud Server Providers	Location	Latency (ms)	Average Bandwidth (Mb/s)
VPS.NET Cloud Server	Hong Kong	75.33	1.10
VPS.NET Cloud Server	Singapore	148	0.49
Elastic Hosts Cloud Server	Hong Kong	75.33	1.22
Elastic Hosts Cloud Server	Australia	656	0.24
Amazon EC2	Australia	476	0.28
Tata Communications Insta Compute	India	223.67	0.3
Tata Communications Insta Compute	Singapore	131	0.71
GMO Cloud	Japan	93.5	1.05
IDC Frontier Cloud	Japan	90.83	1.03

5   Conclusion

The purpose of this research is to help an enterprise to find suitable cloud server providers. This study presents how to find the nearest cloud server providers to reduce the latency problem for improving bandwidth and evaluates the cloud server providers based on the factors and enterprise's weightings. For recommendation function, this paper tracks the enterprise location and recommends the closest cloud server to the enterprise. For the searching function, this study classifies essential factors into two models, basic model and feature model. These models can help enterprises easier to search their needs in the system. The result of the cloud server providers will be analyzed and evaluated based on the factors and weights that enterprises input in the system. The differences between the proposed method and others are the evaluation based on the enterprise point of view. With this evaluation model, CSEV results will become a standard evaluation for cloud server providers. CSEV values will help enterprises to find and select a suitable cloud server provider. In the future, this study will try to include more complex enterprises requirements, such as more customized options, cloud server reliability, cloud provider's rating (social network rating) and other factors that can reduce the latency problem. Data of the cloud server providers also become an important part for recommendation and evaluation. With lots of data, the CSEV and recommendation results will be more accurate.

Acknowledgment. The authors would like to thank the National Science Council of the Republic of China, Taiwan for financially / partially supporting this research under Contract No. NSC102-2221-E-143-004- and NSC101-2221-E-259-005-MY2.

References

1. Velte, A.T., Velte, T.J., Elsenpeter, R.: Cloud Computing a Practical Approach. McGraw-Hill, United States (2010)
2. Ingthorsson, O.: 5 Reasons Cloud Computing Is Key to Business Success (Data Center Knowledge)   (2012), http://www.datacenterknowledge.com/archives/2012/06/25/5-reasons-cloud-computing-is-key-to-businesss-success/ (accessed: June 5, 2013)
3. Paul, F.: 8 Reasons Why Cloud Computing is Even Better for Small Businesses (2012), http://readwrite.com/2012/04/06/8-reasons-why-cloud-computing (accessed: June 5, 2013)
4. Sinnott, R.W.: Virtues of the haversine. Sky and Telescope 68(2), 159 (1984)
5. Abramowitz, M., Stegun, I.A.: Inverse circular functions. In: Handbook of Mathematical Functions with Formulas, Graphs, and Mathematical Tables, 9th printing, pp. 79–83. Dover, New York (1972)
6. The Harvesine Formula, longitude store, http://www.longitudestore.com/haversine-formula.html (accessed: June 20, 2013)
7. Gellert, W., Gottwald, S., Hellwich, M., Kästner, H., Küstner, H.: The vnr concise encyclopedia of mathematics, 2nd edn. Van Nostrand Reinhold, New York (1989)
8. Ireneus Romuald' Marchocki Scibor: Spherical trigonometry. Elementary-Geometry Trigonometry web page (1997)
9. Calculate distance, bearing and more between latitude/longitude points, Movable Type Scripts (2002), http://www.movable-type.co.uk/scripts/latlong.html (accessed: August 2, 2013)
10. Rimal, B.P., Jukan, A., Katsaros, D., Goeleven, Y.: Architectural requirements for cloud computing systems: an enterprise cloud approach. Journal of Grid Computing 9, 3–26 (2011)
11. Chang, R.S., Liu, C.Y.: Choosing Clouds for an Enterprise – Modeling and evaluation. National Dong Hwa University, Hualien, Taiwan, Republic of China (July 2012)
12. Chang, R.S., Fan, C.E.: A Hybrid Users Demand Consideration for Cloud Service Recommendation and Evaluation Standard. National Dong Hwa University, Hualien, Taiwan, Republic of China (2009)
13. Han, S.M., Hassan, M.M., Yoon, C., Lee, H., Huh, E.: Efficient Service Recommendation System for Cloud Computing Market. In: Conference of Interaction Sciences: Information Technology, Culture and Human, November 24-26, pp. 839–845 (2009)

Non-local Denoising in Encrypted Images*

Xianjun Hu, Weiming Zhang, Honggang Hu, and Nenghai Yu

Key Laboratory of Electromagnetic Space Information, Chinese Academy of Sciences,
University of Science and Technology of China, Hefei, China, 230027
hxj2012@mail.ustc.edu.cn, {zhangwm,hghu2005,ynh}@ustc.edu.cn

Abstract. Signal processing in the encrypted domain becomes a desired technique to protect privacy of outsourced data in cloud. In this paper we propose a double-cipher scheme to implement non-local means denoising in encrypted images. In this scheme, one ciphertext is generated by Paillier scheme which enables the mean-filter, and the other is obtained by a privacy-preserving transform which enables the non-local searching. By the privacy-preserving transform, the cloud can search the similar pixel blocks in the ciphertexts with the same speed as in the plaintexts, so the proposed method can be fast executed. The experimental results show that the quality of denoised images in the encrypted domain is comparable to that obtained in plain domain.

Keywords: Paillier homomorphic encryption, Image denoising, Non-Local Means, Johnson-Lindenstrauss Transform.

1 Introduction

Computable cloud is now prevalent in our daily life, by which customers can remotely store their data so as to enjoy the convenient and effective services [9]. More and more sensitive information such as e-mails and finance data are professionally maintained in data centers. Although outsourcing data storage and processing are quite promising, it still faces a large number of basic challenges, for which the first we need to consider about is security [11]. In fact, many corporations and companies are still afraid of outsourcing their data to the cloud server for the reason that their data may be leaked and cloud sever could abuse their data. So it comes that sensitive data has to be encrypted prior for data privacy and combating unsolicited access.

This leads to a need for techniques of signal processing on encrypted data, which obviously is a difficult problem, because we must have a secure encryption

* This work was supported in part by the Natural Science Foundation of China under Grant 61170234 and Grant 60803155, by the Strategic Priority Research Program of the Chinese Academy of Sciences under Grant XDA06030600, by the Funding of Science and Technology on Information Assurance Laboratory under Grant KJ-13-02, by the National Natural Science Foundation of China (61271271), 100 Talents Program of Chinese Academy of Sciences, and the Fundamental Research Funds for the Central Universities in China (WK2101020005).

R.C.-H. Hsu and W. Shangguang (Eds.): IOV 2014, LNCS 8662, pp. 386–395, 2014.
© Springer International Publishing Switzerland 2014

scheme that allows computations in the encrypted domain. In 1978, Rivest et al. [12] proposed to solve this problem by a scheme called homomorphic encryption that keeps the algebraic relations between plaintexts and ciphertexts. After that, several homomorphic encryption schemes [5], [10], [4] were presented, which process encrypted data with only one homomorphic property, such as addition or multiplication. For instance, the Paillier scheme [10] has additive homomorphism that means one can realize the addition of two plaintext signals by some operations on the two corresponding encrypted signals. A scheme is called fully homomorphic encryption (FHE) if it enables additive and multiplicative homomorphisms at the same time. The first secure FHE scheme is proposed by Gentry [6] in 2009, which, from a theoretical perspective, can solves any privacy-preserving computation problem. However, due to the huge computational complexity and cipher context expansion, FHE scheme is too inefficient to be applied in practice. So far, additive homomorphic encryption is the most popular scheme used by privacy protection community. Based on additive homomorphic encryption, some linear computations have been realized in the encrypted domain, such as discrete fourier transform [2], discrete cosine transform[1], discrete wavelet transform [13] [14] and Walsh-Hadamard transform [15].

An interesting and challenge problem is how to do nonlinear computations in encrypted domain without FHE. In the present paper, we will present a framework to solve a problem of encrypted image denoising that involves some nonlinear operations. Image denoising is one of the most popular image processings, and there exists many classical image denoising algorithms, such as Gauss filter, neighborhood filter, and non-local means (NLM) [3]. Among them NLM and its extensions can reach better performance by exploiting the similarity between the non-local pixel blocks with the current block. However, the Computational complexity of NLM algorithm is very high because it needs to search for the similar pixel blocks. Such hardness of computation is suitable for outsourcing to cloud, but the user may hope to prevent the cloud server from getting the content of the images. Therefore, the cloud should implement denoising in the encrypted images.

In this paper, we try to implement the NLM in the encrypted domain, which consists of two operations, i.e., non-local searching and mean-filter. Mean-filter in encrypted domain can be realized based on additive homomorphic cryptosystem such as Paillier scheme [10], while non-local searching is a nonlinear operation that needs FHE. To avoid FHE, we proposed a double-cipher denoising scheme in which we encrypt the image with two cryptosystems and thus outsource two ciphertexts to the cloud. One ciphertext is generated by Paillier scheme [10] which enables the mean-filter, the other is obtained by a privacy-preserving transform which enables the non-local searching. By the privacy-preserving transform, the cloud can search the similar pixel blocks in the ciphertexts with the same speed as in the plaintexts, so the proposed method can be fast executed.

The rest of the paper is organized as follows. In Section 2, we will give some preliminaries about NLM, Paillier cryptosystem and Johnson-Lindenstrauss (JL) transform. In Section 3, we will describe how to perform image denoising in the encrypted domain in detail. Complexity analysis of our proposed scheme will be given in section 4. The experimental results are shown in Section 5 and the paper is concluded with discussion in Section 6.

2 Preliminary

2.1 Non-local Means

The NLM method proposed by Buades et al. [3], was widely used in image denoising. Unlike local smoothing methods which only use the local relativity within pixels, NLM tries to exploit the relativity between the pixels that are not close to each other. We briefly introduce NLM below.

We assume the noise is the additive Gaussian noise with mean zero and variance σ^2. So we can describe a discrete noisy image as follows:

$$v(i) = u(i) + n(i) \tag{1}$$

where i is the pixel index in the set I, $v(i)$ is the observed value, $u(i)$ is the original value, and $n(i)$ is the i.i.d.Gaussian noise.

The denoised pixel value at position i is obtained by

$$NL(i) = \sum_{j \in \Omega} w(i,j)v(j) \tag{2}$$

where Ω is the searching window for the similar pixel. The weights $\{w(i,j)\}_j$ are determined by the similarity between the pixel i and j and satisfy $0 \leq w \leq 1$ and $\sum_j w(i,j) = 1$, and the similarity usually can be calculated by the Euclidean distance between the two blocks centered at the i-th and the j-th pixels respectively, such that

$$w(i,j) = \frac{1}{Z(i)} e^{-\frac{\|v(N_i) - v(N_j)\|_2^2}{h^2}}. \tag{3}$$

Herein, N_i denotes the pixel patch centered at the i-th pixel, $\|\cdot\|_2$ is the Euclidean norm, and h is used to control the decay of the weights. $Z(i)$ is normalizing parameter which is defined as

$$Z(i) = \sum_{j \in \Omega} e^{-\frac{\|v(N_i) - v(N_j)\|_2^2}{h^2}}, \tag{4}$$

2.2 Paillier Cryptosystem

Paillier homomorphic cryptosystem [10], is one of the well-known probabilistic and homomorphic schemes with an additive homomorphic property, which is realized as follows.

Initialization. Compute $N = pq$, which p, q was selected as two large prime numbers. Let $\lambda = lcm(p-1, q-1)$ and $g \in Z_{N^2}^*$ where the order of g is a multiple of N. The public key is (N, g) and the private key is λ.

Encryption. Take a plaintext $m \in Z_N$, and a random number (blinding factor) $r \in Z_N^*$. The corresponding ciphertext is

$$c = E_P(m, r) = g^m r^N \ mod \ N^2 \tag{5}$$

Decryption. Let the ciphertext $c \in Z_{N^2}^*$, so the plaintext m is

$$m = D_P(c) = \frac{L(c^\lambda \ mod \ N^2)}{L(g^\lambda \ mod \ N^2)} \ mod \ N \tag{6}$$

where $L(\phi) = (\phi - 1)/N$.

Homomorphism. The additive homomorphism means that the sum of two plaintexts m_1 and m_2 can be obtained by decrypting the product of corresponding ciphertexts.

$$D(E(m_1, r_1) \cdot E(m_2, r_2)) = D(E(m_1 + m_2, r_1 r_2)) = m_1 + m_2 \tag{7}$$

Moreover, let α be a constant and m be a plaintext, then αm can be calculated by decrypting the power of the ciphertext.

$$D(E(m, r)^\alpha) = D((g^m r^N)^\alpha) = D(E(\alpha m, r^\alpha)) = \alpha m \tag{8}$$

2.3 Johnson-Lindenstrauss Transform

Johnson-Lindenstrauss Transform (JL Transform) [7] is a dimension reduction method preserving Euclidean distance, which comes from the following lemma.

Lemma 1. *Given* $0 < \varepsilon < 1$, *a set* Q *of* n *points in* R^d, *and* $k = \Omega(\frac{\log n}{\varepsilon^2})$, *there exits a linear map* $f : R^d \to R^k$, *for any two vectors* $\alpha, \beta \in Q$, *there exits an inequality below*

$$(1 - \varepsilon)\|\alpha - \beta\|_2^2 \le \|f(\alpha) - f(\beta)\|_2^2 \le (1 + \varepsilon)\|\alpha - \beta\|_2^2 \tag{9}$$

Lemma 1 means that we can map some d-dimensional vectors to k-dimensional vectors, and the Euclidean distance between these d-dimensional vectors can be estimated by corresponding k-dimensional vectors. Usually f is defined by $f(\alpha) = P\alpha$ where $P \in R^{k \times d}$ is a random matrix. When $k < d$, one cannot recover α from $P\alpha$, so JL Transform can be used to conceal the elements in vector α and thus used for privacy protection. Kenthapadi et al. [8] analyzed the security of JL Transform and proposed the following private projection (Algorithm 1) and (Algorithm 2).

3   Image Denoising in the Encrypted Domain

In this section, we describe the double-cipher denoising method. Assume that the owner of one image I wants to denoise I with the NLM method. The owner hopes to outsource this work to a cloud server without leaking the content of I.

Algorithm 1. JL Transform-based Private Projection

Input: d-dimensional vector X; $k \times d$ random matrix P; noise parameter ζ.
Output: The projected k-dimensional vector Z.

1. $Y := PX$
2. Construct a random k-dimensional noise vector Δ based on the noise parameter ζ.
3. $Z := Y + \Delta$

Algorithm 2. JL Transform-based distance recover

Input: two k-dimensional vector α and β published in a privacy-preserving manner;
    Noise parameter ζ;
Output: Estimated squared distance between α and β in the original space.

1. Output $dist^2_{\alpha,\beta} = \|\alpha - \beta\|^2_2 - 2k\zeta^2$.

To do that, the owner encrypts I by JL Transform (Algorithm 1) and Paillier cryptosystem, and gets two encrypted images denoted by $E_J(I)$ and $E_P(I)$ respectively. Then the owner sends $E_J(I)$ and $E_P(I)$ to the cloud. With the help of $E_J(I)$, the cloud executes a non-local filter on $E_P(I)$ and yields a denoised cipher-image $E'_P(I)$ that is sent back to the owner. The owner decrypts $E'_P(I)$ and gets a plain denoised image I'. Next we elaborate the details of each step.

Encryption with JL Transform. When encrypting I with Algorithm 1, the owner takes the random matrix P and noise parameter ζ as the key. For each pixel $v(i)$ of I, take a $s \times s$ block centered at $v(i)$ and permute the block as a s^2-dimensional vector, denoted by N_i. With Algorithm 1, the owner projects N_i into a k-dimensional vector $E_J(N_i)$ which is just the ciphertext of $v(i)$. In other words, by JL Transform, each pixel is encrypted into a k-dimensional vector. For marginal pixels, some elements of the block matrix is blank, so we fill them with the surrounding pixels.

Encryption with Paillier Cryptosystem. For each pixel $v(i)$, take a random number $r_i \in Z_N^*$ and encrypt $v(i)$ by Eq. (5) as

$$E_P(v(i)) = E_P(v(i), r_i) = g^{v(i)} r_i^N \bmod N^2. \tag{10}$$

Denosing in Encrypted Images. As shown in Eq. (2) and Eq. (3), to do non-local filter, the cloud should first calculate the weights $\{w(i,j)\}_j$ that are determined by the Euclidean distance between N_i and N_j. Note that JL Transform preserves Euclidean distance, so the cloud can estimate $\|v(N_i) - v(N_j)\|_2$ by the ciphertexts of $v(i)$ and $v(j)$, i.e., $E_J(v(N_i))$ and $E_J(v(N_j))$. Therefore the weights are estimated by

$$w'(i,j) = \frac{1}{Z(i)} e^{- \frac{\|E_J(v(N_i)) - E_J(v(N_j))\|_2^2}{h^2}}, \tag{11}$$

where h is the decaying parameter and the normalizing parameter $Z(i)$ is obtained by

$$Z(i) = \sum_{j \in \Omega} e^{-\frac{\| E_J(v(N_i)) - E_J(v(N_j)) \|_2^2}{h^2}}. \tag{12}$$

With weights $\{w'(i,j)\}_j$, the cloud filters the other encrypted image $E_P(I)$ as follows. For each ciphertext $E_P(v(i))$, the filtered value $E'_P(v(i))$ is

$$E'_P[v(i)] = \prod_{j \in \Omega} E_P[v(j)]^{w'(i,j)} \tag{13}$$

Collecting all $E'_P(v(i))$, the cloud yields a denoised encrypted image $E'_P(I)$ that is sent back to the owner of I.

Decryption. After receiving $E'_P(I)$, the image owner decrypts it pixel by pixel. According to the homomorphism Eq. (7) and Eq. (8), the pixel $E'_P(v(i))$ is decrypted as

$$NL'(i) = D_P[\prod_{j \in \Omega} E_P[v(j)]^{w'(i,j)}] = \sum_{j \in \Omega} w'(i,j)v(j) \tag{14}$$

Compare Eq. (2) with Eq. (14), we conclude that the denoising result obtained in the encrypted image is similar with that obtained in the plain image because JL Transform can preserve Euclidean distance and thus $w'(i,j)$ is a good estimation of $w(i,j)$.

Note that the wights $\{w'(i,j)\}_j$ are real numbers, but to calculate Eq. (13) and Eq. (14) according to Paillier cryptosystem, the values $\{w'(i,j)\}_j$ have to be quantified as integer numbers. The quantization process can be expressed as

$$W(i,j) = \lfloor Aw'(i,j) \rceil \tag{15}$$

where $\lfloor \cdot \rceil$ is the rounding function and A is the scaling factor. For simplicity, we rewrite Eq. (15) as follow:

$$W(i,j) = Aw'(i,j) + \varepsilon_{w_j} \tag{16}$$

where $|w'(i,j)| \leq 1$ and ε_{w_j} is the error caused by quantization with $|\varepsilon_{w_j}| \leq 1/2$.

Replacing $w'(i,j)$ by $W(i,j)$, the decrypted result Eq. (14) will be changed to

$$NL''(i) = \sum_{j \in \Omega} W(i,j)v(j) = \sum_{j \in \Omega} (Aw'(i,j) + \varepsilon_{w_j})v(j). \tag{17}$$

From $NL''(i)$, the owner of I can estimate $NL'(i)$ by

$$\overline{NL'(i)} = \frac{NL''(i)}{A} = NL'(i) + \frac{\sum_{j \in \Omega} \varepsilon_{w_j} v(j)}{A} \tag{18}$$

The last item $\frac{\sum_{j \in \Omega} \varepsilon_{w_j} v(j)}{A}$ is the error caused by quantization, which can be controlled by selecting a large enough parameter A. Note that, to get the accurate result of $NL''(i)$ by decryption in the Paillier cryptosystem, we have to limit $NL''(i) < N$. In other words, the value of A cannot be as large as possible, and must be chosen properly according to the settings of Paillier cryptosystem.

Table 1. Result of simulation

Index	d	k	PSNR before	PSNR after	Index	d	k	PSNR before	PSNR after
			house					parrot	
(c)	25	-	22.09	32.39	(h)	25	-	22.09	29.03
-	25	20	22.09	30.93	-	25	20	22.09	27.93
-	25	18	22.09	30.54	-	25	18	22.09	27.76
(d)	25	16	22.09	30.03	(i)	25	16	22.09	27.51
-	25	12	22.09	28.83	-	25	12	22.09	26.86
(e)	25	9	22.09	28.08	(j)	25	9	22.09	26.36
			peppers					cameraman	
(m)	25	-	22.09	30.15	(r)	25	-	22.09	29.48
-	25	20	22.09	28.61	-	25	20	22.09	28.45
-	25	18	22.09	28.30	-	25	18	22.09	28.24
(n)	25	16	22.09	27.95	(s)	25	16	22.09	27.94
-	25	12	22.09	27.03	-	25	12	22.09	27.29
(o)	25	9	22.09	26.40	(t)	25	9	22.09	26.82

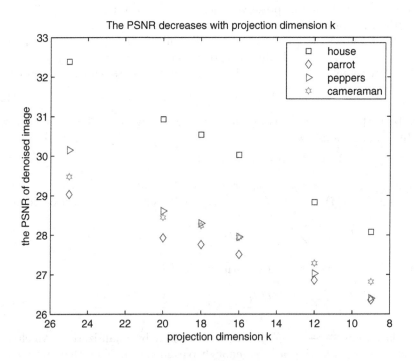

Fig. 1. The PSNR of denoised image decreases with the projection dimension k

4 Complexity Analysis

Now we estimate the computational complexity of our proposed scheme. Our scheme has two parts, first part is non-local searching, and second part is mean-filter in the encrypted domain.

So, we analysis the computational complexity from the first part. Here we refer to the literature [3]. If we use a similarity window of size $s \times s$, so for a image of size $n \times n$, the computational complexity is $n^2 \times s^2 \times n^2 = s^2 \times n^4$. So the computational complexity of the original algorithm is $O(n^4)$. If we also restrict the search of the similarity windows in the size of $L \times L$. The entire computational complexity of the algorithm is $n^2 \times s^2 \times L^2$.

Now we discuss computational complexity of the second part. In the second part we only consider about the Eq. (14), there are only modular exponentiation and modular multiplication operation in the encrypted domain. Hence, we can use the number of modular exponentiation (m_{exp}) and modular multiplication (m_{mul}) to evaluate the computational complexity. As we defined before, for a $n \times n$ image, the similarity window size is $s \times s$, and the size of the search window is $L \times L$. Hence for a single pixel, the number of modular exponentiation is $L^2 \times W(i,j) = L^2 \times Aw'(i,j)$, and the number of modular multiplication is $L^2 - 1$. For the whole image, the computation of modular exponentiation and modular multiplication are $n^2 \times L^2 \times Aw'(i,j)$ and $n^2 \times (L^2 - 1)$, respectively. When the search window size is $n \times n$, the total number of modular exponentiation is $n^2 \times n^2 \times Aw'(i,j) = n^4 \times Aw'(i,j)$ and the total number of modular multiplication is $n^2 \times (n^2 - 1)$ in encrypted domain.

5 Experiments

In our experiments, for security reason, the product of two primes ($N = p \times q$) for the Paillier cryptosystem is longer than 1024 bits. For $A \times NL'(i) < N$, we can get $A < 2^{1024}/255 = 2^{1016}$, For $A = 2^{30}$, the error $\frac{\sum_{j \in \Omega} \varepsilon_{w_j} v(j)}{A}$ can be less than $L^2/2^{23}$, so we set the size of searching window $L \times L = 21 \times 21$, the size of similar block $d = s \times s = 5 \times 5$, Gaussian noise $\sigma = 20$, the decaying parameter $h = 0.75\sigma$, the noise parameter $\zeta = 1$, and the images "house, parrot, peppers, cameraman" are used as an example. In Fig. 2, the first column is the original image sized of 256×256, the second column is the images after adding $(0, 20^2)$ Gaussian noise, the third column is the images denoised in the plaintext, the fourth and fifth column are the images denoised in the encrypted domain with projection dimension $k = 16, 9$, respectively. The peak signal-to-noise ratios (PSNR) of the noisy images and the denoised images are listed in Table 1. It can be seen from Fig. 2 and Table 1, the denoised images in encrypted domain can achieve similar quality as done in plain domain.

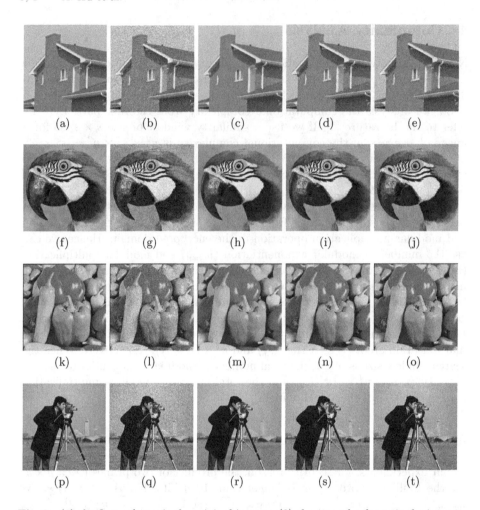

Fig. 2. (1) the first column is the original images; (2) the second column is the images after adding $(0, 20^2)$ Gaussian noise; (3) the third column is the images denoised in the plaintext; (4) the fourth column is the images denoised in the encrypted domain with projection dimension $k = 16$; (5) the fifth column is the images denoised in the encrypted domain with projection dimension $k = 9$.

6   Conclusion and Future Work

In this paper, we propose a double-cipher denosing method in encrypted images, which enables the cloud to implement NLM with the ability of preserving privacy of the image contents. This double-cipher scheme is a novel framework to deal with nonlinear operations in the encrypted domain avoiding FHE. In the present scheme, the nonlinear operation is searching for similar blocks which is realized based on the privacy projection. As shown in Table 1 and Figure 1, the PSNR of denosed image decreases with the projection dimension k. In fact, the secure level of the privacy projection increases with decreasing k. However, because of the limits of pages, the security of the proposed scheme is not analyzed, which will be studied in our further work.

References

1. Bianchi, T., Piva, A., Barni, M.: Encrypted domain dct based on homomorphic cryptosystems. EURASIP Journal on Information Security 2009, 1 (2009)
2. Bianchi, T., Piva, A., Barni, M.: On the implementation of the discrete fourier transform in the encrypted domain. IEEE Transactions on Information Forensics and Security 4(1), 86–97 (2009)
3. Buades, A., Coll, B., Morel, J.: A review of image denoising algorithms, with a new one. Multiscale Modeling & Simulation 4(2), 490–530 (2005)
4. Damgård, I., Jurik, M.: A generalisation, a simplification and some applications of paillier's probabilistic public-key system. In: Kim, K. (ed.) PKC 2001. LNCS, vol. 1992, pp. 119–136. Springer, Heidelberg (2001)
5. ElGamal, T.: A public key cryptosystem and a signature scheme based on discrete logarithms. IEEE Transactions on Information Theory 31(4), 469–472 (1985)
6. Gentry, C.: A fully homomorphic encryption scheme. Ph.D. thesis, Stanford University (2009)
7. Johnson, W., Lindenstrauss, J.: Extensions of lipschitz mappings into a hilbert space. Contemporary Mathematics 26(189-206), 1 (1984)
8. Kenthapadi, K., Korolova, A., Mironov, I., Mishra, N.: Privacy via the johnson-lindenstrauss transform. arXiv preprint arXiv:1204.2606 (2012)
9. Mell, P., Grance, T.: Draft nist working definition of cloud computing. Referenced on June 3, vol. 15 (2009)
10. Paillier, P.: Public-key cryptosystems based on composite degree residuosity classes. In: Stern, J. (ed.) EUROCRYPT 1999. LNCS, vol. 1592, pp. 223–238. Springer, Heidelberg (1999)
11. Ren, K., Wang, C., Wang, Q.: Security challenges for the public cloud. IEEE Internet Computing 16(1), 69–73 (2012)
12. Rivest, R., Adleman, L., Dertouzos, M.: On data banks and privacy homomorphisms. Foundations of Secure Computation 32(4), 169–178 (1978)
13. Zheng, P., Huang, J.: Implementation of the discrete wavelet transform and multiresolution analysis in the encrypted domain. In: Proceedings of the 19th ACM International Conference on Multimedia, pp. 413–422. ACM (2011)
14. Zheng, P., Huang, J.: Discrete wavelet transform and data expansion reduction in homomorphic encrypted domain (2013)
15. Zheng, P., Huang, J.: Walsh-hadamard transform in the homomorphic encrypted domain and its application in image watermarking. In: Kirchner, M., Ghosal, D. (eds.) IH 2012. LNCS, vol. 7692, pp. 240–254. Springer, Heidelberg (2013)

An Adaptive Pre-copy Strategy
for Virtual Machine Live Migration

Ching-Hsien Hsu[1,2], Sheng-Ju Peng[1], Tzu-Yi Chan[1],
Kenn Slagter[3], and Yeh-Ching Chung[3]

[1] Department of Computer Science and Information Engineering,
Chung Hua University, Hsinchu, 30012 Taiwan
{chh,m10102022,b10002099}@chu.edu.tw
[2] School of Computer and Communication Engineering,
Tianjin University of Technology, Tianjin, 300384 China
[3] Department of Computer Science, National Tsing Hua University, Hsinchu, 30013 Taiwan
{kennslagter,ychung}@cs.nthu.edu.tw

Abstract. Live migration technology for virtual machines provides greater flexibility when scheduling tasks in a cloud environment. This flexibility helps increase the utilization of resources within the cloud. A key component of live migration technology is the pre-copy strategy. The pre-copy strategy allows virtual machine to perform live migration without interruption of service. However, in order for live migration to be efficient, it is imperative that virtual machines' memories are not limited by bandwidth and that the downtime of the virtual machines involved is minimal.

This paper presents an adaptive pre-copy strategy for virtual machine live migration called Multi-Phase Pre-Copy (MPP). In iterative pre-copy stage MPP transmits memory pages only when a predefined threshold is met. This strategy significantly reduces unnecessary migration of memory pages.

Keywords: Virtualization, virtual machine, live migration, multi-phase pre-copy.

1 Introduction

Investment by businesses and governments has led to a rapid growth in cloud computing research. Cloud computing applications use a combination of networked computing resources and virtualization techniques and architecture. Virtualization is achieved by having physical machines (called nodes) in the network run virtual machines. These virtual machines can be divided up in different ways and can be asked to perform different tasks.

Virtualization is a key technology in cloud computing. Consequently, effective management of virtual machines and related technologies is required in order to make efficient use of resources on the cloud. One of the ways to make efficient use of the underlying hardware on the cloud is to dynamically transfer virtual machines throughout the network in order to make better use of the resources on the network. Dynamic transfer of virtual machines over the network is known as migration.

R.C.-H. Hsu and W. Shangguang (Eds.): IOV 2014, LNCS 8662, pp. 396–406, 2014.

Live migration technology is based on prevalent virtual machine migration technology. Previous migration techniques required a short downtime of a system whenever a virtual machine gets transferred over the network. The purpose of live migration is to allow virtual machines to migrate elsewhere on the network without any perceivable interruption of a service by the user.

Live migration of virtual machines can be divided into pre-copy and post-copy methods. The most common live migration method is pre-copy. With the pre-copy method a hypervisor copies all the memory pages from the source node to the destination node while the virtual machine is running on the source node. With the post-copy method the virtual machine is paused at the source, and the execution state of the virtual machine is transferred to the target. Once the virtual machine is transferred to the target the virtual machine resumes execution and the source pushes stored memory pages to the target via a technique known as pre-paging.

Migration time for post-copy migration is relatively low compared to pre-copy migration, but the overall downtime of the virtual machine in post-copy is longer than it is for pre-copy. Therefore, this paper focuses on improving pre-copy migration. The Xen hypervisor [1][2] is a well-known open source hypervisor used by industry and academia that implements pre-copy migration. For these reasons, this paper focuses on reducing downtime and total migration time when doing pre-copy migration by the Xen hypervisor.

A drawback of the traditional Xen pre-copy migration process is that it repeatedly copies memory pages and processor (CPU) states across the network. The copying of memory page occurs when the data in the memory page changes, and becomes a dirty page. Xen will send this dirty page to the target even if the dirty page remains unchanged from the last time it was copied. Consequently, this prolongs the overall migration time.

In this paper, we propose a new multi-phase pre-copy method (MPP) that reduces the number of pages being shipped over the network, and reduces overall migration time. MPP transfers pages over the network based on a set of threshold values which determine if a page should be transferred to its target or not.

The rest of this paper is organized as follows. In Section 2 we discuss related work. Section 3 presents some background. In Section 4, we present our proposed technique. In Section 5, we present our performance evaluation. Finally, the conclusion and future work are presented in Section 6.

2   Related Work

Virtual Machine Live Migration (VMLM) has become a hot topic in both academia and industry. Topics on VMLM can be found in both practical applications as well as research papers. Traditionally VMLM migrates the internal memory state, and importantly involves memory image transfer. Some memory transfer research focuses on handling the state of the virtual machine memory [3][4][5]. Additional research by [5][6][7] provides a virtual machine management platform that provides an uninterrupted service when migrating virtual machines.

Pre-copy algorithms [5][7] have been presented that enhance pre-copy efficiency for when machine reads and writes are numerous. These algorithms focus on alleviating the amount of downtime that occurs due to the frequent number of dirty pages created as a consequence. From a different perspective there is also research [8] that looks into how bandwidth can be dynamically adjusted during VMLM in order to limit network traffic.

To further improve the efficiency of the pre-copy algorithm [6] introduces time-series prediction techniques. Time-series prediction is done by updating records and using statistics each time a dirty page is sent from the source to the target. However, the associated formula expects parameters used to define a page to be static even though these parameters can easily change. Furthermore, even though the dirty page threshold in its formula can significantly reduce pre-copy transmission times in iterative rounds, it increases the downtime.

3   Background

Virtual machine migration has become an essential feature in cloud computing. There are various reasons why virtual machine migration may be instigated including: hardware maintenance, lack of resources, and load imbalance. Despite improved or more stable performance after migration, it is best if there is no perceivable interruption of service during migration by the user.

Virtual machine migration can be divided into two distinct categories: offline migration and online migration. Online migration itself can be divided into two distinct subcategories cold migration and live migration. Details of these two subcategories are described below.

According to [9] when one migrates virtual machines on a virtual system one needs to consider downtime and total migration time. Downtime is the time it takes a source host to suspend a virtual machine until the time the virtual machine resumes on the target host. In other words downtime refers to the time when the virtual machine is unresponsive. Total migration time is the time from the start of the migration process on the source host until the end of the migration process, which is after the time the virtual machine resumes on the target host and once the source virtual machine has been deactivated and discarded.

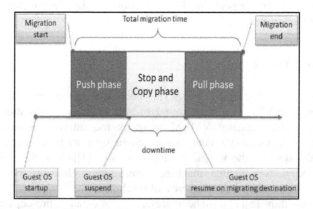

Fig. 1. Virtual Machine Migration Phase Diagram [4]

Figure 1 shows the three different phases that occur during live migration [9], and the relationship they have between each other and their effect on downtime and total migration time. The phases that occur during virtual machine migration are:

1. *Push phase*: The source virtual machine continues to operate while content is moved to the target.
2. *Stop-and-copy phase*: the source virtual machine stops executing. Any remaining content found at the source is removed, following the move, the migrated virtual machine on the target begins to operate.
3. *Pull phase*: a virtual machine system is up and running on the target host during migration. Any content missing on the target is taken (pulled) from the source.

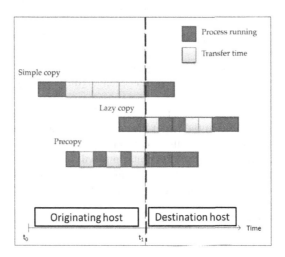

Fig. 2. The three ways migration is performed [4]

In general, there are three common ways that migration is performed [10]:

1. *Simple copy*: also known as "pure stop-and-copy" [11] halts the virtual machine at the source, copies memory pages from the source to the target, and then starts a new virtual machine on the target. The advantage of this approach is that it is the simplest one to implement. However, the disadvantage of this approach is that there must be a significant amount of downtime and overall migration time. How long it takes to migrate depends on the size of the memory used by the virtual machines.
2. *Lazy copy*: also known as "pure demand-migration"[12] uses a short stop-and-copy phase to transfer over any vital kernel data to the target. The target virtual machine is then started. Memory pages are then transferred over the network when used for the first time due as a consequence of a page fault. The advantage of this approach is that it has a much shorter downtime compared to the simple copy method. However, the total migration time is lengthened. Furthermore, the performance of the target virtual machine after migration will likely be poor until a substantial number of pages have been transferred across.

3. *Pre-copy*: balances the concerns found in simple copy and lazy copy methods. It combines an iterative push phase with a typically short stop-and-copy phase. During the iterative push phase pages are transferred in rounds to the virtual machine ready for them to be of use in the subsequent round that needs them. Since every virtual machine has a set of pages that are used often and are a poor candidate for the pre-copy method the number of rounds is bounded based on analysis of a writing working set.

Pre-copy live migration operation can be divided into six stages. Each stage represents a different mode of operation.

1. *Stage 0 Pre-migration*: Prior to migration a host with sufficient resources is selected.
2. *Stage 1 Reservation*: A request is made to migrate from the source to the target host.
3. *Stage 2 Iterative Pre-Copy*: In the first iteration of the round, all source pages are transferred to the host. Any pages that change (dirty pages) are then sent in subsequent rounds.
4. *Stage 3 Stop and Copy*: Stops the virtual machine on the source machine and redirects network traffic to the target machine. CPU state and any dirty memory pages get transferred as well. Both source and target now have a suspended copy of the virtual machine. The source virtual machine will resume if there is a failure.
5. *Stage 4 Commitment*: Target host informs the source host that it has received the complete virtual machine image. The source host can now discard the old virtual machine.
6. *Stage 5 Activation*: The virtual machine will now run as normal on the host machine.

Xen's iterative pre-copy stage categorizes used memory pages into three types of bitmaps. These bitmaps are described as follows:

1. *To_Send*: marks the pages which were dirty on the previous round, this identifies which pages need to be transmitted for the current iteration.
2. *To_Skip*: marks which pages can be ignored for the current iteration.
3. *To_Fix*: marks which pages should have been transmitted in the previous iteration.

These bitmaps represent those memory pages that need to be sent from the source host to the target host. In the first round of the iterative process, the entire page of memory within the virtual machine is sent. Those memory pages that are to be sent are marked. It then determines whether pages that occur in the subsequent round of the iterative process should be sent or skipped.

Xen's iterative pre-copy stage has several termination conditions that ensure it completes the stage in a timely manner. If any of these termination conditions are satisfied the iterative pre-copy stage ends and the stop-and-copy stage begins. The pre-copy termination conditions are as follows:

1. Less than 50 pages were dirtied during the last pre-copy iteration
2. 29 pre-copy iterations have been carried out.

3. More than 3 times the total amount of memory allocated to the VM has been
    copied from the source host to the target host.

If the first termination condition is satisfied there will be a short downtime. This is
because the final iteration will send only a small number of dirty pages from the source
to the target. If the second or third condition is satisfied there will be a longer
downtime. This is because there will be a forced migration, a transition to the
stop-and-copy stage, and a considerable number of dirty pages transferred from the
source to the target host.

The termination conditions used by Xen gives it some advantages to a naïve
implementation of the iterative pre-copy process. Without these termination conditions,
iterative pre-copy would take a long time to terminate. This is because memory
typically has regular periods of intensive reading and writing. Furthermore, workloads
typically have a small set of pages that are frequently accessed. By sending pages when
memory is not undergoing intensive read and write sessions, Xen prevents many
unnecessary page transfers. This in turn prevents long migration times.

4   Multi-phase Virtual Machine Migration

In this section we describe improvements made to the iterative nature of the pre-copy
method. The concept presented here applies lazy pre-copy mechanisms to different
stages of the pre-copy mechanism and then applies different judging criteria to
improve overall efficiency during live migration.

A. Lazy Pre-Copy

Live migration, migrates virtual machines over the network from a source host to a
target host. It is tempting to use available bandwidth as metric as a way to improve
performance of LMVM. Unfortunately, it is impossible to predict what the bandwidth
will be based on data collected from the bandwidth history. Furthermore, an incorrect
prediction is likely to have a negative effect on performance.

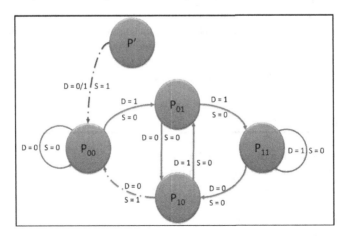

Fig. 3. Lazy Pre-Copy State Diagram

In order to improve bandwidth usage we use a lazy pre-copy mechanism. The lazy pre-copy (LPC) mechanism improves the effective bandwidth by reducing the number of memory pages transmitted over the network. A state diagram for the lazy pre-copy mechanism is presented in Figure 3. A description of the state transitions found in lazy pre-copy is as follows:

1. P' P_{00}: Initialize, send all memory pages (dirty or not) from source host to target host.
2. $P_{00}P_{00}$: pages are *not* dirty, pages are *not* sent from source host to destination host.
3. $P_{00}P_{01}$: pages are dirty, pages are *not* sent from source host to destination host.
4. $P_{01}P_{10}$: pages are *not* dirty, pages are *not* sent from source host to destination host.
5. $P_{01}P_{11}$: pages are dirty, pages are *not* sent from source host to destination host.
6. $P_{11}P_{11}$: pages are dirty, pages are *not* sent from source host to destination host.
7. $P_{11}P_{10}$: pages are *not* dirty, pages are *not* sent from source host to destination host.
8. $P_{10}P_{01}$: pages are dirty, pages are *not* sent from source host to destination host.
9. $P_{10}P_{00}$: pages are *not* dirty, pages are sent from source host to destination host.

Lazy pre-copy improves the migration process by using bandwidth more efficiently. Lazy pre-copy achieves this by waiting an extra round before it transfers data, this reduces the number of retransmissions over the network.

B. Threshold Based Iterative Pre-Copy

To improve the efficiency of lazy pre-copy, a set of criterion is used which decides whether or not to transfer memory pages from the source to the target host. Data transfer is predicated on threshold K, which increases in value on a round by round basis.

While lazy pre-copy is executing the value of K is adjusted and set to one of three thresholds $K_1(\alpha\%)$, $K_2(\beta\%)$, and $K_3(\gamma\%)$. The maximum number of rounds for Xen is 30. These rounds are divided into three stages. The first stage (iterations $0\sim i_1$) uses threshold $K_1(\alpha\%)$, the second stage (iterations $i_{1+1}\sim i_2$) uses threshold $K_2(\beta\%)$ and the third stage (iterations $i_{2+1}\sim i_3$) uses threshold $K_3(\gamma\%)$. The thresholds for the three stages are allocated three different memory sizes. The first stage is allocated 5% of the memory. The second stage is allocated 1% of the memory. The amount of memory allocated in the third stage is defined by LPC which counts the number of dirty pages per round. According to which conditions are met and if they reach the associated threshold value, dirty memory pages are delivered to the target host.

The Multi-Phase Pre-Copy method described above is now presented in the following algorithm:

Algorithm 1: Multi-Phase Pre-Copy

Input:
Set L: the collection of page which is with 1
Set LP: the collection of page which is with 10
Set LPC: the collection of page which is with 100
Begin:
Pre-Migration and Reservation
Set L = Set LP = Set LPC ← NULL

For iteration 1:
   For page j:
      If $(P_j = 1)$ **then** set $L \leftarrow P_j$
For iteration 2:
   For page j:
      If $(P_j = 0$ & P_j in set $L)$ **then** set $LP \leftarrow P_j$
   Reset set L
   For page j:
      If $(P_j = 1)$ **then** $L \leftarrow P_j$
For iteration 3 and afterward:
   Reset set_LPC
   For page j:
      If $(P_j = 0$ & P_j in set $LP)$ **then** set $LPC \leftarrow P_j$
  Reset set LP
   For page j:
      If $(P_j = 0$ & P_j in set $L)$ **then** set $LP \leftarrow P_j$
   Reset set L
   For page j:
      If $(P_j = 1)$ **then** $L \leftarrow P_j$
   If $LPC >$ threshold then **then** send $P_j \in LPC$ to destination host //Pre-Copy
   If one of the termination conditions T1, T2 and T3 hold **then** stop_and_copy ()

5   Performance Analysis

In this section we present the experimental environment and experimental results of the proposed live migration mechanisms. Performance analysis was done by running the proposed algorithm on a simulated physical environment. To simulate the physical environment, multiple virtual machine images were installed and executed on a single physical machine.

A. Experimental Environment

To evaluate the performance of the proposed technique, we implemented the multiphase virtual machine migration algorithm and tested its performance on a physical machine running Xen version 3.1.2. All virtual machines had a single CPU core and tests were performed using different amounts of RAM. The specification of the physical machine used is shown in Table 1. The software environment is presented in Table 2.

Table 1. Physical Machine 1 Hardware Specifications

CPU	AMD Operton 6100 2.0G (8 Core) x1
RAM	8 GB
Disk	500 GB x2 (7200rpm)
Network	1 Gigabit

Table 2. Software Environment

OS	CentOS 6.2 x86_64
Kernel	2.6.32
File system	EXT4

To evaluate the performance of multi-phase pre-copy, we implemented multiphase virtual machine migration and tested its performance against the pre-copy method implementation used by the Xen hypervisor.

The pre-copy methods were tested to see how well they performed with different image sizes and with different dirty memory page rates. Metrics used to evaluate performance include: number of iterations, pre-copy performance (number of pages transferred), downtime and total migration time.

B. Experimental Results

Real-time experimental results for LMVM were performed for Xen and multi-phase methods. Results show that when the the rate dirty pages occur is low, multi-phase pre-copy is able to reduce unnecessary data transfers significantly. When the dirty rate increases the number of dirty pages is higher, therefore the number of necessary data transfers increases. Consequently, the improvement in performance between Xen pre-copy and multi-phase pre-copy is reduced.

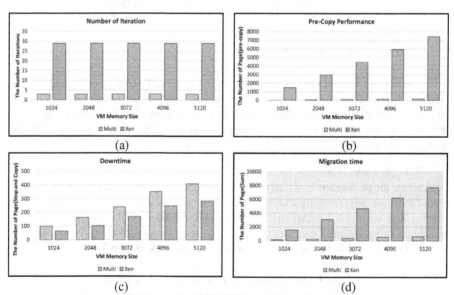

(a) Number of iteration (b) Pre-Copy performance (c) Downtime (d) Migration time

Fig. 4. Impact on Dirty Rate 0.05

Experiments were conducted to compare the performance between multi-phase migration and Xen's iterative pre-copy method. As shown in figure 6(a) regardless of virtual memory size, the number of iterations remains constant. However, In Figure

6(a) the number of iterations is much smaller for multi-phase pre-copy than that of Xen's pre-copy due to an earlier execution of a termination condition. Less iteration does not by itself equate to better performance, however it does mean less pages had to be transferred repeatedly over the network. Figure 6(b) refers to the pre-copy performance. Pre-copy performance refers to the number of data transfers over the network from source to the target host. Figure 6(c) show the downtime for multi-phase pre-copy is slightly longer than Xen's multi-phase pre-copy. However Figure 6(d) show that the total migration time is much less overall.

6   Conclusion

In this paper, we presented a multi-phase pre-copy method for live migration of virtual machines over a network. We show that compared to Xen's pre-copy method, multi-phase pre-copy is able to transfer dirty memory pages more efficiently from a source host to a target host. We show that multi-phase pre-copy can reduce the number of memory page transfers over the network with only a small increase in downtime. We also show that multi-phase pre-copy total migration time is significantly better than Xen's pre-copy method. For future work we intend to further improve live migration downtime and study how our algorithm performs on different network configurations.

References

[1] Barham, P., Dragovic, B., Fraser, K., Hand, S., Harris, T., Ho, A., Neugebauer, R., Pratt, I., Warfield, A.: Xen and the Art of Virtualization. In: SOSP 2003 Proceedings of the Nineteenth ACM Symposium on Operating Systems Principles, vol. 37(5), pp. 164–177 (December 2003)

[2] Xen-org, Xen, http://Xen.org/

[3] Akoush, S., Sohan, R., Rice, A., Moore, A.W., Hopper, A.: Predicting the Performance of Virtual Machine Migration. In: 18th Annual IEEE/ACM International Symposium on Modeling, Analysis and Simulation of Computer and Telecommunication Systems (MASCOTS), pp. 37–46 (August 2010)

[4] Lin, H., Gao, W., Wu, S., Shi, X.-H., Wu, X.-X., Zhou, F.: Optimizing the Live Migration of Virtual Machine by CPU Scheduling. Journal of Network and Computer Applications 34(4), 1088–1096 (2011)

[5] Hines, M.R., Deshpande, U., Gopalan, K.: Post-copy Live Migration of Virtual Machines. ACM SIGOPS Operating Systems Review 43(3), 14–26 (2009)

[6] Hu, B., Lei, Z., Lei, Y., Xu, D., Li, J.: A Time-Series Based Precopy Approach for Live Migration of Virtual Machines. In: IEEE 17th International Conference on Parallel and Distributed Systems (ICPADS), pp. 947–952 (December 2011)

[7] Harney, E., Goasguen, S., Martin, J., Murphy, M., Westall, M.: The Efficacy of Live Virtual Machine Migrations Over the Internet. In: VTDC 2007 Proceedings of the 2nd International Workshop on Virtualization Technology in Distributed Computing, Article, No. 8 (November 2007)

[8]   Goldberg, R.P.: Survey of Virtual Machine Research, vol. 7(9), pp. 34–45. IEEE Computer Society Press, Los Alamitos (1974)

[9]   Kivity, A., Kamay, Y., Laor, D., Lublin, U., Liguori, A.: kvm: the Linux virtual machine monitor. In: Proceedings of the Linux Symposium, pp. 225–230 (2007)

[10] Clark, C., Fraser, K., Hand, S., Hansen, J.G.: Live Migration of Virtual Machine. In: Proceedings of the 2nd Conference on Symposium on Networked Systems Design & Implementation, pp. 273–286 (2005)

[11] Sapuntzakis, C.P., Chandra, R., Pfaff, B., Chow, J., Lam, M.S., Rosenblum, M.: Optimizing the migration of virtual computers. In: Proceedings of the 5th Symposium on Operating Systems Design and Implementation (OSDI 2002), vol. 36(SI), pp. 337–390 (December 2002)

[12] Zayas, E.: Attacking the process migration bottleneck. In: Proceedings of the Eleventh ACM Symposium on Operating Systems Principles, vol. 21(5), pp. 13–24 (November 1987)

Life Support System by Motion Sensor-Based Behavior Monitoring and SNS-Based Information Sharing

Yinghui Zhou[1,*], Yoshio Asano[1], Lei Jing[2], and Zixue Cheng[2]

[1] Graduate School of Computer Science and Engineering, The University of Aizu,
Aizuwakamatu, Fukusima, Japan, 965-8580
[2] School of Computer Science and Engineering, The University of Aizu,
Aizuwakamatu, Fukusima, Japan, 965-8580
{d8131104,m5161159,leijing,z-cheng}@u-aizu.ac.jp

Abstract. Behavior monitoring is an important method for life support of elderly persons. However, current behavior monitoring system is hard to be applied into our lives whether from user side or from supporter side. In this paper, we propose a sensor-based input system that can detect daily activities automatically and provide necessary information to remote supporters. The system adopts a wearable device to obtain activity data and for activity recognize and analysis. Moreover, we develop a rule-based algorithm and employ AHP method for information mining and filtering of daily activities. The filtered information is shared to supporters through cloud to reflect users' behavior and health situations. The system is evaluated by 10 subjects and the result indicates its feasibility and effectiveness.

Keywords: Cloud Computing, Life Support, Behavior Monitoring, Accelerometer.

1 Introduction

The population over 65 is rapidly increasing in world. A survey shows that the elderly persons living alone who need help in some country have reached 64.8% in all elderly persons [8]. Many services have been developed for health care of elderly persons through behavior monitoring system like camera [1], sensor network [2] [3], and cellphone [4]. The systems are helpful for their families or doctors supporting their lives by knowing their activities.

However, these systems are inconvenient for applications in our real lives. From user's point of view, the behaviors can not be detected out of the monitoring scope by using camera and voice detection technologies. From supporter's point of view, it is impossible to monitor the user's situation at all time. In this paper, we propose a sensor-based input system that can get daily activities

---

* Please note that the LNCS Editorial assumes that all authors have used the western naming convention, with given names preceding surnames. This determines the structure of the names in the running heads and the author index.

R.C.-H. Hsu and W. Shangguang (Eds.): IOV 2014, LNCS 8662, pp. 407–415, 2014.

automatically to know living situations of senior citizen and share necessary information through cloud sources like social network systems (SNS). These daily activities can be shared by doctors, their families and neighborhoods.

There are three problems need to be solved in this system. The first one is how to get the activity data from the senior citizen. In order to get his/her daily behavior information like walking, eating, and sleeping, the privacy and convenience of data collection must be considered. The second one is how to analyze these activities to select the proper information because not all data is useful. It is the key point to find out the useful data from daily logs. The last one is how to analyze and share the result to the persons related with the user.

To solve the first problem, we use a wearable device to detect daily activities automatically. It can sense and recognize users' activities based on previous research of our group [5]. To solve second problem, we develop a rule-based algorithm and adopt AHP method for activity information mining and filtering. The necessary and useful information is provided to remote supporters. To solve the last problem, we show the analyzed result of one-day daily behavior and healthy situation through a SNS.

This paper is organized as follows. The related works are discussed in Section 2. The system model is given in Section 3. The system design is introduced in Section 4. The experiments and evaluation of the system are given in Section 5. Finally the conclusions are given in Section 6.

2   Related Works

Many services of behavior monitoring are proposed in various research fields. Generally, two types of approach for behavior detection are adopted including camera-based and sensors-based approach.

Seki et al. detects abnormal behaviors for senior citizen using camera-based technology [1]. They set up cameras in a senior citizen house for study of life style. The camera-based system is effective for behavior monitoring. However, it can only get user information in the scope of cameras. To tackle this problem, Nagai et al. propose a system detecting usersf situations by various sensors including acceleration sensor, GPS sensor, illumination sensor, and smart phone [4]. This system can detect abnormal behaviors correctly but inconveniently because users' situations are input by themselves. Tanaka et al. propose a system that detects abnormal behaviors of senior citizen living along using RFID technology [2]. This system consists of three parts, i.e. behavior recognition part, life pattern generation part, and abnormal situation detection part. This system deals with four behaviors including sleeping, eating, toilet and bathing. Sakai et al. propose a system that can support senior citizen living along using Xport and infrared sensors [3]. They set these sensors in each room to detect users' behaviors. The result is used to verify the safe situation of senior citizens in the room. If the system judges that senior citizens are in danger, it will notify someone by email system.

In our research, we use an accelerometer-based wearable device to recognize human activities. We analyze the recognized result and share necessary information to supporters by a cloud source such as a social network system. It is expected that the system is helpful to improve users' life styles and get real-time help. Compared with other systems, we adopt only one device to detect various activities and share information to remote people in time.

3   System Model

There are various activities in daily living. The rehabilitation field classifies them into ADL (Activities of Daily Living) and IADL (Instrumental ADL) for health evaluation. Not only ADL but also IADL is important for evaluating whether users can live alone or not.

- ADL - Routine activities that people tend to every day without needing assistance. There are six basic ADLs: eating, bathing, dressing, toileting, transferring (walking) and continence. An individual's ability to perform ADLs is important for determining what type of long-term care (e.g. nursing-home care or home care) and coverage the individual need (i.e. Medicare, Medicaid or long-term care insurance) [6].
- IADL - Instrumental activities of daily living are the activities that people do once they are up, dressed, put together. These tasks support an independent life style. Many people can still live independently even though they need help with one or two of these IADL's (e.g. cooking, driving, using the telephone or computer, shopping, managing medication).

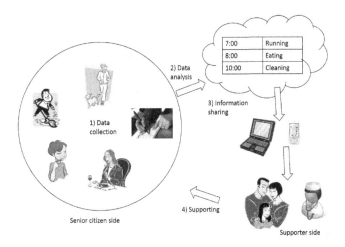

Fig. 1. System Model

The system in this research involves the user side and the supporter side. The user side is senior citizens whose ADLs and IADLs can be monitored by a wearable device. The support side refers to the people who can help senior citizen such as their families, doctors, and neighbors. The system runs by three steps: Data collection, Data analysis, and Data Share shown in Figure 1. Data is collected from senior citizen who wears a wearable device on his/her body. Then, the activity data is transmitted into recognition unit for the activity recognition. The system uploads the detected activities and related information such as time stamp and duration into a local database or cloud for data mining and analysis. Finally, the supporter side shares the information of senior citizen. They can access a cloud source with smart phone or PC to monitor users' activities and health situation.

4   System Design

In our research, we use a wearable device with an accelerometer to monitor daily activities. The motions of hand and arm can be detected and recognized by the device for hand-related activities identification. The recognized activities are saved into a database for data analysis and information sharing.

4.1   Activities Collection

In this system, a wearable device is adopted to detect and recognize daily activities. The device can sense acceleration change from the hand to identify what activities happened. In this research, five types of hand-related daily activities i.e. Eating, Tooth brushing, Running, Writing, and Cleaning are detected by the device. We cluster the five types of daily activity into two classes.

- ADLs: Eating, Tooth Brushing and Running;
- IADLs: Writing and Cleaning.

Data collection and feature extraction are the precondition of activity recognition. In this research, we extract features in time domains and frequency domain for activity recognition. Not all the candidate features can be used for activity recognition. By analyzing the performance of the features, the feature set is generated including mean in time domain, standard deviation in time domain, Energy in time domain, Entropy in time domain, Amplitude in frequency domain, and Spectrum in frequency domain for activity recognition. Three kinds of classifiers, C4.5, K-NN and Naive Bayes are adopted for training and testing.

4.2   Activities Analysis

In this section, Activities are analyzed by using the following four kinds of filter.

- Frequency filter. It analyzes the frequency of each kind of activity occurs in a day.
- Time zone filter. It analyzes the activities time period, and check whether the activities time is normal or not.
- Momentum filter. It analyzes the calorie expenditure.
- Emergence degree filter. It analyzes whether activities are emergence or not.

Frequency filer analyzes the times of activities. If the frequency they did is more than or less than a threshold, this system shares the abnormal information to the supporters. The frequency threshold can be decided by the users, experts in medicine, or their families. For example, if the user eats three times in a day, it is normal. Otherwise, the system considers that is abnormal and informs the supporters. Based on the system, we can notice the unusual life style early.

Time zone filter analyzes the time zone of activities. The user can define what the ideal time zone of an activity is. For example, the eating from 11:00am to 14:00pm belongs to his/her ideal time zone. If the eating time is difference from the setting, the filter considers it is abnormal.

Momentum filter analyzes calorie expenditure of a senior citizen doing exercise in a day. Research [9] find out symptom of body weakening when the momentum of senior citizen goes down. Therefore, the parameter of calorie is important for senior citizen to detect when they need support.

Emergence filter analyzes whether the situation of senior citizen is danger or not. In this system, there are two dangerous situations. One situation is the senior citizen falls down in house. Another situation is that they cannot perform daily activities. By searching activities history, this system detects what activities they are not able to do now and notifies it to the supporters.

All activities information is saved in a database including recognized activities and corresponding information like time stamp. It is useful to not only find activities easily but also reuse past histories information to find symptom of sick.

4.3   Information Sharing

We use AHP method to select proper information for sharing. The AHP (Analytic hierarchy process) is used for organizing and analyzing complex decision, based on mathematics and psychology. There are multiple levels including goal of the analysis, criteria factors, and alternative choices. In this research, we adopt a four level structure as shown in Figure 2.

The final result is obtained on the basis of the pairwise relative evaluations of both the criteria and the options provided by the user. It is assumed that m evaluation criteria are considered, and n options are to be evaluated. In order to compute the weights for the different criteria, the AHP starts creating a pairwise comparison matrix A. The matrix A is $m*m$ real matrix, where m is the number of evaluation criteria considered. Each entry a_{jk} of the matrix A represents the jth criterion relative to the kth criterion. Otherwise, the jth criterion is more important than the kth criterion, when if $a_{jk} < 1$, then the jth criterion is less important than the kth criterion. If two criteria have the same importance, then the entry a_{jk} is 1. The entries a_{jk} and a_{kj} satisfy the following constraint:

$$a_{jk} * a_{kj} = 1 \qquad (1)$$

Obvious, $a_{ij} = 1$ for all j. The relative importance between two criteria is measured according to a numerical scale from 1 to 9, where it is assumed that the jth criterion is equally or more importance between two criteria into numbers. Once

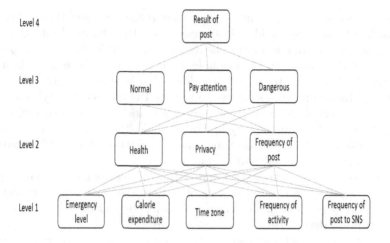

Fig. 2. AHP for behavior analysis

the matrix A is built, it is possible to derive from A the normalized pairwise comparison matrix A_{norm} by making equal to 1 the sum of the entries on each column, i.e. each entry a_{jk} of the matrix A_{norm} is computed as

$$\bar{a}_{jk} = \frac{a_{jk}}{\sum_{l=1}^{m} a_{lk}} \qquad (2)$$

Finally, the criteria weight vector w (that is an m-dimensional column vector) is built by averaging the entries on each row of A_{norm}, i.e.

$$w_j = \frac{\sum_{l=1}^{m} \bar{a}_{jl}}{m} \qquad (3)$$

For a matrix A, a_{ij} denotes the entry in the ith row and the jth column of A. For a vector v, v_i denotes the ith element of v [10]

The matrix of option scores is a $n * m$ real matrix S. Each entry S_{ij} of S represents the score of the ith option with respect to the jth criterion. The vector $s(j)$ contains the score matrix S is obtained as $S = [s(1)\dots s(m)]$ i.e. the jth column of S corresponds to $s(j)$.

The analyzed result is posted into a social network system, Facebook, for information sharing. Facebook has an original News Feed ranking system called edge rank to only show the top-ranked stories for that particular user. Supporters read post of this group, they can know about daily activities of senior citizen and the reason why that activity is selected by AHP method.

5   Experiments and Evaluation

We implement the system on a PC that is taken as a server for activity recognition, activity analysis, and information sharing. A database is created for information storage and history data analysis.

5.1   Filter Design

Aiming at the five daily activities (Eating, Brushing teeth, Running, Writing and Cleaning), we design filters as follows.

The time zone filter is applied to analyze eating and teeth brushing. If the recognition activities time is in appointed time, their activities are not posted. This appointed time is defined by the users firstly. In this system, we define the ideal time zone as following.

– Eating :6;00-9:00,11:00-14:00, 18:00-20:00
– Teeth Brushing : 6;00-9:30,11:00-14:30, 18:00-21:30

The calorie filter is applied to all activities. We save all activities calorie to check user health situations. Calorie is computed according to research [7]. METS (Metabolic equivalents) coefficient is used as a means of expressing the intensity and energy expenditure of activities among persons of different weight.

$$Calorie(kcal) = 1.05 * bodyweight(kg) * METScoefficient * time(h) \quad (4)$$

The frequency filter focuses on two activities. Eating is three times a day, and Teeth brushing is three times a day.

The emergence level filter is applied to ADLs. This filter judges whether user is danger situation or not. In this implementation, if users can't finish ADLs in appointed time, the system post related information right away.

5.2   AHP Analysis

We select important information from activity database for information sharing using AHP method. The structure of AHP is shown in Figure 2. The goal of decision is the contents of post. The optional items are following.

– Post the times of activities;
– Post all calories of activities in appointed time;
– Post time zone of activities;
– Post information right away when user in danger situation;
– No Post

Based on AHP method, the weight of every element is computed as follows.

Table 1. Element Weight

Elements	Health	Privacy	Post Frequency
Health	1	5	3
Privacy	1/5	1	3
Post Frequency	1/3	1/3	1

Then the average weight is shown as follows.

$$(1 + 5 + 3)1/3 = 2.08 \quad (5)$$

$$(1/5 + 1 + 3)1/3 = 1.61 \tag{6}$$

$$(1/3 + 1/3 + 1)1/3 = 1.18 \tag{7}$$

We can get weight of each elements as following

$$\text{Health: } 2.08/(2.08 + 1.61 + 1.18) = 0.42 \tag{8}$$

$$\text{Privacy: } 1.61/(1.21 + 0.54 + 0.44) = 0.33 \tag{9}$$

$$\text{Frequency in post: } 1.18/(1.21 + 0.54 + 0.44) = 0.24 \tag{10}$$

5.3 Evaluation

Ten subjects (5 males and 5 females) in local university took part in the evaluation experiment. After using the system, they were asked to do a questionnaire survey to point out good points and what should be improved in the system. The result is shown in Figure 3.

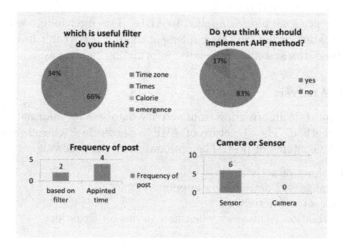

Fig. 3. AHP for behavior analysis

The result indicates that most of subjects think Time Zone filter is the most useful to judge users' health situations. About 83% subjects think AHP method is effective to provide important information to the supporters.

In addition, we also evaluated filtering accuracy using test data. When we start the system, we can get users' activities and analysis information. The results show that three filters have good performance except emergence filter. The reason is that in current system, we did not define detailed emergency patterns so that emergence filter is hard to detect emergency case, which will be solved in future works.

6   Conclusion

We proposed and evaluated an input system that can obtain daily activities of the users for life support. Three problems are solved in this research, which is how to detect daily activities, how to analyze these activities to select the proper information, and how to remotely share the analyzed result to the supporters. To the first problem, a wearable device is adopted to detect activities automatically. To the second problem, four kinds of filters are proposed for data mining of activities. To last problem, the activities are analyzed by AHP method and shared to supporters through a social network system. In future works, we will apply the system to senior citizen for real data collection to improve the usability of the system.

References

1. Seki, H., Hori, Y.: Detection of Abnormal Action Using Image Sequence for Monitoring System of Aged People. The Institute of Electrical Engineers of Japan 122-D, 182–188 (2002)
2. Tanaka, H., Nakauchi, Y.: Senior Citizen Monitoring System by Using Ubiquitous Sensors. The Japan Society of Mechanical Engineers 75, 116–124 (2009)
3. Sakai, A., Kitama, M., Kimura, K., Arisawa, J.: Support System for isolated elderly people using sensors and the network equipment. IEICE Technical Report 110(355), 29–33 (2010)
4. Nagai, M., Suwa, K.: Improvement of Abnormility Detection for Elderly Support System using Smartphone. Medial Journal of Tokyo City University 14, 1–3 (2013)
5. Zhou, Y., Cheng, Z., Hasegawa, T., Jing, L., Huang, T., Wang, J.: Detection of Daily Activities and Analysis of Abnormal Behaviors Based on a Finger-worn Device. In: 5th IET International Conference on Ubi-Media Computing, Xining, China (2012)
6. hActivities of Daily Living - ADL, http://www.investopedia.com/terms/a/adl.asp
7. hCompute Excercise calorie, http://www.kuma-king.net/undou_karori/index.html
8. Mizuho Information and Research Institute: Survey on Support Method or elderly living alone. Technical report (2012)
9. Fujinami, T., Miura, M., Takatsuka, R., Sugihara, T.: A Study of Long Term Tendencies in Residents' Activities of Daily Living at a Group Home for People with Dementia Using RFID Slippers. In: Abdulrazak, B., Giroux, S., Bouchard, B., Pigot, H., Mokhtari, M. (eds.) ICOST 2011. LNCS, vol. 6719, pp. 303–307. Springer, Heidelberg (2011)
10. Saaty, T.L.: Decision making with the analytic hierarchy process. Int. J. Services Sciences 1, 83–98 (2008)

Compression Accelerator for Hadoop Appliance

Sang Don Kim[1], Seong Mo Lee[1], Sang Muk Lee[1], Ji Hoon Jang[1], Jae-Gi Son[2], Young Hwan Kim[2], and Seung Eun Lee[1],*

[1] Dept. of Electronic Engineering,
Seoul National University of Science and Technology, Seoul, Korea
seung.lee@seoultech.ac.kr
[2] Korea Electronics Technology Institute, Seongnam, Korea

Abstract. In this paper, we propose an accelerator for Hadoop appliances. Data servers receive significant data traffic because of several services based on networks. Processing such big data requires sufficient communication bandwidth for big data management. In order to increase communication bandwidth, compression algorithms are adopted in Hadoop appliances, although additional computation overhead is required. Our accelerator compresses data from a PCIe (Peripheral Component Interconnect Express) interface, thus reducing the size of data that should be transmitted through a network. As a result, computation overhead of the main processor in a server is decreased and communication bandwidth is increased.

Keywords: Hadoop, Compression Accelerator, PCI Express, LZ4, FPGA.

1 Introduction

Hadoop [1] is an open source software system developed for big data management that can process 1 TB of data or more per day. Cloud services such as Google drive and Dropbox are popular because of their convenience, safety against losses, and ease of managing personal data. However, such services cause high traffic on data centers and generate big data. Hadoop systems are the proper solution for managing such big data traffic. In a system that processes big data traffic, hardware interconnection bandwidth is important because traditional hardware systems have poor communication speeds.

Various data centers use Hadoop or other big data management systems. Yahoo controls 25 PB of company data using HDFS (Hadoop Distributed File System). HDFS is similar to other distributed file systems. However, the data nodes in HDFS do not use data protection mechanisms [2]. Facebook uses "Hive and Hadoop," which operates Hive-QL (Hive query language) that is similar to SQL. Hive is compiled into a map-reduce process. Moreover, the Hive warehouse has many tables and can retains over 700 TB of data in Facebook [3]. Google designed GFS (Google File System) to

---

* Corresponding author.

R.C.-H. Hsu and W. Shangguang (Eds.): IOV 2014, LNCS 8662, pp. 416–423, 2014.

manage data [4]. Sangwon Seo proposed data processing methods to improve the performance of Hadoop systems. This proposal uses pre-fetching to upgrade data locality and applies pre-shuffling to change maps and accelerate the process [5].

In this paper, we propose a compression accelerator for Hadoop systems. This proposed system includes a PCIe (Peripheral Component Interconnect Express) interface and compression engine. The compression engine compresses data according to a compression algorithm so that data traffic can be reduced. The rest of our paper is organized as follows. First, related work regarding hardware accelerators appears in Section 2, and we introduce compression algorithms and the PCIe interface in Section 3. Section 4 shows the environment of the proposed system and an implemented prototyping system. Finally, Section 5 concludes this paper by outlining the direction for future works on this topic.

2   Related Work

Compression accelerators have been studied in various systems to improving system performance. A GPU-based accelerator was implemented for compression parallelism on an operating system. The accelerator consists of a group of optimized compression algorithms, a compression scheme selection module, and a column-major compression module [6].

A customized RISC (reduced instruction set computing) processor and a compression accelerator that is composed of a 16 x 16 bit storage array similar to the register file was proposed for a body sensor network system. The storage array is used for the proposed lossless compression algorithm. The compression algorithm is executed through an XOR (exclusive or) operation and subtraction. As a result, the embedded compression accelerator requires a smaller execution cycle compared to a standard processor operation [7].

An FPGA (field-programmable gate array)-based accelerator was adopted to compress big data such as log data from Internet searching. In this paper, we use a bitmapping compression/decompression method for processing efficiency. The experimental results show performance improvement on the hardware accelerator to a maximum of 140% utilizing the bitmapping modules [8].

3   Background

3.1   Compression Algorithms

The Hadoop system uses a diverse lossless compression algorithm to improve communication bandwidth and system performance. Gzip is an available compression program based on the deflate algorithm. Gzip has a high compression ratio, but demands much processor resources. Bzip2 and 7zip are also available on the Hadoop system, but they require more computation power to compress than Gzip. When managing big data, compression speed is as important as compression ratio. For this purpose,

Hadoop appliances use the LZ4 algorithm also. LZ4 has high compression speeds compared to other compression programs because it does not use the Huffman algorithm.

When LZ4 compression algorithm is executed on a CPU, it occupies much processor resources. To avoid an increase of unnecessary processor performance, a dedicated compression accelerator could be used. The compression accelerator is composed of an external hardware, and it uses few processor resources. For better performance of data compression, the compression accelerator could be composed of FPGA using Verilog HDL (Hardware Description Language). Although LZ4 has a low compression ratio compared to Gzip or bzip2, it can be implemented in hardware efficiently.

3.2   PCIe Interface

PCIe is a high-speed serial bus standard designed to replace conventional parallel bus standards such as PCI, PCI-X, and AGP (Accelerated Graphics Port). Conventional parallel buses that share physical connections with multiple sources, which are a common set of address, data, and control signals, have limitations in that only one master has access to a bus at a time in the case where multiple masters exist in the bus. In addition, because of synchronous data transmission, a clock of the conventional buses is limited by the slowest peripheral on the bus. In contrast, the PCIe physical link solves these problems by supporting its own point-to-point connection and full-duplex communication between any two PCIe devices. One of the most prospective features of PCIe is connection scalability. PCIe has a dedicated point-to-point connection called a "lane." The PCIe link between two PCIe devices can be extended from one to 32 lanes. Thus, a higher bandwidth can be achieved by increasing the number of lanes in the PCIe system. At the physical level of PCIe, each lane is composed of two unidirectional LVDS (Low-Voltage Differential Signaling) that operate at low power and provide high speeds of approximately 655 Mbps. Figure 1 shows a physical layer interface for PCIe.

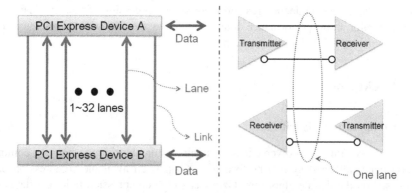

Fig. 1. Physical level interface for PCIe

Another characteristic of PCIe is the packet-based protocol. Basically, the PCIe protocol consists of a physical layer, a data link layer, a transaction layer, and an application layer. The application layer is designed to be compatible with conventional operating systems and PCI device drivers. The PCIe protocol, in contrast with the PCI protocol, presents remarkable difference in three of the layers: the transaction layer, the data link layer, and the physical layer.

The transaction layer is primarily responsible for packetizing and depacketizing TLPs (Transaction Layer Packets); it is also responsible for transmitting TLPs to the data link layer and receiving TLPs from the data link layer. TLPs are composed of header and data, including information for transactions such as read, write, and configuration. Header length ranges from 12 to 16 bytes, and data length ranges from zero to 4,096 bytes. Optionally, ECRC (End-to-End Cyclic Redundancy Check), which has four bytes of data for additional transmission robustness, is checked for all TLPs and added to the TLP. The data link layer serves as an intermediate layer between the transaction layer and the physical layer. The data link layer performs link management, error detection, and error correction. In the data link layer, The LCRC (Link-to-Link Cyclic Redundancy Check) and sequence number is appended to the TLP that originates from the transaction layer. The LCRC has four bytes of data and is used to detect errors in TLPs that are delivered between two PCIe devices. The sequence number has two bytes of data and is used to detect cases where TLPs have been lost. The major roles of the physical layer are parallel-to-serial and serial-to-parallel conversion, impedance matching circuitry, PLL (Phase Locked Loop), and include driver and input buffers. Figure 2 shows a packet flow through these layers.

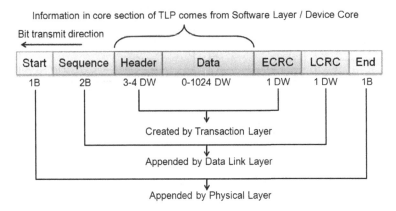

Fig. 2. Packet flow through layers

4   Implementation of Compression Accelerator

Hadoop appliances receive big data from each of the data nodes. This big data can be directly transmitted through a network, stored to a disk drive, or compressed to diminish network traffic. Compression can be processed by a general processor, such as x86, or it can use dedicated hardware such as the proposed system. The compression accelerator for Hadoop appliances uses some processor resources and performs big data compression to reduce traffic. For efficient data compression operations, data input/output speeds are significant. PCIe can be expanded according to data traffic from one lane to 32 lanes; it supports sufficient data bandwidth for Hadoop systems.

The proposed compression accelerator consists of a PCIe module, input/output buffer, and compression engine. Figure 3 illustrates the block diagram of the PCIe module. The PCIe module is comprised of an endpoint IP (Intellectual Property) and an AXI4 interface bridge to manage packets used for PCIe communication. The endpoint IP for PCIe communicates with a network through communication channels that are four lanes with PCIe 2.0 specification. The endpoint IP is also responsible for converting packets to data in the manner of an AXI4 stream interface, and vice versa. The AXI4 interface bridge, which is composed of a TX unit, an RX unit, and a flow controller, interconnects the PCIe module with an AXI4 memory-mapped bus. The RX unit switches from the AXI4 stream interface to the AXI4 memory-mapped interface, whereas the TX unit performs contrary operation of the RX unit. The flow controller indicates data reception completion to the endpoint IP with the configuration interface of PCIe.

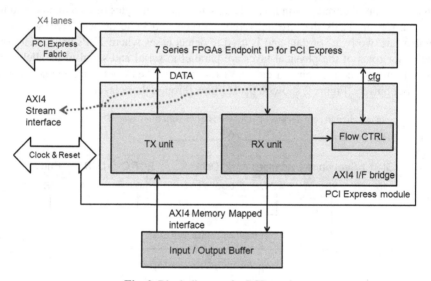

Fig. 3. Block diagram for PCIe engine

Data are stored in the input data buffer until data that are a maximum compression size are received from the PCIe module. When data size exceeds a defined compression size for storing in the input buffer, compression can be started by a compression engine. The compression accelerator supports diverse compression software; the compression engine has multiple compression algorithms. The compression method is selected by the CPU. If the compression engine does not support a specific algorithm, the CPU can compress data. After the compression operation, compressed data can be transferred via a PCIe channel. These data are transmitted through a network or stored in a disk drive or output buffer by the CPU or compression engine. The compression accelerator does not contain a data decompression module because decompression is faster than compression and uses few processor resources. Figure 4 illustrates the block diagram of a compression accelerator.

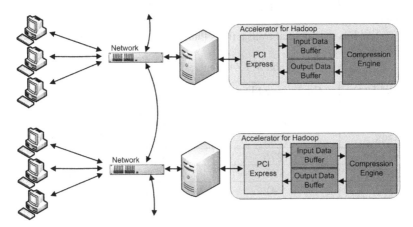

Fig. 4. Architecture for compression accelerator

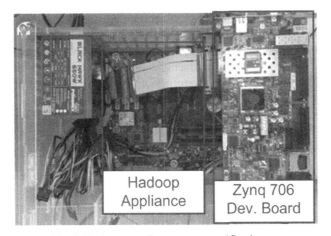

Fig. 5. Environment for prototype verification

The prototype of the compression accelerator was implemented using a development board that supports four lanes of PCIe Interface. Figure 5 shows our prototyping environment; we adopted the Xilinx ZC-706 board to implement the system. The host computer perceives the PCIe device as a memory device through the endpoint block. The compression accelerator system has a Cortex-A9 processor for general purposes. On the proposed system, this processor is used as a compression engine that compresses big data using the LZ4 algorithm. Although the LZ4 algorithm has limitations regarding the compression ratio, it has a fast compression speed. The Gzip program can be used to improve the compression ratio; however, it demands much resource for processing [9]. Therefore, the program selects the proper algorithm according to big data traffic. This general-purpose compression engine can be replaced with dedicated compression hardware for better compression performance.

Table 1 lists the results of the LZ4 compression algorithm used. The average compression ratio is 74%, and it requires 66 μs of compression time. The original data are FX (Forex) margin trading log data composed of ASCII characters. The FX margin trading system has exponential transactions that cause big data traffic.

Table 1. LZ4 Compression results

Original Data (Byte)	Compressed Data (Byte)	Compression Ratio (%)	Compression Time (μs)
3413	654	80.8	56.7
3398	1384	59.3	89.7
3423	1276	62.7	86.6
3387	470	86.1	46.4
3382	590	82.6	54.7

5   Conclusion

In this paper, we presented our prototype of a compression accelerator that includes 4 lane of PCIe interface. The accelerator reduces transferring data size (74% in average) by compressing log data using the LZ4 algorithm. Experimental results demonstrated the feasibility of our proposal for reducing computation overhead of the main processor in a server, thus enhancing the performance of Hadoop appliance.

Acknowledgements. This study was supported in part by the IT R&D program of MSIP and KEIT under contract No. 10047088, Development of open type Hadoop storage appliance to support more than 48 TB per single data node.

References

1. Hadoop: http://hadoop.apache.org/
2. Shvachko, K., Kuang, H., Radia, S., Chansler, R.: The Hadoop Distributed File System. IEEE Mass Storage Systems and Technologies (MSST), 1–10 (2010)
3. Thusoo, A., Sen Sarma, J., Jain, N., Shao, Z., Chakka, P., Zhang, N., Antony, S., Liu, H., Murthy, R.: Hive – A Petabyte Scale Data Warehouse Using Hadoop. In: IEEE Data Engineering (ICDE), pp. 996–1005 (2010)
4. Ghemawat, S., Gobioff, H., Leung, S.-T.: The Google File System. In: The 19th Symposium on Operating Systems Principles, pp. 29–43 (2003)
5. Seo, S., Jang, I., Woo, K., Kim, I., Kim, J.-S., Maeng, S.: HPMR: Prefetching and Pre-shuffling in Shared MapReduce Computation Environment. In: IEEE Cluster Computing and Workshops, CLUSTER 2009, pp. 1–8 (2009)
6. Guo, G., Qui, S., Ye, Z., Wang, B., Fang, L., Lu, M., See, S., Mao, R.: GPU-Accelerated Adaptive Compression Framework for Genomics Data. In: IEEE International Conference on Big Data, pp. 181–186 (2013)

Author Index

7. Kim, H., Choi, S., Yoo, H.-J.: A Low Power 16-bit RISC with Lossless Compression Accelerator for Body Sensor Network System. In: ASSCC Solid-State Circuits Conference, pp. 207–210 (2006)
8. Yan, J., Luo, R., Gao, R., Xu, N.-Y.: An Efficient Lossless Compression Method for Internet Search Data in Hardware Accelerators. In: World Congress on Computer Science and Information Engineering, pp. 453–457 (2009)
9. Chasapis, K., Dolz, M.F., Kuhn, M., Ludwig, T.: Evaluating Power-Performance Benefits of Data Compression in HPC Storage Servers. In: International Conference on Smart Grids, Green Communications and IO Energy-aware Technologies, pp. 29–34 (2014)